WITHDRAWN

TEACHER EFFECTIVENESS

THE GARLAND BIBLIOGRAPHIES
IN CONTEMPORARY EDUCATION
(GENERAL EDITOR: JOSEPH M. MC CARTHY)
VOL. 3

GARLAND REFERENCE LIBRARY
OF SOCIAL SCIENCE
VOL. 116

016.371
P871t

TEACHER EFFECTIVENESS
*An Annotated Bibliography
and Guide to Research*

Marjorie Powell
Joseph W. Beard

GARLAND PUBLISHING, INC. • NEW YORK & LONDON
1984

© 1984 Marjorie Powell and Joseph W. Beard
All rights reserved

Library of Congress Cataloging in Publication Data

Powell, Marjorie, 1942–
  Teacher effectiveness.

  (The Garland bibliographies in contemporary education ;
v. 3) (Garland reference library of social science ;
v. 116)
  Includes index.
  1. Teaching—Bibliography. 2. Teaching—Research—
Bibliography. I. Beard, Joseph W., 1934–   .
II. Title. III. Series. IV. Series: Garland reference
library of social science ; v. 116.
Z5814.T3P68 1984   016.3711'02   81-48423
[LB1025.2]
ISBN 0-8240-9388-7

Printed on acid-free, 250-year-life-paper
Manufactured in the United States of America

CONTENTS

v

CATNov20'84

84-2183

CONTENTS BY CATEGORY

INTRODUCTION: RESEARCH ON TEACHING

The field of research on teaching has expanded dramatically in the fifteen years covered by this bibliography, 1965 through 1980. The expansion has included studies conducted for many purposes; for example, to increase our understanding of life in the classroom, to develop information with which to change the behaviors of teachers, to identify important teaching behaviors which might form the basis for teacher evaluation, and to identify the teacher behaviors and skills which should be taught to prospective teachers in programs of teacher education. This bibliography contains relevant citations to the research which has been conducted for the purposes of increasing our understanding of the science, art and craft of teaching. The existence of research publications has been documented with relevant reference information and brief annotations; there has been no attempt to evaluate the quality of the studies. A brief perusal of the bibliography provides an indication of the range of topics addressed by these studies and also of the variety of studies within a single topic.

I. STRUCTURE OF THE BIBLIOGRAPHY

Topics Covered

The bibliography focuses on teaching in preschool, elementary and secondary schools, of the major subject areas, such as reading, language arts, mathematics, social studies and science. It contains citations covering research on teacher characteristics, expectations, perceptions of teaching and students, teacher behaviors, the influence of teacher behaviors on student behaviors and learning, teacher-student relations, student behaviors and perceptions, a selection of citations on methodological issues and summaries and essays.

The bibliography includes studies with a variety of methodologies. Some studies are based on teacher reports of their behavior, others use tests of teacher personality characteristics and still others report observations of the classroom behaviors of teachers. Over the years covered by the bibliography (1965 through 1980), there have been some changes in the types of research methodologies most frequently used; fashions change in research just as they do in other fields.

There have also been changes in the topics which are most frequently studied. The overview of the history of research on teaching (see Section 2 of this introduction) indicates some of the changes in the topics while the discussion of future directions (see Section 4 of this introduction) indicates some of the current interests and predictions of researcher interests for the next few years.

Topics Not Covered

Several topics which a user might expect to find in a bibliography of research on teaching have been excluded. One major reason for the exclusion of many topics is simply the present length of the bibliography. Each additional topic or group of studies would have increased the size of this volume, and each might well form the basis for future bibliographies.

Studies of post-secondary education have been excluded. Researchers studying elementary and secondary teaching have little communication with the researchers studying teaching at the post-secondary level. Some exceptions exist, e.g., vocational education and studies and reviews of education and training conducted by the military. The conditions of teaching in post-secondary settings, the students and the nature of the instructional content are sufficiently different from those in elementary and secondary schools to warrant separate bibliographies.

Studies of teaching of specialized subjects have also been excluded. Most research on teaching has focused on the major content areas of reading, mathematics, social studies, science and English. Many of the studies of such other content areas as music and physical education have been conducted by re-searchers who are specialists in those content areas and who have limited contact with the rest of the field of research on teaching. Since the nature of the content is sufficiently different, it is not clear how the findings of this research relate to the rest of the field of studies of teaching (a problem not unique to studies of specialized topic areas, as noted in the discussion of methodology and research issues). Thus, studies such as those on the teaching of physical education, foreign language, art and music have been excluded from this bibliography.

Studies which focus on special groups of students, such as students in programs of special and bilingual education, have been excluded for two reasons. First, the fields of special educa-tion and bilingual education are sufficiently distinct and encom-pass a large enough number of studies to warrant separate bibli-ographies. The distinctly different nature of teaching in these fields has been recognized in the requirements for special cre-dentials for their teachers. Second, while many of the teaching techniques for special populations of children are important in teaching any children, it is not possible to assume that the knowledge gained from studies of teaching in special conditions is immediately transferable to teaching in other more typical situations. There are two exceptions to this exclusion. When studies have contrasted teaching in regular and special class-rooms, they have been included in the bibliography because of the information they contain about teaching in regular class-rooms. Studies which address the integration of special needs children into the regular classroom have also been included since they, too, contain information about teaching in regular classrooms.

Another area excluded includes studies of schools and the effects of schools on students. Their inclusion would have in-creased the length of the bibliography to unmanageable propor-tions. However, the more compelling reason for their exclusion is that those studies constitute a separate field of research. It is true that one impetus for studies of teaching has been an un-willingness to accept the conclusions of some school effects studies which have reported that schools do not influence stu-dent learning above and beyond the influence of the home and the socioeconomic level of the students. However, the studies of school effects focus on schools as organizations and address the characteristics of schools. In general, studies of school effects use few and relatively gross distinctions among teachers. As such, they provide little information about the types of teaching which occur or the effects of teachers and have therefore been excluded from this bibliography.

Studies of the education of teachers have also been excluded. While many researchers have conducted studies of both teaching and teacher education, two characteristics argue for the separation of the studies. First, studies of teacher education usually focus on teachers in training, who have not mastered all of the skills which they will use when they actually teach. Many such studies are conducted during the student-teaching period when the student works in, but does not have full responsibility for, a classroom of students. The experiences and understandings of student teachers are sufficiently different from the understandings and perspectives of practicing teachers to warrant excluding these studies from this bibliography. Second, some studies, focusing on retention of learning acquired in a teacher education program, assess the effectiveness of the training methods. These studies have been excluded except when they contain a significant amount of descriptive information about the behaviors of teachers in elementary or secondary school classrooms.

Decisions about the inclusion or exclusion of studies focusing on staff development have followed the rules for studies of teacher education. When the studies provide information about the characteristics or behaviors of teachers or the influence of those characteristics or behaviors on students, they have been included. When the studies contain information about methods of changing the behaviors of teachers, without describing those behaviors, they are excluded.

Studies conducted outside of the United States have been excluded, with the exception of studies conducted in Canada and a few British studies which have had considerable impact on research in the United States and have been reported in U.S. journals. Those studies conducted in other countries and reported in U.S. journals represent a small and undefinable portion of the studies conducted in other countries. The difficulty in describing the relationship between the studies reported in U.S. journals and the total body of research on teaching in other countries warrants the exclusion.

In addition to the above, it is important to note another category of documents excluded from the bibliography. Conference papers which are not generally available from the publication distribution system at the author's institution, through the ERIC system, or through printed conference proceedings have been excluded. While this decision has resulted in the exclusion of some papers which can be argued to be important to the field of research on teaching, documents accessible only by locating the author cannot be considered readily accessible to the average user of the bibliography.

Sources of References

The major index systems reviewed to locate the documents cited were: *Education Index, Dissertation Abstracts*, and both *Resources in Education* (RIE) and *Current Index to Journals of Education (CIJE)* of the Educational Resources Information Center *(ERIC)* system. The specific search terms varied among the indexes, depending upon the nature of the system used to classify documents and the specific terms used within each index.

The search began with the 1965 volume of each index and continued until no citations of documents for 1980 were located in the monthly collections of the index. Since the length of time between the date of a document and the time when it is cited differs among the indexes, the number of volumes searched after the last 1980 volume also differed by index. However, every attempt was made to locate all documents which were published during the years covered by this bibliography.

While some books are cited in *RIE*, a search was also made of *Books in Print*, to insure that major publications reporting research or compiling reports of research were included in the bibliography.

Three additional steps were taken to cross-check the comprehensiveness of the bibliography. Publication lists from the major institutions involved in research on teaching were checked and the reference lists or bibliographies of several major articles were reviewed to identify any documents not already included within the bibliography. Individuals whose work was cited frequently were asked to submit a list of their publications to be cross-checked with the citations in the bibliography.

Types of Documents Included

The bibliography focuses on research, so the majority of the documents in the bibliography are research reports. Among these are technical reports presenting details of the research procedures, data analysis and results and journal articles summarizing the research procedures and findings. Many of these documents were written for submission to funding agencies or to communicate the full research procedures and results to other interested researchers. Some are written in non-technical language to describe the findings for practitioners.

Reviews of research are also included, in both technical report and journal article formats. Reviews provide an overview of the work in the field, often contain a discussion of the quality of the reviewed studies, and synthesize the findings of those studies. Some reviews, particularly the reports of meta-analysis (one technique for statistically summarizing the results of many studies), contain technical discussions. Many provide brief charts summarizing the results of the studies reviewed.

Some essays have been included, particularly when they cite relevant research to document the points made in the essay. Some of these discuss conceptions of teaching and the relationship of these conceptions to research methodologies. Some essays provide summaries which are less formal than full reviews of a set of studies. Other essays indicate new directions which research has taken or should take.

Frequently several documents describe the same study. When the documents are clearly the same, they are cited as a single document, with an indication of the change in title. In other cases, where there are some changes from one document to another, the documents are listed separately. In some few instances the differences between two documents by the same author are very slight.

2. HISTORY OF RESEARCH ON TEACHING

In spite of the proliferation of studies conducted during the fifteen years covered by this bibliography, certain highlights can be identified. These highlights, while not marking definitive breaks in the nature of research on teaching, demonstrate a growing sophistication in conceptualization of research topics and analysis of research data. The past activities form the basis for continuing work in any one or more of these topics. Documents cited throughout this historical discussion are illustrative of the documents presented in the bibliography.

Ratings of Teachers

Many early studies of teachers and teaching sought to identify characteristics of good teachers. Sometimes respondents, such as principals, teachers and even students, were given lists of characteristics and asked to select those they believed to be important for good teachers; other times they were asked to generate their own lists of important characteristics. Occasionally the ratings were correlated with measures of student learning.

Teacher Characteristics

Studies of perceptions of the characteristics of good teachers were followed by studies which actually measured teacher characteristics, usually personality and demographic characteristics. Studies of the degree to which teachers are authoritarian in personality or have an internal or external locus of control or of the number of years of teaching experience are examples. Some of these studies measured one or two personality characteristics while others measured several. Some studies compared the personality characteristics of one group of teachers with another, such as elementary and secondary teachers, science and non-science teachers, or teachers in open and traditional classrooms.

In some instances, the researchers considered the influence of teacher characteristics on teacher attitudes and/or behaviors. Cooper, Hinkel and Good (1980) described a relationship between beliefs and behavior, while Serafino (1978) described a relationship between ficld dependence-independence and behaviors.

In other instances, the researchers described relationships

between teacher demographic and personality characteristics and student learning (e.g., Emmer, Good and Pilgrim, 1972, which looked at the relationship between teacher sex and student learning). Some researchers have investigated student outcomes other than academic achievement, such as Turner and Denny's study (1969) of the effects of teacher characteristics on student creativity.

Many of these studies measured one or a few teacher characteristics and related them to student outcome. Relatively few studies considered the interrelationships among teacher characteristics, and even fewer studies investigated the relationships between complexes of teacher characteristics and student outcomes. In all of these studies there was limited discussion of the ways in which teacher characteristics might affect student learning.

Observations of Teacher Behavior

Recognizing the limitations of earlier studies, researchers turned to studies of teaching as it occurred in the classroom. A variety of methods for observing and recording classroom events were developed. One of the earliest, and perhaps the most influential, was Flanders' Interaction Analysis (see Flanders, 1970, for one summary of the research using this observation instrument). Flanders modified other data collection procedures to develop a system to record, every three seconds, the categories of teacher and student verbal interactions. Various systems were then developed to analyze the coded information, including percentages of talk by teachers and students and the sequence of teacher questions, student responses and teacher reactions to student responses. Several variables, created from combinations of specific categories of verbal statements, were used in a number of studies. For example, several categories of observed verbal interaction have been combined into measures of direct and indirect teaching and many studies investigated the effects of the ratio of indirect to direct teaching. Flanders has studied the dissemination and use of Interaction Analysis (1981). He documented the effect which the observation system has had on both studies of teaching and programs of teacher education.

Once researchers began measuring the behaviors of teachers and students in classrooms, the number of observation instruments expanded dramatically. Researchers developed systems to look at specific teacher and student behaviors and modified existing instruments either by refining existing categories of observed behaviors or by adding new behaviors. In 1967 the majority of available observation instruments were reviewed in a twelve-volume compendium (see Simon and Boyer, 1967). Since then, the number of instruments and modifications of instruments has continued to grow.

In the development of instruments some came to be known as low-inference observation systems because they ask the observer to make simple judgments about the observed behaviors, coding them into mutually exclusive categories. Others more closely fit a category known as high-inference instruments because they ask the observer to make judgments about the purposes of the observed behavior, the reactions of participants to that behavior, or to rate teachers or classes on the basis of behaviors observed over a period of time. The classification of any given instrument may vary depending upon how it is used. The information collected through the use of any one instrument may be analyzed in multiple ways, some remaining closer to the observation data as coded and others collapsing the data into larger and larger categories which the researcher creates, often based on the analysis of the data.

A major issue which developed in the use of observation data was the reliability of the observers, by which researchers mean both the consistency with which an observer codes a behavior within the same category when the behavior is observed at different times and the agreement among observers in the coding of a single event. Several methods for assessing observer reliability have been developed and training of observers typically includes an emphasis on reliability.

Some early studies focused on teacher and student verbal behavior during instruction, describing the behaviors and the proportions of types of verbal exchanges, such as talk by teachers, student-initiated talk and student talk in response to teacher questions. Some studies considered non-verbal behaviors, and a few studies considered the consistency between verbal and non-verbal behaviors.

Researchers have investigated teacher behaviors during a specific subject, such as science or reading (e.g., Spiegel and Rogers's study, 1980, of teacher responses during reading instruction). Uses of classroom time have been studied. For example, Durkin (1978–1979) describes the limited time devoted to instruction in reading comprehension and the behaviors of teachers during that time. Some studies have focused on the cognitive level of teacher questions; others have described teacher use of student ideas and encouragement of student inquiry. In some instances studies have considered teacher use of one or more components of a model of teaching, such as McNair and Joyce's study (1979) which describes most teaching in the classrooms in one elementary school as based on a recitation model of teaching, and Bass's study (1980) of teacher use of some components of a model of direct instruction.

Many specific teaching behaviors have been studied, singly or in clusters. The list includes such behaviors as praise, feedback to students, cognitive levels of questions (e.g., Friedman, 1976), and teacher wait time after asking a question (Rowe, 1974). Many studies report a correlation between specific teacher behaviors and student learning; usually one or more studies also reports a lack of relationship between each teacher behavior and student learning.

Researchers have investigated the consistency of behaviors across types of teachers, such as the consistency of behaviors for male and female teachers, for science and non-science teachers. Rohrkemper and Brophy (1979), for example, studied the consistency of responses to student behavior problems across teachers who differ in their definitions of the teacher role.

Process-Product Studies

Several studies have investigated the processes of teaching in the classroom and related those to the products of teaching, student outcomes. These studies are referred to as process-product studies. Some of these studies have focused on the effects of teacher behavior on student self-concept (see, for example, Van Horn's study, 1976, of the effects of teaching on student concept of self as student). Those few studies generally find that teacher behaviors influence student self-concept, although there is little agreement among studies in the definitions of student self-concept, the aspects of teacher behavior that are studied and the determination of the effects of teacher behaviors on student self-concept.

Other studies have investigated the effects of teacher behavior on student behavior. Among these are studies which look at student disruptive or prosocial behavior in interactions with the teacher and/or with peers (e.g., Borg et al.'s study, 1975, of student behavior). Some of these studies involve training teachers to respond in specific ways to student disruptive behaviors; sometimes student responses are then documented, to determine whether changes in teacher responses result in changes in student disruptive behavior.

Another group of studies relates teacher behaviors to student on-task or engaged behavior. For example, Hess and Takanishi (1973) considered the effects of teaching strategies on the engagement of student in schools serving low-income students. Another cluster of studies consider the effects of teacher behaviors on student academic responses, e.g., Gall's study (1973) of the length and quality of student answers to teacher questions.

A large number of studies have considered the relationship between teacher behaviors and student learning. Usually they span a school year, although some studies occur for shorter periods of time and a few studies have investigated the relationship between teacher behaviors and student learning across multiple school years; for example, Brophy and Evertson (1974) report correlations between teacher behaviors and student learning over two years. The majority of these studies have occurred at the elementary level with a recent increase in the number of studies at the junior and senior high school levels. Some of these studies have investigated the behaviors of teachers with students who have higher and lower levels of achievement, or with students from different socioeconomic backgrounds.

Some studies have considered differences in teacher effectiveness, focusing on teachers who have been nominated as effective or who have had consistently high or low student achievement over a period of time. These studies usually seek to identify differences in the behaviors of the two groups of teachers, differences which can be associated with differences in student outcomes. Amidon and Giammatteo's study (1967) of teachers nominated as effective illustrates this type of study.

These process-product studies vary on several dimensions. Studies have used a variety of measures of student learning, including teacher-made tests for the content covered during the time of the study, teacher grades assigned to the student, researcher-developed tests for the content covered (typically used when the teachers taught a unit prepared by the researcher for the specific purposes of the study), commercially-available standardized norm- or criterion-referenced tests and researcher assessment of work completed by the students during the course of the instruction. Variations also exist in the observation instruments used, the number of classroom observations, the teaching variables studied and the analysis procedures. Sometimes two studies use variables which sound the same, but which are measured differently; other studies use variables which sound different, but which are measured so similarly that they can be thought of as the same variable. Differences in definitions of variables are one cause of inconsistent results across studies. Some reviews consider these differences in synthesizing research findings; others do not, adding to the confusion about consistency of findings across studies.

Sometimes the studies have considered relationships for a single group of students at one grade level and one subject area; other times they describe relationships between teacher behaviors and student learning in several grades or subjects (e.g., Evertson et al., 1980, reporting results in English and math at the junior high school level). Some studies have occurred in special settings, such as within specific educational programs, as illustrated by the Stallings and Kaskowitz (1974) report of relationships between teacher behaviors and student behaviors and academic achievement in Follow Through classrooms. Researchers have also investigated differences in the relationships between teacher behaviors and student learning by differences in student characteristics, such as ability or achievement level (e.g., Good and Beckerman, 1978a).

Over the years, many researchers have sought a set of basic

teaching skills which the correlational studies would demonstrate to be related to all types of student learning, in all subject areas, for all types of students. Reviews of correlational studies have attempted to identify the support for and against a relationship between specific teaching skills and student learning. Results of studies have been compared across content taught and grade levels of students, as well as across other student characteristics and other aspects of teaching, to identify these generic teaching skills. Such syntheses of research results have usually concluded that research on teaching has, to date, not found such generic teaching skills.

Patterns of Behaviors

While a number of studies have focused on single characteristics or behaviors of teachers and related these to other single teacher characteristics or behaviors or to measures of student learning, gradually researchers have come to recognize that single teacher characteristics and behaviors are artifacts of the research method. In natural classroom settings teacher behaviors are always nested within clusters of behaviors. Some behaviors do not appear together, while other behaviors appear together frequently enough that they can be described as consistent patterns of teacher behavior.

Some researchers, such as McDonald (1976), have reported relationships between clusters or patterns of teacher behavior and student learning. Many teacher behaviors and patterns of behaviors have been studied. Berliner (1979) reported a relationship between teacher allocation of instructional time and content coverage and student learning. Rist (1970) described the influence of teacher expectations on patterns of teacher behaviors in interactions with students.

At another level of abstraction, some studies have developed factor scores, based on combinations of measures of teacher behaviors which are statistically related, and then found relationships between those factor scores and student learning. The report by Crawford, et al. (1977) illustrates this type of analysis; factors identified from analysis of observations of teacher behavior were related to measures of student achievement.

Experiments and Training

A still more complex level of research involves the development of models or theories of teaching. The studies of the recitation mode of teaching, Joyce's explication of several models of teaching (1972), and a "Direct Instruction" model are examples of models based on patterns or clusters of behaviors. Several researchers, having identified, in correlational studies, clusters of teaching behaviors which they believe to be related to improved student learning, have conducted experiments or training studies using those teaching behaviors.

Some studies have been conducted in classrooms and others in controlled settings. In early classroom studies, researchers provided training for teachers and then looked for changes in student learning, assuming that the teachers were actually using the behaviors covered in the training. More recent studies have included observations to measure the actual behaviors of the experimental teachers (those who received the training) and control teachers (those who did not receive the training). Ebmeier and Good (1979) reported a study in which teachers were trained to use clusters of behaviors, their use of the behaviors was observed, and the achievement of the students of teachers who did and did not receive the training were compared. In that study, the researchers organized the behaviors of interest into a model of teaching, providing a more coherent picture of the teaching approach than is provided even by clusters or patterns of teaching behaviors. These studies demonstrate that models of teaching can be developed from correlational studies, teachers can implement those models (although usually not in just the ways anticipated by the researchers), and the use of the model leads to increased student learning.

Some experiments and training studies have occurred in laboratory settings, often with volunteer teachers working with small groups of unfamiliar students. The teachers teach special units prepared by the researchers, sometimes teaching from detailed scripts. Many of these studies are designed to assess the effects of varied levels of one or more teacher behaviors. An example of this type of laboratory study is Clark et al. (1979), in which different levels of teacher structuring, reacting and soliciting were related to student learning.

In a still more sophisticated research design, researchers have studied the interrelationship of teaching behaviors and student characteristics. Known as Aptitude-Treatment Interaction (ATI) studies, these almost always occur in a controlled setting, where the researcher can specify the level of the behaviors or treatments of interest. The aptitudes, or characteristics, of the students are measured and often form the basis for assigning students to instructional groups which differ in terms of those aptitudes. For example, Winne (1977) reported the results of a laboratory study where student characteristics influenced the effects of levels of teacher behaviors on student learning.

Many of these studies are of short teaching sequences, often of 30 minutes or less. Since they occur in controlled settings, often on college campuses, they frequently involve teachers-in-training and students who have volunteered to participate, rather than intact classes of students and the teachers assigned to work with them during a school year. Those ATI studies which use practicing teachers are included in this bibliography; the majority of the studies are not included, since they involve student teachers.

Several of these studies have found that levels of teacher behaviors interact with student characteristics to influence student learning. The relationship of the results of these short studies to teaching as it occurs in public school classrooms is an issue which has been raised but not frequently addressed by researchers.

Focus on Context

Gradually, the lessons of the researchers focusing on the interaction of treatment (teaching behaviors) and student aptitude (differences in student characteristics) influenced researchers conducting the process-product correlational studies to consider the importance of the teaching context.

Some of the researchers have studied the consistency of teacher behaviors with different types of students; looking at differences in such characteristics as sex, race, socioeconomic level, ability, personality variables and behavior. Several correlational studies describe differences in teacher behaviors toward high and low achieving students.

Researchers have also investigated the number of observations necessary to obtain a consistent measure of teacher behaviors across instructional contexts, such as subject being taught, types of students and instructional organization.

The effects of differences in instructional setting on teacher behavior have also been considered. Evertson et al. (1977) looked at differences in behaviors of English and math teachers at the junior high school level, while other researchers have studied the differences in the behaviors of the same teachers teaching different subjects (e.g., Filby, 1977). Differences resulting from instructional organization have been studied; e.g., teacher behaviors in open and traditional classrooms. Another large group of studies has assessed the behaviors of teachers with and without new curricula, such as new science programs and computer-assisted instruction.

Some studies have investigated the effects of time on the consistency of teacher behaviors, such as differences in time of day and within the sequence of a lesson. Researchers have studied teaching at the start of the school year and found that some teachers spend a considerable amount of time teaching the routines and standards for behavior expected in the classroom (e.g., Anderson, Evertson and Emmer, 1980). While teachers differ in their patterns of teaching behavior, the context influences the observed behaviors of individual teachers. Factors such as the subject being taught, grade level, time of year and classroom organizational structure effect the consistency of teachers' behaviors.

Ethnographic Studies

Most observational studies use one or more instruments to record the observed classroom behaviors. The coding may be done in the classroom as the events are occurring or from an audiotape or videotape made in the classroom. Researchers, concerned (1) that the observers only recorded information about those events which the researchers had predefined as important and (2) that the complexities of the classroom were condensed into these predefined categories, sought ways to collect classroom information that was not limited and shaped by the researchers' prior expectations. Ethnographic approaches offered an alternative.

A variety of ethnographic methods has been used to study classrooms and teaching. Typically, a researcher spends a long period of time in a classroom, observing as much as possible and trying to find major themes or hypotheses to explain what is observed. The researcher may take detailed notes for later analysis or may make limited notes of events which appear to be important. The researcher may ask the classroom participants to describe what they understand to be happening, or may ask the participants to confirm the researcher's theories or hypotheses. Whatever the specific methods, ethnographic studies, such as Jackson's *Life in Classrooms* (1968) provide a rich collection of descriptive information about teaching and classrooms.

Teacher Perceptions

The ethnographic researcher's concern for classroom participants' perceptions of the classroom events, combined with the researchers' search for new variables to describe classroom events and effective teaching, has led researchers back to teachers. This movement has been reinforced by the concern of teachers and teacher groups for greater teacher involvement in defining and conducting research on teaching. Additionally, concern for the expectations which teachers hold for students, the effects of those expectations on student learning and the nature of the information which teachers use to form those expectations have also lead researchers to a greater interest in teacher perceptions.

Several methods have been used to identify teacher perceptions of teaching and of students. Teachers may describe their experiences or record their thinking during planning activities. Actual teaching may be videotaped and played back to stimulate teachers to describe what they perceive to be happening. Teachers may participate in simulations where their actions are recorded.

The largest group of these studies contains investigations of teacher perceptions of students. Some studies describe the presence or absence of differences in teacher perceptions of and achievement expectations for groups of children, such as boys and girls or children of different cultural or socioeconomic groups. Other studies attempt to identify the cues which teachers use in developing their perceptions of and expectations for students. A variety of student characteristics has been considered as possible factors influencing teacher expectations: student sex, race, and socioeconomic level, physical attractiveness, speech patterns, family structure, speed of response to teacher questions, classroom social behavior and many others.

The influence of teacher characteristics on teacher perceptions of or expectations for student achievement has been studied; Borko and Shavelson (1978), for example, investigated the effects of teacher sensitivity to the quality of information about students on teacher use of that information to predict student achievement. Other researchers have studied the effects of teacher race, socioeconomic level and regional background on teacher predictions of student achievement.

A general conclusion which can be drawn from this group of studies is that most teachers are fairly accurate in predicting student achievement levels for a school year and that teachers use past school academic performance (usually as observed by the teacher during the early days of the school year) as the basis for making the predictions or as the basis for their expectations.

Teacher Planning

In 1975 Shulman and Elstein wrote a review of studies of decision making and problem solving in many fields, applying their conclusions to education, which prompted further focus of research in this area of teacher planning, i.e., how teachers make decisions in preparation for and during their classroom activities. Most of the studies have been descriptive in nature, attempting to document the planning which teachers do. Some of the research has focused on general teacher decision making, such as the decision to use a new curriculum, planning for the school year or planning instruction to meet the diagnosed needs of a group of students. Gil, for example, (1980) reports that teachers used global categories in making diagnostic decisions about students. Some studies have documented the effects of decisions made early in the school year, such as the organizational structure of the classroom and the curricular materials to be used, on later teacher planning. These types of decisions appear to define the parameters within which teachers think and the types of alternative activities which they consider. Some planning studies, growing from studies of teacher expectations, consider the influence of information about students on teacher planning.

Planning for specific lessons, and for specific groups of students, has also been studied. Researchers have found that much teacher planning focuses on the activities in which children will be engaged, rather than instructional objectives. Some research has considered the decisions which teachers make during instruction (e.g., Morine-Dershimer, 1978–1979, which describes teacher decisions and alternatives considered during a lesson), the nature of the information which teachers consider about students and about the instructional sequence during a lesson and the alternatives which teachers think about when making a decision during instruction.

A few studies have considered the relationship between teacher planning and student achievement. Peterson, et al. (1978), for example, related teacher planning to teacher cognitive style and traced the influence of planning on teacher behavior and student achievement.

Students

At least four forces have lead to increased research attention on students. One has been the focus on teacher interactions with students which has lead to studies of student interactions. Another, the concern with the consistency of teacher behavior, has lead to investigations of variations in teachers' behaviors with different students. Studies of teacher perceptions have been paralleled by studies of student perceptions. The search for links between teacher characteristics and behavior and student learning has resulted in increased attention to student behavior in the classroom.

Some studies have described student perceptions of classroom events, including teacher behaviors, interactions between the teacher and the students, the content to be mastered, expectations for student work, and teacher attitudes toward students. Other studies have presented perceptions by type of classroom or subject taught. Others have reported student perceptions for groups of students who differ on one or more characteristics (e.g., Weinstein and Middlestadt, 1979, who described student perceptions of differences in teacher interactions with high- and low-achieving students). Some studies have described student perceptions of specific teaching behaviors, or of the behaviors which students perceive to be related to a general teacher characteristic. For example, Kennedy et al. (1978) describe student perceptions of teacher clarity. Yet another group of studies has related student perceptions of teachers and teacher behaviors to student achievement (e.g., Clark et al., 1976).

Student classroom behaviors have been described. Recent studies of student academic behavior have considered student engagement or on-task behavior (e.g., Good and Beckerman, 1978). Studies of student social behavior have generally focused on student disruptive behavior, with some attention to acceptable student interaction with other students. A few studies have related student behaviors to student characteristics (e.g., Walberg, 1979). However, studies of students are relatively infrequent.

Reviews

Reviews of studies of relationships between teacher behavior and student learning have appeared periodically, as illustrated by Rosenshine (1971, 1979). While Rosenshine's reviews sometimes include studies looking at student achievement in more than one subject area, other reviews focus on student learning within a specific subject area (e.g., Rupley and Blair's 1980 review of studies of reading instruction). Some reviews have included only those studies which meet specified criteria related to qualities of the research design, sample, data collection and/or data analysis. Other reviews have incorporated all studies within a time period or on a specific topic.

The reviews differ in the extent to which they have found consistencies in the research results. This is due in part to differences in the studies included in the reviews, in part to differences in reviewer expectations for consistent results across the reviewed studies, and in part to differences in the methods used to synthesize the results of multiple studies. Most reviews have used a tabulation method where the positive, negative and nonsignificant findings from separate studies have been tabulated to reach a general conclusion about whether a specific teacher behavior is related to student learning. Rosenshine's reviews are examples of this tabulation approach.

The general consensus of reviewers is that some patterns of teaching behaviors are related to increased student learning, but the effectiveness of those patterns may vary by type of students, by content area and by level of student learning. Whether this general consensus, coupled with conclusions about relationships between specific teaching behaviors and specific types of student learning for some types of students, represents a significant impact from research on teaching depends upon the level of expectations for social science research in general and studies of teaching in particular.

Some documents provide overviews of research on teaching. A few histories of research on teaching are available, e.g., Lanier (1978) and Medley (1972). Predictions of future research directions are made occasionally e.g., Koehler (1978) and Gage (1978). A number of documents provide brief summaries of studies of teaching, sometimes citing a small number of studies. Some of the summary documents present models or theories of teaching, such as Bush's discussion (1971) of the roles of teachers and Doyle's descriptions (1977) of models of teaching and the research designs associated with research related to those models. The assumptions underlying the research designs used in most studies of teaching and the resulting approaches to the use of the research findings are discussed in Fenstermacher's article (1978), although such analyses of the research are rare. Other summary documents discuss the implications of several studies, illustrated by Powell's article (1978), which briefly describes the results of several cited studies and then focuses on the implications of the summary information for teachers and for teacher education.

Infrequently an annotated bibliography of a specific topic

will be compiled, such as that which McKenna (1971) compiled on teacher evaluation. More frequently, reviews and reports of individual studies are compiled into books, which may contain new articles (e.g., Borich, 1977) or reprints of articles already published elsewhere (e.g., Amidon and Hough, 1967).

Factors Influencing Increased Study of Teaching

Many factors have influenced the increase in studies of teaching from 1965 through 1980. The federal funding of a number of educational programs provided the impetus for some studies of teaching. The federal programs grew out of a policy concern for quality education for students traditionally not well served by the educational systems, such as disadvantaged, black and handicapped students. With federal money came attention at the state and local levels to effective ways to teach children who had not succeeded within the schools. This concern translated into research and evaluation studies intended to identify effective teaching methods and instructional programs, in the process encouraging studies of teaching (e.g., Stallings and Kaskowitz, 1974).

The growing concern for teacher accountability and the evaluation of teachers also sparked an increase in studies of teaching. To provide the information to support programs of teacher accountability, researchers sought to identify effective teaching behaviors. School districts interested in evaluating teachers, and states seeking an empirical measure of the skills of teachers in order to make decisions about the issuance of teaching credentials, sought information about effective teaching skills. Coker (1976) describes a program of research in Georgia and Powell (1976) describes one in California conducted to provide information relative to teacher certification. The development of Competency-Based Teacher Education programs in which candidates worked to master, and to demonstrate mastery of, specific teaching skills, provided a further impetus to the study of teaching. In all these instances, descriptive information about the behaviors which teachers exhibit was not sufficient; the behaviors needed to be related to changes in student behavior, most frequently to student learning.

3. OVERVIEW OF BIBLIOGRAPHIC TOPICS

The documents cited in this bibliography have been divided into categories, and in most cases into subcategories. A brief description of each of the categories is presented in this section. The categories used form one of many possible sets; they have been chosen because they organize the citations into clusters which are fairly clear-cut and which provide a logical sequence. The nine categories which have been selected are described as follows.

Teacher Characteristics

A number of studies describe teacher characteristics. Some of these focus on demographic characteristics, such as age, sex, years of experience, type of teacher training; others describe teacher personality characteristics. Some studies consider the influence of teacher characteristics on some aspect of teaching, such as teacher attitudes and behaviors and student achievement. Many of these studies measure one or a few teacher characteristics and relate them to student outcomes. Relatively few studies consider the interrelationships among teacher characteristics, and even fewer studies investigate the relationships between complexes of teacher characteristics and student outcomes. Reviews of studies of teacher characteristics are also presented.

Teacher Expectations

One group of studies—of teacher expectations—is unique in that the researchers actively attempted to influence or manipulate the teachers participating in the study. Perhaps the best-known of these is Rosenthal and Jacobson's study (*Pygmalion in the Classroom*, 1968), in which the researchers told teachers that a (randomly selected) group of students would experience a sudden spurt in achievement and the researchers found higher end-of-year achievement scores for those students. Rosenthal and Jacobson's study was the subject of a number of critiques; the most widely cited is the critique by Elashoff and Snow (1971).

Reviews and critiques of this group of studies are included in this section.

A number of studies have tried to measure rather than change teacher expectations for students. These descriptive studies have been classified with a larger group of studies of teacher perceptions.

Teacher Perceptions

Teachers' views of many aspects of education have been studied during the fifteen years covered by the bibliography. Most of these studies are descriptive, although a few try to relate teacher perceptions to behavior. The studies are presented in three subcategories. The first includes studies of teacher perceptions of their schools and districts. Studies of teacher perceptions of their own teaching compose the second subcategory. The third and largest subcategory contains studies of teacher perceptions of students. Many of these investigate the sources of teacher expectations for students, variations in those expectations by student characteristics and the effects of the expectations. A number of reviews of this body of literature are available, e.g., Brophy and Good (1972), and these are cited in the appropriate subcategory.

Teacher Behavior

The development of methods for accurately defining, observing and recording the classroom behaviors of teachers and students resulted in a large number of studies which describe the behaviors of classroom participants. Those studies which describe teacher behavior, both in and out of the classroom, are included within the first subcategory, descriptions of teacher behavior. The second subcategory, consistency of teacher behavior, contains studies which provide information about the consistency of teacher behaviors across various contexts. Some of these studies report on the behaviors of the same teachers with different students or in different teaching situations; other studies describe the behaviors of different teachers. The common thread is a comparison of teacher behaviors. A third subcategory contains studies of teacher planning, before and during instruction, including studies of the sources of information which teachers use in planning, the nature and content of teacher planning activities and the decisions which teachers make during instruction. Studies of the factors which influence teacher behaviors compose a fourth subcategory which includes studies of both teacher characteristics and factors external to the teacher, such as school and student factors. The fifth subcategory includes reviews of studies of teacher behavior.

The Influence of Teacher Behaviors

The largest category of studies in this bibliography is that which includes research on the influence(s) of teacher behaviors. Many studies which describe teacher behaviors are included here because they go beyond description by relating teacher behaviors to student behaviors or learning. The first subcategory in this section contains studies of the influence of teacher behaviors on student behaviors, such as time-on-task or disruptive behaviors and the second subcategory includes studies of the influence on student self-concept. Studies of the influence of teacher behaviors on student achievement compose the third category. The fourth subcategory, experiments and training studies, includes studies in which the researcher has influenced the behaviors of teachers, through training or involvement in an experiment. Again, the last subcategory contains reviews of the studies within this category.

Teacher-Student Relations

Those studies focusing on the interactions between teachers and students, rather than only on the behaviors of teachers or students, are included in this category. Some of these studies describe the sequences of language interactions in the classroom and others describe effects of students on the interactions between teachers and students.

Students

Studies of students which contain information about teachers and describe student responses to teachers are included within two subcategories. The first contains studies which describe the perceptions of students about classroom events, including the interaction between the teacher and the students. The second subcategory contains studies of the behaviors of students in classrooms. For the most part, these studies describe either the academic or the social behavior of students, but not both.

Methodology

Many articles and some books which address methodological issues in the study of effective teaching have been published. No attempt has been made to compile information about all of the potential citations within this category because of the large number of citations and the number of subcategories which would be subsumed under the general category of methodology. Instead, a few key documents have been cited to provide a brief indication of the range of methodological issues which need to be considered in studies of teaching. A few of the entries discuss several methodological issues in research on teaching, perhaps best exemplified by the oft-cited discussion of "Impediments to the Study of Teacher Effectiveness" (Berliner, 1976). Some documents deal with specific methodological issues, such as reliability and generalizability of observations, the unit of analysis for classroom data and issues in the use of ethnographic techniques. Some documents deal with techniques for statistical analysis of observational data. Other documents deal with the relationship between correlational studies and experiments, and the problems of using correlational results to design training studies.

Summaries and Essays

A number of documents provide brief summaries of research on teaching. Unlike reviews, they do not contain a detailed presentation of the results of a comprehensive review of studies or a description of the procedures followed to complete the summarization. They do present the author's summarization of results, sometimes citing a small number of studies. Some of the summary documents present models or theories of teaching. Histories of the study of teaching are also included within this category, as are discussions of the implications of the results of research on teaching.

4. FUTURE DIRECTIONS OF RESEARCH

Future studies of teaching can be expected to take several directions, many of them built upon the work of the recent past. Research on teaching will continue to be conducted for many purposes, e.g., to understand teaching and the interactions between classroom participants; to evaluate teachers or to develop and refine systems used to evaluate teachers; and to provide information to form the basis for inservice and preservice education programs to improve teaching. An increasing number of studies will be conducted to evaluate the effects of inservice education programs, both on the teachers who participate in them and on the students of those teachers.

Studies describing teacher behaviors will be conducted. Some of these will describe the behavior of individual teachers across contexts, such as time, type of lesson or observation occasions. Some studies will investigate small units of behavior, such as teacher academic feedback to students. Some studies will seek reasons for variations in behaviors of teachers, variations among teachers within the same context and variations across contexts, such as with different students, for individual teachers. These studies will address the question of why teachers behave as they do.

Researchers will continue to address questions about relationships between teaching contexts and teaching behaviors. Such studies will investigate many aspects of context, such as the organizational structure of a school, the nature and mix of students in a class, variations across the school year, the influence of the curriculum and teaching methods. Studies of the effects of educational innovations will continue to add to this group of studies of the effects of context on teaching.

The current national focus on basic skills, manifested as a concern for student reading and computational skills, will influence researchers' focus on this area. However, as other portions of the curriculum receive increased attention and if schools demonstrate success in teaching basic tool skills to the majority of students, the attention of some researchers will be directed to additional subject areas. The general tendency to apply knowledge gained in one area (the teaching of basic skills) to other areas (the teaching of other subjects) will also lead to studies of teaching of other subjects.

The large majority of studies of teaching have occurred at the elementary level, for a number of reasons. However, several researchers are studying teaching at the junior and senior high school levels. Some of this is prompted by the concern for student mastery of basic skills at the secondary level, as evidenced by the movement for competency testing as one component of the requirements for high school graduation. Other factors are also at work, including a desire to test the applicability of knowledge about teaching at the elementary level to teaching at the secondary level. This movement to the secondary level will strengthen the movement toward studies of teaching of more subject matter areas, since more defined areas are taught at the secondary level

Researchers will continue to address questions of teacher perceptions of teaching, both their own teaching and their ideals of teaching. This is due in part to a recognition that teachers have conceptions of teaching or practical wisdom about what they do and that knowledge about that wisdom can illuminate the results of other studies. The current emphasis on generating knowledge of teaching to change and, it is assumed, to improve teaching will support the continuation of research on teacher perceptions, since researchers who understand teacher perceptions of the classroom and of teaching will be better able to identify ways of changing teacher behaviors. Other studies will investigate teacher perceptions of other aspects of teaching, such as the curriculum, student behaviors and the role of diagnosis and planning within instruction.

Studies of teacher expectations will continue, with researchers investigating variations among teachers in the ways that teachers form expectations and in the extent to which expectations for students influence both the behaviors of the teachers and the achievement of the students. However, these studies will become more complex investigations of teacher use of information about students to form expectations and to attribute causes for behaviors—a movement away from the earlier, simpler studies in which teachers were given false information about students. Teacher expectation studies using simulation techniques will consider more factors within each study rather than varying only one factor, such as student sex, across the sets of students to whom teachers are asked to respond in the simulation.

Studies of the implementation of instructional innovations, especially new curricula and instructional technologies and the effects of those curricula and technologies on teachers and students will increase. Since the funds available to schools to support innovations will be limited for some period of time, the varied pressures which schools face will provide an impetus to try new programs only if they have been studied and their effects can be described. This will encourage increased attention to teachers and the constraints of teaching in the development and packaging of programs and materials. The influence of technological advances, such as the increasing accessibility of microcomputers, will result in growing attention to their use and potential use by teachers and students.

Studies of the effects of inservice education will continue and will be tied to measures of changes in both the behavior of the teachers participating in the inservice and in the behaviors and academic achievement of their students. Several factors will motivate studies of effects of inservice education programs: the current decline in school enrollments (and potential renewal of growth), the cutbacks in school budgets forcing teacher lay-offs rather than the hiring of newly-trained teachers, and teachers' concerns that evaluation systems lead to programs to improve teaching skills rather than to teacher terminations.

Many of the researchers who have been conducting process-product studies, looking at the relationship between observed teacher behaviors and student learning, have started to conduct training studies; this trend will continue, in keeping with the current emphasis on inservice education. Many of these studies will be conducted in the classroom rather than in the laboratory. These training studies will, more and more, involve models of aspects of teaching developed from the results of correlational studies. The models will be context-specific; they will describe one aspect of effective teaching such as reading for remedial secondary students or classroom management at the start of the school year. In the training studies, teachers will learn both specific behavior patterns and general rules about the conditions in which to use the behavior patterns. This type of model, dependent upon teacher understanding of the model and planning for its application, as opposed to rigid rules to be applied in all situations, will also encourage studies of teacher planning for and understanding of instruction.

Teachers will continue to participate in planning and conducting a small number of studies of teaching. This will be true because of pressures from funding sources, and because access to teachers as research subjects will become even more difficult, leading researchers to offer participation in the research planning and the data analysis as an incentive for teacher and district participation. To the extent that studies of teaching are conducted by or in conjunction with school districts involved in the evaluation of teachers, some teachers will cooperate on the basis of the participation in all stages of the research. However, it is important to note that the involvement of teachers in conducting research on teaching is more difficult than it may sound at first. A variety of problems, not the least of which is the amount of time necessary for teacher participation in all the steps of the research process, will limit the involvement of teachers in research efforts.

Ethnographic studies will increase, as more researchers are trained to conduct such studies and as recognition grows that they can provide information about teaching, especially when they involve teachers in some aspects of the research. At present, studies can be jointly planned to enable clear compilation of results across studies but the synthesis of results across disparate studies is difficult. As the number of separate ethnographic studies increases, researchers will develop and refine procedures to synthesize results across studies.

Studies which follow teachers and students for several years may be conducted. The growing acceptance of studies based on a small number of teachers, the recognition of the importance of context in shaping the behaviors of both teachers and students, and the interest in the consistency or variability of teacher behaviors will all encourage researchers to conduct longitudinal studies. At the same time, the uncertainties associated with research funding make such research difficult to plan and conduct.

Another research method, simulations, will be used in ever-more complex studies, incorporating more variables within a single study. Information will be presented to teachers in a variety of ways, such as through the computer simulations of teacher diagnosis of student reading problems that have been developed at the Institute for Research on Teaching at Michigan State University. Many simulation studies will become more extensive, resembling laboratory studies of teaching in which teachers participate in several teaching steps, such as planning for, conducting and evaluating an instructional sequence. Simulation studies will be used within organized programs of research on teaching to provide the basis for studies of preservice and inservice training of teachers, in the way that microteaching provided one basis for studies of teaching in the classroom.

Attention will be devoted to the synthesis of results across studies. One impetus for increased attention to syntheses of research results is the pressure for documentation of the value of the teaching approaches being taught within pre- and inservice education programs. The inconsistencies in reviews of research on teaching and the increasing number of people familiar with meta-analysis procedures will encourage the use of meta-analysis of collections of studies on teaching. The variety in existing studies, including variety in teacher behaviors, grades, subject matter and student types studied, will also encourage more uses of case study approaches to synthesis. The findings from individual studies will be compiled in terms of the specific characteristics of the studies, to present a coherent picture of the results across different portions of the same general field of study.

Correlational studies will be small, involving a few classrooms within a close geographic area, because of limitations on funds for such studies, and because of the decline in large-scale evaluations of federally-funded educational programs. However, studies will be conducted in local school districts, to investigate the effects of inservice education or teacher evaluation programs. These studies may combine the development of models of teaching to form the basis for inservice training with observations before and after training.

The prediction might be made that researchers will increasingly utilize existing data bases to conduct secondary analyses aimed at answering questions not considered in original studies. This approach would enable researchers to conduct some research without the costs of collecting data. However, a number of factors, including both the costs of documenting existing data sets sufficiently to enable them to be used by other researchers and the absence of mechanisms for the easy exchange of data, will probably preclude increases in secondary analysis within the field of research on teaching, although these authors might hope otherwise.

5. SOURCES OF INFORMATION

There are many sources of information about research on teaching. The *Journal of Classroom Interaction*, formerly called the *Classroom Interaction Newsletter*, is the sole journal devoted exclusively to studies of teaching. It publishes reports of classroom studies, reviews of research and discussions of methodological issues and of future research directions. Research articles appear in many education and educational psychology journals; e.g., *American Educational Research Journal*, *Journal of Educational Research*, *Journal of Educational Psychology*, *Journal of Experimental Education*, *Journal of School Psychology*.

During the years of extensive attention to science education, when the federal government funded a number of programs to improve the teaching of science at both the elementary and secondary school levels, many studies investigated teachers' use of the newly-developed science curricula. Those studies can be found in science education journals, such as *Journal of Research in Science Teaching* and *School Science and Mathematics*. Much research attention is directed to the teaching of reading, and many reports of research are found in reading journals, such as *Reading Improvement* and *Reading Research Quarterly*. Nontechnical reports and summaries of research are found in many educational journals. For example, the *Journal of Teacher Education* includes reports of research which are somewhat less technical than those in the research journals. The *Review of Educational Research* is devoted exclusively to reviews of educational research, including studies of teaching. Some volumes of *Review of Research in Education* and the *Yearbook of the National Society for the Study of Education* contain reviews of research on teaching and/or discussions of methods used to study teaching.

Many publishers have published individual books reporting research or synthesizing results of several studies. A new series, published jointly by the Institute for Research on Teaching at Michigan State University and Longman, Inc., will present results of individual studies. The first volume of the series, (*Student Characteristics and Teaching*, Brophy and Evertson) was published in 1981 and several volumes will be available in 1982.

Many technical reports of research are available through the ERIC system. Computerized search procedures for *Resources In Education* (*RIE*) and *Current Index to Journals in Education* (*CIJE*), allow for quick access to documents reporting and synthesizing research and discussing the implications of that research, although the documents are printed in a variety of sources.

Many studies of teaching are conducted by graduate students as dissertation research. While some of these studies are eventually reported in journals, all of them are more thoroughly described within dissertations and many are never reported in journals. This makes *Dissertation Abstracts* an important source of information about a large group of studies.

Research on teaching is reported at many conferences each year. Major national conferences include the annual meetings of the American Educational Research Association and the American Psychological Association; both groups include many researchers in this field. Other national organizations, such as the Association for Supervision and Curriculum Development, the American Association of Colleges of Teacher Education and the National Education Association, include reports of research within their annual meeting programs. Meetings of subject matter groups, such as the International Reading Association, usually include presentations of research on teaching of the subject around which the association is organized. Many regional associations, such as regional research, educational psychology and subject matter associations, include presentations of research reports within their programs. Many of the papers presented at these conferences are submitted to ERIC, which actively seeks copies from presenters and announces them in *RIE*, making them available to a wide audience.

Many government and other funding sources have, in the past, sponsored studies of teaching which resulted in extensive reports as sources of information. However, in the near future, the majority of the funds for large-scale efforts or for programs of study encompassing a number of individual research efforts, will come from the federal government, through the National Institute of Education of the Department of Education, or its successor in a reorganized education unit within the executive branch of government. Other funds will come from districts interested in studying teacher evaluation or teacher inservice education programs. Some funds will come from developers or publishers seeking information about curricular materials and teacher training programs prior to publication and distribution of those programs. Graduate students are another source of continued study of teaching. Many of the studies cited in this bibliography were conducted as doctoral dissertations and these efforts will continue. Such shifting of funding and effort will make locating relevant research a continuing task of hunt and find.

6. MAJOR INSTITUTIONS

The National Institute of Education of the U.S. Department of Education funds many studies of teaching, through the Division of Teaching and Learning. The studies are conducted in various universities and in NIE-sponsored education research and development laboratories and centers around the country. NIE also funds, or participates in decisions to fund, many studies of other aspects of schooling which incorporate studies of teaching. For example, studies of compensatory education and bilingual education programs include studies of the teaching which occurs in those programs.

The Institute for Research on Teaching (IRT), located at Michigan State University, conducts studies in several areas of teaching, funded both through a basic grant from the National Institute of Education and through competitively-awarded funds for specific research efforts. Areas of particular interest have been teacher diagnosis of reading problems and prescriptions for those problems, studies of teacher planning and perceptions of aspects of teaching, such as student reading interests, factors within and outside the school which influence teacher decisions, teaching of mathematics, science, writing and language arts, as well as methodological issues related to the various ways that researchers study teaching. Reports of research conducted at the IRT are available through publications distributed by the IRT, through journal articles written by researchers affiliated with the IRT, and through research reports submitted to the NIE and available through the ERIC system.

Two of the NIE-supported research and development laboratories have extensive programs of research on aspects of teaching; the Center for Research and Development for Teacher Education at the University of Texas in Austin and the Far West Laboratory for Educational Research and Development in San Francisco. Both of these organizations have been studying teaching for many years and conduct coordinated programs of research and development based on that research. Funding for their programs comes through the basic funding which NIE provides and through competitively-awarded research contracts. Like the IRT, both organizations maintain a distribution office to make research reports available, and submit documents for distribution through the ERIC system, as well as encouraging researchers to publish in various journals.

Focused programs of research on teaching are conducted at other universities, such as at the Center for the Study of Social Behavior at the University of Missouri-Columbia and the Center for the Study of Individualized Schooling at the University of Wisconsin-Madison. A coordinated program of research on teaching, including many experimental laboratory studies, was conducted at the Stanford Center for Research in Teaching, which has now shifted its focus to educational finance and policy issues. The Center for Reading Research at the University of

Illinois at Urbana-Champaign also conducts some studies of teaching within its focus on reading.

Individual researchers work in many universities and private research organizations. A listing of them would be long and probably not useful, as their work can conveniently be located through journals and the ERIC system. As the field of research on teaching grows and expands, more researchers will conduct and publish studies, adding to our knowledge of effective teaching.

REFERENCES

Amidon, Edmund, and Giammatteo, Michael. "The Verbal Behavior of Superior Elementary Teachers," in *Interaction Analysis: Theory, Research and Application*. Edited by Edmund J. Amidon and John B. Hough. pp. 186–188. Reading, Massachusetts: Addison-Wesley Publishing Co. 1967.

Amidon, Edmund J., and Hough, John B., editors. *Interaction Analysis: Theory, Research and Application*. Reading, Massachusetts: Addison-Wesley Publishing Co. 1967.

Anderson, Linda M., Evertson, Carolyn M., and Emmer, Edmund T. "Dimensions of Classroom Management Derived from Recent Research," *Journal of Curriculum Studies 12* (1980): 343–456.

Bass, Jo Ann Scott. Effects of an Inservice Program on Teacher Planning and Student Achievement with Middle School Social Studies Teachers. Ph.D. dissertation. University of Texas at Austin. 1980.

Berliner, David C. "Impediments to the Study of Teacher Effectiveness," *Journal of Teacher Education 27*, No. 1 (1976): 5–13.

Berliner, David C. "Tempus Educare," in *Research on Teaching: Concepts, Findings and Implications*. Edited by Penelope L. Peterson and Herbert J. Walberg. Berkeley, California: McCutchan Publishing Corporation. 1979.

Borg, Walter R., and others. "Teacher Classroom Management Skills and Pupil Behavior," *Journal of Experimental Education 44* (1975): 52–58.

Borich, Gary. *The Appraisal of Teaching: Concepts and Process*. Reading, Massachusetts: Addison-Wesley. 1977.

Borko, Hilda, and Shavelson, Richard J. "Teachers' Sensitivity to the Reliability of Information in Making Causal Attributions in an Achievement Situation," *Journal of Educational Psychology 70* (1978): 271–279.

Brophy, Jere E., and Evertson, Carolyn, M. *Student Characteristics and Teaching*, New York: Longman, Inc. 1981.

Brophy, Jere E., and Evertson, Carolyn M. "The Texas Teacher Effectiveness Project: Presentation of Non-linear Relationships and Summary Discussion." Austin, Texas: Research and Development Center for Teacher Education. University of Texas at Austin. 1974. *ERIC ED* 099 345.

Brophy, Jere E., and Good, Thomas L. "Teacher Expectations: Beyond the Pygmalion Controversy," *Phi Delta Kappan 54* (1972): 276–278.

Bush, Robert. "Redefining the Role of the Teacher," in *Teachers and the Learning Process*. Edited by Robert D. Strom, pp. 142–150. Englewood Cliffs, New Jersey: Prentice-Hall, Inc. 1971.

Byers, J.L., and Evans, T.E. "Children's Reading Interests: A Study of Teacher Judgement." Research Series No. 81. East Lansing, Michigan: Institute for Research on Teaching. Michigan State University. 1980.

Clark, Christopher M., and others. "Student Perceptions of Teacher Behavior as Related to Student Achievement," *Journal of Classroom Interaction 12*, No. 1 (1976): 17–30.

Clark, Christopher M., and Others. "Student Perceptions of Teacher Behavior as Related to Student Achievement," *Journal of Classroom Interaction 12*, No. 1 (1976): 17–30.

Coker, Homer. "Identifying and Measuring Teacher Competencies: The Carroll County Project," *Journal of Teacher Education 27*, No. 1 (1976): 54–56.

Cooper, H.M., Hinkel, G.M., and Good, T.L. "Teachers' Beliefs about Interaction Control and Their Observed Behavioral Correlates," *Journal of Educational Psychology 72* (1980): 345–354.

Crawford, John, and others. "Classroom Dyadic Interaction: Factor Structures of Process Variables and Achievement Correlates," *Journal of Educational Psychology 69* (1977): 761–772.

Doyle, Walter. "Paradigms for Research on Teacher Effectiveness," *Review of Research in Education. Vol. 5* Edited by Lee S. Shulman. pp. 163–198. Itasca, Illinois: F.E. Peacock Publishers, Inc. 1977.

Durkin, Dolores. "What Classroom Observations Reveal about Reading Comprehension Instruction," *Reading Research Quarterly* 14 (1978–1979): 481–533.

Ebmeier, Howard and Good, Thomas L. "The Effects of Instructing Teachers about Good Teaching on the Mathematics Achievement of Fourth Grade Students," *American Educational Research Journal* 16 (1979): 1–16.

Elashoff, Janet D. and Snow, Richard E. *Pygmalion Reconsidered: A Case Study in Statistical Inference: Reconsideration of the Rosenthal-Jacobson Data on Teacher Expectancy.* Worthington, Ohio: Charles A. Jones Publishing Company. 1971.

Emmer, E., Good. T.L., and Pilgrim, G.H. "Effects of Teacher Sex." Austin, Texas: Research and Development Center for Teacher Education. University of Texas at Austin. 1972

Evertson, Carolyn M., and others. "Relationships between Classroom Behaviors and Student Outcomes in Junior High Mathematics and English Classes," *American Educational Research Journal* 17 (1980): 43–60.

Fenstermacher, Gary D. "A Philosophical Consideration of Recent Research on Teacher Effectiveness," in *Review of Research in Education, Vol. 6.* Edited by Lee S. Shulman. pp. 157–185. Itasca, Illinois: F.E. Peacock Publishers, Inc. 1978.

Filby, Nikola N. "Time Allocated to Reading and Mathematics (How It Varies and Why)," *California Journal of Teacher Education* 4, No. 2 (1977): 12–22.

Flanders, Ned A. *Analyzing Teaching Behavior.* Reading, Massachusetts: Addison-Wesley Publishing Company. 1970.

Flanders, Ned A., and Amidon, Edmund J. *A Case Study of an Educational Innovation: The History of Flanders Interaction Analysis.* Oakland, California: 1981.

Friedman, Morton. "Cognitive Emphasis of Geometry Teachers' Questions," *Journal of Research in Mathematics Education* 7 (1976): 259–263.

Gage, N.L. *The Scientific Basis of the Art of Teaching.* New York: Teachers College Press. 1978.

Gall, Meredith D. "What Effect Do Teachers' Questions Have on Students?" 1973. *ERIC ED* 077 882.

Gil, Doron. "The Decision-making and Diagnostic Processes of Classroom Teachers." Research Series No. 71. East Lansing, Michigan: Institute for Research on Teaching. Michigan State University. 1980.

Good, Thomas L., and Beckerman, Terrill M. "An Examination of Teachers' Effects on High, Middle, and Low Aptitude Students' Performance on a Standardized Achievement Test," *American Educational Research Journal 15* (1978a): 477–482.

Good, Thomas L., and Beckerman, Terrill M. "Time on Task: A Naturalistic Study in Sixth Grade Classrooms," *Elementary School Journal 78* (1978b): 193–201.

Hess, Robert D., and Takanishi-Knowles, Ruby. "Teacher Strategies and Student Engagement in Low-income Area Schools." Research and Development Memorandum No. 105. Stanford, California: Stanford Center for Research and Development in Teaching. Stanford University. 1973. *ERIC ED 087 768*.

Jackson, Philip W. *Life in Classrooms*. New York: Holt, Rinehart and Winston, Inc. 1968.

Joyce, Bruce R., and Weil, Marsha. *Models of Teaching*. Englewood Cliffs, New Jersey: Prentice-Hall, Inc. 1972.

Kennedy, John J., and others. "Additional Investigations into the Nature of Teacher Clarity," *Journal of Educational Research 72* (1978): 3–10.

Koehler, Virginia. "Classroom Process Research: Present and Future," *Journal of Classroom Interaction 13*, No. 2 (1978): 3–11.

Lanier, J. E. "Research on Teaching: A Dynamic Area of Inquiry." Occasional Paper No. 7. East Lansing, Michigan: Institute for Research on Teaching. Michigan State University. 1978.

McDonald, Frederick J. "The Effects of Teaching Performance on Pupil Learning," *Journal of Teacher Education 27*, No. 4 (1976): 317–319.

McKenna, Bernard H., and others. "Teacher Evaluation: An Annotated Bibliography." 1971. *ERIC ED 055 988*.

McNair, Kathleen, and Joyce, Bruce. "Teachers' Thoughts While Teaching: The South Bay Study." Part II. Research Series No. 59. East Lansing, Michigan: Institute for Research on Teaching. Michigan State University. 1979.

Medley, Donald M. "Early History of Research on Teacher Behavior," *International Review of Education 18* (1972): 430–439.

Morine-Dershimer, Greta. "Planning in Classroom Reality: An Indepth Look," *Educational Research Quarterly 3*, No. 4 (1978–1979): 83–99.

Peterson, Penelope L., Marx, R.W., and Clark, C.M. "Teacher Planning, Teacher Behavior, and Student Achievement," *American Educational Research Journal 15* (1978): 417–432.

Powell, Marjorie. "Teacher Competencies: California Beginning Teacher Evaluation Study." A paper presented at the American Association of School Administrators, 1976, *ERIC ED* 117 861.

Powell, Marjorie. "Research on Teaching," *Educational Forum 43* (1978): 27–37.

Rist, Ray C. "Student Social Class and Teacher Expectations: The Self-fulfilling Prophecy in Ghetto Education," *Harvard Educational Review 40* (1970): 411–451.

Rohrkemper, Mary M., and Brophy, Jere E. "Influence of Teacher Role Definitions on Strategies for Coping with Problem Students." Research Series No. 51. East Lansing, Michigan: Institute for Research on Teaching. Michigan State University. 1979.

Rosenshine, Barak V. "Content, Time and Direct Instruction," in *Research on Teaching: Concepts, Findings and Implications*. Edited by Penelope L. Peterson and Herbert J. Walberg. Berkeley, California: McCutchan Publishing Corporation. 1979.

Rosenshine, Barak. *Teaching Behaviors and Student Achievement*. London: National Foundation for Educational Research. 1971.

Rosenthal, Robert, and Jacobson, Lenore. *Pygmalion in the Classroom: Teacher Expectations and Pupils' Intellectual Development*. New York: Holt, Rinehart and Winston, Inc. 1968.

Rowe, Mary Budd. "Relation of Wait-time and Rewards to the Development of Language, Logic, and Fate Control: Part II—Rewards," *Journal of Research in Science Teaching 11* (1974): 291–308.

Rupley, William H., and Blair, Timothy R. "Teacher Effectiveness Research in Reading Instruction: Early Efforts to Present Focus," *Reading Psychology 2* (1980): 49–56.

Serafino, Philip Andrew. "Field-dependent and Field-independent Cognitive Style and Teacher Behavior." Ed.D. dissertation. Rutgers University the State University of New Jersey. 1978.

Shulman, Lee S., and Elstein, Arthur S. "Studies of Problem Solving, Judgment, and Decision Making: Implications for Educational Research," in *Review of Research in Education*. Edited by Fred N. Kerlinger. Itasca, Illinois: F.E. Peacock Publishers, Inc. 1975.

Simon, Anita, and Boyer, Gil. *Mirrors for Behavior: An Anthology of Classroom Observation Instruments*. Philadelphia, Pennsylvania: Research for Better Schools, Inc. 1967.

Spiegel, Dixie Lee, and Rogers, Carol. "Teacher Responses to Miscues During Oral Reading by Second-Grade Students," *Journal of Educational Research* 74 (1980): 8–12.

Stallings, Jane A., and Kaskowitz, David H. *Follow Through Classroom Observation Evaluation 1972–1973*. SRI Project URU-7370. Menlo Park, California: Stanford Research Institute. 1974.

Turner, Richard L., and Denny, David A. "Teacher Characteristics, Teacher Behavior, and Changes in Pupil Creativity," *Elementary School Journal* 69 (1969): 265–270.

Van Horn, Royal W. "Effects of the Use of Four Types of Teaching Models on Student Self-concept of Academic Ability and Attitude Toward the Teacher," *American Educational Research Journal* 13 (1976): 285–291.

Walberg, Herbert J. "Physical and Psychological Distance in the Classroom," *School Review* 77 (1979): 64–70.

Weinstein, Rhona Strasberg, and Middlestadt, Susan E. "Student Perceptions of Teacher Interactions with Male High and Low Achievers," *Journal of Educational Psychology* 71 (1979): 421–431.

Winne, Philip H. "Aptitude-Treatment Interactions in an Experiment on Teacher Effectiveness," *American Educational Research Journal* 14 (1977): 389–409.

Teacher Effectiveness

I TEACHER CHARACTERISTICS

A. DESCRIPTION OF CHARACTERISTICS

1. Anderson D.D. "Personality attributes of teachers
   in organizational climates," *Journal of
   Educational Research, 62* (1969): 441-443.

   Describes no differences on most personality
   characteristics between teachers in open and
   traditional schools.

2. Anderson, Gary J. "Effects of course content and
   teacher sex on the social climate of learning,"
   American Educational Research Journal 8 (1971):
   649-663.

   Reports that subject matter, not teacher sex,
   is related to differences in classroom climate.

3. Anonymous. "Combat neurosis in the battered
   teacher," *Science News 114* (1978): 278.

   Describes the symptoms exhibited by many
   teachers as those of combat neurosis.

4. Benell, F.B. "Frequency of misconceptions and
   reluctance to teach controversial topics related
   to sex among teachers," *Research Quarterly of the
   AAHPER 40* (1969): 11-16.

   Reports more misconceptions about social and
   psychological than about biological aspects of
   sex-related topics and that elementary teachers
   have more misconceptions than secondary teachers.

5. Bergman, Janet Lee. Student rights and
   responsibilities: An analysis of student, teacher,
   and administrator knowledge in a school system
   where a well-established policy exists. Ph.D.
   dissertation. University of Maryland. 1979.

   Describes levels of knowledge of
   administrators, teachers and students about

policies related to student rights and
responsibilities; teacher knowledge does not vary
by subject taught and is not related to student
knowledge.

6.   Bridgman, John Northan, Jr. Selected teacher
     characteristics and their relationships with
     certain behavior patterns and teaching
     effectiveness. Ed.D. dissertation. University of
     North Carolina at Chapel Hill. 1967.

          Describes differences in attitudes and
     characteristics of teachers and relationships
     among attitudes and characteristics.

7.   Carter, Phillip Chase. A study of teacher reading
     competency in selected Utah elementary schools.
     Ed.D. dissertation. Brigham Young University.
     1975.

          Describes no difference in reading knowledge
     among categories of educators.

8.   Choate, Joyce S. Elementary classroom teachers of
     Louisiana: Their knowledge of reading,
     professional preparation in reading, experience,
     and ratings by principals and peers. Ed.D.
     dissertation. Memphis State University. 1979.

          Describes teacher knowledge of the teaching of
     reading as greater with more courses and up to ten
     years of experience and related to principal and
     peer ratings of skills.

9.   Clark, Betty Mathis & Creswell, John L.
     "Participants' versus nonparticipants' perception
     of teacher nonverbal behavior," *Journal of
     classroom Interaction 14*, No. 1 (1978): 28-38.

          Describes differences in the order and
     importance of nonverbal cues used in rating
     teacher behaviors and differences in perceptions
     of the behaviors by students and observers.

10. Cortis. G.A. "An analysis of some differences
     between primary and secondary teachers,"
     Educational Research 15, (1973): 109-114.

          Describes personality characteristics of
     elementary and secondary teachers.

11. Crisp, Raymond D. The professional competency of
     Illinois secondary school English teachers: A
     report of the self-evaluations of experienced
     Illinois secondary school English teachers.

Interim report. Urbana, Illinois: Illinois
State-wide Curriculum Center in the Preparation of
Secondary English Teachers. 1968. *ERIC ED* 029
889.

Reports that teacher ratings of their knowledge
are related to demographic characteristics, with
more experienced teachers and teachers with
masters' degrees rating themselves as having more
knowledge than other teachers.

12. Daloisio, Tony Charles. An analysis of the
relationship between cognitive style and the
subject area specialization of secondary teachers
in Connecticut. Ph.D. dissertation. University of
Connecticut. 1980.

Describes differences in cognitive style among
secondary teachers of English, arts, social
studies, science and mathematics.

13. Doty, B.A. A study of the characteristics of women
who begin teaching after age thirty-five. Final
Report. 1968. Naperville, Illinois: North Central
College. 1968. *ERIC ED* 030 585.

Describes higher grades and test scores as well
as more favorable personality characteristics of
women who begin teaching at a later age, compared
with younger female teachers.

14. Eberwein, Lowell D. "The variability of readability
of basal reader textbooks and how much teachers
know about it," *Reading World 18* (1979): 259-272.

Describes teacher knowledge of varying levels
of readability of texts and describes the
readability of certain basal readers.

15. Edelman, Joyce Fleischer. The impact of the
mandated testing program on classroom practices:
Teacher perspectives. Ed.D. dissertation.
University of California, Los Angeles. 1980.

Describes variations across teachers in their
knowledge of tests, preparation of students for
tests, and consistency in teacher reports that
test results do not influence instruction.

16. Ehrlich, Nelson J. A descriptive analysis of
teacher awareness concerning energy sources, use,
and conservation. Ed.D. dissertation. Oklahoma
State University. 1980.

Describes limited knowledge among teachers about energy issues like the production, use and conservation of energy.

17. Eisenberg, Theodore A. "Computational errors made by teachers of arithmetic: 1930, 1973," *Elementary School Journal 76* (1976): 229-237. *ERIC ED* 096 160.

Describes teachers having greater accuracy in arithmetic computations in 1973 than in 1930.

18. Ekstrom, Ruth B. Teacher aptitude and cognitive style: Their relation to pupil performance. 1974. *ERIC ED* 100 496.

Describes teacher knowledge, measured IQ and patterns of thinking.

19. Elbaz, Freema Fayga. The teacher's practical knowledge: A case study. Ph.D. dissertation. University of Toronto, Canada. 1980.

Describes the practical knowledge of one teacher and the structure of that knowledge in terms of five orientations: situational, experiential, theoretical, social and personal.

20. Evans, Thomas E. & Byers, Joe L. Teacher judgement of children's reading preferences. Research Series No. 38. East Lansing, Michigan: Institute for Research on Teaching. Michigan State University. *ERIC ED* 174 955.

Describes characteristics which teachers use to select reading materials for students in relation to student preferences for materials.

21. Fawley, Shirley M. Personality characteristics and job satisfaction among teachers on the elementary, middle, and secondary levels. Ph.D. dissertation. University of South Carolina. 1979.

Describes differences in elementary and secondary teachers in terms of personality characteristics such as empathy and job satisfaction, and differences by teacher sex.

22. Forum, Rhea Ellen Stone. An assessment of classroom teachers' attitudes and knowledge of gifted and talented students. Ph.D. dissertation. University of Oregon. 1980

Describes teacher knowledge about gifted students varying by teacher age and level of graduate education.

23. Frickey, Edward L. A study of the relationships between the critical behavior of teachers, results of the National Teachers Examination and selected socio-economic data. Ph.D. dissertation. Michigan University. 1973.

    Describes a relationship between the National Teachers Examination and grades in high school and college but not teaching behavior during student teaching, sex or socioeconomic level of teacher.

24. Giannangelo, Duane M. & Frazee, Bruce M. "Map reading proficiency of elementary educators," *Journal of Geography 76*, No. 2 (1977): 63-65.

    Describes teachers' limited knowledge of map reading skills.
    25. Gillen, James Robert. A comparison of personality characteristics of teachers in traditional and non-traditional classroom settings. Ed.D. dissertation. University of South Dakota. 1979

    Describes differences in the personality characteristics of teachers teaching in open and traditional classroom settings.

26. Golmon, Metton Eugene. Selected teacher traits characteristic of inquiry science teachers and an analysis of the development of these traits in science methods students. 1972. *ERIC ED* 099 178.
    Describes differences among science teachers based on different philosophies of teaching science but no differences by other background variables.

27. Gordon, Audri. A dynamic analysis of the sexual composition of public school teaching: 1870 to 1970. Ph.D. dissertation. 1980.

    Describes forces which have influenced changes over the past one hundred years in the sexual composition of the population of teachers.

28. Greene, William Washington, Jr. The teaching of anthropology in the first and fourth grades: A comparison of the trained and non-trained teachers as measured by pupil test performance. 1966. *ERIC ED* 055 927.

    Describes differences by teacher training but not by teacher knowledge of anthropology, in student learning of anthropology in first and fourth grades.

29. Griffore, Robert J. & Lewis, Jed. "Characteristics
     of teachers' moral judgement," *Educational
     Research Quarterly 3*, No. 1 (1978): 20-30.

          Describes teachers as supportive of authority,
     democracy and the social contract, and their level
     of moral judgement not related to age, sex, years
     of teaching, degree of training or grade level
     taught.

30. Grover, Shirley Pauline. A study of the conceptual
     levels of teachers in the New England states.
     Ed.D. dissertation. George Peabody College for
     Teachers of Vanderbilt University. 1980.

          Describes conceptual levels of teachers, with
     60% at a level defined as high, with no difference
     by sex, level of training or elementary or
     secondary teaching.

31. Halpin, Gerald & others. "Are creative teachers
     more humanistic in their pupil control ideology?"
     Journal of Creative Behavior 7 (1973): 282-286.

          Describes the relationship between teacher
     creative thinking and authoritarian control
     ideology.

32. Handley, Herbert M. & Bledsoe, Joseph C. "The
     personality profiles of influential science
     teachers, regular science teachers, and science
     research students," *Journal of Research in Science
     Teaching 5* (1968): 95-103. Reprinted in *Current
     research in elementary school science*. Edited by
     David L. Williams & Wayne L. Herman, Jr. pp.
     407-419. New York: The Macmillan Company. 1971.

          Describes the personality characteristics of
     three groups of teachers. For Williams & Herman
     reference see citation No. 3040.

33. Harnischfeger, Annegret. Personal and institutional
     characteristics affecting teacher mobility:
     Schools do make a difference. Stanford,
     California: Stanford Center for Research and
     Development in Teaching, Stanford University.
     1975. *ERIC ED* 106 287.

          Reports that teacher characteristics are
     related to teacher leaves of absence but school
     characteristics are related to teacher transfers.

34. Harris, Charles M. & Smith, Sue W. "Man
     teacher--woman teacher: Does it matter?"
     Elementary School Journal 76 (1976): 285-288.

Describes teacher need for personal power and tendency to establish control of the classroom as differing by teacher sex.

35. Harris, Sherrie Lynn. Health misconceptions of elementary school teachers and teacher aides, Ph.D. dissertation, University of Georgia, 1978.

Describes the knowledge which elementary teachers and aides have about health and health instruction.

36. Hellebust, Gwen LaVerne. Relationship between teachers' knowledge of comprehension and questions asked in third and fifth grade reading classes. Ed.D. dissertation, University of Northern Colorado, 1971.

Describes a slight relationship between the number of college credits and reading comprehension, and the cognitive level of questions which teachers ask during reading instruction.

37. Henney, Maribeth & Mortenson, W. Paul. "What makes a good elementary school teacher," *Journal of Teacher Education 24*, No. 4 (1973): 312-317.

Describes characteristics which have been found to be important for effective teaching.

38. Herr, Edwin L. & others. "Characteristics of students identified by teachers as mature and immature," *High School Journal 55* (1972): 177-186.

Reports that teacher characteristics are related to teacher classification of students as mature or not mature, based on teacher responses to student characteristics.

39. Hesler, Marjorie Walsh. An investigation of instructor use of space. 1972. *ERIC ED* 087 052.

Reports that seating arrangments in classrooms are related to teacher sex and use of space but not to personality ratings of teachers.

40. Hess, Karen Matison. The language attitudes and beliefs of Minnesota elementary and high school English teachers. Volumes 1 & 2. 1968. *ERIC ED* 040 994.

Describes the knowledge of teachers about language and linguistics, based on a survey.

41.   Horton, Terry Dean. Teacher characteristics as related to the acceptance or rejection of new curricular ideas. Ed.D. dissertation, New Mexico State University. 1969.

Finds no relationship between teacher personality characteristics and teacher responses to new curricular ideas.

42.   Hounshell, Paul B. & Dieter, Donn L. "The self-image of outstanding biology teacher," *School Science and Mathematics*, 75. (1975): 284-287.

Describes the self-concept of outstanding biology teachers.

43.   Hutton, Clive Lance. A study of the relationship between teacher motivational need and teacher perception of the ideal leadership style. Ph.D. dissertation, University of Missouri-Kansas City, 1979.

Describes no relationship between teacher personality characteristics and perceptions of principal leadership style.

44.   Ilika, Joseph. A critical review of the teacher readership characteristics research and the implication for performance based teaching. 1974. *ERIC ED* 092 912.

Describes teacher attitudes toward their own reading, which is limited, with some teachers having reading problems.

45.   Jablonsky, Adelaide. The exemplary teacher of the disadvantaged: Two views. ERIC-IRCD Urban Disadvantaged Series Number 30. 1972. *ERIC ED* 064 442.

Describes characteristcs of effective teachers based on a survey of teachers nominated by principals.

46.   Janzen, Henry L., Beeken, Don & Hritzuk, John. "Teacher attitude as a function of locus of control," *Alberta Journal of Educational Research* 9 (1973): 48-54.

Describes teachers who have an internal locus of control wanting more control over the classroom environment than teachers with an external local of control.

47. Jenkins, John Mervin. A study of the
     characteristics associated with innovative
     behavior in teachers. Ed.D. dissertation,
     University of Miami, 1967.

     Reports that innovative teachers differ from
     non-innovative teachers in personality
     characteristics such as flexibility,
     dominativeness, complexity, adventuresomeness.

48. Johnson, David W. "Influences on teachers'
     acceptance of change," *Elementary School Journal*
     70 (1969): 142-153.

     Reviews aspects of schools and studies of
     teacher characteristics and teacher role which
     influence teachers' reluctance or willingness to
     accept change.

49. Johnson, Ernestine H. A study to determine the
     legal knowledge of selected first-year school
     teachers in the State of Alabama. Ed.D.
     dissertation. 1979. University of Alabama.

     Describes the limited knowledge of first year
     teachers about legal issues related to schooling.

50. Johnson, Robert Ellsworth. A study of North Dakota
     public secondary school teachers of English for
     the academic year 1967-68. Ed.D. Dissertation.
     1969. *ERIC ED* 048 261.

     Presents demographic information about the
     teachers and their perceptions of their teaching;
     preferred to teach American literature and found
     composition most difficult to teach.

51. Kerr, R.D. & others. "A study of selected
     characteristcs of secondary mathematics teachers,"
     School Science and Mathematics 69 (1969):
     781-790.

     Describes characteristics of secondary
     mathematics teachers in urban, suburban and rural
     areas.

52. Kimball, Merrritt E. "Understanding the nature of
     science: A comparison of scientists and science
     teachers," *Journal of Research in Science Teaching*
     5 (1967): 110-120. Reprinted in *Current research
     in elementary school science*. Edited by David L.
     Williams and Wayne L. Herman, Jr. pp. 393-407. New
     York: The Macmillan Company. 1971.

     Describes and contrasts teacher and scientist
     knowledge of and perceptions of science, and the

scientific process. For Williams & Herman
reference see citation No. 3040.

53.   Lane, Eunice Rachel Cranford. The relationship
      between selected demographic variables and teacher
      strike participation and between teachers' needs
      levels and their inclination to strike. Ph.D.
      dissertation, University of New Orleans, 1980.

          Reports that background characteristics such as
      sex, tenure status and union membership were
      related to teacher reported willingness to
      strike.

54.   Lapp, Diane Karen. A developmental study of
      elementary teachers' ability to write behavioral
      objectives. Ed.D. dissertation, Indiana
      University, 1970.

          Describes a relationship between teacher years
      of experience and ability to write behavioral
      objectives, with less experience associated with
      greater ability to write objectives.

55.   LeFevre, Carol. "Teacher characteristics and
      careers," *Review of Educational Research 37*
      (1967): 433-447.

          Reviews studies of teacher characteristics,
      attitudes and perceptions of teaching careers.

56.   Lumpkins, Bobby Gene. The relationship between
      experienced elementary school teachers'
      role-preferences and their attitude toward
      behavior problems of children. Ed.D. dissertation.
      North Texas State University. 1970.

          Reports differences by teacher age and years of
      experience in their preferences for teacher roles
      and their ratings of the seriousness of student
      behavior problems.

57.   McCabe, Mary Louise Martinez. The relationships
      between teacher effectiveness, teacher
      self-concept, teacher attitude, and teacher
      knowledge in teaching reading. Ph.D. dissertation.
      East Texas State University, 1978.

          Describes a relationship between teacher
      knowledge of teaching reading and teacher
      self-rating of effectiveness, supervisory rating,
      teacher attitude and self-concept.

58. McKenzie, Frank Lee. Psychological horizontal mobility determiners of male teachers employed in public school work in Missouri 1967-68--1976-77. Ed.D. dissertation. University of Missouri-Columbia. 1979.

    Describes a limited relationship between a number of teacher characteristics and horizontal mobility, with teachers who remain in one place having higher salary increases than those who move.

59. McKenzie, Richard B. "An exploratory study of the economic understanding of elementary school teachers," *Journal of Economic Education 3* (1971): 26-31.

    Describes elementary teachers' knowledge of economics in relation to the number of economics courses they report having taken.

60. McNinch, George, "Teachers' knowledge of word pronunciation skills," *Southern Journal of Educational Research 11*, No. 3 (1977): 99-110.

    Describes teacher level of knowledge about word pronunciation for a sample of teachers.

61. Macomber, Sue Ann. Teacher militancy and propensity to strike: An educational philosophical analysis. Ph.D. dissertation. United States International University. 1980.

    Reports that teacher personality is related to causes for which teachers reported that they would strike, with existentialists willing to strike for issues like instructional programs and pragmatists over salaries and fringe benefits.

62. Main, Cecil Lockwood, Jr. A comparative study of personality and behavior of selected secondary science and non-science teachers. 1971 *ERIC ED* 085 174.

    Describes different personality characteristics of science and non-science teachers.

63. Main, Cecil. "Characteristics of a group of women science teachers," *School Science and Mathematics 73* (1973): 286-290.

    Describes differences in personality characteristics of female science and non-science teachers.

64.   Main, Cecil & Hounshell, Paul B. "A comparative
      study of personality and behavior of science and
      non-science teachers," *Journal of Research in
      Science Teaching 10*, No. 1 (1973): 63-73.
          Describes differences in personality
      characteristics and self-reported behaviors of
      science and non-science teachers.

65.   Mertens, Donna M. & Bramble, William J. Identifying
      formal level functioning in classroom teachers.
      1978. *ERIC ED* 152 703.

          Describes teachers' concrete and formal
      thinking and concludes that teachers'
      manifestations of formal thinking may depend on
      the subject matter in which the teacher is asked
      to demonstrate formal thinking.

66.   Mills, Thomas J. Secondary school science and
      mathematics teachers, characteristics and service
      loads. Washington, D.C.: National Science
      Foundation. 1963. *ERIC ED* 030 573.

          Describes characteristics of junior and senior
      high school science and mathematics teachers from
      a national survey conducted in 1960-1961.

67.   Montgomery, Dexter Wood. A comparison of the
      characteristics of highly effective and effective
      junior high/middle school teachers. Ed.D.
      dissertation. Mississippi State University. 1980.

          Describes proportions of teachers rated highly
      effective and effective, with more highly
      effective teachers having received training to
      teacher at the secondary level.

68.   Mullen, Gail Shepherd. Measurement understanding of
      elementary school teachers. Ed.D. dissertation,
      University of Virginia. 1978.

          Describes teacher knowledge of measurement in
      relation to some teacher characteristics.

69.   Myers, Betty Mae. An empirical investigation of the
      relation of teacher perceived problems to teacher
      personality variables and social-demographic
      variables. Ph.D. dissertation. Ohio State
      University. 1977.

          Reports that teacher characteristics and
      personality are related to teacher identification
      of areas in which they are having problems, such
      as student success, control, use of time.

70. Nachtscheim, N. & Hoy, W.K. "Authoritarian
    personality and control ideologies of teachers,"
    Alberta Journal of Educational Research 22 (1976):
    173-178.

    Describes a relationship between authoritarian
    personality and custodial pupil control ideology.

71. National Education Association Research
    Division. Status of public school teachers, 1965.
    NEA Research Bulletin 43, (1965): 67-71.

    Describes teachers by characteristics such as
    age, sex, years of experience.

72. Neuman, Esther L. Horizontal mobility, professional
    enthusiasm, and personal characteristics of public
    school teachers K-12 in rural and small urban
    schools of the mid/south Willamette Valley of
    Oregon. Ph.D. dissertation. Oregon State
    University. 1979.

    Describes no relationship between teacher
    personal characteristics, mobility and enthusiasm
    for teaching.

73. Nickerson, Suzanne Schultz. A comparison of gay and
    heterosexual teachers on professional and personal
    dimensions. Ph.D. dissertation. University of
    Florida. 1980.

    Describes differences in responses on a scale
    of masculinity/femininity but not on perceptions
    of role and influence between gay and heterosexual
    teachers.

74. Norris, Billy Eugene. A study of the self concept
    of secondary biology teachers and the relationship
    to student achievement and other teacher
    characteristics. Ed.D. dissertation. 1970. *ERIC
    ED* 080 294.

    Describes teacher self concept,
    characteristics, biology knowledge and proficiency
    of biology teachers.

75. Osborn, Clifton Earl. A study of the qualifications
    of Mississippi high school biology teachers and
    the relationship of student achievement in biology
    to the subject matter preparation of the biology
    teacher. Ed.D. dissertation. 1970. *ERIC ED* 053
    973.

    Describes teacher characteristics in relation
    to student achievement in biology.

76. Overstreet, George Clark. A study of teacher characteristics in changing and stable schools. Ed.D. dissertation. University of Kentucky. 1970.

     Reports that teachers in changing schools are more open and creative than teachers in stable schools.

77. Patrick, Opal L. "Ethnic students' perceptions of effective teachers," *Educational Research Quarterly 3*, No. 2 (1978): 67-73.

     Describes personality variables of teachers selected as effective by high school students.

78. Peacock, Jerry Nelson. Teachers' knowledge of essential public school laws and school board policies in selected school districts in southeast Texas. Ed.D. dissertation. University of Houston. 1979.

     Reports that teacher knowledge of laws and school board policy are related to the size of the school where teachers teach but not to size of the district, or years of teaching experience.

79. Peck, Robert & others. Teacher characteristics that influence student evaluations. 1978. *ERIC ED* 189 058.

     Reports that teacher characteristics as rated by elementary students are related to pupil ratings of teacher performance.

80. Perez, Joseph F. "Authoritarianism and teamwork disposition in teacher personality," *Peabody Journal of Education 43* (1977): 215-222.

     Reports that teacher personality, age and sex are related to authoritarianism and to attitude toward teamwork.

81. Peyton, Jimmie Andre. Language theories of Kentucky English teachers. 1966. *ERIC ED* 045 658.

     Reports that teacher theories of language are related to teacher educational background, experience and teaching situation, not to teacher's professional affiliation.

82. Prystupa, Peter. How teachers resolve their job-related learning needs: Towards a phenomenological model. Ph.D. dissertation. University of Manitoba, Canada. 1980.

Based on teacher reports, concludes that teachers develop methods for resolving job-related problems based on teacher characteristics, job conditions and the interpretation of the interrelationship of those two.

83. Pugh, Elouise Gross. A study of standardized test knowledge and interpretation by elementary classroom teachers. Ed.D. dissertation. North Texas State University. 1980.

Reports that elementary teacher knowledge of tests is not influenced by the grade taught, years of experience, highest degree earned, but lower than administration expectations.

84. Quinn, Edward Daniel. An investigation of the relationships among teacher characteristics, the predominant socioeconomic class of students, and teacher effectiveness. Ed.D. dissertation. Indiana University. 1968.

Describes a relationship between principal ratings of teachers on two of several scales and whether the school serves working or middle class students, but not a relationship with teacher experience, age, and other demographic characteristics.

85. Raymond, James Hugh. Teacher receptivity to change and its relationship to perceived risk, local-cosmopolitan orientation, and dogmatism. Ed.D. dissertation. University of Southern California. 1979.

Describes a varied relationship between teacher receptivity to change and dogmatism and local-cosmopolitan orientation, risk, and demographic characteristics.

86. Renault, William Reilly. A comparison of teacher dogmatism with administrators' perceptions of teacher behavior and with teachers' receptivity to change. Ed.D. dissertation, University of Miami. 1973.

Describes a relation between teacher dogmatism and characteristics, such as race, years of experience, and between dogmatism and receptivity to change.

87. Rice, William K., Jr. The effects of task-focused and approval-focused discipline techniques. 1975. *ERIC ED* 108 075.

Reports that in an experiment teachers and students received less-desirable ratings when teachers used person-focused desist techniques than when teachers used task-focused descipline techniques.

88. Robinson, Edward H., III & Schumacher, Richard. "Effects of perceived levels of concreteness on cognitive growth," *Humanist Educator 17* (1978): 64-70.

Describes differences in teachers' abilities to express and communicate feelings.

89. Rubin, Louis J. A study of teaching style. 1971. *ERIC ED* 050 027.

Reports that teachers prefer a teaching style which is matched to the situation but a low structured teaching style may be harmful to students and teachers with high anxiety levels.

90. Ryans, David G. Exploratory cross cultural descriptions of self-reported inventory data derived from Teacher Characteristics Schedule (revised form G-70). 1971. *ERIC ED* 058 169.

Describes teacher self-reported opinions about the characteristics of teachers.

91. Ryans, David G. Teacher evaluation research, part I: Consideration of critical issues, feasibility of collaborative research, and overall design. Final report. *ERIC ED* 055 991.

Describes a two day conference and recommendations for extensive research on teacher and student characteristics and behaviors.

92. Schaeffer, Kenneth Ray. The relationship of teacher and student conceptual system and evaluation of teacher behavior. Ph.D. dissertation. University of Southern California. 1978.

Describes differences in students' conceptual systems and evaluations of teachers but not differences in teacher conceptual systems and evaluations of classes.

93. Scheck, Dennis C. & Rhodes, Gregory A. "The relationship between junior high school teachers' rated competence and locus of control," *Education 100* (1980): 243-248.

Describes junior high teachers with internal locus of control being rated as more competent by evaluators than teachers with external locus of control.

94. Sheppard, Moses Maurice. The relationship of various teacher and environmental factors to selected learnings of ninth-grade science pupils. 1966. *ERIC ED* 020 101.

Describes teachers in schools with higher ninth grade science achievement as having more science courses in college, a greater interest in science, fewer different class preparations, a smaller number of students per class, a greater number of student teachers and other differences.

95. Simmons, Leroy. Preferred approaches to the teaching of social studies as they relate to the personal characteristics, socio-political values and political involvement of secondary teachers in Michigan. Ph.D. dissertation. Florida State University. 1980.

Reports that teacher age, experience and attitude toward traditional socio-political values is related to preferred style of teaching social studies.

96. Slan, Daisy F. A study of the relationship between degree of stress and coping preferences among elementary school teachers. Ed.D. dissertation. George Peabody College for Teachers of Vanderbilt University. 1980.

Describes 32% of the teachers experiencing stress and the varying ways that teachers cope with that stress.

97. Slaper, Trudi Jo. The knowledge of Indiana chemistry teachers related to environmental phenomena. Ph.D. dissertation. Indiana State University. 1980.

Describes factors such as teacher background in chemistry and years of teaching experience as predictors of teachers' ability to teach concepts.

98. Smith, Dan Faye. A study of the relationship of teacher sex to fifth grade boys' sex role preference, general self concept and scholastic achievement in science and mathematics. Ed.D. dissertation. University of Miami. 1970. *ERIC ED* 075 185.

Describes greater student perception of
achievement in mathematics problem solving with
male than with female teachers.

99.   Smith, Earl Pearson. An investigation into the
      relationship between selected personal and
      professional characteristics of teachers and their
      preferences for behavioral objectives. Ph.D.
      dissertation. Syracuse University. 1970.

Describes differences between social studies,
art and math teachers in personality
characteristics but no differences by personality
characteristics and subject matter taught and
preference for student behavioral objectives.

100. Stahl, Robert J. & others. Humanistic and
      behavioristic teachers on the precollege level: A
      second report on the non-existent differences
      between them. *ERIC ED* 166 101.

Describes the attitudes and characteristics of
teachers of high school psychology and no
differences between teachers who describe their
courses as humanistic and behavioristic.

101. Tansey, David Phillips. Altruism and teacher
      behavior. Ed.D. dissertation. University of
      California, Los Angeles. 1968.

Describes no relationship between teacher
dedication and reported values given to teacher
behaviors.

102. Taylor, Loren Eldon. Predicted role of prospective
      activity-centered vs. textbook-centered elementary
      science teachers correlated with sixteen
      personality factors and critical thinking
      abilities. 1972. *ERIC ED* 093 631.

Describes different personality characteristics
and cognitive thinking of teachers who use
activity-centered science teaching.

103. Verma, Sureshrani & Peters, Donald L. Day care
      teacher beliefs and teaching practices. 1974. *ERIC
      ED* 104 516.

Describes different teacher beliefs and
practices within day care settings.

104. Walberg, Herbert J. Teacher personality and
      classroom climate. 1967. *ERIC ED* 014 471.

Describes personality characteristics of male high school physics teachers related to their classroom management; for example, teachers with a high need for dependence, power, order, had formal, subservient classes.

105. Walberg, Herbert J. & Welch, Wayne W. Personality characteristics of innovative physics teachers. 1967 *ERIC ED* 015 888.

Describes similarities between innovative science teachers and research scientists, and describes attitudes as related to values and knowledge of physics.

106. Walker, W.J. "Teacher personality in creative school environments," *Journal of Educational Research 62* (1969): 243-246.

Describes high creative teachers as more adaptive, flexible, outgoing, permissive and nurturant than low creative teachers.

107. Weinfeld, Frederico D. & others. Correlational and factorial analyses of items from the Educational Opportunities Survey teacher questionnaire. 1967. *ERIC ED* 017 996.

Indicates, from an analysis of questionnaire responses, eight factors on which teachers differ: experience, teaching conditions, localism of background, socioeconomic background, training, college attended, activities related to teaching, and preference for student ability level.

108. Wright, Benjamin & Sherman, Barbara. Who is the teacher. *ERIC ED* 013 789.

Describes teacher perceptions of the sources of their personality characteristics in terms of their parents, with three types of mothers reported by teachers, loving and supportive, demanding and prohibitive, and outgoing and independent.

109. Wright, Benjamin D. & Tuska, Shirley A. The childhood romance theory of teacher development. 1967. *ERIC ED* 013 779.

Describes different personality dimensions of elementary and secondary teachers and differences in identification with father and mother.

B. INFLUENCE OF CHARACTERISTICS

1. ON TEACHER ATTITUDES AND BEHAVIORS

110. Ade, William Ervin. A study of the relationships between teacher characteristics and congruity, incongruity, and inconsistency with policy positions of teacher organizations. Ph.D. dissertation. University of Illinois at Urbana-Champaign. 1980.

    Describes relationships between teacher characteristics, such as age, and degree of consistency of opinions with official positions of professional organizations.

111. Bates, Gary C. & Watson, Fletcher J.Predicting learning environments from teacher and student personality. 1976. *ERIC ED* 123 111.

    Relates student, teacher and classroom characteristics to classroom climate in physics classrooms.

112. Bean, James Stevens. Pupil control ideologies of teachers and certain aspects of their classroom behavior as perceived by pupils. Ed.D. dissertation. Rutgers University the State University of New Jersey. 1972.

    Describes teacher sex influencing the relationship between teacher behavior and teacher control ideology, with consistency for male but not female teachers.

113. Bledsoe, Joseph & others. Comparison between selected characteristics and performance of provisionally and professionally certified beginning teachers in Georgia. Final Report. 1967. *ERIC ED* 015 553.

    Describes differences in the characteristics of teachers with two different levels of

23

certification and differences in the ratings given
the two groups of teachers by supervisors, based
on classroom behaviors.

114.   Bonnin, Robert Milton. An assessment of
        relationships between certain personality
        variables and teacher performance in teaching
        assignments of higher and lower difficulty. Ed.D.
        dissertation. University of California, Berkeley.
        1970.

            Describes no difference in personality
        characteristics by teaching assignment but
        differences in personality characteristics by
        higher or lower performance in teaching
        assignment.

115.   Boyles, Sandra Weatherwax. The relationship between
        the personality traits of selected elementary
        school teachers and the organizational climate of
        the school. Ed.D. dissertation. Mississippi State
        University. 1979.

            Describes teacher personality characteristics
        related to teacher perceptions of the school
        climate.

116.   Brown, Bob Burton. An investigation of
        observer-judge ratings of teacher competence.
        Final Report. 1969. *ERIC ED* 027 281.

            Describes relationships between teacher
        beliefs, teacher competence, observer beliefs and
        observer ratings of the competence of the
        teachers.

117.   Calder, Mary & others. An exploratory study of the
        possible relationships between teacher's mood and
        teacher's supportive instructional behavior. Vol.
        1. Research Report. San Francisco, California: Far
        West Laboratory for Educational Research and
        Development. 1978. *ERIC ED* 185 012.

            Describes a study of teacher moods in relation
        to behaviors which are supportive of students.
        Related document, *ERIC ED* 185 013, contains nine
        case studies of teachers.

118.   Carleson, Linda Wainscott. Identification of
        articulation referrals in young children in
        relation to teachers' race and experience. Ph.D.
        dissertation. East Texas State University. 1980.

            Reports that Anglo teachers are more accurate
        than black teachers in identifying students

appropriately for referral from videotapes of
students.

119. Carter, Jack Caldwell. Selected characteristics of
     beginning science and mathematics teachers in
     Georgia. 1967. *ERIC ED* 025 425.

     Describes differences in behaviors of first
     year male and female science teachers, with
     females more business-like, stimulating and
     imaginative and males exhibiting more strict
     control and emotional stability.

120. Chalker, Joan Woods. A study, using Interaction
     Analysis, of the relationship between teacher
     dogmatism and the reflective method of teaching
     social studies. Ed.D. University of Pennsylvania.
     1972.

     Describes teachers who have lower dogmatism
     scores as exhibiting more reflective and indirect
     teaching behaviors.

121. Chiu, Lian-Hwang. "Application of self-anchoring
     scaling for study of teaching effectiveness,"
     Journal of Educational Research 65 (1972):
     317-320.

     Describes differences by teacher sex and years
     of experience in their ratings of their
     effectiveness and reports of their teaching
     behaviors.

122. Cook, C. Thomas & Hughes, Hughie. Openness in
     teacher personality and organizational climate.
     1980. *ERIC ED* 182 308.

     Describes no relationship between teacher
     openness of personality and the organizational
     climate of the school.

123. Cortis, Gerald. "Twelve years on--A longitudinal
     study of teacher behavior continued," *Educational
     Review 31* (1979): 205-215.

     Describes teacher characteristics and
     experiences related to teaching ability and
     satisfaction over several years in a study
     conducted in Great Britain.

124. Cropper, Ardeth Parish. Categories of observed
     teachers behavior as related to reported
     self-concept. Ed.D. dissertation. University of
     Arizona. 1971.

Describes no relationship between teacher reported self concept and observed percentages of democratic procedures or the affective content of teacher classroom behaviors.

125.   Crossan, Donna & Olson, David R. Encoding ability in teacher-student communication games. 1969. *ERIC ED* 028 981.

Reports an experiment which found differences in teacher ability to communicate information to students and that redundancy and clarity increased teachers' ability to communicate, but were not related to other teacher characteristics.

126.   Darrow, Lloyd Lee. An analysis of certain selected characteristics of teachers who are teaching non-innovative and selected innovative science curricula. Ed.D. dissertation. University of Nebraska-Lincoln. 1972. *ERIC ED* 099 177.

Describes differences in teacher attitudes toward innovative science curricula by teacher knowledge.

127.   Dershimer, Elizabeth Lovejoy. A study to identify the characteristics of teachers willing to implement computer-based instruction using microcomputers in the classroom. Ed.D. dissertation. Memphis State University. 1980.

Describes characteristics of teachers willing to implement a program using microcomputers as younger and older than other teachers, as reading more professional journals and as having an advanced degree and having traveled more extensively than other teachers.

128.   Dieken, Earl H. The relationship of teachers' self-perceived personality traits to verbal interaction in the classroom. Ed.D. dissertation. Northern Illinois University. 1969.

Describes teacher characteristics related to observed teacher verbal behaviors.Oz3

129.   Dieken, Earl H. & Fox, Raymond B. "Self-perception of teachers and their verbal behavior in the classroom," *Educational Leadership 30* (1973): 445-449.

Describes a relationship between teacher verbal behaviors and perceptions of themselves.

130. Dove, Wayne Edward. Teacher characteristics and
     their relationship to student markings in high
     schools, United States Dependent Schools, Pacific
     Area. Ed.D. dissertation. University of Southern
     California. 1979.

        Describes no relationship between teacher
     characteristics and the giving of failing grades.

131. Duke, Daniel L. "Environmental influences on
     classroom management," In *Classroom management:
     The 78th yearbook of the National Society for the
     Study of Education. Part II.* edited by Daniel L.
     Duke. pp. 333-362. Chicago: University of Chicago
     Press. 1979.

        Reports that environmental factors have lead to
     an increase in teacher control orientation without
     any accompanying increases in teacher authority.
     For Duke reference see citation No. 2940.

132. Dworkin, Anthony Gary. "The changing demography of
     public school teachers: Some implications for
     faculty turnover in urban areas," *Sociology of
     Education 53* (1980): 65-73.

        Describes teacher class background, but not
     race, as related to plans of inner city teachers
     to remain in or leave the teaching profession

133. Edwards, Patricia Ann. An investigation of English
     teachers' knowledge of reading techniques and
     their observed teaching methods. Ph.D.
     dissertation. University of Wisconsin-Madison.
     1979.

        Describes no relationship between teacher
     knowledge and observed behaviors, but describes
     the behaviors of teachers during reading lessons.

134. Ehman, Lee H. Teaching behavior patterns and
     personal teacher attributes related to success and
     failure in specific social studies teaching tasks.
     1973. *ERIC ED* 079 175.

        Reports that in a laboratory setting teacher
     cognitive complexity and attitude toward pupil
     control are not related to teacher behavior but
     behavior and ratings are related to student
     responses to teachers.

135. Ekstrom, Ruth B. The relationship of teacher
     aptitudes to teaching behavior. Beginning Teacher
     Evaluation Study: Phase II, 1973-74, Final Report:
     Vol. V.1. Princeton, New Jersey: Educational
     Testing Service. 1976. *ERIC ED* 127 370.

Describes a relationship between teacher
characteristics, patterns of information
processing and teaching behaviors.

136.   Evans, Thomas P. "Teacher verbal and nonverbal
       behaviors and their relationship to personality,"
       Journal of Experimental Education 38 (1969):
       38-47.

Describes a low correlation between observed
behaviors of teachers and teacher personality
characteristics.

137.   Farrall, Clayton G. "Pupil adjustment as related to
       sex of pupil and sex of teacher," *Psychology in
       the Schools 5* (1968): 371-374.

Describes no differences in the classroom
environment established by male and female
teachers in grades five and six.

138.   Findley, M. & Cooper, H.M. Nonverbal sensitivity,
       teacher expectations and classroom behavior.
       Technical Report No. 239. Columbia, Missouri:
       University of Missouri-Columbia. 1980.

Describes teacher behavior in terms of teacher
expectations for students and variations among
teachers in their expectations.

139.   Finkelstein, David Elliott. The effect of
       conceptual tempo on teacher-student dyadic
       interaction in the classroom. Ph.D. dissertation.
       University of Southern California. 1976.

Describes teacher cognitive tempo not related
to patterns of teacher questions and teacher
response to student answers, but student
conceptual tempo related to pattern of teacher
questions.

140.   Fisher, Francine Priscilla. A study of the
       relationship between the scarcity of women in
       educational administrative positions and the
       multiple factors which influence the career
       aspirations of women teachers. Ph.D. dissertation.
       Michigan State University. 1978.

Describes career aspirations of teachers and
differences in aspirations by selected factors,
such as sex and age.

141.   Flizak, C. W. Organizational structure of schools
       and its relationship to teachers' psychological,
       sociological and emotional role orientation. 1967.
       ERIC ED 017 001.

        Reports that the organizational climate of the
   school is related to the social psychological
   characteristics of the teachers.

142.   Fleming, James T. "Teachers' understanding of
       phonic generalizations," *Reading Teacher 25*
       (1972): 400-404.

        Reports that teacher knowledge of phonics
   generalizations is related to the utility of the
   generalizations.

143.   Frank, Harry & Brown, Clarence. Teachers' belief
       systems and grading practices. *ERIC ED*072 030.

        Reports a relationship between teacher grading
   practices and the consistency of teacher belief
   systems.

144.   Franson, Joseph Paul. An analysis of the
       relationship between needs satisfaction of the
       teacher and the leadership and managerial talent
       of the principal. Ph.D. dissertation. University
       of Connecticut. 1979.

        Describes a relationship between teacher
   personality characteristics (needs) and different
   patterns of contribution to meeting those needs of
   different principal leadership behaviors.

145.   Friedl, Cindy Gay. The relationship between
       knowledge of and use of Bloom's Taxonomy analyzed
       by selected teacher variables. Ed.D. dissertation.
       Northern Illinois University. 1979.

        Describes teacher knowledge of Bloom's taxonomy
   as not related to its use in their teaching.

146.   Friedman, Marianne K. Behavior analysis of reading
       instruction using forced Q sort methodology. 1977.
       ERIC ED 151 727.

        Describes teacher self-reports of teaching
   behaviors not related to grade or pupils but
   related to years of experience.

147.   Gage, Jimmy Allen. A comparison of male and female
       teachers' approval and disapproval interactions
       with children. Ph.D. dissertation. North Texas
       State University. 1969.

        Describes differences in patterns of teacher
   approval and disapproval of students by student
   and teacher sex.

148.   Gardner, Louis & Butts, David. Teacher concerns and
       competency achievement. 1972. *ERIC ED* 064 079.

           Describes teacher experience and level of
           concern related to the learning of new teaching
           skills.

149.   George, Archie A. & Rutherford, William L. Changes
       in concerns about the innovation related to
       adopter characteristics, training workshops and
       the use of the innovation. Austin, Texas: Research
       and Development Center for Teacher Education.
       University of Texas at Austin. 1980. *ERIC ED* 192
       450.

           Describes a limited relationship between
           teacher and principal demographic and personality
           characteristics and responses to innovative
           programs.

150.   Giebink, John W. "A failure of the Minnesota
       Teacher Attitude Inventory to relate to teacher
       behavior," *Journal of Teacher Education 18* (1967):
       233-239.

           Describes a relationship between observed
           teacher behaviors and principal ratings and
           results of the Minnesota Teacher Attitude
           Inventory.

151.   Giese, Ronald Norman. An analysis of selected
       aspects of the ISCS model of science teaching.
       Part I. Relationships of selected characteristics
       and behaviors of teachers using the Intermediate
       Science Curriculum Study. Ed.D. dissertation.
       Temple University. 1971. *ERIC ED* 091 144.

           Reports that training in the use of the new
           science curriculum materials resulted in changes
           in teacher knowledge but not attitude and that
           knowledge of the content and process was related
           to teacher behaviors.

152.   Goldenberg, Ronald. Pupil control ideology and
       teacher influence in the classroom. 1971. *ERIC ED*
       048 099.

           Describes some differences in the verbal
           behaviors of teachers with custodial and
           humanistic pupil control ideologies, with
           humanistic teachers exhibiting more indirect
           teaching.

153.   Goudinoff, Peter. "High school social studies
       teachers: A research note on the relationship of

sex differences to political socialization and
student race," *Teaching Political Science 2*
(1975): 338-344.

Describes differences by teacher sex in the
role that political socialization plays in the
teaching of social studies.

154. Granderson, George. Measurement of teacher
attitudes towards sanctioned activities in the
Detroit public school system. Ph.D. dissertation.
University of Michigan. 1978.

Describes no relationship between teacher
characteristics and attitudes toward strike
activities.

155. Grapho, M.F. & Fraser, J.A. Relationships of pupil
security characteristics and teacher awareness to
pupil security characteristics. *ERIC ED* 054 487.

Describes differences in consistency of teacher
ratings of pupil security needs and in pupil
responses to teachers by teacher marital status,
sex, interest in individual students, and type of
teaching approach.

156. Grant, A.D. A study of the personality
characteristics of the acceptor and the rejector
of the newer educational media among secondary
teachers of Wisconsin. 1969. *ERIC ED* 044 899.

Describes teacher personality traits of
dominance and aggression as related to teacher
rejection of use of audiovisual materials.

157. Guthrie, Larry Fields. A descriptive analysis of
perception and teaching behavior. Ph.D.
dissertation. University of Illinois at
Urbana-Champaign. 1971.

Describes differences in teacher behavior and
perceptions of behavior by differences in teacher
patterns of perception.

158. Haldeman, Jeanene. Individual teacher-student
interaction when matched and mismatched on
cognitive style and the effect upon student self
concept. Ed.D. dissertation. University of
Connecticut. 1978.

Describes no differences in the interactions of
students with teachers who are matched and
mismatched in terms of cognitive style.

159. Maller, Emil J. "Pupil influence on teacher
      socialization: A socio-linguistic study,"
      Sociology of Education 40 (1967): 316-333.

          Describes some aspects of complexities of
      teacher speech with adults, lower complexity for
      primary than for intermediate teachers, related to
      teacher socioeconomic level.

160. Harders, James Henry Lewis. The relationship
      between selected in-service activities and
      supportive behavior by teachers. Ph.D.
      dissertation. University of Minnesota. 1971.

          Describes statements of female teachers as more
      supportive of in-service education than the
      statements of male teachers, but no differences by
      age.

161. Harmsen, Howard Lee. A study of the comparison
      between the interpersonal values of sixth grade
      pupils and their female teachers. Ed.D.
      dissertation. University of Missouri-Columbia.
      1978.

          Describes a relationship between teacher and
      student personal values, differing by student
      sex.

162. Harty, Henry F. A study of cognitive styles: Field
      dependence field independence and teacher-pupil
      interactions. Ed.D. dissertation. Rutgers
      University the State University of New Jersey.
      1978.

          Reports no relationship between teacher field
      dependence and use of specific teaching behaviors,
      but differences in patterns of field dependence by
      teacher sex.

163. Haywood, Gerald Donald. The relationship of job
      satisfaction, job satisfactoriness and personal
      characteristics of secondary school teachers in
      Georgia. Ed.D. dissertation. University of
      Georgia. 1980.

          Describes job satisfaction related to job
      satisfactoriness and level of teacher
      certification.

164. Helsel, A. Ray. "Personality and pupil control
      behavior," *Journal of Educational Administration
      14* (1976): 78-86. *ERIC ED* 090 193.

Reports that teacher dogmatism is related to teacher behavior through teacher pupil control ideology.

165.   Hollinger, Constance Louise. The effects of student dependency, sex, birth order, and teacher control ideology on teacher-student interaction. Ph.D. dissertation. Case Western Reserve University. 1975.

Describes a relationship between teacher sex, birth order and pupil control ideology and teacher ratings of and interactions with students.

166.   Hughes, Evangelina Pena. An analysis of the relationship between teachers' beliefs and the manner of structuring the classroom physical environment. Ed.D. dissertation. University of Illinois at Urbana-Champaign. 1980.

Reports that teacher degree of dogmatism is not related to teacher structuring of the physical environment or to characteristics such as age.

167.   Jenks, Houston Carter. A study of innovation adoption by teachers from a consortium of schools. 1968. *ERIC ED* 028 076.

Describes a relationship between grade, enrollment, teacher and school characteristics and the adoption of Science—A Process Approach, one of the new science curricula.

168.   Jeter, Jan "Teacher expectancies and teacher classroom behavior," *Educational Leadership 30* (1973): 677-681.

Reports a relationship between teacher expectations and teacher behavior toward students.

169.   Jeter, Jan T. & Davis. O.L., Jr. Elementary school teachers' differential classroom interaction with children as a function of differential expectations of pupil achievement. 1973. *ERIC ED* 074 067.

Describes different verbal interactions with students related to different teacher expectations for those students.

170.   Johnson, Sidney Alvin. An analysis of teacher absence behavior in a metropolitan school district. Ed.D. dissertation. University of Houston. 1979.

          Describes a relationship between teacher
characteristics and absences from work.

171. Kirkwood, Kristian John. An examination of some of
      the determinants affecting teacher absenteeism.
      Ed.D. dissertation. University of Toronto, Canada.
      1980.

          Reports that teacher sex, level of education,
      position in the school hierarchy and job
      satisfaction are related to absenteeism.

172. Koon, Joseph Ransome, Jr. Effects of expectancy,
      anxiety, and task difficulty on teacher behavior.
      Ph.D. dissertation. Syracuse University. 1970.

          Describes differences in the behavior of high
      and low anxious teachers toward students whom they
      expect to be competent and non-competent.

173. Koppelman, Kent L'Roy. An ethnographic
      investigation of teacher behavior as a function of
      cognitive style. Ph.D. dissertation. Iowa State
      University. 1979.

          Describes differences in the behavior of
      teachers by their placement on the continuum of
      field dependence—independence, with field
      independent teachers using more impersonal control
      techniques and asking more analytic questions.

174. Krasno, R.M. Teachers' attitudes: Their empirical
      relationship to rapport with students and survival
      in the profession. 1972. *ERIC ED* 067 388.

          Describes teacher attitudes and the
      relationship between attitudes and interactions
      with students.

175. Kremer, Lya & Ben-Peretz, Miriam. "Teachers'
      characteristics and their reflection in curriculum
      implementation," *Studies of Educational Evaluation*
      6 (1980): 73-82.

          Describes teacher characteristics such as
      dogmatism, attitudes, knowledge, seniority and
      locus of control related to the degree of
      implementation of curriculum, with dogmatism the
      most and attitudes the least related.

176. Kuchinskas, Gloria. "Whose cognitive style makes
      the difference?" *Educational Leadership* 36 (1979):
      269-271.

Describes behaviors of teachers and students in classrooms as resulting from the cognitive style of the teacher.

177. Kuhn, David J. "A study of selected elementary school science teaching competencies," *College Student Journal 8*, No. 3 (1974): 68-75.

Describes a relationship between teacher background and characteristics and teacher level of achievement in science teaching competencies.

178. Lorentz, Jeffrey L. & Coker, Homer. Myers-Briggs types as predictors of observed teacher behavior. 1977. *ERIC ED* 150 186.

Reports that teachers with different personality types tend to teach the same way but that students respond to them differently.

179. McCall, Gerald Joseph. The self-concept as a correlate to teacher performance: An empirical study of the relationship between teacher self-concept as measured by the Tennessee self concept scale and teacher performance as measured by the principal's assessment of a teacher instrument of 119 middle school teachers in Clay County, Florida. Ph.D. dissertation. George Peabody College for Teachers. 1978.

Describes some relationships between teacher self concept and ratings of teacher behaviors in the classroom.

180. MacDonald, James B. & Zaret, Esther. "A study of classroom openness," In *Teaching: Vantage points for study.* Edited by Ronald T. Hyman. pp. 197-208. Philadelphia, Pennsylvania: T.B. Lippincott Company. 1968.

Describes the behaviors of more open and more closed teachers and different percentages of time that they spend in different teaching roles. For the Hyman reference, see citation No. 2973.

181. McNeil, Don Crichton. The relationship between psychological and behavioral characteristics of primary teachers and the concept of classroom psychological climate. Ph.D. dissertation. University of Michigan. 1972.

Describes no relationship between teacher personality, educational beliefs, classroom behavior and perceptions of deviant children, with discrepencies between educational beliefs and classroom behaviors.

182. McNeilly, Charles & Wichman, Harvey. Open and
      traditional teachers: Differences in orientation
      to interpersonal relations. 1973. *ERIC ED* 095
      162.

         Describes a relationship between teacher
      personality characteristics and teaching style.

183. Mahlios, Marc Clifford. An exploratory study of
      teacher-student cognitive style and patterns of
      dyadic classroom interaction. Ph.D. dissertation.
      Arizona State University. 1978.

         Describes differences in teacher behavior by
      field dependence-independence, but no relationship
      between match of teacher and student cognitive
      style and number of interactions.

184. Mallen, Leon Peter, Jr. Teacher characteristics and
      values related to the degree of teacher
      participation in curricular and instructional
      development tasks. Ed.D. dissertation. University
      of Virginia. 1978.

         Reports that teacher characteristics are
      related to the degree of teacher involvement in
      curriculum development work.

185. Medley, Donald M. & Hill, Russell A. Cognitive
      factors in teaching style. 1970. *ERIC ED* 038 380.

         Describes a relationship between the teaching
      behaviors of first year teachers and their scores
      on various parts of the National Teachers
      Examination.

186. Mendoza, S., Good, T. & Brophy, J. The
      communication of teacher expectations in a junior
      high school. 1971. *ERIC ED* 050 038.

         Describes differences in teacher behaviors by
      teacher and student conceptual level, with high
      conceptual teachers using more interdependent
      teaching techniques.

187. Miller, John W. "Teachers' ability to judge the
      difficulty of reading materials," *Reading Horizons*
      19 (1979): 151-158. with Marshall, Francis W.
      1978. *ERIC ED* 159 6127.

         Reports no differences between experienced
      teachers and students in a teacher education
      program in their ability to judge the difficulty
      level of reading materials.

188. Moore, Carol Ann. Styles of teacher behavior under simulated teaching conditions. Ph.D. dissertation. Stanford University. 1973.

    Reports that teacher behaviors are related to sex, age, experience and verbal and analytic abilities.

189. Moore, Carol Ann. Teacher styles in questioning and explaining. Technical Report No. 39. Stanford, California: Stanford Center for Research and Development in Teaching. Stanford University. 1973. *ERIC ED* 087 697.

    Describes different teacher behaviors in a simulation related to teacher characteristics.

190. Moore, Charles Emerson. Understanding and use of principles of learning in selected secondary school teachers. Ph.D. dissertation. University of Nebraska-Lincoln. 1980.

    Reports that teacher characteristics and orientation toward teaching were related to teacher knowledge and use of learning principles.

191. Nami, Peter Busama. Relationship between selected social environmental factors with Chatholic secondary lay teachers' strike behaviors. Ph.D. dissertation. State University of New York at Buffalo. 1979.

    Describes characteristics of teacher associated with strike behavior; age, attitude toward the union, but no differences in commitment to a Catholic school system.

192. Ohnmacht, Fred W. Relationships among field independence, dogmatism, teacher characteristics and teaching behavior of pre-service teachers. 1967. *ERIC ED* 011 525.

    Describes differences by student teacher sex and field dependence-independence in behaviors during teaching.

193. Okon, Edet Etim. A descriptive analysis of classroom management approach preferences. Ed.D. dissertation. University of Houston. 1977.

    Describes behaviors of teachers as related to teacher characteristics.

194. Omerza, Daniel Robert. Elementary school climate, personal orientation of teachers and absenteeism. Ph.D. dissertation. St. John's University. 1979.

Describes teacher absence as related to teacher
personality needs and perceptions of school
climate.

195.   Oswald, Richard Charles & Broadbent, Frank
       W. Conceptual level as a determinant of teacher
       behavior and attitudes in a non-structured type
       learning activity. 1972. *ERIC ED* 061 175. first
       author Ed.D. dissertation. Syracuse University.
       1972.

       Describes differences in teacher success in a
       simulation as related to teacher conceptual level,
       attitudes and behaviors.

196.   Parkay, Forrest W. "Inner-city high school
       teachers: the relationship of personality traits
       and teaching style to environmental stress," *Urban
       Education 14* (1980): 449-470. Ph.D. dissertation.
       University of Chicago. 1978.

       Reports that teacher personality
       characteristics are related to the teaching styles
       that emerge in anxiety-provoking environmental
       conditions.

197.   Petrilla, Fred J., Jr. Grades assigned by teachers
       as biased by teacher experience and student
       characteristics. Ph.D. dissertation. University of
       Kentucky. 1978.

       Reports that teacher grading is related to
       teacher experience and knowledge of students,
       based on a simulation.

198.   Piele, Philip K. A social-psychological study of
       classroom verbal behavior. 1969. *ERIC ED* 027 271.

       Describes close-minded teachers as controlling
       and monopolizing classroom talk through a variety
       of teacher verbal behaviors.

199.   Piele, Philip Kern. The relationship of teacher
       open and closed mindedness to classroom verbal
       behavior. Ph.D. dissertation. University of
       Oregon. 1968.

       Describes differences in the verbal behavior of
       open- and closed-minded teachers in a simulation,
       with closed-minded teachers monopolizing classroom
       talk.

200.   Poston, Mary Anne. Teachers' verbal behavior in the
       classroom as related to teachers' locus of
       control. Ed.D. dissertation. State University of
       New York at Albany. 1971.

Describes no differences in teacher interaction patterns between teachers with internal or external locus of control but differences by subject taught and years of teaching experience.

201. Power, Colin N. "Communication in the science classroom--An empirical study of teacher-pupil interactions," *Australian Science Teachers Journal 18*, No. 3 (1972): 61-64.

Describes student personality, student location in the classroom and similarities in teacher and student personality as related to patterns of interactions between teacher and students.

202. Rathbone, Charles & Harootunian, Berj. Teachers' information handling when grouped with students by conceptual level. 1971. *ERIC ED* 050 025. First author, Ph.D. dissertation. Syracuse University. 1970.

Describes differences in teacher teaching behaviors by conceptual level, with high conceptual level teachers using more interdependent teaching techniques.

203. Regan, Ellen Mary. The relationship between teacher beliefs, teacher classroom verbal behavior, and experts' views of selected child development principles. Ed.D. dissertation. State University of New York at Albany. 1967.

Describes no differences in teacher behaviors by expressed beliefs about education, with beliefs similar to those of child development theorists.

204. Reynolds, Florence Saradell. Teacher beliefs and observed classroom behavior. Ed.D. dissertation. University of Arizona. 1972.

Describes no relationship between teacher behavior, teacher self-acceptance and self-satisfaction and teacher fundamental philosophical beliefs.

205. Richards, Mary Lynne. Elementary teachers' attitudes toward and inclusion of home economics in the elementary school, in relation to previous home economics experience. Ph.D. dissertation. University of Maryland. 1978.

Describes teacher attitudes toward home economics in the elementary school in relation to teacher experience and behaviors.

206.   Richardson, William James. A causal comparative
       study of teacher absenteeism in the Dallas
       Independent School District. Ed.D. dissertation.
       East Texas State University. 1980.

           Reports that absenteeism was greater for female
       and younger teachers and greatest at the end of
       the school year.

207.   Rose, Janet Susan. Relationships among teacher
       locus of control, teacher and student behavior,
       and student achievement. Ph.D. dissertation.
       University of South Carolina. 1978.

           Describes teacher behaviors having some
       relationship to locus of control but no
       relationship to student locus of control or
       behavior.

208.   Rosen, Jacqueline L. "Personality and first-year
       teachers' relationships with children," *School
       Review 76* (1968): 294–311.

           Describes teacher background and personality
       factors related to the degree that observers rated
       students as liking the teacher.

209.   Rosenfeld, Carole Patricia. The relationship of
       kindergarten teachers' awareness of their control
       behavior to control behavior style as determined
       in videotape analysis. PH.D. dissertation. New
       York University. 1974.

           Reports some non-significant differences in
       teacher ability to estimate their controlling
       behavior by personality characteristics.

210.   Ross, Dorene Doerre. Teaching beliefs and practices
       in three kindergartens. Ed.D. dissertation.
       University of Virginia. 1978.

           Describes a relationship between teacher
       beliefs and classroom behavior and identifies
       important aspects of teacher beliefs.

211.   Roth, Robert August. The relationship of verbal
       interaction patterns and teacher-student rapport
       of selected ESCP teachers. 1971. *ERIC ED* 085 205.

           Describes differences in teacher verbal
       behaviors related to differences in teacher
       attitudes toward the Earth Science Curriculum
       Project materials.

212. Saletore, Sudha. The relationships between
      teachers' goal orientation, structure and
      observable classroom behaviors. Ph.D.
      dissertation. University of Idaho. 1980.

          Describes a relationship between level of
      classroom structure and teacher affective response
      to students, with low structure teachers having a
      higher ratio of positive to negative affective
      responses.

213. Sandler, Paul. "Sex of teacher and referral
      frequency of sixth-, seventh-, and
      eighth-graders," *Psychology in the Schools 17*
      (1980): 115-116.

          Reports that female teachers referred
      proportionately more students for special
      education than did male teachers.

214. Sawayer, Audrey Evelyn. Teachers' sense-of-control
      in the school organization and its relationship to
      their attitudes toward open education. Ed.D.
      dissertation. University of Massachusetts. 1979.

          Reports that teacher sense of control, or
      ability to influence decisions in a school, is
      related to some behaviors, such as making changes
      in the curriculum, but not other behaviors, such
      as attendance at in-service sessions, or attitudes
      toward open education.

215. Schluck, Carolyn. Using the MMPI to predict teacher
      behavior. 1971. *ERIC ED* 049 313.

          Describes teacher personality characteristics
      measured by the MMPI related to teacher
      behaviors.

216. Sherman, Thomas Francis. A study of the
      relationships between teacher knowledge of
      motivational principles and practices and the
      application of those principles and practices as
      they apply to reading in the second and fifth
      grade classrooms. Ed.D. dissertation. University
      of Colorado at Boulder. 1980.

          Describes some relationships at grade two but
      not grade five between teacher knowledge of
      motivational techniques, reported use of those
      techniques, and student reports of teacher use of
      motivational techniques.

217. Smart, Rosemary & others. "Teacher factors and
      special class placement," *Journal of Special
      Education 14* (1980): 217-229.

Describes attitudes and personality
characteristics of teachers who had and had not
referred children for special class placement.

218.   Smith, B. Othaniel. "Teaching: Conditions of its
       evaluation," In *The evaluation of teaching.*
       Washington, D.C.: Pi Lambda Theta. 1967.

Discusses aspects of teacher behavior related
to teacher personality characteristics and
cognitive and affective aspects of teacher
behaviors. For Pi Lambda Theta reference see
citation No. 3003.

219.   Smith, Douglas K. A study of contrasting styles of
       teacher behavior. 1978. *ERIC ED* 178 785.

Describes different behaviors of teachers with
students by differences in teacher attitudes
toward student socialization.

220.   Smith, Louise Anne. An investigation of the
       relationship between teacher personality and
       classroom interaction at the secondary level.
       Ph.D. dissertation. St. Louis University. 1972.

Describes no relationship between teacher
characteristics and teacher behavior.

221.   Smith, Robert A. An analysis of selected presage,
       criteria and supervisors appraisal of teachers'
       effectiveness. 1969. *ERIC ED* 029 816.

Reports a relationship between teacher
background variables and supervisor ratings of
teaching.

222.   Smith, Robert Edward. Teacher characteristics,
       observations of classrooms, and recommendations
       for action. Ph.D. dissertation. Washington
       University. 1979.

Describes teacher characteristics such as age
related to observed student misbehavior and types
of recommendations for responses to that
misbehavior.

223.   Southwell, Reba Kirby. Teaching roles in childhood
       education and related belief systems as manifested
       in interactive teaching behaviors. Ed.D.
       dissertation. University of Alabama. 1972.

Describes four different teaching styles which
are related to teacher beliefs about teaching
role.

224. Spector, Barbara Solomon. Curricular innovation and
      teacher role change: An exploratory study. Ph.D.
      dissertation. Syracuse University. 1977.

      Reports that teacher experience is related to
      teacher willingness to try an innovation and
      success with it is related to encouraging other
      teachers to use the innovation.

225. Spring, Martha F. & others. Conceptual complexity
      and teacher-student interaction in alternative and
      traditional classrooms. 1974. *ERIC ED* 114 743.

      Reports that more concrete, rigid teachers have
      more direct and controlling interactions with
      students.

226. Sprinthall, Norman A., Whiteley, John M. & Mosher,
      Ralph L. *Journal of Teacher Education 17* (1966):
      93-106.

      Describes teacher cognitive flexibility related
      to teacher behavior, with more rigid teachers
      using less effective teaching behaviors.

227. Stayrook, Nicholas. Aptitude-treatment interactions
      in a study of teaching basic reading skills in
      secondary school. 1979. *ERIC ED* 172 164.

      Describes different relationships between
      teacher behavior and personality traits for
      trained and untrained teachers, when the training
      focused on aspects of direct instruction.

228. Summers, Jerry Andy. The relationship of
      organizational climate and selected personal
      variables with verbal interaction behavior of
      elementary school teachers. Ph.D. dissertation.
      Southern Illinois University. 1970.

      Describes differences in teacher behavior by
      age, experience, degrees, sex, with teacher
      perceptions of the organizational climate related
      to teacher discipline but not other teacher
      behaviors.

229. Taylor, Azilla L. Teacher dogmatism as related to
      classroom questions and pupil-teacher verbal
      interaction. Ph.D. dissertation. University of
      Washington. 1969.

      Reports no difference in teacher ratio of
      indirect to direct teaching behaviors by the
      degree of teacher dogmatism.

230.   Tolbert, Rodney N. "Should you employ that male
        elementary teacher?" *National Elementary Principal*
        47 (1968): 40-43.

            Describes no difference between male and female
        teachers in grades four through six on fifteen
        teacher competencies but female teachers were
        better at using community resources and male
        teachers at physical activities.

231.   Torrance, E. Paul and Others. "Verbal originality
        and teacher behavior: A predictive validity
        study," *Journal of Teacher Education 21* (1970):
        335-341.

            Describes a relationship between teacher
        creativity as measured by a test and teacher use
        of creative teaching behaviors.

232.   Treanor, Hugh Joseph. An examination of the verbal
        and cognitive behavior patterns of selected
        secondary social studies teachers in West
        Virginia. Ed.D. dissertation. West Virginia
        University. 1971.

            Describes differences in verbal behaviors of
        teachers with high and low scores on the Teaching
        Situation Reaction Test.

233.   Turner, Richard L. Beginning teacher
        characteristics and beginning teacher
        problems--Some predictive relationships. 1966.
        ERIC ED 015 886.

            Reports differences in the principals' ratings
        of teachers with and without student behavior
        problems, in terms of teacher warmth, attitude
        toward self and school, business-like behavior,
        problem solving performance.

234.   Urbina, Otilia. Teacher turnover in an urban
        setting. Ed.D. dissertation. University of
        Houston. 1980.

            Describes characteristics of teachers who left
        teaching and reasons given for leaving by age,
        sex, and other demographic characteristics.

235.   Vann, Marvin John. An assessment of the
        relationship between birth order and classroom
        teaching practices of secondary teachers and a
        bibliography of birth order research 1866-1977
        with index. Ed.D. dissertation. George Washington
        University. 1979.

Reports that secondary teachers include a greater proportion of first-borns but no relationship between birth order and teaching style.

236. Victor, James B. Peer judgements of teaching competency as a function of field-independence and dogmatism. 1973. *ERIC ED* 086 910.

Describes a relationship between teacher field dependence and assessment of teaching skills by peers.

237. Walsh, Thomas Michael, III. The relationship between the open-closed mindedness systems within teachers and the degree of their implementation of an innovative curriculum program. Ph.D. dissertation. University of Minnesota. 1971.

Describes teachers as open-minded but reports that background and personality characteristics are not related to degree of implementation of an innovation.

238. Weaver, Andrew M. & Stansel, Paul L. "Authoritarian-democratic attitudes and practices of retired military personnel employed as secondary school social studies teachers," *High School Journal 62* (1978): 7-12.

Describes differences in the perceived behavior of teachers who are retired military personnel and other teachers.

239. Weinstein, Carol S. & Woolfolk, Anita E. Impression formation and classroom design: The impact of spatial arrangement and neatness on judgements of teachers. 1979. *ERIC ED* 172 717.

Describes teacher personality, teacher behavior and observer ratings of teachers as related to classroom neatness.

240. Whale, Kathleen Bailie. The teaching of writing in an elementary school. Ed.D. dissertation. University of Toronto, Canada. 1980.

Describes aspects of teacher instruction in writing and reports that instruction is related to experiences but not to teacher training.

241. Williams, Paul L. & Callahan, Carolyn M. Cognitive complexity and its relationship to the classroom cognitive behavior of teachers. 1977. *ERIC ED* 135 770.

Describes the development of a measure of cognitive complexity and relationship between teacher cognitive complexity and behavior.

242.   Williamson, John A. "Biographical factors and teacher effectiveness," *Journal of Experimental Education 37*, No. 3 (1969): 85-88.

Describes a relationship between teacher background factors and student ratings of teachers as most and least effective.

243.   Willower, Donald J. The teacher subculture and curriculum change. 1968. *ERIC ED* 020 588.

Describes teachers as more custodial than principals in pupil control ideology and reports that teachers' and principals' concern for community support result in little curriculum change.

244.   Wilson, Alfred P. Personality characteristics of teachers in relation to performance in an individually prescribed instruction program. Final Report. 1970. *ERIC ED* 040 163.

Describes no relationship between personality characteristics, age, years of teaching and success in implementing a program of individually prescribed instruction.

245.   Woodward, John William. A study of relationships between professional characteristics and teacher behaviors which promote critical thinking, problem solving, transfer, and autonomy. Ed.D. dissertation. Indiana University. 1978.

Describes teacher characteristics and attitudes related to teacher behaviors.

246.   Yarger, Gwendolynne Polk. A study of conceptual level, perceived learning style and intended use of teaching materials. 1976. *ERIC ED* 120 187.

Reports that teachers differ by conceptual level in their ability to describe their own learning style and the way they use materials in the classroom

247.   York, L. Jean Netcher. Relationships between problems of beginning elementary teachers, their personal characteristics and their preferences for in-service education. Ed.D. dissertation. Indiana University. 1967.

Describes teacher characteristics related to problems which teachers and their principals

perceive they have, with the problems falling into
several clusters.

248. Young, James R. A discriminant analysis of a
      teaching model using three levels of teaching
      experience. 1979. *ERIC ED* 171 659.

      Describes differences in the motivational and
      instructional techniques used by teachers at three
      levels of teacher experience.

249. Zimmerman, Robert Edgar. Teacher perceptions and
      personality characteristics associated with
      innovation. Ph.D. dissertation. University of
      North Dakota. 1970.

      Describes innovative secondary teachers as more
      assertive, imaginative and risk taking than
      non-innovative teachers.

2. ON STUDENT ATTITUDES AND BEHAVIOR

250. Amato, Josephine A. Teachers' achievement
      expectations: Effects in open and traditional
      classrooms. 1979. *ERIC ED* 179 891.

      Reports no effects of teacher expectations but
      effects of open versus traditional classrooms on
      student achievement, interacting with grade
      level.

251. Anderson, Trudy Lane Spinks. Interactive effects of
      achievement motivation and teaching style on
      academic achievement in eighth-grade science
      classes. Ed.D. dissertation. Auburn University.
      1976.

      Describes a relationship between student
      motivation to achievement, teacher behavior and
      classroom type (reinforcement for conforming or
      independent behavior) and student science
      achievement.

252. Aspy, David N. & Buhler, June H. "The effect of
      teachers' inferred self concept upon student
      achievement," *Journal of Educational Research* 68
      10 (1975): 386-389. By the first author only, *ERIC*
      ED 031 300.

      Describes inferred teacher self concept related
      to student achievement.

253. Aspy, David & Roebuck, Flora. *Kids don't learn from*
      people they don't like. Amherst, Massachusetts:
      Human Resources Development Press, Inc. 1977.

Describes a program to train teachers in interpersonal skills, the effects on teacher behaviors of that program, and the effects of teacher behaviors on students, such as greater student attendance and achievement.

254. Barnett, Werner Joseph. The effects of teacher gender on mathematics achievement of first-grade students. Ed.D. dissertation. Oregon State University. 1980.

Describes differences in the achievement of first grade students in math concepts and computation when taught by male and female teachers, with higher scores for students of male teachers.

255. Bastress, Robert Lewis. A study of the relationships of teacher experience, teacher-student relations, and teacher leadership style with teacher effectiveness in selected secondary school English classrooms. Ph.D. dissertation. University of Maryland. 1980.

Reports that teacher leadership style and years of experience interact to effect student achievement but no interactive effect of leadership style and training.

256. Begle, Edward G. The prediction of mathematics achievement, NLSMA reports, No. 27. Stanford, California: School Mathematics Study Group. Stanford University. 1972. *ERIC ED* 084 129.

Describes teacher and student characteristics related to student math achievement.

257. Begle, Edward G. Teacher knowledge and student achievement in algebra, School Mathematics Study Group Reports No.9. Stanford, California: School Mathematics Study Group. Stanford University. 1972. *ERIC ED* 064 175.

Reports no correlation between teacher knowledge of algebra and student achievement in algebra.

258. Begle, Edward G. & Geeslin, William Edward. NLSMA Reports No. 28, Teacher effectiveness in mathematics instruction. Stanford, California: School Mathematics Study Group. Stanford University. 1972. *ERIC ED* 084 130.

Reports a relationship between teacher characteristics and student achievement but questions the stability of the findings.

259. Bennett, Donald Allison. A comparison of the
      achievement of fifth grade pupils having male
      teachers with those having female teachers. Ed.D.
      dissertation. University of Denver. 1966.

          Reports greater achievement for female students
      and for all students of female teachers in grade
      five.

260. Bohn, Coylene & others. A study of teacher
      characteristics as predictors in the successful
      implementation of an innovative curriculum.
      Austin, Texas: Center for Research and Development
      for Teacher Education. Texas University at Austin.
      1968. ERIC ED 051 140.

          Reports that teacher characteristics account
      for the variance in student achievement in a six
      week unit in Science--A Process Approach.

261. Bond, Guy L. & Dykstra, Robert. The cooperative
      research program in first-grade reading
      instruction," Reading Research Quarterly 2 (1967):
      1-142.

          Reports that teacher characteristics such as
      absence, experience and rating by supervisor were
      not related to student achievement, and presents
      information about the effects of different
      instructional materials.

262. Brantley, Verna Lee. Relationships among teachers
      and pupil self-concept and pupil reading
      achievement at the first grade level. Ph.D.
      dissertation. University of North Dakota. 1976.
      ERIC ED 140 229.

          Describes teacher self-concept, views of
      children as students and views of teaching as
      related to student self-concept and reading
      achievement in grade one.

263. Brewer, Michael Richard. The effectiveness of
      teacher ratings as predictors of first grade
      achievement. Ph.D. dissertation. University of
      Kansas. 1979.

          Describes a relationship between teacher
      characteristics and ratings of student success and
      student achievement.

264. Brophy, Jere E. & Good, Thomas L. "Feminization of
      American elementary schools," Phi Delta Kappan 54
      (1973): 564-566.

Reviews studies and concludes that teachers
don't appear to favor girls, that male teachers
have a slight effect on male student achievement.

265. Buck, Camellus Wilson. A study of teacher-student
      characteristics in selected New Mexico senior high
      schools. Ph.D. dissertation. University of New
      Mexico. 1974.

      Describes some relationships between teacher
      characteristics and attitude and student attitude
      and achievement.

266. Byars, Jackson Abbott. The relationship between
      teacher conformity to a model of teaching behavior
      and student achievement and student attitude in a
      first course in algebra. Ph.D. dissertation.
      University of Nebraska-Lincoln. 1970.

      Reports no differences by teacher
      characteristics such as number of math courses and
      teacher use of behaviors which correspond to a
      model of effective math teaching and student
      achievement.

267. Cafferty, Elsie Irene. An analysis of student
      performance based upon the degree of match between
      the educational cognitive style of the teacher and
      the educational cognitive style of the students.
      Ed.D. dissertation. University of
      Nebraska-Lincoln. 1980.

      Describes higher grade point average in classes
      with greater match between teacher and student
      cognitive style across all subjects for grades ten
      and eleven.

268. Campbell, Raymond McKinley. The educational
      implications of cognitive style and its effects on
      selected indexes of pupil grading and teaching
      behaviors. Ph.D. dissertation. University of
      Michigan. 1974.

      Describes slight difference in teacher-student
      interaction but no differences in student grades
      when students and teacher are matched or
      mismatched in terms of cognitive style.

269. Cantrell, Robert P. & others. "Teacher knowledge,
      attitudes, and classroom teaching correlates of
      student achievement," *Journal of Educational
      Psychology* 69 (1977): 172-179.

      Describes differences in behaviors of teachers
      with high and low levels of knowledge of

behavioral principles and those differences related to student achievement.

270. Cheek, Helen Neely. Teacher/pupil level of field-dependence congruence and mathematics achievement. Ph.D. dissertation. Arizona State University. 1979.

Describes the relationship between congruence and achievement, with higher achievement for field dependent pupils when placed with field dependent teachers.

271. Clapp, Rufus Carvel. The relationship of teacher sex to fifth grade boys' achievement gains and attitudes toward school. Ed.D. dissertation. Stanford University. 1967.

Describes no relationship between teacher sex and measures of teacher "femininity" and boys' attitudes toward school and academic achievement.

272. Clark, Thomas James, Jr. The relationships of teacher characteristics and classroom behaviors recommended by the Intermediate Science Curriculum Study (ISCS) to pupil achievement in the ISCS level one. Ed.D. dissertation. Temple University. 1975.

Reports that teacher knowledge of science content taught and processes of science are related to student achievement, but no relationship between achievement and teacher affective behavior.

273. Clary, Linda Mixon. Teacher characteristics that predict successful reading instruction. 1972. *ERIC ED* 174 961.

Describes a relationship between teacher personality characteristics and knowledge and student reading achievement.

274. Coble, Charles R. & Hounshell, Paul B. "Teacher self-actualization and student progress," *Science Education 56* (1972): 311-316.

Describes no differences in the biology achievement or the criticnal thinking of students with teachers at different levels of self-actualization.

275. Compagnone, Pasquale. The relationship of student achievement in high school chemistry to matched student-teacher cognitive style. Ph.D. dissertation. Boston College. 1980.

Describes no relationship between high school
student chemistry achievement and the match
between student and teacher cognitive style.

276.   Conners, C. Keith & Eisenberg, Leon. The effect of
        teacher behavior on verbal intelligence in
        operation Head Start children. 1966. *ERIC ED* 010
        782.

Describes students responding positively and
having IQ gains when teachers used more verbal
interactions and concentrated on intellectual
activities.

277.   Courtney, Dan & Schell, Leo M. "The effect of male
        teachers on the reading achievement of
        father-absent sixth grade boys," *Reading
        Improvement 15* (1978): 253-256.

Describes no effect of male teachers on reading
achievement of sixth grade boys whose fathers are
absent from the home.

278.   Crumpton, Robert. Teacher-pupil reading achievement
        levels and the organizational climate of urban
        elementary schools. Ph.D. dissertation. University
        of Wisconsin. 1972.

Describes school climate as related to teacher
knowledge of reading and teacher knowledge related
to student achievement in reading.

279.   Curtis, J. & Altmann, H. "The relationship between
        teachers' self-concept and the self-concept of
        students," *Child Study Journal 7* (1977): 17-27.

Describes a relationship between teacher and
student self-concept.

280.   Denton, Jon J. & others. "An evaluation design to
        examine the instructional effects of classroom
        teachers," *Educational Evaluation and Policy
        Analysis 2* (1980): 5-15.

Reports that differences among teachers in
knowledge, skills and teaching experience are
related to differences in class achievement.

281.   Dirnick, Janice Marie Wirth. Effect of teacher
        self-concept on pupil reading achievement. Ed.D.
        dissertation. Ball State University. 1980.

Reports that teacher global self-concept is not
related to student reading achievement in grades
one and two.

282. Doyal, Guy T. & Forsyth, Robert A. "The relationship between teacher and student anxiety levels," *Psychology in the Schools 10* (1973): 231-233.

    Describes teacher anxiety as related to student level of anxiety.

283. Easterday, Kenneth E. & Paul, Oliver Daye. "A study of the relationship of student-teacher compatability on student achievement in algebra," *Southern Journal of Educational Research 14* (1980): 127-143.

    Describes a relationship between student-teacher compatability on personal need for inclusion and student achievement.

284. Edeburn, Carl E. & Landry, Richard G. "Self-concepts of students and a significant other, the teacher," *Psychological Reports 35*, No. 1 part 2. (1974): 505-506.

    Describes a relationship between teacher self-acceptance and student self-concept.

285. Edeburn, Carl E. & Landry, Richard G. "Teacher self-concept and student self-concept in grades three, four, and five," *Journal of Educational Research 69* (1976): 372-375. 1974. *ERIC ED* 088 892.

    Describes changes in student self-concept over a school year related to teacher self-concept.

286. Eisenberg, Theodore A. "Begle revisited: teacher knowledge and student achievement in algebra," *Journal of Research in Mathematics Education 8* (1977): 216-222.

    Describes no relationship between teacher knowledge of math and number of math courses taken and student achievement in algebra.

287. Elias, Patricia J. & Hare, Gail. Special study: Reading difficulties: Videotape test of teachers' diagnostic skills. Beginning Teacher Evaluation Study: Phase II, 1973-74, Final Report: Vol. V. 4. Princeton, New Jersey: Educational Testing Service. 1976. *ERIC ED* 127 373.

    Reports that teachers with greater skill in diagnosing student reading problems had classes with lower student achievement during the school year.

288.   Etaugh, Claire & Harlow, Heidi. "Behaviors of male
       and female teachers as related to behaviors and
       attitudes of elementary school children," *Journal
       of Genetic Psychology 127* (1975): 163-170. 1973.
       ERIC ED 086 345.

           Describes behavior of male and female teachers
       as related to the behavior of male and female
       students, with students rating teachers of the
       same sex higher than teachers of opposite sex.

289.   Evans, Nelson Edward. Competitiveness,
       cooperativeness, and assigning grades in the high
       school classroom. Ed.D. dissertation. Andrews
       University. 1978.

           Describes a relationship between teacher and
       student cooperativeness and student grades, but no
       relationship between other teacher characteristics
       and student cooperativeness and grades.

290.   Farmer, Rodney Bruce. The relationship between
       social studies teacher self-actualization and
       teacher effectiveness. Ph.D. dissertation.
       University of Missouri-Columbia. 1978.

           Reports that teacher characteristics defined as
       self-actualizing are not related to student
       ratings of teacher effectiveness.

291.   Flanigan, Francis B. Teachers' classroom behavior
       as related to open and closed-mindedness. Ph.D.
       dissertation. Kent State University. 1972.

           Describes teacher dogmatism not related to
       teacher behavior or student concept of self as a
       learner.

292.   Flener, Frederick O. "Teacher assistance in problem
       solving," *Educational Research Quarterly 4*, No. 2
       (1979): 43-51.

           Describes a study which showed greater student
       learning of math problem solving with than without
       teacher assistance.

293.   Forslund, M.A. & Hull, R.E. "Teacher sex and
       achievement among elementary school pupils,"
       Education 95 (1974): 87-89.

           Describes no difference in student achievement
       by teacher sex.

294.   Fox, Ronald B. & Peck. Robert F. Personal
       characteristics of teachers that affect student
       learning. Austin, Texas: Center for Research and

Development for Teacher Education. Texas
University at Austin. 1978. *ERIC ED* 156 644.

Describes teacher self-reported personality
characteristics and observed classroom behaviors
as related to student achievement and attitude in
grade six.

295. Fraser, Barry J. "Science teacher characteristics
and student attitudinal outcomes," *School Science
and Mathematics 80* (1980): 300-308.

Describes a relationship between changes in
student attitude and some, but not most, teacher
characteristics.

296. Gehbauer, Sharon Ann. Teacher knowledge and student
reading achievement: Specifically teacher
knowledge, teaching experience and college hours
in reading and their relationship to student
reading achievement. Ed.D. dissertation. Brigham
Young University. 1978.

Describes teacher knowledge and experience as
significantly related to student reading
vocabulary but not comprehension achievement.

297. George, Kenneth D. & Dietz, Sister M. "The
relationship of teacher-pupil critical-thinking
ability," *Science Education 52* (1968): 426-432.

Reports no differences in student critical
thinking in elementary school by teacher level of
critical thinking.

298. Gerety, Maryclaire Ann. A study of the relationship
between the moral judgement of the teacher and the
moral atmosphere in the classroom. Ed.D.
dissertation. Boston University School of
Education. 1980.

Describes a limited relationship between
teacher and student level of moral judgment.

299. Glick, Irvin David. "Does teacher's skin color
matter?" *Integrated Education 9*, No. 5 (1971):
26-30.

Describes a relationship between teacher race
and secondary school students' achievement on a
listening comprehension test.

300. Goodwin, Coy Ronald. The relationship between
junior high school teacher effectiveness and
junior high school teacher personality factors.

Ed.D. dissertation. University of
Missouri-Columbia. 1978.

Describes a relationship between teacher
personality characteristics and student rating of
teacher effectiveness, with more effective
teachers being more reserved, intelligent,
toughminded, conservative.

301. Gullatt, David Elmer. Effects of matching-
      mismatching field-dependent-independent teachers
      and students on student achievement and evaluation
      of teacher attributes. Ph.D. dissertation.
      University of Kansas. 1980.

      Describes no difference in achievement in
      secondary school math when students are matched or
      mismatched with teachers in terms of field
      dependence-independence.

302. Hackett, Jay K. An investigation of the correlation
      between teacher observed and student self-reported
      affective behavior toward science. Ed.D.
      dissertation. University of Northern Colorado.
      1972.

      Reports a correlation between students'
      attitudes toward science as observed by teachers
      and reported by students.

303. Hallam, Kenneth Jerome. The effects of teaching
      styles and pupils' needs on learning, retention,
      and preference. Ph.D. dissertation. American
      University. 1966.

      Describes no differences in immediate learning
      but some differences in delayed retention when
      student personality needs were matched with
      teacher style of teaching.

304. Hanushek, Eric. "Teacher characteristics and gains
      in student achievement: Estimation using micro
      data," *American Economic Review 61* (1971):
      280-288.

      Describes a relationship between teacher
      characteristics and student achievement.

305. Hanushek, Eric. The production of education,
      teacher quality and efficiency. 1970. *ERIC ED* 037
      396.

      Describes a relationship between teacher verbal
      ability, recentness of education and socioeconomic
      level as related to student achievement, based on
      two data sets with limited information about
      teachers.

306. Harris, Albert J. & Others. A continuation of the CRAFT project comparing reading approaches with disadvantaged urban Negro children in primary grades. Final Report. 1968. *ERIC ED* 020 297.

Describes a project using different teaching approaches and limited effects of teacher characteristics on student reading achievement for disadvantaged students.

307. Harrison, Marilyn. "Class achievement and the background and behavior of teachers," *Elementary School Journal 77* (1976): 63-70.

Describes teacher abstract conceptual structure related to teacher behavior and student achievement.

308. Hartlage, Lawrence C. & Schlagel, Judith. "Teacher characteristics associated with student classroom behavior," *Journal of Psychology 86* (1974): 191-195

Describes a relationship between teacher characteristics and student classroom behavior.

309. Hering, William M., Jr. "Student learnings from sociology project materials according to teacher preparation in sociology," *Educational Leadership 30* (1972): 46-54.

Describes no relationship between student achievement and the length of teacher preparation in sociology.

310. Hirsch, Elizabeth S. A study of the influence of the teacher's role upon the social behavior of preschool children: the influence of dominative and socially integrative behavior of teachers upon cohesiveness of preschool class groups. Ph.D. dissertation. New York University. 1967.

Describes differences in the behavior of dominative and integrative teachers but no differences in group cohesiveness of students.

311. Hirsch, Vickie E. A study of instructional approaches to spelling: Student achievement and teacher attitudes. Ed.D. dissertation. University of Cincinnati. 1980.

Reports that teacher attitudes toward two instructional methods were not related to student spelling achievement.

312.   Holle, Ervin F. Teacher effectiveness: A study of
       the relationship between teacher personality
       characteristics and anxiety in elementary pupils.
       Ed.D. dissertation. University of New Mexico.
       1971.

           Describes teachers who score high in anxiety as
       having pupils who score high in anxiety.

313.   Hook, Edward Nicholas. Teacher factors influencing
       pupil achievement in elementary school English.
       Ed.D. dissertation. Colorado State College. 1965.

           Reports that some teacher traits and choice of
       textbook are related to higher student achievement
       in English in grades four through six.

314.   Hooks, Mose Yvonne Brooks. A study of the
       educational, behavioral and psychological
       characteristics of teachers as motivators for
       creative and less creative students. Ed.D.
       dissertation. University of Tennessee. 1973.

           Describes a relationship between teacher
       characteristics such as knowledge of a second
       language and student creativity.

315.   Hunkins, Francis Peter. The influence of analysis
       and evaluation questions on achievement and
       critical thinking in sixth grade social studies.
       Final Report. 1968. *ERIC ED* 035 790.

           Describes a study of the types of questions
       which teachers ask and their relationship to
       student critical thinking.

316.   Hurst, Doyle. The relationship between certain
       teacher-related variables and student achievement
       in third grade arithmetic. Ed.D. dissertation.
       Oklahoma State University.1967.

           Reports no relationship between teacher
       training, experience, and student math
       achievement, but teachers who had taken a math
       course more recently had lower student
       achievement.

317.   Johnson, Darwin B. Teacher knowledge of reading and
       the reading development of students in grades two
       through four. Ed.D. dissertation. Northern
       Illinois University. 1976. *ERIC ED* 127 588.

           Describes differences in teacher knowledge but
       student achievement related to differences in
       teacher expectations and student IQ, not
       differences in teacher knowledge.

318. Kleinfield, Judith. Effective teachers of Indian
      and Eskimo high school students. 1972. *ERIC ED* 068
      246.

          Describes effective teachers as having a high
      level of personal warmth and demandingness.

319. Klumb, Roger & Otto, Wayne. "Effect of three
      teacher—feedback/incentive conditions on pupils'
      reading skill development in an objective-based
      program," *Journal of Educational Research 70*
      (1976): 10–14.

          Describes no differences in pupil achievement
      in three groups where teachers were given
      different forms of feedback about student
      progress.

320. Kuchta, Frank Howard. A study to determine the
      effect of teachers' humanistic behavior on student
      learning behavior. Ed.D. dissertation. University
      of Oklahoma. 1980.

          Reports that students of more humanistic
      teachers had higher achievement gains in reading.

321. Lampela, Roland Mitchell. An investigation of the
      relationship between teacher understanding and
      change in pupil understanding of selected concepts
      in elementary school mathematics. Ed.D.
      dissertation. University of California, Los
      Angeles. 1966.

          Describes no relationship between teacher
      knowledge and coursework in the new math content
      and student achievement gains.

322. Lawrence, Frances. "The relationship between
      science teacher characteristics and student
      achievement and attitude," *Journal of Research in
      Science Teaching 12* (1975): 433–437. *ERIC ED* 161
      679.

          Describes a relationship between teacher
      characteristics and teacher behavior and student
      achievement in science.

323. LeRoy, Jack Arthur. The effects of Interaction
      Analysis and feedback procedures on the verbal
      behavior patterns of teachers and the creative
      thinking ability of their students. Ed.D.
      dissertation. Arizona State University. 1973.

          Reports that when teachers were given feedback
      about their behavior they changed their behavior

but the changes resulted in no changes in student creative thinking ability.

324. Lieberman, J. Nina. Explorations in teacher characteristics: Playfulness in the classroom teacher. *ERIC ED* 083 215.

   Reports that teacher playfulness encouraged student divergent thinking.

325. Lynch, Wallette Coles. Teacher warmth and pupil performance in the urban classroom with reference to two models of teacher education. Ph.D. dissertation. Washington University. 1979.

   Describes teacher warmth perceived by students and related to student achievement after the effects of student socioeconomic level and intelligence have been removed.

326. McLane, Darlene Harris. The relation of teacher empathy, mathematics training, and pedagogical preparation to changes in their students' achievement and attitude. Ed.D. dissertation. University of Houston. 1980.

   Reports that teacher empathy, teacher training and math training are related to students' attitudes and achievement.

327. McNary, Shirley R. The relationships between certain teacher characteristics and achievement and creativity of gifted elementary school students. 1967. *ERIC ED* 015 787; 060 479.

   Describes teacher characteristics related to student achievement and creativity, but none consistently related to all areas of achievement.

328. Masling, Joseph M. & Stern, George G. The pedagogical significance of unconscious factors in career motivation for teachers. 1966. *ERIC ED* 010 178.

   Describes teacher personality factors as not related to teacher behavior or student achievement.

329. Michell, Lynn & Peel, E.A. "A cognitive dimension in the analysis of classroom discourse," *Educational Review 29* (1977): 255-266.

   Describes a relationship between classroom discourse and student thinking.

330. Moore, Robert Ezra. The mathematical understanding of the elementary school teacher as related to pupil achievement in intermediate-grade arithmetic. Ed.D. dissertation. Stanford University. 1965.

Describes greater teacher knowledge of math associated with greater variability of student achievement.

331. Moskowitz, Howard Jay. An investigation of the differential effects of male and female teachers on primary pupils' mathematics and reading achievement. Ph.D. dissertation. University of Toledo. 1980.

Describes differences in reading but not math achievement favoring students with male teachers in grades two and three.

332. Murray, Howard B. & Staebler, Barbara K. "Teacher's locus of control and student achievement gains," *Journal of School Psychology* (1974): 305-309.

Describes greater achievement for male and female grade five students with teachers with internal than external locus of control, regardless of student locus of control.

333. Neumeister, David E. "Differences between fourth grade instructors on intelligence of boys and girls, *Pscychological Reports 26* (1970): 309-310.

Reports that sex and teaching style of teacher have no effect on student IQ scores.

334. Newman, Rita Gray. The impact of teacher experience on the achievement of third-grade students in inner-city schools. Ph.D. dissertation. North Texas State University. 1979.

Describes a relationship between years of teacher experience and student reading but not math achievement scores.

335. Noll, R.L. & others. "Teacher self-actualization and pupil control ideology—behavior consistency," *Alberta Journal of Educational Research 23* (1977): 65-70.

Describes a relationship between teacher level of self-actualization, pupil control ideology and behavior.

336. Olson, Roy Albert, Jr. The effects of teacher educational attitude, school location, and sex on

the incidence of cheating behavior in the test
situation. Ph.D. dissertation. University of Iowa.
1970.

Describes no relationship between teacher
characteristics and student cheating on tests in
grade six.

337.   Paraskevopoulos, Ioannes. "How students rate their
       teachers," *Journal of Educational Research 62*
       (1968): 25-29.

Describes secondary student ratings of teacher
characteristics differing by teacher personality
characteristics such as divergent/convergent
thinking.

338.   Patelmo, Philip Joseph. The relationship of
       selected teacher characteristics and classroom
       behaviors of teachers to critical thinking growth
       in students using the Introductory Physical
       Science (IPS) program as the content vehicle.
       Ed.D. dissertation. Temple University. 1975.

Reports that teacher experience and some
personality traits have a greater relationship to
student critical thinking than teacher cognitive
characteristics.

339.   Patsloff, Patricia Kathryn. Attitude change of
       teachers and students. 1967. *ERIC ED* 017 980.

Describes no relationship between teacher
characteristics and student attitude change if the
teachers are using materials designed to produce
changes in student attitudes.

340.   Peck, Robert R. & Veldman, Donald J. Personal
       characteristics associated with effective
       teaching. 1973. *ERIC ED* 078 038.

Describes a relationship between teacher
characteristics and student achievement gains.

341.   Peery, Criss-Tenna. The prediction of teacher
       effectiveness: A linear regression analysis of
       mean residual student achievement and teacher
       personality characteristics. Ed.D. dissertation.
       West Virginia University. 1979.

Describes a relationship between student
achievement in secondary algebra and three teacher
personality characteristics, tender-mindedness,
conscientiousness, and self-sufficiency.

342. Perham, Bernadette Helen. A study of multiple
     relationships among teacher characteristics,
     teaching behaviors and criterion-referenced
     student performance in mathematics. Technical
     Report No. 286. 1974. Ph.D. dissertation.
     Northwestern University. 1973. *ERIC ED* 167 370.

     Describes teacher characteristics related to
     teacher behaviors, such as structuring comments,
     which in turn are related to student achievement
     in elementary school math.

343. Perkes, Victor Aston. "Junior high school science
     teacher preparation, teaching behaviors,and
     student achievement," *Journal of Research in
     Science Teaching* 5 (1967-68): 121-126. *ERIC ED* 025
     417.

     Describes no relationship between teacher
     background and science courses taken and teacher
     behavior, and no relationship with student recall
     of factual information.

344. Peters, LaVern Ann. A classroom participant
     observation study of the behavior of selected high
     school students with a reading handicap. Ph.D.
     dissertation. Southern Illinois University at
     Carbondale. 1978.

     Describes relationships between teacher
     characteristics and teacher behavior, including
     interactions with students, and student behavior.

345. Phillips, Mark & Sinclair, Robert. Conceptual
     system and educational environment: relationships
     between teacher conceptual systems, student
     conceptual systems, and classroom environment as
     perceived by fifth and sixth grade students. 1973.
     ERIC ED 076 539.

     Describes a relationship between teacher and
     student conceptual similarity and student
     perception of the classroom environment.

346. Phillips, Robert B., Jr. "Teacher attitude as
     related to student attitude and achievement in
     elementary school mathematics," *School Science and
     Mathematics* 73 (1973): 501-507.

     Reports that teacher attitude toward math is
     related to student attitude but not achievement in
     math.

347. Porter, Jeffrey & Cohen, Margaret. Personal
     causation and locus of control: An analysis of
     selected teacher characteristics and their

relations to student achievement. 1977. *ERIC ED* 137 231.

Describes a distinction between personal causation and locus of control among teachers as related to student achievement.

348. Porter, Jeffrey Edward. Person/environment interaction within the classroom setting: A motivational analysis of student achievement. Ph.D. dissertation. Washington University. 1979.

Describes no relationship between degree of match between student personality characteristics and student-teacher relationship and student achievement.

349. Pozzi, Francis Thomas. A study of student and teacher cognitive styles. Ph.D. dissertation. Miami University. 1979.

Describes no difference in student achievement by match or mismatch of teacher and student cognitive style, but differences in student achievement by student cognitive style.

350. Prekeges, Demitrios P. Relationship between selected teacher variables and growth in arithmetic in grades four, five and six. Final report. 1973. Ed.D. dissertation. University of British Columbia, Canada. 1974. *ERIC ED* 090 023.

Describes no relationship between teacher variables such as training, attitude toward and knowledge of new math and student achievement.

351. Racine, Celine S. A study of the relationship between pupil control ideology of high school teachers and principals and alienation and structured role orientation of high school students. Ed.D. dissertation. State University of New York at Albany. 1980.

Reports that student alienation is related to student orientation but not to teacher pupil control ideology.

352. Romano, Anthony W. A study to determine the correlation between secondary teachers' biology knowledge and student achievement in biology. Ph.D. dissertation. University of South Carolina. 1978.

Describes no relationship between teacher knowledge of biology and student achievement.

353.   Rothman, Arthur I. "Teacher characteristics and
       student learning," *Journal of Research in Science
       Teaching* 6 (1969): 340-348.

       Describes a relationship between teacher
       characteristics and personality and student
       achievement in high school physics.

354.   Rothman, Arthur I, Welch, Wayne W. & Walberg,
       Herbert J. "Physics teacher characteristics and
       student learning," *Journal of Research in Science
       Teaching* 6, No. 1 (1969): 59-63.

       Describes teacher attitude and values having a
       greater impact than teacher training on student
       achievement, attitude and interest in physics.

355.   Rouse, William M. A study of the correlation
       between the academic preparation of teachers of
       mathematics and the mathematics achievement of
       their students in kindergarten through grade
       eight. Ph.D. dissertation. Michigan State
       University. 1967.

       Describes no relationship between teacher
       characteristics and student achievement.

356.   Royalty, William Edward. The relationship of
       selected student, teacher characteristics and
       student achievement in science using Science--A
       Process Approach. Ed.D. dissertation. University
       of Virginia. 1979.

       Describes no relationship between teacher
       characteristics and student achievement using the
       new science curriculum materials.

357.   Saracho, Olivia N. & Dayton, C.
       Mitchell. "Relationship of teachers' cognitive
       styles to pupils' academic achievement gains,"
       Journal of Educational Psychology 72 (1980):
       544-549.

       Describes student achievement related to
       teacher cognitive style but not to the congruence
       between teacher and student cognitive style in
       grades two and five.

358.   Sargent, Earl Alvin. A study to determine certain
       characteristics of Earth Science Curriculum
       Project teachers and students in the permissive or
       authoritarian classroom which lead to greater
       academic achievement in these students. 1966. *ERIC
       ED* 021 716.

Describes differences in student achievement by teacher background, such as college majors and number of education courses, but no differences by authoritarian/permissive characteristics.

359. Sass, Edmund J. & Meyer, Marie. Student test anxiety as related to the personality characteristics of their teachers. *ERIC ED* 183 503. By first author only, Ed.D. dissertation. Northern Illinois University. 1977.

Reports a significant relationship between teacher spontaneity and self-regard and student test anxiety among junior high students, with a strong but not significant relationship at the elementary level.

360. Sauls, Charles. "The relationship of selected factors to recreational reading of sixth graders," *Elementary English 51* (1974): 1009-1011.

Describes a relationship between both teacher and student characteristics and student recreational reading in grade six.

361. Schirner, Silas Wesley. A comparison of student outcomes in various earth science courses taught by seventeen Iowa teachers. 1967. *ERIC ED* 031 401.

Describes a relationship between teacher beliefs, teaching behaviors and type of science curriculum and student science achievement, with greater student critical thinking with the ESCP curriculum and indirect teaching.

362. Schofield, Hilary L. "Reading attitude and achievement: Teacher-pupil relationships," *Journal of Educational Research 74* (1980): 111-119.

Describes higher teacher achievement in and attitude toward reading as related to higher pupil achievement in and positive attitude toward reading.

363. Seaton, Hal W. & others. The relationship of self-concept, knowledge of reading, and teacher effectiveness. 1978. *ERIC ED* 165 119.

Describes teacher self-concept and years of experience related to teacher knowledge of reading instruction and in turn related to supervisor ratings of teacher effectiveness.

364. Sellinger, Stuart. An investigation of the effects of organizational climate and teacher anxiety on

test anxiety of elementary school students. Ed.D. dissertation. New York University. 1971.

Reports that student test anxiety was greater in open than in traditional elementary schools and was related to teacher test anxiety.

365.   Sharp, Christopher Samuel. A study of certain teacher characteristics and behavior as factors affecting pupil achievement in high school biology. Ph.D. dissertation. University of Southern California. 1966.

Describes no relationship between teacher characteristics such as preparation for teaching and teacher verbal behaviors and student achievement.

366.   Sheehan, Daniel S. & Marcus, Mary. "Teacher performance on the National Teacher Examinations and student mathematics and vocabulary achievement," *Journal of Educational Research 71* (1978): 134-136.

Describes a relationship between teachers' scores on the National Teachers Examination and teacher race and student achievement.

367.   Sheehan, Daniel S. & Marcus, Mary. "The effects of teacher race and student race on vocabulary and mathematics achievement," *Journal of Educational Research 70* (1977): 123-126.

Describes no relationship between the match of student and teacher race and student achievement, but students had greater vocabulary achievement with black teachers with less than five years experience than with more experienced black teachers.

368.   Shigaki, Irene S. The effects of teacher strength and sensitivity and pupil intelligence and creativity on the production of divergent responses. 1970. *ERIC ED* 041 831.

Describes a relationship between student creativity and divergent thinking but no relationship with teacher strength and sensitivity.

369.   Shively, Joe E. & others. Effects of creativity training programs and teacher influence on pupils' creative thinking abilities and related attitudes. 1971. *ERIC ED* 047 332.

Reports that teacher level of divergent
thinking has little effect on the effectiveness of
the training program and student divergent
thinking.

370.   Smith, Louis M. & Kleine, Paul F. "Teacher
       awareness: Social cognition in the classroom,"
       School Review 77 (1969): 45-256.

       Describes teacher awareness of classroom social
       interactions not related to teacher cognitive
       complexity but related to student positive
       sentiment about the classroom.

371.   Snyder, William R. & Kellogg, Theodore M.
       Preliminary analysis of teacher factors with ISCS
       student achievement. 1970. *ERIC ED* 052 923.

       Describes more effective teachers with the
       Intermediate Science Curriculum Study program
       having more experience with the materials and
       allowing student self-pacing but not a
       relationship with teacher characteristics.

372.   Soar, Robert S. A measure of teacher classroom
       management. 1971. *ERIC ED* 057 890.

       Describes teacher beliefs related to teacher
       behavior and student achievement.

373.   Soeteber, Warren Harvey. Major-minor teaching
       assignments and related pupil achievement. Ed.D.
       dissertation. Colorado State College. 1969.

       Describes teacher knowledge of math, college
       achievement and years of teaching experience, but
       not number of math courses related to greater
       student achievement in advanced algebra.

374.   Sroka, Stephen Roland, II. The relationship of
       teachers' health knowledge to their ninth-grade
       students' health knowledge. Ph.D. dissertation.
       Case Western Reserve University. 1978.

       Describes teacher knowledge not related to
       student achievement in health.

375.   Stanton, H.E. "The relationship between teachers'
       anxiety level and the test anxiety level of their
       students," *Psychology in the Schools 11* (1974):
       360-363.

       Describes less class test anxiety with teachers
       with greater test anxiety and less student test
       anxiety in traditional than in open classrooms.

376. Steele, James Davis. The relationship between teacher sex and the variables of reading achievement, sex-role preference, and teacher-pupil identification in a sample of fourth-grade boys. Ph.D. dissertation. Ohio University. 1967.

Describes differences in sex role preferences of students with male and female teachers but those differences not related to reading achievement.

377. Steiner, Laurie Levine. A study of female kindergarten teachers' sex-role attitudes and their effect on kindergarten girls' sex-typed toy preferences. Ed.D. dissertation. University of Houston. 1980.

Describes traditional teacher attitudes related to their students' greater preferences for sex-stereotyped toys.

378. Stern, Carolyn & Frith, Sandra. Classroom language of teachers of young children. 1970. *ERIC ED* 053 108.

Describes overlap between vocabulary used by the teacher and textbook, with some differences in teacher verbal reinforcement of vocabulary usage by student and teacher race and student socioeconomic level.

379. Stone, Meredith K. Correlates of teacher and student cognitive style. Beginning Teacher Evaluation Study: Phase II, 1973-74. Princeton, New Jersey: Educational Testing Service. 1976. *ERIC ED* 131 120.

Describes teacher cognitive style related to teacher attitude and knowledge but not to teacher behavior which is related to student achievement,

380. Stone, Meredith Knight. "The role of cognitive style in teaching and learning," *Journal of Teacher Education 27*, No. 4 (1976): 332-334.

Describes teacher cognitive style related to student learning, especially during initial skills instruction.

381. Struthers, Joseph A. Developing creative and critical thinking through an elementary school science program. Final report. 1969. *ERIC ED* 056 853.

Describes differences in teacher style and type of curriculum as related to differences in student creative thinking.

382. Sweely, H.D. The effect of the male elementary teacher on children's self-concepts. Ph.D. dissertation. University of Maryland. 1969. 1970. *ERIC ED* 039 034.

Describes no relationship between teacher sex and student self-concept, with no differences across classrooms in average student self-concept.

383. Thoman, John Henry. The relationships between teacher knowledge of science, preparation in science, teaching experience and fifth grade achievement in science. Ph.D. dissertation. University of Wisconsin-Madison. 1978.

Describes a slight correlation between teacher characteristics and student achievement, but not teacher knowledge of science and student science achievement.

384. Torrance, E. Paul. & others. Characteristics of mathematics teachers that affect students' learning. 1966. *ERIC ED* 010 378.

Describes teacher characteristics such as years of experience as not related to student achievement, but student achievement in math related to student attitudes and school climate.

385. Travers, Kenneth J. Non-intellective correlates of under- and overachievement in grades four and six. NLSMA Reports, No. 19. Stanford,California: School Mathematics Study Group. Stanford University. 1971. *ERIC ED* 084 121.

Describes characteristics of classrooms and teachers which are associated with student achievement.

386. Triplett, Suzanne Elaine. Some effects of open classroom instructional styles on certain cognitive and affective characteristics of kindergarten-age children. Ed.D. dissertation. Duke University. 1978.

Describes differences in student achievement and teacher ratings of student behavior by open versus traditional teaching style.

387. Turner, Richard L. & Denny, David A. "Teacher
      characteristics, teacher behavior, and changes in
      pupil creativity," *Elementary School Journal 69*
      (1969): 265-270.

         Describes a relationship between teacher
      characteristics and clusters of teacher behaviors
      and changes in student creativity.

388. Vroegh, Karen S. The relationship of sex of teacher
      and father presence-absence to academic
      achievement. Ph.D. dissertation. Northwestern
      University. 1973. *ERIC ED* 070 026.

         Describes sex of teacher and student and
      presence of the father not related to student
      achievement.

389. Wagner, Richard Carl. Teacher knowledge of reading
      and student achievement at the second, third, and
      sixth grade levels. Ed.D. dissertation. Brigham
      Young University. 1978.

         Describes no relationship between teacher
      knowledge of reading and student achievement.

390. Walberg, Herbert J. & Rothman, Arthur I. "Teacher
      achievement and student learning," *Science
      Education 53* (1969): 253-257.

         Describes a relationship between teacher
      knowledge and achievement and student achievement
      in physics.

391. Wallen, N.E. & Wodtke, K.H. Relationships between
      teacher characteristics and student behavior. Part
      I, II. *ERIC ED* 001 250; 001 257.

         Describes differences in the relationships
      between teacher characteristics and pupil behavior
      across grades but teachers at warm, permissive end
      of the scale had lower student achievement gains.

392. Walter, Glen Herman. The relationship of
      teacher-offered empathy, genuineness, and respect
      to pupil classroom behavior. Ph.D. dissertation.
      University of Florida. 1977.

         Describes teacher characteristics related to
      behavior toward students and student classroom
      behavior.

393. Watson, Larry Wayne. The relationship of the
      mathematical course work of teachers and the SAT-M
      scores of their students. 1969. *ERIC ED* 046 703.

Describes a relationship between the number of math courses teachers had taken and the size of the high school and student math scores on the Scholastic Achievement Test, but no relationship between specific math courses or patterns of math courses teachers had taken and student achievement.

394. Weber, Wilford A. Relationships between teacher behavior and pupil creativity in the elementary school. 1968. *ERIC ED* 028 150.

Describes student verbal creativity fostered by direct teaching and figural creativity fostered by consistent direct or indirect teaching.

395. Weber, Wilford Alexander. Teacher behavior and pupil creativity. Ed.D. dissertation. Temple University. 1967. *Classroom Interaction Newsletter* 3, No. 3: 30.

Describes lower student creativity by inconsistently direct and indirect teaching across four years, and greater verbal creativity with indirect teaching.

396. Wightman, Lawrence Edward. Achievement as a function of interactions between student characteristics and teacher behaviors. Ph.D. dissertation. Cornell University. 1970.

Describes no relationship between teacher warmth, harshness, directiveness and student levels of intelligence, anxiety and impulsivity and student achievement.

397. Wills, Stanley Ewing. A study of the relationship between teacher effectiveness and contacts among faculty members in an elementary school situation. Ed.D. dissertation. Colorado State College. 1966.

Describes no differences in achievement of students when teachers are similar or dissimilar to students in value orientations, but higher student achievement with teachers who contacted colleagues less frequently.

398. Wodtke, Kenneth H. & Wallen, Norman E. "The effects of teacher control in the classroom on pupils' creativity-test gains," *American Educational Research Journal* 2 (1965): 75–82.

Describes teachers who exhibit greater control in the classroom at elementary grades having students who make lower gains in a creativity test than teachers who exhibit less classroom control.

399. Wood, Dennis & Larsen, Gary Y. "The effects of
      different teaching styles on creativity," *Journal
      of Creative Behavior 10* (1976): 220.

      Describes a greater increase in total number of
      responses to a creativity test over the year for
      grade one students in classrooms with indirect
      than with direct teachers.

400. Yando, Regina & others. "The influence of Negro and
      white teachers rated as effective or noneffective
      on the performance of Negro and white lower-class
      children," *Developmental Psychology 5* (1971):
      290-299.

      Describes student performance related to
      teacher characteristics, not teacher race, in a
      classroom task situation.

401. Young, Penelope Lapham. An investigation of
      relationships between teacher attitudes,
      teacher-pupil interaction and pupil achievement
      and attitude toward school. Ph.D. dissertation.
      University of North Carolina at Chapel Hill.
      1973.

      Describes a relationship between teacher
      characteristics and teacher behavior and student
      achievement for black but not white students.

3. ON STUDENT ACHIEVEMENT

402. Beller, E. Kuno. "Research on organized programs of
      early education," In *Second handbook of research
      on teaching.* Edited by Robert M.W. Travers. pp.
      530-600. Chicago: Rand McNally & Company. 1973.

      Reviews various types of programs for and
      research on programs for infants and preschool
      children; includes a review of the influences of
      teacher characteristics and techniques on
      students. For Travers reference see citation No.
      3033

403. Gold, Dolores & Reis, Myrna. Do male teachers in
      the early school years make a difference? A review
      of the literature. 1978. *ERIC ED* 171 387.

      Reviews research on the effects of the sex of
      the teacher on students in the early years of
      school.

404. Gupta, Nina. Some school and classroom antecedents
      of student achievement. 1979. *ERIC ED* 182 815.

Reviews studies of classroom, school, student
and teacher characteristics as they influence
student achievement.

405. Jansen, Mogens, Jensen, Paul Erik, & Mylov,
      Peer. "Teacher characteristics and other factors
      affecting classroom interaction and teaching
      behavior," *International Review of Education 18*
      (1972): 529-540.

      Reviews studies which identify the effects of
      educational settings on teachers and on student
      achievement.

406. Khan, S.B. & Weiss, Joel. "The teaching of
      affective responses," In *Second handbook of
      research on teaching.* Edited by Robert M.W.
      Travers. pp. 759-804. Chicago: Rand McNally &
      Company. 1973.

      Reviews research on student attitudes and
      teachers' attitudes, perceptions of students'
      attitudes and influence on student attitudes. For
      Travers reference see citation No. 3033.

407. Metzner, Seymour. An empirical criterion validation
      study on some psychological inventory findings
      related to elementary school teachers. 1967. *ERIC
      ED* 013 775.

      Reviews studies using the Edwards Personal
      Preference Schedule and relating teacher
      personality characteristics to teacher behaviors.

408. Peck, R.F., Manning, B.A. & Buntain, D.M. The
      impact of teacher and student characteristics on
      student self-concept, attitudes toward school,
      achievement, and coping skills: A review of
      research. Austin, Texas: Center for Research and
      Development for Teacher Education. Texas
      University at Austin. 1977.

      Reviews studies of teacher characteristics as
      they are related to student attitude and
      achievement.

409. Power, Colin N. Somewhere over the
      rainbow--Systematic studies of the environment of
      science classrooms. 1974. *ERIC ED* 091 243.

      Reviews research on the climate of the science
      classroom, influences on that climate such as
      teacher characteristics, and the effects of the
      climate on students.

410. Ryans, David G. "Teacher behavior can be evaluated," *Educational Horizons 45* (1967): 99-120.

Describes assumptions about teacher behavior as influenced by teacher characteristics and the characteristics of the teaching situation, and reviews some studies.

411. Slavin, Robert E. "Classroom reward structure: An analytic and practical review," *Review of Educational Research 47* (1977): 633-650.

Reviews the few available classroom studies that indicate that cooperative classrooms lead to more social connectedness among students while competitive classrooms result in more student achievement, and classrooms which combine cooperation and competition lead to greater social connectedness and achievement.

412. Vroegh, Karen. "Sex of teacher and academic achievement: A review of research," *Elementary School Journal 76* (1976): 389-405.

Reviews studies on the effect of teacher sex on student achievement and concludes that there is no support for greater achievement of boys with male teachers.

413. Washington, Valora. "Noncognitive effects of instruction: A look at teacher behavior and effectiveness," *Educational Horizons 57* (1979): 209-213.

Summarizes research relating teacher characteristics and behaviors to student behavior and attitude.

414. Witkin, H.A., Moore, C.A., Goodenough, D.R. & Cox, P.W. Field-dependent and field-independent cognitive styles and their educational implications," *Review of Educational Research 47* (1977): 1-64.

Reviews studies of field dependence-independence in teachers and students and their effects on student learning, ways that teachers teach, student-teacher interactions, and student interests and achievement.

II TEACHER EXPECATIONS

A. INDUCED

415. Anderson, Thomas Hugh. Are a student's
      school-related behaviors dependent upon what is
      expected of him? Ed.D. dissertation. University of
      Illinois at Urbana-Champaign. 1970

      Describes teachers in a summer program told to
      expect spurts in some students; there were gains
      in teacher ratings of student personality
      variables but not in achievement.

416. Beez, W.V. Influence of biased psychological
      reports on teacher behavior and pupil performance.
      Ph.D. dissertation. Indiana University. 1968. Also
      printed in *Proceedings of the 76th annual
      convention of the American Psychological
      Association.* 3 (1968): 605-606.

      Describes differences in behavior of teachers
      toward students in a summer Head Start program
      with teachers teaching more to students for whom
      teachers were given false IQ information.

417. Claiborn, William Longshore. An investigation of
      the relationship between teacher expectancy,
      teacher behavior and pupil performance. Ph.D.
      dissertation. Syracuse University. 1968.

      Describes no difference in achievement of
      students for whom teachers were given information
      indicating students would show intellectual spurts
      and other students.

418. Claiborn, William L. "Expectancy effects in the
      classroom: A failure to replicate," *Journal of
      Educational Psychology* 60 (1969): 337-383.

      Describes no difference in the achievement of
      children or behaviors of teachers toward children
      whom teachers were told would and would not
      experience a sudden spurt in achievement.

419.   Coon, Lane K., Edwards, Carl N., Rosenthal, Robert
       & Crowne, Douglas. "Perception of emotion and
       response to teachers' expectancy by elementary
       school children," *Psychological Reports 22* (1968):
       27-34.

           Describes greater student achievement over four
       months for students with greater sensitivity to
       emotions among a group of students for whom
       teachers were given reports of anticipated high
       potential for intellectual gains.

420.   Dusek, Jerome B. An investigation of adult
       expectations as they affect children's learning
       and performance. Final Report. Syracuse, New York:
       Syracuse University. 1973. *ERIC ED 096 584.*

           Describes teacher rankings but not expectations
       provided by researcher related to student
       achievement.

421.   Dusek, Jerome B. Teacher and experimenter bias
       effects on children's learning and performance.
       1973. *ERIC ED 083 345.*

           Describes a lack of bias in experiments
       designed to predict student achievement.

422.   Dusek, Jerome B. & O'Connell, Edward J. "Teacher
       expectancy effects on the achievement test
       performance of elementary school children,"
       Journal of Educational Psychology 65 (1973):
       371-377.

           Describes student end-of-year achievement
       related to teacher ranking but not to expectancy
       of achievement created by the researcher through
       provision of information to teachers.

423.   Fiedler, William R., Cohen, Ronald D. & Feeney,
       Stephanie. "An attempt to replicate the teacher
       expectancy effect," *Psychological Reports 29*
       (1971): 1223-1228.

           Describes no difference in achievement over one
       semester between elementary students for whom
       teachers had and had not been given information
       about a potential spurt in achievement.

424.   Fleming, Elyse S. & Anttonen, Ralph C. Teacher
       expectancy or My Fair Lady. 1970. *ERIC ED 038
       183.*

           Describes an experiment in which the level of
       information given to teachers about student IQ

had no effect on student IQ after several months,
but teachers did differ in their opinions about IQ
tests.

425. Gess, Larry Robert. The effects of information
which is provided to teachers concerning students
on the attitudes and the behaviors of the teachers
and the students. Ph.D. dissertation. University
of Michigan. 1970.

Describes no difference in the behavior of
teachers toward students for whom they had and had
not received information about an expected growth
spurt, but teacher post-session expectations were
related to student behavior during the
experiments.

426. Goldsmith, Josephine S. & Fry, Edward. The effect
of a high expectancy prediction on reading
achievement and IQ of students in grade 10. 1971.
ERIC ED 049 901.

Describes no difference in IQ or reading
achievement for expectancy and control students
when teachers were given false expectancy
information.

427. Goodwin, William L. & Sanders, James R. An
exploratory study of the effect of selected
variables upon teacher expectation of pupil
success. 1969. *ERIC ED* 029 826.

Reports that a simulation using information
contained in cumulative records, found that
teacher expectations for students were based upon
student IQ, grades, test results and socioeconomic
status,

428. Grieger, Russell Marvin, III. The effects of
teacher expectancies on the intelligence of
students and the behavior of teachers. Ph.D.
dissertation. Ohio State University. 1970.

Describes no difference in teacher behavior or
student IQ for students for whom the researcher
had told the teacher to expect achievement gains.

429. Henrikson, Harold Arthur. An investigation of the
influence of teacher expectation upon the
intellectual and achievement performance of
disadvantaged kindergarten children. Ed.D.
dissertation. University of Illinois at
Urbana-Champaign.

Describes both teacher predictions for student achievement and expectations provided by researcher related to achievement gains for Negro males in proportion to their measured IQ.

430.   Jose, Jean & Cody, John J. "Teacher-pupil interaction as it relates to attempted changes in teacher expectancy of academic ability and achievement," *American Educational Research Journal 8* (1971): 39-49. Also, by first author only, Ph.D. dissertation. Southern Illinois University. 1969. *ERIC ED* 041 630.

Describes no difference in teacher behavior, assessment of student grades and student behavior for students for whom teacher was given information indicating an expected achievement spurt.

431.   Mahmoudi, Homayoun N. & Snibbe, John R. "Manipulating expectancy in the affective domain and its effects on achievement, intelligence and personality," *Psychology in the Schools 11* (1974): 449-457.

Describes some changes in achievement and affect when teachers and students were given affective expectancy information, told students were "special" individuals with greater respect for others.

432.   Meichenbaum, Donald H., Bowers, Kenneth S. & Ross, Robert R. "A behavioral analysis of teacher expectancy effect," *Journal of Personality and Social Psychology 13* (1969): 306-6316.

Describes differences in the behavior of teachers toward the students for whom they had been given expectancy information, and greater student achievement on objective but not subjective tests.

433.   Mendels, Glen E. & Flanders, James P. "Teacher expectations and pupil performance," *American Educational Research Journal 10* (1973): 203-212.

Describes no differences in many of the measures of achievement between student for whom teachers were and were not told to expect achievement gains.

434.   Moore, J. William & others. Expectancy statements in meaningful classroom learning. 1973. *ERIC ED* 083 347.

Describes expectancy information given to teachers having no effect when it is not credible to teachers.

435. Peng, Samuel Sen-Ming. Teacher class-expectations, instructional behaviors, and pupil achievement. Ph.D. dissertation. State University of New York at Buffalo. 1974. *ERIC ED* 088 833.

Describes no relation between teacher expectation and behavior when the expectation information is not congruent with teacher perceptions of students.

436. Rosenthal, Robert, Baratz, S.S. & Hall, C.M. "Teacher behavior, teacher expectations, and gains in pupils' rated creativity," *Journal of Genetic Psychology 124* (1974): 115-122.

Reports that teachers were told that some students would gain and those students did experience gains in measured creativity and IQ.

437. Rosenthal, Robert & Jacobson, Lenore. *Pygmalion in the classroom: Teacher expectation and pupils' intellectual development.* New York: Holt, Rinehart and Winston, Inc. 1968.

Describes a study in which teachers were told to expect an achievement spurt from randomly selected students and those students had higher achievement at the end of the year.

438. Van Alst, Jane Ann. The effects of influenced teacher and student expectations on student performance in tenth grade science. 1973. *ERIC ED* 094 962.

Describes no difference in achievement by expectancy information given to the teachers.

439. Wilkins, William Edward. The role of teacher expectations in the academic and social behaviors of students. Ph.D. dissertation. Cornell University. 1973.

Describes no differences in teacher interactions with students throughout the school year for whom teachers had and had not been given information about an expected achievement spurt.

440. Wilkins, William E. & Glock, Marvin D. Teacher expectations and student achievement: A replication and extension. Final Report. Ithaca, New York: Cornell University. 1973. *ERIC ED* 080 567.

Describes no difference in teacher behaviors toward students for whom they were and were not told to expect an achievement spurt.

441.   Zanna, Mark P. & others. "Pygmalion and Galatea: The interactive effect of teacher and student expectations," *Journal of Experimental Social Psychology 11* (1975): 288-299.

Describes an experiment which reported an interaction between teacher and student expectations for student achievement.

B. REVIEW OF EXPECTATIONS

442. Bellamy, G. Thomas. "The Pygmalion effect: What teacher behaviors mediate it," *Psychology in the Schools* 12 (1975): 454-460.

    Review finds some relation between teacher expectations for students and teacher behavior toward those students.

443. Braun, Carl. "Johnny reads the cues: Teacher expectation," *Reading Teacher* 26 (1973): 704-712.

    Reviews studies of teacher expectations and finds that they effect student expectations.

444. Braun, Carl. "Teacher expectations: Sociopsychological dynamics," *Review of Educational Research* 46 (1976): 185-213.

    Reviews studies of the factors which influence teacher expectations, differential teacher sensitivity to such influences, their effects of teacher behaviors and student responses to teacher behaviors, and student achievement.

445. Braun, Carl, Neilsen, Allan R. & Dykstra, Robert. "Teacher's expectations: Prime mover or inhibitor?" *Elementary School Journal* 76 (1975): 181-188.

    Reviews studies of teacher expectations and their effects of teacher behaviors.

446. Brophy, Jere E. "Reflections on research in elementary schools," *Journal of Teacher Education* 27 (1976): 31-34.

    Review synthesizes research on teacher expectations and behavior as they relate to student learning, and as they may vary by student characteristics.

447.   Cooper, Harris M. "Pygmalion grows up: A model for
       teacher expectation communication and performance
       influence," *Review of Educational Research 49*
       (1979): 389-410.

           Review develops a model of teacher influence
       through teacher communication of more affective
       feedback to low expectation students and more
       feedback about work to high expectation students
       who therefore work harder.

448.   Cooper, Harris M., Good, T., Blakey, S., Hinkel,
       G., Burger, J. & Sterling, J. Understanding
       Pygmalion: The social psychology of
       self-fulfilling classroom expectations. Columbia,
       Missouri: Center for Research in Social Behavior.
       University of Missouri-Columbia. 1979. *ERIC ED*
       182 642.

           Review presents a theory of teacher
       interaction in which teachers provide different
       types of feedback to students for whom they have
       different expectations.

449.   Dusek, J.B. "Do teachers bias children's
       learning," *Review of Educational Research 45*
       (1975): 661-684.

           Reviews research and concludes that there is
       no strong evidence for teacher bias resulting
       from telling teachers some student will have
       greater gains, but teacher expectations based on
       their own perceptions of students are related to
       student gains.

450.   Elashoff, Janet Dixon & Snow, Richard E. A case
       study of statistical inference: Reconsideration
       of the Rosenthal-Jacobson data on teacher
       expectancy. Stanford, California: Stanford Center
       for Research and Development in Teaching.
       Stanford University. 1970. *ERIC ED* 046 892.

           Critique of *Pygmalion in the Classroom* which
       questions the data collection procedures, date
       analysis, and interpretation of results. See
       citation No. 437 for Rosenthal-Jacobson
       document.

451.   Elashoff, Janet D. & Snow, Richard E. *Pygmalion
       reconsidered: A case study in statistical
       inference: Reconsideration of the
       Rosenthal-Jacobson data on teacher expectancy.*
       Worthington, Ohio: Charles A. Jones Publishing
       Company. 1971.

Review critiques the procedures and results of the Rosenthal-Jacobson study, with the conclusion that the original conclusions are incorrect; teacher expectations did not lead to greater student achievement. See citation No. 437 for Rosenthal-Jacobson document.

452. Finn, Jeremy D. "Expectations and the educational environment," *Review of Educational Research 42* (1972): 387-410.

Review of studies of teacher expectations and their influences on teacher behavior and student learning.

453. Gay, Geneva. "Teachers' achievement expectations of and classroom interactions with ethnically different students," *Contemporary Education 46*, No. 3 (1975): 166-171.

Reviews studies of teacher expectations specifically for children from ethnic minority groups with conclusion that teacher expectations are lower for minority children.

454. Gay, Geneva. "Teacher prejudice as a mediating factor in student growth and development," *Viewpoints in Teaching and Learning 55* (1970): 94-106.

Essay review describes ways that teacher attitudes may influence students and thereby student learning.

455. Gollub, Wendy Leebov & Sloan, Earline. "Teacher expectations and race and socioeconomic status," *Urban Education 13* (1978): 95-106.

Reviews selected studies and concludes that teacher expectations are related to student race and social class.

456. Good, Thomas L. "Classroom expectations: Teacher-pupil interactions," In *The social psychology of school learning*. Edited by J. MacMillan. New York: Academic Press. 1980.

Reviews studies of teacher expectations for students and the effects of those expectations on the interactions between teachers and students. For MacMillan reference see citation No. 2985.

457. Good, Thomas L. "Teacher expectations and student
      perceptions: A decade of research," *Educational
      Leadership 38* (1981): 415-422.

          Reviews research which indicates that teacher
      expectations are related to student achievement
      and that some teachers behave differently toward
      high and low achieving students. Included because
      of its comprehensiveness.

458. Good, Thomas L. & Brophy, Jere E. *Looking in
      Classrooms*. New York. Harper and Row, Publishers.
      1973.

          Describes aspects of teaching, such as
      grouping and management, based on research on
      teaching; includes a discussion of teacher
      expectations.

459. Good, Thomas L. & Brophy, Jere E. "Teachers'
      expectations as self-fulfilling prophecies," In
      Contemporary readings in educational psychology.
      Edited by H. Clarizio, R. Craig & W. Mehrens.
      Boston: Allyn and Bacon. 1977.

          Reviews studies of teacher expectations for
      students and their effects on the behavior of
      teachers and the achievement of students. For
      Clarizio, Craig & Mehrens reference see citation
      No. 2924.

460. Good, Thomas L. & Brophy, Jere E. "The influence
      of teacher attitudes and expectations upon
      classroom behavior," In *Psychological Concepts in
      the Classroom*. Edited by R. Coop & K. White. New
      York: Harper and Row. 1973.

          Reviews studies of teacher attitudes toward
      students and the influence of expectations for
      those students on behaviors of teachers toward
      those students. For Coop & White reference see
      citation No. 2929.

461. Good, Thomas L. & Brophy, Jere E. "The
      self-fulfilling prophecy," *Today's Education 60*
      (1971): 52-53.

          Briefly reviews research on teacher
      expectations which indicates that expectations do
      influence student achievement.

462. Good, Thomas L. & Dembo, M.H. "Teacher
      expectations and classroom life," *School Review
      81*: 247-253.

Discusses research on teacher expectations and their influence on teacher behaviors with students.

463. Hoge, Robert D. The teacher expectation effect: An attempt at clarification. 1979. *ERIC ED* 183 264.

Essay describes teachers as basing their expectations on pupil classroom behaviors and as accurate predictors of future student behavior and achievement, but indicates that it is important to learn how teacher expectations influence student learning.

464. Jeter, Jan T. "Can teacher expectations function as self-fulfilling prophecies," *Contemporary Education 46* (1975): 161-165.

Reviews teacher expectations and their influence on the behavior of teachers with students and on student achievement.

465. Kohn, Paul M. "Relationships between expectations of teachers and performance of students (Pygmalion in the classroom)," *Journal of School Health 93* (1973): 498:503.

Reviews studies of teacher expectations and their influence on teacher behaviors with students.

466. Metzner, Seymour. "Teacher bias in pupil evaluation: A critical analysis," *Journal of Teacher Education 22* (1971): 40-43.

Reviews studies of the influences on teacher grades, such as student sex, race, socioeconomic level.

467. Nash, Roy. *Teacher expectations and pupil learning.* Students library of education series. London: Routledge & Kegan Paul, Ltd. 1967.

Reviews studies of teacher expectations, including experimental studies, studies of effects on student achievement and self-concept, and studies of student expectations.

468. Richey, Harold W. & Richey, Marjorie H. "Nonverbal behavior in the classroom," *Psychology in the Schools 15* (1978): 571-576.

Review concludes that teacher nonverbal behavior may communicate expectations to students.

469.   Rosenthal, Robert. "Teacher expectations and pupil
        learning," In *Teachers and the learning process*.
        Edited by Robert L. Strom. pp. 33-60. Englewood
        Cliffs, New Jersey: Prentice-Hall, Inc. 1971.

        Reviews studies on experimenter expectations
        and concludes that they influence teacher
        expectations and student achievement. For Strom
        reference see citation No. 3029.

470.   Rosenthal, Robert & Rubin, Donald B. Pygmalion
        reaffirmed. Cambridge, Massachusetts: Harvard
        University. 1971. *ERIC ED* 059 247.

        Responds to Elashoff and Snow's critique of
        Pygmalion in the Classroom, responding to each of
        their points. See citation No. 451 for Elashoff
        and Snow document.

471.   Snow, Richard E. "Unfinished Pygmalion,"
        Contemporary Psychology 14 (1969): 197-200.

        Reviews *Pygmalion in the Classroom* with
        criticisms of methodology of the study and the
        presentation of the data in the book.

472.   Weintraub, Samuel. "Teacher expectation and
        reading performance," *Reading Teacher 22* (1969):
        555, 557, 559.

        Reviews studies of teacher expecations and
        their influence on student reading achievement.

473.   West, Charles K. & Anderson, Thomas H. "The
        question of preponderant causation in teacher
        expectancy research," *Review of Educational
        Research 46* (1976): 613-630.

        Reviews studies of teacher expectancy research
        in terms of a model which incorporates
        information, expectancy, teacher behavior,
        student achievement and intelligence, and
        emphasizes the importance of the interactions
        among all five factors.

III TEACHER PERCEPTIONS

A. OF SCHOOL

474. Alutto, Joseph A. & Balasco, James A. "Patterns of teacher participation in school system decision making," *Educational Administration Quarterly 9* (1972): 27-41.

    Describes teacher characteristics (age, sex) and school characteristics related to teacher perceptions of their participation in school decisions.

475. Banks, Floyd Malone. An analysis of the reactions of elementary teachers and principals to the role of disciplinarian as conducted within a selected Chicago public school district. Ed.D. dissertation. Loyola University of Chicago. 1980.

    Describes teacher and principal perceptions of discipline problems and the role of the principal as disciplinarian.

476. Barchi, Barbara. & Others. "Teacher-pupil perceptions of selected dimensions of social studies class activities," *Journal of Social Studies Research 2* (1978): 53-56.

    Describes differences in student and teacher perceptions of classroom activities.

477. Barfield, Vivian & Burlingame, Martin. "The pupil control ideology of teachers in selected schools," *Journal of Experimental Education 42*, No. 4 (1974): 6-11.

    Describes school characteristics related to teacher perceptions of appropriate methods and level of pupil control

478. Bayer, Gerald Allen. The perceptions of parents and teachers regarding school practices related to stages of moral cognitive development. Ed.D. dissertation. Wayne State University. 1980.

Describes consistency between teacher and parent identification of school practices which teach moral lessons but discrepancies in identifying what the lessons teach.

479.   Beam, Kathryn J. & Horvat, Robert E. "Differences among teachers' and students' perceptions of science classroom behaviors, and actual classroom behaviors," *Science Education 59* (1975): 333-344.

Describes teacher perceptions of science classrooms as being more inquiry oriented than observers report.

480.   Beckman, Walter Fay. The variability of social interaction in secondary schools. Ph.D. dissertation. Claremont Graduate School. 1971.

Describes changes in teacher perceptions of social interactions within the school over the school year, to perceptions of more closed interactions.

481.   Berger, Carl F. A comparison of science teaching behavior with a theoretical construct. 1974. *ERIC ED* 091 189.

Describes teacher perceptions of elementary science instruction.

482.   Bosman, Robert Garrott. A comparison between the perceived concerns of elementary school principals and teachers toward mainstreaming. Ed.D. dissertation. Northern Illinois University. 1979.

Describes concerns of teachers and principals in implementing mainstreaming, such as training and instructional approaches.

483.   Caliguri, Joseph P. "Teacher bias in the selection of social studies textbooks," *Journal of Negro Education 40* (1971): 322-329.

Describes teacher reports of the need to update and integrate the illustrations and contents of textbooks.

484.   Davies, Bronwyn. The culture of the child versus the culture of the teacher. 1976. *ERIC ED* 151 692.

Describes differences in teacher and student perceptions of school and school values.

485. DeAngelis, Mary I. An investigation into the reported needs of neophyte teachers and the perceived helpfulness of supervisors. Ph.D. dissertation. Ohio State University. 1979.

Describes attitudes and perceptions by beginning teachers of their supervisors as helpful, devoting time and attention to teachers but not helping in areas in which teachers most need help, so teachers tend to look to other teachers.

486. Duttinger, Linda Rooney. Educational environmental perceptions of secondary school students and their teachers in relation to school size. Ph.D. dissertation. Purdue University. 1979.

Describes perceptions of students and teachers of school environment, with perceptions differing by school size.

487. Floden, R.E. & others. Responses to curriculum pressures—A policy-capturing study of teacher decisions about content. East Lansing, Michigan: Institute for Research on Teaching. Michigan State University. 1980. *ERIC ED* 190 526.

Describes teacher attitudes toward curriculum and awareness of pressures to add but not to drop topics from the curriculum.

488. Forman, Norman. An investigation of personality and situational factors associated with teacher innovativeness. Ed.D. dissertation. Rutgers University the State University of New Jersey. 1971.

Describes no difference between most and least innovative teachers in terms of perceptions of the school, leadership style and cognitive complexity.

489. Freeland, Arthur Linton. A study of the comparison between teacher perceptions of student discipline and the managerial philosophy of Georgia secondary school principals. Ed.D. dissertation. University of Georgia. 1980.

Describes teacher perceptions of discipline and differences in teacher ratings of the quality of discipline by principal's theory of discipline.

490. Fridie, Samuel. "Black teachers inside predominantly white schools: An identification of their problems," *High School Journal 58* (1975): 323-335.

Describes problems which black teachers perceive that they have in white schools.

491. Good, T., Coop, R., Dembo, M., Denton, J. & Limbacher, P. "Teachers' view of accountability: An empirical study," *Phi Delta Kappan 56* (1975): 367-368. Report No. 90. Columbia, Missouri: Center for the Study of Social Behavior. University of Missouri-Columbia. 1974.

Describes teacher views of the concept of and systems for teacher accountability.

492. Goodman, Victor Brian. Teacher absenteeism-stress in selected elementary schools: An assessment of economic and human costs. Ed.D. dissertation. University of California, Los Angeles. 1980.

Describes teachers at white, black and Hispanic schools reporting different patterns of stress, with greater teacher stress in schools with Hispanic students.

493. Grace, Gerald R. *Role conflict and the teacher*. International Library of Sociology. London: Routledge & Kegan Paul, Ltd. 1972.

Describes a study of teacher perceptions of the role of the teacher in one school.

494. Helsel, A. Ray, Aurback, Herbert A. & Willower, Donald J. "Teachers' perceptions of organizational climate and expectations of successful change," *Journal of Experimental Education 38* (1969): 39-44.

Describes teacher perception of the climate of teacher-principal relations related to teacher perceptions of the possibility of change in the school.

495. Ingraham, Murray James. Role conflict of teachers with the principal and team members and the relationship of role conflict to perceived climate and rated effectiveness. Ed.D. dissertation. Boston University School of Education. 1979.

Describes congruence of teachers' and principals' role expectations and teachers' perceptions of school climate and reports similar perceptions across schools.

496. Janesick, Valerie J. An ethnographic study of a teacher's classroom perspective: Implications for curriculum. East Lansing, Michigan: Institute for

Research on Teaching. Michigan State University. 1978. *ERIC ED* 173 302.

Describes teacher perceptions of the influence of behavior on students and teacher shaping of the curriculum, limited by influence of principal and parents.

497. Jorgensen, Gerald W. "An analysis of teacher judgments of reading level," *American Educational Research Journal 12* (1975): 67-75.

Describes teachers differing in judgments of reading level of passages, with urban teachers judging them to be at higher reading levels than suburban teachers.

498. Kabiry, Ghassem. An investigation of organizational climate perceptions between students and teachers. Ph.D. dissertation. George Peabody College for Teachers of Vanderbilt University. 1980.

Describes no relationship between teacher and student perceptions of the organizational climate of classrooms.

499. King-Stoops, Joyce & Meier, Wanda. "Teacher analysis of the discipline problem," *Phi Delta Kappan 59* (1978): 354.

Describes teacher reports of discipline problems and their causes; teacher failure to motivate students, lack of student respect for other students and teacher, and lack of student interest.

500. Kritek, William J. "Teachers' concerns in a desegregated school in Milwaukee," *Integrated Education 17*, No. 1-2. (1979): 19-24.

Describes concerns of teachers in a newly desegrated school relating to problems derived from busing, unfamiliar behavior of black students, disadvantaged family and educational background of black students, wide range of achievement levels, and maintaining discipline.

501. Loucks, Susan F. Concerns expressed by elementary school teachers about the implementation of the SCIS Curriculum. Austin, Texas: Research and Development Center for Teacher Education. University of Texas at Austin. 1977.

Describes concerns of elementary teachers about the use of an innovative science curriculum.

502.   Malone, Janet Lorraine. Decision-making behavior of
       kindergarten teachers. Ph.D. dissertation.
       Oklahoma State University. 1979.

       Describes teacher perceptions of the
       decision-making power which they have and would
       like to have about instruction and student
       assignment.

503.   Oyeshiku, Patricia Delores. The perceived influence
       of black and white teachers on the self-concept
       and learning motivation of black students in
       desegregated classrooms. Ph.D. dissertation.
       United States International University. 1980.

       Describes differences in the ways that teachers
       expect that white and black students will perceive
       teacher influence and the ways that students
       describe the influence of black and white
       teachers.

504.   Packard, John S. & Willower, Donald J. "Pluralistic
       ignorance and pupil control ideology," *Journal of
       Educational Administration 10* (1972): 78-87.

       Describes teachers and principals with
       inaccurate estimates (too high) of the extent that
       others hold a custodial orientation toward pupil
       control.

505.   Rutherford, W.L. A study of the effects of various
       interventions in a two-year implementation effort.
       Report No. 3080. Austin, Texas: Research and
       Development Center for Teacher Education.
       University of Texas at Austin. 1979.

       Describes teacher perceptions of the
       innovations used in one school over a two year
       period.

506.   Rutherford, W.L. An investigation of how teachers'
       concerns influence innovation adoption. Austin,
       Texas: Research and Development Center for Teacher
       Education. University of Texas at Austin. 1977.

       Describes teacher concerns about an innovation
       and relates teacher levels of use of the
       innovation to those concerns.

507.   Rutherford, W.L. "Questions teachers ask about team
       teaching," *Journal of Teacher Education 30*, No. 4
       (1979): 29-30.

       Describes questions which teachers have about
       team teaching and about implementing it as a
       teaching approach.

508. Rutherford, W.L. & Loucks, S. F. Examination of the implementation of a junior high school's new approach to discipline by longitudinal analysis of change in teachers' stages of concern and levels of use. Austin, Texas: Research and Development Center for Teacher Education. Texas University at Austin. 1979.

   Describes levels of use of an innovation by teachers in one junior high school and their changing concerns about the innovation through the period of implementation.

509. Ryan, James J. & Rising, Gerald R. Participant teacher judgements of experimental programs in secondary mathematics. St. Paul, Minnesota: Minnesota State Department of Education. 1966. *ERIC ED* 011 942.

   Describes teachers responding favorably to experimental mathematics programs in junior high school, with teachers perceiving the programs to be better for high ability students.

510. Sanders, James L. An evaluation of interpersonal communications in Flagstaff High School. Flagstaff, Arizona: Northern Arizona Supplementary Education Center. 1970. *ERIC ED* 043 668.

   Describes student and teacher perceptions of communication among all school personnel.

511. Scott, Vera Orriss. An exploratory study to identify the teaching behaviors that are used most frequently and are most crucial in teaching culturally disadvantaged children. Ph.D.dissertation. Michigan State University. 1967.

   Describes teacher ratings of the frequency of teaching events, and differences between inner city and non-inner city teachers.

512. Slater, Marcia Diane. The teacher drops out—Oregon teacher attrition, 1974-1979. Ph.D. dissertation. University of Oregon. 1980.

   Describes a greater proportion of teachers leaving teaching in 1974-1979 than in 1962-1967 and work-related conditions cited more frequently than non-work-related factors as reasons for leaving.

513. Smith, Sidney & Smith, Pat C. An analysis of teacher self-assessment and related student perceptions regarding instructional behavior of

junior high school science teachers. 1973. *ERIC*
ED 079 070.

Describes teacher perceptions changing during
science in-service and related to their
involvement in a science project and to student
perceptions.

514.   Songchaikul, Chiaranai Prugsawan. The awareness by
        Wisconsin elementary school teachers of classroom
        environment. Ph.D. dissertation. University of
        Wisconsin-Madison. 1979.

        Describes low levels of teacher awareness of
        classroom environment.

515.   Tymitz, Barbara L. "Instructional aspects of the
        IEP: An analysis of teachers' skills and needs."
        Educational Technology 20 (Sept. 1980): 13-20.

        Describes teacher views of and problems with
        IEP instructional goals, teacher planning for
        goals and objectives, and areas where teachers
        need training.

B. OF THEMSELVES AND THEIR TEACHING

516. Adams, Ronald D. & others. A developmental study of teacher concerns across time. 1980. *ERIC ED* 189 181.

    Describes levels of concerns of teachers across years of experience and changes over year, with greatest concern being the academic impact on students.

517. Adams, R.S. Teachers and their social relationships. 1969. *ERIC ED* 028 1330.

    Describes the way teachers in the United States, England, Australia and New Zealand think others expect them to behave.

518. Anderson, Mary Beth Godfroy. A study of the differences among perceived need deficiencies, perceived burnout, and selected background variables for classroom teachers. Ph.D. dissertation. University of Connecticut. 1980.

    Describes differences in teachers perceptions of security, with more experienced teachers and elementary and high school teachers reporting greater satisfaction of their security needs.

519. Anglin, Leo W. & Romberg, Thomas A. Results of teacher task surveys. Technical Report No. 9. Madison, Wisconsin: Wisconsin Research and Development Center for Individualized Schooling. University of Wisconsin-Madison. 1976.

    Describes the tasks which teachers perform, including instructional and non-instructional tasks.

520. Bannister, Langston Clinton. A study to identify teachers who are judged to be effective in inner city school. Ed.D. dissertation. University of Massachusetts. 1971.

Describes criteria used by teachers, students and administrators to judge effects inner city teachers; stage presence and process criteria used by teachers and some students.

521.   Berger, Carl Frederick. Predictions of teaching behaviors by teachers of elementary school science. Ed.D. dissertation. University of California, Berkeley. 1971. *ERIC ED* 089 941.

Describes no difference between teachers trained and not trained in using inquiry methods in predicting their teaching behaviors.

522.   Berk, Laura E. & Berson, Minnie P. Acting, interacting and responding in the nursery school--An analysis of observed activities in a preschool classroom. 1971. *ERIC ED* 057 918.

Describes events in one preschool classroom and discrepancies between teachers' expectations and reality in amount of transition time, block play.

523.   Berliner, David C. Using the language of teachers to identify basic teaching skills. 1972. *ERIC ED* 100 910.

Describes use of teacher descriptions of teaching to define important teaching skills.

524.   Beverly, Gene Wright. Elements important in planning for classroom instruction: A study of the perceptions of elementary classroom teachers in the public schools of Prince William County, Virginia. Ed.D. dissertation. George Washington University. 1976.

Describes elements that teachers feel are involved in instructional plans in relation to reported plans.

525.   Biddle, Bruce J. "Teacher roles," In *Encyclopedia of Educational Research*. Edited by Robert L. Ebel. pp. 1437-1446. New York: The McMillan Company. 1969.

Reviews studies of expectations of teachers and others about teacher roles and studies of the performance or behavior of teachers. For Ebel reference see citation No. 2942.

526.   Biddle, Bruce J, Rosencranz, Howard A., Tomich, Edward & Twyman, J. Paschal. "Shared inaccuracies in the role of the teacher," in *Role theory: Concepts and research*. Edited by Bruce J. Biddle

& Edwin J. Thomas. pp. 302-310. New York: John
Wiley & Sons, Inc. 1966.

Describes differences in the behavior within
roles attributed to teachers by teachers,
administrators, parents and the general public and
in the perceptions of those attributions by
members of each group. For Biddel & Thomas
reference see citation No. 2913.

527.   Blackburn, Diane Fischer. An examination of the
relationships among several potential influences
of teachers' perceptions of their own teaching.
Ed.D. dissertation. University of Cincinnati.
1979.

Describes teachers' perceptions of their own
teaching influenced by student but not principal
perceptions, and not related to teachers'
attitudes toward children and school work.

528.   Bledsoe, Joseph C. & Brown, Iva D. "Role
perceptions of secondary teachers as related to
pupils' perceptions of teacher behavioral
characteristics," *Journal of Educational Research
61* (1968): 422-429.

Describes teacher age, sex, subject taught and
years of experience as influencing teachers'
perceptions of various teaching roles and students
having more favorable attitudes toward female
teachers.

529.   Bonekemper, Harold George. Perceptions of teaching
behavior by middle school teachers and pupils in
an open education setting. Ed.D. dissertation.
Lehigh University. 1974.

Describes teacher and student reports of
critical teaching incidents, with teachers'
reports focused on interactions with individual
pupils.

530.   Borg, Walter R. & Brite, Luna R. "Teacher's
perceptions of team teaching," *California Journal
of Educational Research* (1967): 71-81.

Describes the views of team teaching of
teachers who are working in team situations.

531.   Bosco, James. "Individualization--Teachers' views,"
Elementary School Journal 72 (1971): 125-131.

Describes teachers' reports of ideal and actual
behavior in terms of the types of goals for

students, grouping practices, sources of
information used for grouping students for
instruction.

532. Broadbent, Frank W. & Cruickshank, Donald R. The
      identification and analysis of problems of first
      year teachers. 1965. *ERIC ED* 013 786

      Describes the problems which first year
      teachers identified, including problems with
      instructional methods, evaluation of students,
      discipline, parent relations, routines and
      materials and personal problems.

533. Brode, E. Leland. Imitation of supervisors as a
      factor in teachers' classroom behavior. 1967. *ERIC
      ED* 011 524.

      Describes an experiment in which teachers
      ratings of direct and indirect teacher responses
      on a film were related to verbal behavior of the
      researcher in a prior discussion with teachers.

534. Brown, Iva Dunkin. Role perceptions of secondary
      teachers as related to pupils' perceptions of
      teacher behavioral characteristics. Ed.D.
      dissertation. University of Georgia 1965.

      Describes differences in teacher perceptions of
      their role by characteristics such as sex and
      years of experience.

535. Brumberger, Sally Clausen. A comparative study of
      striking and non-striking teachers in selected
      school districts in the United States. Ed.D.
      dissertation. Louisiana State University and
      Agricultural and Mechanical College. 1980.

      Describes characteristics of teachers, their
      reports that pressure came from peers and union to
      strike, that administrators impeded settlement of
      the dispute, that tenure status was not related to
      the decision of whether to strike.

536. Burden Paul Robert. Teachers' perceptions of the
      characteristics and influences on their personal
      and professional development. Ph.D. dissertation.
      Ohio State University. 1979.

      Describes teachers' perceptions of the stages
      in their professional careers and the
      characteristics of those stages.

537.   Burge, G. A survey of training, assignments, and
        attitudes of English teachers in Iowa public
        schools--grades 9-12. Des Moines, Iowa: Iowa State
        Department of Public Instruction. *ERIC ED* 015
        176.

            Describes English teachers' perceptions of work
        load, preferences for training, with one half
        belonging to a professional organization and one
        half attenting a professional conference in the
        past three years.

538.   Burke, Michael. "Perceived needs of elementary
        science teachers," *Science and Children 17* (1980):
        15-17.

            Describes teachers' needs for in-service
        training as reported by teachers in a survey, and
        relates some of those needs to the nature of the
        districts where the teachers work.

539.   Bussis, Anne M., Chittenden, Edward A. & Amarel,
        Marianne. *Beyond surface Curriculum: An interview
        study of teachers' understandings.* Boulder,
        Colorado: Westview Press. 1976.

            Describes teacher perceptions of the
        curriculum, purposes for learning, perceptions of
        students and the resources which they have for
        learning, and the support available to teachers.

540.   Campbell, N. Jo & Schoen, Harold L. "Relationships
        between selected teacher behaviors of prealgebra
        teachers and selected characteristics of their
        students," *Journal of Research in Mathematics
        Education 8* (1977): 369-375.

            Describes a relationship between teacher
        perceptions of teacher behavior and student
        performance.

541.   Caruso, Virginia Mary. Behaviors indicating teacher
        enthusiasm: Critical incidents reported by
        teachers and students in secondary school physical
        education and English classes. Ed.D. dissertation.
        University of Massachusetts. 1980.

            Describes teacher and student perceptions of
        enthusiasm, with teacher emphasis on communication
        of content and student emphasis of interaction.

542.   Chandler, Arnold Marvin. The effect of mathematics
        curriculum materials on the perceived behavior of
        urban junior high school teachers of low
        achievers. Ph.D. dissertation. University of
        Wisconsin. 1971.

Describes no changes in teacher perceptions of their teaching behaviors with a new math curriculum.

543. Charters, W.W., Jr. The effects of the team organization of elementary schools on teacher influence and work attitudes: A replication. *ERIC ED* 152 758.

Describes teaming influencing teachers' communication within the team but not teacher sense of job satisfaction and lower sense of autonomy.

544. Chesler, Mark Arnold. Social structure and innovation in elementary schools. Ph.D. dissertation. University of Michigan. 1966. *ERIC ED* 014 817.

Describes teacher perceptions of self and peers related to teacher use of innovative practices.

545. Christensen, Judith Carol. Wisconsin elementary school teachers' perceptions about their professional development needs. Ed.D. dissertation. Northern Illinois University. 1979.

Describes teachers' perceptions of their developmental needs.

546. Clark, Ernestine Hart. An analysis of occupational stress factors as perceived by public school teachers. Ed.D. dissertation. Auburn University. 1980.

Describes job related stress perceived by teachers to be related to five factors: feelings of professional inadequacy, principal-teacher professional relations, collegial relationship, group instruction, and job overload.

547. Collea, Francis Peter. A study of the intentions, self-perceptions, role perceptions and classroom verbal behavior of first year science teachers. Ph.D. dissertation. Syracuse University. 1970.

Describes changes in teachers' perceptions over the first year of science teaching, perceiving themselves as becoming more direct.

548. Collea, Francis P. "The first year science teacher—A study of his intentions, perceptions and verbal behavior," *School Science and Mathematics* 72 (1972): 159-164.

Describes conflicts in the intentions for behavior and perceptions of role of first year science teachers.

549. Cook, Lynne Harris. The relationship of teachers' training to perceptions of student behavior problems, teaching competence, and the utility of support roles. Ph.D. dissertation. University of Michigan. 1978.

Describes no relationship between teacher training and perception of their responses to behavior problems, but teachers report they need more training in dealing with behavior problems.

550. Crotty, Olga Caroline Watson. A comparative study of experts' and teachers' perceptions of the nature of appropriate/inappropriate teacher classroom behavior. Ed.D. dissertation. George Peabody College for Teachers of Vanderbilt University. 1980.

Describes agreement between teachers and experts on the behaviors which constitute emotional abuse of students.

551. Cruickshank, D.R. & Stiles, R. Perceived problems of teachers in schools serving rural disadvantaged populations and their comparison with problems reported by inner-city teachers. Knoxville, Tennessee: Tennessee University. 1968. *ERIC ED* 027 986.

Reports that teachers' greatest reported concerns were for language arts, followed by concerns for student personality characteristics, family circumstances and school- and classroom-related problems.

552. Cussen, Michael P. A comparative study of student and teacher perceptions regarding decision-making in selected open and traditional classrooms. 1977. *ERIC ED* 150 134.

Describes differences between teachers and students in perceptions of who makes decisions, with teachers perceiving that students make more decisions than students perceive they make.

553. Deck, Ronald Robert. A study of the relationship between organizational climate and the perceived congruence between teachers and principals of teachers' professional responsibilities in the elementary schools of Nassau County. Ed.D. dissertation. St. John's University. 1979.o

Describes a relationship between school climate and congruence of teacher and principal perceptions of teacher responsibilities.

554. Elswick, D.E. & others. Situational factors influencing quality teaching. Exploratory Phase--Teacher identification of factors--conditions, climate, competencies--influencing the teaching-learning process in Kentucky public schools. Frankport, Kentucky. Kentucky State Department of Education. *ERIC ED* 010 705.

Describes factors which teachers report in a survey that they think are important for quality teaching.

555. Eubanks, E. Three most essential teacher attributes needed for success as perceived by teachers in defacto segregated schools. 1972. *ERIC ED* 091 348.

Describes teachers' perceptions of the skills necessary for successful teaching within desgregated schools.

556. Evertson, Carolyn M., Brophy, J.E. & Crawford, J. Texas Teacher Effectiveness Project: An investigation of selected presage-process relationships. Report No. 75-16. Austin, Texas: Research and Development Center for Teacher Education. Texas University at Austin. 1975. *ERIC ED* 147 277.

Describes teachers' self-reports as accurate for some behaviors stressed within teacher education but inaccurate for other behaviors, compared with observations.

557. Gesten, Ellis L., Cowen, Emory L, DeStafano, Michael A. & Gallagher, Richard. "Teachers' judgments of class-related and teaching-related problem situations," *Journal of Special Education* *12* (1978): 171-181.

Describes teacher ratings of the frequency and difficulty of specific problems; those which occurred less frequently were the most difficult.

558. Gilbert, Evelyn Lee. Perceptions of sixth-grade pupils of their teachers' teaching behavior compared to the teachers' own perceptions of their teaching behavior. Ed.D. dissertation. Indiana University. 1978.

Describes differences between teacher and grade six student perceptions of teacher behavior

559. Gillogly, Gilbert John. Inservice education needs of elementary teachers in the Los Angeles Unified School District integration project as perceived by teachers in pair/cluster schools. Ed.D. dissertation. University of Southern California. 1980.

Describes the perceptions of teachers of their needs for inservice education.

560. Gottlieb, David & Brookover, Wilbur B. Social factors in the adoption of new teaching-learning techniques in the elementary school. Acceptance of new education practices by elementary school teachers. 1966. *ERIC ED* 011 958.

Describes teacher perceptions of their role as not involving decisions regarding the acceptance of new innovations within the school.

561. Greenfield, Henry. Congruence of teacher, student, and principal perceptions of the classroom practices of selected high school English teachers. Ph.D. dissertation. Michigan State University. 1978.

Describes general congruence between the perceptions of teachers, students and principals of teacher classroom behavior.

562. Hall, G.E. & Rutherford, W.L. "Concerns of teachers about implementing team teaching," *Educational Leadership 34* (1976): 227-233.

Describes variations in the concerns of teachers about implementing team teaching.

563. Halterman, Richard Jones. A Q-technique study of characteristics of effective science teachers. Salt Lake City, Utah: Utah University. 1969. *ERIC ED* 041 779.

Describes variations of principal, student and teacher ratings of the effectiveness of science teachers.

564. Hamachek, Don. "Characteristics of good teachers and implications for teacher education," *Phi Delta Kappan 50* (1969): 341-345. Reprinted in *Teachers and the learning process*. Edited by Robert D. Strom. pp. 166-174. Englewood Cliffs, New Jersey: Prentice-Hall, Inc. 1971.

Reviews research on characteristics of good teachers based on self-perceptions and the perceptions of others. For Strom reference see citation No. 3029.

565. Harding, Vivian Elizabeth. Question difficulty: A study of the interactions between teacher judgement and actual student performance on questions in a recall and a reinspection testing situation. Ph.D. dissertation. University of Maryland. 1978.

Describes teacher judgements about question difficulty effects by the question type and the testing situation, and question type related to student achievement.

566. Hilliard, Robert Donald. Relationships between selected communication behaviors of teachers and teacher effectiveness as perceived by teachers and their students. Ph.D. dissertation. University of Arkansas. 1973.

Describes a relationship between teacher and student perceptions of teacher communication behaviors.

567. Hook, Colin M. & Rosenshine, Barak V. "Accuracy of teacher reports of their classroom behavior," *Review of Educational Research 49* (1979): 1-12.

Reviews teacher reports of their own behavior and finds them not highly consistent with observations of their behavior.

568. Hudelson, Dorthea Bush. A retrospective analysis of the evolution of an open education teacher with focus on internal and external rewards and demands of the practice of open education. Ed.D. dissertation. University of Massachusetts. 1979.

Describes perceptions of one teacher of teacher role and problems as well as solutions to those problems, and the rewards of open education.

569. Hyman, Ronald Terry. An analysis of high school teaching: The structuring move in the language of selected classrooms. Ed.D. dissertation. Columbia University. 1965.

Describes teachers as speaking most of the structuring moves in secondary classrooms, to set the context for work, give rules and reasons for verbal interaction.

570. James, R. & Hall, G.E. "A study of the concerns of science teachers involved in an implementation of ISCS," *Journal of Research in Science Teaching 18* (1981): 479-488.

     Describes the concerns which teachers have as they implement an innovative science instructional program. Included because it builds upon key prior work.

571. Lamberg, Walter J. Practices and attitudes in providing information on writing performance. 1977. *ERIC ED* 158 276

     Describes discrepancies between teacher perceptions of effective feedback to students about their writing and actual behavior.

572. Lortie, Dan C. "Observations on teaching as work," In *Second handbook of research on teaching*. Edited by Robert M.W. Travers. pp. 474-498. Chicago: Rand McNally & Company. 1973.

     Describes the tasks of teaching and aspects of belonging to the profession, including recruitment, selection and mobility. For Travers reference see citation No. 3033.

573. McClanahan-Devet, Rebecca Lou. The professional opinions, instructional practices, and attitudes of South Carolina public high school teachers of English concerning the teaching of composition. Ph.D. dissertation. University of South Carolina. 1978.

     Describes English teachers' attitudes and self-reported behaviors in teaching composition.

574. Martin, Roy & Keller, Albert. "Teacher awareness of classroom dyadic interactions," *Journal of School Psychology 14* (1976): 47-54. ERIC ED 090 243.

     Describes teachers as not making accurate estimates of the frequency and types of interactions with students.

575. Medley, Donald M. "How valid are expert opinions about effective teaching," *Phi Delta Kappan 62* (1980): 131-134.

     Describes teacher perceptions of important teaching competencies and relates those to teacher behaviors which are correlated with student learning.

576.   Morine-Dershimer, Greta. "Teacher judgements and
       pupil observations: Beauty in the eye of the
       beholder," *Journal of Classroom Interaction 12*,
       No. 2 (1976): 31-50. *ERIC ED* 129 927.

          Describes differences between teachers in
       perceptions of classroom interaction, and between
       teachers and students.

577.   Morine, Greta & Vallance, Elizabeth. A study of
       teacher and pupil perceptions of classroom
       interaction. Special Study B. Technical Report No.
       75-11-6. Beginning Teacher Evaluation Study. San
       Francisco, California: Far West Laboratory for
       Educational Research and Development. 1975. *ERIC
       ED* 146 157.

          Describes four variables in teacher perceptions
       of instruction which are related to achievement of
       students on two week units.

578.   Mulgrew, Edna Catherine Birmingham. Relationships
       and personal development: An ethnomethodological
       study of teachers' perspectives. Ed.D.
       dissertation. University of North Carolina at
       Greensboro. 1979.

          Describes teacher perceptions of contacts with
       students as supportive of student personal
       development but detached and less important than
       teachers once were in student personal
       development.

579.   Newfield, John. "Accuracy of teacher reports:
       Reports and observations of specific classroom
       behaviors," *Journal of Educational Research 74*
       (1980): 78-82,

          Describes teacher reports of their own behavior
       under some conditions being quite accurate, and
       describes some of those behaviors.

580.   Perreault, Conrad Arnold. A comparison of
       indirectness in the teaching of science at the
       elementary, junior high, and high school levels by
       means of Interaction Analysis. 1972. *ERIC ED* 177
       763.

          Describes differences between elementary and
       junior high teachers in amounts of indirectness
       and teacher incorrect estimates of degree of
       indirectness.

581. Pogirski, Alex Joseph. A correlation of teacher self-assessment and student perception of the instructional behavior of high school biology teachers. Ph.D. dissertation. University of Michigan. 1971.

Describes differences in teacher and student perceptions of teacher behavior, with teachers talking 62% of the time in the classroom and 43% of the time in the laboratory.

582. Pogirski, Alex & Voss, Burton. "Evaluating the biology teacher's behavior in the classroom," *American Biology Teacher 34* (1972): 279-281.

Describes a relationship between teacher and student reports of teacher behavior, and observation record.

583. Price, G., Janicki, T., Van Deventer, H. & Romberg, T. Organizational features of IGE schools as correlates of teacher job satisfaction. Technical Report No. 512. Madison, Wisconsin: Wisconsin Research and Development Center for Individualized Schooling. University of Wisconsin-Madison. 1979.

Describes features of IGE schools and relates those to teacher perceptions of their work and their satisfaction with that work.

584. Rice, Eric Michael. Teacher occupational socialization: An exploration in on-the-job norm acquisition. Ph.D. dissertation. University of North Carolina at Chapel Hill. 1979.

Describes a sequence across years during which teachers report mastering various teaching skills.

585. Richey, Harold W. & Richey, Marjorie H. "Attribution in the classroom: How just is the just world?" *Psychology in the Schools 15* (1978): 216-222.

Reviews research on teacher attributions which indicates that teachers attribute events to individual personality characteristics of participants.

586. Rohrkemper, M.M. & Brophy, J.E. Teachers' general strategies for dealing with problem students. Research Series No. 87. East Lansing, Michigan: Institute for Research on Teaching. Michigan State University. 1980.

Describes types of behaviors teachers report they would use in responding to twelve types of student disruptive behavior.

587.   Ryan, Kevin, (Ed.) *Don't smile until Christmas: Accounts of the first year of teaching.* Chicago: University of Chicago Press. 1970

Collection of articles by first year teachers about their experiences during that first year of teaching.

588.   Sankowski, Eleanore Chenoweth. An analysis of perceptual and behavioral data relating to teacher classroom interaction. Ph.D. dissertation. Ohio State University. 1975.

Describes greater agreement between teachers and students about teacher verbal behavior than with observer perceptions of that behavior.

589.   Schwebel, Andrew I. & Cherlin, Dennis L. "Physical and social distancing in teacher-pupil relationships," *Journal of Educational Psychology* 63 (1972): 543-550.

Describes teachers as assigning classroom seats to minimize disruption, with students in front seats more attentive and perceived more positively by teachers and students.

590.   Smith, Louis M. "A perspective on a theory of urban teaching," In *Research into classroom processes: Recent developments and next steps.* Edited by Ian Westbury and Arno A. Bellack, pp. 167-174. New York: Teachers College Press. 1971

Describes interactions and structure of an urban classroom, views of that clasroom of particpants and ways that those views effect interactions. For Westbury and Bellack reference see citation No. 3039.

591.   Stern, William Alvin. Teacher absenteeism at the secondary school level: An investigation of work-related attitudes and demographic correlates. Ph.D. dissertation. Michigan State University. 1980.

Describes teacher perceptions of the causes of absenteeism, such as low job motivation, poor relations with colleagues, perceptions of promotional possibilities.

592. Talmage, Harriet & Ornstein, Allan C. "Teachers'
      perceptions of decision-making roles and
      responsibilities in defining accountability,"
      Journal of Negro Education 42 (1973): 212-221.

          Reports that teacher ethnicity, grade and
      school location affect teacher perceptions of
      their role and responsibilities within the school
      system.

593. Teresa, Joseph Gerald. The measurement of meaning
      as interpreted by teachers and students in
      visuo-gestural channel expressions through nine
      emotional expressions. Ph.D. dissertation.
      University of Michigan. 1971.

          Describes similarites in responses of teachers
      and students to non-verbal commmunications of
      feelings viewed on videotapes.

594. Teresa, Joseph G. & Francis, John B. A
      multi-variate analysis of teacher-student
      interpretations of non-verbal cues: The
      measurement of visuo-gestural channel expressions.
      1972. *ERIC ED* 063 552.

          Describes differences in teacher and student
      perceptions of behavior which communicates fear
      and anger.

595. Wahlstrom, M. & others. Assessment of student
      achievement: Evaluation of student achievement at
      the intermediate level. Final Report. Toronto,
      Canada: Ontario Institute for Studies of
      Education. 1977. *ERIC ED* 152 822.

          Describes teacher reports of their use of
      assessment procedures and teacher desire for more
      standardized instruments and training in their
      use.

596. Waller, Victoria Miller. Differential language use
      by teachers with high and low reading groups.
      Ed.D. dissertation. University of Cincinnati.
      1979.

          Teachers and students identify differences in
      teacher behavior with high and low reading groups
      and give similar reasons for the differences.

597. Watson, Elizabeth P., Marshall, Jon C. & Sokol,
      Alvin P. "Students' role expectations as perceived
      by teachers and students in American studies and
      American history programs," *Educational Leadership
      28* (1971): 397-404.

Describes differences between trained and untrained teachers and their students in their stated, observed and realized expectations for student's role.

598. Webb, Jeaninne Nelson. The effects of training in analysis of classroom behavior on the self-evaluation of teaching performance. Final Report. Tuscaloosa, Alabama: Alabama University. 1970. *ERIC ED* 059 963.

Describes no differences in teacher self-evaluation with and without training in the analysis of teaching behaviors.

599. Wolfson, Bernice J. & Nash, Shirley. "Perceptions of decision-making in elementary-school classrooms," *Elementary School Journal 69* (1968): 89-93.

Describes major differences in teacher and student perceptions with teachers seeing a greater number of pupil decisions than pupils saw.

600. Woog, Pierre. The relationship between elementary school teachers' assignments of educational priorities and their practices: A Q study. Ph.D. dissertation. Hofstra University. 1972. *ERIC ED* 061 176.

Describes no relation between teacher ranking of the importance of objectives and their behaviors in the classroom.

C. OF STUDENTS

601. Adams, Gerald R. "Racial membership and physical attractiveness effects on preschool teachers' expectations," *Child Study Journal 8* (1978): 29-41.

    Reports that Head Start teachers rated boys, unattractive children and black children less favorably than other children, in terms of how they would do in the classroom.

602. Adams, G.R. & Cohen, A.S. "An examination of cumulative folder information used by teachers in making differential judgements of children's abilities," *Alberta Journal of Educational Research 22* (1976): 216-225.

    Describes the influence of sources of information about students on teacher expectations for students.

603. Adams, Gerald R. & Cohen Allan S. "Characteristics of children and teacher expectancy: An extension to the child's social and family life," *Journal of Educational Research 70* (1976): 87-90.

    Describes teachers having different expectations about student personality and family characteristics for attractive versus unattractive and affluent versus unaffluent children, based on teacher responses to cumulative folder information.

604. Adams, Gerald R. & Cohen Allan S. "Children's physical and interpersonal characteristics that effect student-teacher interactions," *Journal of Experimental Education 43* (1974): 1-5.

    Describes physical characteristics which have stronger effects on teacher ratings more during the first weeks of school than later, based on teacher ratings of their students.

605. Adams, Gerald R. & LaVoie, Joseph C. "The effect of student's sex, conduct, and facial attractiveness on teacher expectancy," *Education 95* (1974): 76-83.

Describes teachers influenced in their ratings
of students by student conduct but not facial
attractiveness, after reading descriptions and
seeing pictures.

606.   Airasian, Peter W., Kellaghan, Thomas, Madaus,
       George F. & Pedulla, Joseph J. "Proportion and
       direction of teacher rating changes of pupils'
       progress attributable to standardized test
       information," *Journal of Educational Psychology*
       69 (1977): 702-709.

       Describes fewer than 10% of the teachers who
       received student test results showing shifts in
       ratings of pupil achievement in grade two reading
       and math from fall to spring, a shift in a
       positive direction.

607.   Albro, Harley M. & Haller, Emil J. "Teachers'
       perceptions and their tracking decisions,"
       Administrator's Notebook 20, No. 7 (1972): 1-4.

       Describes the criteria which teachers use in
       recommending ability placements for secondary
       school students.

608.   Algozzine, Bob. "The disturbing child: A matter of
       opinion," *Behavioral Disorders 5* (1980): 112-115.

       Describes regular classroom teachers rating a
       set of student behaviors as more disturbing than
       did special education teachers.

609.   Algozzine, Bob & Curran, Thomas J. "Teachers'
       predictions of children's school success as a
       function of their behavioral tolerances," *Journal
       of Educational Research 72* (1079): 344-347.

       Describes teacher predictions of success for
       students with behavior problems related to teacher
       tolerance for deviant behavior.

610.   Algozzine, Bob & Ysseldyke, James E. "Decision
       makers' prediction of students' academic
       difficulties as a function of referral
       information," *Journal of Educational Research 73*
       (1980): 145-150.

       Describes teachers and psychologists using
       available information in referral simulation and
       their placement decisions varied by the available
       information, with differences in predicted
       problems by reason for referral and student sex.

611. Algozzine, Robert Francis. Attractiveness as a biasing factor in teacher-pupil interactions. Ph.D. dissertation. Pennsylvania State University. 1975.

Describes more teacher interaction with students whom the teachers rate as attractive.

612. Aloia, Stephen Douglas. Regular education and special education teachers' attributions to causality for a handicapped child's performance on arithmetic and physical fitness tests. Ph.D. dissertation. University of California, Riverside. 1970.

Describes no differences in the causes assigned to achievement and physical performance of a sample of hypothetical students between regular and special education teachers; achievement, not physical performance, influences teacher rating.

613. Ames, Russell. "Teachers' attributions of responsibility: Some unexpected nondefensive effects," *Journal of Educational Psychology 67* (1975): 668-676.

Describes teacher assessments of success and assignment of responsibilty to students in mastering one instructional task.

614. Anderson, Charles Joseph. An investigation into teacher perceptions of differences in male and female students in selected Massachusetts elementary schools. Ed.D. dissertation. Northeastern University. 1978.

Describes different teacher behavior in rating the behaviors of boys and girls.

615. Anderson, Linda M. & others. Relationships between teacher and observer adjective descriptions and teacher perceptions of student characteristics. Report No. 75-24. Austin, Texas: Research and Development Center for Teacher Education. Texas University at Austin. 1975. *ERIC ED* 147-015.

Describes teacher rankings of students on specific characteristics related to general descriptions of students given by teachers, with intelligence forming one underlying aspect which has a halo effect on other ratings.

616. Antonoplos, Daniel Peter. Interactions of teacher-pupil sex as expressed by teacher expectations, patterns of reinforcement and

judgements about pupils: A national study.
Ed.D.dissertation. Indiana University. 1971.

Describes teacher ratings as more favorable to
females and white students than blacks and
Spanish—surnamed male students, with white
teachers less extreme in ratings than black and
Spanish—surnamed teachers.

617. Aron, Robert & others. Effects of teacher
      expectancies: Myth or reality? 1975. *ERIC ED* 115
      722.

      Describes student characteristics related to
      teacher predictions of success in a simulation.

618. Baird, Rita Margaret. Teacher—student interpersonal
      relationships and student self—concepts. Ed.D.
      dissertation. Oklahoma State University. 1971.

      Describes no relationship between teacher
      accuracy in perceiving student self—concept and
      student perception of teacher—student
      interaction.

619. Baker, Cynthia Mary. Elementary school teacher's
      perceptions of the typical male, typical female,
      and typical athlete. Ed.D. dissertation.
      University of Northern Colorado. 1979.

      Describes teacher perceptions and attributions
      of traits of competency and warmth—expressiveness
      to males, females, and athletes.

620. Bannai, Hideko. Teachers' perceptions of
      comparisons between the spoken communication
      competencies of Asian American and Caucasian
      students. Ph.D. dissertation. University of
      Southern California. 1980.

      Describes differences between Asian American
      and other teachers in their assessment of the
      language competencies of and attitudes toward
      Asian American students.

621. Baum, M., Brophy, J., Evertson, L., Anderson, L. &
      Crawford, J. Grade and sex differences in
      adjective descriptions of elementary school
      children given by their teachers and by classroom
      observers. Austin, Texas: Research and Development
      Center for Teacher Education. University of Texas
      at Austin. 1975. *ERIC ED* 146 154.

      Describes differences in observer and teacher
      ratings of students, with teachers responding to

characteristics related to student and teacher roles while observers respond to student personal and social characteristics.

622. Beckman, Linda J. Teacher's and parent's attribution of causality for children's performance. 1973. *ERIC ED* 083 498.

Describes teachers assigning different causes and parents not assigning different causes to different student performance.

623. Beckman, Linda. "Teachers' and observers' perceptions of causality for a child's performance," *Journal of Educational Psychology* 65 (1973): 198-204. ERIC ED 061 181, 084 020.

Describes an experiment in which teacher and observer perceptions of student performance and causes for student performance were in agreement, with greater attribution to circumstances when performance was low.

624. Beggs, Donald L. & others. "The effects of various techniques of interpreting test results on teacher perception and pupil achievement," *Measurement and Evaluation in Guidance* 5 (1972): 290-297.

Describes no relationship between the manner in which IQ test results are presented to teachers and later student achievement.

625. Bell, Nancy J. & others. "Teachers' definitions of self-esteem when rating preschool children," *Perceptual and Motor Skills 51* (1980): 292.

Describes a relationship between teacher ratings of high student self-esteem and ratings of students as assertive, athletic and active.

626. Benedict, Joseph A. A comparison of parents' and teachers' expectancy and appraisal of kindergarten children's reading development. Ed.D. dissertation. University of Northern Colorado. 1975. *ERIC ED* 122 235.

Describes differences in fathers', mothers' and teachers' expectations of the reading readiness of kindergarten children.

627. Benson, Doris Jean. Teacher expectations and achievement of students with learning disabilities. Ph.D. dissertation. University of Pittsburgh. 1979.

Describes teacher behavior with and
expectations for students with learning
disabilities.

628.   Benz, Carolyn Ridenour. Sex role expectations of
       classroom teachers grades 1 through 12. Ed.D.
       dissertation. University of Akron. 1980.

       Describes teacher expectations about
       sex-specific student behavior not related to
       expectations for student but high achieving
       students were more apt to be assigned
       characteristics classified as androgynous and
       masculine.

629.   Blattstein, D., Peck, R.F. & Blattstein,
       A. Consistency in self, peer, and teacher ratings
       of student coping skills. Austin, Texas: Research
       and Development Center for Teacher Education.
       Texas University at Austin. 1979.

       Describes consistency in teacher, student and
       peer ratings among ethnic groups of students, but
       variations in the consistency among students
       within ethnic groups.

630.   Bloom, Robert B. "Teacher-pupil compatability and
       teachers' ratings of children's behavior,"
       Psychology in the Schools 13 (1976): 142-145.

       Describes a relationship between teacher
       ratings of pupils with behavior problems and
       student-teacher compatability.

631.   Bognar, Carl Joseph. The effect of dissonant
       feedback about achievement on teachers'
       expectations. Ph.D. dissertation. University of
       Toronto, Canada. 1980.

       Describes teachers as likely to underestimate
       the achievement of students who misbehave, likely
       to over or underestimate achievement of low SES
       students, and not likely to change estimates based
       on test score information.

632.   Bolstad, Orin D. & Johnson, Stephen M. "The
       relationship between teachers' assessment of
       students and the students' actual behavior in the
       classroom," *Child Development 48* (1977): 570-578.

       Describes teacher ratings of students related
       to student behavior in the classroom.

633.   Borich, G.D. & Peck, R.F. Relationships between
       teachers' marks, achievement test scores and

aptitude as a function of grade, ethnicity and
sex. Austin, Texas: Research and Development
Center for Teacher Education. Texas University at
Austin. 1976. *ERIC ED* 132 197.

Describes differences in teacher grades by
student sex as the grades are related to student
achievement measured by standardized tests.

634. Borko, Hilda & Shavelson, Richard J. "Teachers'
sensitivity to the reliability of information in
making causal attributions in an achievement
situation," *Journal of Educational Psychology 70*
(1978): 271-279.

Reports that in a simulation, teachers
attributed positively valued information about
students to ability and effort and negatively
valued information to luck.

635. Boucher, Carol Robin. The influence of information
about handicap labeling and child characteristics
on teacher decision-making appropriate for
individualized education programming. Ph.D.
dissertation. University of Minnesota. 1979.

Describes teacher placement decisions in terms
of label, severity of handicap, whether the
decision is for long or short term placement, and
goals set for child.

636. Boyd, R.S. Student attitudes and teachers judgement
of student attitudes. *ERIC ED* 016 270.

Describes teachers' estimates of student
attitudes most like the attitudes of male and low
achieving students; teachers underestimated
student valuing of school, school work, and
learning.

637. Bredemeier, Mary Elizabeth. Teacher-student
transactions and student growth. Ed.D.
dissertation. Rutgers University the State
University of New Jersey. 1973.

Describes no relationship between teacher and
student perceptions of self and each other and
student achievement for four students.

638. Brittan, Elaine M. "Multiracial education. 2.
Teacher opinion on aspects of school life. Part 2:
Pupils and teachers," *Educational Research 18*, No.
3 (1976): 182-191.

Describes teacher appraisal of students in multiethnic classrooms and the effects of such classrooms on teachers.

639. Brooks, Douglas M. The diagnostic value of psychologically meaningful teaching units as expressed in children's classroom drawings. 1976. *ERIC ED* 131 914.

Describes students' self-reported attitude to school related to teacher ratings of students.

640. Brooks, D.M. & Wagenhauser, Betsy. "Completion time as a nonverbal component of teacher attitude," *Elementary School Journal 81* (1980): 24-27.

The time that students take to complete a task assigned by the teacher may influence teacher perceptions of the student.

641. Brophy, J.E. & Good, T.L. "Teacher expectations: Beyond the Pygmalion controversy, *Phi Delta Kappan* 54 (1972): 276-278. Austin, Texas: Center for Research and Development for Teacher Education. Texas University at Austin. 1972.

Review synthesizes studies using teacher naturally-formed expectations, reveals that teacher expectations can but don't necessarily act as self-fulfilling prophecies.

642. Brophy, Jere E. & Rohrkemper, Mary M. Teachers' thinking about problem students. Research Series No. 68. East Lansing, Michigan: Institute for Research on Teaching. Michigan State University. 1980. *ERIC ED* 186 408.

Describes teacher attribution of student intention and ability to control behavior as varying by the degree teachers felt ownership of student behavior problems.

643. Brophy, J.E. & Rohrkemper, M.M. The influence of problem ownership on teachers' perceptions of and strategies for coping with problem students. Research Series No. 84. East Lansing, Michigan: Institute for Research on Teaching. Michigan State University. 1980.

Describes teacher views of the causes of student disruptive behavior, whether students can control such behavior, and persons with major responsiblity to correct or change the behavior.

644. Byers, J.L. & Evans, T.E. Children's reading
     interests: A study of teacher judgement. Research
     Series No. 81. East Lansing, Michigan: Institute
     for Research on Teaching. Michigan State
     University. 1980.

     Describes teachers and students using the same
     cues about books to judge their level of interest
     to students but weighing the cues differently.

645. Byers, J.L. & Evans, T.E. Using a lens-model
     analysis to identify the factors in teacher
     judgement. Research Series No. 73. East Lansing,
     Michigan: Institute for Research on Teaching.
     Michigan State University. 1980.

     Describes teacher judgements about student
     reading performance and the cues which teachers
     use to make those judgements.

646. Cable, Stella Bartkus. The effect of positive and
     negative statements of pupils' social behaviors on
     recommendations made by teachers. Ed.D.
     dissertation. University of Southern California.
     1971.

     In a simulation different teacher
     recommendations were related to the nature of the
     description of student behavior, with more
     placement recommendations with a large number of
     negative and a small number of positive reported
     behaviors.

647. Cahill, Virginia Mary. The effects of standardized
     test information on teachers' perceptions of their
     students and teachers' perceptions of student
     achievement: A longitudinal study. Ph.D.
     dissertation. Boston College. 1979.

     Reports that, in Ireland, test information
     provided to teachers for the first time did not
     effect teacher views of students.

648. Canzoniero, Michael Joseph. The effects of teacher
     attitudes towards open versus traditional
     education upon the grades received by male and
     female elementary school children. Ph.D.
     dissertation. St. John's University. 1979.

     Describes teacher grades related to teacher
     attitudes and student sex and degree to which
     student exhibited sex-typed behavior.

649. Caplan, Paula J. "The role of classroom conduct in
     the promotion and retention of elementary school

children," *Journal of Experimental Education 41*,
No. 3 (1973): 8-11.

Describes teacher perceptions of behaviors of
girls and boys, with teachers considering behavior
as well as achievement in promotion decisions for
girls.

650. Carter, T.P. & others. Value systems of teachers
      and their perception of self, and of Mexican
      American, Negro, and Anglo children. Symposium on
      applications of psychological principles to the
      classroom. 1969. *ERIC ED* 037 507.

      Describes teacher perceptions of students as
      similar to teacher perceptions of themselves.

651. Catalogna, Lenore & others. An exploratory
      examination of teachers' perceptions of pupils'
      race. 1980. *ERIC ED* 185 197.

      Describes teachers according more positive
      characteristics to white pupils and less positive
      to Puerto Rican pupils in sorting of photographs
      of pupils.

652. Caudry, Robert D. & Wilson, Warner. "A survey of
      what teachers like in students," *Southern Journal
      of Educational Reseach 7* (1973): 1:6.

      Describes characteristics of students which
      teachers like and dislike.

653. Chang, Theresa. The relationship between children's
      self-concepts, teachers' ratings, and academic
      achievement. 1975. *ERIC ED* 106 699.

      Describes correlations between teacher ratings
      of students and student self-concept and
      achievement.

654. Chasen, Barbara. "Sex-role stereotyping and
      prekindergarten teachers," *Elementary School
      Journal 64* (1974): 220-235.

      Describes sex role stereotypes in teacher
      attitudes toward and expectations for students.

655. Cherry, Louis J. & Berman, Linda S. Teacher-student
      interaction and teachers' perceptions of students'
      communicative competence: A cross-sectional study.
      Technical Report No. 473. Madison, Wisconsin:
      Research and Development Center for Individualized
      Schooling. University of Wisconsin-Madison. 1978.
      ERIC ED 166 670.

Describes complex interactions between teacher
expectations, teacher behavior, and measures of
teacher behavior.

656. Choy, Steven J. & Dodd, David
      H. "Standard-English-speaking and nonstandard
      Hawaiian-English-speaking children: Comprehension
      of both dialects and teacher's evaluations,"
      Journal of Educational Psychology 68 (1976):
      184-193.

      Describes teacher evaluation of language
      behavior, academic performance, classroom behavior
      and future success as lower for
      Hawaiian-English-speaking than for standard
      English-speaking students.

657. Clifford, Margaret M. The effect of physical
      attractiveness on teacher expectation. Final
      Report. Iowa City, Iowa: Iowa University. 1971.
      also in *Sociology of Education 46* (1973): 248-258.
      ERIC ED 056 348.

      Describes teacher ratings as higher for more
      than less attractive children.

658. Clifford, Miriam. Relative potency of teacher
      attitudes toward black and retarded children.
      1973. *ERIC ED 088 986.*

      Describes teacher perceptions of black
      non-retarded students like retarded students, with
      higher expectations for white students.

659. Cohen, Libby. Stereotyping of learning disabled and
      remedial reading students by teachers. 1980. *ERIC
      ED* 187 045.

      Describes differences in teacher ratings of
      students by labelled and unlabelled groups
      (remedial reading and learning disabled) but not
      differences in teacher grading of student essays.

660. Cohen, Margaret W. Student influence in the
      classroom. *ERIC ED* 152 750.

      Reports that teacher beliefs about students are
      related to the ways that teachers interact with
      students and the influence that students have in
      the classroom.

661. Cone, Richard Evan. Teachers' decisions in managing
      student behavior: A laboratory simulation in
      interactive decision-making by teachers. Ph.D.
      dissertation. University of California, Los
      Angeles. 1979.

Describes a simulation which identifies factors
which teachers use to identify student behavior
problems and describes teacher management
approaches.

662. Cooper, Harris M. Intervening in expectation
      communication: The "alterability" of teacher
      expectations. 1977. *ERIC ED* 165 079.

      Describes teachers differing in the degree to
      which their expectations are related to student
      sex and IQ and the degree to which student
      achievement gains are related to teacher
      perceptions.

663. Cooper, Harris M. "Some effects of preperformance
      information on academic expectations," *Journal of
      Educational Psychology 71* (1979): 375-380.

      Describes teacher expectations based on
      information in the cumulative record related to
      teacher ratings of student performance.

664. Cooper, Harris M. & Baron, Reuben M. "Academic
      expectations and attributed responsibility as
      predictors of progessional teachers' reinforcement
      behavior," *Journal of Educational Psychology 69*
      (1977): 409-418.

      Describes a relationship between teacher
      behavior toward students and teacher ratings of
      student level of expected achievement and
      acceptance of responsibility.

665. Cooper, H.M. & Burger, J.M. "How teachers explain
      students' academic performance: A categorization
      of free response academic attributions," *American
      Educational Research Journal 17* (1980): 95-109.

      Describes teacher responses which indicate the
      extent to which teachers attribute student
      achievement to teachers, to student effort, and to
      other causes.

666. Cooper, Harris M., Burger, J.M. & Seymour
      G.E. "Classroom context and student ability as
      influences on teacher perceptions of classroom
      control," *American Educational Research Journal
      16* (1979): 189-1976.

      Describes teacher perceptions that they have
      greater control with high ability students and in
      teacher-initiated interactions than with low
      ability students and student-initiated
      interactions.

667. Cornbleth, Catherine & Korth, Williard. "Teacher perceptions and teacher-student interactions in integrated classrooms," *Journal of Experimental Education 48* (1980): 259-263.

Describes teachers perceiving black and white students differently, based on teacher ratings and observations of teacher-student interactions.

668. Cornbleth, Catherine & Korth, Williard. Teachers' perceptions of and interaction with students in multicultural classrooms. 1977. *ERIC ED* 137 227.

Describes teachers interpreting student behavior differently depending upon student race.

669. Coulter, C., Brophy, J., Evertson, C., Anderson, L. & Baum M. Sex and grade level differences in ratings of students by teachers and classroom observers. Austin, Texas: Research and Development Center for Teacher Education. Texas University at Austin. 1975. *ERIC ED* 146 141.

Describes perceptions of teachers and observers of students, both ranking girls more favorably than boys.

670. Crano, William D. & Mellon, Phyllis M. "Causal influence of teachers' expectations on children's academic performance: A cross-lagged panel analysis," *Journal of Educational Psychology 70* (1978): 39-49.

Describes student social performance effects by teacher expectations and teacher expectations having more influence on student achievement than achievement on teacher expectations.

671. Cross, Dolores Evelyn Tucker. The relationship between individualization of instruction and teacher perception of pupil behavior. Ph.D. dissertation. University of Michigan. 1971.

Describes no difference in teacher and student perceptions of students and teacher success in handling student behavior problems by degree of instructional organization.

672. Crowl, Thomas Kenneth. White teachers' evaluations of oral responses given by white and Negro ninth grade males. Ph.D. dissertation. Columbia University. 1970. *ERIC ED* 058 239.

Describes teacher responses to black voices by rating them lower than white voices, but no reliabilty for individual teacher ratings.

673. Crowl, Thomas K. & MacGinitie, Walter H. "The influence of students' speech characteristics on teachers' evaluations of oral answers," *Journal of Educational Psychology 66* (1974): 304–308.

Describes teachers as rating higher the recorded responses of white than of black students, but not differences by teacher age, sex, years of experience, percentage of black students in their class.

674. Cunningham, Patricia M. "Teachers' correction responses to black-dialect miscues which are non-meaning-changing," *Reading Research Quarterly 12* (1976–1977): 637–653.

Describes teacher attitudes to miscues and different perceptions of errors made by black and white students

675. Datta, L. Sex and scholastic aptitude as variables in teachers' ratings of the adjustment and classroom behavior of Negro and other seventh grade students. 1966. *ERIC ED* 028 206.

Describes differences in teacher perceptions by ability level, with no differences in teacher descriptions of high ability Negro and other students, but low ability Negro and male students more often described as maladjusted than low ability female and other ethnic group male students.

676. de Bary, Victoria Gaillard. Who shapes whom in the classroom?: A comparison between teacher reported vs. actual teacher and pupil classroom behaviors. Ph.D. dissertation. Columbia University. 1978.

Describes teacher rates of approval and disapproval of student behavior not related to teacher reports of the student behaviors they find to be annoying or satisfactory.

677. DeFlaminis, John A. Teacher responses to classroom misbehavior: Influence methods in a perilous equilibrium. 1976. *ERIC ED* 121 741.

Describes teacher responses to pupil misbehavior and teacher reasons for those responses.

678.   Desrochers, John Edward. Is off-task behavior
        (observed behavioral inattention) a stable trait
        of individual pupils or is it subject
        matter/teacher specific? Ph.D. dissertation.
        Columbia University. 1978.

        Describes variability by subject and day of
        student off-task behavior and no relationship
        between teacher ratings of student behavior and
        student off-task behavior.

679.   DeMeis, Debra Kanai & Turner, Ralph R. "Effects of
        students' race, physical attractiveness, and
        dialect on teachers' evaluations," *Contemporary
        Educational Psychology 3* (1978): 77-86.

        Describes teachers rating unattractive and
        black-English-speaking students lower than other
        students, based on taped speech samples.

680.   Dietz, S. & Purkey, W. "Teacher expectation of
        performance based on race of student,"
        Psychological Reports 24(1969): 694.

        Describes student race not related to teacher
        ratings of likely scholastic success of students
        based on descriptive vignettes.

681.   Dobson, Russell Lee. The perception and treatment
        by teachers of the behavioral problems of
        elementary school children in culturally deprived
        and middle-class neighborhoods. Ed.D.
        dissertation. University of Oklahoma. 1966.

        Describes different perceptions among teachers
        of the seriousness of behavior problems, with
        ratings of them as less serious for more
        experienced teachers and teachers of disadvantaged
        students.

682.   Domanskis, Francis Constance Laucka. Children's
        attention: The relationship between teacher's
        perceptions and performance on experimental
        measures. Ph.D. dissertation. University of
        Michigan. 1980.

        Describes teacher ratings of attention to task
        related to male student attention on experimental
        tasks, with more consistency across tasks for good
        than poor attenders.

683.   Dorr, Darwin & others. The relationship between
        child and teacher evaluations of self esteem and
        adjustment in fourth and sixth grade children.
        1973. *ERIC ED* 088 969.

Describes a limited relationship between teacher and student perceptions of student self-esteem and adjustment.

684.   Doyle, Wayne J., Hancock, G. & Kifer, E. "Teachers' perceptions: Do they make a difference?" *Journal of the Association for the Study of Perception 7*, No. 2 (1972): 21-30.

Describes a relationship between teacher perceptions of students and student grade one reading achievement.

685.   Driscoll, Anne M. The onset and stability of attachment and achievement expectations: A study of kindergarten teachers. Ed.D. dissertation. University of Houston. 1980.

Describes changes in teacher expectations for and attitudes of attachment to individual students during the first three months of kindergarten.

686.   Dunn, Charleta J. & Kowitz, Gerald T. A statistical analysis of data used in critical decision making by secondary school personnel. Houston, Texas: Bureau of Educational Research and Service. University of Houston. 1967.

Describes a relationship between teacher grades and student achievement measured by standardized tests.

687.   Dunn, Charleta J. & Kowitz, Gerald T. "Teacher perceptions of correlates of academic achievement," *School and Society 98* (1970): 370-2.

Describes the ratings of secondary teachers of the importance of various student personality characteristics for achievement.

688.   Duval, Concetta. "Differential teacher grading behavior toward female students of mathematics," *Journal for Research in Mathematics Education 11* (1980): 202-213.

Describes no difference in teacher grading of four geometry proofs by student sex or ability.

689.   Elijah, David V., Jr. A comparison of teacher rankings of reading readiness, Metropolitan Readiness Test Score rankings, and socioeconomic status rankings of first graders. 1976. *ERIC ED* 119 144.

Describes a relationship between teacher
ranking of readiness, student achievement on
readiness tests, and student socioeconomic level.

690. Elijah, David. "Teacher expectations: determinants
      of pupils' reading achievement," *Reading
      Improvement 17* (1980): 117-121.

      Describes teacher rankings of students in terms
      of reading readiness as related to results of
      student achievement on a test of reading
      readiness.

691. Elijah, David & Legenza, Alice. "Teacher rankings,
      readiness tests, and socioeconomic status,"
      Reading Improvement 17 (1980): 10-13.

      Describes student socioeconomic status as
      related to both teacher perceptions of student
      reading readiness and student scores on a reading
      readiness test.

692. Elmore, Particia B. & Beggs, Donald L. "Consistency
      of teacher ratings of pupil personality traits in
      a classroom setting," *Measurement and Evaluation
      in Guidance 8*, No. 2 (1975): 70-73. *ERIC ED* 066
      685.

      Describes teachers as inconsistent in rating
      student personality traits.

693. Elmore, Patricia B. & Beggs, Donald L. Stability of
      teacher ratings of pupil behavior in a classroom
      setting. 1972. *ERIC ED* 066 685.

      Describes teachers as not stable in their
      ratings of student behavior.

694. Enochs, J. Romily. The relationship between Indian
      teachers' and non-Indian teachers' perception of
      Indian first-graders and student achievement in
      reading. 1977. *ERIC ED* 148 543.

      Describes differences in perceptions of Indian
      students by Indian and non-Indian teachers but
      those differences not related to student
      achievement.

695. Entwisle, Doris R. & Hayduk, Leslie Alec. *Too great
      expectations: The academic outlook of young
      children.* Baltimore, Maryland: Johns Hopkins
      University Press. 1978.

      Describes differences across schools and
      children but a relationship between teacher grades
      and student expectations for the next year.

696. Eubanks, Eugene E. "A study of perceptions of black
      and white teachers in de facto segregated high
      schools," *Education* 95 (1974): 51-57.

      Describes differences in teacher perceptions of
      student-teacher relations, status of white versus
      black high schools and job satisfaction in white
      versus black high schools.

697. Evertson, C., Brophy, J., Anderson, L., Crawford,
      J. & Baum, M. Relationships of grade, sex, and
      teacher rankings to coder ratings on a checklist
      of student behaviors. Austin, Texas: Research and
      Development Center for Teacher Education. Texas
      University at Austin. 1975. *ERIC ED* 150 160.

      Describes consistencies in observer ratings of
      students with student sex, grade and teacher
      rankings.

698. Feldman, David & Altman, Rueben. Effects of teacher
      conceptual system and two pupil variables of EMRs
      on attitudes toward integration. 1978. *ERIC ED* 189
      779.

      Describes teacher responses to mainstreamed
      handicapped pupils related to the behavior and
      race of pupils and the extent to which teacher
      personality is more abstract or concrete.

699. Felsenthal, Helen. Pupil sex as a variable in
      teacher perception of classroom behavior. 1971.
      ERIC ED 050 026.

      Describes teacher perceptions of boys as more
      disruptive and having lower achievement and
      receiving more criticism.

700. Feuquay, Jeffrey Price. Teachers' self-attributions
      and their projections of student attributions
      under varying conditions. Ph.D. dissertation.
      Oklahoma State University. 1979.

      Describes teacher attributions to effect,
      ability, luck and task difficulty as differing for
      success and failure situations and, in failure
      situations, by student race.

701. Fish, Virginia Kemp. The relative contribution of
      perceived parental, science teacher, and best
      friend evaluations of science ability of the
      self-concept of science ability held by eighth
      grade females. Ph.D. dissertation. Western
      Michigan University. 1978.

Describes a relationship between the ratings of
science teachers, parents, and best friends of
student self-concept, with teacher ratings having
the highest relationship with student
self-concept.

702. Fisher, Lawrence. Teacher judgements of competence
      of male junior high school students. 1978. *ERIC*
      ED 180 667.

Describes four stable factors in junior high
school teachers' assessment of male students;
academic competence, intrusiveness, social
avoidance, and dependency/immaturity.

703. Foster, Glen & Keech, Valerie. "Teacher reactions
      to the label of educable mentally retarded,"
      Education and Training of the Mentally Retarded
      12 (1977): 307-311.

Describes regular class teachers rating lower
the videotape of a child labelled educable
mentally retarded than the same tape of a child
labelled a normal fourth grade boy.

704. Foster, Glen & others. "Classroom teacher and
      teacher-in-training susceptibility to
      stereotypical bias," *Personnel and Guidance*
      Journal 59 (1980): 27-30.

Describes teachers rating behavior as normal
but influenced by label of hypothetical child as
normal or emotionally disturbed.

705. Foster, Glen G. & Salvia, John. "Teacher response
      to label of learning disabled as a function of
      demand characteristics," *Exceptional Children 43*
      (1977): 533-534.

Describes teacher ratings of child related to
the label given to the child and instructions
given to the teacher about making the rating from
a videotape.

706. Foster, Glen G, Schmidt, Carl R. & Sabatino,
      David. "Teacher expectancies and the label
      'learning disabilities'," *Journal of Learning*
      Disabilities 9 (1976): 111-114.

Describes the label of learning disabled as
influencing teacher observations and ratings of a
child's behavior, when teachers were given
information about children.

707. Garcia, Augustine. A study of the relationship
      between teacher perceptions and

bicultural/bilingual affective interaction in the
classroom. Ph.D. dissertation. University of New
Mexico. 1972.

Describes teacher perceptions related to the
behavior of bilingual students in classrooms.

708. Gardner, John & Bing, Marion. "The elusiveness of
Pygmalion and differences in teacher-pupil
contacts," *Interchange 4* (1973): 34-42.

Describes differences among teachers in the
relationship of their perceptions to their
behavior toward students.

709. Garrison, Karen R. & Garrison, John P. Elementary
teachers' perceptions of communication
apprehension among their students: A research
note. 1979. *ERIC ED* 175 076.

Describes a moderate relationship between
teacher predictions of student communication
apprehension and measured student apprehension.

710. Garwood, S. Gray. "First-name stereotypes as a
factor in self-concept and school achievement,"
Journal of Educational Psychology 68 (1976):
482-487.

Describes differences in the behavior and
characteristics of students with first names
teachers consider desirable and undesirable.

711. Gay, Helen Kemp. Teacher effectiveness in
identifying children with specific learning
disabilities. Ph.D. dissertation. University of
North Carolina at Chapel Hill. 1980.

Describes teachers as quite accurate in
identifying students whose achievement is
discrepant from expected and who therefore may
have a learning disability.

712. Gerardi, Judith Orenstein. The influence of
information about pupil personal-social behavior,
pupil sex, and order of presentation of
information on teacher expectation. Ph.D.
dissertation. New York University. 1979.

Describes teacher responses to behavior records
and descriptive vignettes of students, with some
differences in expectations for boys and girls,
greater reponse to negative than positive behavior
records, and higher expectations by suburban than
urban teachers.

713. Giesbrecht, Margaret L. & Routh, Donald K. "The influence of categories of cumulative folder information on teacher referrals of low-achieving children for special education services," *American Educational Research Journal 16* (1979): 181-187.

Describes teacher use of information about student behavior in judging student need for special education.

714. Gil, Doron. The clinical problem solving behavior of classroom teachers as they diagnose children's reading performance in experimental and classroom situations. Ph.D. dissertation. Michigan State University. 1979.

Describes teachers showing little agreement on diagnoses, lacking systematic approaches to collecting and considering information, and using the same global diagnostic categories in simulation and when questioned about their behavior with their own students.

715. Gilberts, Richard A., Guckins, J.P. & Leeds, D.S. Teacher perceptions of race, socio-economic status and language characteristics. 1971. *ERIC ED* 052 131.

Describes race, socioeconomic status and language as factors related to teacher ratings of students, with language and socioeconomic status magnifying the effects of race.

716. Glazzard, Peggy. "Kindergarten predictors of school achievement," *Journal of Learning Abilities 12* (1979): 689-694.

Compares kindergarten teacher predictions of achievement, reading readiness test results, and achievement over four years.

717. Goldberg, Miriam L, Passow, A. Harry & Justman, Joseph. *The effects of ability grouping* New York: Teachers College Press. 1966.

Describes a study of the effects of ability grouping on student achievement and self-concept with a description of teacher ratings of ability, task orientation, and social relations related to student ability level.

718. Good, Thomas L., Schmidt, L., Peck, R. & Williams, D. Teacher assessment of pupil potential. Report Series No. 33. Austin, Texas: Research and

Development Center for Teacher Education. Texas University at Austin. 1969. *ERIC ED* 015 589.

Describes teachers as not accurate judges of student over and underachievement.

719. Good, Thomas L., Williams, D., Peck, R. & Schmidt, L. Listening to teachers. Research Series No. 34. Austin, Texas: Research and Development Center for Teacher Education. University of Texas at Austin. 1969. *ERIC ED* 036 456.

Describes teachers as identifying more behavioral than academic problems when discussing student problems, and attributing problems to factors other than their own teaching.

720. Gordon, E.M. & Thomas A. "Children's behavioral style and the teacher's appraisal of their intelligence," *Journal of School Psychology 5* (1967): 292–300.

Describes teacher ratings of intelligence related to kindergarten children's immediate positive or negative reactions to new situations.

721. Gotts, E.E. Factors related to teachers' irratability in response to pupil classroom behaviors. 1967. *ERIC ED* 015 495.

Describes teacher views of irritating student behavior and differences in views between regular classroom teachers and other school personnel.

722. Granger, Robert C. & Ramig, Christopher J. Teacher judgements of the ability of readers with different speech patterns. 1978. *ERIC ED* 153 197.

Describes teachers rating as lower readers those students who make miscues which do not change the meaning of the text, based on audiotapes.

723. Granger, Robert C. & others. "Teacher judgements of the communication effectiveness of children using different speech patterns," *Journal of School Psychology 69* (1977): 793–796.

Describes different teacher ratings of students by race and socioeconomic status, using taped speech samples.

724. Greenfield, Eugene Ronald. Teacher acceptance and perception of behavior of educationally

handicapped pupils transferred from special to regular classes, Los Angeles Unified School District. Ed.D. dissertation. Brigham Young University. 1972.

Describes no difference in teacher ratings of pupils by regular and special class teachers, with regular class teachers recommending that students return to special education classes.

725. Haberman, Martin & Raths, James D. "High, average, low--and what makes teachers think so," *Elementary School Journal 68* (1968): 241-245.

Describes a simulation in which teachers were asked to identify students' needs for enrichment and remedial help, with teachers recommending an equal number of students for each group regardless of the range of scores of the group of students.

726. Haller, Emil J. & Davis, Sharon A. "Does socioeconomic status bias the assignment of elementary school students to reading groups?" *American Educational Research Journal 17* (1980): 409-418.

Describes no relationship between consistency of teacher and student social class and student assignment to reading groups.

727. Hamilton, James T. "Values held by teachers," *Peabody Journal of Education 46* (1969): 278-281.

Describes the attitudes of experienced teachers to a number of statements about students.

728. Harari, Herbert & McDavid, John W. "Name stereotypes and teachers' expectations," *Journal of Educational Psychology 65* (1973): 222-225.

Describes a relationship between teacher expectations for students and evaluation of student work and stereotyped responses to student names.

729. Hardy, Timothy Ashley. Teacher-student dyadic relationships in the elementary classroom: A participant observation study. Ph.D. dissertation. University of Toronto, Canada. 1974.

Describes teacher ideal student, sources of information about students, and theories about student behavior.

730.   Harper, Gregory F. & others. Relationship of two
        measures of classroom behavior to the academic
        achievement of kindergarten, first and second
        grade children. *ERIC ED* 138 636.

        Describes teacher ratings of students and
        observed student behavior accounting for variance
        in student achievement over the influence of IQ.

731.   Harvey, Dale G. & Slatin, Gerald T. "The
        relationship between child's SES and teacher
        expectations: A test of the middle-class bias
        hypothesis," *Social Forces 54* (1975): 140-159.

        Describes teacher expectations related to
        student race and socioeconomic status.

732.   Hassan, James Craig. The relationship of
        socioeconomic status of neighborhood school on
        teacher perception of intellectually gifted sixth
        grade students. Ph.D. dissertation. University of
        Southern California. 1980.

        Describes no relationship between the
        socioeconomic settings of schools and teacher
        perceptions of gifted students.

733.   Hedin, Diane & Conrad, Dan. "Changes in children
        and youth over two decades: The perceptions of
        teachers," *Phi Delta Kappan 61* (1980): 702-703.

        Describes perceptions of experienced teachers
        of changes in students, more assertive and
        outspoken, oriented toward instant gratification
        than they used to be.

734.   Helton, George B. & Oakland, Thomas D. "Teacher's
        attitudinal responses to differing characteristics
        of elementary school students," *Journal of
        Educational Psychology 69* (1977): 261-265.

        Describes student personality characteristics
        related to differences in teacher attitudes toward
        children.

735.   Henderson, Edmund H. When teachers predict success
        in first-grade reading. 1973. *ERIC ED* 094 856.

        Describes teacher predictions of student
        reading achievement as complex and somewhat
        related to student race.

736.   Herbert, G.W. "Teachers' ratings of classroom
        behavior: Factorial structure," *British Journal of
        Educational Psychology 44* (1974): 233-240.

Describes five factors involved in teacher ratings of students based on analysis of teacher ratings.

737. Herson, Phyllis F. "Biasing effects of diagnostic labels and sex of pupil on teacher's views of pupils' mental health," *Journal of Educational Psychology* 66 (1974): 117-122.

Describes greater teacher rating of student incompacity with diagnostic labels than with descriptive information about behavior of students, but no difference by student sex.

738. Holmes, Monica Bychowski & others. Interaction patterns as a source of error in teacher's evaluations of Head Start children. Final Report. 1968. *ERIC ED* 023 453.

Describes behavior of Head Start students whom teachers perceived to be brighter as resembling middle class behavior.

739. Hudgins, Bryce B. "Attending and thinking in the classroom," *Psychology in the Schools* 4 (1967): 211-216.

Describes lack of a relationship between observer and teacher judgement of pupil attending and teacher predictions of subject matter relevance.

740. Humphreys, Lloyd G. & Stubbs, June. "A longitudinal analysis of teacher expectation, student expectation, and student achievement," *Journal of Educational Measurement* 14 (1977): 261-270.

Reports analyses of grades, teacher expectations and student expectations, with student achievement influencing teacher expectations.

741. Iadicola, Peter & Moore, Helen. Ethnic and class bias in teacher expectations of junior high school students: A test of the Bowles and Gintis thesis. 1977. *ERIC ED* 161 821.

Describes teacher expectations related more to teacher perceptions of student cognitive skills than class, presentation of self, and personality characteristics.

742. Irvin, Mari Griffiths. Self, mother, and teacher perceptions of the child as related to academic readiness, sex, and sibling position in

the family. Ed.D. dissertation. Northern Illinois University. 1974.

Describes teacher perceptions of students related to student academic readiness, language ability and visual-perceptual-motor skills.

743. Jackson, Philip W., Silberman, Melvin L. & Wolfson, Bernice J. "Signs of personal involvemen in teachers' descriptions of their students," *Journal of Educational Psychology 68* (1969): 22-27.

Describes teacher perceptions of students, with teachers providing more information about boys and those students whom teachers named first.

744. Jaeger, Richard M. & Freijo, Tom D. "Race and sex as concomitants of teachers' accuracy in evaluative rating of students," *Journal of Educational Psychology 67* (1975): 226-237. *ERIC ED 096 374.*

Describes female and white teachers as most accurate in ratings of white students.

745. Jarvis, Madelyn McKenna. Teacher perceptions of reading-related problems and the effect of inservice education in changing teacher classroom behavior. Ph.D. dissertation. Bowling Green State University. 1978.

Describes teacher characteristics related to their perceptions of student reading problems and teacher evaluation of in-service related to consistency of teacher use of the learned behaviors in the classroom.

746. Jensen, Mary & Rosenfeld, Lawrence B. "Influence of mode of presentation, ethnicity, and social class on teachers' evaluations of students," *Journal of Educational Psychology 66* (1974): 540-547. *ERIC ED 083 358.*

Describes teacher ratings of student audio and video presentations differ by student ethnic and socioeconomic levels.

747. Johnson, Roger A. "Teacher and student perception of student creativity," *Gifted Child Quarterly 20* (1976): 164-167.

Describes teachers as perceiving students to be more creative than students perceived themselves.

748. Kaplan, Susan Diane. The relationship of overt behavior, teacher perception of behavior, and teacher-assigned grades to locus of control in fourth graders. Ph.D. dissertation. Syracuse University. 1980.

    Describes teacher perceptions of differences in behaviors of students with internal and external locus of control.

749. Kay, B.R. & Lowe, C.A. "Teacher nomination of children's problems. A rolecentric interpretation," *Journal of Psychology 70* (1968): 121-129.

    Describes teacher evaluation of student behavior problems related to teacher expectations for self, teacher sex, age, level of education and experience.

750. Kedar-Voivodas, Gita & Tannenbaum, Abraham J. "Teachers' attitudes toward young deviant children," *Journal of Educational Psychology 71* (1979): 800-808. Also by first author only, Ph.D. dissertation. Columbia University. 1977.

    Presents information about student behaviors which influence teacher expectations for present and future school functioning of students, with teachers using more than information about labels, sex, of hypothetical students.

751. Kehle, Thomas J., Bramble, William J. & Mason, Emanuel J. "Teachers' expectations: Ratings of student performance as biased by student characteristics," *Journal of Experimental Education 43* (1974): 54-60.

    Describes teacher expectations in a simulation related to student sex, sex in interaction with attractiveness, and other student characteristics.

752. Kelly, Thomas J. & others. Teachers' perceptions of behavioral disorders in children. 1974. *ERIC ED* 097 319.

    Describes teacher perceptions of students within categories of identified behavioral problems.

753. Klein, Andrea Rubinstein. Hyperactive and active boys in the classroom: A naturalistic assessment of teacher ratings, classroom behaviors, peer interactions and perceptions, and subtypes

of hyperactives. Ph.D. dissertation. Indiana
University. 1978.

Describes differences in teacher ratings of
active and hyperactive students.

754.   Klein, Andrea Rubinstein & Young, Richard
       David. "Hyperactive boys in their classroom:
       Assessment of teacher and peer perceptions,
       interactions, and classroom behaviors," *Journal of
       Abnormal Child Psychology 7* (1979):425-442.

       Describes both teacher and students perceiving
       hyperactive boys as different from other boys in
       the classroom.

755.   Kleinfield, Judith. "The relative importance of
       teachers and parents in the formation of Negro and
       white students' academic self-concept," *Journal of
       Educational Research 65* (1972): 211-212.

       Describes teacher evaluation of student ability
       as greater than parent evaluation for black but
       not white high school students.

756.   Knafle, June D. "The relationship of behavior
       ratings to grades earned by female high school
       students," *Journal of Educational Research 66*
       (1972): 106-110.

       Describes a relationship between teacher
       assignment of grades and good behavior ratings.

757.   Knudsen, Janice Eileen. The relationships among
       teacher perception, student achievement
       motivation, and Metropolitan Readiness Test scores
       of kindergarten boys. Ph.D. dissertation.
       University of Florida. 1978.

       Describes teacher perceptions and student
       motivation as related to student achievement, with
       student motivation the stronger predictor of
       achievement.

758.   Langsdorf, Richard & others. "Ethnicity, social
       class, and perceptions of hyperactivity,"
       Psychology in the Schools 16 (1979): 293-298.

       Describes teacher ratings of student
       hyperactivity related to student ethnicity, with
       more black and fewer Mexican American children
       rated as hyperactive.

759.   Laosa, Luis M. & others. "Cognitive and personality
       characteristics of high school students

as predictors of the way they are rated by their teachers: A longitudinal study," *Journal of Educational Psychology 67* (1975): 866–872.

Describes differences in teacher ratings of students by grade, with teachers focusing on different aspects of students at different grades.

760. LaVoie, J.C. & Adams, G.R. "Teacher expectancy and its relation to physical and interpersonal characteristics of the child," *Alberta Journal of Educational Research 20* (1974): 122–132

Describes effects of student sex, conduct and physical attractiveness on teacher expectations.

761. Lawlor, Francis X. & Lawlor, Elizabeth P. "Teacher Expectations: A study of their genesis," *Science Education 57* (1973): 9–14.

Describes student teachers selecting top and bottom ten students from videotapes of students with agreement among themselves, but not being able to identify the cues that they used to select students.

762. Leiter, Kenneth C.W. "Teachers' use of background knowledge to interpret test scores," *Sociology of Education 49* (1976): 59–65.

Describes teachers interpretations of test scores in light of subjective information which they have about students.

763. Lewis, Lois Matheson. The relationship of achievement to reported self-concept and behavior ratings by teachers. Ph.D. dissertation. Wayne State University. 1968.

Describes teacher ratings of student behavior and student reports of self-concept related to achievement for male but not female black students.

764. Lockheed, Marliane E. Some determinants and consequences of teacher expectations concerning pupil performance. Beginning Teacher Evaluation Study: Phase II, 1973–74, Final Report: Volume V.2. Princeton, New Jersey: Educational Testing Service. 1976. *ERIC ED* 127 371.

Describes teacher expectations as not biased by student sex, race, but higher teacher expectations related to higher student achievement.

765. Lockheed, Marliane E. "Some causes and consequences
      of teacher expectations concerning pupil
      performance," *California Journal of Teacher
      Education 4*, No. 2 (1977): 40-52.

      Describes teacher expectations related to
      student achievement but prior student achievement
      related strongly to teacher expectations.

766. Lockheed, Marliane E. & Morgan, William R. A causal
      model of teachers' expectations in elementary
      classrooms. Princeton, New Jersey: Educational
      Testing Service. 1979.

      Describes student characteristics as
      influencing teacher and student expectations and,
      at grade five, information about students' current
      achievement influencing teacher expectations.

767. Loeb, Roger C. & Horst, Leslie. "Sex differences in
      self- and teachers' reports of self-esteem in
      preadolescents," *Sex Roles: A Journal of Research
      4* (1978): 779-788.

      Describes differences in student and teacher
      ratings of student self-esteem by student sex for
      female but not male students.

768. Long, Barbara H. & Henderson, Edmund H. "Certain
      determinants of academic expectancies among
      southern and non-southern teachers," *American
      Educational Research Journal 11* (1972): 137-147.

      Describes student test scores, activities and
      attention related to teacher ratings of reading
      achievement in a simulation, concluding that
      expectations may be realistic, not prejudiced.

769. Long, Barbara H. & Henderson, Edmund H. The effect
      of pupils' race, class, test scores, and classroom
      behavior on the academic expectancies of southern
      and non-southern white teachers. 1972. *ERIC ED* 063
      422.

      Reports a study of teacher ratings of student
      achievement biased by pupil characteristics.

770. Long, Barbara H. & Henderson, Edmund H. "teachers'
      judgements of black and white school beginners,"
      Sociology of Education 44 (1971): 358-368. *ERIC
      ED* 038 708.

      Describes greater variability in teacher
      ratings of white than of black students and
      student sex and socioeconomic level related to
      ratings.

771. Lowichik, Thomas Carl. The effects of three selected variables on the reading achievement of elementary school children. 1975. *ERIC ED* 116 121.

   Describes teachers having favorable perceptions of children and of the support services available to assist children in learning to read.

772. Luce, Sally R. & Hoge, Robert D. "Relations among teacher rankings, pupil-teacher interactions, and academic achievement: A test of the teacher expectancy hypothesis," *American Educational Research Journal 15* (1978): 489-500.

   Describes no relation between teacher expectations, teacher behavior with students, and student achievement.

773. McHugh, Linda Marie. Consistency in diagnosing reading problems and prescribing remedial programs among reading specialists, learning disabilities teachers, Title I teachers, and fourth grade classroom teachers. Ph.D. dissertation. University of Wisconsin, Madison. 1980.

   Describes consistency in the diagnosis of reading problems and prescriptions for those problems across teacher job groups.

774. McKinley, Bettie Jean Sanders. A comparison study of pupils' reading interests as depicted by individual pupils, their teachers, and in their basal readers. Ph.D. dissertation. Southern Illinois University at Carbondale. 1978.

   Describes teacher ratings of student reading interests in relation to student reports of reading interest.

775. Maddox-McGinty, Ann. Children's non-verbal behavior in the classroom and teachers' perceptions of teachability: An observational study. Ph.D. dissertation. University of California, Los Angeles. 1979.

   Describes agreement among teachers in rating a student as teachable but different behavior patterns of teachers with students rated as high and low teachable.

776. Magee, John Wesley, III. An aptitude-by-treatment interaction anaysis of teacher attitudes and the reduction of labeling bias. Ph.D. dissertation. Pennsylvania State University. 1978.

Describes teacher prediction of student off-task behavior as related to setereotyped responses to label (learning disabled and emotionally disturbed) and effected by training.

777. Mahaffey, L., Brophy, J.E., Evertson, C.M., Crawford, J. & Baum, M. The Student Attributes Study: Relationships between classroom observation measure with teacher attitudes of attachment, rejection, and concern. Austin, Texas: Center for Research and Development for Teacher Education. Texas University at Austin. 1975. *ERIC ED* 113 378.

Describes attributes of groups of students toward whom teachers feel attachment, rejection or concern.

778. Mahaffey, L, Brophy, J.E., Evertson, C.M., Crawford, J. & Baum, M. The Student Attributes Study: A preliminary report (abbreviated version). Austin, Texas: Center for Research and Development for Teacher Education. Texas University at Austin. 1976. *ERIC ED* 121 799.

Describes student characteristis which are related to teacher attitude toward and expectation for students.

779. Malowitzky, Noah. Peer, teacher, self, parent perception as they affect school achievement. Ph.D. dissertation. Yeshiva University. 1979.

Describes differences in perceptions by teachers, parents, and selves of higher and lower achieving students in grades two through five.

780. Marshall, John C. & Sokol, Alvin P. "Characteristics of students perceived by teachers to be self-directed and not-self-directed," *Education 91* (1970): 41-49.

Describes characteristics of those students whom teachers perceive to be good and not good students.

781. Martinek, Thomas J. "Stability of teachers' expectations for elementary school aged children," *Perceptual and Motor Skills 51* (1980): 1269-1270.

Describes stable ratings of students over eight weeks in physical performance, peer relations, cooperative behavior and ability to reason.

782. Marwit, Karen L., Marwit, Samuel J. & Walker,
     Elaine. "Effects of student race and physical
     attractiveness on teachers' judgements of
     transgressions," *Journal of Educational Psychology*
     70 (1978): 911-915.

     Describes teachers as rating negative behavior
     by attractive students more severely than by
     unattractive students.

783. Mason, Emanuel J. "Teachers' observations and
     expectations of boys and girls as influenced by
     biased psychological reports and knowledge of the
     effects of bias," *Journal of Educational
     Psychology* 65 (1973): 238-243.

     Describes factors influencing teacher
     expectations by student sex.

784. Mason, Emanuel J. & Larimore, David L. "Effects of
     biased psychological reports on two types of
     teachers' ratings," *Journal of School Psychology*
     12 (1974): 46-50.

     Describes differences in teacher ratings of
     student characteristics but not performance from
     videotape when given false information.

785. Mayfield, Betty. "Teacher perception of creativity,
     intelligence and achievement," *Gifted Child
     Quarterly* 23 (1979): 812-817.

     Describes teacher perceptions of student
     performance and actual student performance on
     intelligence, achievement and creativity tests.

786. Megiveron, Gene E. "Relevancy and morale of
     students," *NASSP Bulletin* 59 (1975): 46-49.

     Describes teacher predictions of student
     attitudes toward school, homework and rules as
     less positive than actual attitudes.

787. Merz, William R. & Rutherford, Brent
     M. "Differential teacher regard for creative
     students and achieving students," *California
     Journal of Educational Research* 23 (1972): 83-90.

     Describes a slight relation between teacher
     judgement of and measures of student creativity
     and achievement.

788. Metz, Mary Haywood. Teachers' adjustments to
     students' behaviors: Some implications for the
     process of desegregation. 1978. *ERIC ED* 155 294.

Describes teacher attitude influenced by
behavior of students and teachers in desegregated
schools, with differences in teacher behavior
related to achievement level of students, not
teacher beliefs about desegregation.

789.   Mikulecky, Larry J. Teacher prediction of students'
reading attitudes: An examination of teacher
judgement compared to student-peer judgement in
assessing student reading attitude and habit.
1978. *ERIC ED* 163 429.

Describes teacher and student perceptions of
student reading attitude related more to student
English grades than to actual student attitude.

790.   Moles, Oliver & Perry, Esther. Sources of teacher
expectations early in first grade. National
Institute of Education. 1975. *ERIC ED* 106 000.

Describes teacher expectations related to prior
student learning, parent involvement in schooling,
and socioeconomic level.

791.   Morine-Dershimer, Greta. "The anatomy of teacher
prediction," *Educational Research Quarterly 3*, No.
4 (1978-1979): 59-65.

Describes teacher predictions related to
student test results, with predictions quite
accurate in terms of reading achievement but not
so accurate in other areas.

792.   Mossaddad, Seyed Ali Asghar. Attribution conflict
between teachers and students regarding students'
academic achievement. Ph.D. dissertation.
University of California, Los Angeles. 1980.

Describes teachers' attributions of causes of
student achievement differing by level of student
achievement and differing from student
attributions.

793.   Murray, Howard B & others. "The effects of locus of
control and pattern of performance on teacher's
evaluation of a student," *Psychology in the
Schools 10* (1973): 345-350. 1971. *ERIC ED* 073
403.

Describes student initial performance having a
greater influence on teacher evaluation than later
student performance, with no differences by
teacher locus of control.

794. Nagler, Sylvia, & Hoffnung, Robert. Teacher expectations, children's perceived powerfulness and school performance. 1971. *ERIC ED* 049 335.

   Describes those children perceived as having high power being viewed more favorably by teachers, as having higher test scores and fewer behavior problems.

795. Naremore, Rita C. "Teachers' judgements of children's speech: A factor analytic study of attitudes," *Speech Monograph 38* (1971): 17-27.

   Describes four types of teachers in terms of their different ratings of students from audiotapes.

796. Nash, Roy. *Classrooms observed: The teacher's perception and the pupil's performance.* London: Routledge & Kegan Paul, Ltd. 1973.

   Reports studies of elementary and secondary schooling in England, including teacher perceptions of students, student perceptions of themselves, student friendships and interactions with other students.

797. Natriello, Gary James. An experimental study of the effects of student characteristics on teacher standards and warmth. Ph.D. dissertation. Stanford University. 1979.

   Describes teacher responses to student behavior and academic problems in a simulation related to student characteristics.

798. O'Connell, Edward J., Dusek, Jerome B. & Wheeler, Richard J. "A follow-up study of teacher expectancy effects," *Journal of Educational Psychology 66* (1974): 325-328.

   Describes a two year study which concludes that teachers do not bias student learning with their expectations but are good predictors of student achievement.

799. Oliver, Jo Ellen & Arnold, Richard. "Comparing a standardized test, an informal inventory and teacher judgement on third grade reading," *Reading Improvement 15* (1978): 56-59.

   Describes a relationship between teacher judgement, student results on an informal reading inventory and standardized test scores.

800. Palardy, J. Michael. The effect of teachers'
      beliefs on the achievement in reading of
      first-grade boys. Ph.D. dissertation. Ohio State
      University. 1968.

           Describes a relationship between teacher
      beliefs about student reading and actual
      achievement of first grade students.

801. Palardy, J. Michael. "What teachers believe--What
      children achieve," *Elementary School Journal 69*,
      No. 7 (1969): 370-374.

           Describes teacher beliefs about student
      achievement by sex related to achievement of their
      students by sex.

802. Palmer, Douglas. "The effect of educable mental
      retardation descriptive information on regular
      classroom teachers' attributions and instructional
      perceptions," *Mental Retardation 18* (1980):
      171-175.

           Describes changes in teacher ratings and
      prescriptions for instruction, resulting from the
      cumulative effects of information about EMR
      status, rather than the specific types of
      information.

803. Parker, Robin Nell. Teacher expectancy behavior:
      The impact of several salient student
      characteristics upon expectations and causal
      attributions. Ph.D. dissertation. Stanford
      University. 1979.

           Describes teachers' expectations for
      performance and grades related to information
      about student ability while expectations for
      social success were related to personality in a
      simulation.

804. Paulauskas, Stana L. & Campbell, Susan B.
      Goodman. "Social perspective-taking and teacher
      ratings of peer interaction in hyperactive boys,"
      Journal of Abnormal Psychology 7 (1979): 483-493.

           Describes teachers as rating hyperactive boys
      differently than students rate their peers, and
      older hyperactive boys rated as more deviant than
      younger ones.

805. Peck, R.F., Blattstein, D., Blattstein, A. & Fox,
      R. "Comparison of self, peer, and teacher ratings
      of student coping as predictors of achievement,
      self-esteem, and attitudes," *Journal of Teacher
      Education 31* (1980): 45-46.

        Describes a relationship between self, peer and
teacher ratings and student coping, with teacher
ratings showing the strongest relationship of the
three sets of ratings.

806. Pelzer, Inge Anna Elizabeth. Teacher identification
      of impulsivity-reflectivity in low, average, and
      high achievers. Ph.D. dissertation. University of
      California, Riverside. 1979.

        Describes some consistency in teacher rating of
children on a scale of impulsive-reflective when
descriptions of behavior were provided, with
teachers more apt to rate boys as impulsive.

807. Petrilla, Linda Kay. Teachers' perceptions of
      students they nominate as high-motivated and
      low-motivated. Ph.D. dissertation. University of
      Kentucky. 1979.

        Reports that teachers use classroom behavior,
grades, achievement scores, appearance and
socioeconomic status as cues to student
motivation.

808. Phillips, Ruthellen Hill. Teachers' reported
      expectations of children's sex-roles and
      evaluations of sexist teaching practices. Ed.D.
      dissertation. West Virginia University. 1980.

        Describes teacher expectations of children's
sex roles differing by child sex, with boys
expected to be more aggressive and girls more
emotional.

809. Post, Eleanor Victoria. The effects of increasing
      amounts of information and training on elementary
      teachers' ability to identify verbally gifted
      children. Ph.D. dissertation. University of Texas
      at Austin. 1980.

        Describes teachers in a district with high
socioeconomic status homes not identifying as
gifted all the students who were so identified by
a test.

810. Prawat, Richard S. & Jarvis, Robert. "Gender
      differences as a factor in teachers' perceptions
      of students," *Journal of Educational Psychology*
      72 (1980): 734-749.

        Describes teacher ratings of students more
strongly related to student ability and
achievement than to student sex.

811.   Prieto, Alfonso G. & Zucker, Stanley H. The effects
       of race on teachers' perceptions of educational
       placement of behaviorally disordered children.
       1980. *ERIC ED* 188 427.

           Describes teachers selecting for special class
       placement more often those hypothetical children
       identified as Mexican American than as Caucasian.

812.   Pringle, Celestine Ann. The effects of teachers'
       attitudes toward dialects on their expectations
       for students' academic competence. Ph.D.
       dissertation. Kent State University. 1980.

           Describes teachers as rating dialect speakers
       lower in academic competence than speakers of
       standard English, with elementary teachers less
       negative than junior high teachers.

813.   Pugh, Lee G. Teacher attitudes and expectations
       associated with race and social class. 1974. *ERIC
       ED* 094 018.

           Reports that teachers perceived white students
       more favorably than black students, from
       videotapes, with greater differences for black
       than white teachers, and no difference by social
       class.

814.   Purgess, Patricia Jane. Teacher expectancy for
       academic success in relation to label, sex, and
       pupil behavior. Ph.D. dissertation. Fordham
       University. 1979.

           Describes lower teacher ratings for student
       success in a simulation for those students with
       disruptive behavior and labelled as having an
       educational problem.

815.   Raffaniello, Eileen Mary. Determinants of
       diagnostic labeling and educational placement
       judgements by teachers. Ph.D. dissertation.
       University of Texas at Austin. 1979.

           Describes teachers making fewer decisions for
       mainstreaming of students when label information
       was given to teachers before the placement
       decision, in a simulation.

816.   Rich, Jordan. "Effects of children's physical
       attractiveness on teachers' evaluations," *Journal
       of Educational Psychology 67* (1975): 599-609.

           Describes teachers rating attractive students
       as having more desirable personalities

but teachers regarding misbehavior as less serious
for less attractive students.

817. Richmond, Bert O. & White, William F. "Predicting
      teachers' perceptions of pupil behavior,
      "Measurement and Evaluation in Guidance 4 (1971):
      71-78.

      Describes a relationship between teachers'
      ratings of students and student characteristics,
      with lower ratings for students with lower
      self-concepts.

818. Rivers, James Edward. Older siblings as bases of
      teacher expectations. Ph.D. dissertation.
      University of Kentucky. 1979.

      Describes little variance in student
      achievement and no relation to teacher
      expectations based on achievement of older
      siblings.

819. Robinson, Gloria Jean. Analysis of teacher
      expectations and reading in first grade. Ed.D.
      dissertation. Ball State University. 1975. *ERIC
      ED* 124 933.

      Describes low achieving students making greater
      gains in classses of teachers who did not expect
      student background to be related to reading
      achievement.

820. Roeber, Edward Dean. The influence of information
      about students on the expectations of teachers.
      Ph.D. dissertation. University of Michigan. 1970.

      Describes teacher ratings influenced by student
      test scores, record of achievement and comments of
      past teacher, but not race or socioeconomic level,
      based on teacher readings of descriptions of
      students.

821. Rose, Bruce J. A cognitive and communications
      system of behavior. 1977. *ERIC ED* 137 287.

      Reports that data from teacher ratings of
      videotapes of students indicating teachers use new
      information to readjust their expectations for
      students.

822. Rosenthal, Rita Sharon. Differences in teacher
      behavior in mainstreamed vs. non-mainstreamed
      schools. 1977. Ph.D. dissertation. Yeshiva
      University. 1977.

Describes no differences in teachers' attitudes
toward and perscriptions for students from
videotapes of students for teachers in
mainstreamed and non-mainstreamed schools.

823.   Rotter, George S. The effect of sex identification
upon teacher evaluation of pupils. 1967. *ERIC ED*
013 793.

Describes differences in teacher ratings of
student behavior by sex of child, with boys seen
as more active, gregarious, dirtier, and leaders.

824.   Rotter, Naomi G. The influence of race and other
variables on teachers' ratings of pupils. Ph.D.
dissertation. New York University. 1974.

Describes teachers basing their expectations on
previous performance when that information was
available.

825.   Safran, Stephen Philip. Resource teacher
communication and regular educator's initial
expectations of handicapped children. Ph.D.
dissertation. University of Virginia. 1980.

Describes effects of different types of
communication from a resource teacher upon
classroom teachers' perceptions of a hypothetical
student.

826.   Salvia, John & others. "Attractiveness and school
achievement," *Journal of School Psychology 15*
(1977): 60-66.

Describes a relationship between the rated
attractiveness of elementary students and their
grades and achievement test scores.

827.   Sandler, Paul Stewart. Male and female teachers'
ratings of children's behavior. Ed.D.
dissertation. University of Georgia. 1979.

Describes differences in teacher ratings of
student behavior by student sex.

828.   Santrock, John W. & Tracy, Russel L. "Effects of
children's family structure status on the
development of stereotypes by teachers," *Journal
of Educational Psychology 70* (1978): 754-757.
1976. *ERIC ED* 162 192.

Describes teachers shown a videotape of a
student as rating the boy reported to be from a
divorced family lower on happiness, emotional

adjustment and coping with stress than a boy
reported to be from a two-parent family.

829. Saracho, Olivia. "The relationship between
      teachers' cognitive style and their perceptions of
      their students' academic achievements,"
      Educational Research Quarterly 5, No. 3 (1980):
      40-49.

      Describes teachers as more accurate in their
      rankings of student academic achievement if
      teachers and students are at the same end of the
      field-dependence-independence continuum.

830. Saunders, Bruce T. & Ditullio, William M. "The
      failure of biased information to affect teacher
      behavior ratings and peer sociometric status of
      disturbing children in the classroom," *Psychology
      in the Schools 9* (1972): 440-445.

      Describes teachers as not changing their
      perceptions of students when given information
      that students were emotionally disturbed.

831. Saur, Rosemary Eklund. The teacher expectancy
      phenomenon: A decision-making perspective. Ph.D.
      dissertation. University of California, Santa
      Barbara. 1978.

      Describes teacher perceptions of students as
      related to student characteristics and presents a
      model of teacher perceptions of students.

832. Schlosser, Linda & Algozzine, Bob. "Sex, behavior,
      and teacher expectancies," *Journal of Experimental
      Education 48* (1980): 231-236.

      Reports that elementary teachers in discussing
      theoretical children viewed sex-inappropriate
      behavior less favorably than sex-appropriate
      behavior.

833. Schumer, Harry & Royer, James M. Student
      achievement gains as a function of teacher
      predications. 1974. *ERIC ED 096 316*.

      Describes greater student gains for those
      students for whom teachers over several years
      predicted success in achievement.

834. Schwebel, Carol Rose. Teacher's versus student's
      perception of a children's book. Ph.D.
      dissertation. Ohio State University. 1979.

Describes teacher perceptions of student
understanding of a book in comparison with student
understanding, with teacher estimates higher than
actual student understanding.

835.   Sebastian, Carolyn Bryam. Teachers' understandings
        of the behavior of Mexican-American children.
        Ed.D. dissertation. University of Southern
        California. 1972.

        Describes teachers not identifying ethnic and
        socioeconomic factors as influencing the behavior
        of Mexican-American children.

836.   Selig, H., Brophy, J. & Willis, S. Causal
        inferences of first grade teachers. Austin, Texas:
        Center for Research and Development for Teacher
        Education. Texas University at Austin. 1976. *ERIC
        ED* 126 063.

        Describes teacher statements of expectations
        for students in terms of levels of student
        achievement.

837.   Shavelson, Richard J., Caldwell, Joel, & Izu,
        Tonia. "Teachers' sensitivity to the reliability
        of information in making pedagogical decisions,"
        American Educational Research Journal 14 (1977):
        83-97.

        Describes teachers using different kinds of
        information about students to form estimates of
        student ability and to make decisions about
        instruction.

838.   Shore, Alfred Lewis. Confirmation of expectancy and
        changes in teachers' evaluations of student
        behavior. Ph.D. dissertation. University of
        Southern California. 1969.

        Reports that teacher expectations for students
        changed with information which confirmed or
        contradicted their expectations.

839.   Silberman, Melvin L. "Behavioral expression of
        teachers' attitudes toward elementary school
        students," *Journal of Educational Psychology 60*
        (1969): 402-407.

        Describes some teachers' attitudes toward
        students related to differences in behavior of
        students, and student predictions of teacher
        behavior toward them related to actual teacher
        behavior toward them.

840. Silvern, Louis E. "Masculinity-femininity in children's self-concepts: The relationship to teachers' judgements of social adjustment and academic ability, classroom behaviors and popularity," *Sex Roles: A Journal of Research 4* (1978): 929-949.

Describes teacher attitude toward student behavior as related to teacher views of traits as masculine or feminine.

841. Simmons, Barbara. "Sex role expectations of classroom teachers," *Education 100* (1980): 249-253.

Describes differences in teacher and student expectations for the behavior of girls and boys, with boys viewed as more aggressive and physically adept due to cultural factors and girls more emotional, intuitive due to biological factors.

842. Simmons, Cassandra Anae. Racial bias of teachers and counselors in the assignment of incoming seventh graders to ability groups within a desegregated school district. Ph.D. dissertation. Michigan State University. 1979.

Describes race as not related to decisions of the level at which to place students in the seventh grade language arts and math, based on teacher and counselor decisions for hypothetical students.

843. Smith, Mieko Kotake. The relationships between mother and teacher expectations and child academic and behavioral performance. Ph.D. dissertation. Case Western Reserve University. 1980.

Reports that teachers and mothers differed in expectations for children by socioeconomic level and sex of students, with teacher expectations for middle and upper class minority students higher than for white students.

844. Smith, Mildred B. "Interpersonal relationships in the classroom based on the expected socio-economic status of sixth grade boys," *Teachers College Journal 36* (1965): 200-206.

Describes differences in teacher behavior toward boys by teacher expectations of boys' achievement in adult occupations, and teacher predictions of adult status based on student behavior.

845.   Sobel, David Allen. Relationships among
        internality-externality, teacher perceptions of
        pupils behaviors and pupil behavior. Ph.D.
        dissertation. Case Western Reserve University.
        1970

            Describes no relation between external/internal
        control of the teachers and teachers' perceptions
        of the behavior of external boys.

846.   Solomon, Daniel & Kendall, Arthur J. "Dimensions of
        children's classroom behavior as perceived by
        teachers," *American Educational Research Journal*
        14 (1977): 411-421. *ERIC ED* 132 065.

            Describes teacher ratings of students as
        discriminating accurately between students by
        student approach to learning, as perseverant,
        autonomous, intellectual.

847.   Sorotzken, Feige, Fleming, Elyse S. & Anttonen,
        Ralph, G. "Teacher knowledge of standardized test
        information and its effect on pupil IQ and
        achievement," *Journal of Experimental Education*
        43 (1974): 79-85.

            Describes no difference in student achievement
        by type of test information given to teachers, but
        differed by teacher sex and attitude toward
        standardized tests.

848.   Spencer, Richard Paul. Demographic investigation of
        elementary school teachers' perception of mildly
        handicapped children. Ph.D. dissertation.
        University of Connecticut. 1979.

            Describes differences by geographic location
        and student type in teacher ability to identify
        types of students in a simulation.

849.   Stanton, M. "Teachers' assessments of various forms
        of social behavior," *Journal of Moral Education 2*
        (1973): 137-144.

            Describes differences in teacher judgements of
        student behavior by type of behavior and sex of
        students.

850.   Stockton, William Simms. Social control in a
        multi-cultural inner-city junior high school
        classroom. Ph.D. dissertation. University of
        Minnesota. 1980.

            Describes teacher's views of relationships
        between teacher and students in the classroom,

teacher expectations for students and strategies for interactions with students.

851. Stone, Brenda G. "Relationship between creativity and classroom behavior," *Psychology in the Schools* *17* (1980): 106-108.

Describes no relationship between teacher identification of students as behavior problems and a measure of student creativity.

852. Strickmeier, Henry Bernard, Jr. An analysis of verbal teaching behaviors in seventh grade mathematics classes grouped by ability. Ph.D. dissertation. University of Texas at Austin. 1970.

Describes differences in teacher expectations for students by ability level of the class, but no differences in teacher behavior.

853. Sundby, Dianne Yvonne. The relationship of teacher-child perception similarities and teacher-ratings, and the effect of teachers' similarity expectancies on children's self-perceptions and teacher-ratings. Ph.D. dissertation. Purdue University. 1971.

Describes teacher ratings of student progress in reading and math as related to achievement, with somewhat more favorable ratings for female students.

854. Taft, Rhonda Susan. Teacher language and perception of behavior problems in children: The influences of Massachusett General Law, Chapter 766, Acts, 1972. Ed.D. dissertation. Boston University School of Education. 1979.

Describes teacher descriptions of student behavior, the aspects of student behavior that teachers use in judging behavior and teacher recommendations for actions in response to that behavior.

855. Therrien, S. "Teachers' attributions of student ability," *Alberta Journal of Educational Research* *22* (1976): 205-215.

Describes teacher perceptions of student ability as related to the source and order of information about students, in a simulation.

856. Touliatos, John & Lindholm, Byron W. "Teachers' perceptions of behavior problems in children from

intact, single-parent, and stepparent families,
"Psychology in the Schools 17 (1980): 266-269.

Describes differences in teacher ratings of
children in terms of behavior problems by type of
home-family structure.

857.   Treffinger, Donald J., Feldhusen, John F. & Thomas,
Susan Bahlke. "Relationship between teachers'
divergent thinking abilities and their ratings of
pupils' creative thinking abilities," *Measurement
and Evaluation in Guidance 3* (1970): 169-176.

Describes teachers differing in ability to
predict student divergent thinking and those
predictions related to student IQ and divergent
thinking scores.

858.   Tymitz, Barbara Sladcik. The relationship of
differentiated teacher/learner interactions on
teachers' frame of reference in understanding
children's cognitions and behaviors. Ph.D.
dissertation. University of Illinois at
Urbana-Champaign. 1977.

Describes the aspects of children that teachers
attend to in diagnosing children's learning needs,
with aspects differing by teacher, and not related
to teacher years of experience.

859.   Vinsonhaler, J.F. The consistency of reading
diagnosis. Research Series No. 28. East Lansing,
Michigan: Institute for Research on Teaching.
Michigan State University. 1979.

Describes limited agreement among teachers and
reading specialists in diagnosing reading problems
of students.

860.   Wagner, Bruce Elliot. An analysis of the academic
and personality characteristics of colorless
children who are responded to with indifference in
the classroom environment. Ph.D. dissertation.
University of Southern California. 1979.

Describes lower achievement for those students
whom teachers identify as hard to get to know and
colorless than students whom teachers describe as
easy to get to know and a randomly selected
group.

861.   Wang, Margaret C. "The accuracy of teacher's
predictions on children's learning performance,"
Journal of Educational Research 66 (1973):
462-465.

Describes variability in teacher skill in evaluating student achievement by informal methods.

862. Wang, M.C. & Weisstein, W.J. "Teacher expectations and student learning," In *Achievement motivation: Recent trends in theory and research.* Edited by Leslie J. Fyans. New York: Plenum Publications. 1980.

Describes information which influences teacher expectations and the effects of those expectations on student achievement. For Fyans reference see citation No. 2949.

863. Warder, Sally Loy. The sex-role perceptions of teachers and their relationship to the reading achievement of first grade boys and girls with appropriate and inappropriate sex-role preferences. Ph.D. dissertation. University of Iowa. 1978,

Describes no differences in teacher perceptions of the behaviors of boys and girls in terms of adult-assigned sex roles.

864. Warren, Sue Allen, Gardner, David C. & Hogan, David W., Jr. "Teacher nominations of minority and low SES students for special education," *Education 96* (1975): 57-62.

Describes characteristics of students nominated by teachers for special education services, with greater than expected numbers nominated within certain groups, such as vocational education students and students receiving free lunches.

865. Wasik, John L. "Teacher perceptions of behaviors associated with creative problem solving performance," *Educational and Psychological Measurement 34* (1974): 327-341.

Describes cues teachers use in rating students in terms of problem-solving ability and teacher ratings related to abilities measured by scholastic aptitude test.

866. Weinberg, Dorothy R. The racially changing school: Negative teacher perceptions of Afro-American students as a response to change, rather than "cultural difference". 1976. *ERIC ED* 123 293.

Describes no differences in the categories teachers use in thinking about elementary students in stable white and black schools.

867. Weinshank, A. Investigations of the diagnostic reliability of reading specialists, learning disabilities specialists, and classroom teachers: Results and implications. Research Series No. 88. East Lansing, Michigan: Institute for Research on Teaching. Michigan State University. 1980.

Describes low reliability in diagnosis of reading problems made by teachers and specialists, with simulations of student problems.

868. Weinshank, A.B. An observational study of the relationship between diagnosis and remediation in reading. Research Series No. 72. East Lansing, Michigan: Institute for Research on Teaching. Michigan State University. 1980.

Describes observations of reading teachers' diagnosis of reading problems and the lack of systematic procedures consistent across cases and specialists.

869. White, William F. & Simmons, Margaret. "First-grade readiness predicted by teachers' perceptions of students' maturity and students' perception of self," *Perceptual and Motor Skills 39* (1974): 395-399.

Describes a relationship between teacher judgement of student academic maturity and reading readiness.

870. Wilborn, Bobbie LaRue. The relationship between teacher attitudes and teacher ratings of pupil behavior. Ph.D. dissertation. University of Missouri-Columbia. 1971.

Describes no relationship between teacher personality and teacher ratings of student behavioral maturity.

871. Wilkerson, Mary Alice. The effects of sex and ethnicity upon teachers' expectations of students. Ed.D. dissertation. East Texas State University. 1980.

Describes teacher expectations for students by teacher and student characteristics, with highest expectations for white female and Mexican-American male students.

872. Willerman, M. "A study of the effect of objective student information on teacher perception of

culturally disadvantaged children," *Illinois School Research 8* (1971): 33-36.

Describes a study of teacher use of information about students in planning for instruction for those students.

873. Williams, Frederick & Naremore, Rita C. "Language attitudes: An analysis of teacher differences," *Speech Monographs 41* (1974): 391-396.

Describes five types of teachers in terms of the way they rated students from audiotapes of students.

874. Williams, Frederick & others. Attitudinal correlates of children's speech characteristics. Final Report. Austin, Texas: Center for Communication Research. Texas University at Austin. 1971. *ERIC ED* 052 213.

Reports a study in which teacher expectations for child were based in part on ethnicity and use of non-standard English and related to expectations for performance in languauge arts classes, after teachers listened to taped speech samples.

875. Williams, Frederick & Whitehead, Jack L. "Language in the classroom: Studies of the Pygmalion effect," *English Record 21*, No. 4 (1971): 108-113.

Describes teacher attitudes toward students as based on student speech and visual characteristics.

876. Williams, Frederick, Whitehead, Jack L & Miller, Leslie M. "Relations between language attitudes and teacher expectancy," *American Educational Research Journal 9* (1972): 263-277.

Describes teacher evaluation of students as related to ethnicity of the teacher and student; teacher ratings of speech samples were most accurate in terms of achievement when the ratings related to language arts.

877. Williams, Trevor. Students, teachers, and educational expectations: Reciprocal effects at three points in time. Toronto, Canada: Ontario Institute for Studies in Education. 1972. *ERIC ED* 063 250.

Reports that student effects on teachers are greater than teacher expectancy effects on students, since teacher expectancy effects are negative.

878. Williams, Trevor. Teacher discrimination and self-fulfilling prophecies. 1975. *ERIC ED* 106 185.

Describes teacher expectancies for students related to student classroom behavior.

879. Williams, Trevor. "Teacher prophecies and the inheritance of inequality," *Sociology of Education* 49 (1976): 223-236.

Describes teacher expectations related not to student learning but related to school certification of the amount of student learning.

880. Willis, Sherry Lynn. Formation of teachers' expectations of first grade student's academic performance. Ph.D. dissertation. University of Texas at Austin. 1972. *ERIC ED* 078 902.

Describes teacher rankings of students as stable over time and student characteristics and behavior related to teacher rankings.

881. Willis, Sherry & Brophy, Jere E. "Origins of teachers' attitudes toward young children," *Journal of Educational Psychology* 66 (1974): 520-529.

Describes student characteristics and attributes associated with teacher ratings of student personality.

882. Wong, Morrison G. "Model students? Teachers' perceptions and expectations of their Asian and white students," *Sociology of Education* 53 (1980): 236-246.

Describes greater expectations for Asian than for white students, even white students of a higher socioeconomic level.

883. Woodworth, W.D. & Salzer, R.T. "Black children's speech and teacher's evaluation," *Urban Education* 6 (1971): 167-173.

Reports that teachers preferred material read by and reportedly written by white rather than black children, after listening to tapes.

884. Wunderlich, Elaine & Bradtmueller, Mary. "Teacher estimates of reading levels compared with IRPI instructional level scores," *Journal of Reading* 14 (1971): 303-308, 336.

Reports that teachers under-rate good readers, over-rate poor readers in terms of defining student reading levels.

885. Yee, A.H. "Interpersonal attitudes of teachers and advantaged and disadvantaged pupils," *Journal of Human Resources* 3 (1968): 327-345.

Reports that teacher attitudes toward students vary by student social class and ethnicity, teacher sex, years of experience and grade level, with teachers of middle class children more warm, sympathetic than teachers of lower class children.

886. Yoshida, Roland K. & Meyers, C. Edward. "Effects of labeling as educable mentally retarded on teachers' expectancies for change in a student's performance," *Journal of Educational Psychology* 67 (1975): 521-527.

Reports that teacher ratings of likely student achievement in concept formation were not related to label as regular class or EMR student but evaluations of students over time were related to student behavior.

887. Ysseldyke, James E. & Foster, Glen G. "Bias in teachers' observations of emotionally disturbed and learning disabled children," *Exceptional Children* 44 (1978): 613-615.

Reports that teachers rated students differently by label, when given the same information for hypothetical students except for the label.

888. Zach, L. & Price, M. "The teacher's part in sex role reinforcement," *Research in Education* (1973). *ERIC ED* 070 513.

Describes teacher responses to characteristics of children as varying by sex and ability/achievement levels of children.

889. Zehm, Stanley J. "Teacher expectations: A key to reading success," *Reading Improvement* 12 (1975): 23-26.

Describes teacher expectations related to student reading achievement.

IV TEACHER BEHAVIOR

A. DESCRIPTIONS OF

890. Acheson, Elizabeth. Responses of teachers to
pupils' dependent behavior and the reactions of
pupils to these responses. Ed.D. dissertation.
Temple University. 1969.

Describes behavior of students and teachers in
Head Start classrooms, the number of dependent
behaviors by student sex and differences in
teacher responses to those behaviors by student
sex.

891. Achilles, C.M. & Crump, H.B. Comparison of teacher
verbal/nonverbal communications to various pupil
groups. 1979. ERIC ED 171 667.

Describes different observed patterns of
teacher and student verbal and nonverbal behaviors
associated with differences in student demographic
variables.

892. Achilles, Charles M. & French, Russell L. (Eds.)
Inside classrooms: Studies in verbal and nonverbal
communication. Knoxville, Tennessee: Tennessee
University. ERIC ED 143 046.

Presents thirteen articles which describe
teacher verbal and nonverbal behaviors in
interactions with students in public school and in
other settings.

893. Adams, Raymond S. "Location as a feature of
instructional interaction," *Merrill-Palmer
Quarterly 15* (1969): 309-321.

Describes the concentration of classroom
communication in the front of the room, in
elementary and secondary classrooms, across
grades, subjects, and age of the teacher.

894. Adams, Raymond S. & Biddle, Bruce. *Realities of
teaching* New York: Holt, Rinehart & Winston, Inc.
1970.

Describes a study of classrooms and the acitivities and behaviors of teachers and students, in non-technical language, including a discussion of student and teacher roles.

895. Allington, Richard L. Are good and poor readers taught differently? Is that why poor readers are poor readers? 1978. *ERIC ED* 153 192.

Reports that teachers interrupt poor readers more than good readers, with the type and location of teacher interruptions related to student reading level.

896. Allington, Richard L. Poor readers don't get to read much. Occasional Paper No. 31. East Lansing, Michigan: Institute for Research on Teaching. Michigan State University. 1980. *ERIC ED* 186 883.

Reports differences in the number of words read by poor and good readers with poor readers reading less in the same amount of instructional time and describes differences in teacher responses to errors by poor and good readers.

897. Allington, Richard L. "Teacher interruption behaviors during primary-grade oral reading," *Journal of Educational Psychology 72* (1980): 371-377.

Describes teachers as more apt to interrupt poor than good readers and differences in the types of interruptions by student reading level.

898. Alpert, Judith Landon. "Teacher behavior across ability groups: A consideration of the mediation of Pygmalion effects," *Journal of Educational Psychology 66* (1974): 348-353.

Describes behaviors of teachers with top and bottom reading groups as not related to teacher expectations for student achievement.

899. Alpert, Judith L. & Hummel-Rossi, Barbara. "Differences in teacher behavior toward boys and girls in third grade classrooms," *Educational Research Quarterly 1* (1976): 29-39.

Describes no differences in the response opportunities and teacher reactions to student responses for boys and girls in grade three reading and math.

900. Alpert, Judith L. & Hummel-Rossi, Barbara. Teacher's communication of differential

performance expectations for boys and girls. 1975.
ERIC ED 103 360.

Describes no differences by student sex in the
behaviors of teachers during reading and math
instruction.

901. Amick, Beverly Tanis. Selected social studies
materials and classroom verbal interaction
patterns. Ed.D. dissertation. Rutgers University
the State University of New Jersey. 1971.

Describes no differences in teacher verbal
behaviors with materials designed to make use of
student experiences and materials not so
designed.

902. Anderson, Beth & others. A study of the utilization
of teacher times free of students during the
student day. South Bend, Indiana: Indiana
University. 1974. *ERIC ED* 091 316.

Describes differences among elementary schools
in the amount of teacher time without students,
teacher desire for more such time, and percentages
of that time that teachers spend in specific
activities.

903. Anderson, Charles Ward. An observational study of
classroom management and information structuring
in elementary school science lessons. Ph.D.
dissertation. University of Texas at Austin.
1979.

Reports results of an observational study of
how elementary teachers handle classroom
management and the structuring of information
during science, and teacher preferences for
approaches which simplified both.

904. Anderson, C.W. & Barufaldi, J.P. Research on
elementary school science teaching: A study using
short-term outcome measures. Occasional Paper No.
37. East Lansing, Michigan: Institute for Research
on Teaching. Michigan State University. 1980.

Describes behaviors of elementary teachers
teaching science, and limitations on the types of
teaching which occurs by the limits of teacher
planning time.

905. Anderson, Harold H. "The measurement of domination
and of socially integrative behavior in teachers'
contacts with children," in *Interaction Analysis:
Theory, research and application.* Edited by

Edmund J. Amidon & John B. Hough. pp. 4-13.
Reading, Massachusetts: Addison-Wesley, Inc. 1967.

Describes differences in dominative and
integrative interaction with children of three
kindergarten teachers. For Amidon & Hough
reference see citation No. 1638.

906. Anderson, Linda M. & Evertson, Carolyn M. Classroom
organization at the beginning of school: Two case
studies. Austin, Texas: Research and Development
Center for Teacher Education. University of Texas
at Austin. 1978. *ERIC ED* 166 193.

Describes teachers who are nominated as more
effective managers spending time at the start of
the school year teaching students the rules of
classroom behavior.

907. Anderson, Lorin & others. Teachers' use of
potentially reinforcing behaviors and students'
task-oriented behavior. 1977. *ERIC ED* 146 489.

Describes most teacher behavior as neutral, not
reinforcing and no relationship between
potentially reinforcing teacher behavior and the
level of orientation to task of the class.

908. Aronson, Edward. A dramatistic analysis of language
in the high school English classroom. Ph.D.
dissertation. Northwestern University. 1976. *ERIC
ED* 137 831.

Describes the behavior of four English
teachers, all nominated as excellent teachers,
with teachers using preplanned lessons, with
little student questioning, considerable teacher
talk, and little talk between students.

909. Aspy, David N. & Hutson, Barbara. "Promotion of
student success," *Journal of Educational Research*
66 (1972): 57-60.

Describes behaviors which differentiate
teachers rated as high and low in promoting
student success; use of praise, avoidance of
criticism, use of student-initiated ideas,
awareness of the meaning of the situation for
students, genuine responses to students and
showing positive regard for students.

910. Baker, Chrostopher John. The nature and
distribution of sustaining teacher feedback
communicated during oral reading instruction in a
dyadic context. Ph.D. dissertation. University of
Texas at Austin. 1980.

Describes teachers' responses to student miscues in oral reading as occurring within three seconds of the miscue, associated with miscues which made a change in the meaning of the materials, and were related to student rather than teacher identification of the miscued word.

911. Bartolome, P. "Teachers' objectives and questions in primary reading," *Reading Teacher 23* (1969): 27-33.

Describes teacher statements of objectives as vague, but pointing to analysis-level student work, but questions asked of students required recall, with higher cognitive level questions occurring more often in individualized than in basal reader programs.

912. Battaglia, Marguerite. Mainstreaming from plan to program: From the perspective of the regular classroom teacher. 1977. *ERIC ED* 139 230.

Reports one teacher's description of the process of mainstreaming a handicapped student.

913. Beaulieu, Roderic Aldege. Patterns of verbal behavior in secondary school geometry classes. Ed.D. dissertation. Teachers College Columbia University. 1979.

Describes behaviors of teachers and students in secondary classrooms.

914. Blackwood, Ralph O. The control of anti-social behavior in inner-city classrooms through the use of verbally mediated self control (Teaching verbally mediated self control in the classroom). Final Report. 1971. *ERIC ED* 062 502.

Describes a study of teacher use of behavior modification techniques to assist students to control their social behaviors.

915. Bloom, Richard D. & Wilensky, Harold. Four observational categories for describing teacher behavior. 1967. *ERIC ED* 013 238.

Describes differences among four teachers in their verbal behavior, with 46% of their time spent in giving information, 33% in eliciting student responses, and 14% in feedback to students.

916. Bolvin, John O. Evaluating teacher functions. 1967. *ERIC ED* 020 573.

Describes teacher behaviors in developing a
prescription for students in an individualized
instructional program, relying on pre-unit tests,
and on aspects of the resources available to
teachers, such as materials.

917.   Bondi, Joseph. "Verbal patterns of teachers in the
       classroom," *Elementary School Principal* 50 (1971):
       60-61.

       Describes the verbal behaviors of teachers in
       the classroom.

918.   Borg, Walter R. "Teacher effectiveness in team
       teaching," *Journal of Experimental Education* 35
       (1967): 65-70.

       Describes the behaviors of teachers who are and
       are not effective in team teaching situations.

919.   Bosch, Albert C. Relationships of teaching patterns
       to indices of classroom verbal interaction
       behavior: A further analysis and synthesis of
       classroom verbal interaction data using
       descriptive indices of behavior and teaching
       pattern analysis. Ph.D. dissertation. New York
       University. 1972. *ERIC ED* 065 331.

       Describes no relationship between patterns of
       teacher behavior and measures of teachers as
       direct or indirect.

920.   Boser, Judy & Poppen, William A. "Identification of
       teacher verbal response roles for improving
       student-teacher relationships," *Journal of
       Educational Research* 72 (1978): 90-94.

       Describes teachers who are rated as having good
       relations with students frequently using one of
       five response roles with students.

921.   Brandt, Richard M. An observational investigation
       of instruction and behavior in an informal British
       infant school. Final Report. 1972. *ERIC ED* 073
       823.

       Describes the activities and behaviors of
       participants in an open British infant schools,
       and teacher expectations for behavior, with
       students spending about 30% of their time
       interacting with teachers.

922.   Bredo, Eric. "Collaborative relations among
       elementary school teachers," *Sociology of
       Education* 50 (1977): 300-309.

Describes varying degrees of collaboration among elementary teaching teams.

923. Brighouse, Verna Lee & Snyder, Neil Carl. Teacher-controlling behavior as related to selected pupil and classroom variables. Ed.D. dissertation. University of Southern California. 1977.

Describes teacher control behaviors representing a large percentage of teacher behaviors, but not related to other teacher characteristics, student achievement, student self-concept.

924. Brooks, Douglas M. The contextual application of observation schedules within naturalistic classrooms. 1977. *ERIC ED* 152 800.

Describes teacher nonverbal behaviors in responses to student-initiated questions.

925. Brophy, Jere E. Teacher praise: A functional analysis. Occasional Paper No. 28. East Lansing, Michigan: Institute for Research on Teaching. Michigan State University. 1979. *ERIC ED* 181 013.

Describes teacher praise statements as often not actually reinforcing, but the meaning is dependent upon the context, and the frequency of teacher praise is related to teacher perceptions of student need rather than the quality of the student response.

926. Brophy, J., Anderson, L., Greenhalgh, C., Ogden, J. & Selig, H. An instructional model for first grade reading groups. Austin, Texas: Research and Development Center for Teacher Education. University of Texas at Austin. 1976.

Describes a model of reading instruction based on research and describes the behaviors of teachers using that model in teaching reading.

927. Bush, Andrew J., Kennedy, J.J. & Cruickshank, D.R. "An empirical investigation of teacher clarity," *Journal of Teacher Education 28*, No. 2 (1977): 53-58. *ERIC ED* 137 234.

Describes teacher clarity and relates measures of teacher clarity to observed behaviors of teachers.

928. Bulter, Thomas Albert. A descriptive study of teacher verbal behavior in an inquiry approach,

laboratory-oriented secondary science course.
Ed.D. dissertation. University of Rochester.
1971.

Describes behaviors of teachers as not related
to their philosophy of innovation in science
teaching.

929. Camfield, Marvin A. Teaching style and classroom
      seating arrangements in East Tennessee middle
      schools. Ed.D. dissertation. University of
      Tennessee. 1980.

      Describes teacher teaching style and patterns
      of seat assignment and change of seat assignment,
      based on teacher self-report, and finds a limited
      relationship between teaching style and seating
      arrangements.

930. Carew, Jean V. & Lightfoot, Sara L. First grade: A
      multi-faceted view of teachers and children. Final
      Report. 1977. *ERIC ED* 148 495.

      Describes classroom behavior, planning and
      attitudes toward students and teaching of four
      elementary teachers.

931. Carll, Carol G. & Davis, O.L., Jr. Verbal teaching
      behaviors of teachers of mathematics in second and
      fifth grades. Austin, Texas: Center for Research
      and Development for Teacher Education. Texas
      University at Austin. 1970. *ERIC ED* 051 135.

      Describes behaviors of teachers in classrooms,
      with more teacher talk by second than fifth grade
      teachers.

932. Cazden, Courtney B. "How knowledge about language
      helps the classroom teacher--or does it: A
      personal account," *Urban Review 9* (1976): 74-90.

      Describes experiences and behavior of one
      researcher who spent a year as a classroom
      teacher.

933. Clark, Richard M. A study of teacher behavior and
      attitudes in elementary school with high and low
      pupil achievement. 1975. *ERIC ED* 110 925.

      Describes differences in the behavior and
      attitudes of teacher toward students in schools
      with high and low achieving students.

934. Clark, Richard M. A micro-study of teacher behavior
      in outlier schools. 1976. *ERIC ED* 126 071.

Describes differences in the behavior of teachers in schools with high and low achieving students.

935. Cline, Marvin D. & others. Observers in the classroom. A case study of an innovative program. Boston, Massachusetts: Head Start Evaluation and Research Center. Boston University. 1970. *ERIC ED* 046 876.

Describes teachers establishing barriers to the use of information from observers, to maintain teacher control of the classroom.

936. Clinefelter, David Lee. Analysis of the interaction between students, teachers, and materials in intermediate grade mathematics classes. Ph.D. dissertation. Ohio State University. 1978.

Describes teacher use of curriculum materials in a small number of classrooms.

937. Cogan, John I. "Elementary teachers as nonreaders," *Phi Delta Kappan 56* (1975): 495-496.

Reports that elementary teachers read practical journals to which their schools subscribe, with younger teachers reading less.

938. Colbert, C. Dianne. Classroom teacher behavior and instructional organization patterns. 1979. *ERIC ED* 170 280.

Describes behavior of experienced teachers in using classroom organizational patterns to cope with the multiple events which occur and to organize classrooms into manageable units.

939. Collins, James L. & Seidman, Earl. Language and secondary schooling: The struggle for meaning. 1978. *ERIC ED* 155 709.

Describes teachers' shaping of meaning through classroom talk and limitations in student talk.

940. Coombs, Jerrold R. "The logic of teaching," In *Teaching: Vantage points for study*. Edited by Ronald T. Hyman. pp. 420-427. Philadelphia, Pennsylvania: T.B. Lippincott Company. 1968. reprinted in: *High School Journal 50* (1966): 22-29.

Describes units of verbal behaviors of teachers in presenting lessons and in responding to students. For Hyman reference see citation No. 2973.

941. Cooney, Thomas James. An analysis of teachers'
      verbal behavior using the theory of relations.
      Ph.D. dissertation. University of Illinois at
      Urbana-Champaign. 1969.

      Describes behaviors of teachers in helping
      students organize their cognitive knowledge.

942. Cooper, H.M., Hinkel, G.M. & Good, T.L. "Teachers'
      beliefs about interaction control and their
      observed behavioral correlates," *Journal of
      Educational Psychology 72* (1980): 345-354.

      Describes the beliefs of teachers about
      procedures to control student interactions with
      the teacher and the consistency of observed
      teacher behaviors with those beliefs.

943. Cosper, Wilma Baker. An analysis of sex differences
      in teacher-student interaction as manifest in
      verbal and nonverbal behavior cues. Ed.D.
      dissertation. University of Tennessee. 1970.

      Describes teacher behaviors, with more
      encouraging than restricting behaviors, and
      differences in teacher behaviors by sex of student
      toward whom the behaviors are directed.

944. Cruickshank, Donald R., Kennedy, J.J., Bush, A. &
      Meyers, B. "Clear teaching: What is it?" *British
      Journal of Teacher Education 5* (1979): 27-33.

      Describes behaviors of teachers which are
      defined as clear teaching.

945. Davis, Sharon A. & Haller, Emil J. Socioeconomic
      segregation within elementary school classrooms
      and teachers' own socioeconomic background: Some
      contrary evidence. 1975. *ERIC ED* 106 394.

      Describes student placement in reading groups
      related to student race, socioeconomic level and
      teacher attitudes toward students.

946. Davis, Sharon A. Students' SES as related to
      teachers' perceptions and ability grouping
      decisions. 1974. *ERIC ED* 090 487.

      Describes teacher placement of students in
      reading groups on the basis of student perceived
      ability, achievement, and work habits, with some
      misplacement related to student social class.

947. Dennis, Virginia C. Patterned teaching behavior: A
      study of dyadic infracommunication. 1973. *ERIC ED*
      076 576.

Describes patterns of teacher behaviors in
interacting with students.

948. Denton, Drew Allen. Analysis of the interaction
between students, teachers, and materials in
intermediate grade reading classes. Ph.D.
dissertation. Ohio State University. 1978.

Reports the behavior of teachers with students,
in describing students to others, and in using
curriculum materials during instruction.

949. Dishaw, Marilyn. Descriptions of allocated time to
content areas for the A-B period. Technical Note
IV-2a. Beginning Teacher Evaluation Study. San
Francisco, California: Far West Laboratory for
Educational Research and Development. 1977. *ERIC
ED* 146 163.

Describes teacher allocation of instructional
time to reading and math in a sample of grade two
and five classrooms from October to January

950. Dishaw, Marilyn. Description of allocated time to
content areas for the B-C period. Technical Note
IV-2b. Beginning Teacher Evaluation Study. San
Francisco, California: Far West Laboratory for
Educational Research and Development. 1977. *ERIC
ED* 150 109.

Describes teacher allocation of instructional
time to reading and math in a sample of second and
fifth grade classrooms from January through May.

951. Dodl, Normal Richard. Pupil questioning behavior in
the context of classroom interaction. Ed.D.
dissertation. Stanford University. 1965.

Describes teacher domination of the classroom
with control of questions and most questions
related to content; few student questions.

952. Doyle, Walter. *Classroom Management*. West
Lafayette, Indiana: Kappa Delta Pi. 1980.

Describes the behaviors of teachers in managing
classrooms and student activities and effects of
teacher behaviors on student behaviors.

953. Driver, Beth. Children's negotiation of answers to
questions. Working papers in sociolinguistics. No.
51. Austin, Texas. Southwest Educational
Development Laboratory. 1978. *ERIC ED* 165 491.

Describes three steps in a question-answer sequence used by teachers, with question, student answer, and teacher's indication of evaluation of the answer.

954. Duffy, Gerald G. & McIntyre, Lonnie D. A qualitative analysis of how various primary grade teachers employ the structured learning component of the direct instruction model when teaching reading. Research Series No. 80. East Lansing, Michigan: Institute for Research on Teaching. Michigan State University. 1980. *ERIC ED* 184 085.

Describes behaviors of teachers as aimed toward activities, not objectives, as responding to students and oriented toward recitation rather than toward providing assistance to students.

955. Durkin, Dolores. "What classroom observations reveal about reading comprehension instruction," *Reading Research Quarterly 14* (1978-1979): 481-533. Technical Report No. 106. Urbana, Illinois: Center for the Study of Reading. Illinois University. 1978. *ERIC ED* 162 259.

Describes behaviors of teachers in teaching reading, with the major focus on word attack and little time spent in comprehension instruction.

956. Eberle, Jeanne. A descriptive study of teacher-pupil verbal interaction in informal classrooms. Ed.D. dissertation. State University of New York at Buffalo. 1978.

Describes behavior of teachers and students in informal classrooms.

957. Eccles, Priscilla J. "Teacher behavior and knowledge of subject matter in sixth grade science," *Journal of Research in Science Teaching 3* (1965): 345.

Describes the observed behaviors of teachers and their levels of knowledge of the science content.

958. Eccles, Priscilla J. "Teaching behavior and lesson effectiveness for a specific science objective," *Journal of Research in Science Teaching 5* (1967-68): 397-404.

Describes behavior and information processing of teachers and students while teaching a specific science lesson, with some teachers having greater achievement with a new group of students than with their normal class of students.

959. Edelmann, Anne M. & Furst, Norma F. Changing
      teacher response behavior to those more consistent
      with good mental health practices. 1969. *ERIC ED*
      025 478.

      Describes differences in teacher responses to
      "difficult" classroom behavior, and fewer teacher
      responses which tend to diminish the student after
      teacher training.

960. Eisenhart, Margaret. Maintaining control: Teacher
      competence in the classroom. 1977. *ERIC ED* 154
      098.

      Describes teacher control techniques,
      arrangement of the physical space and people, and
      use of time, rewards and recognition of students.

961. Elias, Patricia J. & others. The reports of
      teachers about their mathematics and reading
      instructional activities. Beginning Teacher
      Evaluation Study: Phase II, 1973-74, Final Report:
      Vol. V.5. Princeton, New Jersey: Educational
      Testing Service. 1976. *ERIC ED* 127 374, 131 116.

      Describes teacher behavior and the classroom
      organizational system for reading and math
      instruction.

962. Elias, Patricia & Wheeler, Patricia. "Instructional
      activities as reported by teachers," *Journal of
      Teacher Education 27*, No. 4 (1976): 326-328.

      Describes the instructional behaviors of
      teachers and the organization of the classroom for
      reading and math instruction.

963. Epstein, Joyce L. Field search: Practitioners
      inform research on authority structures. Report
      No. 277. Baltimore, Maryland: Center for the
      Social Organization of Schools. John Hopkins
      University. 1979. *ERIC ED* 178 518.

      Describes the structures which teachers report
      using to give students a decision-making role and
      authority, in grades one through twelve.

964. Etkind, Alan Andre. An analysis of teacher-used and
      pupil activities assigned junior high school
      social studies students. Ed.D. dissertation.
      Syracuse University. 1980.

      Describes the activities which teachers use in
      social studies instruction in junior high school
      classes.

965. Evans, J. Daryll. "Oral communication in biology,"
      Journal of Biological Education 10 (1976):
      280-290.

      Describes the verbal communication in high
      school and college biology classes, with teachers
      dominating the communication and limited
      discussion.

966. Evans, Thomas P. & Balzer, LeVon. "An inductive
      approach to the study of biology teacher
      behaviors," *Journal of Research in Science
      Teaching 7* (1970): 47-56.

      Describes the instruction development and the
      observed behavior of one teacher.

967. Evertson, Carolyn M. & Anderson, Linda M. Beginning
      school. Research and Development Report No. 6007.
      Austin, Texas: Center for Research and Development
      for Teacher Education. Texas University at Austin.
      1979. *ERIC ED* 178 541.

      Describes teachers who are good managers
      preventing problems from occurring by establishing
      and teaching management routines early in the
      year.

968. Evertson, Carolyn M. & Anderson, Linda
      M. "Beginning School," *Educational Horizons 57*,
      No. 4 (1979): 164-168.

      Describes the behaviors of effective teachers
      as teaching patterns of classroom behaviors and
      classroom rules during the first weeks of school

969. Evertson, C.M., Emmer, E.T. & Brophy, J.E.
      "Predictors of effective teaching in junior high
      mathematics classrooms," *Journal of Research in
      Mathematics Education 11* (1980): 167-178.

      Describes differences in the behaviors of three
      highly and six less effective mathematics teachers
      in time use, management, interaction styles, and
      personal characteristics.

970. Fagot, Beverly I. Teacher reinforcement of
      feminine-preferred behavior revisited. 1975. *ERIC
      ED* 116 809.

      Describes teachers reinforcing female-preferred
      behavior in boys and girls in preschool, and
      responding equally to boys and girls.

971. Fagot, Beverly I. & Patterson, Gerald R. "An in
      vivo analysis of reinforcing contingencies

for sex-role behaviors in the preschool child,"
Developmental Psychology 1 (1969): 563-568.

Describes differences in types of behavior
which teachers reinforce; feminine-type, with more
reinforcement for boys who exhibited opposite-sex
behaviors.

972. Fair, J.W. & others. Teacher interaction and
observation practices in the evaluation of student
achievement. 1980. *ERIC ED* 190 527.

Describes the ways that teachers use
observations of students to assess levels of
student learning.

973. Far West Laboratory for Educational Research and
Development. Instructional time allocation in
fifth grade reading. Technical Report II-5.
Beginning Teacher Evaluation Study. San Francisco,
California: Far West Laboratory for Educational
Research and Development. 1976. *ERIC ED* 145 412.

Describes differences in patterns of teacher
allocation of instructional time to areas of
reading instruction.

974. Feldman, Robert S. "Nonverbal disclosure of teacher
deception in interpersonal affect," *Journal of
Educational Psychology 68* (1976): 807-816.

Describes teacher nonverbal behavior as
indicative of teacher truthfulness, with
differences by the publicness of the interaction.

975. Felker, Roberta Mary. The relationship between
teacher implementation of an innovation and
decisional participation in the elementary school.
Ph.D. dissertation. University of Wisconsin.
1980.

Describes teacher participation in decision
making in implementing an educational innovation
and problems with methods for studying teacher
uses of innovations.

976. Fereday, Linda Presnell. Investigation of teacher
behaviors and characteristics related to frequency
of student disciplinary referrals. Ed.D.
dissertation. University of Oklahoma. 1979.

Describes behavior of teachers in a middle
school with high and low numbers of student
discipline referrals.

977.   Ferren, Ann Speidel. Teacher survival behaviors
       within the school organization. 1971 *ERIC ED* 061
       174. Under title, An exploratory study of teacher
       survival techniques within the school
       organization. Ed.D. dissertation. Boston
       University. 1971.

              Describes a wide range of adaptive behaviors of
       teachers in secondary schools, used in response to
       the demands of the organizations in which they
       teach.

978.   Filby, Nikola N. Description of patterns of
       teaching behavior within and across classes during
       the A—B period. Technical Note IV—3a. Beginning
       Teacher Evaluation Study. San Francisco,
       California: Far West Laboratory for Educational
       Research and Development. 1977. *ERIC ED* 156 637.

              Describes five categories of behaviors of
       teachers during the first half of the school year,
       including assessing student needs, planning,
       presenting, monitoring and providing feedback.

979.   Filby, Nikola N. & Fisher, Charles W. Description
       of patterns of teaching behaviors within and
       across classes during the B—C period. Technical
       Note IV—3b. Beginning Teacher Evaluation Study.
       San Francisco, California: Far West Laboratory for
       Educational Research and Development. 1977. *ERIC
       ED* 156 641.

              Describes five categories of behaviors of
       teachers during the second half of the school
       year, including assessing student needs, planning,
       presenting, monitoring and providing feedback.

980.   Filby, Nikola N., Marliave, Richard S. & Fisher,
       Charles W. Allocated and engaged time in different
       content areas of second and fifth grade reading
       and mathematics curriculum. 1977. *ERIC ED* 137
       315.

              Describes teacher allocation of time to content
       areas and student engagement in instructional
       tasks.

981.   Fleming, James T. "Teachers' ratings of urban
       children's reading performance," *Child Study
       Journal 1* (1970—1971): 80—99.

              Describes teachers as often confusing different
       student speech patterns with errors in reading.

982. Florio, Susan. The problem of dead letters: Social perspectives on the teaching of writing. Research Series No. 34. East Lansing, Michigan: Institute for Research on Teaching. Michigan State University. 1978.

     Describes one classroom and the procedures the teacher used to make writing meaningful and to integrate writing and other lessons.

983. Fox. John Maurice. A study of teacher activity and involvement in the NASSP Model Schools Project. Ed.D. dissertation. Catholic University of America. 1978.

     Describes the behaviors of teachers in 23 schools implementing the NASSP model of instructional organization.

984. Franklin, Josephine Elizbeth Seaton. Teacher competence and effective reading instruction (in the middle elementary grades). 1975. *ERIC ED* 117 667.

     Describes the behavior and attitudes of teachers nominated as superior reading teachers.

985. French, Russell Lee. A study of communication events and teacher behavior: Verbal and nonverbal. Ph.D. dissertation. Ohio State University. 1968.

     Describes teacher verbal and nonverbal behavior in the classroom within communication events and the development of an observation instrument.

986. Friedman, Lora Ruth. An investigation of certain teaching behaviors of and influences upon new elementary teachers. Ed.D. dissertation. University of Florida. 1967.

     Describes differences in behaviors of beginning teachers, teachers in a laboratory school, and college professors, but no differences between the behaviors of beginning teachers and their cooperating teachers.

987. Friedman, Morton. "Cognitive emphasis of geometry teachers' questions," *Journal of Research in Mathematics Education* 7 (1976): 259-263.

     Describes the levels of questions used by geometry teachers, with more questions at the meaning and application levels than at higher levels.

988.   Gaite, A.J.H. "Teachers' attitudes," *Instructor 84*,
        No. 1 (1975): 30.

        Describes the behaviors of teachers with
        students toward whom the teachers hold different
        attitudes.

989.   Gallagher, James J. "Expressive thought by gifted
        children in the classroom," In *The nature of
        teaching: A collection of readings.* Edited by Lois
        N. Nelson. pp. 170-179. Waltham, Massachusetts:
        Blaisdell Publishing Company. 1969. reprinted from
        Language and the higher thought processes.
        Champaign, Illinois: National Council of Teachers
        of English. 1965.

        Describes the classroom statements of teachers
        and students in terms of their cognitive levels.
        For Nelson reference see citation No. 2997.

990.   Galloway, Charles M. "Nonverbal communication in
        teaching," In *Teaching: Vantage points for study.*
        Edited by Ronald T. Hyman. pp. 70-77.
        Philadelphia, Pennsylvania: T.B. Lippincott
        Company. 1968 reprinted from *Educational
        Leadership 24* (1966): 55-63.

        Describes three studies which report complex
        patterns of communication, verbal and nonverbal,
        between teacher and students. For Hyman reference
        see citation No. 2973.

991.   Garrity, Joseph Peter. Analysis of pedagogical
        communication in individualized computer-oriented
        mathematics classrooms. Ed.D. dissertation.
        Teachers College Columbia University. 1979.

        Describes behaviors of teachers and students in
        grade five and twelve classrooms where students
        were studying computer programming and
        mathematics.

992.   George, A.A. & Hord, S.M. Monitoring curriculum
        implementation: Mapping teacher behaviors on a
        configuration continuum. Austin, Texas: Research
        and Development Center for Teacher Education.
        University of Texas at Austin. 1980. *ERIC ED* 192
        451.

        Describes the behaviors of teachers using a
        specific mathematics curriculum, in terms of their
        consistency with the curriculum specifications.

993. Gigante, Lucille Mary. The use of the question by teachers of literature. Ed.D. dissertation. Florida Atlantic University. 1980.

Describes teacher questioning behavior, reliance on procedural and lower cognitive level questions among secondary teachers of literature.

994. Gil, Doron & Freeman. D.J. Diagnosis and remediation of reading difficulties in the classroom. Research Series No. 78. East Lansing, Michigan: Institute for Research on Teaching. Michigan State University. 1980.

Describes teacher diagnostic procedures as fitting a global, not specific, view of reading diagnosis.

995. Gil, D. & Heller, P.S. Classroom discipline: Toward a diagnostic model integrating teachers' thoughts and actions. Occasional Paper No. 13. East Lansing, Michigan: Institute for Research on Teaching. Michigan State University. 1978.

Describes teacher diagnosis in a model which incorporates a child's social and work behavior.

996. Goebel, Laurence Gayhart. An analysis of teacher-pupil interaction when programed instruction materials are used. Ed.D. dissertation. University of Maryland. 1966.

Describes differences in the amount of teacher direct verbal behavior and individualized instruction when teachers are using traditional and programmed materials.

997. Good, T.L., Grouws, D.A. & Beckerman, T. "Curriculum pacing: Some empirical data in mathematics," *Journal of Curriculum Studies 10* (1978): 75-81.

Describes the pacing of content presentation and coverage in math lessons.

998. Goslin, David A. *Teachers and testing*. New York: Russell Sage Foundation. 1967.

Describes a study of teachers' use of test information, their perceptions of the role of testing, their attitudes toward, experience with and training related to testing.

999. Graeber, Anna, Rim, Eui-do & Unks, Nancy. A survey of classroom practices in mathematics: Report

of first, third, fifth, and seventh grade teachers
in Delaware, New Jersey, and Pennsylvania.
Philadelphia, Pennsylvania: Research for Better
Schools, Inc. 1977.

Describes the teaching of mathematics as
reported by teachers, with information about
materials, methods.

1000.   Grannis, Joseph C. The Columbia Classroom
Environment Project—Third progress report, May
1971. New York: Institute for Pedagogical Studies.
Columbia University. 1971. *ERIC ED* 123 289.

Describes the behaviors of teachers which
establish the environment of the classroom, and
the development of a data collection instrument.

1001.   Grannis, Joseph C. The Columbia Classroom
Environment Project—Fifth progress report, May
1972. New York. Institute for Pedagogical Studies.
Columbia University. 1972. *ERIC ED* 123 291.

Describes behaviors of teachers and students in
varied classroom climates.

1002.   Grant, Barbara M. & Hennings, Dorothy G. *The
teacher moves: An analysis of non-verbal
activity.* Theory and Research in Science Series.
New York. Teachers College Press. 1971.

Describes the non-verbal behaviors of five
experienced classroom teachers, including
instructional and personal motivations and the
relationship of teacher non-verbal behaviors and
teaching style.

1003.   Groves, John Thomas. A description of student-cuing
behaviors, teacher-management responses, and
self-reported teacher management conceptions in an
elementary classroom. Ph.D. dissertation. Michigan
State University. 1979.

Reports that observations in one classroom
revealed three categories of student behavior
(on-task, talking with neighbor, aimless walking)
with teacher management behaviors directed toward
maintaining behavior to avoid potential
disruptions and different teacher emphases in the
morning and afternoon.

1004.   Gump, Paul V. The classroom behavior setting—Its
nature and relation to student behavior. Final
Report. 1967, *ERIC ED* 015 515.

Describes behavioral units and subunits of teachers and students and interdependencies of actions within the units and describes the various portions of the classroom day.

1005. Gump, Paul V. "What's happening in the elementary classroom?" In *Research into the classroom processes: Recent developments and next steps.* Edited by Ian Westbury and Arno A. Bellack. pp. 155-165. New York: Teachers College Press. 1971.

Describes classroom events in terms of their organization and emphasis on maintaining the environment, i.e., social and procedural concerns. For Westbury & Bellack reference see citation No. 3039.

1006. Guszak, Frank James. A study of teacher solicitation and student response interaction about reading content in selected second, fourth, and sixth grades. Ph.D. dissertation. University of Wisconsin. 1966.

Describes teacher questions, with about 75% focusing on literal comprehension of materials read, and student responses, with about 10% incongruent with teacher questions, and limited teacher follow-up of questions and responses.

1007. Haffner, Herbert M. & Slobodian, June J. "An analysis of teacher-pupil interaction patterns," *International Reading Association Conference Proceedings, 13 Part I.* (1968): 763-767.

Describes the behaviors of teachers while using a basal reader for reading instruction.

1008. Hall, Gene Erwin. A comparison of the teaching behaviors of second grade teachers teaching *Science--A Process Approach* with second grade teachers not teaching a recently developed science curriculum. Ph.D. dissertation. Syracuse University. 1968.

Describes differences in the teaching behaviors of teachers using and not using the new science curriculum.

1009. Hall, Gene E. Longitudinal and cross-sectional studies of the concerns of users of team teaching in the elementary school and instructional modules at the college level. Austin, Texas: Research and Development Center for Teacher Education. University of Texas at Austin. 1976.

Describes the behaviors and attitudes of
teachers using innovative instructional
approaches.

1010.   Hall, Gene E. "Teacher-pupil behaviors exhibited by
two groups of second grade teachers using
Science—A Process Approach," *Science Education*
54 (1970): 325-334.

Describes differences in the behaviors of
teachers and students using the new science
curriculum materials.

1011.   Hall, Gene. "The concerns-based approach to
facilitating change, "*Educational Horizons 57*, No.
4 (1979): 202-208.

Describes the steps teachers go through in
implementing an innovation and their feelings and
concerns.

1012.   Harvey, Mary R. "Public school treatment of
low-income children: Education for passivity,"
Urban Education 15 (1980): 279-323.

Describes the behaviors of teachers interacting
with students, the classroom organization,
curriculum in urban low income grade two classes.

1013.   Hassard, John Russell. An investigation of teacher
and student behavior in earth science classrooms.
Ph.D. dissertation. Ohio State University. 1969.

Describes behaviors of teachers and the
relations between teachers and students in science
classes.

1014.   Haupt, Dorothy. Relationship between children's
questions and nursery school teachers' responses.
1966. *ERIC ED* 046 507.

Describes teachers responding differently to
questions from boys and girls, and teachers
reinforcing their role as the source of
information.

1015.   Hautala, Lynda W. & Aaron, Robert L. Time-use: A
variable in teacher effectiveness. 1977. *ERIC ED*
147 790.

Describes the behavior of teachers in reading
groups and relates reading instructional behavior
to behavior during other times of the school day.

1016.   Hautala, Lynda W. & Mason, George E. "In search of
        success," *Southern Journal of Educational Research*
        12 (1978): 235-248.

        Describes the behaviors of elementary teachers
        with high achieving students.

1017.   Hawkins, Michael L. Mobility of students in reading
        groups. Newark, Delaware: International Reading
        Association. 1966. *ERIC ED* 013 727.

        Describes teacher reports of student changes of
        reading groups over seventeen weeks; 41% of the
        teachers reported no changes in groups, with less
        change at the upper grades.

1018.   Herman, Wayne L., Jr. "The use of language arts in
        social studies lessons," *American Educational
        Research Journal 4* (1967): 117-124.

        Describes the verbal behavior of teachers and
        students in a sample of fifth grade classrooms,
        with teachers talking and students listening.

1019.   Hess, William George. A description of the oral
        communication interactions in two first grade and
        two second grade classrooms in a midwestern
        community. Ph.D. dissertation. University of Iowa.
        1974.

        Describes the verbal behavior of teachers and
        students, based on several short observations.

1020.   Hester, Joy & Ligon, Glynn. Where does the time go?
        A study of time use in public schools. 1978. *ERIC
        ED* 153 307.

        Describes the patterns of time use in schools
        with and without compensatory education programs,
        with up to 50% of the day devoted to instructional
        activities.

1021.   Hickerson, Robert Leslie. Classroom behavior as a
        function of activity setting. Ed.D. dissertation.
        Yeshiva University. 1977.

        Describes the behavior of students and
        teachers, the climate, and the acceptance of
        handicapped students in regular and special
        education classrooms.

1022.   Hiller, Jack H., Fisher, Gerald A. & Kaess,
        Walter. "A computer investigation of verbal
        characteristics of effective classroom lecturing,"
        American Educational Research Journal 6 (1969):
        661-675.

Describes the behavior of secondary social studies teachers during lectures, using factors identified through computer analysis of the content of lectures to describe the teacher behaviors.

1023.   Hough, John B. "Classroom interaction and the facilitation of learning: The source of instructional theory," In *Interaction Analysis: Theory, research, and application.* Edited by Edmund J. Amidon & John B. Hough. pp. 375-387. Reading, Massachusetts: Addison Wesley Publishing Co. 1967.

Describes the behaviors which learning theory predicts reinforce students and relates those behaviors to observed behaviors of teachers. For Amidon & Hough reference see citation No. 1638.

1024.   Howard, Rose Ann. An investigation of discipline techniques used by effective teachers. Ph.D. dissertation. George Peabody College for Teachers. 1978.

Describes the discipline techniques which teachers selected as effective in working with students.

1025.   Hudgins, Bryce B. & Ahlbrand, William P., Jr. "Some properties of formal teacher and pupil classroom communication," *Psychology in the Schools 7* (1970): 265-268.

Describes the verbal behaviors of teachers and students in the classroom.

1026.   Huebner, Dwayne. "Curricular language and classroom meanings," In *Teaching: Vantage points for study.* Edited by Ronald T. Hyman. pp. 353-356. Philadelphia, Pennsylvania: T.B. Lippincott Company. 1968. reprinted from *Language and Meaning.* Edited by James B. McDonald & Robert R. Leeper. Washington, D.C.: Association for Supervision and Curriculum Development. 1966.

Essay discusses the instructional language used in the classroom and its meaning within the classroom context. For Hyman reference see citation No. 2973.

1027.   Hyman, Ronald T. Questioning in the classroom. 1977. *ERIC ED* 138 551.

Describes teacher questioning behavior, which is more apt to be a sequence of questions to

be answered by individual students than a
discussion.

1028.   Ivany, J.W. George & Oguntonadi, Christopher
         B. "Verbal explanation in physics classes,"
         Journal of Research in Science Teaching 9 (1972):
         353-359.

         Describes the verbal behaviors of teachers in
         explaining content in physics classes.

1029   Jackson, James E. "Reading in the secondary school:
         A survey of teachers," *Journal of Reading 23*
         (1979): 229-232.

         Reports the results of a survey of high school
         teachers, with many reporting that they do teach
         reading.

1030.   Jackson, Philip W. *Life in classrooms* New York:
         Holt, Rinehart and Winston, Inc. 1968.

         Describes classrooms and teaching from the
         perspective of the teacher, the student, and the
         observer, based on the author's studies and some
         references to other research.

1031.   Jackson, Philip W. "The student's world," In
         Teachers and the learning process. Edited by
         Robert D. Strom. pp. 130-141. Englewood Cliffs,
         New Jersey: Prentice-Hall, Inc. 1971. reprinted
         from *Elementary School Journal 66* (1966):
         345-357.

         Describes the classroom environment created by
         the teacher, the classroom rules and teacher
         behaviors, from the perspective of the students.
         For Strom reference see citation No. 3029.

1032.   Jackson, Philip W. "The way teaching is," in *The
         way teaching is.* pp. 7-27. Washington. D.C.:
         Association for Supervision and Curriculum
         Development. 1965. *National Education Association
         Journal 54* (1965): 10-13.

         Describes what occurs in classrooms, in terms
         of the public nature of teacher behavior and the
         types of activities in which teachers are engaged.
         For Association for Supervision and Curriculum
         Development reference see citation No. 2905.

1033.   Joyce, Bruce & McNair, Kathleen. Teaching styles at
         South Bay School: The South Bay Study, Part I.
         Research Series No. 57. East Lansing, Michigan:
         Institute for Research on Teaching. Michigan State
         University. 1979. *ERIC ED* 187 666.

Describes the patterns of behavior among
teachers in one school, and the frequency of
teacher use of the recitation mode, with a focus
on presentation of factual information.

1034.   Karr, P.J. & Beatty, Michael. "Effects of
verbal-vocal message discrepancy on teacher
credibility," *Educational Research Quarterly* 4,
No. 1 (1979): 76-80.

Describes discrepancies between teacher vocal
cues and content of teacher messages as related to
teacher lack of credibility.

1035.   Kaye, Mildred. Patterns of verbal interaction in
classes for disadvantaged high school students.
Ed.D. dissertation. Columbia University. 1970.

Describes teacher talk and student responses in
social studies lessons as focusing on factual
information.

1036.   Kean, John M. "Teachers' language analysis," *High
School Journal* 51 (1967): 32-38.

Describes the language use of a sample of
teachers, with no differences among teachers but
some relationships among types of language use.

1037.   Keith, L. Thomas, Tornatzky, L.G. & Pettigrew,
L.E. "An analysis of verbal and nonverbal
classroom teaching behaviors," *Journal of
Experimental Education* 42, No. 4 (1974): 30-38.

Describes the verbal and nonverbal behaviors of
teachers and students.

1038.   Korth, Willard W. & others. A study of the
relationships between measures of teacher-pupil
verbal interaction and student assessment of
classroom practices. 1971. *ERIC ED* 055 798.

Describes verbal behavior in the classroom,
with teachers dominating and inquiry composing a
small portion of the classroom talk.

1039.   Kounin, Jacob S. "An analysis of teachers'
managerial techniques," *Psychology in the Schools*
4 (1967): 221-227.

Describes several dimensions of teacher
management of the classroom; withitness,
overlapping (handling two or more things at one
time).

1040.   Kounin, Jacob S. "Observing and delineating
        technique of managing behavior in classrooms,"
        Journal of Research and Development in Education
        4 (1970): 62-72.

        Describes the behaviors of teachers who are
        good managers of children, having withitness;
        overlapping; momentum and smoothness; few mistakes
        in timing, fragmentation and overdwelling; group
        alerting and accountability to maintain students'
        focus.

1041.   Kounin, Jacob S. & Doyle, Patrick H. "Degree of
        continuity of a lesson's signal system and the
        task involvement of children," *Journal of
        Educational Psychology 67* (1975): 159-164.

        Describes differences in techniques for signal
        continuity for both individual construction and
        reading and demonstration lessons; within the
        lesson format, greater signal continuity is
        associated with greater student task involvement.

1042.   Kounin, J.S. & Gump, P.V. "Signal systems of lesson
        settings and the task-related behavior of
        pre-school children," *Journal of Educational
        Psychology 66* (1974): 554-563.

        Describes teacher events in terms of
        consistency of the signal system in relation to
        student attentive behavior.

1043.   Kounin, Jacob S. and Gump, Paul V. "The ripple
        effect in discipline," In *Discipline and learning:
        An inquiry into student-teacher relationships.*
        (Revised edition). pp. 100-104. Washington, D.C.:
        National Education Association. 1977. Reprinted
        from *Elementary School Journal 59* (1958):
        158-162.

        Describes three teacher control techniques
        observed in classrooms, clarity, firmness and
        roughness. For National Education Association
        reference see citation No. 1080.

1044.   Kroul, Lola Zita. A decade of reading 1969-1979: An
        analysis of the nature of information sources used
        by elementary teachers for professional growth.
        Ed.D. dissertation. Hofstra University. 1980.

        Describes sources and differences in sources of
        professional information and growth identified by
        teachers, specialists, and administrators, with
        teachers reporting local conferences, faculty
        meetings, and public and school libraries.

1045.   Kruger, John Mott. Interaction patterns of
        industrial arts teachers in laboratory type
        situations at the junior high school level. 1971.
        ERIC ED 049 379.

        Describes the behaviors of teachers, including
        the large amount of teacher talk.

1046.   Kyle, Diane Wells. Life-as-teacher: The disclosure
        of teachers' activities and emergent problems.
        Ed.D. dissertation. University of Virginia. 1979.

        Describes the activities of two second grade
        teachers, the problems they encounter, the effects
        of activities on the teachers and on the
        curriculum as taught.

1047.   LeCompte, Margaret Diane. Teacher behavior and the
        presentation of a work ethic. 1975. *ERIC ED* 103
        354.

        Describes behaviors of teachers which reinforce
        task involvement, the use of time, order and
        authority norms which are rooted in the school
        culture.

1048.   Licata, Joseph W. Custodial teacher social types.
        1980. *ERIC ED* 190 518.

        Describes two methods of custodial teacher
        behaviors, the "screamers" and the "cold" types,
        based on pupil perceptions of teachers.

1049.   Lindvall, C.M. & Bolvin, John O. "The role of the
        teacher in individually prescribed instruction,"
        Educational Technology 10 (1970): 37-41.

        Describes the tasks of teachers in managing
        individualized instruction and in interacting with
        students.

1050.   Lockwood, James Riley. An analysis of teacher-
        questioning in mathematics classrooms. Ph.D.
        dissertation. University of Illinois at Urbana-
        Champaign. 1970.

        Describes two types of teacher responses to
        student responses to questions; teachers either
        proceeded with the next question or activity to
        move the lesson on or they modified the question
        to be more specific.

1051.   Loftis, Larraine. Differential behaviors of male
        teachers as related to ability, social class and
        sex differences of students at the sixth

grade level. Ph.D. dissertation. Washington
University. 1971.

Describes the behavior of male teachers to
students, with differences by student; teachers
favored the high ability male students.

1052. Lortie, Dan C. *School Teacher*. Chicago: University
of Chicago Press. 1975.

Describes aspects of the work of teachers,
attitudes and characteristics of people who enter
teaching and their attitudes toward their work.

1053. Louisell, Robert Daniel. What teacher educators
miss: Patterns in the classroom behavior of
elementary teachers. Ed.D. dissertation.
University of Illinois at Urbana-Champaign. 1979.

Describes teacher behaviors as directed toward
instruction and, more frequently, toward
maintaining a context in which learning could
occur, which teachers defined to include
socializing the child.

1054. McCully, Thomas Michael. Curriculum planning:
teacher concerns in affective learning. Ed.D.
dissertation. State University of New York at
Buffalo. 1979.

Describes teacher attitude, planning and
self-reported behavior dealing with student
affective growth.

1055. McGreal, Shirley Springer. Teacher questioning
behavior during classroom discussions of short
stories. Ph.D. dissertation. University of
Illinois at Urbana-Champaign. 1976. *ERIC ED* 132
608.

Describes teachers using distinct patterns of
questions and a greater number dealing with
content than with form of the stories.

1056. McKay, A. An exploration of the relationship
between teacher thought processes and behavior.
1979. *ERIC ED* 171 684.

Describes a relationship between teacher
thought and decisions during instruction and
teacher classroom behavior, based on teacher
stimulated recall.

1057.   McKeon, Helen M. Book selection criteria of
        children's book editors and elementary classroom
        teachers. 1975. *ERIC ED* 116 136.

        Describes criteria teachers use to select
        reading books and differences between their
        criteria and editors' criteria.

1058.   McNair, Kathleen. "Capturing inflight decisions:
        Thoughts while teaching," *Educational Research
        Quarterly 3*, No.4 (1978-1979): 26-42.

        Describes teachers responding to cues from
        students while teaching in the recitation mode.

1059.   McNair, Kathleen & Joyce, Bruce. Teachers' thoughts
        while teaching: The South Bay Study. Part II.
        Research Series No. 59. East Lansing, Michigan:
        Institute for Research on Teaching. Michigan State
        University. 1979.

        Describes teacher behaviors while teaching and
        their thoughts about their teaching as they are
        related to those behaviors.

1060.   McNeil, John D. Performance tests: assessing
        teachers of reading. 1971. *ERIC ED* 054 200.

        Describes teacher performance tests and the
        information which they provide about teacher
        behaviors, and teacher resistance to their use.

1061.   Madsen, Ronald Joseph. A study of the congruence
        between selected generic teaching behaviors
        derived from the consensus method and the observed
        behaviors of successful classroom teachers. Ed.D.
        dissertation. State University of New York at
        Albany. 1979.

        Describes a comparison of the behaviors of
        successful teachers of English and social studies
        with a list of generic behaviors, common across
        the two subjects.

1062.   Maehara, Oei. The behavior controls used the by
        Honolulu kindergarten teachers and the development
        of self-discipline. Ed.D. dissertation. New York
        University. 1969.

        Describes the behavior control moves that
        kindergarten teachers use with students.

1063.   Marliave, Richard S. Findings of clinical field
        observations. Technical Note I-4. Beginning
        Teacher Evaluation Study. San Francisco,

California: Far West Laboratory for Educational
Research and Development. 1976. *ERIC ED* 146 161.

Describes observations of teacher and student
behavior in a small sample of classrooms and the
consistency of teacher reports of behavior with
observer descriptions.

1064. Martin, Oneida L. An analysis of classroom
management behaviors used by selected secondary
English teachers. Ed.D. dissertation. University
of Tennessee. 1980.

Describes the management behaviors used by
teachers, the most frequent being organizing,
planning, decision-making, maintaining, and
discipline, to manage classroom time, students and
materials.

1065. Matthews, C. EIE Elementary School Science Project
evaluation report. Tallahassee, Florida: Florida
State University. 1969. *ERIC ED* 035 553.

Describes behavior of teachers and students in
elementary science classes; teachers tended to
interact with groups of more than six children, to
give information and directions and to spend time
observing without responding to children.

1066. Medley, Donald M. Studying teacher behavior with
the OScAR technique. Berkeley, California: Far
West Laboratory for Educational Research and
Development. 1966.

Describes OScAR and two studies of its use and
the behaviors which teachers were observed to use
in the classroom.

1067. Mehan, Hugh. *Learning lessons: Social organization
in the classroom.* Cambridge, Massachusetts:
Harvard University Press. 1979.

Describes the behavior of one teacher and the
primary grade children over the course of a year,
and the effects of the classroom organization on
the behaviors of teachers and students.

1068. Mehlenbacher, Sandra & Mehlenbacher, Earl. J.J.
O'Keefe's': A particiant-observation study of
teachers in a bar on Friday afternoon. 1980. *ERIC
ED* 185 051.

Describes behavior of teachers in a bar and
relates these to constraints on adult interactions
in school settings.

1069.   Melendy, Ward Tinker. Cognitive meaning of
        teacher-child verbal interaction in a fourth grade
        classroom. Ed.D. dissertation. Oregon State
        University. 1968.

        Describes verbal behaviors of teachers in one
        classroom.

1070.   Miller, G.W. Some aspects of teacher behavior.
        Ottawa, Ontario, Canada: Canadian Council for
        Research in Education. 1968. *ERIC ED* 026 672.

        Describes a model and collection of data to
        describe behaviors of teachers and the sequences
        of interactions with students.

1071.   Molnar, S.R. Teachers in teams: Interaction,
        influence, and autonomy. Stanford, California:
        Stanford Center for Research and Development in
        Teaching. Stanford University. 1971. *ERIC ED* 058
        177.

        Describes behavior of teachers in team teaching
        situations, ways of working together, influencing
        other teachers, and resolving conflicts.

1072.   Montague, Earl J., (Ed.) Research and curriculum
        development in science education. 3. Science
        teacher behaviors and student affective and
        cognitive learning. Austin, Texas. Science
        Education Center. Texas University at Austin.
        1971. *ERIC ED* 124 404.

        Presents a collection of fifteen papers which
        describe the behaviors of teachers teaching
        science.

1073.   Moore, Barbara Ann Bair. Classroom teachers' use
        and modification of instructional materials for
        mainstreamed, handicapped students and perceived
        need for assistance and training. Ed.D.
        dissertation. American University. 1980.

        Describes teacher use of materials, with print
        materials used most; differences in use with
        regular and mainstreamed students, and teacher
        reports of need for assistance in use of materials
        with handicapped students.

1074.   Morgan, Edward P. "Effective teaching in the urban
        high school," *Urban Education 14* (1979): 161-181.

        Describes the behaviors of one social studies
        teacher identified as being effective.

1075. Morris, Marian. Identifying and analyzing communication patterns of classroom management which characterize levels of role acquisition. Ed.D. dissertation. University of Pittsburgh. 1980.

Describes teachers spending time on organization and management, controlling the amount of time for and topics of discussion and varying in their management behaviors by the way they view their role.

1076. Moskowitz, Gertrude & Hayman, John L., Jr. "Interaction patterns of first-year, typical, and 'best' teachers in inner-city schools," *Journal of Educational Research 67* (1974): 224-230.

Describes the initial contact between teachers and students, with the best teachers devoting time to setting standards; differences between teachers and administrators in concerns for first contacts between teachers and students.

1077. Mueller, Doris E. "Teacher questioning practices in reading," *Reading World 12* (1972): 136-145.

Describes the questioning behaviors of teachers, who emphasize cognitive memory questions.

1078. Mueller, Doris Land. An analysis of instructional material and verbal behavior in fourth grade reading groups. Ph.D. dissertation. Washington University. 1971.

Describes teacher behavior in reaction to student responses in reading instruction.

1079. Mueller, Doris Land. "The second-round question (or how teachers react to student responses)," *Urban Education 8* (1973): 153-165.

Describes teacher responses to adequate and inadequate student responses, with a large number of types of responses but a small number used frequently by teachers.

1080. National Education Association. *Discipline and learning: An inquiry into student-teacher relationships.* (revised edition). Washington, D.C. National Education Association. 1977.

Presents a collection of brief articles on aspects of discipline in the classroom, including Kounin & Gump, citation No. 1043.

1081. Newcastle, Helen Phyllis. Oral interrogatory
       soliciting and responding behaviors of selectd
       elementary school teachers. Ph.D. dissertation.
       University of Arizona. 1970.

       Describes questioning behaviors of teachers,
       with evaluation questions underemphasized but
       memory questions not overemphasized.

1082. Nickerson, Jacquelyn Ruth. A participant
       observation study of teachers' affective
       interaction in racially and culturally diverse
       classrooms. Ph.D. dissertation. Michigan State
       University. 1980.

       Describes the behaviors of two teachers
       nominated as especially capable in the affective
       domain and teacher provision for student
       interactions across racial groups in grade six.

1083. Oakley, Wayne F. & Crocker, Robert K. "An
       exploratory study of teacher interventions in
       elementary science laboratory groups," *Journal of
       Research in Science Teaching 17* (1980): 407–418.
       ERIC ED 139 608.

       Describes behavior of teachers and pupils in
       science classes, with use of a large number of
       student work groups.

1084. Okey, James R. & Humphreys, Donald W. Measuring
       teacher competence. 1974. *ERIC ED* 090 060.

       Describes methods to measure outcomes and
       relates those to three categories of teacher
       behavior.

1085. Payne, David A. & others. The impact of instruc-
       tional television teacher aides on teacher
       behavior and student learning. 1972. *ERIC ED* 060
       638.

       Describes an evaluation of different manuals
       for use with television programs, and teachers
       using little pre and post program teaching.

1086. Pendergrass, R.A. An analysis of the verbal
       interaction of small group discussion members in
       secondary, social studies classes. Ed.D.
       dissertation. Washington State University. 1973.

       Describes teacher domination of small groups,
       with more than 50% of the talk by teachers, and
       student talk not evenly distributed among
       students.

1087.   Pierce-Jones, John & others. Outcomes of individual
        and programmatic variations among project Head
        Start centers, summer, 1965. Final Report. 1966.
        ERIC ED 014 325.

        Describes the behaviors of teachers as one
        portion of the evaluation of Head Start centers.

1088.   Porter, Andrew C., Schwille, J.R., Floden, R.E.,
        Freeman, D.J., Knappen, L.B., Kuhs, T.M. &
        Schmidt, W.H. Teacher autonomy and the control of
        content taught. Research Series No. 24. East
        Lansing, Michigan: Institute for Research on
        Teaching. Michigan State University. 1979. *ERIC
        ED* 181 006.

        Describes math content covered in elementary
        classrooms, teacher reports of what content they
        would choose in a simulation, and the content
        presented by textbooks and recommended by various
        persons.

1089.   Rencher, Alvin C. & others. "A discriminant
        analysis of four levels of teacher competence,"
        Journal of Experimental Education 46 (1978):
        46-51.

        Describes behaviors of teachers, identifying
        four levels or patterns of behaviors.

1090.   Resnick, Lauren B. "Teacher behavior in the
        informal classroom," *Journal of Curriculum Studies
        4* (1972): 99-109.

        Describes the observed behaviors of teachers
        and young students in open classrooms.

1091.   Rist, Ray C. On the social and cultural milieu of
        an urban black school: An ethnographic case study.
        1972. *ERIC ED* 066 523.

        Describes teaching, the classroom environment,
        and the environment of the school.

1092.   Rist, Ray C. "Social distance and social inequality
        in a ghetto kindergarten classroom: An examination
        of the 'cultural gap' hypothesis," *Urban Education
        7* (1972): 241-261.

        Describes the behaviors of teachers and
        students in a black urban school and different
        teacher responses to children by child
        characteristics.

1093.   Robertson, Ina Herbrig. An investigation of the use
        of children's non-fiction-informational trade
        books in selected fourth-, fifth-, and sixth-grade
        classrooms in Illinois. Ph.D. dissertation.
        University of Illinois at Urbana-Champaign. 1980.

        Describes teacher use of nonfiction trade books
        in grades 4-6, most frequently for social studies,
        for research reports and free choice reading.

1094.   Robitaille, David F. & Sherrill, James M. British
        Columbia mathematics assessment, 1977. Report
        Number 2; Teacher questionnaire--Instructional
        practices. Vancouver, British Columbia, Canada:
        British Columbia University. 1977. *ERIC ED* 152
        526.

        Describes teacher organization and use of
        materials for math instruction, based on teacher
        self-reports.

1095.   Roderick, Jessie A. & Vawter, Jacquelyn. A category
        system to describe the nonverbal behavior of
        teachers and students: An interim report.
        Occasional Paper No. 2. College Park, Maryland:
        Center for Young Children. Maryland University.
        1972. *ERIC ED* 094 874.

        Describes behavior of teachers and students in
        prekindergarten through secondary classrooms.

1096.   Rodriguez-Brown, Flora V. & others. Language
        interaction in a bilingual classroom: An
        observational study. 1976. *ERIC ED* 129 883.

        Describes behavior and language use of teachers
        and Spanish-speaking children in a grade one
        classroom.

1097.   Roehler, Laura & others. How do teachers spend
        their language arts time? Research Series No. 66.
        East Lansing, Michigan: Institute for Research on
        Teaching. Michigan State University. 1979. *ERIC
        ED* 189 620.

        Describes ways that instructional time is
        allocated to language arts and reading over a
        three month period in six elementary classrooms.

1098.   Rosenberg, Eileen Popkoski. Embattled species: A
        case study of high school teachers in contemporary
        suburbia. Ed.D. dissertation. Boston University
        School of Education. 1979.

        Describes the attitudes and behaviors of
        teachers in out-of-classroom task settings.

1099. Rothenberg, Marilyn & Rivlin, Leanne G. An
       ecological approach to the study of open
       classrooms. 1975. *ERIC ED* 132 209.

       Describes classroom operation, teacher
       behaviors and student behaviors in open
       classrooms.

1100. Rowe, Mary Budd. "Reflections on wait-time: Some
       methodological questions," *Journal of Research in
       Science Teaching 11* (1974): 263-279.

       Describes teacher use of wait time after asking
       questions and some methodological issues in
       measuring and analyzing wait time.

1101. Rowe, Mary Budd. "Relation of wait-time and rewards
       to the development of language, logic, and fate
       control: Part II--Rewards, *"Journal of Research in
       Science Teaching 11* (1974) 291-308.

       Describes the frequency (about one fourth of
       all teacher speech) of verbal rewards, differences
       in patterns for high and low students, and
       differences in students responses to rewards.

1102. Rowe, Mary Budd. "Wait-time and rewards as
       instructional variables, their influence on
       language, logic, and fate control: Part
       I--Wait-time," *Journal of Research in Science
       Teaching 11* (1974):81-94.

       Describes teacher wait-time for student
       response after a question, typically less than
       three seconds but different by level of student
       achievement, and reports changes in student
       behavior when wait-time is increased.

1103. Rowe, Mary Budd. "What research says," *Science and
       Children 18* (1980): 19-21.

       Presents data which show a decline in time that
       teachers allocate to elementary science
       instruction, declines in teacher knowledge of
       science and teacher views of student interest in
       science.

1104. Rubinstein, Dahta Louise. A study of verbal
       communications of teachers and students in small
       groups for personal and interpersonal growth in
       the classroom. Ed.D. dissertation. Teachers
       College Columbia University. 1979.

       Describes behaviors of teachers and students in
       small group settings.

1105.   Russo, Lillian Norma. Classroom language
        analysis--A study of reacting moves in the
        language of selected classrooms. 1968. *ERIC ED* 037
        471.

        Describes teacher reacting moves in secondary
        social studies classrooms.

1106.   Searle, Dennis & Dillon, David. "Responding to
        student writing: What is said or how it is said,"
        Language Arts 57 (1980): 773-781.

        Describes alternative ways of responding to
        children's writing, responses to form and/or
        content and teacher emphasis on the basics of
        usage and grammar.

1107.   Seif, Elliott. "What are teachers like who use a
        personalized approach?" *Educational Leadership 37*
        (1979): 262-264.

        Describes the behaviors of eight successful
        teachers with individualized personalized learning
        program.

1108.   Shafer, Robert E. A comparative study of successful
        practices and materials for teaching reading in
        the primary schools as viewed by teachers in
        England and the United States. 1976. *ERIC ED* 145
        364.

        Describes perceptions of teachers in England
        and Los Angeles in open education programs about
        materials and teacher uses of materials.

1109.   Sharpe, Donald M. Studying teacher classroom
        behavior to determine how paraprofessionals can
        help in the classroom. 1969. *ERIC ED* 033 897.

        Describes teacher time spend in different
        teaching roles in secondary school classrooms.

1110.   Shultz, Jeffrey & Florio, Susan. "Stop and freeze:
        The negotiation of social and physical space in a
        kindergarten/first grade classroom," *Anthropology
        and Education Quarterly 10* (1979): 166-181.
        Occasional Paper No. 26. East Lansing, Michigan:
        Institute for Research on Teaching. Michigan State
        University. 1979. *ERIC ED* 181 008.

        Describes the teacher role in socializing child
        to school in kindergarten and grade one, in terms
        of the child's social competence.

1111.   Slater, B.C. & Thomas, J.J. "Science teachers
         described--A new method for the understanding of
         individual differences," *School Science Review 59*,
         No. 206. (1977): 49-57.

         Describes behaviors of five science teachers
         while teaching science.

1112.   Slicker, Clyde Charles. An investigation of
         kindergarten teachers' verbal behavior. Ed.D.
         dissertation. Columbia University. 1970.

         Describes similarities in teacher verbal
         behavior in interactions with students.

1113.   Smith, John P. "Classroom profiles of three ESCP
         teachers," *Journal of Geological Education 21*
         (1973): 168-172.

         Describes behaviors of teacher and students
         using new science curriculum as not actually
         implementing the Earth Science Curriculum Project
         materials.

1114.   Smith, John Preston. The development of a classroom
         observation instrument relevant to the Earth
         Science Curriculum Project. 1969. *ERIC ED* 043
         502.

         Describes actual and expected behavior of
         teachers using the Earth Science Curriculum
         Project instructional materials.

1115.   Smith, Paul M., Jr. & Pindle, Viola. "The
         culturally disadvantaged pupil on the cumulative
         record," *Journal of Negro Education 38* (1969):
         78-81.

         Describes a greater number of negative than
         positive remarks by teachers on student cumulative
         records, with more favorable comments on girls'
         than boys' records.

1116.   Smith, Stanley Ferris. The identification of
         teaching behaviors descriptive of the contstruct:
         Clarity of presentation. Ph.D. dissertation.
         Syracuse University. 1978.

         Describes behaviors of teachers which are
         subsumed under the label "clarity of
         presentation".

1117.   Sparks, Patricia May. Scheduled teacher preparation
         time as perceived by superintendents, principals,
         and teachers in secondary schools accredited

by North Central Association. Ed.D. dissertation.
Ball State University. 1980.

Describes the availability of preparation time
for secondary teachers and ways that teachers use
the time to work with students, such as student
conferences.

1118. Spiegel, Dixie Lee & Rogers, Carol. "Teacher
responses to miscues during oral reading by
second-grade students," *Journal of Educational
Research 74* (1980): 8-12.

Describes responses of grade two teachers to
miscues in oral reading, within eight categories,
50% of responses told child the word and 5% used
meaning clues to help the child identify the
word.

1119. Sprague, Nancy Frietag. Social issues classroom
discourse: A study of expository, inquiry-
nonprobing, and inquiry-probing classes. Ph.D.
dissertation. University of Michigan. 1970.

Describes three types of discussion patterns of
secondary social studies teachers, expository,
inquiry-probing and inquiry-nonprobing, and
differences in student evaluations by type of
discussion pattern.

1120. Stallings, Jane A. "How to change the process of
teaching reading in secondary schools,"
Educational Horizons 57, No. 4 (1979): 196-201.

Describes the patterns of behaviors of
successful secondary teachers of remedial reading,
in organizing for instruction and in interacting
with students.

1121. Steffy, Betty Eileen. Analysis of group member
characteristics and interaction of elementary
teaching teams: Implications for leadership. Ed.D.
dissertation. University of Pittsburgh. 1978.

Describes behaviors of teachers in teaching
teams in terms of the characteristics of
teachers.

1122. Stuchin, Jacqueline B. A study of third grade
pupils as related to their teachers' communication
of positive and negative personal information.
Ed.D. dissertation. New York University. 1971.

Describes the limited variety of behaviors
which communicate personal information about
teachers to students.

1123. Sword, Jeane-Marie Hilma. Factors related to kindergarten teachers' book selection. Ed.D. dissertation. University of Illinois at Urbana-Champaign. 1979.

Describes the criteria which teachers use to select books to read to students, and patterns of reading to students, with 80% of teachers reporting that they read to students in whole-class settings.

1124. Thomas, John D. & others. "Natural rates of teacher approval and disapproval in grade-seven classrooms," *Journal of Applied Behavioral Analysis 11* (1978): 91-94.

Describes rates of teacher verbal approval and disapproval of student behaviors.

1125. Tidwell, Clyde D. Teacher behavior and democratic processes. Ed.D. dissertation. University of Arizona. 1971.

Describes behavior of one teacher, the author, using democratic processes in the classroom.

1126. Tighe, Mary Ann. A survey of the teaching of composition in the English classroom and in the content areas of social studies and science. Ph.D. dissertation. University of Pittsburgh. 1979.

Describes teacher self-reports of teaching activities for student writing in the content courses and in English classes.

1127. Tisher, Richard P. "Verbal interaction in science classes," *Classroom Interaction Newsletter 8* (1971): 1-8. reprinted as "A study of verbal interaction in science classes and its association with pupils' understanding of science," *University of Queensland Papers 1* 31-75.

Describes the verbal behaviors of teachers and students and teacher-student interaction in science classes.

1128. Tom, C.L. What teachers read to pupils in the middle grades. Ph.D. dissertation. Ohio State University. 1969. *ERIC ED* 041 887

Describes teacher patterns of reading to students; teachers who value such reading read more fiction than non-fiction, choices of books are dependent on what's easily available and teachers have limited knowledge of contemporary children's literature.

1129.   Tway, Eileen. "Teacher responses to children's
        writing," *Language Arts 57* (1980): 763-772.

        Reports one writing lesson as a case study of
        ways that a teacher responds to children's writing
        and relation of student needs in communication to
        teacher teaching of writing skills and
        conventions.

1130.   Vartuli, Sue Ann. The correlation between preschool
        teacher self-concept and teacher-child
        interaction. Ph.D. dissertation. Ohio State
        University. 1979.

        Describes the greater frequency of positive
        than negative teacher behavior in preschool
        classrooms, not related to teacher reported
        self-concept.

1131.   Velazquez, Clara. Teacher student interaction in
        the Puerto Rican school system. 1977. *ERIC ED* 142
        602.

        Describes the behaviors of teachers in
        English-as-a-second-language classrooms in Puerto
        Rico.

1132.   Veldman, Donald J. & Peck, Robert F. The Pupil
        Observation Survey; Teacher characteristics from
        the student's viewpoint. Austin, Texas: Center for
        Research and Development for Teacher Education.
        Texas University at Austin. 1967. *ERIC ED* 055
        980.

        Describes behaviors of a large sample of
        teachers and the perceptions of students of those
        behaviors.

1133.   Warren, Richard L. Teacher encounters: A typology
        for ethnographic research on the teaching
        experience. Stanford, California: Stanford Center
        for Research and Development in Teaching. Stanford
        University. 1969. *ERIC ED* 028 988.

        Describes a typology based on in- and
        out-of-class encounters, which reports that events
        which happen infrequently may cause stress, such
        as interactions with parents.

1134.   Warren, R.L. The teaching experience in an
        elementary school: A case study. *ERIC ED* 080 512.

        Describes the behaviors of one teacher in
        elementary school.

1135. Washington, Valora. "Teachers in integrated classrooms: Profiles of attitudes, perceptions, and behaviors," *Elementary School Journal 60* (1980): 192-201.

Describes the attitudes and behaviors of a small number of teachers in integrated elementary classrooms.

1136. Welch, Wayne W. & Walberg, Herbert J. "Are the attitudes of teachers related to declining percentage enrollments in physics," *Science Education 51* (1967): 436-442.

Describes teacher reports of texts used, teaching methods and objectives of high school physics.

1137. Wells, Reese. "Teacher survival in the classroom," *Journal of Research and Development in Education 11*, No. 2 (1978): 64-73.

Describes problems in discipline, student misbehavior and violence and teacher reactions.

1138. Willerman, Marvin. "Interruption behavior in the elementary classroom," *Illinois School Research 11* (1975): 19-27.

Describes numbers and types of classroom interruptions throughout the school day.

1139. Woodward, Donald Dean. A study of the verbal language styles of Head Start teachers and teacher aides. Ph.D. dissertation. University of South Dakota. 1977.

Describes the verbal behaviors of teachers and aides when speaking with children in a sample of Head Start centers.

1140. Worsham, Murray E. & Evertson, Carolyn M. Systems of student accountability for written work in junior high English classes. Austin, Texas: Center for Research and Development for Teacher Education. Texas University at Austin. 1980.

Describes behaviors which teachers use to hold students accountable for assigned written work.

1141. Zahorik, John A. "Classroom feedback behavior of teachers," *Journal of Educational Research 62* (1968): 147-150.

Describes behavior of elementary teachers giving feedback to students on current events lesson, with a large number of methods used occasionally but only a few used frequently, and type used is related to value of student response.

1142.   Zahorik, John A. "Pupils' perception of teachers' verbal feedback," *Elementary School Journal 71* (1970): 105-114.

Describes types of teacher feedback to students and student perceptions of that feedback; typically feedback provides some reinforcement-motivation but little cognitive information to the student.

1143.   Zimmerman, Barry J. & Bergan, John R. "Intellectual operations in teacher question-asking behavior," *Merrill-Palmer Quarterly of Behavior and Development 17* (1971): 19-26.

Describes the various types of teacher processes involved in asking questions.

B. CONSISTENCY OF

1144. Ahtman, Harold. "Teacher-student interaction in inner-city and advantaged classes using the Science Curriculum Improvement Study," Ed.D. dissertation. University of California, Los Angeles. *Classroom Interaction Newsletter* 6, No. 1 (1970): 5-16.

Describes inner-city teachers using more procedural talk and teachers of advantaged students using more cognitive talk and two times the amount of student initiated talk as in inner-city classrooms.

1145. Amidon, Edmund & Giammatteo, Michael. "The verbal behavior of superior elementary teachers," In *Interaction Analysis: Theory, research and application.* Edited by Edmund J. Amidon & John B. Hough. pp. 186-188. Reading, Massachusetts: Addison-Wesley Publishing Company. 1967. Reprinted from *Elementary School Journal* 65 (1965): 283-285.

Describes differences in the patterns of verbal behavior of teachers nominated as superior and a random sample of average teachers, including superior teachers spending less class time talking, using more praise and acceptance of student feelings. For Amidon & Hough reference see citation No. 1638.

1146. Anderson, Linda M., Evertson, Carolyn M. & Brophy, Jere E. Context effects and stability of teacher behaviors in an experimental study of first grade reading group instruction. Research and Development Report No. 4091. Austin, Texas: Center for Research and Development for Teacher Education. Texas University at Austin. 1978. *ERIC ED* 177 485.

Describes stability of teacher behavior in selection of students to respond to questions, feedback in response to student answers, workbook activities and in assigning students to read new information from texts.

1147.   Anderson, Linda M. & others. Dimensions of
        classroom management derived from recent research.
        Research and Development Report No. 6006. Austin,
        Texas: Center for Research and Development for
        Teacher Education. Texas University at Austin.
        1979. ERIC ED 175 860.

        Describes behavior of effective managers in
        identifying and teaching the tasks related to the
        functioning of the classroom and the coordination
        of student tasks.

1148.   Armstrong, Stephen W., Algozzine, Bob, & Sherry,
        Lee. "Perceived brightness and classroom
        interactions," Educational Research Quarterly 4
        (1979): 54-60.

        Describes behavior of teachers in classrooms
        with no differences in the number of negative
        interactions with children perceived as "bright"
        and "dull" but a greater number of positive
        interactions with children perceived to be
        "bright".

1149.   Arnold, Virginia Ann. The nature of teacher-pupil
        interaction in informal and traditional
        classrooms. Ph.D. dissertation. Ohio State
        University. 1972.

        Describes more student initiated and more
        individual interactions in informal classrooms,
        with those teachers emphasizing student inquiry,
        divergence, and free verbal exchange.

1150.   Attridge, Carolyn Bernice. Teacher and student
        behavior and its environmental context in diverse
        classroom settings. Ph.D. dissertation. University
        of Toronto, Canada. 1975.

        Describes similarities of student and teacher
        behavior across classes, but differences by task
        groupings.

1151.   Ayers, Jerry B. A longitudinal study of teachers.
        1980. ERIC ED 189 146.

        Describes an evaluation of teachers over
        several years and reports no differences over the
        years by teaching level.

1152.   Babb, Charles Worthy. Some selected relationships
        between the concerns of elementary school teachers
        and their verbal behavior in the classroom. Ed.D.
        dissertation. University of Alabama. 1971.

Describes teachers with high concerns about
teaching as no less direct in their verbal
behavior and as spending more time praising and
encouraging students than teachers with low
concerns.

1153.   Bailey, Gerald Douglass. "Verbal behavior models:
        Identifying change and direction of teacher
        interaction pattern styles," *College Student
        Journal 8*, No. 3 (1974): 18-24.

        Describes changes in teacher behavior from less
        to more flexible verbal behavior from student
        teaching to second year of teaching.

1154.   Baker, Robert Morris. A study of the effects of a
        selected set of science teaching materials
        (Elementary Science Study) on classroom
        instructional behaviors. Ed.D. dissertation.
        University of Rochester. 1970. *ERIC ED* 077 645.

        Describes differences in teacher behaviors by
        the types of science curriculum material being
        used.

1155.   Baldwin, Thelma L. & Johnson, Thomas J. Teacher
        behavior and effectiveness of reinforcement. 1966.
        ERIC ED 010 511.

        Describes differences in behaviors of punative
        and nonpunative teachers, with nonpunative
        teachers responding to students with greater
        reinforcement for student behaviors.

1156.   Balzer, A.L. An exploratory investigation of verbal
        and non-verbal behaviors of BSCS teachers and
        non-BSCS teachers. Ph.D. dissertation. Ohio State
        University. 1968. *ERIC ED* 027 197.

        Describes differences between teachers but not
        between groups of teachers using and not using the
        new science curriculum materials in how they
        controlled the laboratory setting, facilitated
        communication, taught the scientific process and
        expressed affect.

1157.   Balzer, LeVon. "Nonverbal and verbal behaviors of
        biology teachers," *American Biology Teacher 31*
        (1969): 226-229.

        Describes behaviors of biology teachers using
        and not using a new science curriculum, with about
        half the teacher behavior directed toward
        management and giving directions, and goal setting
        and affective behaviors about 1% each of all
        teacher behaviors.

1158. Barchi-McBroom, Barbara Ann. Teacher use of new
       social studies skills and behaviors and sixth
       grade students' perceptions of class activities.
       Ph.D. dissertation. University of Michigan. 1975.

       Describes teachers not consistently using the
       teaching behaviors of the new curriculum and
       student perceptions of teacher behavior not
       related to teacher behavior.

1159. Barnes, Willie J. "Teachers in desegregated high
       schools in Texas," *Integrated Education 17*, No.
       1-2 (1979): 25-26.

       Describes observations of white teacher
       behaviors with white and black students, with no
       differences in most behaviors but the differences
       which do exist show that teachers have lower
       expectations for black students.

1160. Batchelder, Ann Streeter. Process objectives,
       observed behaviors, and teaching patterns in
       elementary math, English, and physical education
       classes. Ed.D. dissertation. Boston University
       School of Education. 1976.

       Describes similarities and differences in
       teacher behavior in math, English and physical
       education and differences between teacher behavior
       and teacher process objectives.

1161. Becker, Jerome & others. School Days. 1967. *ERIC
       ED* 012 710.

       Describes differences in classroom environment
       and behaviors of teachers in urban, suburban and
       rural classrooms.

1162. Biber, Henry, Miller, Louise B. & Dyer, Jean L.
       "Feminization in the preschool," *Developmental
       Psychology 7* (1972): 86. *ERIC ED* 045 196.

       Describes teachers providing more contact and
       more positive reinforcement for instructional
       activities in preschool classrooms to girls.

1163. Blumberg, Arthur & Perry, Roger. "A comparison of
       human relations problem diagnostic tendencies of
       elementary and secondary teachers," *Journal of
       Educational Research 67* (1974): 207-209. *ERIC ED*
       075 439.

       Describes differences in responses of
       elementary and secondary teachers to problems in
       human relations within the classroom.

1164. Bogener, Jerry Dean. The application of the verbal interaction analysis to seven independent approaches to teaching reading in the elementary school. Ed.D. dissertation. University of Kansas. 1967.

Describes differences among teachers in patterns of behavior, but behavior for each teacher stable across lessons.

1165. Borgeson, Don Raymond. A comparative study of work-related activities of elementary school classroom teachers in selected Minneapolis public schools. Ed.D. dissertation. University of Minnesota. 1979.

Describes activities of teachers, time allocation and differences among teachers by types of school program.

1166. Borman, Kathryn Matey. Social control and the process of schooling: A study of socialization of kindergarten children in two settings. 1977. *ERIC ED* 140 932.

Describes variations in the behaviors of teachers and students in kindergarten by season, teacher, school and sex of student.

1167. Brickner, Sally Ann Mary. Observed classroom behaviors and personality types of 178 beginning teachers. Ph.D. dissertation. Michigan State University. 1970.

Describes differences in teacher behavior by sex, grade level taught but not by personality type.

1168. Brooks, Douglas M. & Wilson, Barry J. "Teacher verbal and nonverbal behavioral expression toward selected pupils," *Journal of Educational Psychology 70* (1978): 147-153.

Describes no differences in behavior of teachers toward students by teacher types.

1169. Brophy, Jere E. A study to determine if teachers communicated differential performance expectations to students. Final Report. Austin, Texas: Center for Research and Development for Teacher Education. Texas University at Austin. 1972. *ERIC ED* 067 379.

Describes stability of teacher behaviors across subject areas and student ability levels.

1170.   Brophy, Jere E. & Coultier, C., Crawford, J.,
        Evertson, C. & King, C. "Classroom observation
        scales: Stability across time and context and
        relationships with student learning gains,"
        Journal of Educational Psychology 67 (1975):
        873-881.

            Describes stability of observed teacher
        behavior across years, not stability in the
        relationship between teacher behavior and student
        achievement.

1171.   Brophy, Jere E., Evertson, C., Crawford, J., King,
        C. & Senior, K. Stability measures of classroom
        process behaviors across three different contexts
        in second and third grade classrooms. Austin,
        Texas: Center for Research and Development for
        Teacher Education. Texas University at Austin.
        1975.

            Describes different patterns of stability of
        behavior across three classroom contexts, morning,
        afternoon, and reading groups.

1172.   Brophy, Jere E. & Good, Thomas L. "Teachers'
        communication of differential expectations for
        children's classroom performance: Some behavioral
        data," *Journal of Educational Psychology 61*
        (1970): 365-374.

            Describes some differences in teacher behavior
        toward students related to student behaviors and
        some to teacher expectations, with teachers
        demanding greater performance and giving greater
        praise to high expectation students.

1173.   Brophy, Jere E. & others. The Texas Teacher
        Effectiveness Study: Student sex, grade, and
        socioeconomic status differences in classroom
        process measures. Austin, Texas: Center for
        Research and Development for Teacher Education.
        Texas University at Austin. 1975. *ERIC ED* 150
        159.

            Describes differences in behaviors of teachers
        in classrooms with students from low and middle
        socioeconomic levels.

1174.   Brown, Lorraine Hayes, Willower, Donald J. & Lynch,
        Patrick D. "School socioeconomic status and
        teacher pupil control behavior," *Urban Education
        9* (1974): 239-246. By first author only, Ph.D.
        dissertation. Pennsylvania State University.
        1973.

Describes no differences in pupil control behavior of teachers in lower and middle socioeconomic status secondary schools.

1175.   Brown, William E. & others. "Praise, criticism, and race," *Elementary School Journal 70* (1970): 373-377.

Describes greater teacher praise for students when the race of the teacher differs from the race of the student.

1176.   Buck, Crayton LaRue. Mathematics teaching behavior of selected intermediate grade teachers utilizing the OScAR (EM) for systematic observation. Ed.D. dissertation. Pennsylvania State University. 1967.

Describes behaviors of teachers teaching math, with no differences by the achievement level of students or the years of experience of the teachers.

1177.   Buttery, Thomas J. & Powell, Jack V. "Teacher verbal feedback during primary basal reading instruction," *Reading Improvement 15* (1978): 183-189.

Describes teacher questioning, frequency of student responses and teacher feedback differing by the student reading group.

1178.   Cabeceiras, James. "Observed differences in teacher verbal behavior when using and not using the overhead projector," *A V Communication Review 20* (1972): 271-280. Ph.D. dissertation. Syracuse University. 1968.

Describes no difference with and without an overhead projector in teacher allocation of time to content, in indirect teacher behavior.

1179.   Cadwell, Joel. Regression models of teacher judgement and decision-making. Ph.D. dissertation. University of California, Los Angeles. 1979.

Describes two regression models tested on three sets of data describing teacher decision making and reports variation between teachers in such decision making.

1180.   Calkins, Dick & Others. "Generalizability of teacher behaviors across classroom observation systems," *Journal of Classroom Interaction 13*, No. 1 (1977): 9-22.

Describes variation in teacher behavior across classrooms and across observation systems.

1181.   Campbell, James Reed. "A longitudinal study in the stability of teachers' verbal behavior," *Science Education 56* (1972): 89-96.

Describes wide fluctuations in teacher use of indirect teaching behaviors over a two year period in junior high school science classes.

1182.   Campbell, James Reed. "Can a teacher really make a difference?" *School Science and Mathematics 74* (1974): 657-666.

Describes variations in the verbal behavior of teachers with high and low ability junior high students in science classes, and by science subject taught.

1183.   Campbell, James Reed. "Cognitive and affective process development and its relation to a teacher's interaction ratio: An investigation to determine the relationship between the affective and cognitive development of junior high low achievers and the interaction ratio employed by their instructors, *"Journal of Research in Science Teaching 8* (1971): 317-324. Ph.D. dissertation. New York University. 1968.

Describes differences in amounts of teacher indirect behavior in junior and senior high science classes, with more indirect behavior related to higher student cognitive achievement and scientific curiosity.

1184.   Chai, Henry Keonaona. The effect of knowledge of student's beliefs and attitudes on the teacher's attitude and behavior toward that student. Ed.D. dissertation. Arizona State University. 1979.

Describes an experiment which demonstrated no differences in the attitude and behavior of teachers toward students when teachers did and did not have information about student attitudes and beliefs.

1185.   Chapman, Robert B. & others. "Interactions of first-grade teachers with learning disordered children," *Journal of Learning Disability 12* (1979): 225-230.

Describes behaviors of teachers with low, average, and high achievement students and students labelled as learning disordered.

1186. Cherry, Louise Joan. Sex differences in preschool teacher-child verbal interaction. Ed.D. dissertation. Harvard University. 1974.

Describes difference in patterns of teacher verbal behavior by student sex.

1187. Cohen, Martin Abraham. Teacher questioning behavior and pupil critical thinking ability: A study of the effects of teacher-questioning behavior on pupil critical thinking ability in three academic subjects offered in a suburban high school. Ph.D. dissertation. New York University. 1972. *ERIC ED* 084 136.

Describes differences between science and non-science teachers in the use of questions at the translation and application levels but not in the use of questions at higher cognitive levels.

1188. Colbert, C. Diane. "Instructional organization patterns of fourth grade teachers," *Theory into Practice 18* (1979): 170-173.

Describes differences by context in teacher behavior, with lesson type, size of group, subject and time influencing, and differences in teacher management on different days of the week but consistency for the same day each week.

1189. Colbert, C. Diane. "Teacher instructional management patterns," *Illinois School Research and Development 15*, No. 3 (1979): 85-92.

Describes differences in teacher behavior related to four context factors; lesson type, *subject matter, size of instructional group and time within the day and week.

1190. Conner, James B. A study of the extent of teacher absence in selected school districts in Colorado. Ph.D. dissertation. University of Colorado at Boulder. 1979.

Describes differences in teacher absence rates, within categories, by district, day of the week, weeks of year and for some categories of absence by teacher sex and teaching level.

1191. Connors, Judith Margaret. The application of a specific questioning model to two-hundred thirteen teacher-pupil conferences in individualized reading in three elementary schools. Ed.D. dissertation. University of Massachusetts. 1974.

Describes differences in areas covered by
teacher questions with those teachers who used
student conferences the most often covering more
lower level skills than other teachers in
conference questions.

1192. Copeland, Robert McDaniel. A comparative study of
visually perceived teacher nonverbal behavior and
the formation of student affect among members of
three different ethnic groups. Ph.D. dissertation.
Oregon State University. 1974.

Describes differences in teacher nonverbal
behavior by student ethnic group, and differences
in student interpretation of teacher behavior by
student ethnic group.

1193. Cornbleth, Catherine. "Expectations for pupil
achievement and teacher-pupil interaction," *Social
Education 38* (1974): 54-68.

Describes different teacher behaviors toward
students for whom teachers expect high and low
achievement.

1194. Cornbleth, Catherine & others. Teacher-pupil
interaction and teacher expectations for pupil
achievement in secondary social studies classes.
1972. *ERIC ED* 068 402.

Describes differences in teacher behavior
toward students for whom teachers have
expectations for high and low achievement.

1195. Cortez, Jesus, Jr. Miscue corrections by bilingual
and monolingual teachers when teaching bilingual
children to read: A comparative survey of Wales,
Spain, and two regions of the United States. Ph.D.
dissertation. University of Washington. 1980.

Describes differences in the behavior of
bilingual and monolingual teachers in correcting
errors in student oral reading.

1196. Crawford, W. John & others. Texas Teacher
Effectiveness Project: Stability correlations
between first and second year data. Austin, Texas:
Center for Research and Development for Teacher
Education. Texas University at Austin. 1975. *ERIC
ED* 150 158.

Describes variations in the consistency from
year to year of teacher behavior and factors which
appear to influence that consistency.

1197. Crispin, David. "Discipline behaviors of different
       teachers," *Contemporary Education* 39 (1968):
       164-167.

       Describes differences among teachers in the
       number of disciplinary acts, but teachers
       consistent across classes and subject matter.

1198. Crump, Harriet & Achilles, C.M. "Teacher
       communications toward different groups of
       students," *Catalyst for Change* 5 (1975): 8-11.

       Describes different patterns of teacher verbal
       behavior with different students.

1199. Dalton, William B. The relations between classroom
       interaction and teacher ratings of pupils: An
       exploration of one means by which a teacher may
       communicate her expectancies. Peabody papers in
       human development. George Peabody College for
       Teachers. 1969. *ERIC ED* 036 468.

       Describes greater teacher direct, versus
       indirect, interaction and more criticism with
       pupils whom teachers rated as lower in
       achievement.

1200. Davidson, Charles W. & others. "Relationships
       between class intelligence quotient means and
       teacher behavior," *Southern Journal of Educational
       Research 10* (1967): 99-104.

       Describes different patterns of behaviors of
       teachers by the average IQ of the class.

1201. Davidson, Jane Louise. The relationship between
       teachers' questions and pupils' responses during a
       directed reading activity and a directed
       reading-thinking activity. Ph.D. dissertation.
       University of Michigan. 1970.

       Describes differences in the types of questions
       which teachers ask with different types of
       instructional units using a basal reader, with
       more interpretation questions asked during
       directed thinking activity units than directed
       reading activity units.

1202. Delefes, Peter, & Jackson, Barry. "Teacher-pupil
       interaction as a function of location in the
       classroom," *Psychology in the Schools 9* (1972):
       119-123.

       Describes differences in teacher behavior by
       student characteristics and sex, with no

single location in the room having the maximum
amount of teacher contact or student response.

1203.   Denero, Sharon Blattner. A study of the influence
of high-ability and low-ability groups of teacher
behavior. Ed.D. dissertation. University of
Georgia. 1971.

Describes a relationship between teacher
behavior and the ability level of students, with
more indirect teaching with higher ability
groups.

1204.   Dispenziere, Joseph Anthony. The relationship of
the supportive behavior of teachers and their
instructional organization patterns and years of
experience. Ph.D. dissertation. Lehigh University.
1972.

Describes no differences by years of
experience, open versus traditional classrooms,
and teacher supportive behavior as measured in a
simulation.

1205.   Emmer, E., Evertson, C. & Anderson, L.M. "Effective
classroom management at the beginning of the
school year in junior high classes," *Elementary
School Journal 80* (1980): 219-231.   Austin, Texas:
Center for Research and Development for Teacher
Education. Texas University. 1980. *ERIC ED* 178
542.

Describes the behaviors at the start of the
school year of effective and less effective
managers of the classroom, as effective managers
teach students the rules of the classroom.

1206.   Emmer, Edmund T. & others. The first weeks of
class...and the rest of the year. Research and
Development Report No. 6005. Austin, Texas: Center
for Research and Development for Teacher
Education. Texas University at Austin. 1979. *ERIC
ED* 175 861.

Describes the behaviors of effective and
ineffective classroom managers, with effective
managers spending the first weeks of the year
teaching classroom routines and rules.

1207.   Erickson, Edsel L. & others. A study of the effects
of teacher attitude and curriculum structure on
preschool disadvantaged children. Annual Progress
Report 1. 1968. *ERIC ED* 027 079.

Describes teachers using Bereiter-Engelmann program as more alike and less like other teachers in their classroom behavior and attitudes toward instruction.

1208. Erlich, Oded & Borich, Gary. Generalizability of teacher process behaviors during reading instruction. Austin, Texas: Center for Research and Development for Teacher Education. Texas University at Austin. 1976. *ERIC ED* 142 586.

Describes differences in teacher-student interactions in reading and other instruction, in the proportion of public versus private questions, the nature of the questions asked, teacher feedback, pupil involvement and question difficulty.

1209. Erlich, Oded & Shavelson, Richard J. "The search for correlations between measures of teacher behavior and student achievement: Measurement problem, conceptual problem, or both?" *Journal of Educational Measurement 15* (1978): 77-89.

Describes the extent to which measures of teacher behaviors are generalizable across the same teachers teaching different subjects and across different time periods, with the most generalizable behaviors being those related to checking of student learning, positive feedback, probing, and most global ratings of teachers.

1210. Evans, Judith T. Characteristics of open education: Results from a classroom observation rating scale and a teacher questionnaire. Newton, Massachusetts: Education Development Center, Inc. 1971. *ERIC ED* 058 160.

Describes differences in the behaviors of teachers in open and traditional classroom across student socioeconomic levels.

1211. Evertson, C. Differences in instructional activities in high and low achieving junior high classes. Austin, Texas: Center for Research and Development for Teacher Education. Texas University at Austin. 1980.

Describes differences in the behavior of teachers teaching low and high achieving classes.

1212. Evertson, Carolyn M., Anderson, L., Edgar, D., Minter, M. & Brophy, J. Investigations of stability in junior high school math and English classes: The Texas Junior High School

Study. Research and Development Report No. 77-3. Austin, Texas: Center for Research and Development for Teacher Education. Texas University at Austin. 1977. *ERIC ED* 143 692.

Describes greater stability across two sections of a course and across courses in two subjects with high inference ratings than with frequency counts of behaviors.

1213. Evertson, Carolyn M. & Veldman, Donald J. Changes over time in process measures of classroom behavior. Research and Development Report No. 4060. Austin, Texas: Center for Research and Development for Teacher Education. Texas University at Austin. 1979. *ERIC ED* 189 072.

Describes behaviors of teachers and junior high school students in English and math classes over a school year.

1214. Fanselow, John F. I can't. I'm talking with the lady. Feedback in teaching and non-teaching settings. 1973. *ERIC ED* 155 926.

Describes the feedback which teachers give to students in English-as-a-second-language classrooms and other settings.

1215. Farley, George T. & Clegg, Ambrose A., Jr. Increasing the cognitive level of classroom questions in social studies: An application of Bloom's taxonomy. 1969. *ERIC ED* 034 732.

Describes differences in levels of questions between trained and untrained teachers, in terms of Bloom's taxonomy.

1216. Felsenthal, Helen Martha. Sex differences in teacher-pupil interaction and their relationships with teacher attitudes and pupil reading achievement. Ph.D. dissertation. University of Iowa. 1969.

Describes teachers interacting more with boys than girls in reading instruction, but no differences in rates of praise by student sex or level of reading group.

1217. Filby, Nikola N. "Time allocated to reading and mathematics (How it varies and why)," *California Journal of Teacher education 4*, No. 2 (1977): 12-22.

Describes teacher allocation of instructional time varying by subject and student.

1218. Fish, Enrica. The relationship of teachers' assigned marks to tested achievement among elementary grade, racially divergent lower socio-economic status boys and girls. 1969. *ERIC ED* 059 990.

Describes no differences in teacher grades for minority and white students when student socioeconomic level is held constant.

1219. Fitzgerald, John & others. The effects of subject of instruction on the behavior of teachers and pupils. Toronto, Ontario, Canada: Toronto Board of Education. *ERIC ED* 151 323.

Describes markedly different teacher behaviors in reading and math instruction, with more whole class instruction in math.

1220. Freeman, Robert Noble. An observational study of teacher interaction with successful and unsuccessful pupils. Ed.D. dissertation. University of Tennessee. 1977.

Describes differences in teacher behavior by student sex, grade level and level of success, with more positive teacher behaviors with more successful students.

1221. Freeman, Robert N. Life in classrooms: Teacher interaction with successful and unsuccessful pupils. 1980. *ERIC ED* 187 044.

Describes differences in teacher behaviors with successful and unsuccessful students, with greater physical distance and less interaction with unsuccessful students.

1222. Freiberg, Harvey Jerome. An investigation of the effect of verbal teacher-student interaction of similar and different ability groups in secondary classrooms. Ed.D. dissertation. University of Massachusetts. 1972.

Describes teachers as using more direct teaching behaviors with low ability groups, and perceiving themselves as more effective with low ability groups.

1223. Freiberg, H. Jerome. The effects of ability grouping on interaction in the classroom. 1970. *ERIC ED* 053 194.

Describes differences in teacher verbal behavior by the ability level of the class.

1224. Friedli, Robert LeRoy. A comparison of teacher's
       verbal behavior in selected self-contained and
       team-taught classrooms. Ph.D. dissertation.
       University of Utah. 1970.

       Describes no differences in the behavior of
       teachers in team and self-contained classrooms.

1225. Friedman, Philip. "Comparisons of teacher
       reinforcement schedules for students with
       different social class backgrounds," *Journal of
       Educational Psychology 68* (1976): 286-292.

       Describes differences in the frequencies of
       nonverbal but not verbal reinforcement which
       teachers give to middle and lower class students.

1226. Friedman, Philip. Frequency of teacher
       reinforcement and its relationship to peer group
       interaction. Ph.D. dissertation. Northwestern
       University. 1971.

       Describes differences in teacher reinforcement
       of students by student grade, socioeconomic level
       and ethnic group, and relationship between rate of
       teacher and of peer reinforcement of students.

1227. Friedman, Philip & Friedman, Harvey. Frequency and
       types of teacher reinforcement given to lower and
       middle class students. 1973. *ERIC ED* 074 185.

       Describes more teacher reinforcement for middle
       than for lower class students.

1228. Frizzi, Richard John. A comparative analysis of
       student-teacher interaction during episodes of
       classroom reading instruction. Ed.D. dissertation.
       Hofstra University. 1972. *ERIC ED* 076 938.

       Describes differences in behavior of most and
       least effective teachers during reading
       instruction.

1229. Furst, Norma & Amidon, Edmund. "Teacher-pupil
       interaction patterns in the elementary school," In
       *Interaction Analysis: Theory, reading and
       application.* Edited by Edmund J. Amidon & John B.
       Hough. pp. 167-175. Reading, Massachusetts:
       Addison-Wesley Publishing Co. 1967.

       Describes differences in the behaviors of
       teachers at primary and intermediate levels, with
       primary teachers using more question and answer
       interactions and intermediate teachers doing more
       lecturing. For Amidon & Hough reference see
       citation No. 1638.

1230. Furst, Norma & Amidon, Edmund. "Teacher-pupil
       interaction patterns in the teaching of reading in
       the elementary school," *Reading Teacher 18* (1965):
       283-287.

       Describes differences in behavior of reading
       and other teachers by grade, in amount of teacher
       talk, praise, ratio of indirect to direct
       teaching, responses to student talk.

1231. Gallagher, James J. "Three studies of the
       classroom," In *Classroom observation*. American
       Educational Research Association Monograph Series
       on Curriculum Evaluation. Edited by James J.
       Gallagher, Graham A. Nuthall & Barak Rosenshine.
       pp. 74-108. Chicago: Rand McNally & Company.
       1970.

       Describes three studies of classroom
       interaction which describe the behaviors of
       teachers and the content of instruction and
       differences by subject matter. For Gallagher,
       Nuthall & Rosenshine reference see citation No.
       1675.

1232. Galloway, Elizabeth Anne. A descriptive comparison
       of teacher questions. Ph.D. dissertation.
       Claremont Graduate School. 1979.

       Describes similar patterns of teacher
       questioning behavior in primary classrooms for
       regular students, aurally impaired students and
       visually impaired students, and reports
       similarities in secondary classrooms.

1233. Garrison, Ronald Joseph. Comparison of verbal
       behaviors of teachers and pupils in lessons
       designed to achieve creative response. 1971. *ERIC
       ED 088 669.*

       Describes differences in student and teacher
       verbal behavior during different lessons.

1234. Gay, Geneva. Differential dyadic interactions of
       black and white teachers with black and white
       pupils in recently desegregated social studies
       classrooms. A function of teacher and pupil
       ethnicity. Final Report. 1974. *ERIC ED 091 489.*

       Describes differences in behavior of black and
       white teachers toward black and white students,
       with less interaction with black students.

1235.   Gold, Louis Lance. Verbal interaction patterns in
        the classrooms of selected science teachers:
        Biology. Ph.D. dissertation. Ohio State
        University. 1966. *ERIC ED* 031 400.

        Describes differences in patterns of behavior
        but not individual behaviors of more and less
        effective science teachers.

1236.   Good, Ronald Glenn. An analysis of the
        self-perceptions and other selected
        characteristics of effective and ineffective
        teachers: A study based on the educational
        philosophy of the fifth-year program in teacher
        education at the University of North Carolina.
        Ph.D. dissertation. University of North Carolina
        at Chapel Hill. 1968.

        Describes the behavior and characteristics of
        teachers identified as effective by teacher
        education teams, as compared with those identified
        as ineffective.

1237.   Good, Thomas L. "Which pupils do teachers call on?"
        Elementary School Journal 70 (1970): 190-198.

        Describes teachers as giving brighter students
        more chances to answer than the slower students.

1238.   Good, Thomas L. & Brophy, Jere E. "Do boys and
        girls receive equal opportunity in first grade
        reading instruction?" *Reading Teacher 25* (1971):
        247-252. Report No. 24, Austin, Texas: Research
        and Development Center for Teacher Education.
        University of Texas at Austin. 1969.

        Reports that differences in the behaviors of
        teachers toward boys results from more disruptive
        behaviors by boys, but that higher student
        achievement is related to preferential teacher
        behavior in some instances.

1239.   Good, Thomas L. & Brophy, Jere E. "Questioned
        equality for grade one boys and girls," *Reading
        Teacher 25* (1971): 247-252.

        Describes no observed differences in behavior
        of teachers toward boys and girls in reading
        instruction.

1240.   Good, Thomas L, Cooper, H.M. & Blakey,
        S. "Classroom interaction as a function of teacher
        expectations, student sex, and time of year,"
        Journal of Educational Psychology 72 (1980):
        378-385.

Describes variations in teacher interactions by
time of year and sex of students and reports
teacher focus on socialization of students at the
start of the year.

1241. Good, Thomas L, Ebmeier, H. & Beckerman,
T. "Teaching mathematics in high and low SES
classrooms: An empirical comparison," *Journal of
Teacher education 29*, No. 5 (1978): 85-90.

Describes differences in teacher behavior by
student socioeconomic level, with more supervision
of seatwork and student social interaction with
low SES students and more praise and relaxed
classroom climate in higher SES classes.

1242. Good, Thomas L. & Grouws, Douglas A. "Teacher
rapport: Some stability data," *Journal of
Educational Psychology 67* (1975): 179-182.

Describes stability over a year in the ratings
of teacher affective behavior with students.

1243. Gufford, Joseph Lafayette, Jr. A comparison of
verbal environments: Verbal behaviors displayed in
mathematics and social studies lessons in
self-contained fifth grade classrooms. Ed.D.
dissertation. University of Florida. 1975.

Describes no differences in the verbal behavior
of teachers in lessons in two different subjects.

1244. Guszak, Frank J. "Teacher questioning and reading,"
Reading Teacher 21 (1967): 227-234.

Describes differences in teacher questioning
behavior, with greater emphasis on inference
questions in upper elementary grades, patterns of
teacher questions and pupil responses.

1245. Harlan, Jean Durgin & Leyser, Yona. "Head Start
teachers' use of verbal encouragement,"
Exceptional Children 46 (1980): 290-292.

Describes differences in the verbal
encouragement of teachers to handicapped and
nonhandicapped students and within categories of
student handicap but not differences in
criticism.

1246. Hartnett, Barbara M. & Rumery, Robert E. Mark chain
analysis of classroom interaction data. 1973. *ERIC
ED* 083 133.

Describes differences in the chains or
sequences of teacher behavior by teacher
training.

1247. Heines, Barbara A. & Hawthorne, Richard
       D. Sibling-related teacher expectancies and their
       possible influence on classroom behaviors and
       achievement levels in seventh grade English
       classes. 1978. *ERIC ED* 151 324.

       Describes differences in teacher use of praise
       with high and low expectancy students and by the
       mean achievement level of the group of students.

1248. Heller, Marc Stephen. Teacher approval and
       disapproval by ability grouping. 1973. *ERIC ED* 108
       902.

       Describes differences in teacher rate of
       approval by ability level of class, with more
       disapproval with lower ability classes.

1249. Heller, Marc S. & White, Mary Alice. "Rates of
       teacher verbal approval and disapproval to higher
       and lower ability classes," *Journal of Educational
       Psychology 67* (1975): 796-800.

       Describes differences in teacher behavior by
       ability level of class, with more disapproval and
       more management behavior with lower ability
       classes.

1250. Helliesen, Mary Tillotson. A study of the
       relationship between the importance of certain
       feedback sources and classroom teacher
       performance. Ed.D. dissertation. College of
       William and Mary in Virginia. 1978.

       Describes differences between effective and
       less effective teachers, based on principals'
       ratings, in types of feedback to students about
       classroom behavior.

1251. Henderson, Judith E. & Ward, Ted W. Teaching in the
       inner city: Identification of educational
       practices of competent elementary teachers of
       culturally disadvantaged youths. 1966. *ERIC ED* 050
       006.

       Describes the behaviors of teachers in inner
       city and suburban classes and two models of the
       appropriateness of that behavior.

1252. Herman, Wayne L., Jr. "An analysis of the
       activities and verbal behavior in selected
       fifth-grade social studies classes," *Journal of
       Educational Research 60* (1967): 339-345.

Describes more teacher democratic and
student-centered behavior with higher achieving
groups, but little teacher provision for
individual student differences and for the social
and physical needs of students in grade five
social studies classes.

1253. Hopkins, Layton Janet Kay. The relationships
between student achievement and the
characteristics of perceived leadership behavior
and teacher morale in minority, low
socio-economic, and urban schools. Ed.D.
dissertation. University of Houston. 1980.

Describes less teacher absenteeism in the more
successful schools.

1254. Horak, Willis J. An analysis and comparison of
elementary pre-service and in-service teacher's
beliefs about science teachers' classroom
behaviors. 1980. *ERIC ED* 184 889.

Describes specific types of science teachers
and science teachers at the junior and senior high
school levels, among samples of elementary
teachers and student teachers.

1255. Hoyle, Jonathan Vernon. An exploratory study of
differences in teacher and principal perceptions
of teacher roles, school goals and actual
classroom practices. Ed.D. dissertation.
University of North Carolina at Chapel Hill.
1971.

Describes differences in the behaviors of
teachers with and without experience in the school
but not differences between teachers of grades two
and five and no differences in perceptions of
teacher role.

1256. Huffine, Susan, Silvern, Steven B. & Brooks,
Douglas M. "Teacher responses to contextually
specific sex type behaviors in kindergarten
children," *Educational Research Quarterly 4*, No. 2
(1979): 29-35.

Describes different teacher responses to
disruptive behavior of boys and girls with greater
teacher discipline for verbally disruptive
behavior of boys and aggressive behavior of
girls.

1257. Humphrey, Frank Maurice. "Shh!": A sociolinguistic
study of teachers' turn-taking sanctions in
primary school lessons. Ph.D. dissertation.
Georgetown University. 1979.

Describes differences in the styles of four
teachers in sanctions relative to teaching
turn-taking in kindergarten and third grade.

1258.   Jackson, Gregg & Cosca, Cecilia. "The inequality of
educational opportunity in the southwest: An
observational study of ethnically mixed
classrooms." *American Educational Research Journal*
11 (1974) 219-229.

Describes differences in behavior of teachers
toward Anglo and Mexican American students, with
more praise, acceptance of student ideas,
questioning, and positive feedback toward Anglo
students.

1259.   Jeter, Jan Thomason. Elementary social studies
teachers' differential classroom interaction with
children as a function of differential
expectations of pupil achievement. Ph.D.
dissertation. University of Texas at Austin.
1972.

Describes differences in teacher behavior with
students for whom they have high and low
expectations, such as more sustaining feedback
after wrong answers and less criticism for high
expectation students.

1260.   Johnson, David L. Teacher-pupil interaction in
bilingual elementary school classrooms. 1974. *ERIC*
ED 089 900.

Describes differences in teacher behaviors with
different students.

1261.   Johnson, Rudolph. Teacher collaboration, principal
influence, and decision making in elementary
schools. Technical Report No. 48. Stanford,
California: Stanford Center for Research and
Development in Teaching. Stanford University.
1976. *ERIC ED* 126 083.

Describes greater teacher involvement in school
management when teachers are involved in team
teaching.

1262.   Kaplan, Charles H. & White, Mary Alice. "Children's
direction-following behavior in grades K-5,"
Journal of Educational Research 74 (1980): 43-48.

Describes similarities in teacher directions
from kindergarten through grade five, involving
one behavior and one qualifying statement setting
conditions on the behavior, and correct student
responses to directions.

1263. Kean, John M. A comparison of the classroom
       language of second- and fifth-grade teachers.
       1967. *ERIC ED* 018 777.

       Describes no differences between teachers in
       grades two and five in the number of words used,
       diversity of vocabulary, use of subordinant
       clauses and other normal adult speech patterns.

1264. Kelly, Inga K. The effects of differentiated
       instruction in visuo-motor skills on developmental
       growth and reading readiness at kindergarten
       level. Final Report. 1971. *ERIC ED* 053 821.

       Describes teacher use of language, with 40% of
       teacher vocabulary not within the expected
       vocabulary of students, with differences in the
       vocabulary used by teacher and student race and
       student socioeconomic level

1265. Kendall, Arthur J. & Solomon, Daniel. Classroom
       dimensions and classroom types. 1975. *ERIC ED* 114
       337.

       Describes behaviors of teachers in three types
       of classrooms, open, traditional, and combined.

1266. Kennedy, Emily R. Kindergarten teachers' individual
       integrative and dominative contact patterns with
       children and their relation to teacher assessments
       of children. 1976. *ERIC ED* 124 291.

       Describes more teacher integrative contacts
       with those children whom teachers assess as more
       likely to succeed in school.

1267. Kester, Scott W. & Letchworth, George A.
       "Communication of teacher expectations and their
       effects on achievement and attitudes of secondary
       school students," *Journal of Educational Research*
       66 (1972): 51-55.

       Describes teachers spending more time with
       students whom the teachers think are more able
       students.

1268. Khleif, Bud B. "Role distance of classroom teachers
       of slow learners," *Journal of Research and
       Development in Education* 9 (1976): 69-73.

       Describes differences in the behaviors of
       teachers with classes of slow, average and fast
       learners, with more sarcasm, shaming, tight
       control and antagonistic behavior with classes of
       slow learners.

1269. Klitzkie, Lourdes Palomo. Multiethnic teacher-pupil
       classroom interaction. Ph.D. dissertation. Utah
       State University. 1980.

       Describes no differences in the frequencies of
       positive, neutral and negative verbal behavior of
       teachers of three ethnic backgrounds to students
       of the same ethnic backgrounds in Guam.

1270. Kondo, Allan Kiichi. A study of the questioning
       behavior of teachers in the Science Curriculum
       Improvement Study teaching the unit on material
       objects. Ed.D. dissertation. Columbia University.
       1968.

       Describes more differences between teachers
       than between different lessons by the same teacher
       in the frequency and complexity of types of
       teacher questions

1271. Kranz, Patricia L. & others. The relationships
       between teacher perception of pupils and teacher
       behavior toward those pupils. ERIC ED 038 346 By
       first author only, Ph.D. dissertation. Syracuse
       University. 1970.

       Describes more managerial behaviors directed
       toward students whom teachers perceive to have low
       ability and more substantive interactions with
       students whom teachers perceive to have high
       ability.

1272. Krenkel, Noel. Teacher attitude and interaction
       with gifted culturally different children. Ed.D.
       dissertation. University of Southern California.
       1980.

       Describes slight but not statistically
       different behaviors of teachers with culturally
       different students.

1273. Kysilka, Marcella Louise. The verbal teaching
       behaviors of mathematics and social studies
       teachers in eighth and eleventh grades. Ph.D.
       dissertation. University of Texas at Austin.
       1969.

       Describes differences in teacher behavior by
       grade and subject taught.

1274. Ledesma, Consuelo Pablo. The use of Interaction
       Analysis in assessing the verbal behavior of
       Filipino elementary teachers and pupils. Ed.D.
       dissertation. Boston University School of
       Education. 1973.

Describes differences in teacher behavior by the subject and language of instruction, with more student talk in classrooms of teachers trained in Interaction Analysis.

1275. Lee, Patrick C. "Male and female teachers in elementary schools: An ecological analysis," *Teachers College Record 75* (1973): 24-29.

Describes differences in teacher behaviors by teacher sex, with more differences at the elementary than the secondary level, and some teacher responses to students related to sex roles.

1276. Leinhardt, Gaea, Seewald, Andrea M. & Engel, Mary. "Learning what's taught: Sex differences in instruction," *Journal of Educational Psychology 71* (1979): 432-439.

Describes greater teacher contact with girls during reading instruction and boys during math instruction.

1277. Lenz, Joan B. & Gallimore, Ronald. "A behavioral comparison of two 'good' teachers," In *Focus on classroom behaviors: Readings and research.* Edited by W. Scott McDonald. & others. pp. 36-44. Springfield, Illinois: Charles C. Thomas, Publisher. 1973.

Describes the different behaviors of two teachers nominated as good, with differences in interactions with students, such as the cognitive level of quesions. For McDonald et al. reference see citation No. 2821.

1278. Lesniak, Robert J., Lohman, Ernest E. & Churukian, George A. "Verbal behavior differences between inner-city and suburban elementary teachers: A pilot study," *Urban Education 7* (1972): 41-48.

Describes differences in the verbal behaviors of teachers in inner-city and suburban classes, with less student talk in inner-city classes.

1279. Ligon, Mary Jean Faris. A study of the questioning behavior of classroom teachers during reading instruction to good and poor readers. Ph.D. dissertation. Georgia State University. 1980.

Describes differences in teacher questioning behavior with good and poor readers and between primary and intermediate elementary students.

1280.   London, Forestene L. Black and white observers'
        perceptions of teacher verbal and nonverbal
        behaviors. 1976. *ERIC ED* 120 162.

            Reports that black and white observers record
        the same verbal but different nonverbal teacher
        behavior, when observing black and white
        teachers.

1281.   Lujan, James LeeRoy. Teacher warmth and student
        effort for high and low status students. Ph.D.
        dissertation. Stanford University. 1980.

            Describes greater teacher warmth, related to
        academic and nonacademic interactions, to low
        status students at the elementary levels, with
        greater teacher warmth perceived by low status
        secondary school students.

1282.   McGinley, Pat & McGinley, Hugh. "Reading groups as
        psychological groups," *Journal of Experimental
        Education 39* (1970) 36-42.

            Describes differences in the behaviors of
        teachers and students in low and high achieving
        groups.

1283.   McNelis, Joanne Smith. An analysis of the verbal
        influence of the kindergarten teacher in the
        coeducational classroom. Ph.D. dissertation.
        University of Alabama. 1979.

            Describes a greater amount of teacher
        interaction and a greater amount of direction
        verbal influence with male than female students.

1284.   Marshall, Hermine H. & Green, Judith L. Classroom
        verbal behavior: Contextual purpose and
        situational factors. 1976. *ERIC ED* 129 774.

            Describes variations in teacher verbal behavior
        by the context, including subject matter and
        classroom structure.

1285.   Marshall, Hermine H. & others. "Everyone's smart in
        our class": Relationships between classroom
        characteristics and perceived differential teacher
        treatment. 1980. *ERIC ED* 186 404.

            Describes differences in teacher behavior
        toward students by achievement level, with more
        negative feedback, information about rules, and
        orientation to work for low achieving students.

1286. Marshall, Hermine H. & others. "Stability of
       classroom variables as measured by a broad range
       observational system," *Journal of Educational
       Research 70* (1977): 304-311. 1976. *ERIC ED* 127
       348.

       Describes differences in teacher behavior and
       instructional strategy by the subject and
       classroom structure.

1287. Martin, Jeanne & others. "Within-class analyses of
       relationships between student achievement and
       teacher behavior," *American Educational Research
       Journal 17* (1980): 479-490. Austin, Texas: Center
       for Research and Development for Teacher
       Education. Texas University at Austin. 1980. *ERIC
       ED* 190 671.

       Describes different patterns of significant
       relationships between teacher behaviors and
       student achievement when the analyses were
       conducted within instructional groups and for the
       whole class, indicating the importance of the
       reading group as an instructional context.

1288. Martin, Roy. "Student sex and behavior as
       determinants of the type and frequency of
       teacher-student contracts," *Journal of School
       Psychology 10* (1972): 339-347.

       Describes a greater number of teacher-student
       interactions for those boys whom teachers report
       as having behavior problems than for other boys
       and all girls.

1289. Martinello, Marian Letitia. A study of first and
       fourth grade teachers' instructional role
       enactment during verbal interaction with high and
       low achievers. Ed.D. dissertation. Columbia
       University. 1971.

       Describes similarities in teacher verbal
       behavior across grades, with slight differences by
       student achievement level.

1290. Mathews, Jack Gibson. A study of the teaching
       process in the classroom of selected physics
       teachers. 1968. *ERIC ED* 028 079.

       Describes significant similarities and
       differences in the behaviors of non-science
       teachers and teachers using the PSSC (Physical
       Science Study Committee) physics curriculum.

1291.   Matthews, Horace. Attitudes and classroom behaviors
        of Virginia middle school English teachers
        regarding black English and certain other usages.
        Ed.D. dissertation. University of Virginia. 1980.

        Reports that teachers are more critical of
        black English than of other usages but correct all
        usages equally, although urban teachers correct
        black English more than do rural teachers.

1292.   Mayes, Bea. What do reading teachers teach in first
        grade classes?: A study of questions teachers ask.
        1977. *ERIC ED* 158 253.

        Describes differences in the behavior of
        teachers with students when teachers are using
        Distar insructional materials and traditional
        basal readers.

1293.   Meckes, Richard C. A study to ascertain the
        instructional index and questioning strategy of
        mathematics teachers in grade 6, and to determine
        their relationship to professional characteristics
        and situational factors. Ph.D. dissertation.
        Southern Illinois University. 1971.

        Describes teachers with more experience and in
        rural schools as more indirect and as spending
        more time giving information than inner-city and
        inexperienced teachers.

1294.   Meyer, William J. & Lindstrom, David. The
        distribution of teacher approval and disapproval
        of Head Start children. Final Report. 1969. *ERIC
        ED* 042 509.

        Describes no differences in teacher approval
        and disapproval by student sex, race, or index of
        motivation.

1295.   Moore, J. William & Schant, Judith A. "Stability of
        teaching behavior, responsiveness to training and
        teaching effectiveness," *Journal of Educational
        Research* 69 (170): 360-363.

        Describes a relationship between stability of
        teacher behaviors and teacher effectiveness and
        responses to training.

1296.   Morine-Dershimer, Greta. Teacher plan and classroom
        reality: The South Bay Study, Part IV. Research
        Series No. 60. East Lansing, Michigan: Institute
        for Research on Teaching. Michigan State
        University. 1979.

              Describes teacher decisions during instruction
              as related to the extent that the lesson goes in
              accordance with the teacher's plan for the
              lesson.

1297. Moskowitz, Gertrude & Hayman, Jon L., Jr. "Success
       strategies of inner-city teachers: A year-long
       study," *Journal of Educational Research 69* (1976):
       283-289.

              Describes differences in behaviors of "best"
              and first year teachers in setting classroom
              climate in the fall, in reinforcing student
              behavior during the year, in control, discipline
              and motivation.

1298. Mulawka, Edward John. Sex role typing in the
       elementary school classroom as reinforcement of
       sex role stereotypes learned at home. Ph.D.
       dissertation. Wayne State University. 1972.

              Describes no differential teacher responses to
              inappropriate student sex role behaviors.

1299. Myers, Joan Silver. Teacher language and
       expectancies for retarded and nonretarded pupils.
       Ph.D. dissertation. Yeshiva University. 1979.

              Describes teachers differing in their verbal
              behavior toward students in their class, toward
              similar but unknown students and toward students
              from EMR classes, but no differences in student
              achievement by teacher verbal behavior.

1300. Nelson, Hal & others. Southeast alternatives: A
       working paper on comparative school culture
       studies. 1975. *ERIC ED* 139 869.

              Describes differences in teacher and student
              behavior and attitude and the curriculum in four
              types of elementary schools.

1301. Nelson, Lois N. "Teacher leadership: An empirical
       approach to analyzing teacher behavior in the
       classroom," *Journal of Teacher education 17*
       (1966): 417-425. Reprinted in *The nature of
       teaching: A collection of readings.* Edited by Lois
       N. Nelson. pp. 29-38. Waltham, Massachusetts:
       Blaisdell Publishing Co. 1969.

              Describes stable teacher behaviors over
              observations but different patterns of teacher
              behavior related to the goals of two different
              language arts programs. For the Nelson reference
              see citation No. 2997.

1302.   Neujahr, James L. An analysis of teacher
        communications to individual pupils when
        instruction is individualized. 1971. *ERIC ED* 048
        107.

        Reports that the frequency of teacher
        interaction with students varies across students
        but not by the function of the interaction.

1303.   Neujahr, James L. "Analysis of teacher-pupil
        interaction in individualized instruction," *A V
        Communication Review 22* (1974): 69-77. *ERIC ED* 079
        022.

        Describes differences in the behaviors of
        teachers using individualized instruction from the
        reported behaviors of teachers in traditional
        classrooms.

1304.   Newcastle, Helen. A study of teachers' classroom
        questioning and responding techniques. *ERIC ED* 079
        260.

        Reports that teachers in grades two and five
        are almost alike in their techniques for
        responding to students.

1305.   Norwood, Elizabeth R. Effects of open and
        traditional education on curriculum, social
        environment, and behavioral interaction of
        students and teachers in third grade classrooms.
        Ed.D. dissertation. West Virginia University.
        1973.

        Describes differences in teacher-student
        interactions in open and traditional classrooms,
        in student behavior, use of materials, student
        cooperation and teacher interaction with
        students.

1306.   Nowak, Arlene Theresa. The use of time-lapse
        photography to record teacher-pupil contacts,
        teacher supervisory behavior, and teacher travel
        in the classroom. Ed.D. dissertation. Wayne State
        University. 1970.

        Describes different patterns of teacher contact
        labelled extended and alternating, and teachers
        spending large amounts of time supervising and
        little time in interactions with individual
        students.

1307.   Oliveira, Arnulfo Luis. A comparison of the verbal
        teaching behaviors of junior high school Mexican
        American and Anglo American teachers of social

studies and mathematics with classes of
predominantly Spanish-speaking children. Ph.D.
dissertation. University of Texas at Austin.
1970.

Describes differences in the verbal behavior of
teachers and students with Mexican American and
Anglo American teachers and Spanish-speaking
students.

1308. Oppenlander, Lester Christen. The relative
influence of the group of pupils and of the
teacher as determinants of classroom interaction.
Ph.D. dissertation. Indiana University. 1969.

Describes changes in teacher behavior over a
school year, with more indirect teaching with the
low achieving group and more direct teaching with
the high achieving group.

1309. Pankratz, Roger. "Verbal interaction patterns in
the classrooms of selected physics teacher," In
*Interaction Analysis: Theory, research and
application.* Edited by Edmund J. Amidon and John
B. Hough. pp. 189-209. Reading, Massachusetts:
Addison Wesley Publishing Co. 1967.

Describes differences in the observed verbal
behaviors of groups of teachers ranked high and
low by principals and students on relationships
with students, with high teachers using more
praise, skill and cognitive clarification and
acceptance. For the Amidon & Hough reference see
citation No. 1638.

1310. Pankratz, Roger Sam. Verbal interaction patterns in
the classrooms of selected science teachers:
Physics. Ph. D. dissertation. Ohio State
University. 1966.

Describes differences in the behaviors of
teachers, with those ranked high in relationships
with students using more praise, acceptance, less
commands, criticism, rejection.

1311. Pate, Robert T. Inquiry patterns in elementary
teaching. Final Report. 1969. *ERIC ED* 034 738.

Describes each teacher using a unique pattern
of questions, with no general pattern across
teachers.

1312. Payne, James Irvin. Analysis of teacher-student
classroom interaction in Amish and non-Amish
schools, Ed.D. dissertation. Pennsylvania

State University. 1970. *Social Problems 19* (1971): 79-90.

Describes the behavior of Amish teachers as consistent with Amish philosophy, and using more direct teaching than non-Amish teachers.

1313. Peck, Robert F., Olsson, G. & Green, J. The consistency of individual teaching behavior. Austin, Texas: Center for Research and Development for Teacher Education. Texas University at Austin. 1978. *ERIC ED* 156 645.

Describes stability of several aspects of teacher behavior across years, subject matter, observers and students.

1314. Peek, Anita Perkins. Comparison of awareness and interpretation of teacher verbal behavior revealed through self-analysis and Flanders system analysis of teacher behavior. Ph.D. dissertation. East Texas State University. 1970.

Describes differences in teacher self-reported and observed behavior, and differences by teacher sex, grade and years of experience.

1315. Peek, Don Adolphus. A comparison of the verbal behaviors of teachers and pupils in a predominantly Negro high school with the verbal behaviors of teachers and pupils in a predominantly white high school. Ph.D. dissertation. East Texas State University. 1970.

Describes differences in teachers' behaviors, with the teachers of black students using more indirect teaching.

1316. Perez, Gretchen S. The verbal sanctioning behavior of teachers in an open classroom environment: A descriptive time sampling study. Ed.D. dissertation. 1973.

Describes no differences in teacher verbal sanctioning behaviors by grade, teacher experience, but differences by student sex in sanctions for concepts/skills and social/procedural.

1317. Pfeiffer, Isobel L. Teaching in ability grouped English classes: A study of verbal interaction and cognitive goals. Ph.D. dissertation. Kent State University. 1966. *Journal of Exceptional Education 36* (1967): 33-38.

Reports that teachers described different instructional goals by class ability level, with more indirect teaching with their preferred ability level, but teachers reported less teacher talk than actually occurs.

1318. Pollack, Barbara Lee. Effects of behavior modification consultations on teacher behavior. Ph.D. dissertation. Columbia University. 1971.

Describes decreasing proportions of teacher time spent teaching over three observations, with attention to principles of behavior modification resulting in greater attention to appropriate behavior but no increase in teaching time.

1319. Powell, Marjorie. "Time allocations: Teachers help determine curriculum," *Educational Horizons 57* (1979): 175-177.

Describes variations in teacher allocation of time to reading and math instruction across classrooms.

1320. Powell, Marjorie. "Variable teaching behaviors: The importance of considering context in understanding teaching," *Educational Research Quarterly 4* (1979): 36-42.

Describes some teacher behaviors, such as academic feedback, which occur infrequently and other behaviors which vary by self-paced or other-paced instructional settings.

1321. Premazon, Judith Aline. A study examining teacher decisions, as exhibited by teachers' behaviors, and their relationship to teacher concerns. Ed.D. dissertation. University of Houston. 1975.

Describes differences in the concerns and the behaviors of elementary and secondary teachers but no relationship between teacher concerns and behavior.

1322. Prescott, Elizabeth & Jones, Elizabeth. Patterns of teacher behavior in preschool programs. 1969. *ERIC ED 075 092.*

Describes some stability for some teacher behaviors, with teachers using encouragement or restraint with students, but not both, related to the space of the center, the staff and the students.

1323. Quirk, Thomas J. & others. Comparison of teacher
       behavior at different grade levels within Project
       PLAN: A program of individualized instruction.
       1970 *ERIC ED* 039 185.

            Describes primary teachers spending more time
       in individualized instruction than upper
       elementary grade teachers, but no differences in
       the amount of student discussion time.

1324. Rains, Ohren Willis. A study of teacher-pupil and
       pupil-pupil interactional differences between
       inquiry centered science and traditional science
       in elementary schools. Ed.D. dissertation.
       Oklahoma State University. 1970. *ERIC ED* 077 649.

            Describes greater teacher-student and
       student-student interaction in traditional than
       inquiry science methods, and more interaction
       between teachers and male than female students.

1325. Rajendra-Prasad, Teli John. A study of the
       responding behaviors of junior high school
       mathematics teachers in simulated and real
       classroom problem solving situations. Ph.D.
       dissertation. University of Illinois at Urbana:
       Champaign. 1975.

            Describes behavior of teachers toward students
       in problem-solving situations with no differences
       by student ability level.

1326. Ramirez, Judith Valla. Teacher behavior in
       role-playing: A study in Interaction Analysis.
       Research and Development Memorandum No. 43.
       Stanford, California: Stanford Center for Research
       and Development in Teaching. Stanford University.
       1969. *ERIC ED* 028 998.

            Describes behavior of teachers using
       role-playing with grade six students in comparison
       with the behaviors of teachers with students in
       general discussion groups.

1327. Randhawa, Bikkar S. "Instructional quality as a
       function of locale, grade, and subject,"
       Educational Research Quarterly 2, No. 3 (1977):
       29-39. *ERIC ED* 135 771.

            Describes differences in the behavior of
       teachers by grade and subject taught and
       geographic location of the school (urban, rural).

1328. Raney, Joseph F. An observational study of
       classroom control. Final Report. 1968. *ERIC ED* 033
       065.

Describes no differences in ratings for
teachers who differed in their classroom control
behaviors.

1329. Ray, Vivian Derricotte. Modifications of language
input by preschool teachers as a function of young
children's language competencies. Ph.D.
dissertation. Temple University. 1980.

Describes differences in teacher language in
interactions with preschool children at different
levels of language development.

1330. Ribble, James Mark. A description of
teacher-student interaction from a developmental
perspective. Ph.D. dissertation. Washington State
University. 1976. *ERIC ED* 135 033.

Describes different communication patterns
among teachers, based on their analyses of
comments during discussion lessons.

1331. Roberts Linda G. Observation and analysis of
first-graders' oral reading errors and
corrections, and the accompanying teacher response
and teacher-pupil interaction. Ed.D. dissertation.
University of Tennessee. 1973.

Describes different patterns of teacher
behavior in response to student reading errors by
reading group level, with teacher behavior related
to student self-correction.

1332. Robitaille, David F. "Criteria for assessing the
effectiveness of teachers of secondary school
mathematics," *Journal of Research in Mathematics
Education* 6 (1975): 77-87.

Describes differences in the behavior and
knowledge of teachers judged to be effective and
ineffective math teachers.

1333. Robitaille, David Ford. Selected behaviors and
attributes of effective mathematics teachers.
Ph.D. dissertation. Ohio State University. 1969.

Describes differences in the behaviors of
effective and non-effective secondary school math
teachers.

1334. Rohrkemper, Mary M. & Brophy, Jere E. Classroom
Strategy Study: Investigating teacher strategies
with problem students. Research Series No. 50.
East Lansing, Michigan: Institute for Research on
Teaching. Michigan State University. 1979. *ERIC
ED* 175 857.

Describes different teacher behaviors by type
of student problem, with more intense and less
effective teacher responses to disruptive behavior
than to learning problems.

1335.   Rohrkemper, Mary M. & Brophy, Jere E. Influence of
        teacher role definitions on strategies for coping
        with problem students. *ERIC ED* 179 522. Research
        Series No. 51. East Lansing, Michigan: Institute
        for Research on Teaching. Michigan State
        University. 1979.

        Describes teacher responses to student behavior
        in a simulation as more influenced by student
        behavior than by teacher definition of role as
        instruction or socialization and by teacher
        ability.

1336.   Rosemond, Bruce Earle. Teacher behavior and teacher
        expectations as they relate to pupil achievement.
        Ph.D. dissertation. University of Michigan. 1976.

        Describes some differences in teacher behavior
        by expectations but not by pupil sex or
        socioeconomic status.

1337.   Rosenthal, Ted L., Underwood, Billie, & Martin,
        Marion. "Assessing classroom incentive practices,"
        Journal of Educational Psychology 60 (1969):
        370-376.

        Describes behaviors of teachers in normal
        classrooms and with a program for disadvantaged
        students.

1338.   Ross, Grady. An assessment of absenteeism of
        certificated teacher staff in the Robles School
        District of California, 1978-1979 school year.
        Ed.D. dissertation. University of Northern
        Colorado. 1980.

        Describes differences in patterns of teacher
        absences by day of the week, month of the year,
        but not after holidays.

1339.   Rothbart, Myron, Dalfen, Susan & Barrett,
        Robert. "Effects of teacher's expectancy on
        student-teacher interaction," *Journal of
        Educational Psychology* 62 (1971): 49-54.

        Describes greater teacher attentiveness to high
        expectancy students in a simulation of teacher
        interviews with students.

1340.   Rupley, William H. Relationship between selected
        areas of teacher emphases and student achievement
        in reading. Ph.D. dissertation. University of
        Illinois at Urbana-Champaign. 1975. *ERIC ED* 116
        169.

        Describes differences in areas of reading
        instruction emphasized in grades three and six but
        no differences between higher and lower achieving
        classes.

1341.   Rutherford, W.L. Team teaching—How do teachers use
        it? Austin, Texas: Center for Research and
        Development for Teacher Education. Texas
        University at Austin. 1975.

        Describes behaviors of teachers at various
        levels of use of team teaching.

1342.   Sandefur, J.T. & others. Teaching experience as a
        modifier of teaching behavior. Final Report. *ERIC*
        ED 035 598.

        Describes differences in behaviors of first
        year teachers, experienced teachers and student
        teachers.

1343.   Sanford, J. Beginning the school year at a low SES
        junior high: Three case studies. Austin, Texas:
        Center for Research and Development for Teacher
        Education. Texas University at Austin. 1980.

        Describes the initial management behavior of
        three teachers who differ in effectiveness in
        terms of student achievement.

1344.   Schaffer, Diane Maximoff. Variability in observed
        teacher behavior: An investigation of the
        generalizability of selected low-inference
        measures. Ph.D. dissertation. Stanford University.
        1977.

        Describes differences in behaviors of teachers
        across observations, but same rank ordering of
        teachers by behaviors, with differences not
        related to subject being taught.

1345.   Schalock, H. Del. & Beaird, James H. Increasing
        prediction of teachers' classroom behavior through
        use of motion picture tests. Final Report. 1968.
        ERIC ED 021 809.

        Reports a study using a film test of teaching
        situations to predict behaviors of teachers, with
        experienced and first year teachers.

1346.   Scott, Myrtle. Some parameters of teacher
        effectiveness as assessed by an ecological
        approach. 1969. *ERIC ED* 032 928.

        Describes behaviors of teachers rated as
        effective and ineffective, with effective teachers
        showing more smooth continuity, more directly
        involved and in control of situation, more
        spontaneous.

1347.   Sego Lily Elementary School. A study of teacher
        behavior with and without the use of programmed
        books. author. Lehi, Utah: *ERIC ED* 024 269.

        Describes differences in behaviors of teachers
        with and without Sullivan programmed readers, with
        teachers with programmed texts spending more time
        with individual students and having more knowledge
        about student abilities.

1348.   Serbin, Lisa & others. "A comparison of teacher
        response to the preacademic and problem behavior
        of boys and girls," *Child Development 44* (1973):
        796–804.

        Describes teachers responding more frequently
        to boys than to girls.

1349.   Shapiro, Edythe R. Influence of addressee and
        activity on kindergarten teachers' directives.
        1979. *ERIC ED* 182 648.

        Describes decreases in teacher directives in
        kindergarten classes from September to December,
        but consistent clarity of directives.

1350.   Sheriff, Friyal. Comparison of classroom
        interactions in three different preschools. Ph.D.
        dissertation. University of Michigan. 1972.

        Describes differences in the behaviors of
        teachers and students and their interactions in
        three types of preschool programs.

1351.   Sherman, Deaconess Ann. The relationship of teacher
        behavior and child behavior of four and five year
        old black disadvantaged children during Distar and
        during non-Distar sessions. Ed.D. dissertation.
        University of Virginia. 1971.

        Describes differences in the behaviors of
        teachers and students with and without the Distar
        reading materials.

1352.   Shirley, Don. Verbal interaction patterns of
        elementary school teachers and students during

the story review phase of the guided reading
activity. Final Report. 1970. *ERIC ED* 040 033.

Describes no differences in the behaviors of
first year and experienced teachers during the
story review portion of a guided reading lesson.

1353.   Shutes, Robert Eugene. Verbal behaviors and
instructional effectiveness. Ph.D. dissertation.
Stanford University. 1969.

Describes differences in behaviors of teachers
by instructional content for teachers with high
and low student achievement.

1354.   Sikes, Joseph Neville. Differential behavior of
male and female teachers with male and female
students. Ph.D. dissertation. University of Texas
at Austin. 1971.

Describes differences in male and female
teacher behavior toward male and female students,
with more interactions with male students.

1355.   Sloan, Fred A. & Pate, Robert
Thomas. "Teacher-pupil interaction in two
approaches to mathematics," *Elementary School
Journal* 67 (1967) : 161-167.

Describes the behaviors of teachers using the
School Mathematics Study Group curriculum,
differing from other math teachers in the types of
questions asked of students.

1356.   Slobodian, June Jenkinson. An analysis of certain
dimensions of teacher behavior during reading
instruction in the first grade. Ph.D.
dissertation. Kent State University. 1966.

Describes no differences in the behaviors of
teachers toward boys and girls but differences in
student perceptions of teacher behavior toward
boys and girls.

1357.   Smith, Douglas K. "Teacher styles of classroom
management," *Journal of Educational Research 71*
(1978): 277-282.

Describes differences in teacher behaviors
toward students by student sex, with more
punishment for males.

1358.   Smith, George Wilson. The development of an
instrument to record the interaction between
teacher and pupil in the classroom and

the correlation of certain factors with
achievement. Ed.D. dissertation. University of
Maryland. 1971.

Describes differences in the behavior of
teachers when working with students at different
achievement levels, and differences in student
involvement in tasks by patterns of classroom
organization.

1359.   Snider, Ray Merrill. A project to study the nature
of physics teaching using the Flanders method of
Interaction Analysis. Ph.D. dissertation. Cornell
University. 1966.

Describes teacher behaviors varying among
activities, with little use of inquiry methods and
no single measure of teacher behavior related to
student achievement.

1360.   Snyder, William Ray. The question-asking behavior
of gifted junior high school science students and
their teachers. Ph.D. dissertation. University of
Illinois. 1966.

Describes similarities and differences in
behaviors across teachers and for the same teacher
across different content units, and greater
differences across teachers than for a single
teacher.

1361.   Soar, Robert S. & others. Change in classroom
behavior from fall to winter for high and low
control teachers. 1973. *ERIC ED* 083 152.

Describes changes in teacher control and other
behaviors during the course of the school year.

1362.   Sprague, Nancy Frietag. Inquiry dialogue in the
classroom. 1971. *ERIC ED* 049 143.

Describes more questions and student
interaction in inquiry than in traditional
secondary social studies classes, and describes
teacher influence through teacher questions.

1363.   Stallings, Jane. What happens in the Follow Through
program? Implications for child growth and
development. 1972. *ERIC ED* 071 755.

Describes differences in the behavior of
teachers and students in Follow Through and
non-Follow Through classrooms.

1364.   Stowe, Robert S., Jr. A comparison of teacher
behavior in disadvantaged and advantaged

elementary schools. Ph.D. dissertation. University of Connecticut. 1971.

Describes some differences in the behavior of teachers with advantaged and disadvantaged students and a low correlation between teacher behaviors and teacher attitudes.

1365. Stuck, G. & Wyne, M. "Study of verbal behavior in special and regular elementary school classrooms," *American Journal of Mental Deficiency 75* (1971): 463-469.

Describes behaviors of regular and special class teachers, and reports no differences in behaviors.

1366. Taylor, Denelene. Second grade reading instruction: The teacher-child dyadic interactions of boys and girls of varying abilities. Ma. Thesis. Rutgers University the State University of New Jersey. 1977. *ERIC ED* 142 952.

Describes greater teacher sensitivity to child needs and more praise for student success with low achieving than higher achieving children in reading groups.

1367. Thomas, Jean L. A comparison of the verbal behavior patterns of black and white teachers. Ed.D. dissertation. Temple University. 1973.

Describes no differences in the behavior of black and white teachers with black and integrated classes and by attitudes of teachers toward teaching.

1368. Tinsley, Drew C. & others. Cognitive objectives revealed by classroom questions in "Process-oriented" and "Content-oriented" secondary social studies programs. 1970. *ERIC ED* 040 895.

Describes no differences between classes in the number of questions asked, with teachers asking three times as many questions as students and most questions at a low cognitive level.

1369. Townsend, Darryl Raymond. A comparison of the classroom interaction patterns of bilingual early childhood teachers. Ph.D. dissertation. University of Texas at Austin. 1974.

Describes different patterns of teacher behavior when teaching in English and Spanish, with more indirect teaching in Spanish and more student responses during instruction in Spanish.

1370.   Tyo, Alexina M. A comparison of the verbal
        behaviors of teachers in interaction with students
        they perceived as migrant and non-migrant. Ph.D.
        dissertation. Syracuse University. 1972. ERIC ED
        075 160.

        Describes fewer teacher positive and neutral
        interactions and an equal number of negative
        interactions with migrant than non-migrant
        students.

1371.   Urbach, Floyd D. A study of recurring patterns of
        teaching. Ph.D. dissertation. University of
        Nebraska. 1966. ERIC ED 028 153.

        Describes consistency in verbal instructional
        techniques for each of three teachers but not
        consistent patterns across the three teachers.

1372.   U.S. Commission on Civil Rights. "Teachers and
        students: Differences in teacher interaction with
        Mexican American and Anglo students, Report V:
        Mexican American Education Study, A report of the
        U.S. Commission on Civil Rights." Journal of
        Comparative Cultures 1 (1973): 195-258. ERIC ED
        073 881.

        Describes differences in teacher verbal
        interaction with Mexican American and Anglo
        students in classrooms in the southwest.

1373.   Wahab, Zaher. Teacher-pupil transactions in
        bi-racial classrooms: Implications for
        instruction. 1973. ERIC ED 092 294.

        Describes differences in teacher behavior by
        student ethnicity and sex.

1374.   Walberg, Herbert J. & Thomas, Susan Christie. "Open
        education: An operational definition and
        validation in Great Britain and United States,"
        American Educational Research Journal 9 (1972):
        197-207. Also in Educational Psychology: A
        Developmental Approach. Edited by N. Sprinthall.
        Reading, Massachusetts: Addison-Wesley Publishing
        Company. 1974. Foundations of Education. Edited by
        E.F. Thibadean. New York: Kendall Hull. 1973.
        Environments for Learning. Edited by Kevin
        Marjoribanks. London: National Foundation for
        Educational Research. 1974.

        Describes differences in teacher reports of
        behavior and observer ratings of classrooms
        between open and traditional classrooms. For
        Sprinthall reference see citation No. 3027.

1375. Wallen, Susan Stimac. Teacher control behaviors as a function of teacher experience and differential behavioral descriptions of students. Ph.D. dissertation. University of Minnesota. 1975.

Describes differences in management behavior of experienced teachers and student teachers but no differences in teacher behavior toward students for whom the teachers had and did not have various types of information.

1376. West, Betsy. "Patterns of sex and race of teachers and students in disciplinary referrals, *Action in Teacher Education 1* (1978): 67-75.

Describes teacher referral of students for behavior problems related to teacher and student sex and race.

1377. Whittemore, Judith Duncan. An examination of the relationship between the cognitive level of teacher questions and selected student placement and teacher variables. Ed.D. dissertation. University of Virginia. 1979.

Describes the cognitive level of questions which teachers ask students during a reading lesson as related to the student grade level, the level of the reading group, and teacher experience, training and race.

1378. Williams, Edward Wesley. Teacher and student behaviors in multiethnic high school classrooms: An analysis using socioeconomic stratification of students. Ph.D. dissertation. University of Texas at Austin. 1975.

Describes differences in teacher behavior by socioeconomic level of students within ethnic groups.

1379. Willis, Bill J. The influence of teacher expectations on teacher's classroom interaction with selected children, Ph.D. dissertation. George Peabody College for Teachers. 1969.

Describes different teacher responses to the behavior of students for whom teachers have high and low expectations.

1380. Workman, Susan Harms. Teacher verbal strategies and the social interaction of blind children in an integrated preschool program. Ed.D. dissertation. Syracuse University. 1980.

Describes verbal behaviors of teachers toward
blind children (direct prompts) and sighted
children (indirect prompts) which result in
greater interaction between blind and sighted
children.

1381. Wright, Donald Leroy. Teaching patterns: A study
analyzing classroom teaching processes of
secondary and elementary school teachers. Ed.D.
dissertation. University of Kansas. 1971.

Describes more pupil talk and teacher praise in
secondary than in elementary classrooms but no
differences in other categories of interactions.

1382. Wuhl, Gloria Bleier. Sex differences in teachers'
gender expectations about reading and their
relationship to teacher-student interaction and
first grade reading achievement. Ph.D.
dissertation. University of Pennsylvania. 1976.

Describes differences in teacher behavior
toward boys and girls related to teacher
expectations for reading achievement by student
sex, and expectations related to actual
achievement.

1383. Zahorik, John A. "Individual instruction and group
instruction: A case study," *Journal of Educational
Research 62* (1969):

Describes differences in teacher behavior by
group and individual instruction, with more
teacher talk and lower cognitive levels of
questions in individualized instruction.

C. PLANNING

1384. Barr, R. & Duffy, G. Teachers' conceptions of
       reading: The evolution of a research study.
       Research Series No. 17. East Lansing, Michigan:
       Institute for Research on Teaching. Michigan State
       University. 1978.

       Describes teacher conceptions of reading, that
       teachers follow administrative directions but
       manage to adjust their teaching to match their own
       beliefs.

1385. Bawden, Robert, Buike, S. & Duffy G. Teacher
       conceptions of reading and their influence on
       instruction. Research Series No. 47. East Lansing,
       Michigan: Institute for Research on Teaching.
       Michigan State University. 1979. *ERIC ED* 174 952.

       Reports that teachers have more than one
       conception of reading instruction, they differ in
       complexity and vary in stability of conceptions,
       and the variations are related to the grade level
       and student ability level the teachers are
       teaching.

1386. Belli, Gabriella, Blom, G. & Reiser, A. Teachers'
       concerns and conceptions of reading and the
       teaching of reading: A literature review.
       Occasional Paper No. 1. East Lansing, Michigan:
       Institute for Research on Teaching. Michigan State
       University. 1977. *ERIC ED* 161 018.

       Reviews teacher attitudes toward, knowledge of
       and approaches to the teaching of reading.

1387. Blase, Joseph John. On the meaning of being a
       teacher: A study of the teachers' perspective.
       Ph.D. dissertation. Syracuse University. 1980.

       Describes teacher views of what it means to be
       teacher and problems in instructional management
       and social relations areas.

1388. Borko, Hilda. Factors contributing to teachers'
       preinstructional decisions about classroom

management and long-term objectives. Ph.D.
dissertation. University of California, Los
Angeles. 1978.

Describes teacher perceptions of student
attitude and teacher plans for student instruction
and cues teachers use in a simulated situation to
make decisions about instruction.

1389.   Borko, Hilda, Cone, Richard, Russo, Nancy Atwood &
Shavelson, Richard J. "Teachers' decision making,"
In *Research on teaching: Concepts, findings and
implications*. Edited by Penelope L. Peterson &
Herbert J. Walberg. Berkeley, California:
McCutchan Publishing Corporation. 1979.

Describes four experimental studies of ways
teachers plan for instruction and classroom
organization. For Peterson & Walberg reference
see citation No. 3001.

1390.   Bower, Eli M. Teachers talk about their feelings,
1973. *ERIC ED* 083 155.

Describes teacher thoughts and feelings about
teaching and the conditions of teaching.

1391.   Brophy, Jere E. Teachers' cognitive activities and
overt behaviors. Occasional Paper No. 39. East
Lansing, Michigan: Institute for Research on
Teaching. Michigan State University. 1980.

Reviews research on teacher thinking and
planning and discusses teacher focus on activities
and curriculum.

1392.   Bruckner, Marion Wood. Educational objectives in
the affective domain: The aims and methods of
twenty-eight elementary school teachers. Ph.D.
dissertation. University of Colorado at Boulder.
1978.

Describes erratic teacher plans and objectives
for affective education, dependent on the
interests and good intentions of the teacher.

1393.   Buchmann, Margaret. Practitioners' concepts: An
inquiry into the wisdom of practice. East Lansing,
Michigan: Institute for Research on Teaching.
Michigan State University. 1980. *ERIC ED* 187 667.

Describes the role of teacher "folk wisdom" in
defining the choices available to teachers and in
influencing teachers' choices.

1394. Buike, Sandra. A study of teacher decision making in reading classrooms. Ph.D. dissertation. Michigan State University. 1980.

Reports that a year's observations indicate teacher decisions are concerned with effective classroom management rather than instruction and are dependent on the context in which decisions occur.

1395. Buike, Sandra. Teacher decision making in reading instruction. Research Series No. 79. East Lansing, Michigan: Institute for Research on Teaching. Michigan State University. 1980.

Reports that teacher decisions are preactive, interactive or proactive, but primarily concerned with materials and not related instructional issues.

1396. Buike, Sandra & Duffy, Gerald G. Do teacher conceptions of reading influence instructional practice? East Lansing, Michigan: Institute for Research on Teaching. Michigan State University. 1979. *ERIC ED* 170 729.

Reports that teacher conceptions of reading are not simply related to instruction but are related to other conceptions, but teachers do not work from a theory of reading.

1397. Burdman, Jacqueline B. Teacher competencies which enhance self-concept in children with learning problems and learning disabilities. Ed.D. dissertation. State University of New York at Buffalo. 1978.

Describes teacher perceptions of important teaching competencies.

1398. Carlson, Dennis Lynn. Constructing classroom order: A phenomenological analysis of commonsense knowledge in the classroom. Ph.D. dissertation. University of Wisconsin-Madison. 1979.

Describes the meanings created for events and activities, roles and responsibilities within Individually Guided Education classrooms.

1399. Chappell, Luthene Bruinsma. A descriptive study of how three teachers developed and modified their reading conceptions over time. Ph.D. dissertation. Michigan State University. 1980.

Describes variations in teacher conceptions of
reading, with two of three teachers having
multiple conceptions, and factors which teachers
identify as influenced their conceptions.

1400.   Clark, Christopher M. Choice of a model for
research on teacher thinking. Research Series No.
20. East Lansing, Michigan: Institute for Research
on Teaching. Michigan State University. 1978. *ERIC
ED* 166 135.

Describes two models of teacher thinking,
decision making and information processing.

1401.   Clark, Christopher M. & Elmore, Janis M. Teacher
planning in the first weeks of school. Research
Series No. 56. East Lansing, Michigan: Institute
for Research on Teaching. Michigan State
University. 1979. *ERIC ED* 186 407.

Describes three categories of teacher planning
during the first weeks of school, for the physical
environment, placement of students and classroom
structures, and establishing routines and
activities.

1402.   Clark, C.M. & Joyce, B.R. "Teacher decision making
and teacher effectiveness," In *Flexibility in
teaching*. Edited by Bruce Joyce. New York: Longman
Green. 1979.

Describes research on teacher decision making
before and during instruction in relation to
student learning.

1403.   Clark, Christopher M. & Yinger, Richard
J. "Research on teacher planning: A progress
report," *Journal of Curriculum Studies 11* (1979):
175–177.

Describes six teachers' planning for units in
writing instruction, with teachers thinking about
the resources which are readily available and
about activities, not objectives.

1404.   Clark, Christopher M. & Yinger, Richard
J. "Research on teacher thinking," *Curriculum
Inquiry 7* (1977): 279–304. Also in *Research on
teaching: Concepts, findings and implications*.
Edited by Penelope L. Peterson and Herbert J.
Walberg. Berkeley, California: McCutchan
Publishing Corporation. 1979.

Reviews both studies and the methods of
research used to study teacher thinking. For
Peterson & Walberg reference see citation No.
3001.

1405. Clark, C.M. & Yinger, Richard J. The hidden world of teaching: Implications of research on teacher planning. Research Series No. 77. East Lansing, Michigan: Institute for Research on Teaching. Michigan State University. 1980.

Reviews research on teacher planning, the importance of planning to teachers, differences between actual planning and theories of planning, use of routines once developed.

1406. Clark, Christopher M. & Yinger, Robert J. Three studies of teacher planning. Research Series No. 55. East Lansing, Michigan: Institute for Research on Teaching. Michigan State University. 1979. *ERIC ED* 175 855.

Reports a survey of teacher planning, teacher judgements about activities and case studies of teacher planning, implementation and evaluation of activities.

1407. Conrad, Robert James. A study of the relationship between lesson planning and teacher behavior in the secondary classroom. Ed.D. dissertation. University of Utah. 1969.

Describes no difference in the quantity and quality of teacher planning and flexibility, but the more teacher planning the less teacher talk during instruction.

1408. Dienes, Barbara & Connelly, F. Michael. A case study of teacher choice and deliberation. Analysis of deliberate sessions. 1973. *ERIC ED* 081 771.

Describes teacher thinking about curriculum, based on teacher discussions.

1409. Doyle, Walter. How do teacher effects occur? Research Report No. 4101. Austin, Texas: Research and Development Center for Teacher Education. Texas University at Austin. 1979. *ERIC ED* 178 543.

Describes types of academic tasks and student reactions, ways that students manage risks and ambiguity in the classroom and the influence of student behaviors on teacher planning.

1410. Doyle, Walter & Ponder, Gerald A. "The practicality ethic in teacher decision-making," *Interchange 8*, No. 3 (1977-1978): 1-12.

Reviews research on teacher decision making and
identifies a thread of teacher focus on practical
issues in the several studies.

1411.   Duffy, G.G. & Metheny, W. Measuring teachers'
beliefs about reading. Research Series No. 41.
East Lansing, Michigan: Institute for Research on
Teaching. Michigan State University. 1979

Describes teacher beliefs about reading and the
development of an instrument to measure those
beliefs.

1412.   Dunn, Frank. Decision making behaviors of teachers
in preplanning a unit of instruction from a
computer generated resource guide. Ed.D.
dissertation. State University of New York at
Buffalo. 1971.

Describes nine elements which influence teacher
decisions, including learner characteristics, the
learner in society, school resources, societal
problems, educational aims of the school, methods
and content, available materials, and field trip
policies.

1413.   Fairbrother, R.W. "The reliability of teachers'
judgement of the abilities being tested by
multiple choice items," *Educational Research 17*
(1975): 202-210.

Describes variations in teacher judgements of
student abilities and similarities and differences
between those judgements and student abilities
measured by test items.

1414.   Falk, Julia S. The Teachers' Conceptions of Reading
Project. East Lansing, Michigan. Institute for
Research on Teaching. Michigan State University.
1977. *ERIC ED* 136 218.

Describes teacher thinking about reading
instruction based on four sources of information
collected over a school year, and variations in
conceptions of reading.

1415.   Gil, Doron. The decision-making and diagnostic
processes of classroom teachers. Research Series
No. 71. East Lansing, Michigan: Institute for
Research on Teaching. Michigan State University.
1980. *ERIC ED* 189 575.

Describes teacher use of global categories
about students in making diagnostic decisions, but
also an absence of systematic approaches and
little agreement among teachers.

1416.   Gil, Doron, Vinsonhaler, J.F. & Sherman,
        G. Defining reading diagnosis: Why, What and How?
        Research Series No. 46. East Lansing, Michigan.
        Institute for Research on Teaching. Michigan State
        University. 1979.

        Reviews literature on diagnosis to identify
        teacher views, but finds limited discussion of
        effective diagnosis of reading problems.

1417.   Hardesty, Margaret Ann. A study of elementary
        teachers' perceptions regarding selected social
        studies concepts. Ph.D. dissertation. University
        of Iowa. 1980.

        Describes teacher concepts of what is important
        to teach and concludes that teachers are not
        following the curriculum.

1418.   Harootunian, Berj. "Teacher effectiveness: The view
        from within," *Theory into practice 19* (1980):
        266-270.

        Essay discusses differences in the variables
        studied by researchers and the ways that teachers
        think of teaching and argues that teacher
        characteristics need to be considered if research
        results are to be useful in changing teachers'
        behaviors.

1419.   Hawthorne, Richard Darryl. A model for the analysis
        of teachers' verbal pre-instructional curricular
        decisions and verbal instructional interaction.
        Ph.D. dissertation. University of Wisconsin.
        1968.

        Presents a model and analysis of teacher
        planning by coding teacher verbal planning into
        categories developed from the model.

1420.   Hirabayashi, Richard Shinolu. An observational
        study of teacher decisions in a primary classroom.
        Ph.D. dissertation. University of Illinois at
        Urbana-Champaign. 1978.

        Describes patterns of teacher decisions in
        primary classrooms, based on observations of
        teacher behaviors.

1421.   Holland, Ann Kirschberg. Characteristics of
        information teachers perceive as necessary in
        adopting a curriculum. Ph.D. dissertation. Kent
        State University. 1980.

Describes nine factors teachers report using in making decision about the adoption of curriculum and teacher perceptions that people within their districts have the necessary information.

1422. Hyman, Beverly. The dominant models and metaphors with which teachers report they function in the classroom environment. Ph.D. dissertation. New York University. 1980.

Presents the metaphors teachers use in describing the classroom environment, with 37% of the teachers describing going on a journey and 37% describing the imposing of order on chaos.

1423. Jackson, Philip W. & Belford, Elizabeth. "Private Affairs in public settings: Observations on teaching in elementary schools," *School Review 75* (1967): 1972-1986.

Describes teacher views about teaching, including the immediacy of events, different interpretations given to slight variations in student behavior, and other views of the tasks of teaching.

1424. Janesick, Valerie Jeanette. An ethnographic study of a teacher's classroom perspective. Ph.D. dissertation. Michigan State University. 1977.

Describes five elements of one teacher's classroom perspective, including a need to maintain a strong sense of groupness, respect and cooperation with classroom goals, to plan and organize the school day.

1425. Johnston, Michelle H. Conceptions of reading: The REP test. Research Series. No. 7. East Lansing, Michigan. Institute for Research on Teaching. Michigan State University. 1978. *ERIC ED* 162 261.

Describes a test which identifies teacher conceptions of reading and relates those concepts to teacher beliefs about instruction.

1426. Johnson, Sharon Fogelquist. A cognitive study of an elementary teacher's first experience teaching a "new science" unit and its relevance to the implementation of science programs. Ph.D. dissertation. University of Illinois at Urbana-Champaign. 1979.

Reports a case study of the behavior and cognitive processes, beliefs about science and about the teaching of science of one teacher as that teacher implements a science unit.

1427. Jones, Howard L. & others. "How teachers perceive
       similarities and differences among various
       teaching models," *Journal of Research in Science
       Teaching 17* (1980): 321-326.

       Describes the ways teachers perceive aspects of
       instructional models in terms of three factors,
       affective orientations, application emphasis and
       aspects of the environmental structure.

1428. Joyce, Bruce. "Toward a theory of information
       processing in teaching," *Educational Research
       Quarterly 3*, No. 4 (1978-1979): 66-77.

       Describes teacher information processing as
       effecting long-term decisions about the classroom,
       the flow of activities, and the selection of
       materials.

1429. Koenke, Karl. ERIC/RCS: One view of improving the
       teaching of reading," *Reading Teacher 34* (1980):
       90-92.

       Describes several studies of reading diagnosis
       and remediation and teacher's conceptions of
       reading.

1430. Kuhs, Therese. Elementary school teachers'
       conceptions of mathematics content and the
       potential effect on classroom instruction. Ph.D.
       dissertation. Michigan State University. 1980.

       Describes elementary teachers as primarily
       concerned with teaching content and the decisions
       they make regarding content result in variations
       in the content taught across classrooms.

1431. Kuhs, Theresa M. & Freeman, Donald J. The potential
       influence of textbooks on teachers' selection of
       content for elementary school mathematics.
       Research Series No. 48. East Lansing, Michigan:
       Institute for Research on Teaching. Michigan State
       University. 1979. *ERIC ED* 175 856.

       Describes the core curriculum as following
       current trends while the selection of additional
       options requires a high level of teacher knowledge
       of mathematics.

1432.   Lee, A. & Weinshank, A. Case production and
        analysis: CLIRIR pilot observation study. Research
        Series No. 14. East Lansing, Michigan: Institute
        for Research on Teaching. Michigan State
        University. 1978.

        Describes ways that teachers as diagnositicians
        identify student reading problems, based on
        teacher analysis of simulated cases.

1433.   Libbey, Patricia Miller. Teachers' conceptions of
        discipline: A cognitive-developmental framework.
        Ph.D. dissertation. University of Minnesota.
        1980.

        Describes a taxonomy of discipline and
        punishment based on teachers' discussions of
        discipline and punishment.

1434.   Lynch, William W. CATTS (Computer Assisted Teacher
        Training System) technology in analyzing
        observational data from public school classrooms:
        A study of interactive tasks and decisions of
        teachers. *ERIC ED* 137 774.

        Presents information from the observed behavior
        of teachers and from stimulated recall which
        suggests a method of teacher information
        processing and decision making.

1435.   MacKay, D.A. & Marland, P. Thought processes of
        teachers. *ERIC ED* 151 328.

        Describes thoughts of teachers during
        instruction as focusing on lesson tactics, past
        events in the lesson, expectations for students
        and predictions of future lesson developement.

1436.   McCutcheon G. "How do elementary school teachers
        plan? The nature of planning and influences on
        it," *Elementary School Journal 81* (1980): 4-23.

        Describes teacher planning for various time
        periods, the effects of planning on curriculum and
        the influences on teacher planning.

1437.   McKinney, Mabel Corinne. Study of factors related
        to teacher decisions of students placement in
        school curriculum. Ed.D. dissertation. University
        of Illinois at Urbana-Champaign. 1979.

        Reports that teachers make greater use of
        personality than academic information in decisions
        about readiness of students to proceed with
        specific aspects of the elementary curriculum.

1437A. McRae, Brenda B. Individualization: An exploration of teaching models and instructional strategies in selected junior high school teachers. Ed.D. dissertation. Temple University. 1979.

Describes behaviors of teachers as they plan for, develop and implement models of individualized instruction in junior high school classes.

1438. Mazurkiewicz, Albert J. "What do teachers know about phonics?" *Reading World 14*, No. 3 (1975): 165-177.

Describes teachers as not skilled at defining the terms and concepts that they teach.

1439. Metheny, William. The influence of grade and pupil ability levels on teachers' conceptions of reading. East Lansing, Michigan: Institute for Research on Teaching. Michigan State University. 1979. *ERIC ED* 182 713.

Describes teacher conceptions of reading by socioeconomic level of students and reports that teachers view low SES students as poor readers.

1440. Miller, Donald M. & others. Elementary school teachers' viewpoints of classroom teaching and learning. Madison, Wisconsin: Instructional Research Laboratory. University of Wisconsin. *ERIC ED* 046 904.

Reports that teachers think about teaching in units which are defined by teaching procedures.

1441. Mintz, Susan Levy. Teacher planning: A simulation study. Ph.D. dissertation. Syracuse University. 1979. *ERIC ED* 170 276.

Reports that in a simulation teachers seek information about student background, use basal manuals, plan for groups and include activities and content in their planning.

1442. Morine, Greta & Vallance, Elizabeth. A study of teacher planning. Special Study C. Beginning Teacher Evaluation Study. Technical Report Series. San Francisco, California: Far West Laboratory for Educational Research and Development. 1976. *ERIC ED* 146 160.

Describes four variables which distinguish between the planning of teachers who have greater and lesser student learning on two week instructional units.

1443.   Morine-Dershimer, Greta. "How teachers 'see' their
        pupils," *Educational Research Quarterly 3*, No. 4
        (1978-79): 43-52..

        Describes time of year and the curriculum
        management system as influencing the information
        which teachers have about students.

1444.   Morine-Dershimer, Greta. "Planning in classroom
        reality: An indepth look," *Educational Research
        Quarterly 3*, No. 4 (1978-79): 83-99.

        Reports that the amount of discrepancy between
        a plan and the actual less is critical to the
        information processing of teachers in evaluating
        the plan.

1444.   Morine-Dershimer, Greta. What's in a plan? Stated
        and unstated plans for lessons. *ERIC ED* 139 739.

        Describes similarities and differences in
        teacher plans and relates those to student
        achievement, with greater attention to cognitive
        aspects of the lesson related to greater student
        learning.

1446.   Muneno, Ronald Hiroshi. The relationship between
        teacher attribution of student performance and
        conceptual level of teachers. Ph.D. dissertation.
        University of Southern California. 1979.

        Describes an experiment in which teachers with
        lower conceptual levels used a greater number of
        defensive attributions about student learning than
        did teachers with higher conceptual levels.

1447.   Murphy, Patricia D. & Brown, Marjorie M.
        "Conceptual systems and teaching styles," *American
        Educational Research Journal 7* (1970): 529-540. By
        first author only, *ERIC ED* 039 190.

        Describes teacher conceptual system as related
        to teacher processing of information and use of
        sanctions with students.

1448.   O'Connell, Joseph M. A study of instructional
        objectives as related to the dynamics of the
        teaching-learning situation--A descriptive study.
        Ed.D. dissertation. State University of New York
        at Buffalo. 1971.

        Describes different types of emergent
        objectives during an instructional unit, with
        teachers differing in their focus on student needs
        versus the content of the subject.

1449. Peterson, Penelope L. & Clark, Christopher
M. "Teachers' reports of their cognitive processes
during teaching," *American Educational Research
Journal 15* (1978): 555-565.

Describes teacher reports of their thoughts
while teaching as related to teacher cognitive
styles.

1450. Peterson, Penelope L., Marx, R.W. & Clark,
C.M. "Teacher planning, teacher behavior, and
student achievement," *American Educational
Research Journal 15* (1978): 417-432.

Describes teacher planning as differing by
teacher cognitive style and ability in planning as
related to teacher behavior and student
achievement.

1451. Phelps, Carol McEwel. The nature and etiology of
the educational decision-making of two preschool
teachers. Ph.D. dissertation. Ohio State
University. 1979.

Describes five major themes in decision making:
conflicts and their resolution, rules, responses
to accomplishment, responses to hurt children,
responses to pleas for help.

1452. Prosak, Leslie Ann. A study and investigation of
the perception of the reading process of
preservice and inservice teachers. Ph.D.
dissertation. University of Toledo. 1980.

Describes perceptions of teachers of the
process of reading and relates perceptions to sex,
age and educational background.

1453. Quisenberry, Larry Dee. A study of semantic
congruency between school administrators and
teachers in use of educational terms. Ph.D.
dissertation. University of Missouri-Columbia.
1978.

Describes the meaning given to, and consistency
between groups in the meaning given to,
educational terms by teachers and administrators.

1454. Rubin, Joseph Bernard. A descriptive study of
teachers' conceptions of language as affecting the
decision-making in planning and evaluating
students' writing in grades four, five, and six.
Ph.D. dissertation. Michigan State University.
1980.

Describes teachers as having undefined concepts
of language and being unaware of any relationships
between concepts of language and the evaluation
oif student writing.

1455.   Russo, Nancy Atwood. The effects of student
        characteristics, educational beliefs and
        instructional tasks on teachers' preinstructional
        decisions in reading and math. Ph.D. dissertation.
        University of California, Los Angeles. 1978.

        Reports that in a simulation teachers used
        information about students to form reading and
        math groups, which in turn influenced teachers'
        planning.

1456.   Saphier, Jonathan Donald. The parameters of
        teaching: An empirical study using observations
        and interviews to validate a theory of teaching by
        linking levels of analysis, levels of knowing and
        levels of performance. Ed.D. dissertation. Boston
        University School of Education. 1980.

        Describes teacher conceptions of important
        aspects of teaching and ways the concepts can be
        used to study and describe teaching.

1457.   Sarver, Edward James. An exploratory analysis of
        the relationship of experienced secondary
        teachers' cognitive profiles and the complexity of
        their instructional planning. Ph.D. dissertation.
        University of Pittsburgh. 1980.

        Describes differences in cognitive profiles of
        teachers and relates those differnces to
        differences in the complexity of teacher
        instructional plans.

1458.   Scheille, John & others. Factors influencing
        teachers' decisions about what to teach:
        Sociological perspectives. Research Series No. 62.
        East Lansing, Michigan: Institute for Research on
        Teaching. Michigan State University. 1979. *ERIC*
        ED 190 550.

        Reviews research on the factors influencing
        curriculum decisions, like teacher beliefs,
        parental attitudes, tests and textbooks.

1459.   Shavelson, Richard J. "Teachers' decision making,"
        In *The psychology of teaching methods. 75th*
        Yearbook of the National Society for the Study of
        Education. Edited by N.L. Gage. pp. 372-414.
        Chicago: University of Chicago Press. 1976.

Describes models of decision making, applies them to teaching, and discusses types of decisions which teachers make when planning for and during instruction, citing relevant research. For Gage reference see citation No. 1674.

1460. Shavelson, Richard J. "Teachers' estimates of student 'states of mind' and behavior," *Journal of Teacher Education 29*, No. 5 (1978): 37-40.

Describes teachers using estimates of students' states of mind in deciding what to teach.

1461. Shavelson, Richard J., Atwood, Nancy & Borko, Hilda. "Experiments on some factors contributing to teachers' pedagogical decisions," *Cambridge Journal of Education 7* (1977): 51-70.

Describes studies of several factors which influence teacher decisions about student instructional needs and plans for instructional activities

1462. Shavelson, Richard J. The basic teaching skill: Decision making. Stanford, California: Stanford Center for Research and Development in Teaching. Stanford University. 1973. *ERIC ED* 073 117.

Presents a model of decision making in teaching, including types of decisions and sources of information, cites relevant studies and describes research methods.

1463. Shavelson Richard J. & Borko, Hilda. "Research on teachers' decisions in planning instruction," *Educational Horizons 57*, No. 4 (1979): 183-189.

Summarizes research on teacher planning for yearly and daily instruction and the influences on that planning.

1464. Shirley, Fehl L. Professional values from reading: The influence of reading on the instructional methodology of teachers. 1977. *ERIC ED* 137 748.

Describes teacher reports that reading books and periodicals influenced their reading instruction, with more new than experienced teachers reporting being influenced.

1465. Shulman, Lee S. & Elstein, Arthur S. "Studies of problem solving, judgment, and decision making: Implications for educational research," In *Review of Research in Education Vol. 3*. Edited by Fred N.

Kerlinger. Itasca, Illinois: F.E. Peacock
Publishers, Inc. 1975.

Reviews studies of decision making and
judgement and relates them to teacher decision
making roles such as diagnosis and development of
expectations for students. For the Kerlinger
reference see citation No. 2977.

1466.   Smith, Jeffrey K. Teacher planning for instruction.
Chicago, Illinois: ML-GROUP for Policy Studies in
Education. CEMREL, Inc. 1977.

Describes teacher planning for allocation of
time to subject areas, content and emphasis of
tasks and organization of pupils for instruction.

1467.   Smith, Jeffrey Keniray. Teacher planning processes
and outcomes. Ph.D. dissertation. University of
Chicago. 1977.

Describes teacher planning for the school year,
including major decisions about time allocated to
various subjects and the influence of factors such
as the curriculum series.

1468.   Stein, Paula Judith. A participant observer study
of team teacher planning behavior in a middle
school setting. Ph.D. dissertation. Michigan State
University. 1978.

Describes the planning activities of a grade
seven teaching team.

1469.   Sweet, Robert Arthur. An investigation of the
relationship between teachers' attitudes and their
curriculum planning decisions in primary reading
instruction: An application of the Fishbein model.
Ed.D. dissertation. University of British Columbia
(Canada). 1978.

Describes teacher planning as related to
teacher personality and training.

1470.   Thompson, Bruce. "The instructional strategy
decisions of teachers," *Education 101* (1980):
150-157.

Describes teacher beliefs as related to teacher
decisions about instructional methods.

1471.   Wade, Priscilla Malpass. A comparative study of the
responses of the teachers in the Title I federally
funded and state supported kindergartens in
Alabama in reading readiness. Ed.D. dissertation.
Auburn University. 1980.

Describes no significant differences in teacher
reports of their instruction and materials
selection for reading readiness.

1472. Ware, J.Gilbert. Teacher awareness and application
of teaching theory. Ph.D. dissertation. Miami
University. 1979.

Describes teacher awareness of educational
psychology and teacher focus on intellectual
rather than personal and social aspects of
teaching, but lack of teacher understanding of
teaching theories.

1473. Willis, Katherine Phelan. Knowledge and practices
of teachers and librarians in instructional design
and in audio-visual media selection and
utilization. Ph.D. dissertation. University of
Michigan. 1979.

Describes limited teacher knowledge of theories
of uses and effects of media on learning and
limited planning to use media.

1474. Yarger, Gwendolynne Polk & Harootunian,
Berj. Teacher's use of classroom materials. 1978.
ERIC ED 151 361.

Describes use of materials in reading
instruction and limited teacher decisions
regarding use of materials.

1475. Yinger, Robert J. A study of teacher planning:
Description and a model of preactive decision
making. Research Series No. 18. East Lansing,
Michigan: Institute for Research on Teaching.
Michigan State University.

Describes a model of teacher planning
illustrated with examples from observed teacher
planning.

1476. Yinger Robert Johnston. A study of teacher
planning: Description and a model of preactive
decision making. Ph.D. dissertation. Michigan
State University. 1977. *ERIC ED* 152 747.

Describes an ethnographic study and teacher
reports of planning decisions and argues for a
distinction between planning for instructional
activities and the use of teaching routines.,

1477. Yinger, Robert. "Routines in teacher planning,"
Theory into Practice 18 (1979): 163-169.

Describes seven features of instructional
activities, location, structure and sequence,
duration, participants, acceptable student
behavior, instructional moves, content and
materials.

1478.   Zahorik, John A. "The effect of planning on
teaching," *Elementary School Journal 71* (1970):
143-151.

Describes some differences in teachers'
sensitivity to students by whether teaching from
their own or the researcher's plan.

D. FACTORS INFLUENCING

1. TEACHER CHARACTERISTICS

1479. Aspy, David N. "An investigation into the
        relationship between teachers' factual knowledge
        of learning theory and their classroom
        performance," *Journal of Teacher Education 23*, No.
        1 (1972): 21-24.

        Describes little relationship between teacher
        knowledge of learning theory and the observed
        behaviors of teachers.

1480. Aspy, David N. & Roebuck, Flora N. "An
        investigation of the relationship between student
        levels of cognitive functioning and the teacher's
        classroom behavior," *Journal of Educational
        Research 65* (1972): 365-368.

        Describes teacher regard for students as
        related to teacher behavior and the level of
        cognitive functioning of students.

1481. Aspy, David N., Roebuck, Flora N. & Black,
        Bob. "The relationship of teacher-offered
        conditions of respect to behaviors described by
        Flanders' Interaction Analysis," *Journal of Negro
        Education 41* (1972): 370-372.

        Describes a relationship between teacher
        respect for individual students and the observed
        behavior of teachers with students.

1482. Ayers, Jerry B. & others. "Human relations skills
        and teacher characteristics," *Education 100*,
        (1980): 348-351.

        Describes a relationship between teacher
        characteristics and teacher human relations
        skills.

1483. Babb, Charles W. Relationships between concerns and
        verbal behavior in elementary school teachers.
        1972. *ERIC ED* 075 366.

Describes the concerns of teachers related to
the behavior of teachers.

1484.   Bane, Robert King. Relationships between measures
of experimental, cognitive, and affective teaching
behavior and selected teacher characteristics.
Ed.D dissertation. University of Florida. 1969.

Describes a relationship between teacher
beliefs and behavior, but not teacher
characteristics and behavior.

1485.   Bassett, Jimmy Floyd. An analysis of the oral
questioning process and certain causal
relationships in the elementary school science
classroom. 1971. *ERIC ED* 070 568.

Describes teacher characteristics as related to
teacher questioning practices.

1486.   Bates, Sara Jane. Hemisphericity and teachers: A
study of the relationship between brain dominance
and teaching style of junior high/middle school
teachers. Ed.D dissertation. Brigham Young
University. 1980.

Describes no relationship between brain
dominance (right and left brain) and teaching
style, teaching speciality, sex, years of
experience.

1487.   Baum, Michael, Brophy, Jere E., Evertson, Carolyn
M., Anderson, Linda M. & Crawford, W. John. "Sex
and grade level of student as context variables in
elementary school teaching," *Journal of Classroom
Interaction 14* (1979): 11-17. Also Report No.
4048. Austin, Texas: Research and Development
Center for Teacher Education. University of Texas
at Austin. 1976. *ERIC ED* 147 260.

Describes subtle differences in the behaviors
of teachers toward boys and girls, with a shift
over the grades with more public interactions at
higher grades.

1488.   Biberstine, Richard Doyle. A study of selected
areas of teacher influence upon the written
compostion of fourth graders. Ph.D. dissertation.
University of Illinois. 1967. *ERIC ED* 030 648.

Describes teacher writing abilities in relation
to behaviors in teaching others to write.

1489.   Biddle, Bruce J. & Adams, Raymond S. An analysis of
classroom activities. A final report. Columbia,

Missouri: Missouri University. 1967. *ERIC ED* 015 357.

Describes classroom events differentially affected by age and sex of teacher, subject matter, grade leve.

1490. Bird, Robert Carl. An investigation of teacher dogmatism and teacher behavior in science instruction. Ph.D. dissertation. Florida State University. 1970. *ERIC ED* 086 447.

Describes different behavior of open- and closed-minded teachers.

1491. Bloland, Paul A. & Selby, Thomas J. "Factors associated with career change among secondary school teachers: A review of the literature," *Educational Research Quarterly 5*, No. 3 (1980): 13-24.

Reviews studies of research on teachers leaving teaching and reports that studies have considered institutional and teacher demographic variables but not teacher affective and personality issues.

1492. Bolden, Bernadine Mildred Johnson. The relationship between teacher attitudes and observed classroom behavior. Ph.D. dissertation. University of Florida. 1977.

Describes teacher characteristics as related to teacher behavior, but no relationship between teacher attitudes and behavior.

1493. Bowman, Benjamin Phillip. Teacher interpersonal behavior and classroom control. Ed.D. dissertation. University of California, Berkeley. 1967.

Describes teacher behavior in the classroom as related to teacher behavior outside of the classroom with other people and responses to "life in general".

1494. Brophy, J.E., Evertson, C.M., Harris, T. & Good, T.L. Communication of teacher expectations: fifth grade. Austin, Texas: Research and Development Center for Teacher Education. University of Texas at Austin. 1973.

Describes the behaviors of teachers in interactions with students in terms of teacher expectations for those students.

1495.   Brophy, Jere E. & Good, Thomas L. *Teacher-student relationship: Causes and consequences*. New York: Holt, Rinehart & Winston. 1974.

Reviews research which shows that teachers behave differently toward students based on teacher perceptions of student characteristics.

1496.   Bruck, Margaret & Shultz, Jeffrey. An ethnographic analysis of the language use patterns of bilingually schooled children. Working papers on bilingualism. No. 13. Toronto, Canada: Bilingual Education Project. Ontario Institute for Studies in Education. 1977. *ERIC ED* 140 664.

Describes increasing use of English over the year and teacher language dominance related to patterns of language use in bilingual pull-out programs in grade one.

1497.   Carbonari, Joseph P. An investigation of relationships among instructional mode, teacher needs, and students' personalities. 1973. *ERIC ED* 076 563.

Describes a relationship between the instructional mode used by the teacher, student personality, and teacher needs.

1498.   Dadey, William Joseph. An investigation of the relationship between perceived classroom verbal behavior of teachers and frequency of discipline problems. Ph.D. dissertation. Syracuse University. 1971.

Describes a relationship between actual number of discipline problems which teachers refer and ranking of perceived number of discipline problems, related to teacher characteristics.

1499.   Dischel, Phyllis Isaacs. Teacher anxiety level, personality style and classroom teaching style: A study of the relationships among level of trait anxiety, hesteroid and obsessoid personality style and dominative and integrative teacher behavior. Ph.D. dissertation. New York University.

Reports a slight relationship between teacher personality and behavior, with teachers with greater levels of anxiety showing less integrative behavior in the classroom.

1500.   Dobson, Russell & Elsom, Bill. "Elementary teachers' philosophies of human nature and nonverbal communication patterns, *"Journal*

of the Student Personnel Association for Teacher
Education 11 (1973): 98-101.

Describes a relationship between teacher
behavior and teacher philosophy of human
behavior.

1501. Dobson, Russell, Goldenberg, Ron & Elsom,
Bill. "Pupil control ideology and teacher
influence in the classroom," *Journal of
Educational Research* 66 (1972): 76-80.

Reports that teachers with more humanistic
ideology of control of pupil behavior exhibited
greater use of indirect questions and responses to
students than teachers with more custodial control
ideology.

1502. Dobson, Russell & others. "Congruence of verbal and
nonverbal behavior of elementary school teachers
with differing beliefs about the nature of man,"
*Journal of Student Personnel Association for
Teacher Education* 12 (1974): 157-163.

Describes no clear relationship between teacher
philosohy of human nature and degree of congruence
between verbal and nonverbal behavior.

1503. Downey, Loren Willard. The relationship of teaching
patterns to organizational climate and teacher
belief system. Ed.D. dissertation. University of
Arizona. 1966.

Describes no influence of open or traditional
school or teacher personality characteristics on
the behavior of teachers.

1504. Doyle, W. & Olszewski, R. "Colleague interaction
and teacher performance," *Education* 95 (1975):
276-279.

Describes levels of teacher interactions with
other teachers and relates those levels to
measures of teacher performance on teaching
tasks.

1505. Earl, Robert Duane. The science teacher's inclusive
behavior as related to certain personality
characteristics. Ed.D. dissertation. Oklahoma
State University. 1976.

Describes no relationship between teacher
personality and "inclusive" behavior as perceived
by pupils.

1506.   Ekstrom, Ruth B. "Teacher aptitudes, knowledge,
        attitudes, and cognitive style as predictors of
        teaching behavior," *Journal of Teacher Education*
        27 (1976): 329-331.

        Describes a relationship between teacher
        attitude and knowledge and observed behavior of
        elementary teachers.

1507.   Ellner, Carolyn Lipton. Psychophysiological
        correlates of female teacher behavior and
        organizational outputs. Ph.D. dissertation.
        University of California, Los Angeles. 1968. *ERIC*
        ED 033 888.

        Describes a relationship between autonomic
        balance and teacher emotional behavior, reported
        teaching behavior, perceived stress in teaching
        and teaching effectiveness.

1508.   Evans, Thomas Parker. An exploratory study of the
        verbal and non-verbal behaviors of biology
        teachers and their relationships to selected
        personality traits. Ph.D. dissertation. Ohio State
        University. 1968.

        Describes a relationship between teacher
        behaviors and teacher personality
        characteristics.

1509.   Everston, C.M., Brophy, J.E. & Good, T.L.
        Communication of teacher expectations : First
        grade. Austin, Texas: Research and Development
        Center for Teacher Education. University of Texas
        at Austin. 1972.

        Describes teacher expectations as not related
        to interactions between teacher and students in
        the observed classrooms.

1510.   Evertson, C.M., Brophy, J.E. & Good, T.L.
        Communication of teacher expectations: Second
        grade. Austin, Texas: Research and Development
        Center for Teacher Education. University of Texas
        at Austin. 1973.

        Describes teacher expectations for student
        achievement as not related to teacher interactions
        with students.

1511.   Frankiewicz, R.G. & Merrifield, P.R. Student
        teacher preferences as predictors of their
        teaching behavior. *ERIC ED* 011 255.

Describes a relationship between teacher perceptions of the teacher's role and observed behaviors.

1512. Gibson, Edgar Lee. Relationships among measures of personality, teacher performance, and classroom verbal interaction patterns of selected elementary school teachers. Ed.D. dissertation. University of Southern Mississippi. 1972.

Describes no difference in behaviors of teachers by age, experience, principal rating, but differences by teacher personality characteristics.

1513. Golden, Carol Johnson. A survey of the personal reading habits of a selected group of elementary classroom teachers. Ed.D. dissertation. Indiana University. 1979.

Describes limited general and professional reading by elementary teachers and a relationship between reading habits and teacher personality characteristics, and family background.

1514. Goldenberg, Ronald. Pupil control ideology and teacher influence in the classroom. 1971. *ERIC ED* 048 099.

Describes differences in teacher pupil control ideology as related to teacher behavior.

1515. Greenwood, G.E. & Soar, R.S. "Some relationships between teacher morale and teacher behavior," *Journal of Educational Psychology 64* (1973): 105-108.

Describes relationships between measures of teacher morale within schools and teacher observed behaviors.

1516. Gregory, John William. A study of the impact of the verbal environment in mathematics classrooms on seventh grade students' logical abilities. Final Report. Columbus, Ohio: Research Foundation. Ohio State University. 1972. *ERIC ED* 064 178.

Describes no interaction between teacher math ability and frequency of teacher conditional moves in the classroom.

1517. Guerrieri, Sandra Irene. Teacher personality characteristics in selected open and non-open elementary schools. Ed.D. dissertation. University of Arizona. 1980.

Describes teacher personality characteristics
as related to their observed behavior and job
satisfaction in open and traditional schools.

1518.   Harrow, Mitchell Scott. The behavioral connection
between "teacher morale" and teacher rates of
emitted classroom verbal approval and disapproval.
Ph.D. dissertation. Columbia University. 1979.

Describes a relationship between teacher morale
and teacher verbal approval and disapproval of
student behavior and work in the classroom.

1519.   Harste, Jerome C. Teacher behavior and its
relationship to pupil performance in reading.
1977. *ERIC ED* 141 750.

Describes teacher theories of reading
instruction as consistent with their pretutorial
planning and behavior in reading instruction.

1520.   Harvey, O.J. Teachers belief systems and preschool
atmospheres. Boulder, Colorado: Colorado
University. 1965. *ERIC ED* 014 320.

Describes a relationship between the
abstractness or concreteness of teachers' belief
systems and their observed behavior.

1521.   Harvey, O.J. & others. Teachers' beliefs, classroom
atmosphere, and student behavior. *ERIC ED* 011
888.

Describes a relationship between the
abstractness of teacher beliefs and the observed
behavior of teachers and students in the
classroom.

1522.   Harvey, O.J. & others. Teachers' beliefs, classroom
atmosphere and students behavior. Final Report.
Boulder, Colorado: Colorado University. 1967. *ERIC
ED* 018 249.

Reports a replication of a previous study
finding a relationship between teacher belief
system and teacher behavior in the classroom.

1523.   Harvey, O.J., Prather, Misha, White, B. Jack &
Hoffmeister, James K. "Teachers' beliefs,
classroom atmosphere and student behavior,"
American Educational Research Journal 5 (1968):
151–166.

Describes teachers' concreteness or
abstractness of belief system as related to

resourcefulness, dictatorialness, and punitiveness
in the classroom.

1524. Hoetker, William James. Analyses of the
subject-matter related verbal behavior in nine
junior high school English classes. Ed.D.
dissertation. Washington University. 1967.

Describes specific teaching moves related to
rates of teacher factual errors made while
teaching, and teacher risk-taking related to use
of recitation and lower rates of factual errors.

1525. Hunt, Edith Joan. The critical thinking ability of
teachers and its relationship to the teachers'
classroom verbal behavior and perceptions of
teaching purposes. Ph.D. dissertation. University
of Maryland. 1967.

Describes differences in the number of higher
but not lower cognitive comments by level of
teacher critical thinking.

1526. LeCompte, Margaret D. "Establishing a workplace:
Teacher control in the classroom," *Education and
Urban Society 11* (1978): 87-106.

Describes few differences in teacher management
behavior and those few related to teacher
personality and philosophy.

1527. Lightfoot, Sara Lawrence. "Politics and reasoning:
Through the eyes of teachers and children,"
Harvard Educational Review 43 (1973): 197-244.

Describes teacher views of education and levels
of political consciousness related to teaching
practices and their effects of the development of
children's thinking abilities.

1528. Lucio, William H. & others. Psychophysiologial
correlates of female teacher behavior and
emotional stability: A seven-year longitudinal
investigation. Los Angeles, California: Center for
the Study of Evaluation. University of California,
Los Angeles. 1967. *ERIC ED* 021 786.

Describes a relationship between teacher
autonomic nervous system and teacher behavior,
health, and emotional stability.

1529. McCaskill, Robert Hugh. The relationship between
teacher knowledge of adolescent development,
teacher warmth, and teacher educational ideology
with teacher overt verbal behavior in selected

junior high classrooms. Ed.D. dissertation.
University of Maryland. 1979.

Describes teacher characteristics such as
warmth related to behaviors of junior high school
teachers.

1530. McDaniel, Ernest. Some relationships among teacher
observation data and measures of self concept and
attitude toward school. 1976. *ERIC ED* 138 887.

Describes a relationship between observed
behavior of teachers and teacher attitude and
exhibition of "warmth" toward students.

1531. McGhan, Barry Robert. Teachers' use of authority
and its relationship to socioeconomic status,
race, teacher characteristics, and educational
outcomes. 1978. *ERIC ED* 151 329.

Describes teacher openness and use of authority
as related to teacher and student
characteristics.

1532. MacNaughton, Dolores Elaine. An analysis of
language arts teaching practices in grade six.
1972. *ERIC ED* 124 993.

Describes no relationship between teacher
reports of practices and teacher characteristics.

1533. McNair, Kathleen & Joyce, Bruce. "Thought and
action: A frozen section—The South Bay Study,"
Educational Research Quarterly 3, No. 4
(1978-1979): 10-15.

Describes a relationship between teacher
behaviors and teacher cognitive processing of
information.

1534. Mager, Gerald Martin. An analysis of the conditions
which influence a teacher in initiating contact
with parents. Ph.D. dissertation. Ohio State
University. 1978.

Describes teacher characteristics related to
teacher initiation of contacts with parents of
students.

1535. Mager, Gerald M. "The conditions which influence a
teacher in initiating contact with parents,"
Journal of Educational Research 73 (1980):
276-282.

Reports that teachers who have more contact
with parents feel more responsible for initiating

contact and more comfortable with parents but have less support from parents.

1536. Morris, Jeanne B. "An analysis of the perceived behaviors of early childhood education teachers on selected characteristics," *Illinois School Research and Development 14* (1978): 65-72.

Describes a relationship between teacher characteristics and role perceptions and teacher behaviors.

1537. Myers, Betty, Kennedy, John J. & Cruickshank, Donald R. "Relationship of teacher personality variables to teacher perceived problems," *Journal of Teacher Education 30,* No. 6 (1979): 33-41.

Describes a relationship between teacher personality characteristics and the problems of teaching which they experience.

1538. Pavlovich, Natalie Sophie. Cognitive types of teachers and pupils in relation to classroom interaction. Ph.D. dissertation. University of Michigan. 1970.

Describes no relationship between teacher reflective/impulsive characteristics, direct/indirect teaching behavior, flexible teaching behavior.

1539. Roebuck, Flora N. & Aspy, David N. "Grade level contributions to the variance of Flanders' Interaction categories," *Journal of Experimental Education 42* (1974): 86-92.

After differences in teacher characteristics are accounted for, differences in teacher behavior measured by Flanders' Interaction Analysis are related to the subject being taught during the observation.

1540. Rogers, Robert Earl. Classroom verbal behavior as related to teachers' perception of pupils in fifth-grade science classes. Ph.D. dissertation. Ohio State University. 1970. *ERIC ED* 079 036.

Describes differences in teacher behavior related to teacher perceptions of pupils and describes differences in the behavior of students in inner and outer city schools.

1541. Semmens, Ronald L. The relationship of elementary science classrooms to selected teacher and student variables. 1970. *ERIC ED* 092 319.

Describes a relationship between teacher ideal and observed behavior in science, with a stronger relationship for teachers trained in science teaching.

1542.   Serafino, Philip Andrew. Field-dependent and field-independent cognitive style and teacher behavior. Ed.D. dissertation. Rutgers University the State University of New Jersey. 1978.

Reports that the degree of field dependence is related to some, but not other, teacher behaviors.

1543.   Shepard, Robert Gene. An analysis of teacher non-verbal behaviors as exhibited toward pupils representing three social classes. Ed.D. dissertation. University of Tennessee. 1971.

Describes an interaction between teacher sex and the socioeconomic level of students in relation to teacher verbal behaviors in the classroom.

1544.   Treanor, Hugh J. & Murray, C. Kenneth. Verbal and cognitive behavior patterns in the classrooms of selected social studies teachers. 1971. *ERIC ED* 067 306.

Reports that the behaviors of teachers are similar at the lower levels of cognitive complexity but different among teachers at the higher levels of cognitive complexity.

2.   EXTERNAL FACTORS

1545.   Abramowitz, Susan. The effects of mini-school size on the organization and management of instruction. Washington, D.C.: Rand Corporation. 1976. *ERIC ED* 122 396.

Describes the effects of school size on teacher behaviors and attitudes.

1546.   Anderson, James G. "Strategies of control and their effects on instruction," *Journal of Research and Development in Education 9* (fall 1975): 115-122.

Reports that greater bureaucratic control of instruction results in teachers spending less time with individual students and using more impersonal instructional behaviors in junior high schools.

1547. Anderson, Linda M, Evertson, Carolyn M. & Brophy,
       Jere. "An examination of classroom context:
       Effects of lesson format and teacher training on
       patterns of teacher-student contacts during
       small-group instruction," *Journal of Classroom
       Interaction 15*, No. 2 (1980): 21-26. *ERIC ED* 189
       075.

       Reports that both lesson format and teacher
       training were related to classroom processes in an
       experiment.

1548. Black, D.B. & others. "The effects of teacher aides
       on teacher teaching behavior," *Alberta Journal of
       Educational Research 22* (1976): 140-148.

       Describes a relationship between the
       availability of aides and teacher behavior.

1549. Bolchazy, Marie Carducci. Classroom verbal
       interaction, teachers' perceptions of students'
       self-concept and autonomy, and reading group
       placement. Ed.D. dissertation. State University of
       New York at Albany. 1979.

       Describes teacher verbal behavior as related to
       teacher perceptions of student self-concept and
       autonomy.

1550. Booth, Terry Michael. An analysis of teacher morale
       and absenteeism in a declining enrollment school
       district. Ph.D. dissertation. Western Michigan
       University. 1980.

       Describes no relationship between program
       cutbacks and teacher absenteeism and between
       teacher morale and absenteeism.

1551. Borg, Walter R. "The minicourse as a vehicle for
       changing teacher behavior: A three-year followup,"
       Journal of Educational Psychology 36 (1972):
       572-579.

       Describes the behaviors of teachers after
       training in the use of specific behaviors through
       a minicourse.

1552. Bossert, Steven T. "Tasks, group management, and
       teacher control behavior: A study of classroom
       organization and teacher style," *School Review 85*
       (1977): 552-565.

       Describes three patterns of classroom task
       organization and the effects on the behavior of
       teachers and students, such as teacher control,
       and differences in the behavior of teachers.

1553.   Bush, Robert N. The status of the career teacher:
        Its effect upon the teacher dropout problem.
        Stanford, California: Stanford Center for Research
        and Development in Teaching. Stanford University.
        1969. *ERIC ED* 029 858.

        Describes the status of career teachers in
        general society and the ways that young teachers
        report that the status of teachers effects their
        decisions to leave teaching.

1554.   Clayback, Thomas J. A summary of research related
        to teacher behavior resulting from the use of
        computer assisted planning. 1970. *ERIC ED* 040
        141.

        Describes greater individualized instruction
        and more change for secondary than elementary
        teachers when teachers were given a curriculum
        guide than when they worked without one in using
        computers for instruction.

1555.   Colbert, C. Dianne & Wang, Margaret C. A study of
        teacher behaviors in an adaptive learning
        environment. 1978. *ERIC ED* 155 153.

        Describes the effects of contexts, such as
        group size and subject matter, on teacher
        behaviors.

1556.   Conran, Patricia C. & Beauchamp, George A.
        Relationships among leadership, climate, teacher,
        and student variables in curriculum engineering.
        1976. *ERIC ED* 119 330.

        Describes a relationship between teacher
        behavior, classroom climate, curriculum, student
        behaviors and the leadership behavior of the
        principal.

1557.   Copeland, Willis D. "Teaching-learning behaviors
        and the demands of the classroom environment,"
        Elementary School Journal 80 (1980): 163-177.

        Describes the effects of elementary classroom
        environment on the teaching and learning behaviors
        of classroom participants.

1558.   Costantino, Peter Samuel. A study of differences
        between middle school and junior high school
        curricula and teacher-pupil classroom behavior.
        Ed.D. dissertation. University of Pittsburgh.
        1968.

Describes no differences in the curriculum and in teacher behavior in junior high and middle schools.

1559. Crandall, Nelson David. Relationship of teacher aides and teacher behavior in selected areas. Ed.D. dissertation. University of Southern California. 1970.

Reports that teachers with aides spent a greater proportion of the teaching time working with small groups, giving supportive verbal expressions, and other differences in behavior.

1560. Daily, Frances M. & Phillips, James A., Jr. Phenomena and methodology of studying social structures in the classroom. *ERIC ED* 073 052.

Describes a correlation between teacher behaviors and the social structures of the classroom.

1561. Daniel, K. Fred. A catalog of analysis of variance pilot studies employing data from the official Florida Teacher Evaluation Form. Part II. Tallahassee, Florida: Florida State Department of Education. 1967. *ERIC ED* 018 863.

Describes analyses of factors related to principal ratings of teacher performance, with only level of instruction accounting for differences in ratings.

1562. Derhammer, John Loren. The effects of training on increased incidence of, and correlation between, higher order classroom and test questioning behavior. Ed.D. dissertation. University of Tennessee. 1971.

Describes no relationship between the percentage of higher cognitive level questions asked by teachers in class and on tests before training and changes in behavior after training.

1563. Dillon, Michael Joseph. A descriptive study of teacher utilization of mathematics objectives checklists. Ed.D. dissertation. Pennsylvania State University. 1980.

Describes differences among teachers in use of a student checklist, with younger teachers and those involved in development of the checklist making greater use of it.

1564. Dockery, Elston Ray. A study of the effects of
       atmospheric conditions related to teacher and
       student behaviors. Ed.D. dissertation. University
       of Tennessee. 1975.

       Describes non-significant differences in
       teacher and student behavior during stable and
       unstable atmospheric conditions.

1565. Doyle, Walter. "Helping beginning teachers manage
       classrooms," *NASSP Bulletin 59* (1975): 38-41.

       Describes some management techniques that
       teachers can use, based on studies of teacher
       behaviors in organizing and managing student
       tasks.

1566. Doyle, Walter. "Learning the classroom environment:
       An ecological analysis of induction into
       teaching," *Journal of Teacher Education 28*
       (Nov.-Dec, 1977): 51-55.

       Describes the influence on behavior of teachers
       and students of the classroom environment.

1567. Dolye, Walter. "The uses of nonverbal behaviors:
       Toward an ecological model of classrooms,"
       Merrill-Palmer Quarterly 23, No. 3 (1977):
       179-192.

       Review and essay reports that classroom
       environments, teacher and student performance all
       shape and limit the range of teacher behavior
       options.

1568. Doyle, W. & Redwine, J. "Effect of intent-action
       discrepancy and student performance feedback on
       teacher behavior change," *Journal of Educational
       Psychology 66* (1974): 750-755.

       Describes teacher behaviors, differences
       between plans and actual lessons, and the effects
       of those discrepancies and feedback from student
       behavior on teacher behaviors.

1569. Duckworth, Kenneth & Jovick, Thomas. Task
       interdependence, communication, and team
       management among elementary school teachers.
       Eugene, Oregon: Center for Educational Policy and
       Management. Oregon University. 1978. *ERIC ED* 152
       743.

       Reports that teaming results in greater teacher
       communication with other teachers but not

in shared responsibility for management of working conditions.

1570. Dunkum, William Washington. Achievement and student-teacher verbal interactions in high school physics lectures with and without computer simulated demonstration experiments. Ph.D. dissertation. American University. 1979.

Describes teacher behavior but not student achievement as influenced by the use of a computer in high school physics classes.

1571. Edwards, Peter. An interaction-network instrument to assess pupil-interaction and movement in open-area learning situations. Vancouver, British Columbia, Canada: Vancouver Board of School Trustees. 1973. *ERIC ED* 086 741.

Describes student moves and the role of the teacher in open and traditional schools.

1572. Feldman, Carol & Wertsch, Jim. Analysis of syntactic and semantic elements found in the classroom speech of teachers. Washington, D.C.: National Institute of Education. 1972. *ERIC ED* 142 077.

Describes differences in some of the parameters of the speech of teachers in and out of the classroom.

1573. Feldman, Carol Fleisher & Wertsch, James V. "Context dependent properties of teachers' speech," *Youth and Society* 7 (1976): 227-258.

Describes differences in teacher language with adults and with students, indicating differences in the social distances which teachers maintain with students and with other adults.

1574. Freed, Alfred Sherwood. A descriptive study of the relationship of organizational structure and teacher professional orientation to teachers' grievances. Ed.D. dissertation. New York University. 1979.

Describes greater principal latitude to teachers resulting in more teacher grievances.

1575. Gitlin, Andrew David. Understanding the work of teachers. Ph.D. dissertation. University of Wisconsin, Madison. 1980.

Describes the ways that the structure of the
school using Individually Guided Instruction
limits the work of teachers, such as the nature of
the curriculum influencing the types of tasks in
which teachers are engaged.

1576.   Green, Martha Mackie. An investigation of the
permanence of certain teacher classroom behaviors
exhibited by trained teachers in the DISCUS
project. Ed.D. dissertation. University of
Florida. 1971.

Reports that teachers continued to use the
behaviors needed to teach with innovative science
materials when the materials were no longer
available.

1577.   Hall, Gene E. The effects of "change" on teachers
and professors--Theory, research, and implications
for decision-makers. Research report No. 3012.
Austin, Texas: Research and Development Center for
Teacher Education. University of Texas at Austin.
1975. *ERIC ED* 128 338.

Describes the effects of change in teaching
situations on the behaviors and attitudues of
teachers and professors, and the sequence of
responses to change.

1578.   Hall, Gene E. & Loucks, Susan F. A longitudinal
investigation of individual implementation of
educational innovations. Austin, Texas: Research
and Development Center for Teacher Education.
Texas University at Austin. 1977.

Describes changes in the behavior of teachers
as they implement team teaching in elementary
schools and in universities.

1579.   Halleen, Owen Paul. Teacher behavior in a
modular-flexible scheduled school: A comparative
study. Ph.D. dissertation. University of
Minnesota. 1972.

Describes differences in teacher reports of
role satisfaction and use of time in traditional
and flexible scheduled schools.

1580.   Hannum, James W. & others. Changing the evaluative
self-thoughts of two elementary teachers. Research
and Development Memorandum No. 122. Stanford,
California: Stanford Center for Research and
Development in Teaching. Stanford University.
1974. *ERIC ED* 092 519.

Describes some change in the behavior of teachers after observing their own teaching.

1581. Harvley-Felder, Thomas William. The use of specialists and teacher authority in the third grade. Ph.D. dissertation. University of North Carolina at Chapel Hill. 1978.

Describes teacher decision making behavior as related to the presence of aides and specialists.

1582. Hawkins, Warren. "Research on the determinants of classroom processes," *Classroom Interaction Newsletter 11*, No. 1 (1975): 15-17.

Describes studies of teacher behavior and concludes that teacher behaviors are related to class size.

1583. Hendricks, C. Gaylong & others. Effects of behavioral self-observation on elementary teachers and students. Research and Development Memorandum No. 121. Stanford California: Stanford Center for Research and Development in Teaching. Stanford University. 1974. *ERIC ED* 092 520.

Reports that teachers who observed their teaching with 40% to 80% accuracy changed their behavior which resulted in changes in student behavior, but changes did not last beyond the observation period.

1584. Hines, Vynce A. & Alexander, William M. High School self-evaluations and curriculum change. Final Report. Gainesville, Florida: University of Florida. 1967. *ERIC ED* 017 971.

Describes more curriculum change in high schools where teachers participated in a self-study for accreditation, but no greater teacher openness to curriculum change.

1585. Hite, Herbert. Follow-up study: Long-term effects of modified internship for beginning elementary teachers. 19681 *ERIC ED* 022 715.

Describes small gains in the performance of teachers from preservice through the second year of teaching.

1586. Hovey, Larrry Michael. Measuring Science Curriculum Improvement Study teachers' attitudinal changes toward science. 1970. *ERIC ED* 085 195.

Reports that training in use of new science curriculum effected the attitudes of teachers toward use of the program but the changes disappeared after use of the curriculum in the classroom.

1587.   Huenecke, Dorothy. "Knowledge of curriculum works: its relation to teaching practice." *Journal of Teacher Education 21* (1970): 478-483.

Describes differences in the cognitive level of teacher questions by teacher familiarity or not with several curriculum texts.

1588.   Hummel-Rossi, Barbara & Merrifield, Philip. "Student personality factors related to teacher reports of their interactions with students," *Journal of Educational Psychology 69* (1977): 375-380.

Describes differences in teacher behavior toward students by student personality, including greater supervision of aggressive and apprehensive students.

1589.   Hunter, Elizabeth. "Talk in first grade classrooms," *Urban Review 4* (1969): 39-42.

Describes the behaviors of teachers trained and not trained in a new elementary science program; the trained teachers talked less and their students talked more.

1590.   Jocobs, Joseph H. "Insight learning through structured observations of classroom interaction," *Journal of Research in Science Teaching 10* (1973): 213-220.

Describes patterns of teacher and student talk and changes in those patterns after teacher training in the use of an observation system, but the changes not related to changes in student behavior.

1591.   Jeffs, George A. & others. The effects of training in Interaction Analysis on the verbal behavior of teachers. 1968. *ERIC ED* 023 621.

Describes changes in the behaviors of teachers after training in the use of Interaction Analysis, such as greater use of student comments.

1592.   Jones, John Carl. The effect of feedback on the verbal behavior of beginning teachers. Ed.D. dissertation. University of Oregon. 1969.

Describes the behavior of first year teachers and no differences by the type of feedback provided to one group of teachers.

1593. Kaminsky, Sally. An analysis of teacher behavior in variously structured second grade classrooms. Ed.D. dissertation. Columbia University. 1974.

Describes a relationship between teacher classroom concerns and teacher controlling behavior.

1594. Kardatzke, Howard Holbrook. Cultural-institutional and teacher influences upon social studies curriculum and instruction: An exploratory study. Ph.D. dissertation. Michigan State University. 1968. *ERIC ED* 055 928.

Describes most cultural, institutional and teacher personal variables not related to teacher behaviors.

1595. Kozuch, Joyce A. "The influence of structure and technology on teacher work performance," *Educational Research Quarterly 4*, No. 2 (1979): 58-65.

Describes how the conditions of a school influence the behaviors of the teachers in the school.

1596. Lamb, Morris Lynn. The effects of different classroom observation conditions on questioning patterns of teachers. Ed.D. dissertation. University of Oklahoma. 1970.

Describes no difference in the questioning behaviors of teachers when the purposes of the observations vary among administrative decision making, instructional evaluation, and in-service education.

1597. Larkin, Ralph W. "Research notes: Contextual influences of teacher leadership," *Sociology of Education 46* (1973): 471-479.

Describes the influence of school organizational variables on the leadership style of teachers.

1598. Lichtenstein, Lynn Ellen. The socialization of first year teachers in secondary school. Ph.D. dissertation. University of Illinois at Urbana-Champaign. 1980.

Describes the processes by which first year
secondary teachers are socialized into teaching.

1599.   Loucks, Susan & Melle, Marge. Implementing a
        district-wide science curriculum: The effects of a
        three-year effort. 1980. *ERIC ED* 204 181.

        Describes the effects of a new science
        curriculum and teacher concerns about its use
        related to the level of teacher use of the
        curriculum.

1600.   Marshall, Robert Edward Kessler. The effect of
        classroom organization and teacher-student
        interaction on the distribution of status in the
        classroom. Ph.D. dissertation. University of
        Chicago. 1978.

        Describes differences in the behaviors of
        teachers and students by the degree of
        centralization of the classroom.

1601.   Miklos, Erwin. Organizational structure and teacher
        behavior. 1969. *ERIC ED* 030 963.

        Describes characteristics of influential and
        noninfluential teachers within the structure of
        the school and reviews studies which consider
        influences on the behaviors of teachers.

1602.   Miller, James Lee. A comparison of how first grade
        classroom teachers with and without full time
        teacher aides utilize instructional time and the
        effect of aide utilization upon academic
        performance of children. 1970. *ERIC ED* 043 595.

        Describes no consistent pattern of aide or
        teacher behavior, but teachers with aides do more
        clerical work and more whole-class instruction.

1603.   Miller, Robert Joseph. An investigation of the
        cognitive and affective verbal behavior of
        selected groups of physical science teachers.
        Ph.D. dissertation. University of Texas at Austin.
        1970. *ERIC ED* 107 456.

        Describes different behavior of teachers
        trained and not trained in science with nontrained
        teachers having more consistent verbal behavior
        across years.

1604.   Mitchell, Katherine Ann. "Patterns of
        teacher-student responses to oral reading errors
        as related to teachers' previous training in
        different theoretical frameworks," *Research on*

the Teaching of English 14 (1980): 243-263. Ph.D. dissertation. New York University. 1979.

Describes behavior of teachers in oral reading with remedial students, and some differences by types of teacher training.

1605. Moon, Thomas C. "A study of verbal behavior patterns in primary grade classrooms during science activities," *Journal of Research in Science Teaching 8* (1971): 171-177. Also Ph.D. dissertation. Michigan State University. 1969. *ERIC ED* 043 482.

Describes verbal behavior of science teachers and differences between trained and untrained teachers.

1606. Moore, Jean Ralph. An analysis of teacher and pupil verbal behavior and teacher procedural and evaluative behavior in relation to objectives unique to the PSSC and Non-PSSC physics curricula. Ph.D. dissertation. University of Michigan. 1968.

Describes little difference in the behavior of physics teachers after training in the new curriculum, and the differences related to differences in teacher personality.

1607. Morine-Dershimer, Greta. Teachers' conceptions of pupils--an outgrowth of instructional context: The South Bay Study, Part III. Research Series No. 59. East Lansing, Michigan: Institute for Research on Teaching. Michigan State University. 1979. *ERIC ED* 180 988.

Describes three aspects of instructional context which influence teacher information processing and the concepts which teachers use in thinking about students.

1608. Newport, John & McNeil, Keith. "A comparison of teacher-pupil verbal behaviors evoked by Science--A Process Approach and by textbooks," *Journal of Research in Science Teaching 7* (1970): 191-195.

Describes behaviors of teachers with two types of science instruction materials and some differences by training in use of the innovative science materials.

1609. Olszewski, Ronald W. & Doyle, Walter. "Environmental influences on professional behavior: A case of elementary teaching," *Journal of Research in Education 70* (1976): 55-59.

Describes teachers who are dependent on other teachers, in a team teaching situation, as sharing a greater number of common teaching patterns than do teachers working alone.

1610. Perry, Gail. Cross-cultural study on the effect of space and teacher controlling behavior. *ERIC ED* 131 351.

Describes teachers in classrooms with inadequate space using greater controlling behavior toward students than teachers in classrooms with adequate space.

611. Pflaum, Susanna W. & others. "The influence of pupil behaviors and pupil status factors on teacher behaviors during oral reading lessons," *Journal of Educational research 74* (1980): 99-105.

Reports that pupil behaviors during oral reading have a greater influence on teacher responses than do student characteristics.

1612. Poe, Arthur Maurice. A study of the antecedent and subsequent verbal behaviors of teachers in classrooms exhibiting high and low student-initiated response. Ed.D. dissertation. University of Oregon. 1979.

Describes differences in behaviors of teachers before and after student initiation of interaction in classrooms which have high and low levels of student initiation of interactions.

1613. Porterfield, Denzil Ray. Influence of preparation in Science Curriculum Improvement Study on questioning behavior of selected second and fourth grade reading teachers. Ed.D. dissertation. University of Oklahoma. 1969.

Describes different types of questions asked during reading by teachers trained and not trained in using Science Curriculum Improvement Study materials.

1614. Rubovits, Pamela C. & Maeha, Martin L. "Pygmalion analyzed: Toward an explanation of the Rosenthal-Jacobson findings," *Journal of Personality and Social Psychology 19* (1971): 197-204. *ERIC ED* 048 108.

Describes no differences in the amount but differences in the quality of interaction with students by the IQ information about students which was given to teachers.

1615. Samph, Thomas. "Observer effects on teacher verbal classroom behavior," *Journal of Educational Psychology 68* (1976): 736-741.

Describes teacher behavior as more like teachers' ideal behavior when an observer is present in the classroom.

1616. Samph, Thomas. Observer effects on teacher behavior. Ph.D. dissertation. University of Michigan. 1968. *ERIC ED* 029 843. also under title "Observer effects of teacher verbal classroom behavior," *Journal of Educational Psychology 68* (1976): 736-741.

Describes teacher behavior as more like teacher perceived ideal teacher behavior when an observer is present in the classroom.

1617. Serwer, Blanch L. & Harris, Albert J. How first-grade teachers spend their time teaching language arts to disadvantaged urban youth. 1966. *ERIC ED* 019 195.

Reports that teachers spend different amounts of time on various language arts areas, in accordance with differences in the types of curriculum.

1618. Shapiro, Sylvania. "Preschool ecology: A study of three environmental variables," *Reading Improvement 12* (1975): 236-241. Also Ed.D. dissertation. Columbia University. 1971.

Describes effects of class size, physical space and activity centers on the behavior of teachers and students.

1619. Smith, Howard A. "Nonverbal communication in teaching," *Review of Educational Research 49* (1979): 631-672.

Reviews research on non-verbal communication in terms of environmental factors, proxemics, kinesics, touching behavior, physical characteristics, paralanguage and artifacts.

1620. Solomon, Daniel & Kendall, Arthur J. "Teachers'
       perceptions of and reactions to misbehavior in
       traditional and open classrooms," *Journal of
       Educational Psychology 67* (1975): 528-530.

       Describes differences in teacher reactions to
       student behavior by the setting in which it
       occurs.

1621. Steen, Margaret T. & Lipe, Dewey. Teacher behavior
       in PLAN and control classroom using the PLAN
       Teacher Observation Scale. 1970. *ERIC ED* 045 586.

       Describes differences in the behaviors of
       teachers who had and had not been trained to use
       PLAN instructional materials and procedures.

1622. Stolt, Harold E. An analysis of the individual
       reading conference in the fourth, fifth, and sixth
       grades. 1970. *ERIC ED* 063 607.

       Reports that teachers who had been trained in
       Interaction Analysis and in the use of reading
       conferences exhibited more of the expected
       behaviors during reading conferences with
       students

1623. Streitberger, Horst Eric. Teacher
       influence-behaviors and teacher-student
       interaction patterns in selected Oregon chemistry
       classes. Ph.D. dissertation. Oregon State
       University. 1970.

       Describes no differences in CHEM and
       traditional chemistry classes in teacher behavior,
       with more teacher than student talk in all
       classes.

1624. Strickler, Darryl J. Effects of training with
       "Minicourse 18" on inservice and preservice
       teacher behavior and pupil performance. 1974. *ERIC
       ED* 089 237.

       Describes observed changes in teacher behavior
       after training.

1625. Tardif, Robert F. Modification of the verbal
       behavior of teachers: Its impact on the verbal
       behavior of pupils. 1971. *ERIC ED* 065 457.

       Reports that after observation of their
       teaching and training, teachers changed their
       teaching behaviors.

1626. Tjosvald, Dean & Kastelic, Ted. "Effects of student
       motivation and principal's values on teacher

directiveness," *Journal of Educational Psychology*
68 (1976): 768-774.

Describes the influence of other teacher and
principal attitudes about pupil control on teacher
efforts at student control.

1627. Tovey, Duane R. "Teachers' perceptions of
children's reading miscues," *Reading Horizons 19*
(1979): 302-307.

Describes teacher objections to student reading
miscues related to student dialect.

1628. Townsend, Darryl R. & Zamora, Gloria L. "Differing
interaction patterns in bilingual classrooms,"
Contemporary Education 46 (1975): 196-202.

Describes verbal and nonverbal behavior of
teachers and aides in bilingual classrooms as they
use both languages.

1629. Tuckman, Bruce, Cochran, D. & Travers, E.
Evaluating the open classroom. 1973. *ERIC ED* 080
177.

Describes teachers in open space classrooms as
more flexible in their use of space and classroom
activities and more creative, warm and accepting
than teachers in traditional classrooms.

1630. Turner, Richard L. "The acquisition of teaching
skills in elementary school settings: A research
report," *Indiana University School of Education
Bulletin 41* (1965): 1-94.

Describes relationships between teacher
characteristics and teaching contexts which
influence the extent to which teachers exhibit the
behaviors which they have been trained to use.

1631. Vavrus, M.J. The relationship of teacher alienation
to school workplace characteristics and career
stages of teachers. Research Series No. 36. East
Lansing, Michigan. Institute for Research on
Teaching. Michigan State University. 1979.

Describes teacher alienation from the workplace
and limited believes in opportunities to
participate in decisions within the school and for
professional growth.

1632. Ward, Beatrice A. & Tikunoff, William J. "Utilizing
nonteachers in the instructional process," in
*Classroom management: The 78th Yearbook of the
National Society for the Study of Education.*

Part II. Edited by Daniel L. Duke. pp. 281-300.
Chicago: University of Chicago Press. 1979.

Reports that the use of nonteachers modifies
the roles of students and teachers, including the
distribution and use of authority, assigment of
instructional tasks, monitoring of student
performance and student self-direction. For the
Duke reference see citation No. 2940.

1633.   Wilson, John H. "The 'new' science teachers are
asking more and better questions," *Journal of
Research in Science Teaching* 6 (1969): 49-53.

Describes differences in the questioning
behaviors of science teachers by whether they had
training in innovative teaching methods for
science.

1634.   Wright, Delivee L. Verbal behaviors occurring in
biology classes engaged in inquiry learning. 1973.
ERIC ED 089 942.

Describes differences in the verbal behavior of
teachers in inquiry and non-inquiry teaching
settings.

1635.   Zahorik, John A. "Teacher verbal feedback and
content development," *Journal of Educational
Research* 63 (1970): 419-423.

Describes differences in the types of feedback
which teachers provide to students in the middle
and end phases of lessons and by the purposes of
discussions.

1636.   Zigarmi, P., Goldstein, M. & Rutherford, W.L.
"Implementing a new approach to discipline in a
junior high school: A two-year study of
interventions in a Teacher Corps project," *Journal
of Classroom Interaction 14*, No. 1 (1978): 19-27.

Describes teacher levels of use of a new
discipline approach over two years and relates
levels of use to the efforts of facilitators
working with teachers.

E. REVIEWS

1637. Adams, Raymond S. "A sociological approach to classroom research," In *Research into Classroom Processes: Recent developments* Edited by Ian Westbury & Arno A. Bellack. pp. 101-117. New York: Teachers College Press. 1971.

Describes several studies of research on teaching and summarizes their results. For Westbury & Bellack reference see citation No. 3038.

1638. Amidon, Edmund J. & Hough, John B. (Eds.). *Interaction Analysis: Theory, research and analysis*. Reading, Massachusetts: Addison-Wesley Publishing Company. 1967.

Presents a collection of articles about teacher behaviors, including Amidon & Flanders, citation No. 2282; Amidon & Giammatteo, citation No. 1145; Amidon & Hunter, citation No. 2417; Anderson, citation No. 905; Cogan, citation No. 2701; Flanders, citation No. 1666; Flanders, citation No. 2441; Flanders, citation No. 2568; Furst & Amidon, citation No. 1229; Hough, citation No. 1023; Pankratz, citation No. 1309; and Soar, citation No. 2230.

1639. Amidon, Edmund & Simon, Anita. "Teacher-pupil interaction," *Review of Educational Research 35* (1965): 131-139.

Reviews research to date on the observed behaviors of teachers in classrooms, describing the research methods and the teacher behaviors reported by the studies.

1640. Anastasiow, Nicholas J. "Teaching: The interaction of performance and personality," *Indiana University School of Education Bulletin 45*, No. 4 (1969): 1-46.

Reviews studies of characteristics and behaviors of teachers, specifically as they related to teachers' implementation of innovative programs.

1641.   Atkin, J. Myron & Burnett, R. Will. "Science
        education," In *Encyclopedia of educational
        research.* edited by Robert L. Ebel. pp. 1192-1206.
        Toronto, Canada: The MacMillan Company. 1969.

        Reviews content and methods of science
        education at the elementary, secondary and college
        levels, including a review of studies of the
        teaching of science. For Ebel reference see
        citation No. 2942.

1642.   Balzer, A.L. & others. A review of research on
        teacher behavior relating to science education.
        1973. Columbus, Ohio. ERIC Information Analysis
        Center for Science, Mathematics and Environmental
        Education. *ERIC ED* 087 638.

        Reviews studies of science teacher behaviors,
        systems for observing teacher behavior during
        science instruction, and studies of behaviors of
        teachers of other subjects.

1643.   Balzer, LeVon. Review, appraisal, and
        recommendations concerning research on classroom
        behavior in science. 1970. *ERIC ED* 059 874.

        Reviews twenty studies of science teaching,
        with a focus on teacher behaviors and the
        consistency of behaviors across teachers,
        classroom settings and the nature of the science
        training of the teachers.

1644.   Beisenharg, Paul C. Research in teacher questioning
        behavior: Past, present, and future. 1972. *ERIC
        ED* 074 051.

        Reviews studies of teacher questioning,
        describing both methods of study and results of
        the research.

1645.   Biddle, B.J., Jameson, R.E., Kang, J. & Marcus,
        F.M. A bibliography on the role of the teacher.
        Technical Report No. 27. Columbia, Missouri:
        University of Missouri-Columbia.

        Reviews studies of the role of the teacher, in
        terms of instructional and other tasks.

1646.   Blosser, Patricia E. Review of research: Teacher
        questioning behavior in science classrooms. 1979.
        Columbus, Ohio. ERIC Information Analysis Center
        for Science, Mathematics and Environmental
        Education. *ERIC ED* 184 818.

Reviews studies and concludes that science teacher questions are primarily at the cognitive-memory level and that teachers vary by the grade level at which they teach in their receptivity to training in different questioning behaviors.

1647. Braddock, Richard. "English composition," In *Encyclopedia of educational research.* Edited by Robert L. Ebel. pp. 443-461. Toronto, Canada: The MacMillan Company. 1969.

Reviews the history of teaching English composition, aspects of curriculum, and research on teaching and learning composition. For Ebel reference see citation No. 2942.

1648. Brooks, Douglas M. "Ethnographic analysis of instructional methods," *Theory into Practice 19* (1980): 144-147.

Essay reviews research and concludes that teaching behaviors can be defined at various levels of specificity.

1649. Brophy, Jere E. & Putnam, Joyce G. "Classroom management in the elementary grades," In *Classroom management: The 78th yearbook of the National Society for the Study of Education. Part II.* Edited by Daniel L. Duke, pp. 182-216. Chicago: University of Chicago Press. 1978. Research Series No. 32. East Lansing, Michigan: Institute for Research on Teaching. Michigan State University. 1978.

Describes classroom management, including classroom climate and group management, citing relevant research. For Duke reference see citation No. 2940.

1650. Bush, Robert N. & Gage, N.L. Center for Research and Development in Teaching. 1968. *ERIC ED* 026 297.

Describes prior research at the Center, including observations of teacher behaviors, teacher personality variables inferred from test results, and the institutional variables which influence teaching, such as social, technological and administrative areas.

1651. Carver, Fred D. & Sergiovanni, Thomas J. (Eds.) *Organization and human behavior: Focus on schools.* New York: McGraw-Hill Book Company. 1969.

Presents a collection of readings on human
behavior in schools and factors which influence
such behavior.

1652.   Cazden Courtney B. Learning to read in classroom
        interaction. 1976. *ERIC ED* 155 654.

        Reviews observational studies of teacher
        behaviors in early reading instructin.

1653.   Cohen, Elizabeth G., Intili, Jo-Ann K. & Robbins,
        Susan Hurevitz. "Task and authority: A
        sociological view of classroom management," In
        *Classroom management: The 78th yearbook of the
        Natonal Society for the Study of Education. Part
        II.* Edited by Daniel L. Duke. pp. 116-143.
        Chicago: University of Chicago Press. 1979.

        Discusses order and management in relation to
        the task complexity in classrooms and describes a
        concept of management and changes in the teacher
        role, citing relevant research. For Duke
        reference see citation No. 2940.

1654.   Corno, Lynn "Classroom instruction and the matter
        of time," In *Classroom management: The 78th
        yearbook of the National Society for the Study of
        Education. Part II.* Edited by Daniel L. Duke. pp.
        245-280. Chicago: University of Chicago Press.
        1979.

        Describes studies of time use and conceptions
        of the role of time in instruction, including
        student engagement. For Duke reference see
        citation No. 2940.

1655.   Dessart, Donald J. & Frandsen, Henry. "Research on
        teaching secondary-school mathematics," In *Second
        handbook of research on teaching.* Edited by Robert
        M.W. Travers. pp. 1177-1195. Chicago: Rand McNally
        & Company. 1973.

        Reviews studies of secondary mathematics
        instruction with a major focus on students and a
        brief review of the use of student and teacher
        time. For Travers reference see citation No.
        3033.

1656.   Doyle, Walter. "Making managerial decisions in
        classrooms," In *Classroom management: The 78th
        yearbook of the National Society for the Study of
        Education, Part II.* Edited by Daniel L. Duke. pp.
        42-74. Chicago: University of Chicago Press.
        1979.

Describes the structure, tasks and activities of the classroom, including teacher information processing, teacher classroom knowledge as it relates to planning and monitoring classroom activities, with citations of relevant research. For Duke reference see citation No. 2940.

1657. Dreeben, Robert. "The school as a workplace," In *Second handbook of research on teaching.* Edited by Robert M.W. Travers. pp. 450-473. Chicago: Rand McNally & Company. 1973.

Reviews research on aspects of the work of teachers, including the power and authority arrangements and the workplace, the classroom. For Travers reference see citation No. 3033.

1658. Dwyer, Carol A. "Sex differences in reading: An evaluation and a critique of current theories," *Review of Educational Research 43* (1973): 455-467.

Reviews research on sex differences including a review of studies of differences in teacher interactions with girls and boys.

1659. Emmer, Edmund T. & Evertson, Carolyn M. "Synthesis of research on classroom management," *Educational Leadership 38* (1981): 342-343, 345-347.

Review indicates that important instruction in classroom procedures and expectations for student behavior occurs during the first weeks of the school year. Included because of nontechnical discussion of research results.

1660. Emmer, E.T., Good, T.L., & Pilgrim, G.H. Effects of teacher sex. Austin, Texas: Research and Development Center for Teacher Education. University of Texas at Austin. 1972

Reviews research on the effects of teacher sex on interactions with students in the classroom.

1661. ERIC abstracts: A collection of ERIC document resumes on evaluating teacher effectiveness. ERIC Abstracts Series No. 20. ERIC Clearinghouse on Educational Administration. 1971. *ERIC ED* 055 311.

Presents an annotated bibliography of ERIC documents on teacher evaluation.

1662. Flesenthal, Helen. Factors affecting reading achievement. Philadelphia, Pennsylvania: Research for Better Schools, Inc. 1978.

Describes several factors, including teacher
behaviors, which correlate with student learning.

1663. Findley, Warren G. Effective use of teacher time in
the elementary school--teaching assistant, teacher
aides, etc., Abstracts of research pertaining to.
1966. *ERIC ED* 017 051.

Summarizes each of fourteen research reports on
effective use of teacher time and use of aides
from 1960-1964.

1664. Finkelstein, Barbara Joan. Governing the young:
Teacher behavior in American primary schools.
1820-1880. A documentary history. Ed.D.
dissertation. Columbia University. 1970.

Describes teachers during the period from 1820
to 1880 as educators and disciplinarians.

1665. Flanders, Ned A. *Analyzing teaching behavior.*
Reading, Massachusetts: Addison-Wesley Publishing
Company. 1970. Reprinted from *Theory and Research
in Teaching.* Edited by A. A. Bellack. New York:
Teachers College Press. 1963.

Describes the process of observing teacher and
student behavior using Flanders Interaction
Analysis and discusses conceptions of teaching,
variations in teaching behaviors, and reviews some
studies of teacher effectiveness.

1666. Flanders, Ned A. "Teacher influence in the
classroom," In *Interaction Analysis: Theory,
research and analysis.* Edited by Edmund J. Amidon
& John B. Hough. pp. 103-116. Reading,
Massachusetts: Addison-Wesley Publishing Company.
1967. Also printed in *The nature of teaching: A
collection of readings.* Edited by Lois N. Nelson.
Waltham, Mass.: Blaisdell Publishing Company.
1969.

Reviews studies of teachers behaviors which
create the climate in the classroom and studies
of direct and indirect teaching behaviors. For
Amidon & Hough reference see citation No. 1368.
For Nelson reference see citation No. 2997.

1667. Fuller,, Frances F. & others. Creating climates for
growth. Austin, Texas: Center for Research and
Development for Teacher Education. Texas
University at Austin. *ERIC ED* 013 989.

Reviews studies and describes teacher concerns
about themselves, teaching, methods for dealing

with student problems, methods for collecting
information about students, for using classroom
resources and seeking help from the
administration.

1668. Gage, N.L. (Ed.). NIE conference on studies in
teaching: Panel 3, Teaching as behavioral
analysis. Washington, D.C.: National Institute of
Education. 1974. *ERIC ED* 111 804.

Presents results of a panel of researchers
convened to discuss the status of knowledge about
research on teacher behaviors and directions for
future research.

1669. Gage, N.L. (Ed.). NIE conference on studies in
teaching: Panel 4, Teaching as skill performance.
Washington, D.C.: National Institute of Education.
1974. *ERIC ED* 111 805.

Presents results of a panel of researchers
convened to discuss the status of knowledge about
teaching as the performance of a set of skills and
directions for future research.

1670. Gage, N.L. (Ed.). NIE conference on studies in
teaching: Panel 5, Teaching as a linguistic
process in a cultural setting. Washington, D.C.:
National Institute of Education. 1974. *ERIC ED*
111 806.

Presents results of a panel of researchers
convened to discuss the status of knowledge about
the linguistic aspects of teaching and the effects
of the culture of the school and the cultures of
teachers and students and directions for future
research.

1671. Gage, N.L. (Ed.). NIE conference on studies in
teaching: Panel 6, Teaching as clinical
information processing. Washington, D.C.: National
Institute of Education. 1974. *ERIC ED* 111 807.

Presents results of a panel of researchers
convened to discuss the status of knowledge about
the information processing of teachers and the
decisions which teachers make and the directions
of future research.

1672. Gage, N.L. (Ed.). NIE conference on studies in
teaching: Panel 7, Instructional personnel
utilization. Washington, D.C.: National Institute
of Education. 1974. *ERIC ED* 111 808.

Presents results of a panel of researchers
convened to discuss the status of knowledge about
the roles and uses of multiple personnel and
directions of future research.

1673.   Gage, N.L. "Teaching methods," In *Encyclopedia of
educational research*. Edited by Robert L. Ebel.
pp. 1446-1458. Toronto, Canada: The MacMillan
Company. 1969.

Describes studies of various methods of
teaching, including observational studies of
teacher behaviors and reviews of these studies.
For Ebel reference see citation No. 2942.

1674.   Gage, N.L. (Ed.). *The psychology of teaching
methods: 75th yearbook of the National Society for
the Study of Education. Part I.* Chicago:
University of Chicago Press. 1976.

Chapters dealing with the psychology and
learning basis for teaching, specific methods, a
review of research on teaching and a discussion
teacher decision making, including Rosenshine,
citation No. 2483 and Shavelson, citation No.
1459.

1675.   Gallagher, James J., Nuthall, Graham A. &
Rosenshine, Barak. *Classroom observation.* American
Educational Research Association Monograph on
Curriculum Evaluation. Chicago: Rand McNally &
Company. 1970.

Presents a series of articles and reprints of
studies using classroom observation methods,
instruments, analysis procedures, including
Gallagher, citation No. 1231 and Nuthall, 1689.

1676.   Gil, Doron, Hoffmeyer, E., Van Roekel, J. &
Weinshank, A. Clinical problem solving in reading
theory and research. Research Series No. 45. East
Lansing, Michigan: Institute for Research on
Teaching. Michigan State University. *ERIC ED* 179
914.

Describes a number of studies, including
classroom observations and simulations, which
describe teacher behaviors while addressing
problems in reading instruction.

1677.   Goodlad, John J. & Shane, Harold G. (Eds.). *The
elementary school in the United States: the 72nd
yearbook of the National Society for the Study of
Education. Part II.* Chicago: University of Chicago
Press. 1973.

Presents a series of articles on aspects of elementary schools, including Morine & Morine, citation No. 1688.

1678. Gordon, Ira J. & Jester, R. Emile. "Techniques of observing teaching in early childhood and outcomes of particular procedures," In *Second handbook of research on teaching*. Edited by Robert M.W. Travers. pp. 184-217. Chicago: Rand McNally & Company. 1973.

Describes various methods for observing in classrooms and presents results of studies using the various techniques to observe classroom interactions. For Travers reference see citation No. 3033.

1679. Hanley, Edward M. "Review of research involving applied behavior analysis in the classroom," *Review of Educational Research 49* (1970): 597-625.

Reviews studies of teacher behavior in which teacher behaviors are changed by applying principles of behavior modification, and results of such attempts to change teacher behaviors.

1680. Harvard University. Bibliography on teaching. Supplement. Cambridge, Massachusetts: Harvard University. 1966. *ERIC ED* 011 306.

Presents a bibliography of documents from 1960 to 1966 in a number of areas, including teacher evaluation, games and teaching materials, not annotated.

1681. Howard, Norma K. (Comp.). Discipline and behavior: An abstract bibliography. Urbana, Illinois: ERIC Clearinghouse on Early Childhood Education. 1974. *ERIC ED* 092 243.

Presents an annotated bibliography of ERIC documents on discipline and the use of behavior modification techniques in teaching.

1682. Kliebard, Herbert M. The observation of classroom behavior--Some recent research. Washington, D.C.: Association for Supervision and Curriculum Development. Reprinted in *The way teaching is*. Washington, D.C.: Association for Supervision and Curriculum Development. pp. 45-76. 1965. *ERIC ED* 028 112. Related citations are *ERIC ED* 003 273; 015 164; 003 285.

Reviews six recent studies of teaching and summarizes the results to describe the behaviors

of teachers and students in the classroom.   For
Association for Supervision and Curriculum
Development reference see citation No. 2905.

1683. Kounin, Jacob S. *Discipline and group management in
classrooms.* New York: Holt, Rinehart and Winston,
Inc. 1970.

Describes studies of classroom management at
all levels of education and several variables
which define effective management, such as
withitness, overlapping and group alerting.

1684. McCaleb, Joseph L. & White, Jacqueline A. "Critical
dimensions in evaluating teacher clarity," *Journal
of Classroom Interaction 15*, No. 2 (1980): 27-30.

Reviews studies of teacher clarity which reveal
that clarity is composed of understanding,
structuring, sequencing, explaining and
presenting.

1685. Massialas, Byron G. "Citizenship and political
socialization," In *Encyclopedia of educational
research.* Edited by Robert L. Ebel. pp. 124-141.
Toronto, Canada: The MacMillan Company. 1969.

Discusses, within a review of student
development of knowledge and attitudes, and the
influences on that development, studies of teacher
presentation of political views in the classroom.
For Ebel reference see citation No. 2942.

1686. Mathieson, Moira B. Beginning teachers in the inner
city: A study of the literature on their problems
and some possible solutions. 1971 *ERIC ED* 050
028.

Reviews research and other literature on the
problems faced by beginning teachers and ways to
resolve those problems.

1687. Medley, Donald M. & Crook, Patricia R. "Research in
teacher competency and teaching tasks," *Theory
into Practice 19* (1980): 294-301.

Reviews studies and identifies five tasks which
teachers perform: maintaining pupil task
involvement, teaching in large groups, minimizing
disruptive pupil behavior, managing small group
activity, and supervising pupil seatwork.

1688. Morine, Greta & Morine, Harold. "Teaching," In *The
elementary school in the United States: The 72nd
yearbook of the National Society for the Study*

of Education. Part II. Edited by John J. Goodlad & Harold G. Shane. pp. 272-298. Chicago: University of Chicago Press. 1973.

Discusses instructional roles of teachers as systems manager, model, reporter, problem solver, counselor, and some research related to those roles. For Goodlad reference see citation No. 1677.

1689.   Nuthall, G.A. "A review of some selected recent studies of classroom interaction and teaching behavior," In *Classroom observation.* American Educational Research Association Monograph Series on Curriculum Evaluation. Edited by James J. Gallagher, Graham A. Nuthall, & Barak Rosenshine. pp. 6-29. Chicago: Rand McNally & Company. 1970. Reprinted from *New Zealand Journal of Educational Studies 3*, No. 2 (1968).

Reviews types of observation systems and studies which describe differences in teacher verbal behavior by grade, subject, and within the same curriculum. For Gallagher, Nuthall & Rosenshine reference see citation No. 1675.

1690.   Peltier, Gary L. "Sex differences in the school: Problem and proposed solution," *Phi Delta Kappan 50* (1968): 182-185.

Essay cites some studies of the differences in behaviors of boys and girls and of teachers toward girls and boys.

1691.   Power, Colin. "A critical review of science classroom interaction studies," *Studies in Science Education 4* (1977): 1: 30.

Reviews studies of teacher behaviors during science instruction, with a summary of results and critique of methods.

1692.   Rashid, Martha & others. The teacher, teacher style, and classroom management. Proceedings of the Head Start Research Seminars; Seminar No. 2, The teacher and classroom management (Washington, D.C. 1968). Princeton, New Jersey: Educational Testing Service. 1968. *ERIC ED* 035 463.

Reviews studies of teacher classroom management and discusses areas needing further study, with bibliography.

1693.   Riedesel, C. Alan & Burns, Paul C. "Research on the
        teaching of elementary-school mathematics," In
        Second handbook of research on teaching. Edited by
        Robert M.W. Travers. pp. 1149-1176. Chicago: Rand
        McNally & Company. 1973.

        Reviews studies of elementary school
        mathematics dealing with the learner, the
        curriculum and teaching, including the use of time
        and teaching strategies.   For Travers reference
        see citation No. 3033.

1694.   Rudman, H.C., Kelly, J.L., Wanous, D.S., Mehrens,
        W.A., Clark, C.M. & Porter, A.C. Integrating
        assessment with instruction: A review (1922-1980):
        Research Series No. 75. East Lansing, Michigan:
        Institute for Research on Teaching. Michigan State
        University. 1980.

        Describes limited research about teacher
        attitudes toward and use of information about
        students from various types of tests.

1695.   Ryans, David G. "Teacher behavior can be
        evaluated," In *The evaluation of teaching.*
        Washington, D.C.: Pi Lambda Theta. 1967.

        Describes assumptions about teacher behavior
        which influence the conditions under which it is
        evaluated and reviews studies which describe
        teacher behavior.   For Pi Lambda Theta reference
        see citation No. 3003.

1696.   Ryans, David G. "Teacher behavior theory and
        research: Implications for teacher education," In
        Teaching: Vantage points for study. Edited by
        Ronald T. Hyman. pp. 32-43. Philadelphia: T.B.
        Lippincott Company. 1968. Reprinted from *Journal
        of Teacher Education 14* (1963): 274-293.

        Discusses teacher behavior in terms of the
        processing of information and describes the
        Teacher Characteristics Study in terms of teacher
        uses of information.   For Hyman reference see
        citation No. 2973.

1697.   Shavelson, Richard J. The theory of directed
        graphs: Some applications to research on teaching.
        Stanford, California: Stanford Center for Research
        and Development in Teaching. Stanford University.
        1971. *ERIC ED* 049 192.

        Describes a theory of information processing
        and relates that theory to selected studies of
        teaching.

1698. Spady, William G. & Mitchell, Douglas E. "Authority
        and the management of classroom activities," In
        *Classroom management: The 78th yearbook of the
        National Society for the Study of Education. Part
        II.* Edited by Daniel L. Duke. pp. 75-115. Chicago:
        University of Chicago Press. 1979.

        Describes models of classroom management and
        use of authority within the goal structure of
        schools, citing relevant research. For Duke
        reference see citation No. 2940.

1699. Vinsonhaler, J.F., Wagner, C.C. & Elstein, A. The
        inquiry theory: An information-processing approach
        to clinical problem-solving research and
        application. Research Series No. 1. East Lansing,
        Michigan: Institute for Research on Teaching.
        Michigan State University. 1978.

        Review synthesizes research on clinical problem
        solving in terms of measurement of problem-solving
        performance, clinical simulation and case
        simulation.

1700. Wang, Margaret C. (Ed.). *The use of direct
        observation to study instructional-learning
        behaviors in school settings.* Pittsburgh,
        Pennsylvania: Learning Research and Development
        Center. Pittsburgh University & The Ford
        Foundation. 1974. *ERIC ED* 100 798.

        Describes the processes of observing in
        classrooms and studies of teacher and student
        behaviors.

1701. Wisniewski, Richard. *New teachers in urban schools:
        An inside view.* New York: Random House. 1968.

        Presents a collection of articles about urban
        education, including two reports of first year
        teaching in an urban high school.

V INFLUENCE OF TEACHER BEHAVIOR

A. ON STUDENT SELF-CONCEPT

1702. Albert, Raymond Patrick. Self-esteem of the
        elementary school child as affected by
        teacher-pupil conferences. Ed.D. dissertation.
        Northern Illinois University. 1970.

        Describes no difference in the self-concept of
        students whose teachers were trained to conduct
        student conferences.

1703. Ascione, F.R. & Borg, W.R. "Effects of a training
        program on teacher behavior and handicapped
        children's self-concepts," *Journal of Psychology*
        104 (1980): 53-75.

        Describes the behaviors of teachers, changes in
        behaviors after training, and the effects of
        teacher behaviors on student self-concept.

1704. Bartch, Marian R. The influence of teacher-led
        discussion of children's reading on children's
        self-concept development. Ph.D. dissertation.
        University of Toledo. 1974.

        Reports that teacher-led discussions influence
        student self-concept in terms of academic
        abilities but not in other areas of self-concept.

1705. Brody, Gene H. & Zimmerman, Barry J. "The effects
        of modeling and classroom organization on the
        personal space of third and fourth grade
        children," *American Educational Research Journal*
        12 (1975): 157-168.

        Describes a relationship between teacher
        behavior and classroom organization and children's
        sense of personal space.

1706. Burrows, Richard Charles. The effect of level of
        teacher approval on student disruptive behavior
        and self concept. Ph.D. dissertation. University
        of Washington. 1971.

Describes variations in teacher approval in an experiment not related to changes in student self-concept.

1707.   Cross, Lawrence H. & Cross, Gail M. "Teachers' evaluative comments and pupil perception of control," *Journal of Experimental Education 49* (1980): 68-70.

Reports that when teachers provided written comments on tests and assignments students had a greater sense of internal locus of control.

1708.   Dawson, Paul. Fatherless boys, teacher perceptions, and male teacher influence: A pilot study. Final Report. 1971. *ERIC ED* 048 616.

Describes better social and emotional development, self confidence, feelings of worth, ability to accept responsibility, for fatherless boys with male teachers.

1709.   Deci, Edward L., Sheinman, Louis, Wheeler, Lynne & Hart, Robert. "Rewards, motivation, and self-esteem," *Educational Forum 44* (1980): 429-433.

Describes a strong relationship between teacher style of rewards and control and student perceptions of their own competence and student intrinsic motivation.

1710.   Del Polito, Carolyn M. Teacher communication in the classroom: Effects on student self-concept. 1980. *ERIC ED* 184 148.

Reviews the effects of teacher communication on student self-concept.

1711.   Doebler, L.K. & Eicke, F.J. "Effects of teacher awareness of the educational implication of field-dependent/field-independent cognitive style on selected classroom variables," *Journal of Educational Psychology 71* (1979): 226-232.

Reports that when teachers received information about student and teacher cognitive style and training in implications for education, the students of those teachers showed increased self-concept and attitude toward school, compared with students of other teachers.

1712.   Evertson, Carolyn M., Anderson, Charles W., Anderson, Linda M. & Brophy, Jere E. "Relationships between classroom behaviors and student outcomes in junior high mathematics and English classes," *American Educational Research Journal 17* (1980): 43-60.

Describes behaviors of teachers related to student achievement in mathematics, but no consistent pattern of relations in English classes.

1713. Fagan, Michael John. Student, teacher and classroom level variables as determinants of self concept among elementary school students. Ph.D. dissertation. University of Toronto, Canada. 1980.

Describes a limited relationship between teacher and classroom variables and student self-concept.

1714. Hogan, Ermon O. & Green, Robert L. "Can teachers modify children's self-concepts?" *Teachers College Record 72* (1971): 423-426.

Reports a greater increase in student self-concept for control students than for students of teachers who had been trained to support student self-concept.

1715. Kash, M.M. & Borich, G.D. *Teacher behavior and pupil self-concept.* Reading, Massachusetts: Addison Wesley Publishing Company. 1978.

Describes the process of development of students' self-concept and reviews research on effects of teacher behavior on students' self-concept.

1716. King, Martha, Wolf, Willavene, Huck, Charlotte, Ellinger, Bernice & Gansneder, B. Observations of teacher-pupil verbal behavior during critical reading lessons. 1967. *ERIC ED* 011 819.

Reports that teacher level of question and expectations for student response are related to the level of student response.

1717. Morris, Joseph Ridell. Teacher-pupil classroom interaction and the relationship to the self-concept. Ph.D. dissertation. University of Michigan. 1975.

Describes a non-significant trend for teacher verbal behavior to be related to student self-concept and changes in student self-concept to result in changes in teacher behavior.

1718. Nummela, Renate Margarete. The relationship of
       teacher-effectiveness training to pupil
       self-concept, locus of control and attitude. Ph.D.
       dissertation. University of Florida. 1978.

           Reports greater student self-concept and
       attitude but no difference in locus of control for
       students of teachers who received training in
       effective teaching behaviors.

1719. Poris, Marilyn Abby. The relationships among
       specific teacher behaviors, student self-concept,
       and student divergent production. Ph.D.
       dissertation. Hofstra University. 1977.

           Reports that greater teacher affective behavior
       is related to increased student self-concept and
       divergent production in grades three through six.

1720. Soar, Robert S. & Soar, Ruth M. "Pupil subject
       matter growth during summer vacation," *Educational
       Leadership 26* (1969): 577-587.

           Describes different patterns of behavior of
       teachers associated with student achievement
       during the school year and continued gains in
       achievement over the summer vacation.

1721. St. John, Nancy. "Thirty-six teachers: Their
       characteristics, and outcomes for black and white
       pupils," *American Educational Research Journal 8*
       (1971): 635-648. *ERIC ED* 048 101.

           Describes different relationships between
       teacher behavior and student self-concept for
       black and white students.

1722. Van Horn, Royal W. "Effects of the use of four
       types of teaching models on student self-concept
       of academic ability and attitude toward the
       teacher," *American Educational Research Journal
       13* (1976): 285-291.

           Describes differences in student self-concept
       of academic ability but not attitude toward the
       teacher by differences in teacher teaching style.

1723. Woolfolk, Robert Lee, IV. The effects of
       systematically varied teacher verbal and nonverbal
       evaluative behavior upon student perceptions and
       attitudes. Ph.D. dissertation. University of Texas
       at Austin. 1972.

           Reports no differences in student self-esteem
       by types of teacher evaluative comments.

B. ON STUDENT BEHAVIOR

1724. Alderman, Terry Wayne. The relationship between affective teacher behavior and teacher ability to modify the behavior of students through the use of approval. Ed.D. Dissertation. University of Tennessee. 1979.

Describes teachers low in affective behavior having greater influence on student behavior through the use of approval and describes changes in teacher behavior.

1725. Anderson, Lorin W. & Scott, Corinne C. "The relationship among teaching methods, student characteristics, and student involvement in learning," *Journal of Teacher Education 29*, No. 3 (1978): 52-57.

Describes differences in patterns of student on-task behavior for different types of students in high schools with different teaching methods.

1726. Ankney, Robert Francis. Effects of classroom spatial arrangement on student behavior. Ph.D. Dissertation. Ohio State University. 1974.

Describes more on-task behavior of retarded students but no differences in teacher-student interactions with seats in a horseshoe rather than in rows.

1727. Arnold, Daniel S., Atwood, Ronald, & Rogers, Virginia M. "Question and response levels and lapse time intervals," *Journal of Experimental Education 43* (1974): 11-15.

Describes differences in wait time by the cognitive level of teacher question but not a direct increase in wait time with higher level questions, and a relationship of level of question and level of student response.

1728. Arnold, Daniel S. & others. "An investigation of relationships among question level, response level and lapse time, *School Science and Mathematics 73* (1973): 591-594.

317

Describes teacher level of questions and wait
time related to the cognitive level of student
responses.

1729. Aronson, Elliot, & others. *The Jigsaw classroom*.
       Beverly Hills, California: Sage Publications.
       1978.

       Describes changes in classroom structure, with
       children in groups and group tasks resulting in
       changes in teacher and student behavior.

1730. Aschwald, Howard Bernard. Some relationships
       between teacher cognitive verbal behavior and
       student cognitive verbal response in secondary
       school social studies classes. Ph.D. dissertation.
       University of Oregon. 1969.

       Describes the cognitive level of teacher
       questions and information related to the level of
       student questions and statements, with no
       relationship between teacher indirectness and the
       cognitive level of student statements.

1731. Aspy, David N. & Roebuck, Flora N. "The
       relationship of teacher-offered conditions of
       meaning to behaviors described by Flanders
       Interaction Analysis," *Education 95* (1975):
       216-222.

       Describes teacher empathy as related to student
       involvement in tasks.

1732. Atyeo, Marilyn J. "The influence of an adult model
       on behavior and attitudes of young children,"
       Journal of Educational Research 66 (1972):
       147-149.

       Describes teacher behavior toward the least
       preferred doll resulting in changes in the
       behavior of preschool children in selecting
       dolls.

1733. Ayllon, T. & McCullen, G. Academic objectives in
       classroom management. Atlanta: Georgia State
       University. 1970. *ERIC ED* 059 510.

       Describes a study of teacher behavior related
       to student disruptive behavior and increases in
       student and teacher academic work in special class
       settings.

1734. Balzer, LeVon. "Teacher behaviors and student
       inquiry in biology," *American Biology Teacher 32*
       (1970): 26-28.

Describes a relationship between teacher
behavior and student inquiry, with teacher
behavior limiting student inquiry.

1735.   Barbour, Nita Hale. "Relationship of change in
        child language to nursery school climate as
        determined by teacher verbal behavior," *Probe 1*,
        No. 6 (1974): 52-54. Also Ph.D. dissertation.
        University of Maryland. 1973.

Describes a relationship between teacher
directive verbal behavior and greater complexity
in student language.

1736.   Barbour, Nita Hale. Teacher verbal behavior and its
        relationship to growth in child language. *ERIC ED*
        133 087.

Describes a greater change in student use of
complex sentences with teachers using directive
verbal behavior.

1737.   Bartlett, Carol Ann Hansen. The effects of oral
        reading of literature by teachers on the reading
        attitudes of fourth-grade students. Ed.D.
        dissertation. University of Northern Colorado.
        1980.

Describes no effects on attitudes of boys and
girls toward reading of teachers' reading to
students.

1738.   Beatty, Michael J. & Behnke, Ralph R. "Teacher
        credibility as a function of verbal contents and
        paralinguistic cues," *Communication Quarterly 28*
        (1980): 55-59.

Describes a relationship between teacher vocal
cues and verbal message and teacher credibility to
students.

1739.   Bell, Michael L. & Davidson, Charles W.
        "Relationships between pupil-on-task-performance
        and pupil achievement," *Journal of Educational
        Research 69* (1976): 172-176.

Describes differences in the behaviors of
teachers in classrooms where the relationship
between pupil-on-task-performance was and was not
statistically significant.

1740.   Blattstein, A. & Peck, R.F. Teachers do affect
        student self-esteem--but so do the students.
        Austin, Texas: Research and Development Center for
        Teacher Education. Texas University at Austin.
        1979.

        Describes a relationship between teacher
behavior and student attitude, which varied by
student characteristics.

1741.   Blue, Terry W. The effect of written and oral
        student evaluation feedback and selected teacher
        and student demographic and descriptive variables
        on the attitudes and ratings of teachers and
        students. 1977. *ERIC ED* 135 855.

        Describes teacher and student characteristics
        as related to the effects of teacher feedback to
        students on student attitudes.

1742.   Bollinger, G. Kip. The effect of teachers'
        behaviors on biology students' development of
        positive science attitudes. Ed.D. dissertation.
        Temple University. 1979.

        Describes a relationship between teacher
        behavior and student attitude toward science based
        on observations of teacher behavior.

1743.   Borg, W.R. & Ascione, F.R. "Changing on-task,
        off-task, and disruptive pupil behavior in
        elementary mainstreaming classrooms," *Journal of
        Educational Research 72* (1979): 243-252.

        Describes the effects of teacher behaviors and
        management approaches on student behavior.

1744.   Borg, Walter R. & others. "Teacher classroom
        management skills and pupil behavior." *Journal of
        Experimental Education 44* No. 2 (1975): 52-58.

        Describes a relationship between teacher
        training based on materials designed to change
        teacher behavior and changes in student on-task
        and disruptive behavior.

1745.   Bossert, Steven T. *Tasks and social relationships
        in classrooms.* New York: Cambridge University
        Press. 1979.

        Describes behaviors of teachers and the
        influence of teacher behaviors and the patterns of
        interactions which teachers establish on the
        behaviors of students.

1746.   Broden, Marcia, Bruce, Carl, Mitchell, Mary Ann,
        Carter, Virginia, & Hall, R. Vance. "Effects of
        teacher attention on attending behavior of two
        boys at adjacent desks," *Journal of Applied
        Behavior Analysis 3* (1970): 205-211.

Describes reinforcing behavior of teachers for pupil attending behavior and resulting changes in the attending behavior of two disruptive second-grade boys.

1747. Brogan, Joseph John. Teacher behavior, classroom verbal interaction, and pupils' science interest and achievement: An investigation of teacher effectiveness in high school biology and chemistry teaching using the Flanders method of Interaction Analysis and a pupil science inventory with experimentally adjusted contrasting classroom climates. Ph.D. dissertation. New York University. 1971.

Describes no differences in the behavior of teachers in science and chemistry classrooms and a relationship between teacher indirect behavior and student interest in science.

1748. Brooks, Douglas M. & Bowers, Norman D. The relationship between teacher nonverbal behaviors and selected teacher-pupil attitudes and behaviors. Ph.D. dissertation. Northwestern University. 1974. *ERIC ED* 104 888.

Describes teacher nonverbal behavior and its relationship to student attitude toward school.

1749. Brophy, J.E. & Senior, K. "Praise and group competition as motivating incentives for children," *Psychological Reports 32* (1973): 951-958.

Describes relationships between both teacher praise and use of competition and student motivation for academic tasks.

1750. Bruni, Stephanie Leeds. The class and them: Social interaction of handicapped children in integrated primary classes. Ph.D. dissertation. Syracuse University. 1980.

Describes the influence of teacher interventions and teacher assignments of seats and control of aspects of the classroom on the interactions between retarded and normal children in primary classrooms.

1751. Buys, Christian J. "Effects of teacher reinforcement on elementary pupils' behavior and attitudes," *Psychology in the Schools 9* (1972): 278-288.

Describes changes in behavior of teachers toward disruptive students resulting in changes in the behavior and attitudes of the students.

1752. Chesney, Barbara Haack. Relationships among teacher-student conceptual tempo compatibility, student attitude toward school, and student attitude toward the self. Ph.D. dissertation. Case Western Reserve University. 1970.

Describes no relationship between student and teacher tempo and student attitude toward school and self.

1753. Clay, Marie M. Theoretical research and instructional change: A case study. Pittsburgh, Pennsylvania: Learning Research and Development Center. University of Pittsburgh. *ERIC ED* 155 629.

Describes the behavior of teachers and students as teachers guide student learning and as students develop self-limiting and self-improving strategies for learning to read, in New Zealand.

1754. Coleman, Lee Murphy. Behavioral contrast between classrooms. Ph.D. dissertation. University of Georgia. 1975.

Describes a change in teacher behavior in one class resulting in a change in the behavior of the students in that class in the next teacher's classroom.

1755. Cooper, Margaret & Thomson, Carolyn. The observation of reinforcement behavior of teachers in Head Start classrooms and the modification of a teacher's attending behaviors. Report No. 1. Lawrence, Kansas: Head Start Evaluation and Research Center. University of Kansas. 1967. *ERIC ED* 021 633.

Describes changes in teacher behavior in attending to and reinforcing student behavior and changes in student behavior.

1756. Cormier, William Henry. Effects of teacher random and contingent social reinforcement on the classroom behavior of adolescents. Ed.D. dissertation. University of Tennessee. 1969.

Describes an experiment in which different student behavior resulted from different teacher reinforcement of student behavior.

1757. Cormier, William H. & Wahler, Robert G. The application of social reinforcement in six junior high school classrooms. 1971. *ERIC ED* 051 109.

   Describes the use of contingent praise and ignoring of inappropriate behavior with eighth grade students and the effects of changes in teacher behaviors.

1758. Crockenberg, Susan & Bryant, Brenda. Helping and sharing behavior in cooperative and competitive classrooms. 1973. *ERIC ED* 081 497.

   Describes teacher behavior as related to student behavior and attitudes in classrooms characterized as cooperative and competitive.

1759. Cunningham, William G. "The impact of student-teacher pairings on student orientation toward school related tasks," *Journal of Educational Research 68* (1975): 378-381.

   Describes the greater impact on student task orientation of one particular type of teacher with one type of student.

1760. Daily, Frances M. & Phillips, James A., Jr. Teacher verbal behavior and classroom social structure. *ERIC ED* 075 389.

   Reports a relationship between patterns of teacher verbal behavior and peer relationships of students in classrooms.

1761. Daniels, Ursula P. An analysis of the cognitive behavior of preschool children and teachers during free play. Ed.D. dissertation. New York University. 1976.

   Describes a relationship between teacher and student level of cognitive functioning in free play, but no relationship between degree of teacher contact and student level of cognitive functioning.

1762. Davidson, Roscoe L. "Teacher influence and children's level of thinking," *Reading Teacher 22* (1969): 702-704.

   Describes teacher questions as related to level of student response.

1763. Denovellis, Donna Marie. Relationships between selected classroom process variables and social acceptance in early elementary classroom groups. Ed.D. dissertation. University of Florida. 1978.

Describes a relationship between teacher
behavior toward students and student behavior
toward other students.

1764.   Devany, Tommy Wayne. An examination of the
relationships between the variety of classroom
activities and observable student responses. Ed.D.
dissertation. University of Tennessee. 1978.

Describes teacher behavior as related to
student behavior, with variations in the
relationship by teacher characteristics.

1765.   DeVault, Marjorie L. & others. Schooling and
learning opportunities. Interim Report. St. Ann,
Missouri: Central Midwest Regional Laboratory.
ERIC ED 155 157.

Describes student time spent on content areas
and the types of observed behaviors of teachers.

1766.   Dickson, Neil S. Student attitudes towards
mathematics: A study concerning teacher influence
and subject content. Ed.D. dissertation. Brigham
Young University. 1978.

Describes teacher influence as rated by
students related to student attitude toward
mathematics

1767.   Dillon, James Thomas. Duration of responses to
teacher questions and statements during periods of
class discussion. Ph.D. dissertation. University
of Chicago. 1078.

Describes teacher behavior, characteristics and
student characteristics as not related to the
length of secondary student responses to teacher
questions.

1768.   Docteur, Kenneth Everett. The effects of increased
verbal and nonverbal contingent teacher
reinforcement on the level of attentive student
behavior. Ed.D. dissertation. University of
Rochester. 1979.

Describes teacher behavior in response to
student disruptions and responses of students to
teacher behavior; when teachers were trained to
exhibit different behavior, students changed their
behavior.

1769.   Douglas, Earl McGrath. A study of relationships
between teacher classroom behavior and concurrent
student interest in classroom activities. Ph.D.
dissertation. University of New Mexico. 1972.

Describes differences in teacher and student behavior and a relationship between teacher behavior and student involvement in classroom activities.

1770. Edwards, Clifford H. & Surma, Michael. "The relationship between type of teacher reinforcement and student inquiry behavior in science," *Journal of Research in Science Teaching 17* (1980): 337-341.

Describes teacher verbal reinforcement and mimicry of students' responses as reducing student inquiry behaviors.

1771. Elkins, Keith & Porter, Martha. Classroom research on subgroup experiences in a U.S. History class. Publication 114. Lafayette, Indiana: Social Science Education Consortium. Purdue University. 1966. *ERIC ED* 014 002.

Describes an experiment in which students had different reactions to instructional group sizes by the level of class ability and achievement.

1772. Emmer, Edmund T. The effect of teacher use of student ideas on student initiation. Austin, Texas: Research and Development Center for Teacher Education. Texas University at Austin. 1968. *ERIC ED* 022 732.

Reports an increase in student initiation of interaction when teachers make greater use of student ideas in two twenty minute lessons after the initial observations.

1773. Engel-Bland, Alice. Some effects of teacher approval or disapproval on elementary school children's perceptions of peers. Ph.D. dissertation. Duke University. 1979.

Describes an experiment in which teacher approval had a positive and disapproval a negative effect on student perceptions of the social acceptability of their peers.

1774. Evertson, Carolyn, Anderson, Linda & Brophy, Jere E. The Texas Junior High School Study: Final report of process-outcome relationships. Report No. 4061. Austin, Texas: Research and Development Center for Teacher Education. University of Texas at Austin. *ERIC ED* 173 744.

Describes high and low inference measures of teacher behaviors related to student behaviors and student achievement.

1775.   Feldhusen, John. "Problems of student behavior in
        secondary schools," In *Classroom management: The
        78th yearbook of the National Society for the
        Study of Education, Part II.* Edited by Daniel L.
        Duke. pp. 217-244. Chicago: University of Chicago
        Press. 1979

            Describes the behavior of students and teachers
        associated with lower rates of student disruptive
        behavior. For Duke reference see citation No.
        2940.

1776.   Filby, Nikola & Cahen, Leonard S. Teaching behavior
        and Academic Learning Time in the A-B period.
        Technical Note V-1b. Beginning Teacher Evaluation
        Study. San Francisco, California: Far West
        Laboratory for Educational Research and
        Development. 1977.

            Describes the behaviors of teachers in relation
        to their allocation of instructional time and
        student engagement on tasks during the first half
        of the school year.

1777.   Filby, Nikola N. & Cahen, Leonard S. Teaching
        behavior and Academic Learning Time in the B-C
        period. Technical Note V-2b. Beginning Teacher
        Evaluation Study. San Francisco, California: Far
        West Laboratory for Educational Research and
        Development. 1978.

            Describes the behaviors of teachers in relation
        to their allocation of instructional time and the
        engagement of students on assigned tasks during
        the second half of the school year.

1778.   Filby, Nikola N. & Marliave, Richard. Descriptions
        of distribution of ALT within and across classes
        during the A-B period. Technical Note IV-1a.
        Beginning Teacher Evaluation Study. San Francisco,
        California: Far West Laboratory for Educational
        Research and Development. 1977. *ERIC ED* 156 642.

            Describes teacher allocation of instructional
        time, level of task difficulty for individual
        students, and student engagement in grades two and
        five during the fall.

1779.   Fisher, Charles W., Filby, Nikola N. & Marliave,
        Richard S. Description of distributions of ALT
        within and across classes during the B-C period.
        Technical Note IV-1b. Beginning Teacher Evaluation
        Study. San Francisco, California: Far West
        Laboratory for Educational Research and
        Development. 1977. *ERIC ED* 156 638.

Describes teacher allocation of instructional time, level of task difficulty for individual students, and student engagement for the second half of the school year.

1780. Fowler, Thaddeus W. An investigation of the teacher behavior of wait-time during an inquiry science lesson. 1975. *ERIC ED* 108 872.

Describes teachers who were trained to wait longer for student responses having more interaction among students.

1781. Friedman, Philip. Imitation of a teacher's verbal behavior as a function of teacher and peer reinforcement. 1971. *ERIC ED* 050 010.

Describes more grade one student imitation of high than of low rewarding teachers.

1782. Friedman, Philip. "Relationship of teacher reinforcement to spontaneous student verbalization within the classroom," *Journal of Educational Psychology* 65 (1973): 59-64.

Describes a relationship between teacher reinforcement and student initiation of classroom interaction.

1783. Friedman, Philip. "Student imitation of a teacher's verbal style as a function of natural classroom reinforcement," *Journal of Educational Psychology* 64 (1973): 267-273.

Describes greater student imitation of rewarding than of non-rewarding teachers.

1784. Friedman, Philip & Bowers, Norman D. Pupil imitation of a rewarding teacher's verbal behavior. 1969. *ERIC ED* 038 376.

Reports that student sex and grade as well as teacher verbal behavior influenced the degree that students imitated teacher verbal behavior.

1785. Gaasholt, Marie Goff Peters. Teacher and pupil behaviors related to classroom organization and management. Ed.D. dissertation. University of Oregon. 1972.

Describes a relationship between teacher and student behavior but no relationship between teacher planning and evaluation and student behavior.

1786. Gall, Meredith D. What effect do teachers'
       questions have on students. San Francisco,
       California: Far West Laboratory for Educational
       Research and Development. 1973. *ERIC ED* 077 882.

       Describes student response to teacher questions
       in terms of the length and quality of questions.

1787. Gallagher, Betty. "Teachers' attitudes and the
       acceptabilty of children with speech defects,"
       Elementary School Journal 69 (1969): 277-281.

       Describes student attitudes toward students
       with speech defects as related to teacher
       statements, with more positive student attitude
       associated with no teacher statements about the
       speech defect.

1788. Garigliano, Leonard Joseph. The relation of
       wait-time to student behaviors in Science
       Curriculum Improvement Study lessons. Ed.D.
       dissertation. Columbia University. 1972.

       Describes a relationship between teacher
       wait-time and student response length in science
       lessons, with longer wait time resulting in longer
       responses and fewer, "I don't know," responses.

1789. George, Pamela G. & Gallagher, James J. The
       relationship of lesson properties and teacher
       communication to the task-related attention of
       learning disabled children. Final Report. Chapel
       Hill, North Carolina: Frank Porter Graham Center.
       North Carolina University. 1978. *ERIC ED* 182 880.

       Describes specific teacher behaviors and
       characteristics of the task related to the task
       involvement behaviors of learning disabled
       students.

1790. George, Thomas W. "Teacher- versus student-choice
       of learning activities," *Educational Research
       Quarterly 2*, No. 1 (1977): 22-29.

       Reports that students had equal performance on
       teacher and student selected tasks but students in
       classrooms where teachers assigned tasks completed
       more of the curriculum.

1791. Gillett, Maxwell Harry. Effects of teacher
       enthusiasm on at-task behavior of students in
       elementary classes. Ph.D. dissertation. University
       of Oregon. 1980.

       Describes increases in teacher enthusiasm after
       training resulting in increases in student on-task
       behavior.

1792. Goldenson, Dennis. "An alternative view about the role of the secondary school in political socialization: A field-experimental study of the development of civil liberties attitudes," *Theory and Research in Social Education* 6 (1978): 44-72.

Describes teacher credibility and student political attitudes affected by classroom discussions.

1793. Goldstein, Jane McCarthy. Managerial behaviors of elementary school teachers and student on-task behavior. Ed.D. dissertation. University of Houston. 1979. *ERIC ED* 173 315.

Describes the use of group processes and managerial behaviors as related to classroom socioemotional climate and student on-task behaviors.

1794. Goldstein, Jane McCarthy & Weber, Wilford A. Teacher managerial behaviors and student on-task behavior. 1979. *ERIC ED* 178 484.

Describes the managerial behaviors of teachers and their relationship to student on-task behavior.

1795. Golladay, Wendy M. Maintaining student behavior by increasing and maintaining teacher contingent reinforcement rate. Ed.D. dissertation. University of Virginia. 1973.

Describes the effects of three teaching methods on student on-task behavior, with more on-task behavior with greater teacher use of praise.

1796. Good, Thomas L. & Brophy, Jere E. "Changing teacher and student behavior: An empirical investigation," *Journal of Educational Psychology* 66 (1975): 390-405.

Describes changes in teacher behavior and the behavior of target students after training, and changes in behavior of students to whom teacher did not direct changed teacher behavior.

1797. Goodwin, Dwight Lawrence. Training teachers in reinforcement techniques to increase pupil task-oriented behavior: An experimental evaluation. Ph.D. dissertation. Stanford University. 1966.

Describes some changes in teacher behavior after training and no differences in the

attentive behavior of students of teachers
receiving and not receiving the training.

1798.   Grannis, Joseph C. "Task engagement and the
        consistency of pedagogical controls: An ecological
        study of differently structured classroom
        settings," *Curriculum Inquiry 8* (Spring 1978):
        3-36. Urban Diversity Series. No. 57. New York:
        ERIC Clearinghouse on the Urban Disadvantaged.
        Columbia University. *ERIC ED* 169 167.

            Describes consistency of control in pacing and
        feedback from materials and/or peers as related to
        higher student engagement.

1799.   Graves, Robert Bradley. The effectiveness of using
        workbooks in the teaching of eighth-grade English
        grammar. 1969. *ERIC ED* 048 268.

            Describes no differences in student behaviors
        when teachers use drill or workbooks in teaching
        English grammar.

1800.   Gregory, John W. & Casteel, J. Doyle. Verbal
        environment correlates with student growth in
        logical reasoning ability. Final Report Summary.
        Gainesville, Florida: Florida State University.
        Institute for Development of Human Resources.
        1975. *ERIC ED* 121 631.

            Describes a relationship between teacher use of
        conditional statements and student logical
        thinking, differing between math and social
        studies.

1801.   Gregory, John W. & Osborne, Alan R. "Logical
        reasoning ability and teacher verbal behavior
        within the mathematics classroom," *Journal of
        Research in Mathematics Education 6* (1975):
        26-36.

            Describes teacher use of conditional statements
        as related to student ability to apply the
        principles of logic.

1802.   Grubb, Richard Dale. Verbal instructions and
        feedback to teachers on cooperative behavior of
        kindergarten pupils. Ph.D. dissertation.
        University of Illinois at Urbana-Champaign. 1971.

            Describes daily feedback to teachers resulting
        in changes in the behavior of children in the
        teachers' classrooms.

1803.   Gumbiner, Jann & others. Relations of classroom
        structures and teacher behaviors to social
        orientation, self-esteem, and classroom climate
        among Anglo American and Mexican American
        children. 1979. *ERIC ED* 177 426.

        Describes teacher behavior related to a
        positive classroom climate, use of
        culturally-relevant patterns and related to the
        self-esteem and social orientation of children.

1804.   Hall, Gloria Jean. A descriptive study of reading
        in a first grade traditional classroom. Ph.D.
        dissertation. Ohio State University. 1980.

        Describes the behavior and attitudes of one
        teacher teaching reading in grade one and the
        responses of individual students to the teacher's
        emphasis on hard work to master the difficult task
        of learning reading skills.

1805.   Hall, R. Vance, & others. Modification of disputing
        and talking out behaviors with the teacher as
        observer and experimenter. Lawrence, Kansas:
        Bureau of Child Research. Kansas University. 1970.
        ERIC ED 039 298.

        Describes teachers observing disruptive
        behavior of students, recording that behavior, and
        changing their responses, resulting in changes in
        student behavior.

1806.   Hamachek, Don E. *Motivation in teaching and
        learning. What research says to the teacher*.
        Washington, D.C.: National Education Association.
        1968. *ERIC ED* 029 845. Also published as "What
        research tells us about the characterstics of
        'good' and 'bad' teachers," In *Human dynamics in
        Psychology and Education*. Edited by Don Hamachek.
        Boston: Allyn & Bacon. 1968.

        Reviews studies on motivation, including
        teacher and student variables, and teacher
        techniques related to student motivation.   For
        Hamachek reference see citation No. 2967.

1807.   Hamilton, V. Jane & Gordon, Donald A.
        "Teacher-child interactions in preschool and task
        persistence," *American Educational Research
        Journal 15* (1978): 459-466.

        Describes teacher praise related to more, and
        teacher criticism related to less, student task
        persistence.

1808.   Hardy, Robert Earl. The effects of praise on
        selected variables in secondary school classrooms:
        A behavior modification approach. Ed.D.
        dissertation. Western Michigan University. 1971.

        Describes no relationship between experimental
        use and non-use of praise and student hand raising
        and student perceptions of the teacher.

1809.   Harre, Ruthanne. An investigation of the
        interactive effects among student types and
        treatment types on time-on-task behavior in eighth
        grade mathematics classes. Ph.D. dissertation.
        University of Missouri-Columbia. 1980.

        Reports that the on-task behavior of eighth
        grade students varied by type of instructional
        program, with more on-task behavior when teachers
        used an instructional approach based on
        correlational studies of effective math teaching.

1810.   Harris, Florence R. & others. Effects of adult
        social reinforcement on child behavior. 1974. *ERIC
        ED* 019 997.

        Describes an experiment in which the teacher
        attended to the child when the child exhibited
        positive behavior and ignored negative behavior,
        and children increased their positive behavior.

1811.   Hassler, Donni Marie Kawa. A study to investigate
        the effects of wait-time and questioning
        strategies on the oral language behaviors of
        teachers and students during children's literature
        discussions in language arts. Ed.D. dissertation.
        Pennsylvania State University. 1980.

        Describes teacher use of longer wait time after
        a question before calling on student and after
        student response and teacher use of higher level
        questions as related to higher level student
        responses, length of student response and student
        alternate responses.

1812.   Haught, Evelyn Hunt. Students' patterns of thinking
        in teacher-led large group discussions and
        student-led small group discussions of literature.
        1970. *ERIC ED* 055 091.

        Describes more discussion in student-led small
        groups than teacher-led large groups and different
        types of student thinking in the two group types.

1813.   Hawn, Joyce & others. The effects of active and
        quiet activities upon subsequent attending of
        preschool children. 1973. *ERIC ED* 135 471.

Describes children as more attentive to story reading in a large group when the reading is preceeded by active rather than quiet behavior.

1814.   Heitgerd, Helen Anita. Teacher and student characteristics as determined by pace in an elementary school mathematics program. Ph.D. dissertation. University of Missouri-Columbia. 1978.

Reports that teacher behaviors in a Conceptually Oriented Mathematics Program are related to student attitude toward math but not to involvement in math activities.

1815.   Herman, Wayne L., Jr. Teacher behavior in elementary school social studies," *Theory and Research in Social Education 5*, No. 3 (1977): 39-63.

Reviews seven studies on classroom activities in social studies, including teacher verbal behavior and student interest.

1816.   Hess, Robert D. & Takanishi-Knowles, Ruby. Teacher strategies and student engagement in low-income area schools. Research and Development Memorandum No. 105. Stanford, California: Center for Research and Development in Teaching. Stanford University. *ERIC ED* 087 768.

Describes large variations in student engagement rates and teacher behaviors to encourage engagement and greater student engagement in smaller instructional groups.

1817.   Hess, Robert D. & Takanishi, Ruby. The relationship of teacher behavior and school characteristics to student engagement. Technical Report No. 42. Stanford, California: Center for Research and Development in Teaching. Stanford University. 1974. *ERIC ED* 098 225.

Describes teacher behaviors as related to student engagement, and classroom architecture as related to interaction but not to student engagement.

1818.   Hollis, Roy Estes. Effects of direct vs. indirect teacher verbal behaviors on third-grade children's I E locus of control. Ph.D. Dissertation. Boston College. 1976. *ERIC ED* 134 336.

Describes no relationship between teacher direct/indirect verbal behavior and student

1819.   Holt, John. *How children fail*. New York: Pitman
        Publishing Corporation. 1968.

        Describes student behaviors in response to
        behaviors of teachers, the structure and climate
        of the school and the tasks demanded of students,
        based on the author's teaching and analysis of
        schools.

1820.   Hoosein, Abdool Nazir. The effect of teacher
        behavior modification training upon the level of
        student inquiry. Ed.D. dissertation. University of
        Missouri-Columbia. 1972.

        Describes changes in teacher behavior as
        related to student questioning and inquiry
        behavior.

1821.   Houser, Betsy B. Student compliance and attitude: A
        function of classroom control techniques. 1977.
        ERIC ED 151 625.

        Describes teacher control techniques as related
        to student compliance behavior and attitude toward
        teacher.

1822.   Houser, Mary-Elizabeth Bosak. An examination of
        student compliance and attitude as a function of
        gender and classroom control technique. Ed.D.
        dissertation. University of California, Los
        Angeles. 1977.

        Describes different student behavior and
        attitude toward the teacher by type of power-base
        strategy used by the teacher.

1823.   Hoy, Robert V. & others. Developmental differences
        in reactions to combinations of expectancy and
        feedback statements. 1973. *ERIC ED* 097 111.

        Describes differences in responses of second
        and fourth grade students to adult verbal rewards
        and feedback.

1824.   Huebner, Robert Walter. Interactions between
        patterns of individual differences in sensory
        modalities of students and methods of classroom
        instruction. Ph.D. dissertation. University of
        Maryland. 1969.

        Describes no difference in preferred student
        modality by the instructional modality used by the
        teacher.

1825.   Hunter, Dianne Lulie. Student on-task behavior
        during second grade reading group meetings. Ph.D.
        dissertation. University of Missouri-Columbia.
        1978.

            Describes a relationship among teacher
        behavior, student past achievement and student
        behavior in reading group.

1826.   Jacobs, Joseph H. An investigation of structured
        observation experiences as a self-improvement
        technique for modifying teachers' verbal
        behaviors. 1971. *ERIC ED* 085 173.

            Describes modifications in teacher verbal
        behaviors and increases in student participation.

1827.   Johns, Joseph Penberthy. "The relationship between
        teacher behaviors and the incidence of
        thought-provoking questions by students in
        secondary schools," *Journal of Educational
        Research 62* (1968): 117-122. Ph.D. dissertation.
        University. of Michigan. 1966.

            Describes greater student thought-provoking
        questions in classrooms with more indirect teacher
        behavior.

1828.   Johnson, David L. "A conceptual model of teacher
        and student classroom interaction and observed
        student verbal creativity," *Psychology in the
        Schools 10* (1973): 475-481.

            Describes teacher verbal interaction with
        students related to student creativity.

1829.   Johnson, Neal Lane. The association between certain
        student responses and certain teacher behaviors in
        classroom settings. Ed.D. dissertation. Northeast
        Louisiana University. 1979.

            Describes teacher praise, questioning, threats,
        as related to student responses, with differences
        by achievement level of students.

1830.   Joy, Athalie Doris. Classroom organization and
        classroom behavior: A study of children's behavior
        in differentially organized classroom types. Ph.D.
        dissertation. State University of New York at
        Buffalo. 1977.

            Describes differences in classroom structure as
        related to differences in some but not other
        student behaviors.

1831. Kameen, Marilyn C. & Brown, Jeannette A. The
       relationship of teacher affective behavior to
       pupil affective behavior. *ERIC ED* 112 284.

           Describes a positive change in teacher
       affective behavior as related to a positive change
       in student affective behavior.

1832. Kanov, Jeffrey Francis. The effects of
       teacher-determined and student-determined
       contingencies of reinforcement on academic
       response rate. Ph.D. dissertation. University of
       Florida. 1972.

           Describes no difference in the correct response
       rate when the teacher or the student selected the
       schedule of reinforcement.

1833. Kaplan, Sheldon Jay. The effects of verbal
       reprimands on high school students' incorrect
       responses in grammatical exercises. 1973. *ERIC ED*
       091 684.

           Describes a difference in student error rate,
       with lower error rate with more teacher
       reprimands.

1834. Kelly, Joseph Richard. Visually perceived nonverbal
       behaviors of teachers and their relationship to
       affective responses of students. Ed.D.
       dissertation. Oregon State University. 1973. *ERIC
       ED* 080 309.

           Describes student differences by sex in
       affective responses to teacher nonverbal
       behaviors.

1835. Kelly, Thomas Joseph. Physical proximity: An
       important variable in pupil-teacher interactions.
       Ed.D. dissertation. University of Kansas. 1971.

           Describes the proximity of teacher to student
       as related to more attention to task for some
       students but not the whole class, while the
       teacher at his/her desk resulted in more attention
       to task for the whole class.

1836. Key, Paula LeAnn. Effect of teacher roles and
       organizational systems upon secondary student
       attitudes toward educational climate. Ph.D.
       dissertation. University of Southern California.
       1977.

       Describes the organizational system of the
school as significantly related, but teacher role
not related, to student attitude toward some
aspects of the school

1837. Kooi, Beverly Yvonne. An experimental analysis of
       the effects of teacher-pupil interaction cues upon
       learning. Ph.D. dissertation. Arizona State
       University. 1966.

       Reports that an experiment demonstrates
       different student responses to different teacher
       cues in preschool classrooms.

1838. Krantz, Murray & Scarth, Linda. "Task persistence
       and adult assistance in the preschool," *Child
       Development 50* (1979): 578-581.

       Describes adult assistance behavior as related
       to student task persistence in preschool settings
       where students select the tasks.

1839. Lake, John Heath. The influence of wait-time on the
       verbal dimension of student inquiry behavior.
       Ed.D. dissertation. Rutgers University the State
       University of New Jersey. 1973.

       Describes more and cognitively more complex
       student responses with longer teacher wait time.

1840. Lamb, George S. "Teacher verbal cues and pupil
       performance on a group reading test," *Journal of
       Educational Psychology 58* (1967): 332-336.

       Describes girls as more responsive to teacher
       verbal cues to work more accurately and rapidly
       than boys in grades two and three.

1841. Lebby, Andrew Miller. The interactive effect of
       teacher behavior and student attitude on
       productivity and morale in a classroom setting.
       Ph.D. dissertation. Syracuse University. 1977.

       Describes an experiment in which variations in
       the structure of classroom groups are not related
       to student morale or productivity.

1842. Levine, Michael M. The role of redundancy in the
       assessment of the effectiveness of teacher
       communication. *ERIC ED* 079 249.

       Describes teacher redundant behavior in
       communicating information to students in the
       classroom and the amount of redundancy related to
       the messages that students receive.

1843.   Lietz, Jeremy Jon. "Comparing school grades with
        deportment and attendance for the disadvantaged
        elementary pupil," *Education 96* (1976): 291–296.

            Describes a relationship between teacher
        behavior and grading of students and the behavior
        of students.

1844.   Loucks, Susan F. The adaptation of the Stanford
        Research Institute Classroom Observation
        Instrument for use in studying teacher variations
        in innovation implementations. Research Report No.
        3052. Austin, Texas: Research and Development
        Center for Teacher Education. University of Texas
        at Austin. 1978. *ERIC ED* 189 194.

            Describes variations in classroom behaviors of
        teachers implementing an innovative instructional
        program.

1845.   McDaniel, Ernest D. The impact of multi-level
        materials on teaching behavior and learning
        outcomes. Lexington, Kentucky: Kentucky Research
        Foundation. 1971. *ERIC ED* 016 284.

            Describes differences in student use of inquiry
        process but not in student preference for method
        of instruction with an experiment involving the
        use of inquiry methods in seventh grade history.

1846.   McFadden, Craig L. "Academic achievement motivation
        as a function of classroom responsiveness,"
        Journal of Experimental Education 46, No. 4
        (1978): 41–44.

            Describes teacher and student behavior related
        to student motivation to learn.

1847.   Madsen, C.H., Jr., Becker, W.C. & Thomas,
        D.R. "Rules, praise, and ignoring: Elements of
        elementary classroom control," *Journal of Applied
        Behavioral Analysis 1* (1968): 139–150.

            Describes teachers varying their behavior in
        terms of reinforcing classroom rules and describes
        the resulting changes in the behavior of
        individual students.

1848.   Manley, Barry Lee. The relationship of the learning
        environment to student attitudes toward chemistry.
        1978. *ERIC ED* 167 349.

            Describes teacher behavior as of more
        importance than the curriculum in determining
        students' attitudes toward science.

1849. Mann, John S. "Authority styles in a project for Negro children," *Journal of Negro Education 37* (1968): 160-163.

Describes different observed behavior of students to teachers with different styles of expressing teacher authority over the students.

1850. Marino, Martin Francis. The effectiveness of teacher-centered versus case-centered consultation in the reduction of classroom management errors and negative classroom behavior of students. Ph.D. dissertation. Temple University. 1976.

Describes an experiment in which two methods of consultation with teachers resulted in changes in the management methods of the teachers but non-significant decreases in the disruptive behavior of students.

1851. Markell, Clark Stephen. A search for optimum relationships between student perceptions of and attitudes toward the frequency with which science teachers employ instructional moves. Ph.D. dissertation. Ohio State University. 1973.

Describes student reactions to a number of teacher instructional strategies.

1852. Masemann, V. "Ethnography of the bilingual classroom," *International Review of Education 24* (1978): 295-307.

Describes teaching style as one influence on the use of two languages by students in bilingual classrooms.

1853. Maxwell, Diana Kathleen. Relationships between child-teacher interactions and preschool children's play levels. Ph.D. dissertation. University of Maryland. 1980.

Describes relationships between positive teacher-child interactions and child play but no differences in the number of interactions by child sex or age.

1854. Medland, Michael Bancroft. An applied behavior analysis of generalization in the classroom setting. Ph.D. dissertation. Michigan State University. 1978.

Describes a relationship between the behavioral consequences used by teachers and student on-task behavior.

1855.   Medoff, Fay S. A study of seventh-year classes in
        science, mathematics, English, and social studies
        to determine the relation of the verbal
        interaction with pupil ability, pupil self-image,
        and level of questioning. Ph.D. dissertation. New
        York University. 1973.

           Describes the ratio of teacher direct to
        indirect behavior and the subject matter, but not
        student ability, related to student participation
        in lesson activities.

1856.   Middleman, Ruth & Hawkes, Thomas H. An experimental
        field study of the impact of nonverbal
        communication of affect on children from two
        socio-economic backgrounds. Philadelphia,
        Pennsylvania: Temple University. 1972. *ERIC ED* 061
        550.

           Describes an experiment in which student
        responses to different teacher nonverbal
        communications differed by student socioeconomic
        level.

1857.   Miller, Louise B. Situational determinants of
        behavior in preschool classrooms. 1975. *ERIC ED*
        115 401.

           Describes a relationship between teacher
        behavior and the classroom setting and student
        behavior.

1858.   Miller, Robert Pennington. The relationship between
        teacher strikes and student attendance behavior
        and parental attitudes and student interest in
        school and learning. Ph.D. dissertation.
        Pennsylvania State University. 1980.

           Describes students in districts with strikes as
        having lower attendance rates after the strikes,
        as feeling that their parents had less favorable
        attitudes toward the school and reporting less
        favorable attitudes themselves.

1859.   Moore, J. William, Schant, Judith & Fritzges,
        Charles.   "Evaluation of the effects of feedback
        associated with a problem-solving approach to
        instruction on teacher and student behavior,"
        Journal of Educational Psychology 70 (1978):
        200-208.

           Describes two experiments which demonstrate
        that when teachers were given information about
        their behavior and suggestions for changes, they
        changed their behavior and students increased
        their rate of attention.

1860.   Morrison, Sherry B. & Oxford, Rebecca L.   Classroom
        ecology and kindergarten students' task-related
        behaviors: An exploratory study. *ERIC ED* 153 744.

            Describes student behavior, especially task
        engagement, related to the structure of the
        activity, the group size, role of pupil within the
        activity, and whether there is any pupil choice.

1861.   Morrison, Thomas L. "Classroom structure, work
        involvement, and social climate in elementary
        school classrooms," *Journal of Educational
        Psychology 71* (1979): 71-77.

            Describes high structure classrooms with
        greater student involvement, combined with low
        teacher control to produce less student disruptive
        behavior.

1862.   Morton, A.R. The impact of changes in selected
        teacher strategies on expressive student
        engagement. Stanford, California: Stanford Center
        for Research and Development in Teaching. Stanford
        University. 1973. *ERIC ED* 076 550.

            Describes the effects of teacher behaviors and
        changes in those behaviors on the engagement of
        students in tasks.

1863.   Mulcahey, Donna Ann. Implementing humanistic
        education: Some observable teacher behaviors.
        Ed.D. dissertation. University of Massachusetts.
        1975.

            Describes some relationships between teacher
        behavior and the attitudes of teachers and
        students.

1864.   Mulligan, Glenn Franklin. The relation of selected
        teacher characteristics and pupil-teacher
        interaction in the classroom. Ed.D. dissertation.
        Indiana University. 1970.

            Describes relationships between teacher
        characteristics and patterns of interaction with
        students, such as more warm-spontaneous teachers
        have greater student participation.

1865.   Multhauf, Arleen P. & others. "Teacher
        pupil-control ideology and behavior and classroom
        environmental robustnesss," *Elementary School
        Journal 79* (1978): 40-46.

            Describes a relationship between teacher
        beliefs and behavior and student perceptions of
        the qualities of the classroom environment.

1866. Newman, Deena Rosenfeld. Matched student/teacher
       academic engagement in direct and nondirect
       instructional settings. Ph.D. dissertation.
       Syracuse University. 1979.

           Describes an experiment in which different
       rates of student engagement were associated with
       different teacher behaviors and the relationship
       of student engagement varied by degree of direct
       instruction and prior student achievement.

1867. Nickse, Ruth Speirs. Social interaction,
       performance ability, attitudes and process
       education: An exploratory investigation of
       students' behaviors while engaged in a
       process-oriented curriculum. Ph.D. dissertation.
       Cornell University. 1972.

           Describes three weeks of a process-oriented
       curriculum resulting in greater social equality of
       status of students, greater participation, but no
       difference in social cohesiveness of students.

1868. Noble, Carol G. & Nolan, John D. "Effect of student
       verbal behavior on classroom teacher behavior,"
       Journal of Educational Psychology 68 (1976):
       3422-346.

           Describes a relationship between student
       volunteering and teacher questioning behavior and
       teacher response to students.

1869. Noli Pamala Morgan. Changing the academic learning
       time of elementary school students: Three staff
       development approaches. Ed.D. dissertation.
       University of San Francisco. 1980.

           Describes increases in student task engagement
       with changes in teacher behavior resulting from
       staff development, with differences in teacher
       behavior changes by type of staff development.

1870. Nolli, David B. Alternative path analytic models of
       student-teacher influence: The implications of
       different strokes for different folks," *Sociology
       of Education 46* (1973): 417-426.

           Describes the lack of influence of teacher
       behavior on the behavior of black students.

1871. Norris, Roger Alan. The relationships among
       learning style, teaching style, and student
       perception of teacher effectiveness. Ph.D.
       dissertation. University of Idaho. 1977.

Describes no relationship between classroom style, student conceptual level and student rating of teacher.

1872. O'Leary, K. Daniel & Becker, Wesley C. "The effect of the intensity of a teacher's reprimands on children's behavior," *Journal of School Psychology* 7 (1968-1969): 8-11.

Describes the types of teacher responses to student disruptive behavior during rest time related to the frequency of that disruptive behavior.

1873. Olson, David R. & others. The teacher as communicator: An aspect of teacher effectiveness. 1969. *ERIC ED* 040 146.

Describes an experiment which identified differences among teachers and between teachers and students in ability to encode and decode information, and found student ability related to quality of message sent.

1874. Omori, Sharon & others. A study of time spent working at learning centers. Technical Report No. 17. Kamehameha Schools. Honolulu, Hawaii. 1974. *ERIC ED* 158 842.

Describes proportionately less student time on-task during time spent in learning centers than in other instructional settings.

1875. Oppenlander, Lester. Classroom interaction and pupil affect. 1970. *ERIC ED* 038 342.

Describes more and less direct teacher behavior as not related to student affect, but differences by student achievement in preferences for types of classroom interactions.

1876. Otteson, James P. & Otteson, Carol Rodning "Effect of teacher's gaze on children's story recall," *Perceptual and Motor Skills 50* (1980): 35-42.

Describes a positive relationship between teacher gaze during reading of a story and student recall of story, especially for boys.

1877. Oxford, Rebecca L. & others. "Classroom ecology and off-task behavior of kindergarten students," *Journal of Classroom Interaction 15*, No. 1 (1979): 34-40.

Describes continuity of signal stimulus to
students in kindergarten classroom as related to
student on-task behavior.

1878.   Ozgener, Esen Sever. Kindergarten students' verbal
responses in relation to teachers' verbal
questions. Ed.D. dissertation. George Peabody
College for Teachers. 1971.

Describes a strong relationship between the
cognitive level of teacher questions and the
cognitive level of student responses.

1879.   Page, Vilma Huggins. The effect of encouragement
techniques by teachers on the disturbing behaviors
of students. Ph.D. dissertation. University of
South Carolina. 1974.

Describes training of teachers resulting in
less student disturbing behavior.

1880.   Peck, R.F., Blattstein, A. & Blattstein, D. Teacher
and student influence on student attitude toward
school. Austin, Texas: Research and Development
Center for Teacher Education. University of Texas
at Austin. 1979.

Describes student characteristics and teacher
behavior effecting student attitude toward school,
and changes in effects of teacher behaviors by
student characteristics.

1881.   Pedersen, Eigil. "The lifelong impact of a
first-grade teacher,' *Instructor 89*, No. 5 (1979):
62-63, 66.

Describes effects of one first grade teacher on
the adult status of her students.

1882.   Pedersen, Eigil & others. "A new perspective on the
effects of first-grade teachers on children's
subsequent adult status," *Harvard Educational
Review 48* (1978): 1-31.

Describes the influence of one first-grade
teacher on the adult status and lives of her
students, including higher educaton, work and self
concept.

1883.   Penick, John E. & Shymansky, James A. "The effects
of teacher behavior on student behavior in
fifth-grade science: A replication," *Journal of
Research in Science Teaching 14* (1977): 427-432.

Describes teacher behavior, materials, space as
related to student behavior in science lessons.

1884. Petersen, Wretha Lanore Kline. An investigation of variables associated with the observed responses to teacher directions of first graders designated as relatively ineffective in listening and responding behavior. Ed.D. dissertation. George Washington University. 1971.

Describes student listening and responding behavior as related to teacher behavior, being clear, concise, getting student attention, providing opportunities to listen in small groups.

1885. Petrie, Thomas A. & others. Diffentiated staffing and non-teamed organizational structures as they affect elementary school teacher-pupil interaction. Fredonia, New York. State University of New York. 1973. *ERIC ED* 075 090.

Describes more student choice and individual prescription in teamed schools but more information processing in non-teamed schools.

1886. Pickhardt, Carl E. "Fear in the schools: How students make teachers afraid," *Educational Leadership 36* (1978): 107-112.

Describes patterns of student behavior which intimidate teachers.

1887. Potter, Ellen F. Sex differences in classroom participation. 1978. *ERIC ED* 160 911.

Describes classroom participation of girls compared with boys, not related to differences in teacher behavior.

1888. Pouler, Chris A. & Wright, Emmett. The effect of intensive instruction in hypothesis generation upon hypothesis forming and questioning behaviors of ninth grade students. 1977. *ERIC ED* 135 661.

Describes greater student production of hypotheses with reinforcement, greater quality of hypothese with knowledge of criteria for evaluating hypotheses, within an experiment.

1889. Prentice, Barbara Sympson. The effectiveness of group versus individual reinforcement in shaping attentive classroom behavior. Ph.D. dissertation. University of Arizona. 1970.

Describes an experiment in which there was no difference in the behavior of students with different patterns of reinforcement.

1890.   Pusser, Henry Ellison. Modeling and the incidental
        transmission of teaching behaviors in the
        elementary classroom. Ph.D. dissertation. Emory
        University. 1972.

            Describes student use of different teaching
            styles, with greater use of their own teacher's
            style.

1891.   Reed, Marilyn Davis. Children's and teachers'
        recall and reactions to read aloud books. Ph.D.
        dissertation. Ohio State University. 1980.

            Reports that the more teachers read to students
            and the more choice students had in reading
            materials the more students read on their own and
            expressed interest in literature.

1892.   Reimanis, Gunars. Social approval and achievement
        striving in the kindergarten. Stanford,
        California: Stanford Center for Research and
        Development in Teaching. Stanford University.
        1968. *ERIC ED* 054 845.

            Describes a relationship between teacher
            approval, student achievement striving and student
            dependency behavior.

1893.   Reimanis, Gunars. "Teacher—pupil interaction and
        achievement striving in the kindergarten,"
        Psychology in the Schools 7 (1970): 179—183.

            Describes achievement striving of kindergarten
            students as related to the ratio of teacher
            approval to disapproval statements

1894.   Reiss, Douglas J. & others. The effects of
        contingent use of recess activities on the
        academic performance of a third grade classroom.
        1974. *ERIC ED* 091 371.

            Describes a management system with rewards for
            student work, in which students preferred recess
            activities as rewards.

1895.   Rich, H. Lyndall & Bush, Andrew J. "The effect of
        congruent teacher—student characterstics on
        instructional outcomes," *American Educational
        Research Journal 15* (1978): 451—457.

            Describes teacher and student congruence in
            direct/indirect behavior and student social—
            emotional development resulting in greater student
            affective development, achievement, and task
            persistence.

1896. Richey, Linda S. Children's judgments based on their perceptions of teacher characteristics. Ph.D. dissertation. University of Florida. 1979.

Describes differences in responses of emotionally handicapped and regular students to teacher behavior.

1897. Richter, Frederick Douglas. The effects of pupil-teacher planning on elementary school children. Ed.D. dissertation. Pennsylvania State University. 1978.

Describes an experiment in which student and teacher planning resulted in greater student motivation, achievement, prosocial behavior, and attitude toward school.

1898. Rieck, Billie Jo. "How content teachers telegraph messages against reading," *Journal of Reading 20* (1977): 646-648.

Describes teacher responses to questions about required reading and perceptions of students whose teachers report that students don't complete reading assignments that teachers don't encourage or require the reading.

1899. Riehm, Carl Lee. The effects of increased pupil-teacher verbal interaction on oral language development in disadvantaged first grade children. Ed.D. dissertation. University of Florida. 1969. *ERIC ED* 056 007.

Describes no difference in student verbal behavior after a program of verbal interaction with teachers.

1900. Robertshaw, Carroll Stuart. An investigation of attention to task behavior, arithmetic performance and behavior problems in first grade children. Ed.D. dissertation. University of Kansas. 1971.

Describes teacher behavior using behavior modification as resulting in changes in student attention to task.

1901. Rodeheffer, Martha Ann. Effects of two types of communication training on the classroom verbal behavior of elementary school teachers. Ph.D. dissertation. Arizona State University. 1972.

Describes the behavior of teachers as dominating the verbal interaction in classrooms but a greater amount of student talk after teacher training.

1902.   Rollins, Howard A., McCandless, Boyd R., Thompson,
        Marion & Brassell, William R. "Project Success
        Environment: An extended application of
        contingency management in inner-city schools,"
        Journal of Educational Psychology 66 (1974):
        167-178.

        Describes behavior of teachers trained in
        reinforcement of positive behavior and greater
        student on-task behavior, less disruption and less
        teacher discipline and punishment.

1903.   Saba, Robert G. "The effect of unsolicited
        attention on frequency of misbehavior in grade
        levels K-post secondary," *Humanist Educator 16*
        (1977): 19-25.

        Describes teacher behavior intended to redirect
        the misbehavior of students.

1904.   Scanlon, Robert G. Factors associated with a
        program for encouraging self-initiated activities
        by fifth and sixth grade students in a selected
        elementary school emphasizing individualized
        instruction. Ph.D. dissertation. University of
        Kansas. 1973.

        Describes changes in student writing resulting
        from teacher feedback in the experimental group.

1905.   Schwarz, J. Conrad. Effects of teacher behavior
        modification on unresponsive students. Final
        Report. 1971. *ERIC ED 063 051.*

        Describes different teacher behaviors
        resulting in different adjustment of shy students
        to nursery school.

1906.   Scott, Alvin Thomas. A study of the effects of
        planned classroom teacher verbal behavior and
        resulting classroom pupil verbal behavior on the
        achievement of classroom pupils. Ed.D.
        dissertation. University of Tennessee. 1973.

        Describes the effects of planned classroom
        behavior on the actual classroom behavior of
        teachers and some differences in student
        behavior.

1907.   Serbin, Lisa A. & others. "Sex-stereotyped and
        nonstereotyped introductions of new toys in the
        preschool classroom: An observational study of
        teacher behavior and its effects," *Psychology of
        Women Quarterly 4* (1979): 261-265.

Describes teacher behavior in introducing toys and teacher bias toward sex-type of toys as possibly contributing to sex-typing of activities.

1908. Shaffer, Virginia Faye. The categorization of student inquiries and the responses made within the context of classroom interaction. Ed.D. dissertation. University of Illinois. 1966.

Reports that gifted students' inquiries are related to the topics and types of student inquiries.

1909. Shapiro, Edythe R. Children's comprehension of teachers' directives: Effects of development, clarity and context. 1980. *ERIC ED* 184 707.

Describes differences in children's interpretations of teacher directives varying by children's age, with children using the supporting context to interpret directions.

1910. Shepardson, Richard Donald. An analysis of teacher questioning and response behaviors and their influence on student participation during classroom discussion. Ph.D. dissertation. University of Texas at Austin. 1972

Reports that student responses to students and teacher questions account for a large part of the variance in student participation in classroom interactions.

1911. Shepardson, Richard D. Praise and criticism--A sticky issue. *ERIC ED* 107 649.

Reports that praise has different effects by student, that praise decreases and criticism increases in effect over the school year.

1912. Shores, Richard E. & others. "The effects of amount and type of teacher-child interaction on child-child interaction during free-play," *Psychology in the Schools 13* (1976): 170-175,

Describes differences in student social behavior under different conditions of teacher involvement.

1913. Shymansky, James A. "How is student performance affected by the one-to-one teacher-student interactions occurring in an activity-centered science classroom?" *Journal of Research in Science Teaching 13* (1976): 253-258.

Describes a relationship between teacher
classroom behavior and student behavior in
elementary science lessons.

1914. Shymansky, James A. & others. "A study of
self-perceptions among elementary school students
exposed to contrasting teaching strategies in
science," *Science Education 58* (1974): 331-341.

Describes a relationship between teacher
behavior patterns and student perceptions of
science.

1915. Sie, Maureen A., Baker, George A. & Voelkner, Alvin
R. "Observations of classroom activities in two
social studies programs," *High School Journal 56*
(1973): 233-240.

Describes differences by grade and between
innovative and traditional programs and group size
in the classroom activities of students.

1916. Slaby, Ronald G. & Crowley, Christy G.
"Modification of cooperation and aggression
through teacher attention to children's speech,"
Journal of Experimental Psychology 23 (1977):
442-458.

Describes student verbal behaviors changing as
teachers focused on verbal aggressive or
cooperative student behaviors in two preschool
experiments.

1917. Sleven, Selma Rita. Teachers' communication of
content: From practice to theory. Ed.D.
dissertation. University of California, Los
Angeles. 1979.

Reports that students spent more time and
applied content better when teachers linked new
material to materials already learned rather than
to structure of the content discipline.

1918. Smothergill, Nancy L. & others. "The effects of
manipulation of teacher communication style in the
preschool," *Child Development 42* (1971):
1229-1239. *ERIC ED* 034 598.

Reports effects of teacher elaborative and
nonelaborative teaching styles on the behavior of
nursery school children.

1919. Solomon, Richard & Tyne, Thomas F. "A comparison of
individual and group contingency systems in a
first-grade class," *Psychology in the Schools 16*
(1979): 193-200.

Reports a reduction in student disruptive behaviors when teachers used individual and group contingency reinforcement systems.

1920. Spaulding, Robert L. & Showers, Beverly, Applications of the Spaulding system of classroom behavioral analysis in field settings. 1974. *ERIC ED* 091 399.

Describes teachers who received training having less student behavior which is defined as poor coping behavior.

1921. Steiner, Harrel Edwin, Jr. A study of the relationships between teacher practices and student performance of selected inquiry process behaviors in the affective domain in high school biology classes. Ph.D. dissertation. University of Texas at Austin. 1970.

Describes several teacher behaviors correlated with student inquiry and student performances within the affective domain.

1922. Stiltner, Barbara. Group development in the classroom. 1973. *ERIC ED* 128 670.

Describes differences in student responses in junior high classrooms when teachers use techniques designed to foster group development.

1923. Stumme, James Milton. An approach to changing teachers' positive and negative verbalizations, and its effect on student attending behavior. Ed.D. dissertation. Drake University. 1979.

Describes changes in teacher verbalization related to changes in student percentage of time on task.

1924. Szczesnowicz, Roma Krystyna. The relationship between children's levels of interest and freedom of choice in first-grade classrooms. 1975. *ERIC ED* 116 799.

Reports that teachers who restrict student activities have students with a higher level of interest in common classroom activities than teachers who accommodate more to student behavior.

1925. Thomas, Don R., Becker, Wesley C. & Armstrong, Marianne. "Production and elimination of disruptive classroom behavior by systematically varying teacher's behavior," *Journal of Applied Behavior Analysis 1* (1968): 35-45.

Describes patterns of student behavior and
changes to more disruptive behavior when the
teacher lowered her reinforcing responses to
positive student behaviors.

1926.   Thomson, Carolyn L. & Cooper, Margaret L. The
modification of teacher behaviors which modify
child behaviors. Progress Report. 1969. *ERIC ED*
,042 499.

Describes a training program to change the
behaviors and the resulting changes in the
behaviors of students who had been disruptive.

1927.   Tjosvold, Dean & Santamaria, Philip. The effects of
cooperation and teacher support on student
attitudes toward classroom decision-making. 1977.
ERIC ED 139 777.

Reports an experiment in which teacher support
and cooperative interaction resulted in more
positive student attitude toward making classroom
decisions.

1928.   Tuck, Russell Raymond, Jr. Some relationships
between teachers' encouragement of students to
assume more responsibility for their own learning
and the patterns of verbal interaction in their
classrooms. Ph.D. dissertation. George Peabody
College for Teachers. 1971.

Reports different teacher verbal behaviors
associated with high and low encouragement for
students to assume responsibility for their
learning, with high teachers talking less.

1929.   Vinelli, Jose L. & others. "A comparative study of
the effects of two teaching strategies in an
activity-centered science program on middle school
students' need-affiliation and teacher dependency
behaviors," *Journal of Research in Science
Teaching 16* (1979): 159-165.

Describes differences in student dependence
behavior during student-centered and
teacher-centered activities.

1930.   Vlietstra, Alice G. "Effects of adult-directed
activity, number of toys, and sex of child on
social and exploratory behavior in young
children," *Merrill-Palmer Quarterly 26* (1980):
231-238.

Describes differences in student responses when
adult direction varies.

1931. Vorreyer, Donald Field. An analysis of teacher classroom behavior and role. Ed.D. dissertation. University of Maryland. 1965.

Describes the number and variety of teacher behavior patterns exhibited within a time period as related to children's orientation to academic work.

1932. Walker, Robert Kirk, Jr. Variables related to the literary response style preferences of high school English teachers. Ph.D. dissertation. George Peabody College for Teachers. 1979.

Describes teacher stated preferences for and observed behavior styles and discrepancies between styles, which in turn were related to student attitudes.

1933. Wang, Margaret C. "Maximizing the effective use of school time by teachers and students," *Contemporary Educational Psychology 4* (1979): 187-201. Publication Series 1976/23. Pittsburgh, Pennsylvania: Learning Research and Development Center. University of Pittsburgh.

Reports that students using self-scheduling spent more time on task, completed more tasks and had more instructional and fewer management interactions with the teacher than other students.

1934. Wang, Margaret C. "The development of student self-management skills: Implication for effective use of instruction and learning time," *Educational Horizons 57*, No. 4 (1979): 169-174.

Describes research on student self-management and teacher and classroom aspects which result in greater student use of instructional time.

1935. Wang, Margaret C. "Verbal prompting and young children's descriptive language," *Language Sciences 25* (1973): 27-31. Publications Series 1973/7. Pittsburgh, Pennsylvania: Learning Research and Development Center. University of Pittsburgh.

Describes children's language and variations in language by types of adult verbal prompting.

1936. Weinrott, Mark R. & Jones, Richard R. "Differential effects of demand characteristics on teacher and pupil behavior," *Journal of Educational Psychology 69* (1977): 724-729.

Describes teacher influence on the withdrawn
behaviors but not other undesirable behaviors of
selected children.

1937. Weinstein, Carol. The effect of a change in the
physical design of an open classroom on student
behavior. 1976. *ERIC ED* 122 429.

Describes changes in the physical aspects of
the classroom resulting in changes in the behavior
of the students in one open classroom.

1938. Welander, Gary Brent. A descriptive study of the
relationships between classroom verbal interaction
and students' school-related attitudes. Ed.D.
dissertation. Oregon State University. 1980.

Describes teacher behaviors of encouragement,
reception of student ideas and feelings related to
positive student attitudes toward school, teachers
and themselves.

1939. Wickersham, Phillip Hynes. Classroom interaction
patterns: Differential effects and relationships
between sixth-grade children's self concepts and
locus of control of reinforcements. Ph.D.
dissertation. University of Illinois at
Urbana-Champaign. 1970.

Describes differences by student sex and amount
of teacher direct verbal behavior in student
assumption of responsibility for negative events.

1940. Wilensky, Harold. Observational techniques in
preschool classrooms. 1966. *ERIC ED* 100 511.

Describes teacher behavior related to student
attention throughout the school day.

1941. Willower, Donald J. & others Teacher pupil control
ideology and behavior and classroom environmental
robustness. 1978. *ERIC ED* 153 982.

Describes teacher permissiveness resulting in
greater student sense of excitement about the
class, with female but not male teachers.

1942. Wodtke, Kenneth H. & Wallen, Norman E. "Teacher
classroom control, pupil creativity, and pupil
classroom behavior," *Journal of Experimental
Education 34* (1965): 59-65.

Describes little difference between high and
low control teachers in disruptive behavior of

students and no differences in disruptive and
nonconforming behavior of creative and
non-creative students.

1943. Woolfolk, Anita E. & Woolfolk, Robert L. "Student
self-disclosure in response to teacher verbal and
nonverbal behavior," *Journal of Experimental
Education 44* (1975): 36-40.

Describes teacher behavior related to student
disclosure of personal information.

1944. Woolfolk, Robert L. & others. "Nonverbal behavior
of teachers: Some empirical findings,"
Environmental Psychology and Nonverbal Behavior 2
(1977): 45-60.

Describes the effects of teacher verbal and
nonverbal behavior on student attitude and
perceptions.

1945. Workman, Edward A. & others. "The consultative
merits of praise-ignore versus praise-reprimand
instruction," *Journal of School Psychology 18*
(1980): 373-380.

Describes more rapid changes in student
behaviors and slightly greater improvement in
behaviors with a praise-soft reprimand approach
than with a praise-ignore approach.

1946. Yando, Regina M. & Kagan, Jerome. "The effect of
teacher tempo on the child," *Child Development 39*
(1968): 27-34.

Describes changes in student response time over
a year related to student reflective/impulsive
behavior, with increase in response time for
children with experienced, reflective teachers.

1947. Yanoff, Jay Myron. The effects of open teaching
styles on involvement and inquiry activity of
elementary school children. 1973. *ERIC ED* 093 66.

Describes no difference in student involvement
in an open classroom by teaching method.

1948. Yeoh, Oon Chye. An exploratory study of the effect
of the class-teacher's behavior associated with
televised science instruction. Ph.D. dissertation.
Stanford University. 1973.

Describes teacher behavior influencing student
verbal behavior during a televised science
program.

1949.   Zahavi, Shoshana & Asher, Steven R. "The effect of
         verbal instructions on preschool children's
         aggressive behavior," *Journal of School Psychology
         16* (1978): 146–152.

             Describes teacher discussion of the results of
         aggression with students resulting in lower
         student aggression.

1950.   Zimmerman, Barry Joseph. "The relationship between
         teacher classroom behavior and student school
         anxiety levels," *Psychology in the Schools 7*,
         (1970): 89–93. Ph.D. dissertation. University of
         Arizona. 1969.

             Describes a relationship between teacher use of
         general or specific verbal reinforcement and
         student school anxiety.

C. ON STUDENT ACHIEVEMENT--DESCRIPTIVE

1951. Aagaard, Stanley A. Oral questioning by the
teacher: Influence on student achievement in
eleventh grade chemistry. Ph.D. dissertation. New
York University. 1973.

Describes greater achievement of students in
classes with higher cognitive levels of teacher
questions.

1952. Aarestad, Janna Serina. Analysis of teacher
selection/retention and student achievement as
related to Selection Research Incorporated's
Teacher Perceiver Interview. Ph.D. dissertation.
University of Minnesota. 1980.

Describes no relationship between 12 aspects of
teacher philosophy and student math achievement
but differences in philosophy from grade 1 to
grade 6.

1953. Acland, Henry. A study of teacher effects based on
students' achievement scores. 1975. *ERIC ED* 109
064.

Describes teacher effects on student
achievement composed of one part which is stable
and one part which varies from year to year.

1954. Acland, Henry. "Are there great teachers?"
Educational Research Quarterly 1, No. 1 (1976):
38-42. 1977. *ERIC ED* 011 879.

Describes achievement of students by teacher
over two years, with a small number of teachers
having high student achievement both years, who
can be described as great teachers.

1955. Acland, Henry. "Stability of teacher effectiveness:
A replication," *Journal of Educational Research*
69 (1972): 289-292.

Reports that gain scores for students in a
teacher's class from year to year had a slight to
moderate relationship, or teachers were slightly
consistent in terms of student achievement.

1956.   Ahern, Thomas J. A study of the relationships
        between local/cosmopolitan characteristics of
        teachers, teacher-pupil interaction and student
        creativity. Ed.D. dissertation. State University
        of New York at Buffalo. 1974.

        Describes teacher behavior and teaching methods
        related to student creativity.

1957.   Allen, Graham. Teaching behavior and pupils' number
        development. 1973. *ERIC ED* 086 548.

        Describes teacher behavior related to student
        learning of number concepts.

1958.   Alpert, Judith Landon. "Teacher behavior and pupil
        performance: Reconsideration of the mediation of
        Pygmalion effects," *Journal of Educational
        Research* 69 (1975): 53-57.

        Describes changes in teacher behavior but no
        changes in the achievement of students in the
        bottom reading group.

1959.   Alschuler, Marjorie Dion Traxler. The relationship
        of teacher characteristics and behaviors to pupil
        growth in the SCIS program. Ph.D. dissertation.
        Northwestern University. 1980.

        Describes behaviors of teachers, leadership
        flexibility, good classroom management and
        consideration, related to greater gains in science
        achievement; while lack of discipline hampered
        student achievement.

1960.   Anderson, Barry D. School bureaucratization and
        student achievement: Towards modeling
        administrative behavior in teachers. Final Report.
        St. Louis, Missouri: Washington University. 1975.
        ERIC ED 105 629.

        Describes an imperfect fit of observational
        data about teacher behavior and its relationship
        to student achievement and a statistical model of
        teaching.

1961.   Anderson, Enid R. A study of observed teacher
        behavior as a predictor of philosophy, attitude
        and first grade reading achievement. Ph.D.
        dissertation. University of Utah. 1972. *ERIC ED*
        075 780.

        Describes no relationship between observed
        teacher behavior, teacher philosophy and student
        reading achievement.

1962.   Anderson, Harry E., Jr., White, William F. &
        Stevens, John C. "Student creativity,
        intelligence, achievement, and teacher classroom
        behavior," *Journal of Social Psychology 78* (1969):
        99-107.

        Describes teacher behavior having a low to
        moderate correlation with student achievement and
        creativity, with democratic leadership and
        knowledge of subject matter related to student
        learning.

1963.   Anderson, John Robert. Classroom interaction,
        academic achievement and creative performance in
        sixth grade classrooms. Ph.D. dissertation.
        Michigan State University. 1972.

        Describes a relationship between classroom
        interaction, teacher use of student ideas, and
        student problem solving and creativity.

1964.   Anderson, L. Evertson, C. & Brophy, J. The
        First-grade Reading Group Study: Technical report
        of experimental effects and process-outcome
        relationships. Vols. I & II. Austin, Texas: Center
        for Research and Development for Teacher
        Education. Texas University at Austin. 1978. *ERIC
        ED* 177 464.

        Describes results of a study of teacher
        behavior, teacher-student interactions and student
        learning, with tables in volume 2.

1965.   Anderson, Robert H. & Ritsher, Cynthia. "Pupil
        progress," In *Encyclopedia of educational
        research.* Edited by Robert L. Ebel. pp. 1050-1062.
        Toronto, Canada: The Macmillan Company. 1969.

        Reviews methods for assessing student progress
        and the influences of teachers on that progress,
        longitudinal studies of child development and
        methods of reporting student progress. For the
        Ebel reference see citation No. 2942.

1966.   Anderson, W. Thomas, Jr. & others. "A comparative
        analysis of student-teacher interpersonal
        similarity/dissimilarity and teaching
        effectiveness," *Journal of Educational Research
        71* (1977): 36-44.

        Describes a relationship between similarity of
        teacher and student personality and teacher
        effectiveness.

1967.   Applegate, Mary De Konty. The effects on reading
        comprehension of questions to aid students in
        focusing attention on underlying concepts while
        establishing purposes for reading. Ed.D.
        dissertation. Temple University. 1979.

            Describes differences in student reading
        achievement when teachers give them different
        purposes for reading, but the differences varied
        by the reading achievement level of the students.

1968.   Arce, Aaron Hilario. Classroom management approach
        preferences of teachers as related to the reading
        achievement of their respective students. Ed.D.
        dissertation. University of Houston. 1978.

            Describes no relationship between teacher
        self-reported management approaches and student
        achievement.

1969.   Archer, N. Sidney & Woodlen, Milton C. The teacher,
        programed materials, and instructional
        interaction--An assessment of five selected
        conditions of teacher and program integration.
        Final Report. Harrisburg, Pennsylvania:
        Pennsylvania State Department of Public
        Instruction. 1967. *ERIC ED* 019 009.

            Describes no differences in student achievement
        in algebra and attitude with five difference
        conditions of programmed instruction, but teacher
        attitude and student reading scores related to
        student achievement.

1970.   Armento, Beverly Jeanne. Selected correlates of
        effective teacher behavior during concept
        instruction: Their design, utility and
        limitations. 1977. *ERIC ED* 137 290.

            Describes teacher behaviors measured by high
        inference observations related to student learning
        outcomes in grades three, four and five.

1971.   Asher, Steven R. & Gottman, John M. "Sex of teacher
        and student reading achievement," *Journal of
        Educational Psychology 65* (1973): 168-171.

            Describes no difference in student reading
        achievement by teacher sex.

1972.   Aspy, David N. "The effect of teacher-offered
        conditions of empathy, positive regard and
        congruence upon student achievement," *Florida
        Journal of Educational Research 11* (1969): 39-48.

Reports that the level of teacher empathy, unconditional positive regard and congruence is related to student achievement in reading.

1973. Beard, Joseph Walser. Teacher effectiveness and style as related to participation in a science curriculum workshop. Ph.D. dissertation. Stanford University. 1969.

Describes differences in behaviors of teachers and relates those differences to student learning.

1974. Becker, Rhoda McShane. "Teacher behaviors related to the mathematical achievement of young children," 1978. *Journal of Educational Research* 73 (1980): 336-340. *ERIC ED* 164 247.

Describes more indirect teaching and active involvement of the learner as related to greater student achievement in math for low socioeconomic status four and five year olds.

1975. Bemis, Katherine Anna Soucek. Relationships between teacher behavior, pupil behavior, and pupil achievement. Ph.D. dissertation. University of New Mexico. 1969. with Luft, Max. 1970. *ERIC ED* 038 189.

Describes relationships between observed teacher instructional behaviors, pupil behavior in the classroom and pupil achievement.

1976. Bentler, Eugenie J. Effects of movement, posture, proximity, and touch on student achievement. Ed.D. dissertation. Rutgers University the State University of New Jersey. 1978.

Describes differences in patterns of relationships of teacher behavior and student achievement for grades four and six.

1977. Berliner, David C. "Tempus Educare," In *Research on teaching: Concepts, findings, and implications.* Edited by Penelope L. Peterson and Herbert J. Walberg. Berkeley, California: McCutchan Publishing Corporation. 1979.

Describes teacher allocation of time, level of task difficulty and student engagement and their relationship to student achievement in reading and mathematics. For the Peterson & Walberg reference see citation No 3001.

1978. Berliner, David C. & Tikunoff, William J. "The
       California Beginning Teacher Evaluation Study:
       Overview of the ethnographic study," *Journal of
       Teacher Education 27*, No. 1 (1976): 24-30. *ERIC
       ED* 128 338.

          Describes observed behaviors of teachers and
       classroom climate related to levels of student
       achievement.

1979. Blackwelder, Evelyn McWhorter. An investigation of
       the effects of teacher-student conferences on the
       reading achievement, attitude toward reading and
       amount of reading by elementary children. Ph.D.
       dissertation. University of Southern California.
       1976.

          Describes differences in student attitude,
       achievement, and student sex related to the amount
       of student reading and the influence of reading
       conferences with the teacher on student reading.

1980. Blair, Timothy R. "Comparison of reading
       achievement with teacher's effort," *Reading
       Improvement 14* (1977): 112-115.

          Describes a relationship between teacher effort
       in teaching reading and student reading
       achievement.

1981. Blair, Timothy Rawlings. Relationship of teacher
       effort and student achievement in reading. Ph.D.
       dissertation. University of Illinois at
       Urbana-Champaign. 1975. *ERIC ED* 110 932.

          Describes teacher effort in teaching reading
       and a relationship between effort and student
       learning.

1982. Blair, Timothy R. The successful teacher of
       reading: An optimistic explainer of variance.
       1975. *ERIC ED* 117 661.

          Describes a study which relates teacher effort
       in reading instruction to student reading
       achievement.

1983. Boak, R. Terrance R. & Conklin, Rodney C. "The
       effect of teachers' levels of interpersonal skills
       on junior high school students' achievement and
       anxiety," *American Educational Research Journal
       12* (1975): 537-543.

          Describes a relationship between teacher
       behavior in interaction with students and student
       achievement.

1984. Bonney, Lewis Alfred. Relationships between content experience and the development of seriation skills in first grade children. Final Reports. Tucson, Arizona: Arizona University. 1970. *ERIC ED* 040 970.

Describes relationships between some but not other seriation skills in first grade children and no change in the relationships resulting from instruction.

1985. Borg, Walter R. "Teacher coverage of academic content and pupil achievement," *Journal of Educational Psychology 71* (1979): 635-645.

Describes two studies where content coverage was related to achievement of students, with student ability and socioeconomic status controlled.

1986. Botti, James Anthony. The comparative effects of congruent and incongruent teacher verbal behavior on higher level learning outcomes of secondary biology students during discovery/inquiry laboratories. Ph.D. dissertation. Pennsylvania State University. 1979.

Describes no difference in student knowledge of science but higher scores on understanding and ability to use science as a process for students whose teachers used verbal behaviors congruent with science as a inquiry process.

1987. Brophy, Jere E. "Stability of teacher effectiveness," *American Educational Research Journal 10* (1973): 245-252. 1972. *ERIC ED* 066 438.

Describes a number of teacher behaviors related to student achievement for teachers whose effects were consistent over several years.

1988. Brophy, Jere E. Teacher behaviors related to learning by low vs. high socio-economic status early elementary students. Report No. 75-5. 1975. *ERIC ED* 146 143.

Describes differences in the behaviors of teachers related to student achievement by student socioeconomic status.

1189. Brophy, Jere E. & Evertson, Carolyn M. Appendix to first year data of Texas Teacher Effectiveness Project: Complex relationships between teacher process variables and student outcome measures.

Austin, Texas: Center for Research and Development
for Teacher Education. Texas University at Austin.
1974. *ERIC ED* 095 173.

Describes differences in the patterns of
teacher behaviors related to student achievement
by the socioeconomic level of students and for
some relationships the most effective pattern
involves moderate amounts of some teacher
behaviors.

1990.   Brophy, Jere E. & Evertson, Carolyn M. Context
variables in research on teaching. Report No.
4046. Austin, Texas: Research and Development
Center for Teacher Education. University of Texas
at Austin. 1976.

Describes the effects of several contexts on
the relationship between teacher behaviors and
student achievement, relationships which would not
have been identified without considering the
varied effects of contexts such as grade level,
pace of lessons, group size.

1991.   Brophy, Jere E. & Evertson, Carolyn M. *Learning
from teaching: A developmental perspective.*
Boston: Allyn & Bacon. 1976.

Reports results of Texas Teacher Effectiveness
Study, a large two year observational study of
teacher effectiveness, in a non-technical manner,
covering aspects such as teacher attitudes, class
management, student response opportunities, and
related research.

1992.   Brophy, Jere E. & Evertson, Carolyn M.
Low-inference observational coding measures and
teacher effectiveness. Austin, Texas: Center for
Research and Development for Teacher Education.
Texas University at Austin. 1973. *ERIC ED* 077
879.

Describes a relationship between observed
teacher behaviors and consistent student
achievement.

1993.   Brophy, Jere E. & Evertson, Carolyn M.
Process-product correlations in the Texas Teacher
Effectiveness Study: Final Report. Austin, Texas:
Center for Research and Development for Teacher
Education. Texas University at Austin. 1974. *ERIC
ED* 091 394.

Describes a relationship between observed
teacher behavior and student achievement, with

different patterns of teacher behavior related to student learning by student socioeconomic level.

1994. Brophy, Jere & Evertson, Carolyn. Teacher behavior and student learning in second and third grades. Report No. 4015. Austin, Texas: Research and Development Center for Teacher Education. University of Texas at Austin. 1975. *ERIC ED* 146 143.

Describes teachers' behaviors and observers' ratings of teachers as related to student achievement, with the patterns of relationships varying by student socioeconomic level.

1995. Brophy, J. & Evertson, C. Teacher education, teacher effectiveness, and developmental psychology. Austin, Texas: Center for Research and Development for Teacher Education. Texas University at Austin. 1975. *ERIC ED* 118 257.

Describes relationships between teacher behavior and student achievement, relationship which differ between low and high SES students.

1996. Brophy, Jere E. & Evertson, Carolyn M. "Teaching young children effectively," *Classroom Interaction Newsletter 9*, No. 2 (1974): 3-8.

Describes a study relating teacher behaviors in early education programs to the learning goals for students within those programs.

1997. Brophy, Jere E. & Evertson, Carolyn M. The Texas Teacher Effectiveness Project: Presentation of non-linear relationships and summary discussion. Report No. 74-6. Austin, Texas: Center for Research and Development for Teacher Education. Texas University at Austin. 1974. *ERIC ED* 099 345.

Describes different patterns of teacher behavior and student-teacher interactions related to student achievement by student socioeconomic level and grade, and some relationships non-linear.

1998. Byars, Jackson A. Development of a behavioral model for teachers of algebra. 1971. *ERIC ED* 048 000.

Describes a model of the behaviors of algebra teachers and relationships between teacher behavior and student achievement, but no relationship between teacher characteristics such as years of experience and student achievement.

1999.   Calfee, Robert & Brown, Roger. "Grouping students
        for instruction," In *Classroom management: the
        78th Yearbook for the National Society for the
        Study of Education. Part II.* Edited by Daniel L.
        Duke. pp. 144-181. Chicago: University of Chicago
        Press. 1979.

            Describes types of classroom groups and the
        effects on teachers and students, on student
        achievement, of the structure of classroom groups.
        For Duke reference see citation No. 2940.

2000.   Calfee, Robert & Calfee, Katherine Hoover. Reading
        and Mathematics Observation System: Description
        and analysis of time expenditures. Beginning
        Teacher Evaluation Study: Phase II. 1973-74. Final
        Report: Vol. III. 2. Princeton, New Jersey:
        Educational testing Service. 1976. *ERIC ED* 127
        367; 131 115.

            Describes percentages of teacher time spent in
        various instructional roles and relates that time
        to student achievement.

2001.   Calfee, Robert & Calfee, Kathryn Hoover. "Reading
        and Mathematics Observation System: Description
        and measurement of time usage in the classroom,"
        Journal of Teacher education 27, No. 4 (1976):
        323-325.

            Describes behaviors of teachers and the
        relationship between those instructional behaviors
        and student achievement.

2002.   Calkins, Dick S., Godbout, R.C., Poynor, L.H. &
        Kingle, C.L. Relationships between pupil
        achievement and characteristics of observed
        teacher behavior distributions. Research Reports
        No. 6. Austin, Texas: Center for Research and
        Development for Teacher Education. Texas
        University at Austin. 1976. *ERIC ED* 147 276.

            Describes few relationships between ratings of
        teachers based on observed teacher behavior and
        student achievement.

2003.   Callaway, Byron & others. A comparison of five
        methods of teaching language arts: Second year.
        1974. *ERIC ED* 092 929.

            Describes greater student achievement in
        language arts when teachers do not use a program
        of integration of reading and language arts.

2004. Chall, Jeanne S. & Feldmann, Shirley C. "First-grade reading--An analysis of the interactions of professed methods, teacher implementation, and child background," *Reading Teacher 19* (1966): 567-573. *ERIC ED* 010 036.

   Reports that both teacher descriptions of instructional methods, observations of teacher behaviors, and appropriate level of difficulty of lesson are related to student achievement in reading.

2005. Citron, Irvin M. & Barnes, Cyrus W. "The search for more effective methods of teaching high school biology to slow learners through Interaction Analysis, Part I. The effects of varying teaching patterns," *Journal of Research in Science Teaching 7* (1970): 9-19.

   Describes a study in which several patterns of teacher behavior were related to student achievement in biology using the Biological Sciences Curriculum Study materials.

2006. Citron, Irvin M. & Barnes, Cyrus W. "The search for more effective methods of teaching high school biology to slow learners through Interaction Analysis, Part II. The effects of various constant teaching patterns," *Journal of Research in Science Teaching 7* (1970): 21-28.

   Describes the effects of constant patterns of teacher behaviors on the science achievement of slow learners, using the Biological Sciences Curriculum Study materials.

2007. Clements, B. The relationship of teacher perceptions to classroom processes and student outcomes. Austin, Texas: Center for Research and Development for Teacher Education. Texas University at Austin. 1980.

   Describes teacher reports of teacher behavior in managing the classroom as related to student learning.

2008. Cohen, Jean. The interaction of teacher guidance and sequence of instruction on mathematics achievement in field dependent and field independent students. Ph.D. dissertation. University of Maryland. 1979.

   Describes the influence of teacher level of guidance and type of sequence of presentation of math content on student learning in relation to

the position of the student on a continuum from
field dependent to field independent.

2009.   Coker, Homer. "Identifying and measuring teacher
        competencies: The Carroll County Project," *Journal
        of Teacher Education 27*, No. 1 (1976): 54-56.

        Describes relationships between observed
        teacher behavior which teachers have identified as
        important and student achievement at the
        elementary level

2010.   Coker, Homer & Lorentz, Jeffrey L. An examination
        of student coping style, teacher control and
        student achievement in reading. *ERIC ED* 155 190.

        Reports that the pre test predicted most of the
        post test reading score variance, leaving little
        to be explained by teacher control and student
        coping style.

2011.   Coker, Homer & Lorentz, Jeffrey L. Observed
        patterns of teacher-pupil classroom behavior as
        predictors of student growth in reading. *ERIC ED*
        150 553.

        Describes observed student and teacher behavior
        as contributing to student achievement in reading
        above the contribution of the pretest score to the
        variance in reading achievement.

2012.   Cole, Shirley Ann. Teacher behaviors associated
        with mathematics achievement in third grade
        students. Ph.D. dissertation. University of
        Arizona. 1978.

        Describes teacher behavior related to student
        reading achievement.

2013.   Collins, Cathy. "Sustained silent reading periods:
        Effect on teacher's behaviors and students'
        achievement," *Elementary School Journal 81* (1980):
        108-114.

        Describes no increase in student achievement
        but an increase in the rate of completion of basal
        readers and in the number of comments that
        teachers are able to make about student reading
        interests after fifteen weeks of sustained silent
        reading.

2014.   Cook, Robert Earl. The effect of teacher
        methodology upon certain achievements of students
        in secondary school biology. Ph.D. dissertation.
        University of Iowa. 1967.

Reports that the more a teacher uses indirect teaching the higher the achievement of students on tests of critical thinking, understanding of the methods of science, and mastery of Biological Sciences Curriculum Study materials.

2015. Cooley, William W. & Leinhardt, Gaea. The Instructional Dimensions Study: The search for effective classroom processes. Final Report. Pittsburgh, Pennsylvania: Learning Research and Development Center. University of Pennsylvania. 1978. *ERIC ED* 167 580.

Describes student opportunities to learn materials covered on achievement tests as related to student achievement; what is taught is more important than how it is taught.

2016. Cooper, J.G. & Bemis, Katherine. Teacher personality, teacher behavior and their effects upon pupil achievement. *ERIC ED* 012 707.

Describes personality characteristics of urban middle class teachers of grade four as related to teacher behaviors and student learning.

2017. Coulter, Mary M. The open classroom: A comparison of teaching effectiveness in the open classroom and the self-contained classroom in a junior high school reading program. Ed.D. dissertation. Brigham Young University. 1979.

Describes no differences in the reading achievement of students taught in open and traditional classrooms

2018. Crawford, John, Brophy, Jere, Evertson, Carolyn, & Coultier, Cynthia. "Classroom dyadic interaction: Factor structures of process variables and achievement correlates," *Journal of Educational Research 69* (1977): 761-772.

Describes relationships between factor scores developed from measures of teacher behavior and student achievement.

2019. Crawford, John, Evertson, Carolyn, Anderson, Linda, & Brophy, Jere. Process-product relationships in second and third grade classrooms. Report No. 76-11. Austin, Texas: Center for Research and Development for Teacher Education. Texas University at Austin. 1976. *ERIC ED* 148 888.

Describes different patterns of relationships between teacher behavior and student achievement

by the socioeconomic level of students in the
school and the context of classroom instruction.

2020.   Crawford, W. John, King, C., Evertson, C. & Brophy,
J. Error rates and question difficulty related to
elementary children's learning. Report No. 75-8.
Austin, Texas: Center for Research and Development
for Teacher Education. Texas University at Austin.
1975. *ERIC ED* 147 275.

Describes differences in the optimal student
error rates for questions for high and low
socioeconomic status students.

2021.   Creamer, Mary & Lorentz, Jeffrey L. Effect of
teacher structure, teacher affect, cognitive level
of questions, group size and student social status
on reading achievement. *ERIC ED* 185 517.

Describes greater student achievement with more
participation in small group activities, and
higher achievement for low SES students with more
questions at a low cognitive level.

2022.   Creemers, Bert P.M. The relationship between
tasksetting teaching behavior and pupil
achievement. 1976. *ERIC ED* 121 785.

Describes a relationship between teacher task
setting behavior and student achievement in
reading and performance in physical education.

2023.   Cromack, Theodore R. Reinforcing and questioning
behavior of teacher as a measure of teacher
effect. Final Report. *ERIC ED* 085 372,

Describes differences in teacher behavior and
the effects of those differences on student
achievement.

2024.   Cunningham, William G. "The impact of student-
teacher pairings on teacher effectiveness,
"*American Educational Research Journal 12* (1975):
169-189.

Describes congruence in teacher teaching style
and student learning style related to student
learning.

2025.   Darer, Evelyn. The relationship between the degree
of openness in classroom organization and selected
aspects of cognitive achievement. Ph.D.
dissertation. New York University. 1978.

Describes open classes and no relationship
between most measures of teacher behavior and
student achievement in elementary open
classrooms.

2026. Davidoff, Stephan H. The development of an
instrument designed to secure student assessment
of teaching behaviors that correlate with
objective measures of student achievement.
Philadelphia, Pennsylvania: Philadelphia School
District. 1970. *ERIC ED* 039 170.

Describes the development of an instrument to
collect student assessments of teacher behavior,
and reports that the teacher behaviors are not
related to student science achievement.

2027. Davidson, Charles W. & Bell, Michael L.
"Relationships between pupil-on-task-performance
and teacher behavior," *Southern Journal of
Educational Research 9* (1975): 223-235.

Describes a relationship between teacher
behavior and student attention to task and student
achievement.

2028. Dimeolo, James Richard. An experimental study
relating elementary classroom teaching behavior to
student achievement. Ed.D. dissertation. Case
Western Reserve University. 1968.

Describes strong non-significant relationships
between teacher behavior and student achievement
in mathematics.

2029. Dixon, George Matthew. Trends in the relationships
between democratic teacher behaviors and student
achievement. Ph.D. dissertation. Georgia State
University. 1980.

Describes no relationship between teacher
democratic behavior and student achievement in
reading and math.

2030. Downing, Diane E. & others. From teacher to
teacher: Relationships between junior high English
teachers' instructional self-reports and student
"amount of learning". (The Texas Junior High
School Study). Austin, Texas: Center for Research
and Development for Teacher Education. Texas
University at Austin. *ERIC ED* 175 001.

Describes teacher reports of their
instructional behavior and the relationship of
those behaviors to student learning.

2031.   Drenchko, Elizabeth K. The comparative
        effectiveness of two methods of teaching grade
        school science. 1966. *ERIC ED* 014 429.

        Describes no differences in student problem
        solving and work study skills with recitation,
        group project and individual project approaches to
        teaching science.

2032.   Dunkin, Michael J. & Doenau, Stanley J. "A
        replication study of unique and joint
        contributions to variance in student achievement,"
        Journal of Educational Psychology 72 (1980):
        394-403.

        Describes instructional content coverage
        related to student achievement in sixth grade
        social studies.

2033.   Duffey, James B. & Martin, Roy P. "The effects of
        direct and indirect teacher influence and student
        trait anxiety on the immediate recall of academic
        materials," *Psychology in the Schools 10* (1973):
        233-237.

        Describes greater achievement for high anxious
        students when teachers use indirect teaching
        behaviors.

2034.   Easton, John Q, Muirhead, R. Scott, Frederick,
        Wayne C. & Vanderwicken, Sara. Relationship among
        student time on task, orientation of teachers, and
        instructional grouping in elementary reading
        classes. 1979. *ERIC ED* 169 503.

        Reports less student engagement in tasks with
        two or more reading groups, and student engagement
        related to student reading achievement.

2035.   Ebert, Dorothy Jo Williamson. Oral language, sex
        and socio-economic status as predictors of reading
        achievement. Ph.D. dissertation. University of
        Texas at Austin. 1974.

        Describes teacher behavior, student
        characteristics and student prior achievement
        related to student reading achievement.

2036.   Eggert, Wallace. Teacher process variables and
        pupil products. 1978. *ERIC ED* 166 174.

        Describes a positive relationship between
        direct instruction and student achievement, but
        not student attitude.

2037.   Ellett, Chad D. & others. Teacher performance and
        pupil achievement on teacher-made tests. 1980.
        ERIC ED 185 022.

        Describes teacher skills measured by the
        Teacher Performance Assessment Instrument (TPAI)
        related to student learning measured by
        teacher-made tests.

2038.   Elrod, Ianelle Abercrombie. A study of teachers'
        frequency of oral expressions of logic and
        critical thinking ability and their relationship
        to students' geometry achievement and critical
        thinking ability. Ed.D. dissertation. Auburn
        University. 1979.

        Describes teacher thinking and verbal behavior
        and relates those to student thinking ability and
        achievement in geometry.

2039.   Emmer, Edmund T., Evertson, C. & Brophy, J.
        "Stability of teacher effects in junior high
        classrooms," *American Educational Research Journal*
        16 (1979): 71-75.

        Describes teacher effects differing by subject
        matter and the entering achievement level of the
        class.

2040.   Emmer, Edmund T. & Peck, Robert F. "Dimensions of
        classroom behavior," *Journal of Educational*
        Psychology 64 (1973): 223-240.

        Describes teacher behavior and relates it to
        student achievement.

2041.   Evans, Judith T. & Rosenthal, Robert. Interpersonal
        self-fulfilling prophecies: Further extrapolations
        from the laboratory to the classroom. Cambridge,
        Massachusetts: Harvard University. 1969. *ERIC ED*
        034 276.

        Describes teachers having greater expectations
        for gains in reasoning IQ for boys, greater gains
        for girls in verbal IQ.

2042.   Evertson, Carolyn M. Relationship of teacher praise
        and criticism to student outcomes. Report No.
        75-7. *ERIC ED* 146 155.

        Describes differences in the effects of teacher
        praise on student achievement by student
        socioeconomic level, with low praise related to
        learning for low SES students.

2043.   Evertson, C.M. Teacher behavior, student
        achievement and student attitudes: Descriptions of
        selected classrooms. Austin, Texas: Center for
        Research and Development for Teacher Education.
        Texas University at Austin. 1979.

        Describes differences in the behavior of
        teachers and students in classrooms with high and
        low student achievement.

2044.   Evertson, C.M., Anderson, C.W., Anderson, L.M. &
        Brophy, J.E. Predictors of student outcomes in
        junior high mathematics and English classes.
        Austin, Texas: Center for Research and Development
        for Teacher Education. Texas University at Austin.
        1979.

        Describes teacher behavior and relates it to
        student achievement; with elements of both direct
        and indirect instruction related to student
        learning in math classes, but English results are
        not so consistent.

2045.   Evertson, Carolyn M., Anderson, Linda & Brophy,
        Jere. Process-outcome relationships in the Texas
        Junior High School Study: Volume I & Compendium.
        Report No. 4061. Austin, Texas: Center for
        Research and Development for Teacher Education.
        Texas University at Austin. 1968. *ERIC ED* 166 192,
        173 744.

        Describes greater relationships between teacher
        behavior and student achievement in math than in
        English classes, probably because there is greater
        agreement on and consistency in student outcomes
        in math than in English.

2046.   Evertson, Carolyn M. & Brophy, Jere E.
        High-inference behavioral ratings as correlates of
        teaching effectiveness. Austin, Texas: Center for
        Research and Development for Teacher Education.
        Texas University at Austin. 1973. *ERIC ED* 078 042;
        095 174.

        Describes a relationship between ratings of
        teachers based on observations of teacher
        behaviors and student achievement.

2047.   Evertson, C., Lambert, D. & Anderson, L. A time to
        learn: A selected review of research with
        implications for instructional time in schools.
        Austin, Texas: Research and Development Center for
        Teacher Education. University of Texas at Austin.
        1977.

Reviews studies and describes conclusions for
teacher management and use of istructional time.

2048. Evertson, C.M., Sanford, J. & Brophy, J.E. Texas
Junior High School Study: Teacher self reports and
student outcomes. Volumes I, II, III, appendix,
executive summary. Austin, Texas: Center for
Research and Development for Teacher Education.
Texas University at Austin. 1980.

Describes teacher reports of their behavior and
the relation of those reported behaviors to
student achievement and attitude. Vol. I is the
narrative report; II and III are tables; appendix
contains the instruments; the executive summary
reports the results without tables of data.

2049. Farnsworth, Briant Jacob. A quantitative study of
student interaction and levels of instruction as
related to teacher effectiveness. Ed.D.
dissertation. Brigham Young University. 1974.

Describes higher pupil interaction (40% to 70%
of the time) associated with higher student
achievement at the end of a short unit of
instruction.

2050. Farnsworth, Briant & Daines, Delva. "A quantitative
study of cognitive instructional levels as related
to pupil achievement," *Reading Improvement 15*
(1978): 69-73.

Reports a relationship between the cognitive
level of lessons and the cognitive level of
student achievement.

2051. Felsenthal, Helen & Kirsch, Irwin. Variations in
teachers' management of and time spent on reading
instruction: Effects on student learning. 1978.
ERIC ED 159 614.

Reports differences in teacher management and
scheduling and student engaged time in reading but
no relationship between them and student reading
achievement.

2052. Finn, Jeremy D. & others. "Teacher expectations and
pupil achievement: A naturalistic study," *Urban
Education 10* (1975): 175-197.

Describes factors which are related to the
expectations which teachers develop for student
achievement and the relationship between
expectations and actual achievement.

2053. Firestone, Glenn & Brody, Nathan. "Longitudinal
       investigation of teacher-student interactions and
       their relationship to academic performance,"
       Journal of Educational Psychology 67 (1975):
       544-550.

       Describes a relationship between teacher
       interactions with kindergarten students and grade
       one achievement of those students.

2054. Fisher, Charles W., Berliner, D.C., Filby, N.N.,
       Marliave, R.S., Cahen, L.S., Dishaw, M.M. & Moore,
       J.E. Teaching and learning in the elementary
       school: A summary of the Beginning Teacher
       Evaluation Study. Technical Report VII-1.
       Beginning Teacher Evaluation Study. San Francisco,
       California: Far West Laboratory for Educational
       Research and Development. 1978. *ERIC ED* 165 322.

       Describes teacher behavior influencing student
       engagement and teacher allocation of instructional
       time, student engagement and teacher behaviors
       related to student achievement.

2055. Fisher, Charles W., Berliner, David C., Filby,
       Nikola N., Marliave, Richard, Cahen, Leonard &
       Dishaw, Marilyn M. "Teaching behaviors, Academic
       Learning Time, and student achievement: An
       overview," In *Time to Learn*. Edited by Carolyn
       Denham & Ann Lieberman. Washington, D.C.: U.S.
       Government Printing Office. 1980.

       Describes relationships between teacher
       allocation of instructional time and teaching
       behaviors and student engagement, task difficulty
       and achievement. For Denham & Lieberman reference
       see citation No. 2933.

2056. Fisher, Charles W., Filby, N.N., Marliave, R.S.,
       Cahen, L.S. Moore, J.E. & Berliner, D.C. A study
       of instructional time in grade 2 reading.
       Technical Report II-4. Beginning Teacher
       Evaluation Study. San Francisco, California: Far
       West Laboratory for Educational Research and
       Development. 1976. *ERIC ED* 145 414.

       Describes a slight relationship between time
       allocation and student achievement, and describes
       variations in rates of student engagement in
       instructional tasks.

2057. Fisher, Charles W., Filby, Nikola N. & Marliave,
       Richard S. "Instructional time and student
       achievement in elementary school," *California
       Journal of Teacher Education 4*, No. 2 (1977):
       23-39.

Describes teacher allocation of instructional time and the relationship of that time allocation to student achievement in reading and math.

2058. Fisher, Charles W., Filby, N.N., Marliave, R.S., Cahen, L.S., Dishaw, M.M., Moore, J.E. & Berliner, D.C. Teaching behaviors, Academic Learning Time and student achievement: Final Report of Phase III-B, Beginning Teacher Evaluation Study. Technical Report V-1. Beginning Teacher Evaluation Study. San Francisco, California: Far West Laboratory for Educational Research and Development. 1978. *ERIC ED* 183 525.

Describes a relationship between teacher behavior and student engagement in assigned tasks and student achievement in the spring and throughout the school year.

2059. Fisher, Charles W., Marliave, R.S., Filby. N.N., Cahen, L.S., Moore, J.E. & Berliner, D.C. A study of instructional time in grade 2 mathematics. Technical Report II-3. Beginning Teacher Evaluation Study. San Francisco, California: Far West Laboratory for Educational Research and Development. 1976. *ERIC ED* 147 186.

Describes time allocated to math and student engaged time in six classes and the relationship of time and student engagement to student achievement.

2060. Fleming, Elyse S. & Anttonen, Ralph G. Teacher expectancy as related to the academic and personal growth of primary-age children. *Monographs of the Society for Research in Child Development 36*, No. 5 (1971): 1-31.

Describes differences in teacher expectations for students and lack of a relationship between those expectations and student achievement

2061. Flowers, Brenda Mae Gupton. The effects of a teacher's instructional behavior on black students' mastery of standard English. Triple "T" Project Mongraph Series, No. 3. Ed.D. dissertation. Temple University. 1974. *ERIC ED* 092 488.

Describes several teacher behaviors which are related to student achievement on a standardized test after twenty days of instruction.

2062. Foat, Classie M. Teacher instructional processes related to black pupils' achievement. Ph.D. dissertation. Stanford University. 1980.

Describes differences in behaviors of teachers
in classrooms with high and low ability students
and identifies structured teaching behaviors as
more effective for black pupils.

2063. Forster, Fred & Carpenter, James. Classroom by
classroom analysis of the impact of a compensatory
education program. 1973. *ERIC ED* 078 094.

Describes a relationship between teacher
behavior and achievement of students in
compensatory programs.

2064. Fox, Ronald B., Peck. R. & Blattstein, D. Effects
of peer-rated coping and teacher structure on
achievement. 1978. *ERIC ED* 168 712.

Describes a relationship between teacher
organizing behavior and student achievement, but
influenced by student coping skills.

2065. Fox, Ronald, Peck, R. & Blattstein, A. Tracing
teacher effects through student behavior to
learning outcomes. 1978. *ERIC ED* 169 039.

Describes teacher behavior in one sixth grade
class as related to student on-task behavior and
in turn to student achievement.

2066. Frederick, Wayne C., Walberg, Herbert J. & Rasher,
Sue Pinzur. "Time, teacher comments, and
achievement in urban high schools," *Journal of
Educational Research 73* (1979): 63-65.

Describes lower loss of instructional time and
more teacher use of positive reinforcement in high
schools with greater student achievement.

2067. Friedman, Morton. "Teachers' cognitive emphasis and
pupil achievement," *Educational Research Quarterly
2*, No. 1 (1977): 42-47.

Describes greater student achievement on
memory-level questions in classrooms where
teachers ask a greater number of memory-level
questions, with no difference in achievement on
comprehension questions, and teachers not observed
to ask synthesis questions.

2068. Fritz, George Robert. High school achievement and
course satisfaction associated with student
ratings of actual-ideal teacher behavior. Ph.D.
dissertation. St. Louis University. 1972.

Describes greater congruence between teacher behavior and student perceptions of ideal teacher behavior related to greater student achievement.

2069. Funderburg, Craig Slaton. A study of first-graders' reading achievement as a function of teacher-student expectancy. Ph.D. dissertation. University of Alabama. 1980.

Describes greater student achievement when teacher and student expectancy is equal or when teachers have greater expectations than students for student achievement.

2070. Furst, Norma Fields. The multiple languages of the classroom: A further analysis and a synthesis of meanings communicated in high school teaching. Ed.D. dissertation. Temple University. 1967.

Describes a study where teachers used special units and there was greater student achievement with more indirect teaching.

2071. Gallagher, James J. A model for studying teacher instructional strategies. 1966. *ERIC ED* 044 359.

Describes a system which relates different amounts of student talk to student achievement, with more talk related to higher achievement.

2072. Gallo, Donald R. "Journal reading and selected measures of teaching effectiveness," *Research in the Teaching of English 4* (1970): 45-50.

Describes teachers who read journals having greater student achievement in poetry on tests, but teachers who do not read journals are rated by students and observers as better teachers of poetry.

2073. Gardner, James Wise. A study of the effect of pupil-teacher interaction on student achievement. Ed.D. dissertation. McNeese State University. 1973.

Describes indirect teaching related to student achievement in social studies, language arts, arithmetic and reading but not science, based on observations of ten classes.

2074. Gersten, Russell M. & Carnine, Doug. Measuring implementation of the Direct Instruction model in an urban school district: An observational approach. 1980. *ERIC ED* 189 188.

Describes levels of teacher implementation of a model of direct instruction and relates the components of the model to student achievement, with low relationships for pacing and lesson format and moderate relationships for other components of the model.

2075.   Gilman, Ann Coombs. The effects of teacher behaviors on the performance of preschool children. Ed.D. dissertation. Northern Illinois University. 1974.

Describes no difference in student achievement or on-task behavior when teacher initiates and when teacher waits for the student to initiate contact.

2076.   Ginther, John R. "A model for strategies of instruction," In *Research into Classroom Processes: Recent developments and next steps.* Edited by Ian Westbury & Arno A. Bellack. pp. 139-153. New York: Teachers College Press. 1971.

Describes a model which relates aspects of instruction and teaching to student learning and describes a study of that model. For Westbury & Bellack reference see citation No. 3039.

2077.   Gleason, Walter Peterson. An examination of some effects of pupil self-instruction methods compared with the effects of teacher-led classes in elementary science on fifth grade pupils. Ed.D. dissertation. Boston University School of Education. 1965.

Describes no differences in student achievement on tests of science facts, general knowledge and liking of science for teacher- and student-led units.

2078.   Good, Thomas L. "The role of rewards and reinforcements in early education programs: The use of concrete rewards," *Journal of School Psychology 10* (1972): 253-261.

Describes the effects on student behavior and learning of concrete and verbal rewards, in early education programs.

2079.   Good, Thomas L. & Grouws, Douglas A. "Process-product relationships in fourth grade mathematics classrooms," *Journal of Teacher Education 28*, No. 3 (1977): 49-54. 1975. *ERIC ED* 125 907.

Describes patterns of teacher behaviors, not single behaviors, related to student achievement.

2080. Good, T. & Grouws, D. "Teaching effectiveness in fourth-grade classrooms," In *The appraisal of teaching: Concepts and process.* Edited by Gary Borich. Reading, Massachusetts: Addison-Wesley. 1977.

Describes teacher behaviors in mathematics instruction in grade four and relates those behaviors to student achievement, developing a model of effective math instruction. For Borich reference see citation No. 2916.

2081. Good, Thomas & Power, Colin. "Designing successful environments for different types of students," *Journal of Curriculum Studies 8* (1976): 45-60. Report No. 102. Columbia, Missouri: Center for Research in Social Behavior. University of Missouri-Columibia.

Reports that both teacher behaviors and student characteristics are related to student achievement and that effective teaching varies by student characteristics.

2082. Hammer, George J "Experimental study of prolonged teacher silence," *Social Science Record 23*, No. 2 (1976): 32-34.

Describes no differences in student learning from teacher verbal presentations after normal teacher speaking and after prolonged teacher silence.

2083. Hannaman, Jo Eva Peak. The relationship between teacher practices in developmental reading instruction and student achievement. Ph.D. dissertation. University of Georgia. 1979.

Describes no relationship between observed teacher practices in developmental reading or supervisor rating and student reading achievement when past student achievement is held constant.

2084. Harris, Albert J. & Serwer, Blanche L. Comparison of reading approaches in first-grade teaching with disadvantaged children (The Craft Project). New York: Research Foundation. City University of New York. Cooperative Research Project No. 2677. USOE. 1966. *ERIC ED* 010 037.

Describes four different methods of reading instruction with grade one disadvantaged

students and reports small inconclusive
differences with the different approaches.

2085.   Harris, Albert J. & Serwer, Blanche L. "The Craft
Project: Instructional time in reading research,"
Reading Research Quarterly 2 (1966): 27-56.

Reports that the amount of time that teachers
allocated to reading instruction was related to
student reading achievement.

2086.   Hastings, Hiram Irving, Jr. A study of the
relationship between teacher-pupil verbal
interaction and pupil achievement in elementary
school science. 1970. *ERIC ED* 079 035.

Reports no differences in achievement of
students with teachers using direct and indirect
teaching, but boys seem to have greater success
with indirect teachers.

2087.   Herman, Wayne L., Jr., Potterfield, James E.,
Dayton, C. Mitchell & Amershek, Kathleen G. "The
relationship of teacher-centered activities and
pupil-centered activities to pupil achievement and
interest in 18 fifth-grade social studies
classes," *American Educational Research Journal 6*
(1979): 227-239.

Describes no differences in student achievement
with student- and teacher-centered classroom
activities.

2088.   Hett, Geoffrey G. The modification and maintenance
of attending behavior for second-, third-, and
fourth-grade children. Ph.D. dissertation.
University of Oregon. 1973.

Describes behavior modification techniques
related to increased student attention to task but
not achievement.

2089.   Honeycutt, Joan K. & Soar, Robert S. The effects of
verbal rewards and punishment on subject-matter
growth of culturally disadvantaged first grade
children. 1970. *ERIC ED* 062 499.

Describes no relationship between teacher
verbal behavior and student achievement.

2090.   Horton, Phillip Bernard. Teacher characteristics
and student achievement in bilingual ISCS. Ph.D.
dissertation. Florida State University. 1979.

Describes a relationship between five teacher behaviors and student achievement in a science unit, but no difference in student achievement by degree of teacher bilinguality or the presence of a bilingual aide.

2091. Hudgins, Bryce B. & Ahlbrand, William P., Jr. A study of classroom interaction and thinking. Interim Report. St. Ann, Missouri: Central Midwestern Regional Educational Laboratory. 1967. *ERIC ED* 026 344.

Describes teacher and student thoughts and verbal interactions and a relationship between teacher level of thinking and level of student thinking in junior high school English.

2092. Hughes, Stuart William. A comparison of the relative effectiveness of a student-directed versus a teacher-directed program of high school environmental science in changing student attitudes toward the environment. Ed.D. dissertation. Temple University. 1979.

Describes greater student attitude and achievement in a teacher-planned and directed science course than in a student-planned and directed course.

2093. Hull, Ray Edward. A study of the relationship of teacher style and pattern of interaction to cognitive level of interaction as measured by content interaction analysis. Ed.D. dissertation. University of Oregon. 1969.

Describes a tendency for direct teaching to be more effective for student learning at lower cognitive levels and indirect teaching more effective at higher cognitive levels.

2094. Hunkins, Francis P. "The influence of analysis and evaluation questions on achievement in sixth grade social studies," *Educational Leadership 25* (1968): 326-332.

Reports greater social studies scores for students when teachers use more questions at higher cognitive levels.

2095. Hunter, Dale Stuart. The relationship of selected teacher behaviors to student achievement and to student attitude in the United States Dependents Schools, European Area. Ed.D. dissertation. University of Southern California. 1974.

Describes the degree of teacher indirect teaching related to student achievement but not attitude.

2096.   Hutcheson, Carol Edmundson. The relationship of student-teacher compatability on student achievement in sixth grade language arts. Ed.D. dissertation. Auburn University. 1979.

Describes no differences in student achievement by degree of match or mismatch in the desired behaviors of teachers and students.

2097.   Ienatsch, Grant Peter. The effectiveness of teacher interaction on televised instruction designed to supplement a reading program for second-graders. Ph.D. dissertation. University of Iowa. 1973.

Describes greater student achievement when teachers interact with students about the *Electric Company* TV program than when students watch the program without interaction and from a program of instruction with basal reader, but no TV.

2098.   Inglis, Sidney A. "The BTES: What makes the difference?" *Thrust for Educational Leadership 9*, No. 4 (1980): 24-26.

Discusses implications of teacher behaviors which are related to student achievement in reading and mathematics.

2099.   Inventasch, Harvey. A comparison of the effects of teacher-directed and self-directed problem solving on attitudes and understandings in science. Ph.D. dissertation. New York University. 1968.

Describes no differences in student achievement with teacher-directed and student-directed problem solving activities.

2100.   Jackson, Gareld L. The relationship between the observed classroom behavior of high school teachers of English and the growth of pupils in knowledge of grammar skills. Ed.D. dissertation. University of Northern Colorado. 1967.

Describes no relationship between observer ratings of teachers and student achievement.

2101.   Jester, R. Emile & Bear, Nancy R. Preliminary results from relationship between teachers' vocabulary usage and the vocabulary of kindergarten and first grade students. 1969. *ERIC ED* 032 135.

Describes student knowledge of vocabulary that teachers' use quite high for kindergarten and first grade children, but varying by student race, grade, and social class.

2102.   John, Alex, Jr. An analysis and comparison of the effects of student sex, student race, teacher behavior, and teacher race upon the achievement of tenth grade English students. Ed.D. dissertation. Northeast Louisiana University. 1972.

Describes a relationship between the ratio of teacher indirect to direct behaviors and student achievement, which varies by student sex, race, and ability group.

2103.   Johnson, David W., Johnson, Roger T. & Scott, Linda. "The effects of cooperative and individualized instruction on student attitudes and achievement," *Journal of School Psychology* *104* (1978): 207-216.

Reports that when teachers work with students in groups to set objectives for math instruction in advanced math for grades five and six, the students achieve more than when the teachers work with individual students to set goals.

2104.   Johnson, Mary Hill. A comparative study of teacher effectiveness and student achievement of target teachers and students of the response to educational needs project and non target teachers and students of Region 1 of the District of Columbia Public Schools. Ed.D. dissertation. University of Maryland. 1978.

Describes behavior of teachers implementing a staff development plan and some differences in achievement of students with those and other teachers.

2105.   Johnson, Nancy Plattner. Mathematics problem solving and classroom environment. Ph.D. dissertation. University of Wisconsin-Madison. 1979.

Describes greater student achievement in math problem solving in open than in traditional classrooms but no relation to student locus of control.

2106.   Jolly, Pauline E. Student achievement in biology in terms of cognitive styles of students and teachers. Ph.D. dissertation. Louisiana State University and Agricultural and Mechanical College. 1980.

Describes higher achievement in biology for
students who were more field-independent and for
students of more field-independent teachers, but
no greater achievement when teachers and students
were matched on field dependence.

2107. Jones, G.A. & Romberg, T.A. Three "time on task"
studies and their implications for teaching and
teacher education. Project Paper No. 79-6.
Madison, Wisconsin: Research and Development
Center for Individualized Schooling. University of
Wisconsin-Madison. 1979.

Describes three studies of student time on task
and teacher behaviors related to time on task as
related to student achievement.

2108. Keefe, Paul Henry. A study of the relationship of
indirect teaching behavior to the self-concept and
reading achievement of third-, fourth-, fifth-,
and sixth-grade pupils. Ed.D. dissertation.
University of Miami. 1974.

Describes greater student achievement in the
middle elementary grades with more indirect
teaching, but no effect on student self-concept.

2109. Kerr, William. Classroom verbal interaction
patterns of secondary school teachers who are
perceived as most effective. Ed.D. dissertation.
Lehigh University. 1973.

Describes differences in the classroom
behaviors of teachers perceived to be more and
less effective, with more effective teachers using
more praise, being more accepting of student ideas
and feelings.

2110. Kidder, Steven J., O'Rielly, Robert P. & Kiesling,
Herbert J. Quantity and quality of instruction:
Empirical investigations. 1975. *ERIC ED* 110 417.

Reports that instructional time is related to
achievement when student, school and teacher
background are controlled, but the relationship
varies by student ability.

2111. Kim, Byong Sung. Teachers' instructional climate,
mastery model strategy and student achievement at
different grade levels. Ph.D. dissertation.
Michigan State University. 1980.

Describes teacher-created environment and
teacher expectations related to student
achievement, with expectations having the stronger
relationship.

2112.   Kleinman, Gladys S. "Teachers' questions and
        student understanding of science," *Journal of
        Research in Science Teaching 3* (1965): 307-317.

        Describes differences in teachers' use of
        critical thinking questions, with greater student
        understanding of science with more frequent use of
        critical thinking questions.

2113.   Kochendorf, Leonard Hjalmar. A comparative study of
        the classroom practices and teaching rationale of
        high school biology teachers using different
        curriculum materials. 1966. *ERIC ED* 020 125.

        Describes differences in the behaviors of
        teachers using and not using Biological Sciences
        Curriculum Study materials and resulting
        differences in student understanding of the nature
        of scientific work.

2114.   Kovaly, Marlene Joan. Predicting algebra one
        success using grade eight mathematics performance,
        teacher predictions, and a prognostic test. Ph.D.
        dissertation. University of Florida. 1979.

        Three predictor variables account for the
        differences in algebra 1 achievement, grade eight
        math performance, grade eight teacher's prediction
        of final course grade in ninth grade math, and
        results of a math test.

2115.   Kugle, C.L. & Calkins, Dick S. The effect of
        considering student opportunity to learn in
        teacher behavior research. Research Report No. 7.
        Austin, Texas: Center for Research and Development
        for Teacher Education. Texas University at Austin.
        1976. *ERIC ED* 189 059.

        Describes teacher behaviors not significantly
        related to student achievement after a period of
        instruction when student opportunity to learn
        material is considered.

2116.   Lamanna, Joseph B., Jr. The effect of teacher
        verbal behavior on pupil achievement in problem
        solving in sixth grade mathematics. Ed.D.
        dissertation. St. John's University. 1968.

        Describes no relationship between teacher
        verbal behavior with students and student problem
        solving, but indirect teaching related to greater
        student achievement for high ability students.

2117.   Lambert, Nadine M. & Hartsough, Carolyn. "APPLE
        observation variables as measures of teacher

performance," *Journal of Teacher Education 27*, No. 4 (1976): 320-323. *ERIC ED* 131 114.

Describes teacher behaviors and relates them to grade level and student achievement.

2118.   Lambert, Nadine M. & Hartsough, Carolyn S. APPLE observation variables and their relationship to reading and mathematics achievement. Beginning Teacher Evaluation Study: Phase II, 1973-74. Final Report: Vol. III.1. Princeton, New Jersey: Educational Testing Service. 1976. *ERIC ED* 127 366.

Describes behaviors of teachers in grades two and five teaching reading and math and relates those behaviors to student achievement.

2119.   Lambeth, Charlotte Reed. Teacher invitations and effectiveness as reported by secondary students in Virginia. Ed.D. dissertation. University of Virginia. 1980.

Describes relationships between teacher behaviors and student learning, with student perceptions of teacher caring as the best predictor of student achievement.

2120.   Land, M.L. "Low-inference variables of teacher clarity: Effects on student concept learning," *Journal of Educational Psychology 71* (1979): 795-799.

Describes teacher clarity related to student achievement but not to student retention of learned material.

2121.   Land, M.L. & Smith, L.R. "The effect of low inference teacher clarity inhibitors on student achievement," *Journal of Teacher Education 30*, No. 3 (1979): 55-57.

Describes teacher clarity of presentation related to student achievement.

2122.   Larrivee, Barbara Ann. The effects of individualization, teacher-directiveness, and learner support on first-grade reading achievement. Ed.D. dissertation. University of Massachusetts. 1976.

Describes behavior of teachers in three areas, with greater student achievement with low teacher directiveness and high support for students.

2123. Larsen, Jean M. "Effects of increased teacher support on young children's learning," *Child Development 46* (1975): 631–637.

Describes a relationship between teacher support for students and student achievement of cognitive and motor skills.

2124. La Shier, William S., Jr. & Westmeyer, Paul. "The use of Interaction Analysis in BSCS Laboratory Block classrooms," *Journal of Teacher Education 18* (1967): 439–446.

Reports that students in classrooms with indirect teaching have higher achievement than students with direct teaching on a six week science unit.

2125. Lawlor, Francis Xavier. The function of verbal rewards in the science classroom. 1970. *ERIC ED* 038 326.

Reports that students experienced with a new science curriculum worked faster with no teacher rewards while students not familiar with the curriculum worked faster with rewards from the teacher.

2126. Leinhardt, Gaea. Applying a classroom process model to instructional evaluation. 1977. *ERIC ED* 150 197.

Describes a relationship between clusters of teacher behaviors and student achievement in two classrooms.

2127. Levy, Alan William. The effects of teacher verbal behavior on the language development of Head Start children. Ph.D. dissertation. Case Western Reserve University. 1968. *ERIC ED* 046 945.

Reports that teachers have higher student achievement when they are more skilled at eliciting student verbal behavior, reward students appropriately, maintain positive social-emotional relations with students and model verbal behavior.

2128. Linz, Ludwig William. The relative effectiveness of inductively and deductively sequenced modes of teacher-centered presentation in high school chemistry. Ed.D. dissertation. University of Maine. 1972.

Describes greater student achievement on units in high school chemistry with a deductive instructional sequence, but student sex and IQ interacted with instructional method to effect student learning.

2129.   Lorentz, Jeffrey L. The development of measures of teacher effectiveness from multiple measures of student growth. 1977. *ERIC ED* 137 403.

Describes a relationship between student achievement and observed behaviors of teachers.

2130.   Lorentz, Jeffrey L. & Coker, Homer. Empirically derived dimensions of classroom behavior as predictors of student achievement. 1980. *ERIC ED* 186 490.

Describes a number of teacher behaviors and classroom organizational variables which are related to one or more measures of student achievement.

2131.   Lorentz, Jeffrey L. & Coker, Homer. The relationships between low-inference measures of classroom behavior and pupil growth: A cross-validation. 1979. *ERIC ED* 177 192.

Describes behaviors of teachers related to student achievement, based on four observation instruments.

2132.   Lorentz, Jeffrey L. & others. The Georgia Assessment of Teacher Effectiveness (GATE) as a predictor of reading achievement. 1978. *ERIC ED* 169 075.

Describes six dimensions of teacher behavior which are related to student achievement in elementary school.

2133.   Loucks, S.F. An exploration of levels of use of an innovation and the relationship to student achievement. Austin, Texas: Center for Research and Development for Teacher Education. Texas University at Austin. 1976. *ERIC ED* 123 805.

Describes behaviors of teachers using individualized instruction in reading and math and the relationship of the use of the innovation to student achievement.

2134.   Loudermilk, Gloria Neubert. Determining the effectiveness of a student-centered method of instruction for teaching an independent comprehension strategy. Ph.D. dissertation. University of Maryland. 1978.

Describes two methods of instruction with different effects on student learning by levels of student prior achievement.

2135. Low, Lana Wiles, The enduring effects of first-grade teachers on subsequent achievement of their students. Ph.D. dissertation. Virginia Polytechnic Insitute and State University. 1980.

Reports decreases in achievement in subsequent grades of students who as first-graders were in a single class with higher achievement than other first grade classes.

2136. Lucking, Robert Alfred. A study of the effects of a hierarchically-ordered questioning technique on adolescents' responses to short stories. Ph.D. dissertation. University of Nebraska-Lincoln. 1975.

Describes greater student achievement in interpretation of short stories when teachers use a sequence of questions in hierarchical order by cognitive level.

2137. McConnell, John William. Relationships among high-inference measures of teacher behaviors and student achievement and attitude in ninth grade algebra classes. Ph.D. dissertation. Northwestern University. 1978. *ERIC ED* 141 118.

Describes a relationship between some observed teacher behaviors and student ratings of teachers and those related to student attitude and achievement.

2138. McConnell, John W. & Bowers, Norman D. A comparison of high-inference and low-inference measures of teacher behaviors as predictors of pupil attitudes and achievements. 1979. *ERIC ED* 171 780.

Describes a relationship between high and low inference measures of teacher behavior and student attitude and achievement, although the relation-ships are not strong.

2139. McDonald, Frederick J. Summary Report. Beginning Teacher Evaluation Study: Phase II, 1973-74. Princeton, New Jersey: Educational testing Service. 1976. *ERIC ED* 127 375.

Summarizes the results of observations of teachers, and reports relationships between patterns of teacher behaviors and student achievement in reading and mathematics.

2140.   McDonald, Frederick J. "Report on Phase II of the Beginning Teacher Evaluation Study," *Journal of Teacher Education 27*, No. 1 (1976): 39-42.

Describes a relationship between patterns of teacher behaviors and student achievement, with different patterns by grade and subject area.

2141.   McDonald, Frederick J. "The effects of teaching performance on pupil learning," *Journal of Teacher Education 27*, No 4 (1976): 317-319. also titled "A report on the results of Phase II of the Beginning Teacher Evaluation Study: The effects of teaching performance on pupil learning," 1976. *ERIC ED* 131 117.

Describes relationships between teacher behaviors and student achievement, with different patterns of relationships by subject and grade.

2142.   McDonald, Frederick J. & Elias, Patricia. "A report on the results of Phase II of the Beginning Teacher Evaluation Study: An overview," *Journal of Teacher Education 27*, No. 4 (1976): 315-316.

Describes patterns of teacher behaviors related to student achievement.

2143.   McDonald, Frederick J. & Elias, Patricia. Executive Summary Report. Beginning Teacher Evaluation Study, Phase II, 1973-74. Princeton, New Jersey: Educational Testing Service. 1976. *ERIC ED* 142 592.

Describes patterns of teacher behavior related to student learning of reading and math in grades two and five.

2144.   McDonald, Frederick J. & Elias, Patricia. The effects of teaching performances on pupil learning. Beginning Teacher Evaluation Study: Phase II, 1973-74: Vol. I. Princeton, New Jersey: Educational Testing Service. 1976. *ERIC ED* 127 364.

Describes patterns of teacher behaviors related to student learning, with a discussion of the variations by student grade and subject matter.

2145. Mahaffey, Linda L. & others. Teacher feedback to children's answers: Process-product relationships. Report No. 75-9. Austin, Texas: Research and Development Center for Teacher Education. University of Texas at Austin. 1975. *ERIC ED* 146 153.

Describes effective teaching behaviors varying by student socioeconomic level, with effective teachers with low SES students staying with one student until that student gets a right answer.

2146. Manning, Diane. "The reading and mathematics achievement of remedial middle school students taught by teachers versus paraprofessionals," *Reading Improvement 16* (1979): 35-42.

Describes no difference in student achievement related to whether the student was instructed by a teacher or a paraprofessional.

2147. Marcus, Irwin M. "The influence of teacher-child interaction on the learning process," *Journal of the American Academy of Child Psychiatry 10* (1971): 481-500.

Describes a relationship between teacher race and teaching style and student achievement in summer school.

2148. Markin, Mary Bailey. The relationship between the employment of teacher aides in kindergarten classrooms and the improvement of student academic achievement. Ph.D. dissertation. Florida State University. 1978.

Describes a relationship between the amount of time that aides are used, student sex, student socioeconomic level and student achievement.

2149. Marliave, Richard S., Fisher, Charles W. & Dishaw, Marilyn M. Academic Learning Time and student achievement in the A-B period. Technical Note V-1a. Beginning Teacher Evaluation Study. San Francisco, California: Far West Laboratory for Educational Research and Development. 1977.

Describes the effects of time allocation, task difficulty level and student engagement on student learning during the first half of the school year.

2150. Marliave, Richard S., Fisher, Charles W. & Dishaw, Marilyn M. Academic Learning Time and student achievement in the B-C period. Technical

Note V-2a. Beginning Teacher Evaluation Study. San Francisco, California: Far West Laboratory for Educational Research and Development. 1978.

Describes effects of time allocation, task difficulty level and student engagement on student learning during the second half of the school year.

2151.   Marsh, David D. "The classroom effectiveness of Teacher Corps graduates: A national assessment," *Journal of Classroom Interaction 15*, No. 1 (1979): 25-33.

Describes a relationship between several classroom process variables and student growth in reading and self-concept.

2152.   Marshall, Hermine H. Variations in classroom structure and growth in reading. *ERIC ED* 146 553.

Describes a relationship between student achievement and classroom openness, student involvement and student responsibility for learning.

2153.   Martin, Jack. "Effects of teacher higher-order questions on student process and product variables in a single-classroom study," *Journal of Educational Research 72* (1979): 183-187.

Describes teacher use of higher order questions related to classroom processes but not to student achievement.

2154.   Martin, Jeanne. Differences in teacher-student interactions within reading groups. Austin, Texas: Center for Research and Development for Teacher Education. Texas University at Austin. 1979. *ERIC ED* 188 128.

Describes teacher ratings of student behavior and teacher behavior in interaction with students during reading instruction as related to student reading achievement.

2155.   Martinez, David Herrera. A comparison of the behavior, during reading instruction, of teachers of high and low achieving first grade classes. Ed.D. dissertation. University of Oregon. 1973.

Describes no differences in the behavior of two teachers with high and low student achievement.

2156. Massialas, Byron G. & others. Structure and process of inquiry into social issues in secondary schools, Vol. 3, social issues classroom discourse: A study of expository, inquiry non-probing, inquiry-probing classes. 1970. *ERIC ED* 052 124.

   Describes behaviors of teachers classified into three categories with greater student achievement on a test of critical thinking and student ratings of the class when teachers exhibited probing behaviors in class discussions.

2157. Mattson, Robert H. & Buckley, Nancy K. Teacher effectiveness in control of child behavior. Section Three. Interim report. 1968. *ERIC ED* 027 567.

   Describes a relationship between teacher ratings as effective and smoothness of transition periods and teacher involvement in outside activities.

2158. Mendoza, Sonia M., Brophy, Jere E. & Good, Thomas L. Who talks in junior high classrooms? Report No. 68. Austin, Texas: Research and Development Center for Teacher Education. University of Texas at Austin. 1972. *ERIC ED* 150 125.

   Describes quantitative but not qualitative differences in teacher interactions with students at three levels of achievement.

2159. Miller, Lewis Jerold. Fostering interest in children's literature: Selected teachers' practices and competencies. Ed.D. dissertation. Indiana University. 1969.

   Describes differences in reading levels of grade five and six students in classrooms with teachers who were rated as high and low in specified teaching practices and competencies.

2160. Moody, William Braun. An investigation of the relationship between fifth-grade student and teacher performance on selected tasks involving nonmetric geometry. 1968. *ERIC ED* 028 933.

   Describes greater post-test achievement for classes taught by teachers than using self-instructional materials and a relationship between teacher score and student scores on test of instructional content.

2161.   Morine-Dershimer, G, Galluzzo, G. & Fagal, F. Rules
         of discourse, classroom status, pupil
         participation, and achievement in reading. Final
         Report Part II. Syracuse University. 1980.

             Describes student participation in verbal
         interactions as related to student achievement.

2162.   Morrison, Betty Mae. The reactions of internal and
         external children to patterns of teaching
         behavior. Ph.D. dissertation. University of
         Michigan. 1966. *ERIC ED* 039 180.

             Describes no difference in achievement for
         internal and external students with the same level
         of teacher reinforcement, but more reinforcement
         is related to more achievement.

2163.   Mottillo, Joseph Louis. A comparative analysis of
         achievement and attitudes of twelfth grade PSSC
         physics students when they receive as opposed to
         when they do not receive behavioral objectives
         prior to instruction. Ed.D. dissertation. Wayne
         State University. 1973.

             Describes greater student achievement with PSSC
         physics materials when students are provided with
         instructional objectives.

2164.   Mullinix, Darrel D. "Teacher behavior and student
         learning in 15 BSCS green version biology
         classes," *School Science and Mathematics 78*
         (1978): 400-407.

             Describes a weak relationship between teacher
         use of indirect teaching and student classroom
         behavior and student achievement in biology using
         the Biological Sciences Curriculum Study
         materials.

2165.   Neill, Robert D. The effects of selected teacher
         variables on the mathematics achievement of
         academically talented junior high school pupils.
         Ed.D. dissertation. Teachers College, Columbia
         University. 1966.

             Describes student characteristics as having a
         greater relationship than teacher characteristics
         to student achievement.

2166.   Nelson, Rosemary Orlene. The effect of different
         types of teaching methods and verbal feedback on
         the performance of beginning readers. Ph.D.
         dissertation. State University of New York at
         Stony Brook. 1972.

Describes the effects of teacher feedback about performance on student reading performance.

2167. Nikoloff, Sayra Elizabeth Benson. The relationship of teacher standards to the written expression of fifth and sixth grade children. Ed.D. dissertation. State University of New York at Buffalo. 1965.

Describes no differences in the writing produced by fifth and sixth grade students in classrooms with strict and less strict teachers in terms of standards for students.

2168. O'Brien, Mary Catherine. The effect of specific classroom organizational and teacher-mediated practices on teacher perceptions, student achievement, and self-concept. Ed.D. dissertation. Boston University School of Education. 1977.

Describes teachers using the behaviors included in the Individually Guided Education model but those behaviors not related to greater student achievement.

2169. Ohberg, Hjordis G. Achievement of LSE black children with teachers of different sex and ethnic identity. 1970. *ERIC ED* 083 219.

Reports no relationship between teacher sex and ethnic identity and teacher behaviors toward students and student achievement.

2170. Ouzts, Danny Terrell. The effects of learning modality grouping and instruction on total reading achievement and word recognition for first grade students. Ph.D. dissertation. University of South Carolina. 1979.

Describes the characteristics of auditory learners and the relationship of those characteristics to effective instruction.

2171. Peck, Robert F. How do teachers and students interact to create the outcomes of education? Austin, Texas: Center for Research and Development for Teacher Education. Texas University at Austin. 1975. *ERIC ED* 128 336.

Describes factors in interactions between teachers and students within instructional settings in terms of the effects of those interactions on student learning.

2172.   Peck, Robert F., Fox, R.B. & Marston, P.T. Teacher
        effects on student achievement and self-esteem.
        1977. *ERIC ED* 141 723.

        Describes a relationship between teacher
        behavior and student achievement, with
        interactions with student characteristics and
        non-linear relationships, with moderate amounts of
        some teacher behaviors more effective than higher
        or lower levels.

2173.   Peck, Robert F. & others. Student evaluation of
        teaching: A multivariate validation study. Austin,
        Texas: Center for Research and Development for
        Teacher Education. Texas University at Austin.
        1978. *ERIC ED* 169 128.

        Describes student ratings of teachers as
        related to teacher personality and behavior and to
        student achievement.

2174.   Peck, R.F. & Veldman, D.J. Effects of teacher
        characteristics on cognitive and affective gains
        of pupils. Austin, Texas: Center for Research and
        Development for Teacher Education. Texas
        University at Austin.1973.

        Reports that for teachers who had consistent
        student achievement gains over four years, those
        behaviors which were related to greater student
        achievement were also related to decreases in
        student attitude, although the relationship varied
        by student SES level.

2175.   Peng, Samuel S. & Ashburn, Elizabeth A. "Teacher
        affect in relation to pupil achievement," *Journal
        of Teacher Education 29*, No. 4 (1978): 76-79.

        Describes a negative relationship for low SES
        students between reported positive teacher affect
        and student achievement.

2176.   Penick, John E. "Creativity in fifth-grade science
        students: The effects of two patterns of
        instruction," *Journal of Research in Science
        Teaching 13* (1976): 307-314.

        Describes greater student gains on a creativity
        test with more indirect teaching, but not
        differences in student cognitive gains between
        teachers who are more direct and indirect.

2177.   Penick, John E. & others. "Studying the effects of
        two quantitatively defined teaching strategies on
        student behavior in elementary school science

using macroanalytic techniques," *Journal of Research in Science Teaching 13* (1976): 289-296. 1974. ERIC ED 091 244.

Describes patterns of teacher direct and indirect teaching related to student learning.

2178. Perales, Alonso. The effects of teacher-oriented and student-oriented strategies on self-concept, English language development and social studies achievement of fifth grade Mexican American students. Ph.D. dissertation. University of Texas at Austin. 1979.

Describes greater student achievement and self concept with student-oriented than with teacher-oriented social studies lessons over a school year.

2179. Peterson, Penelope L. "Interactive effects of student anxiety, achievement orientation, and teacher behavior on student achievement and attitude," *Journal of Educational Psychology 69* (1977): 779-792.

Describes interactions between student personality and teacher instructional treatment and their influence on student achievement on a two week social studies unit.

2180. Peterson, P.L. & Janicki, T.C. "Individual characteristics and children's learning in large-group and small-group approaches," *Journal of Educational Psychology 71* (1979): 677-687.

Reports that student achievement varied by group size and initial student ability, with higher ability students doing better in small and lower ability students in larger groups.

2181. Petit, Virginia Marie. An analysis of the teaching behaviors of PSSC and N-PSSC physics teachers and their effect on student cognitive achievement in physics and student understanding of the process of science. Ph.D. dissertation. University of Michigan. 1969.

Describes differences in teacher behavior, with a greater number of higher cognitive level questions for the PSSC physics teachers and those questions related to greater student achievement, but little inquiry in either set of classrooms.

2182.   Phillips, Barbara Riley. The effects of teachers on the achievement of black, inner city, elementary school children. Ph.D. dissertation. University of Pennsylvania. 1979.

Describes a relationship between teacher characteristics and behavior and the language arts achievement of students.

2183.   Piestrup, Ann McCormick. Black dialect interference and accommodations of reading instruction in first grade. Monograph No. 4. Berkeley, California: Language and Behavior Research Laboratory. University of California, Berkeley. 1973. *ERIC ED* 119 113.

Describes teacher characteristics and behavior related to reading achievement of black students who speak black dialect.

2184.   Pinney, R.H. Teacher presentational behaviors related to student achievement in English and social studies. 1970. *ERIC ED* 046 895.

Describes behaviors of teachers presenting content to be learned and relates those behaviors to student achievement.

2185.   Pitts, Marcella Rosalie. The relationship of classroom instructional characteristics and writing performance in required composition classrooms. Ed.D. dissertation. University of California, Los Angeles. 1979.

Describes behaviors of teachers which are related to the competency level of the students in the instructional group and to the achievement of those students in writing.

2186.   Politzer, Robert L. "Requesting in elementary school classrooms," *TESOL Quarterly 14* (1980): 165-174.

Reports that student improvement in language is related to teacher use of imperatives during instruction in elementary classrooms.

2187.   Politzer, Robert L. & Lewis, Shirley A.R. The relationship of the Black English Tests for teachers and selected teaching behaviors to pupil achievement. 1978. *ERIC ED* 153 215.

Describes a relationship between teacher behavior in the classroom and student achievement.

2188. Popham, W. James. Development of a proficiency test of teaching proficiency. Final Report. Los Angeles, California: University of California, Los Angeles. 1967. *ERIC ED* 013 242.

Describes no difference in achievement of students taught short lessons by teachers and other adults without training as teachers.

2189. Popham, W.J. "Teaching skill under scrutiny," *Phi Delta Kappan 52* (1971): 599-602.

Describes the development of a teaching performance test and no differences in the levels of performance on the test between trained teachers and other groups without teacher training.

2190. Popham, W. James. Validation results: Performance tests of teaching proficiency in vocational education. 1969. *ERIC ED* 027 260.

Describes no difference in student achievement in a ten hour high school unit taught by teachers and non-teachers.

2191. Powell, Evan Rhys. "Teacher behavior and pupil achievement," *Curriculum and Instruction Newsletter 3*: 23. Ph.D. dissertation. Temple University. 1968.

Describes student achievement with three years of indirect teaching and gains in the fourth year with some direct as well as the indirect teaching.

2192. Powell, Glen Huel. The relationship of teacher reinforcement to pupil behavior and reading achievement. Ph.D. dissertation. University of Georgia. 1979.

Describes teacher and pupil behavior affected by prior student achievement, but pupil on-task and teacher reinforcing behavior not related to student achievement.

2193. Poynor, L.H., Calkins, D.S. & Kugle, C.L. An investigation of the effects of classroom contextual variables in analyses of relationships between teacher behaviors and pupil achievement. Austin, Texas: Center for Research and Development for Teacher Education. Texas University at Austin. 1976.

Describes different relationships between teacher behavior and student achievement by context variables, such as the presence of ability grouping, extent of individualized instruction, pupil sex, and teacher age and years of experience.

2194.   Pratt, H., Winters, W. & George, A.A. The effects of a concerns-based implementation plan on the achievement of elementary science students. Austin, Texas: Research and Development Center for Teacher Education. University of Texas at Austin. 1980. *ERIC ED* 192 446.

Describes a relationship between teacher use of a new science program and student achievement, with greater student achievement for higher ability students.

2195.   Quirk, Thomas J. & others. The classroom behavior of teachers and students during compensatory reading instruction. No. PR-74-5. Princeton, New Jersey: Educational Testing Service. 1973. *ERIC ED* 100 965.

Describes teacher behaviors and relates those behaviors to student behavior and reading achievement.

2196.   Rich, H. Lyndall. The effects of teaching style on student behaviors as related to social-emotional development. 1973. *ERIC ED* 075 376.

Describes greater student achievement when teachers use direct or indirect teaching styles which are matched to student level of devlopment.

2197.   Richey, Betty Jean Bowery. An analysis of selected administrative, teaching, and student learning variables related to reading in the elementary schools in the state of Mississippi. Ph.D. dissertation. University of Southern Mississippi. 1980.

Describes teacher effectiveness but not teacher and principal expectations and leadership behavior related to student gains in reading achievement.

2198.   Rim, Eui-Do & Coller, Alan R. In search of nonlinear process-product functions in existing schooling effects data: I. A reanalysis of the first grade reading and mathematics data from the Stallings and Kaskowitz Follow Through study. Philadephia, Pennsylvania: Research for Better Schools, Inc. 1978. *ERIC ED* 179 289.

Reports that a number of relationships between teacher behavior and student achievement are curvilinear, in which there is some optimal level of the teacher behavior and more or less of the behavior is not as effective; some relationships are more complex, as in quadratic relationships.

2199. Rist, Ray C. "Student social class and teacher expectations: The self-fulfilling prophecy in ghetto education," *Harvard Educational Review 40* (1970): 411-451.

Describes relationships between teacher behavior and the classroom behavior and learning of poverty students.

2200. Rist, Ray C. *The urban school: A factory for failure. A study of education in American society.* Cambridge, Mass.: MIT Press. 1973. *ERIC ED* 086 781.

Describes the interactions of teachers and students in one urban school and documents the ways that teachers' behaviors encourage student failure to learn.

2201. Ritter, William Robert Myron. A comparison of achievement--for two methods of instruction, with the use of behavioral objectives. Ed.D. dissertation. University of Pennsylvania. 1975.

Describes no differences in achievement but differences in rate of completion of materials with student self-paced and teacher-paced instruction.

2202. Robitaille, D.F. "Classroom personality patterns of teachers of secondary mathematics," *Alberta Journal of Educational Research 21* (1975): 249-254.

Describes a relationship between patterns of teacher behaviors and student success in secondary math.

2203. Rosenbloom, Paul C. & others. Characteristics of mathematics teachers that affect student learning: Final Report. Minneapolis, Minnesota: Minnesota School Mathematics and Science Center. University of Minnesota. 1966. *ERIC ED* 021 707.

Describes most effective teachers as having a greater variety of ideas about success and failure in their teaching and a greater variety of ways of teaching math concepts.

2204.   Rosenshine, Barak V. "How time is spent in
        elementary classrooms," *Time to Learn*. Edited by
        Carolyn Denham and Ann Lieberman. pp. 127-138.
        Washington, D.C.: U.S. Government Printing Office.
        1980.

        Describes patterns of teacher allocation of
        instructional time in reading and mathematics in
        grades two and five. For Denham & Lieberman
        reference see Citation No. 2933.

2205.   Rupley, William H. Stability of teacher effect on
        pupils' reading achievement over a two year period
        and its relation to instructional emphasis. *ERIC
        ED* 145 394.

        Describes some teachers who are effective over
        two years as having greater emphasis on diagnosis
        of student reading\problems, on comprehension
        following reading, on structured reading
        activities and on application of reading skills.

2206.   Rupley, Willliam H. "Teacher instructional emphasis
        and student achievement in reading," *Peabody
        Journal of Education 54* (1977): 286-291.

        Describes student achievement as related to
        teacher behaviors and instructional strategies.

2207.   Rupley, William H. & McNamara, James
        F. Longitudinal investigation of the effects of
        teachers' reading instructional emphasis and pupil
        engaged time in reading instruction on pupils'
        reading achievement. 1978. *ERIC ED* 185 497.

        Describes differences in reading instructional
        behavior between grade three and six teachers and
        patterns of teacher behavior related to student
        achievement.

2208.   Ryan, Frank L. "The effects on social studies
        achievement of multiple student responding to
        different levels of questioning," *Journal of
        Experimental Education 42*, (1974): 71-75.

        Describes a relationship between high and low
        levels of teacher questioning and frequency of
        student response to questions and student
        achievement.

2209.   Samph, Thomas. "Teacher behavior and the reading
        performance of below-average achievers," *Journal
        of Educational Research 67*, No. 6 (1974):
        268-270.

Describes indirect teacher behaviors as related to greater student language skill development and positive attitudes.

2210. Sandoval, Jonathan. The evaluation of teacher behavior through observation of videotape recordings. Beginning Teacher Evaluation Study: Phase II, 1973-74, Final Report: Vol. III.3. Princeton, New Jersey: Educational testing Service. 1976. *ERIC ED* 127 368.

Describes teacher behaviors during instruction measured through coding of videotapes and relates those behaviors to student achievement.

2211. Schramm, Charles F. Relating teacher threat to academic achievement in educationally deprived children. 1976. *ERIC ED* 123 317.

Describes more teacher use of threats with students as related to less presentation of instructional content, resulting in lower student achievement.

2212. Schroeder, Thomas Steven. The effects of positive and corrective written teacher feedback on selected writing behaviors of fourth grade children. Ph.D. dissertation. University of Kansas. 1973.

Describes changes in student writing resulting from teacher feedback, such as increased uses of descriptive passages.

2213. Schuck, Robert F. "A determination of the influence of set induction upon pupil perception of effective teaching, achievement, and retention in a unit of respiration in the BSCS curricula," *Psychology in the Schools 7* (1970): 228-231. Ed.D. dissertation. Arizona State University. 1968. *ERIC ED* 031 389.

Reports that teacher behaviors as well as course content influence student learning in a Biological Sciences Curriculum Study course.

2214. Sears, Pauline & others. Effective reinforcement for achievement behavior in disadvantaged children: The first year. Technical Report No. 30. Stanford, California: Stanford Center for Research and Development in Teaching. Stanford University. 1972. *ERIC ED* 067 442.

Describes teacher behavior related to student achievement, self concept, and locus of control.

2215.   Shields, Kathleen Hamilton. Effects of teaching
        approach on self-concept and academic achievement
        in fifth grade students. Ph.D. dissertation.
        University of Denver. 1979.

             Describes no difference in achievement and self
        concept of student with open and traditional
        teachers, defined by observation of teacher
        behaviors and teacher responses to a
        questionnaire.

2216.   Shinedling, Martin M. & Pedersen, Darhl M. "Effects
        of sex of teacher and student on children's gain
        in quantitative and verbal performance," *Journal
        of Psychology 76* (1970): 79-84.

             Describes an interaction between student and
        teacher sex and student achievement, with male
        students doing best in the quantitative area with
        male teachers and worst in the verbal area with
        female teachers.

2217.   Short, Robert Allen. The relationship of teachers'
        classroom behavior to the achievement of junior
        high school students and the effect of Interaction
        Analysis feedback on teachers' classroom behavior.
        Ph.D. dissertation. University of Washington.
        1968.

             Describes no relationship between teacher
        verbal behavior and student achievement, with
        feedback from analysis of teacher-student
        interaction resulting in different changes in
        teacher behaviors by the type of feedback.

2218.   Shymansky, James Andrew & Mathews, C.C. "A
        comparative laboratory study of the effects of two
        teaching patterns on certain aspects of the
        behavior of students in fifth grade science,"
        Journal of Research in Science Teaching 11 (1974):
        157-168. By first author only, Ph.D. dissertation.
        Florida State University. 1972.

             Describes a relationship between
        direct/indirect teaching and student behavior,
        with indirect teaching resulting in greater
        student achievement.

2219.   Siegel, Martin A. & Rosenshine, Barak. Teacher
        behavior and student achievement in the
        Bereiter-Engelmann Follow Through Program. 1973.
        ERIC ED 076 564.

             Describes four specific teaching behaviors

related to greater student learning, following the
format, requiring 100% criterion responding,
correcting mistakes and presenting signals.

2220.   Slatton, Thomas D. A comparison of three strategies
and teacher influence on beginning reading skill
achievement. Ph.D. dissertation. University of
North Carolina at Greensboro. 1977.

Describes no differences in reading achievement
by the instructional method but differences in
achievement by teacher.

2221.   Smith, Howard A. Nonverbal behavior and student
achievement in the elementary classroom. 1979.
ERIC ED 181 000.

Describes some relationships between student
achievement and classroom space, student movement
around the room, proxemics and kinesic teacher
behavior.

2222.   Smith, Lyle R. "Task-oriented lessons and student
achievement," *Journal of Educational Research 73*
(1979): 16-19.

Describes a high amount of class activity
dealing with the lesson content as related to
student achievement in algebra.

2223.   Smith, Lyle R. & Cotten, Mary Linda. "Effect of
lesson vagueness and discontinuity on student
achievement and attitudes," *Journal of Educational
Psychology 72* (1980): 670-675.

Describes teacher vagueness and lesson
discontinuity effecting student learning in
seventh grade mathematics, with teacher vagueness
related to student perception of lesson
effectiveness.

2224.   Smith, T.C., Jr. The utility of an evaluative model
in judging the relationship between classroom
verbal behavior and student achievement in three
selected physics curricula. Ed.D. dissertation.
University of Houston. 1971.

Describes a relationship between teacher verbal
behavior, curriculum, student ability level and
student achievement, with three methods of
teaching physics.

2225.   Smorodin, Theodore Martin. A study of the
relationship of measures of student perception of
teacher behavior to student performance and

characteristics. Ph.D. dissertation. Washington
University. 1973.

Reports that teacher behavior accounts for a
large portion of the small classroom effect on
student achievement.

2226.   Soar, Robert S. An integrative approach to
classroom learning. Philadelphia, Pennsylvania:
Temple University. 1966. *ERIC ED* 033 749.

Describes student achievement as related to
teacher behaviors and reports limited effects of
teacher sensitivity training on student
achievement.

2227.   Soar, Robert S. Follow Through classroom process
measurement. Gainesville, Florida. Institute for
Development of Human Resources. Florida
University. *ERIC ED* 113 288.

Describes some teacher behavior factors,
developed from observations of teacher behaviors,
related to all levels of complexity of student
learning, others to specific complexity levels.

2228.   Soar, Robert S. Follow Through classroom process
measurement and pupil growth (1970-71). Final
Report. Gainesville, Florida: Institute for
Development of Human Resources. Florida
University. 1973. *ERIC ED* 106 297.

Describes a greater relationship between
teacher behavior and student gains in measures of
skill than in measures of concrete or abstract
learning.

2229.   Soar, Robert S. "Optimal teacher-pupil interaction
for pupil growth," *Educational Leadership 26*
(1968): 275-280.

Describes non-linear relationships in which
medium levels of teacher behaviors, including
indirectness, are associated with more pupil
achievement than are high or low levels of
behaviors.

2230.   Soar, Robert S. "Pupil needs and teacher-pupil
relationships: Experiences needed for
comprehension in reading," In *Interaction
analysis: Theory, research and application.* Edited
by Edmund J. Amidon and John B. Hough. pp.
243-250. Reading, Massachusetts: Addison-Wesley.
1967. Also in *Reading and Inquiry.* Edited by

J.A. Figurel. Newark, Delaware: International Reading Association. 1965.

Reports greater vocabulary gains for students when teachers provide for greater freedom of expression and less direct teacher control. For Amidon & Hough reference see citation No. 1638.

2231. Soar, Robert S. "Research findings from systematic observation," *Journal of Research and Development in Education 4* (1970): 116-22.

Describes relationships between teacher behavior and student achievement, and the complexity of student learning, with curvilinear relationships in which moderate levels of teacher behaviors are most effective.

2232. Soar, Robert S. & others. Using process/product relationships as the basis of describing effective teacher behavior. 1977. *ERIC ED* 139 735.

Reports little relationship between observed teacher behaviors which are based on teacher-derived competencies and student achievement.

2233. Soar, Robert S. & Soar, Ruth M. "An empirical analysis of selected Follow Through programs: An example of a process approach to evaluation," In *Early childhood education: The 71st Yearbook of the National Society for the Study of Education. Part II.* Edited by Ira J. Gordon. pp. 229-259. Chicago: The University of Chicago Press. 1972.

Describes behaviors of teachers and students and the relationship of some teacher behaviors to student achievement, including a distinction between structure and teacher control of student activities, and a non-linear relationship in which a moderate amount of effective teaching behaviors is association with more student achievement than higher and lower amounts. For Gordon reference see citation No. 2965.

2234. Sokol, Alvin P. & Marshall, Jon C. The congruence of teacher expectations. Inquiry into innovations Series. Research Report 4. 1969. *ERIC ED* 036 473.

Describes relationships between student and teacher expectations and behaviors in traditional and process-oriented American history classes, but not related to teacher effectiveness.

2235. Soli, Sigfried D. & Devine, Vernon T. "Behavioral
       correlates of achievement: A look at high and low
       achievers," *Journal of Educational Psychology 68*
       (1976): 335-341.

       Describes differences in patterns of student
       and teacher behavior related to achievement for
       high and low achieving students.

2236. Solomon, Daniel & Kendall, Arthur J. "Individual
       characteristics and children's performance in
       'open' and 'traditional' classroom settings,"
       Journal of Educational Psychology 68 (1976):
       613-625.

       Describes differences in student achievement
       related to differences in student characteristics
       interacting with differences in the classroom
       behaviors of teachers.

2237. Solomon, Daniel & Kendall, Arthur J. Individual
       characteristics and children's performance in
       varied educational settings. Rockville, Maryland:
       Montgomery County Public Schools. 1976.

       Describes grade four children with different
       characteristics having different patterns of
       achievement in classrooms which differed in terms
       of teacher control, student initiation of
       activity, emotional tone.

2238. Spaulding, Robert L. Achievement, creativity, and
       self-concept correlates of teacher-pupil
       transactions in elementary school classrooms.
       USOE. Cooperative Research Project No. 1352. 1965.
       ERIC ED 024 463.

       Describes the presence and absence of
       relationships between teacher behaviors and
       student achievement and self-concept and
       identifies more effective teachers.

2239. Stallings, Jane A. "Allocated Academic Learning
       Time revisited, or beyond time on task,"
       Educational Researcher 9 (1980): 11-16.

       Describes time allocated to instruction and
       several classroom and school procedures which
       influence the use of instructional time.

2240. Stallings, Jane A. "Effective teaching and learning
       in urban schools," in *What do we know about
       teaching and learning in urban schools*. Vol. 10.
       St. Louis, Missouri: CEMREL, Inc. 1979.

Describes behaviors of effective teachers of disadvantaged children, in terms of their effects on student learning. Volume reference is citation No. 2512.

2241. Stallings, Jane A. "How instructional processes relate to child outcomes in a national study of Follow Through," *Journal of Teacher Education 27*, No. 1 (1976): 43-47.

Describes relationships between teacher behavior, student achievement, student absence and behavior in the classroom.

2242. Stallings, Jane A. "Implementation and child effects of teaching practices in Follow Through classrooms," *Monograph of the Society for Research in Child Development, Vol 40.* 1975.

Describes various Follow Through educational models, teacher use of those models and relations between teacher behavior and student behavior and achievement.

2243. Stallings, Jane. Relationships between classroom instructional practices and child development. Menlo Park, California: Stanford Research Institute. 1975. *ERIC ED* 110 200.

Reports that teacher behavior, teacher use of classroom time and classroom organization are related to student achievement.

2244. Stallings, Jane A. & Kaskowitz, David H. Follow Through classroom observation evaluation 1972-1973. SRI Project URU-7370. Menlo Park, California: Stanford Research Institute. 1974. *ERIC ED* 104 969.

Describes relationships between teacher behavior and student behavior and achievement in primary grade classrooms.

2245. Stallings, Jane A. & Kaskowitz, David H. Follow Through classroom observation evaluation 1972-1973. Executive Summary. SRI Project URU-7370. Menlo Park, California: Stanford Research Institute. 1974. *ERIC ED* 104 970.

Summarizes the results of a study which relates teacher behaviors to student classroom behaviors and student achievement.

2246. Stallings, J.A., Needles, M. & Stayrook, N. How to change the process of teaching basic reading skills in secondary schools, Phase II and Phase III. Menlo Park, California: SRI International. 1979.

Describes behaviors of teachers in teaching remedial reading, relations between those behaviors and student learning and effects on teacher behaviors and student learning of in-service education.

2247. Stevenson, Andrew. "Student-teacher mutual effects upon learning in physical science," *School Science and Mathematics 70* (1970): 382-394.

Describes grouping of students as related to science achievement, with greater achievement for low ability students when placed with higher ability students, and differences in the ratio of indirect to direct teaching related to achievement.

2248. Swanson, Walter Lee. Effects of two types of individualized instruction on language arts achievement of ninth grade students with varying self concepts. Ed.D. dissertation. University of Missouri-Columbia. 1978.

Describes no differences in student achievement and self-concept in individualized programmed or individualized group instruction.

2249. Tharp, Roland G. & Gallimore, Ronald. The uses and limits of social reinforcement and industriousness for learning to read. Technical Report No. 6. Honolulu, Hawaii. Kamehameha Schools. 1976. *ERIC ED* 158 861.

Describes differences in teacher behaviors in the KEEP program, with greater teacher use of praise, but no differences in student achievement.

2250. Thompson, Donald L. & Nesselroad, Elizabeth M. Teacher verbalization and the verbal development of Head Start children. 1971. *ERIC ED* 053 180.

Reports that the quantity of teacher verbalization was related to student achievement in Head Start classrooms, but that the quality had no relationship.

2251. Tikunoff, William J., Berliner, David C. & Rist, Ray C. Special Study A: An ethnographic study of the forty classrooms of the Beginning

Teacher Evaluation Study known sample. Technical
Report 75-10-5. Beginning Teacher Evaluation
Study. San Francisco, California: Far West
Laboratory for Educational Research and
Development. 1975. *ERIC ED* 150 110.

Describes the characteristics of classrooms and
the behaviors of teachers which distinguish
between more and less effective teachers.

2252.   Tobin, Kenneth George. The effects of variations in
teacher wait-time and questioning quality on
integrated science process achievement for middle
school students of differing formal reasoning
ability and locus of control. Ed.D. dissertation.
University of Georgia. 1980.

Describes teacher behaviors and student
characteristics as related to student engagement
in tasks and student engagement related to
achievement.

2253.   Toney, JoAnne Stanley. The effectiveness of
individual manipulation of instructional materials
as compared to a teacher demonstration in
developing understanding in mathematics. Ed.D.
dissertation. Indiana University. 1968.

Reports no relationship between teacher
provision for the use of manipulative materials
and student achievement.

2254.   Trismen, Donald A. & others. A descriptive and
analytic study of compensatory reading programs.
Final Report. Vol. II. Princeton, New Jersey:
Educational Testing Service. 1976. *ERIC ED* 190
613.

Describes characteristics of classrooms which
were more and less effective in reading
instruction, including student autonomy,
adult-centered classroom, teacher warmth,
charisma, teacher/classroom flexibility,
structure, teacher-student interaction.

2255.   Tuchman, Bruce W. A study of the effectiveness of
directive versus non-directive vocational teachers
as a function of student characteristics and
course format. Final Report. 1968. *ERIC ED* 028
990.

Describes differences in the characteristics of
students in terms of their ratings of their
satisfaction with direct and indirect secondary
vocational and non-vocational teachers, and

differences in patterns of student grades by
teacher differences.

2256.   Turner,P.H. & Durrett, M.E. Teacher level of
questioning and problem solving in young children.
1975. *ERIC ED* 105 997.

Describes teachers teaching units which varied
in the cognitive level of questions and greater
student verbal problem solving after the unit with
the higher cognitive level of questions.

2257.   Tychsen, Alfred Balmer. An experimental comparison
of teacher-paced instruction and student-paced
instruction in the teaching of mathematics in the
public elementary schools in Greenwich,
Connecticut. Ph.D. dissertation. University of
Connecticut. 1971.

Describes no difference in student achievement
but a slightly higher attitude toward math in
student-paced groups than teacher-paced groups.

2258.   Veldman, Donald J. & Brophy, Jere E. "Measuring
teacher effects on pupil achievement," *Journal of
Educational Psychology* 66 (1974): 319-324. 1973.
ERIC ED 076 708.

Describes teacher behavior related to student
achievement, with greater teacher effects in Title
I schools, based on a study of teachers with
consistent levels of student achievement.

2259.   Wallace, Waymon Lether. Effects of individualized
instruction on attendance and achievement in
biology among frequently absent tenth grade
students. Ed.D. dissertation. University of
Cincinnati. 1978.

Describes greater student achievement with
individualized instruction than with traditional
instruction and greater student attendance among
students with a history of absences in
individualized classrooms.

2260.   Wallen, Norman E. Relationship between teacher
characteristics and student behavior--Part III.
USOE Cooperative Research Program 2628. Salt Lake
City, Utah: University of Utah. 1966. *ERIC ED* 010
390.

Describes greater student achievement
associated with some teacher behaviors, such as
greater teacher-pupil interaction, teacher warmth
and support for students.

2261.   Ward, Beatrice A. Independent mathematics learning
        as a function of teacher behaviors. San Francisco,
        California: Far West Laboratory for Educational
        Research and Development. 1971. *ERIC ED* 048 002.

            Describes differences in teacher behavior and
        greater use of individualized that group learning
        as related to greater student achievement.

2262.   Ward, Beatrice A. & Tikunoff, William J. "The
        Effective Teacher Education Program: Application
        of selected research results and methodology to
        teaching," *Journal of Teacher Education 27*, No. 1
        (1976): 48-52.

            Describes relationships between teacher
        behaviors and student achievement based on studies
        of teaching described in the article.

2263.   Warner, Jack Bruce. A comparison of students' and
        teachers' performances in an open area facility
        and in self-contained classrooms. Ed.D.
        dissertation. University of Houston. 1970.

            Describes no differences in the interactions of
        teachers and students and in student achievement
        in open and traditional elementary schools.

2264.   Warshaw, Mimi Blau. Effects of differential teacher
        comments on pupil performance and attitude. Ed.D.
        dissertation. University of California, Los
        Angeles. 1976.

            Describes differences in teacher feedback to
        students during spelling lessons related to
        differences in student attitude but not
        achievement.

2265.   Weidenhamer, Robert Gerald. Affective teacher-pupil
        interactions: Their effect on cognitive and
        affective test scores. Ed.D. dissertation. Brigham
        Young University. 1978.

            Describes teacher-student interactions as
        related to student achievement in reading and math
        but not student attitudes.

2266.   Welch, Wayne W. & Bridgham, Robert G. "Physics
        achievement gains as a function of teaching
        duration," *School Science and Mathematics 68*
        (1968): 449-454.

            Describes no relationship between length of
        time spent on a unit and student ability and
        between time and student achievement.

2267.   Westing, Marilyn Bernice. Class achievement and the
        background and behavior of teachers. Ph.D.
        dissertation. Claremont Graduate School. 1973.

            Describes successful teachers, in terms of
        student achievement, having a more independent
        attitude and more abstract conceptual structure
        but preferring concrete accomplishments to the
        pursuit of ideas.

2268.   Whaley, Leatrice Joy. Precision teaching and its
        effects on sixth grade students' reading
        achievement. Ed.D. dissertation. Wayne State
        University. 1978.

            Describes greater student achievement with
        precision teaching, which is related to the
        behaviors of teachers and the allocation of
        instructional time.

2269.   Wheeler, Patricia & Elias, Patricia J. Historical
        data study. Beginning Teacher Evaluation Study:
        Phase II, 1973-74, Final Report: Volume V.3.
        Princeton, New Jersey: Educational Testing
        Service. 1976. *ERIC ED* 127 372.

            Describes stability of teacher effects on
        student achievement over years, based on available
        student achievement test information.

2270.   Wiener, Craig Bernard. The effects on second and
        third grade mathematics achievement of a teacher's
        intra-class grouping, lesson activity and written
        work assignments. Ed.D. dissertation. Clark
        University. 1979.

            Describes different relationships in grades two
        and three between time, instructional grouping,
        type of assignments and extent of review of
        assignments and student achievement.

2271.   Wilen, William Wayne. The preferences of American
        history students for the cognitive level of
        teachers' verbal questioning behavior and the
        relationship of preferences to achievement. Ed.D.
        dissertation. Pennsylvania State University.
        1974.

            Describes four types of students in terms of
        their preferences for teacher question types and
        no relationship between teacher questions and
        student achievement.

2272.   Wilkins, William E. Teacher expectations and
        classroom behaviors. 1972. *ERIC ED* 090 236.

Describes no observed differences in teacher behavior and student achievement by the level of teacher expectations for students.

2273.   Wolfson, Morton L. "A consideration of direct and indirect teaching styles with respect to achievement and retention of learning in science classes," *Journal of Research in Science Teaching 10* (1973): 285-290. 1970. *ERIC ED* 085 197.

Describes greater student achievement and retention with indirect than with direct teacher behaviors.

2274.   Wong, Harry K. Behavioral objectives, teacher help, and academic achievement. Ed.D. dissertation. Brigham Young University. 1980.

Reports some increase in student achievement when students are given instructional objectives at the start of science lessons.

2275.   Woolfolk, Anita E. "Student learning and performance under varying conditions of teacher verbal and nonverbal evaluative communication," *Journal of Educational Psychology 70* (1978): 87-94.

Describes teacher behavior and teacher sex as related to student achievement.

2276.   Wrape, John Albert. Classroom interaction, academic motivation, and IQ as variables in the cognitive and affective outcomes of fourth, fifth, and sixth grade students. Ph.D. dissertation. University of Miami. 1971.

Describes no differences in teacher verbal behavior to students who differ by achievement, IQ and motivation, and direct teaching behavior associated with greater student achievement for low ability students.

2277.   Wright, Clifford J. & Nuthall, Graham. "Relationships between teacher behaviors and pupil achievement in three experimental elementary science lessons," *American Educational Research Journal 7* (1970): 477-491.

Reports that, in a study in New Zealand, greater student achievement was associated with teacher behaviors such as more direct questions, providing summary information, and involving pupils by redirecting questions when one student could not answer.

2278.   Yager, Robert E. "Teacher effects upon the outcomes
        of science instruction," *Journal of Research in
        Science Teaching 4* (1966): 236-242.

        Describes differences in student attitude
        toward course and achievement in science and
        critical thinking; attitude toward course is
        associated with differences in teacher behaviors.

2279.   Young, Timothy Wallace. A study of the
        relationships of certain teacher characteristics
        and the achievement of secondary Spanish surname
        students. Ph.D. dissertation. Indiana University.
        1980.

        Reports that observed teacher behavior was
        stable over three observations and teacher time
        spent on academic tasks and teacher-centered
        instruction were related to increased student
        achievement, while higher teacher level of
        education was associated with lower student
        achievement.

2280.   Young, Timothy W. "Teacher stability in seventh and
        eighth grade classrooms," *Journal of Classroom
        Interaction 16*, No. 1 (1980): 30-32.

        Reports stability of teacher behaviors and
        relates teacher time allocated to instructional
        tasks and teacher-centered instruction related to
        student achievement.

D. ON STUDENT ACHIEVEMENT--EXPERIMENTS AND TRAINING

2281. Alster, Edgar Stuart. A study of student questions
that elicit factual responses from teachers of
fifth grade classes. Ed.D. dissertation. Rutgers
University the State University of New Jersey.
1978.

Reports that teacher dogmatism is related to
responses to training and resulting changes in
student questioning behavior but not student
achievement.

2282. Amidon, Edmund & Flanders, Ned A. "The effects of
direct and indirect teacher influence on
dependent-prone students learning geometry," In
*Interaction Analysis: Theory, research and
application*. Edited by Edmund J. Amidon and John
B. Hough. pp. 210-216. Reading, Massachusetts:
Addison Wesley Publishing Company. 1967. Reprinted
from *Journal of Educational Psychology 52* (1961):
286-291.

Reports that, in a laboratory study, students
of indirect teachers learned more than students of
direct teachers but there were no differences by
clarity of presentation or instructional goals.
For Amidon & Hough reference see citation No.
1638.

2283. Anderson, Linda M. Classroom-based experimental
studies of teaching effectiveness in elementary
schools. Austin, Texas: Center for Research and
Development for Teacher Education. Texas
University at Austin. 1979. *ERIC ED* 178 540.

Describes a study in which teachers who were
trained to use the behaviors found in
correlational studies to be related to student
achievement changed their behavior and had greater
student achievement than untrained teachers.

2284. Anderson, Linda Mahaffey & Brophy, Jere E. An
experimental investigation of first grade reading
group instruction. Report 76-3. 1976. *ERIC ED* 124
921.

419

Describes greater achievement for students of teachers trained than not trained to use behaviors identified in correlational studies as related to student learning.

2285.   Anderson, Linda M. & Brophy, Jere E. An experimental study of reading group instruction: Data from teacher interveiws. Research and Development Report No. 4073. East Lansing, Michigan: Institute for Research on Teaching. Michigan State University. 1979. *ERIC ED* 177 486.

Describes teacher descriptions of their behavior after training as related to the behaviors covered in the training but not to student achievement.

2286.   Anderson, Linda, Evertson, Carolyn & Brophy, Jere. Analysis of treatment effects in an experimental study of first-grade reading groups. *ERIC ED* 177 463.

Describes a model of reading instruction, changes in the behaviors of teachers after training, and changes in student achievement.

2287.   Anderson, Linda M., Evertson, Carolyn M. & Brophy, Jere E. "An experimental study of effective teaching in first-grade reading groups," *Elementary School Journal 79*, No. 4 (1979): 193-223. *ERIC ED* 201 788.

Describes differences in the behaviors of teachers trained and untrained to implement a model of teaching based on correlational studies, and greater student reading achievement related to those behaviors which teachers implemented from the model.

2288.   Arehart, John Edwin. The relationship between ninth and tenth grade student achievement on a probability unit and student opportunity to learn the unit objectives. Ed.D. dissertation. University of Virginia. 1978.

Reports that, in experimental lessons, time to learn was related to student learning, and teachers accurately reported both content emphasis and student learning.

2289.   Armento, Beverly Jeanne. Correlates of teacher effectiveness in social science concept instruction. 1977. *ERIC ED* 148 660.

Describes greater student achievement gains in a two-lesson experiment when teachers defined concepts and gave examples with enthusiasm, and instruction was related to objectives.

2290. Armento, Beverly Jeanne. "Teacher verbal behaviors related to student achievement on a social concept test," *Journal of Teacher Education 28*, No. 2 (1977): 46-52. 1976. *ERIC ED* 126 145.

Describes a limited relationship between teacher behavior and student achievement on one social studies concept taught in two lessons.

2291. Au, Kathryn H. Relationships between selected teacher behaviors and pupil academic achievement: Preliminary observations (Sample project A). The effect of teacher input on student performance (Sample project B). Technical Report No. 35. Honolulu, Hawaii: Kamehameha Schools. *ERIC ED* 158 853.

Describes different behaviors of teachers by type of classroom organization (individual instruction versus small group) but no difference in student achievement over a short time period.

2292. Austad, Charles A. "Personality correlates of teacher performance in a micro-teaching laboratory," *Journal of Experimental Education 40*, No. 3 (1972): 1-5.

Describes a relationship between teacher personality, teaching strategy and student learning in an experimental setting.

2293. Avila, John Vernon. The effects of selected teaching competencies on secondary student achievement. Ed.D. dissertation. University of Southern California. 1979.

Reports greater student achievement and retention with teachers trained in selected behaviors, teaching English and social studies.

2294. Baker, Eva Lee. The differential effect of behavioral and nonbehavioral objectives given to teachers on the achievement of their students. Ed.D. dissertation. University of California, Los Angeles. 1967.

Describes no difference in achievement of students or responses of teachers to a questionnaire for teachers and students in three groups working with different types of objectives.

2295.   Baker, Katherine D. & Snow, Richard E. Teacher
        differences as reflected in student
        aptitude-achievement relationships. Stanford,
        California: Stanford Center for Research and
        Development in Teaching. Stanford University.
        1972. *ERIC ED* 062 311.

            Describes a relationship between student
        achievement and aptitude and teacher behaviors,
        but no consistent patterns of relationships.

2296.   Baldwin, E.D. & Hite, Herbert. The effectiveness of
        different forms of supplementation as adjuncts to
        programmed learning, a follow-up study. Olympia,
        Washington: State Superintendent of Public
        Instruction. 1963. *ERIC ED* 014 218.

            Describes greater student achievement with some
        of five types of teacher supplements to programmed
        materials.

2297.   Bass, Jo Ann Scott. Effects of an inservice program
        on teacher planning and student achievement with
        middle school social studies teachers. Ph.D.
        dissertation. University of Texas at Austin.
        1980.

            Describes an increase in teacher use of direct
        instruction after training and increased student
        achievement.

2298.   Batty, Barbara Dawn. The effects of advance
        organizers on the learning of the students in the
        study of oceanography in eighth grade earth
        science classes in an inner city school. Ph.D.
        dissertation. University of Texas at Austin.
        1978.

            Describes greater achievement for all the
        students of one teacher but no differences for the
        experimental classes where teachers used advance
        organizers in comparison with the control classes
        where the same teachers did not use advance
        organizers.

2299.   Bedwell, Lance Eugene. The effects of training
        teachers in question-asking skills on the
        achievement and attitudes of elementary pupils.
        Ed.D. dissertation. Indiana University. 1974.

            Describes teachers who were trained asking more
        higher cognitive level questions than untrained
        teachers, but no differences in student learning.

2300. Berger, Florence Cohen. Sex-differential patterns of verbal interaction in fourth, seventh and tenth grade mathematics classrooms. Ph.D. dissertation. Cornell University. 1979.

Describes difference in behaviors, grades and plans to take more mathematics as related to differences in teacher and student behavior and characteristics.

2301. Berliner, David C., Filby, Nikola N., Marliave, Richard S. & Weir, Christina D. An intervention in classrooms using the Beginning Teacher Evaluation Study model of instruction. Technical Note VI-1. San Francisco, California: Far West Laboratory for Educational Research and Development. 1978.

Describes procedures to modify teacher and student behavior and resulting changes in teacher behavior and student time on task.

2302. Borg, Walter R. "Changing teacher and pupil performance with protocols," *Journal of Experimental Education 45* (1977): 9-18.

Describes training of teachers and changes in teacher and student behavior based on use of protocols describing teaching and classroom events

2303. Borg, Walter R. "Protocol materials as related to teacher performance and pupil achievement," *Journal of Educational Research 69* (1975): 23-30.

Describes the use of protocol materials in teacher training, the behaviors of the trained teachers, and the effects of the training on student learning.

2304. Bracht, Glenn Herbert. The relationship of treatment tasks, personological variables, and dependent variables to aptitude-treatment interactions. Ph.D. dissertation. University of Colorado. 1969.

Describes no interactions between teaching methods during one instructional unit and student learning.

2305. Brady, May Ella. Effects of teacher responses to pupil miscues on pupil strategies of decoding and comprehending. Ph.D. dissertation. Indiana University. 1979.

Describes differences in student reading
achievement by initial reading levels, not by four
methods of teacher responses to reading errors
which change the meaning of the material.

2306.   Branch, Robert Charles. The interaction of
cognitive style with the instructional variables
of sequencing and manipulation to effect
achievement of elementary mathematics. Ph.D.
dissertation. University of Washington. 1973.

Describes a relationship between use of
manipulative materials, inductive teaching
approach, student cognitive style and immediate
retention in a sequence of four short lessons

2307.   Breed, George. Nonverbal behavior and teaching
effectiveness. 1971. *ERIC ED* 059 182.

Describes experiments in which changes in
teacher behaviors during lectures are related to
changes in student attitude and retention

2308.   Browning, Bobby Donald. Effects of reality therapy
on teacher attitudes, student attitudes, student
achievement, and student behavior. Ed.D.
dissertation. North Texas State University. 1978.

Describes different behaviors after training in
reality therapy classroom management techniques
and greater achievement for the experimental than
the control classes.

2309.   Buggey, L. JoAnne. A study of the relationship of
classroom questions and social studies achievement
of second-grade children. 1972. *ERIC ED* 066 391.

Describes greater student achievement in
classes where teachers asked questions at higher
cognitive levels than knowledge level, in a six
week study.

2310.   Cardarelli, Aldo Francis. An investigation of the
effect on pupil achievement when teachers are
assigned and trained in the use of behavioral
objectives. Ph.D. dissertation. Syracuse
University. 1971.

Describes no difference in student achievement
with teachers trained and not trained in the use
of behavioral objectives.

2311.   Carline, John Louis. An investigation of the
relationships between various verbal strategies of
teaching behavior and achievement of elementary

school children. Ph.D. dissertation. Syracuse
University. 1969. *ERIC ED* 038 345.

Describes changes in teacher behavior with
training in the use of various verbal strategies
but no differences in the achievement of students
with trained and nontrained teachers.

2312.   Carnes, Phyllis E. An experimental study in the use
of programmed materials for seventh-grade
open-ended laboratory experiences. 1966. *ERIC ED*
010 081.

Describes greater achievement for the
non-programmed than the programmed instruction
group in a six lesson series in general science.

2313.   Carroll, Booker Theodore. Effects of diagnostic-
prescriptive teaching on the reading achievement
of eighth grade students in an urban junior high
school. Ed.D. dissertation. University of
California, Berkeley. 1978.

Describes greater student learning over seven
months with the diagnostic-prescriptive method
than the traditional reading instruction method in
junior high school.

2314.   Carroll, John. A comparison of the effects of
teacher, peer, and self-evaluation on the creative
thinking performance of elementary school
children. Ph.D. dissertation. University of
Georgia. 1979.

Describes a greater effect of teacher
evaluation than peer or self evaluation on student
creative thinking.

2315.   Carry, Laroy, Ray. Interaction of visualization and
general reasoning abilities with instructional
treatment in algebra. Ph.D. dissertation. Stanford
University. 1968.

Describes no interaction by student aptitude
and instructional method for general achievement
scores but some interactions with specific test
items.

2316.   Citron, Irvin M. The search for more effective
methods of teaching high school biology to slow
learners through Interaction Analysis: An
investigation to determine the value of
Interaction Analysis in the adaptation of biology
instruction to the needs of slow learners at the
secondary school level. Ph.D. dissertation. New
York University. 1969. *ERIC ED* 043 504.

Describes teachers changing behavior as
directed and the influences of teacher-student
interactions on student concept formation and
problem solving.

2317.   Clark, Christopher Michael. The effects of teacher
        practice on student learning and attitudes in
        small group instruction. Ph.D. dissertation.
        Stanford University. 1975. Technical Report No.
        47. Stanford, California: Stanford Center for
        Research and Development in Teaching. Stanford
        University. 1976. *ERIC ED* 120 145.

        Describes no changes in teacher behavior or in
        the relationship of teacher behavior with student
        achievement in three experimental lessons.

2318.   Clark, Christopher M., Gage, N.L., Marx, R.,
        Peterson, P.L., Stayrook, N.G. & Winne, P.A. "A
        factorial experiment on teacher structuring,
        soliciting, and reacting," *Journal of Educational
        Psychology 71* (1979): 534-552. Research and
        Development Memorandum No. 147. Stanford,
        California: Stanford Center for Research and
        Development in Teaching. Stanford University.
        1976. *ERIC ED* 135 591.

        Describes an experiment in which low teacher
        structuring and reacting resulted in lower student
        achievement but other uncontrolled teacher
        behavior also influenced student achievement.

2319.   Coladarci, Theodore Tilton. A classroom-based
        experiment assessing the impact of teacher
        behavior and student achievement of a
        direct-instruction approach to teaching. Ph.D.
        dissertation. Stanford University. 1980.

        Describes no change in teacher classroom
        behavior or increase in student achievement from
        teacher use of mailed training packets.

2320.   Crocker, Robert K. & others. A comparison of
        structured and unstructured modes of teaching
        science process activities. 1974. *ERIC ED* 092
        360.

        Describes an experiment which resulted in
        greater student achievement and preference for a
        structured mode of teaching science.

2321.   Crocker, Robert K. & others. An experimental study
        of teacher control in sixth grade science classes.
        1977. *ERIC ED* 139 607.

Describes no difference by treatment in student achievement but differences in student preference for instructional mode, based on an eighteen week experiment.

2322.   Crocker, Robert K. & others. "Treatment and ATI effects for pupil achievement and preference under two experimental conditions of teacher control in sixth grade science classes," *Journal of Research in Science Teaching 16* (1979): 105-121.

Describes differences in treatment by student characteristics related to student achievement and preference for science learning.

2323.   Davidson, Roscoe Levette. The effects of an interaction analysis system on the development of critical reading in elementary school children. Ed.D. dissertation. University of Denver. 1967.

Describes changes in teacher behaviors and resulting changes in student critical thinking during reading.

2324.   Dittmer, Robert Michael. The effects of various levels of teacher/student verbal interaction on geometry students. Ed.D. dissertation. University of Missouri-Columbia. 1978.

Describes an experiment in which the level of teacher-student interaction was related to student learning as measured by the unit tests.

2325.   Dorminey, Ralph Jau Don. An investigation of interaction between selected aptitudes and two methods of presenting a unit in secondary school mathematics. Ed.D. dissertation. University of Georgia. 1972.

Describes a study which found no significant relationship between student aptitudes and instructional methods in a three lesson math unit.

2326.   Ebeling, Thomas Harry. The effects of three teaching strategies on the development of environmental attitudes of selected New Jersey high school students. Ed.D. dissertation. Temple University. 1978.

Describes greater achievement for the experimental than the control group, and achievement related to student attitude and locus of control

2327. Ebmeier, Howard Henry. An investigation of the
       interactive effects among student types, teacher
       types, and treatment types on the mathematics
       achievement of fourth grade students. Ph.D.
       dissertation. University of Missouri-Columbia.
       1978.

           Describes student achievement related to
       student characteristics and teacher behavior, with
       low achieving and dependent students achieving
       more with moderate class structure and direction.

2328. Ebmeier, Howard & Good, Thomas L. "The effects of
       instructing teachers about good teaching on the
       mathematics achievement of fourth grade students,"
       American Educational Research Journal 16 (1979):
       1-16.

           Describes changes in teacher behaviors as a
       result of training in the use on an instructional
       model and resulting changes in student
       achievement.

2329. Egelston, Judy Cobb. An observational investigation
       of classroom behavior under the inductive and
       traditional methods of teaching high school
       biology laboratories. Ed.D. dissertation. State
       University of New York at Buffalo. 1971.

           Describes different behavior, classroom climate
       and student achievement in inductive classrooms,
       with lower achievement at first but eventually an
       increase in student independent behavior.

2330. Fisher, David Lawrence. Effects of classroom
       schedules upon pupil performance. Ed.D.
       dissertation. Boston College. 1978.

           Describes no differences in achievement by
       differences in the schedule of the number and
       length of time blocks provided for classes.

2331. Fox, James Harold, Jr. A study of the relationship
       between program-centered and teacher-centered
       instruction in the social studies. Ed.D.
       dissertation. George Washington University. 1971.

           Describes equal achievement for the students in
       the program-centered and the teacher-centered
       instructional approaches over a months' time.

2332. Gabel, Glen Jay. The effect of behavioral
       objectives use on third grade reading achievement.
       Ed.D. dissertation. Northern Arizona University.
       1977.

Describes an experiment in which students had greater reading achievement when teachers used behavioral objectives than when they did not.

2333. Gage, N.L. "A factorially designed experiment on teacher structuring, soliciting, and reacting," *Journal of Teacher Education 27*, No. 1 (1976). 35-38.

Describes an experiment in which teachers used different behaviors and the different behaviors had a low relationship to differences in student learning.

2334. Gall, Meredith D. & others. "Effects of questioning techniques and recitation on student learning," *American Educational Research Journal 15* (1978): 175-199.

Reports that, in an experiment, teacher behaviors were related to student achievement, with recitation having a greater effect than probing questions or redirecting questions to another student.

2335. George, Thomas William. An investigation of teacher- vs. learner-control of learning activities: Effects on immediate achievement, progress rate, delayed recall, and attitudes. Ed.D. dissertation. University of Tennessee. 1973.

Describes no difference in student achievement or rate of achievement with teacher or student control of the rate of content coverage, but students preferred student control of rate.

2336. Goldberg, Gale. Effects of nonverbal teacher behavior on student performance. Ed.D. dissertation. Temple University. 1971.

Describes differences by student characteristics in response to and the effects of different teacher nonverbal responses to students.

2337. Good, Thomas L. "Teaching mathematics in elementary schools," *Educational Horizons 57*, No. 4 (1979): 178-182.

Describes procedures to teach mathematics based on research on effective math instruction, teacher behaviors when trying to follow those procedures and resulting increases in student achievement.

2338.   Good, Thomas L. The Missouri Mathematics
         Effectiveness Poject: A program of naturalistic
         and experimental research. Technical Report No.
         140. Columbia, Missouri: Center for Research on
         Social Behaviors. University of Missouri. 1978.
         ERIC ED 159 056.

         Describes teacher behaviors identified in a
         correlational study as related to student learning
         forming the basis for a teacher training program,
         with the students of trained teachers having
         higher achievement than the students of untrained
         teachers.

2339.   Good, Thomas L. & Grouws, Douglas A. "Teaching and
         mathematics learning," *Educational Leadership 37*
         (1979): 39-45.

         Describes an experiment in which teachers were
         taught procedures for teaching math identified as
         effective through correlational studies, teachers
         used many of the behaviors after the training, and
         their students had greater achievement than the
         students of untrained teachers.

2340.   Good, Thomas L. & Grouws, Douglas A. "The Missouri
         Mathematics Effectiveness Project: An experimental
         study in fourth-grade classrooms," *Journal of
         Educational Psychology 71* (1979): 355-362.

         Describes changes in teacher behavior after
         training in a model of mathematics teaching and
         the resulting increases in student learning.

2341.   Hecht, Michael & Strum, Irene. The self-fulfilling
         prophecy: An adaptation. 1974. *ERIC ED* 135 464.

         Describes an experiment with greater student
         accomplishment of tasks with teacher use of verbal
         motivation statements than with simple assignment
         of tasks.

2342.   Heeney, Patricia Plaza. An investigation of the
         correlates of effective teaching for a second
         grade unit on following directions and word
         structure for students of high, medium, and low
         achievement. Ph.D. dissertation. University of
         Maryland. 1979.

         Describes a relationship between several
         teacher behaviors and student achievement on an
         experimental teaching unit, with direct
         individualized instruction being the most
         effective.

2343.   Homme, Lloyd E. A demonstration of the use of
        self-instructional and other teaching techniques
        for remedial instruction of low-achieving
        adolescents in reading and mathematics. Technical
        Progress Report No. 2. Albuquerque, New Mexico:
        TMI Institute. 1968. *ERIC ED* 018 111.

        Describes lack of effect of a programmed
        instructional unit based on a contingency contract
        and ascribes the lack of effect to communication
        problems.

2344.   Janicki, Terence Chester. Aptitude-treatment
        interaction effects of variations in direct
        instruction. Ph.D. dissertation. University of
        Wisconsin-Madison. 1979. *ERIC ED* 187 690.

        Describes no differences in student achievement
        for two variations of direct instruction, but
        differences by student locus of control and
        positive attitude.

2345.   Kalish, Daniel Miles. The effects on achievement of
        using behavioral objectives with fifth grade
        students. Ph.D. dissertation. Ohio State
        University. 1972.

        Describes no difference in student achievement
        in a unit with and a unit without behavioral
        objectives shared with students.

2346.   Klesius, Janell Putnal. The effect of teacher
        feedback instruction and student self-directed
        instruction on developing reading comprehension in
        sixth grade students. Ph.D. dissertation. Florida
        State University. 1980.

        Describes no difference in student
        comprehension with teacher feedback and student
        self-directed instruction for sixth grade low
        achieving students.

2347.   Kline, Arlyn Arthur. A study of the relationship
        between self-directed and teacher-directed
        eighth-grade students involved in an open-ended
        ESCP laboratory block. Ed.D. dissertation.
        University of Colorado. 1970.

        Describes no differences in the achievement or
        attitudes of students in teacher-directed and
        student-directed laboratory units in science

 348.   Land, M.L. "Teacher clarity and cognitive level of
        questions: Effects on learning," *Journal of
        Experimental Education 49* (1980): 48-51.

Describes an experiment in which neither the cognitive level of teacher questions nor the interaction of cognitive level of questions and teacher clarity were related to student achievement.

2349.   Land, M.L. & Smith, L.R. Low inference teacher clarity variables: effects on student achievement. 1979. *ERIC ED* 179 499.

Describes three experiments with scripted lessons in which there was a slight increase in student achievement with greater teacher clarity.

2350.   Langley, Bettye Ann Richardson. The effect of four specified teacher behaviors on the academic achievement of kindergarten pupils. Ph.D. dissertation. University of Southern Mississippi. 1977.

Describes an experiment in which teacher behavior is related to student achievement.

2351.   Lashier, William Stanley. An analysis of certain aspects of the verbal behavior of student teachers of eighth grade students participating in a BSCS laboratory block. 1965. *ERIC ED* 013 208.

Describes student achievement and attitude related to indirect teaching, as implemented by trained student teachers in an inquiry science laboratory setting.

2352.   Long, Joe Clark. The effects of a diagnostic-prescriptive teaching strategy on the achievement and attitudes of high school biology students. Ed.D. dissertation. University of Georgia. 1978.

Describes an experiment in which different patterns of teacher behavior were related to student achievement.

2353.   Luckett, Robert Daniel, Sr. Differences in sight vocabulary achievement of dependent and independent first grade children taught by direct and indirect teaching methods. Ed.D. dissertation. Montana State University. 1979.

Describes no difference in the achievement of students taught by the two teaching approaches.

2354.   Lynch, William W. & others. Effects of teachers' cognitive demand styles on pupil learning. 1973. *ERIC ED* 076 566.

Describes the effects of different teaching objectives, resulting in different teacher behaviors and different student achievement on recall but not concept tests in a laboratory experiment.

2355.   McKnight, Philip C. A study of behavioral responsiveness in teachers' verbal interaction with students. Ph.D. dissertation. Stanford University. 1970. *ERIC ED* 062 296.

Describes an experiment in which student teachers were trained to respond to students and to summarize material presented in short lessons, but no differences were found in student achievement with trained and untrained teachers.

2356.   Malvern Kathryn T. The effect of higher cognitive questioning techniques on student achievement after teacher retraining in questioning strategies. Ed.D. dissertation. Rutgers University the State University of New Jersey. 1980.

Describes differences in teacher behaviors; trained teachers asked more higher cognitive level questions and their students had higher comprehension scores than untrained teachers.

2357.   Martikean, Alexandria. The levels of questioning and their effects upon student performance above the knowledge level of Bloom's taxonomy of educational objectives. A research paper. 1973. *ERIC ED* 091 248.

Describes an experiment in which there was no difference in student achievement by level of teacher questions.

2358.   Matheny, Kenneth B. & Edwards, C. Randall. "Academic improvement through an experimental classroom management system," *Journal of School Psychology 12* (1974): 222-232.

Describes the degree to which teachers have implemented a class management system related to the degree of increase in student achievement.

2359.   Miller, George L. "Collaborative teaching and pupil thinking," *Journal of Teacher Education 17* (1966): 337-358. Under title, An investigation of teaching behavior and pupil thinking, Ed.D. dissertation. University of Utah. 1964.

Describes the behaviors of teachers following two models of teaching and the resulting

differences in levels of pupil understanding
during classroom discussions.

2360.   Morris, Phil. A study of teacher influence and
pupil achievement in a public school district.
Ph.D. dissertation. Texas Agricultural &
Mechanical University. 1977.

        Describes an experiment with one thirty-minute
lesson in which teacher interaction with students
was related to student learning only for the high
ability group.

2361.   Na, Younsoon Cho. Interaction effects between
Piagetian cognitive developmental stage (pre and
concrete) and teaching strategies (inductive and
deductive) for concept acquisition. Ph.D.
dissertation. Florida State University. 1977.

        Describes an experiment in which teaching
strategy interacted with pupil stage of
development to influence pupil acquisition of
concepts.

2362.   Nuthall, Graham. "An experimental comparison of
alternative strategies for teaching concepts,"
American Educational Research Journal 5 (1968):
561-584.

        Describes differences in teaching strategies,
such as drawing comparisons for students, which
were related to differences in secondary school
student acquisition of social studies concepts in
an experiment.

2363.   Ojala, William Truman. Aptitude-treatment
interactions in student achievement of grammar.
Ph.D. dissertation. Florida State University.
1969.

        Describes greater student achievement with
teachers using a traditional than a modern
programmed text for English grammar.

2364.   Oliver, Donald W. & Shaver, James P. "Teacher style
and the analysis of the student-teacher dialogue,"
In *Teaching: Vantage points for study*. Edited by
Ronald T. Hyman. pp. 404-420. Philadelphia,
Pennsylvania: T.B. Lippincott Company. 1968.

        Describes teachers who used two different
styles, recitation and the Socratic method,
teaching short units to seventh grade government
students, with equal levels of student
achievement. For Hyman reference see citation No.
2973.

2365. Oner, Necla Palamutlu. Impact of teacher behavior
       and teaching technique on learning by anxious
       children. Ph.D. dissertation. University of
       Minnesota. 1971.

       Describes differences in teacher behaviors with
       a programmed text but no differences in student
       achievement, and no differences by student sex and
       anxiety.

2366. Oppong, Jacob Emmanuel. A study of the advance
       organizer and its effects on achievement of ninth
       grade social studies students. Ed.D. dissertation.
       University of Georgia. 1978.

       Describes greater achievement in the classes in
       which teachers used advance organizers than in the
       classes in which they did not.

2367. Pagano, Arnold Robert. A comparison of the effects
       of four teaching strategies on the acquisition,
       retention, and transfer of selected science
       concepts in the sixth grade. 1970. *ERIC ED* 079
       037.

       Describes differences in the effects of teacher
       summarizing or not summarizing materials presented
       by students, but not by student sex.

2368. Pescosolido, John R. A comparative study between a
       structured and thematic approach in spelling, the
       Stanley-Vance spelling experiment. *ERIC ED* 018
       429.

       Describes no differences in student spelling
       achievement with three approaches to instruction.

2369. Peterson, John F. A demonstration study to
       determine the effect on academic performance of
       giving high school teachers background information
       on high-potential low-achieving students. *ERIC ED*
       020 975.

       Describes an experiment in which there was no
       difference in the achievement of students in three
       groups, with some teachers given detailed
       information, others general information and others
       no information about student background.

2370. Peterson, Penelope Loraine. "Interactive effects of
       student anxiety, achievement orientation, and
       teacher behavior on student achievement and
       attitude," *Journal of Educational Psychology 69*
       (1977): 779-792. Ph.D. dissertation. Stanford
       University. 1976.

Describes a two week experiment in which
student achievement orientation and teaching
behaviors were related to student anxiety level.

2371.   Peterson, Penelope L., Janicki, Terence C. & Swing,
        Susan R. Aptitude-Treatment Interaction effects of
        three teaching approaches: Lecture-recitation,
        inquiry, and public issues discussion. Madison,
        Wisconsin: Research and Development Center for
        Individualized Schooling. University of Wisconsin.
        1979. *ERIC ED* 186 427.

Describes the lecture-recitation approach as
best with experimenter-constructed tests but an
interaction between student ability and teaching
approach when the student outcome measures are
based on the objectives of the instructional
approaches.

2372.   Piatt, Robert George. An investigation of the
        effect the training of teachers in defining,
        writing and implementing educational behavioral
        objectives has on learner outcomes for students
        enrolled in a seventh grade mathematics program in
        the public schools. Ed.D. dissertation. Lehigh
        University. 1969.

Describes an experiment in which there were
some differences in the math achievement of
students of teachers trained and not trained to
use behavioral objectives, but also differences by
student sex and ability group.

2373.   Politzer, Robert L. & Lewis, Shirley A. Teacher
        workshops, black English test for teachers, and
        selected teaching behaviors and their relation to
        pupil achievement. Stanford, California: Stanford
        Center for Research and Development in Teaching.
        Stanford University. 1979. *ERIC ED* 174 986.

Describes the behaviors of teachers in a
teaching situation related to student learning,
and describes some changes in teacher behaviors as
a result of the workshop.

2374.   Porteus, Ann Wilson. Teacher-centered vs.
        student-centered instruction: Interactions with
        cognitive and motivational aptitudes. Ph.D.
        dissertation. Stanford University. 1976.

Describes differences by subject and time of
year, but a relationship between teaching method
and student characteristics and student learning.

2375. Ray, Charles Lester. A comparative laboratory study
of the effects of lower level and higher level
questions on students' abstract reasoning and
critical thinking in two non-directive high school
chemistry classrooms. Ph.D. dissertation. Florida
State University. 1979.

    Describes an experiment over 29 weeks which
demonstrated greater student achievement in
critical thinking with more teacher questions at
higher cognitive levels

2376. Reavis, Charles A. & Derlega, Valerian J. "Test of
a contingency model of teacher effectiveness,"
Journal of Educational Research 69 (1976):
221-225. 1972. *ERIC ED* 131 063.

    Describes an experiment in which the
relationship between teacher behaviors and student
achievement varied by the favorableness of the
situation for teaching.

2377. Renken, Albert Frank. The relationship between
teachers' marks, modifications in grouping
patterns and instructional behavior patterns.
Ed.D. dissertation. New York University. 1972.

    Describes changes to more indirect
instructional behaviors and to heterogeneous
grouping of students resulting in changes in the
achievement of low ability black students.

2378. Roberson, E. Wayne. Effects of teacher in-service
on instructional learning. Tucson, Arizona: EPIC
Evaluation Center. 1969. *ERIC ED* 037 383.

    Describes changes in teacher-student
interaction resulting from teacher in-service
training and resulting in changes in student
achievement.

2379. Romane, Julian J.P. & Taylor, Bob L. "A comparison
of an expository-deductive model of teaching with
an inquiry-inductive model of teaching in the
social studies," *Colorado Journal of Educational
Research 13*, No. 3 (1974): 32-35.

    Describes no differences in student achievement
when teachers use the two different methods of
instruction.

2380. Rosenshine, Victor Barak. Behavioral predictors of
effectiveness in explaining social studies
material. Ph.D. dissertation. Stanford University.
1968.

Describes differences in the verbal behaviors
of teachers whose students had high and low
scores, with teachers with high student scores
using more explaining and connecting terms.

2381.   Ryan, Frank L. "Differentiated effects of levels of
questioning on student achievement," *Journal of
Experimental Education 41*, No. 3 (1973): 63-67.

Describes differences in achievement for
students who received instruction using high and
low levels of questions, with greater cognitive
achievement with higher cognitive level of
questions, over nine days.

2382.   Savage, Tom Verner, Jr. A study of the relationship
of classroom questions and social studies
achievement of fifth-grade children. Ph.D.
dissertation. University of Washington. 1972.

Describes no differences in achievement by the
cognitive level of teacher questions during a six
week experiment.

2383.   Schuck, Robert F. "The effects of set induction
upon pupil achievement, retention, and assessment
of effective teaching in a unit on respiration in
the BSCS curricula," *Educational Leadership 26*
(1969): 785-793. Under the title An investigation
to determine the effects of set induction upon the
achievement of ninth grade pupils and their
perceptions of teacher effectiveness in a unit on
respiration in the BSCS curricula. Ph.D.
dissertation. Arizona State University. 1967.

Describes greater student achievement and
student views of teachers as more effective for
those teachers trained in teaching a unit on set
induction.

2384.   Seymour, Lowell A. & others. The measurement of
program implementation and students' cognitive,
affective, and social performance in a field test
of the inquiry role approach (1972-73). I.
Implementation: Its documentation and relationship
to student inquiry development. *ERIC ED* 091 240.

Describes teacher training resulting in greater
implementation and some differences in student
achievement and affective response to the
instructional method.

2385.   Siegel, Martin Alan. An experimental investigation
of teacher behavior and student achievement in the
Distar instructional system. Ph.D. dissertation.

University of Illinois-Champaign. 1973. *ERIC ED* 097 120.

Describes teachers trained in the Distar instructional program using more correcting and repeating behaviors and those behaviors related to student achievement.

2386.   Siegel, Martin A. Teacher behaviors and curriculum packages: Implications for research and teacher education. Technical Report No. 9. Champaign, Illinois: Center for the Study of Reading. University of Illinois. *ERIC ED* 134 932.

Describes teacher implementation of the Distar reading curriculum and a relationship between teacher behaviors and student achievement.

2387.   Siegel, Murray Harvey. The effects of student participation on the learning of statistical concepts in the middle grades. Ph.D. dissertation. Georgia State University. 1978.

Describes no relationship between the instructional method teachers were taught to use, their behaviors and student achievement.

2388.   Sistrunk, David Francis. The effect of lecture and project methods of instruction upon specific teacher and student behaviors in the classroom and achievement in social studies. Ed.D. dissertation. Mississippi State University. 1976.

Describes differences in teacher and student behavior in a six week experiment with lecture and project instructional approaches and teacher direction resulting in greater student achievement.

2389.   Smith, Lyle R. "Aspects of teacher discourse and student achievement in mathematics," *Journal for Research in Mathematics Education 8* (1977): 195-204.

Describes teacher behavior related to student achievement in one lesson in secondary math classes.

2390.   Stallings, Jane A. Teaching basic reading skills in secondary schools. 1978. *ERIC ED* 166 634.

Describes teacher behavior as related to student achievement in secondary reading, with teachers who received special training having decreased student negative behavior and increased student oral reading.

2391.   Strother, David B. & others. The effects of
        instruction in nonverbal communication on
        elementary school teacher competency and student
        achievement. Final Report. 1971. *ERIC ED* 056 005.

        Describes changes in teacher behavior after
        training but no changes in student achievement.

2392.   Swank, Earl Wayne. A comparison of selected
        strategies for the teaching of mathematics
        concepts. 1973. *ERIC ED* 091 180.

        Describes an experiment in which students had
        different achievement levels when teachers used
        high and low levels of frequency of concept
        presentation.

2393.   Thomas, David Charles. The effects of the
        interaction of response mode and teacher role
        during programmed instruction in "normal"
        classroom situations. Ph.D. dissertation.
        University of Oregon. 1966.

        Describes an experiment in which students had
        higher achievement without teacher assistance and
        with no written responses to programmed
        materials.

2394.   Thornton, Carol Dodd. "An evaluation of the
        mathematics-methods program involving the study of
        teaching characteristics and pupil achievement in
        mathematics," *Journal for Research in Mathematics
        Education 8* (1977): 17-25.

        Describes teacher behaviors, including clarity,
        questioning, and student involvement, as related
        to student achievement.

2395.   Tracy, Diana. A comparison of the effectiveness of
        teacher-directed study and learner-directed study.
        Ed.D. dissertation. Lehigh University. 1968.

        Describes equal achievement for students of
        above average ability with teacher and student
        directed units.

2396.   Trask, Marvin Wellington. A study on interaction
        between aptitudes and concrete vs. symbolic
        teaching methods as presented to third-grade
        students in multiplication and division. Ph.D.
        dissertation. University of Oklahoma. 1972.

        Describes no differences in student achievement
        with two different methods of instruction.

2397. Travis, William Douglas. The selected effects of an in-service teaching skills program on teaching performance of elementary school social studies teachers. Ed.D. dissertation. Boston University School of Education. 1980.

Describes some observed changes in teacher behavior after training and some increase in achievement of students in the classrooms of the trained teachers.

2398. Trinchero, Robert L. "The longitudinal measurement of teacher effectiveness: Gains in overall class performance versus changes in pupil aptitude-performance relationships, "*California Journal of Educational Research 25* (1974): 121-127.

Describes no differences in student achievement and student reports of rapport with teachers by level of teacher use of positive reinforcement, but greater use of teacher reinforcement associated with a smaller correlation between student aptitude and achievement.

2399. Twelker, Paul A. Two types of teacher-learner interaction in learning by discovery. Final Report. 1967. *ERIC ED* 018 117.

Describes no differences in student learning or transfer of skills from a three week experiment with different levels of teacher reinforcement for student behaviors involving searching for and using information.

2400. Tyler, June Florence. A study of the relationship of two methods of question presentation, sex, and school location to the social studies achievement of second grade children. Ph.D. dissertation. University of Washington. 1971.

Describes greater student achievement in grade two social studies when teachers read questions than when students read questions silently.

2401. Valerious, Barbara Hoban. Improving student learning through changing teacher behavior: The helping/supportive student-teacher relationship. Ed.D. dissertation. Nova University. 1977. *ERIC ED* 139 778.

Describes the changes in teacher behavior which result from training resulting in changes in student behavior and achievement.

2402.   Varano, Samuel Peter. The effects of advanced
        organizers and behavior objectives on the
        facilitation of learning and retention of a
        biology unit. Ed.D. dissertation. Pennsylvania
        State University. 1977.

            Describes no differences in student achievement
        and retention with and without behavioral
        objectives and advanced organizers within
        lessons.

2403.   Washbon, Carolynn Ann. A study of the effects of
        varying percentages of time devoted to types of
        instructional activity to teaching elementary
        school students the distributive algorithm for
        division. Ph.D. dissertation. University of
        Maryland. 1978.

            Describes an experiment in which teachers used
        different fixed percentages of time for different
        types of instruction by objectives with no
        differences in student achievement.

2404.   Webb, A. Bert & Cormier, William H. Effects of the
        use of behavioral objectives and criterion
        evaluation on classroom progress in adolescents.
        ERIC ED 064 631.

            Describes changes in teacher behaviors for two
        teachers associated with changes in student
        behaviors.

2405.   Webb, Leland Frederick. Interaction effects between
        selected cognitive abilities and instructional
        treatment in algebra. Ph.D. dissertation.
        University of Texas at Austin. 1971.

            Describes no relationship between two methods
        of presentation of material and student
        achievement in algebra.

2406.   Weber, Margaret B. "The effect of learning
        environment on overt learner involvement and on
        relevant achievement," *Journal of Teacher
        Education 29* (1978): 81-85. 1977. *ERIC ED* 152
        791.

            Describes an experiment in which high levels of
        student task involvement and highly structured
        materials resulted in greater student achievement
        in algebra.

2407.   Widell, Waldo R. & others. The study of student
        achievement as a result of modification of

certain identifiable teacher behaviors. 1969. *ERIC ED* 053 062.

Describes changes in teacher behavior over five weeks in one U.S. history class with no changes in student achievement.

2408. Willis, Roe Elmer. The impact on teacher behavior and pupil performance of an information feedback system. Ph.D. dissertation. University of Colorado. 1973.

Describes no changes in teacher behavior or student achievment in an experiment in which teachers were provided with feedback about their behavior.

2409. Wilson, Leonard James. Relationship of diagnostic-cooperative teaching approach to mathematics achievement and personal-social adjustment of inner city intermediate students. Ed.D. dissertation. Wayne State University. 1978.

Reports greater student achievement and social and personal adjustment when teachers used a diagnostic rather than a competitive instructional approach.

2410. Winne, Philip H. "Aptitude-treatment interactions in an experiment on teacher effectiveness," *American Educational Research Journal 14* (1977): 389-409. Ph.D. dissertation. Stanford University. 1976.

Describes student aptitude as predicting the effects of teacher behaviors, instructional treatment and the interaction of treatment and student aptitude on student achievement in experimental lessons.

2411. Woolfolk, Anita E. The impact of teacher nonverbal behavior upon student learning and performance. 1977. *ERIC ED* 137 238.

Describes an experiment in which negative teacher nonverbal behavior was related to greater student achievement, but the relationship was influenced by student and teacher sex.

2412. Wright, David P. Interactions between aptitudes and instructional strategies. 1977. *ERIC ED* 145 288.

Describes an experiment in which deductive reasoning ability was most consistently related to the effectiveness of two instructional approaches, from among five cognitive aptitudes.

2413. Wright, David Paul. Interactions between
       instructional methods and individual aptitudes in
       the teaching of critical thinking in social
       studies. Ph.D. dissertation. University of
       California, Berkeley. 1975.

       Describes an experiment in which the effects of
       programmed instruction on student achievement
       varied by the method of programmed instruction
       used by the teacher and by student
       characteristics.

E. ON STUDENT ACHIEVEMENT--REVIEWS

2414. Aiken, Lewis R., Jr. "Language factors in learning
       mathematics," *Review of Educational Research 42*
       (1972): 359-385.

           Review includes a brief discussion of some
       studies which relate teacher verbal behavior to
       student achievement.

2415. Amidon, Edmund J. & Flanders, Ned. A *The role of
       the teacher in the classroom: A manual for
       understanding and improving teacher classroom
       behavior.* Minneapolis, Minnesota: Association for
       Productive Teaching. 1971.

           Manual describes the use of Interaction
       Analysis, with a review of studies of teacher
       behavior and their influences on student
       outcomes.

2416. Amidon, Edmund & Hunter, Elizabeth. *Improving
       Teaching: The analysis of classroom verbal
       interaction.* New York: Holt, Rinehart and Winston,
       Inc. 1966.

           Describes aspects of teaching based on studies
       of teacher-student verbal interaction, such as
       motivating students, informing, disciplining,
       planning, illustrated with narratives of classroom
       interaction.

2417. Amidon, Edmund & Hunter, Elizabeth. "Interaction
       Analysis: Recent developments," *In Teaching
       practice: Problems and perspectives.* Edited by E.
       Stone and S. Morris. London: Muthuen and Co. Ltd.
       1972. Reprinted from *Interaction Analysis: Theory,
       research and application.* Edited by E. Amidon and
       J.B. Hough. Reading, Massachusetts: Addison Wesley
       Publishing Co. 1972.

           Reviews studies of teacher behaviors using
       Interaction Analysis and refinements in the
       observation procedure. For Amidon & Hough
       reference see citation No. 1638.

2418.   Amidon, Edmund & Simon, Anita. "Teacher-pupil
        interaction," *Review of Educational Research 25*
        (1965): 130-140.

        Describes instruments, studies and results of
        observational studies of teaching in terms of
        teaching patterns, achievement, climate, teacher
        personality, teacher and student perceptions and
        teacher education.

2419.   Artley, A. Sterl. "The teacher variable in the
        teaching of reading," *Reading Teacher 23* (1969):
        239-248.

        Reviews studies relating teacher behaviors to
        student reading achievement, with a summary of how
        teachers should behave to improve student
        achievement.

2420.   Aspy, David N. "The relationship between selected
        student behavior and the teacher's use of
        interchangeable responses," *Humanist Educator 14*
        (1975): 3-10.

        Reviews literature on teacher empathy and
        concludes that teachers with greater empathy have
        greater student achievement.

2421.   Baldwin, Clara P. "Naturalistic studies of
        classroom learning," *Review of Educational
        Research 35* (1965): 107-113.

        Reviews studies of teacher behavior, student
        achievement, and student self-esteem and some
        relations among them.

2422.   Bank, Barbara J., Biddle, Bruce J. & Good, Thomas
        L. "Sex roles, classroom instruction and reading
        achievement," *Journal of Educational Psychology
        72* (1980): 119-132.

        Reviews research and concludes that some
        combination of four hypotheses probably explains
        differences in rates of achievement of male and
        female students in reading and math;
        discrimination, feminization of reading,
        differential responses, sex-relevant teaching
        styles.

2423.   Begle, E.G. & others. Review of the literature on
        team-teaching in mathematics. Teacher Corps
        Mathematics work/study team. Working Paper No. 3.
        Stanford, California: Stanford University. 1975.
        ERIC ED 138 548.

Reviews studies of team teaching of mathematics and concludes that most studies find greater student attitude, achievement and teacher attitudes in traditional rather than team teaching classrooms.

2424.   Bennett, Neville. *Teaching styles and pupil progress*. Cambridge, Massachusetts: Harvard University Press. 1976.

Reviews research on teaching and describes a study in England of teachers with progressive and traditional teaching styles, with students in formal classrooms more frequently engaged in work and demonstrating greater achievement.

2425.   Biddle, Bruce J. & Adams, Raymond S. "Teacher behavior in the classroom context," In *Instruction: Some contemporary viewpoints*. Edited by Lawrence Siegel. pp. 99-136. San Francisco, California: Chandler Publishing Company. 1967.

Describes influences on the behavior of teacher and students in the classroom and the influence of teacher behaviors on student learning, including a review of several studies and emphasis on the need for more observational studies. For Siegel reference see citation No. 3021.

2426.   Blaney, Robert L. "Effective teaching in early childhood education," *Elementary School Journal 80*, No. 3 (1980): 128-132.

Reviews research on effective teaching of young children and discusses implications of results.

2427.   Borg, Walter R. "Time and school learning," In *Time to learn*. edited by Carolyn Denham & Ann Lieberman. pp. 33-72. Washington, D.C.: U.S. Government Printing Office. 1980

Describes studies of the relationship of instructional time allocation and to student achievement. For Denham & Lieberman reference see citation No. 2933.

2428.   Borich, Gary D. "Implications for developing teacher competencies from process-product research," *Journal of Teacher Education 30*, No. 1 (1979): 77-86. *ERIC ED* 186 374.

Reviews process-product studies and identifies teacher behaviors and skills which the studies find to be correlated with student learning.

2429.   Borich Gary D., Kash, M.M. & Kemp, F.D. What the
        teacher effectiveness research has to say about
        teaching practices and student performance.
        Research and Development Report No. 5069. Austin,
        Texas: Southwest Educational Development
        Laboratory and Research and Development Center for
        Teacher Education. University of Texas at Austin.
        ERIC ED 189 077

           Describes a number of teacher behaviors with
        positive and negative relations to student
        achievement, based on several studies.

2430.   Brophy, Jere. "Achievement correlates," In
        Evaluating educational performance. Edited by
        Herbert J. Walberg. Berkeley, California:
        McCutchan Publishing Corporation. 1974.

           Reviews studies of teacher behavior related to
        student achievement, identifying a number of
        important behaviors.

2431.   Brophy, Jere E. "Advances in teacher effectiveness
        research," *Journal of Classroom Interaction 15*
        (1979): 1-7. Occasional Paper No. 18. East
        Lansing, Michigan. Institute for Research on
        Teaching. Michigan State University. *ERIC ED* 173
        340.

           Summarizes several studies which identify
        relationships between teacher behavior and student
        learning.

2432.   Brophy, Jere E. & Evertson, Carolyn M. "Context
        variables in teaching," *Educational Psychologist
        12* (1978): 310-316.

           Reviews four studies in which instructional
        contexts influenced the relationship between
        teacher behaviors and student achievement,
        including such contexts as grade level, pace of
        lesson, group size, and public versus private
        contacts between the teacher and the students.

2433.   Chaudhari, U.S. "Questioning and creative thinking:
        A research perspective," *Journal of Creative
        Behavior 9*, No. 1 (1974): 30-34.

           Reviews studies of the effects of teacher
        questioning on student creative thinking.

2434.   Cooper, Shirley Howard. "Hope for the future: A
        view of research in teacher effectiveness," *Quest
        Monograph 28* (1977): 29-37.

Reviews studies which describe teacher behavior and relationships to student learning.

2435. Cronbach, Lee J. & Snow, Richard E. Individual differences in learning ability as a function of instructional variables. Final Report. Stanford, California: Stanford University School of Education. 1969. *ERIC ED* 029 001.

Reviews past research on Aptitude Treatment Interaction and the state of current knowledge as a guide to future research.

2436. Doyle, Walter. "Classroom Effects," *Theory into Practice 18* (1979): 138-144.

Describes the behaviors of teachers and students and their interactions, and the effects of interactions on student behavior, work and achievement.

2437. El-Nemr, Medhat Ahmed. Meta-analysis of the outcomes of teaching biology as inquiry. Ph.D. Dissertation. University of Colorado. 1979.

Describes results of meta-analysis indicating greater effects of inquiry teaching on student science process skills, scientific attitudes, critical thinking, achievement and laboratory skills.

2438. Evans, Thomas P. Flanders system of Interaction Analysis and science teacher effectiveness. 1970. *ERIC ED* 059 094.

Reviews studies using Flanders Interaction Analysis to study science teaching but finds no clear relationship between teaching style and teacher effectiveness.

2439. Evertson, Carolyn & Anderson, Linda. Issues in educating disadvantaged students: A review of classroom research. Research and Development Report 4056. Austin, Texas: Research and Development Center in Teacher Education. Universtiy of Texas at Austin. 1977.

Reviews studies of teacher effects on students and discusses the results of studies with low socioeconomic status students.

2440. Fey, James. "Classroom teaching of mathematics," *Review of Educational Research 39* (1969): 535-551.

Reviews studies of teacher behavior and teaching methods related to student learning of mathematics.

2441.   Flanders, Ned A. "Some relationships among teacher influence, pupil attitudes and achievement," In *Interaction Analysis: Theory, research and application*. Edited by Edmund J. Amidon and John B. Hough. pp. 217-242. Reading, Massachusetts: Addison Wesley Publishing Co. 1967.

Presents results of a series of studies of the effects of direct and indirect teaching on the attitudes and achievement of students, and the conditions which influence the study of teaching. For Amidon & Hough reference see citation No. 1638.

2442.   Flanders, Ned A. "Teacher influence in the classroom," In *Teachers and the learning process*. Edited by Robert D. Strom. pp. 272-286. Englewood, Cliffs, New Jersey: Prentice-Hall, Inc. 1971. Reprinted from *Theory and research in teaching*. Edited by Arno A. Bellack. pp. 37-52. New York: Teachers College Press. 1963.

Reviews studies of teacher effects on pupil academic learning and discusses a theory of teacher influence. For Strom reference see citation No. 3029.

2443.   Flanders, Ned A. Teacher influence patterns and pupil achievement in the second, fourth, and sixth grade levels. 1969. *ERIC ED* 051 123.

Describes the behavior of teachers and the relationship of that behavior to student achievement.

2444.   Flanders, Ned A. *Teacher influence, pupil attitudes and achievement*. Cooperative Research Monograph No. 12. Washington, D.C.: U.S. Department of Health, Education and Welfare. 1965. Reprinted in *Teaching: Vantage points for study.* Edited by Ronald T. Hyman. pp. 251-264. Philadephia, Pennsylvania: T.B. Lippincott Company. 1968.

Describes a study of the relationship of teacher behavior to student achievement in secondary mathematics and social studies, during two week units. For Hyman reference see citation No. 2973.

2445.   Fortune, Jimmie C. & others. Use of classroom distributions of student achievement test scores

to evaluate the instructional effectiveness of
teachers. 1975. *ERIC ED* 117 170.

Describes teacher effectiveness as potentially
varying by the type of students and the subject
taught.

2446.   Gage, N.L. Four cheers for research on teaching.
1978. *ERIC ED* 178 460.

Reviews studies of teacher effects on student
achievement, summarizing state of knowledge.

2447.   Gage, N.L. *Teacher effectiveness and teacher
education: The search for a scientific basis.* Palo
Alto, California: Pacific Books, Publishers.
1972.

Presents a series of chapters on teacher
effectiveness, including discussion of conceptions
of teaching, research approaches and cognitive
aspects of teaching, reviews of research on
teaching and teacher education.

2448.   Gage, N.L. "The scientific basis of the art of
teaching," *Phi Delta Kappan 60* (1978): 229-235.
Also, New York: Teachers College Press. 1978.

Discusses research on teaching and reviews
studies, including studies of direct and open
teaching, with summary statements and need for
future research.

2449.   Gage, N.L. & others. An experiment on teacher
effectiveness and parent-assisted instruction in
the third grade. Stanford, California: Stanford
Center for Research and Development in Teacher
Education. Stanford University. 1978. *ERIC ED* 160
648.

Reviews five correlational studies and
identifies teacher behaviors related to student
achievement, and reports that teachers trained to
use those behaviors did use them and reports a
relationship between those behaviors and student
achievement.

2450.   Good, Thomas L. A study of fourth grade mathematics
classrooms: Some process-product data. Technical
Report No. 105. Columbia, Missouri: Center for
Research in Social Behavior. University of
Missouri-Columbia.

Describes relationships between teacher
instructional behaviors and student achievement in
math.

2451.   Good, Thomas L. "Teacher effectiveness in the
        elementary school," *Journal of Teacher Education
        30*, No. 2 (1979): 52-64.

            Reviews studies of teacher behavior related to
        student learning and includes a discussion of
        class management, direct instruction, and varied
        effects by student and teacher.

2452.   Good, Thomas L. & Beckerman, Terrill M. "An
        examination of teachers' effects on high, middle,
        and low aptitude students' performance on a
        standardized achievement test," *American
        Educational Research Journal 15* (1978): 477-482.
        Research Report No. 113. Columbia, Missouri:
        Center for Research in Social Behavior. University
        of Missouri-Columbia. 1976.

            Describes effective teachers as having student
        achievement gains at all levels of student
        achievement, with ineffective teachers ineffective
        at all levels of student ability.

2453.   Good, Thomas L, Biddle, Bruce & Brophy, Jere
        E. *Teachers make a difference*. New York: Holt,
        Rinehart and Winston. 1971. *ERIC ED* 104 863.

            Summarizes many studies in the context of a
        discussion of what constitutes effective
        teaching.

2454.   Good, Thomas L. & Dembo, Myron H. "Teacher
        expectations: Self-report data," *School Review 81*
        (1973): 247-253. Research report No. 64.
        Columbia, Missouri: Center for Research in Social
        Behavior. University of Missouri-Columbia.

            Describes teacher expecctations for student
        achievement related to past and future student
        achievement.

2455.   Good, Thomas L. & Grouws, Douglas A. "Teaching
        effects: A process-product study in fourth grade
        mathematics," *Journal of Teacher Education 28*
        (1977): 49-54.

            Describes patterns of teacher behaviors, not
        single behaviors, related to student achievement.

2456. Gray, James Braden. The effects of teacher structure on disadvantaged preschool children. Ed.D. dissertation. University of Alabama. 1978.

Describes both teacher structure and student ability as related to student achievement.

2457. Greenberg, Selma Betty. *Selected studies of classroom teaching: A comparative analysis.* Scranton, Pennsylvania: International Textbook Company. 1970.

Reviews six studies of teaching to identify areas of agreement and divergence in the studies by Bellack, Flanders, Hughes, Smith and Taba, and identifies some issues which should be resolved in future studies.

2458. Hall, Vernon C. Review of research on classroom communication patterns, leading to improved student performance. 1976. *ERIC ED* 127 292.

Reviews studies, summarizes major findings across studies and discusses the limitations found in many studies, i.e., too few teachers or observations of teachers.

2459. Hargie, Owen D.W. "The importance of teacher questions in the classroom," *Educational Research* 20 (1978): 99-102.

Review research on teacher questioning and concludes that questioning is important but more research is needed, probing by teachers is important, oral questions are better than written ones.

2460. Harnischfeger, Annegret & Wiley, David E. Teaching-learning processes in elementary school: A synoptic view. Technical Report 75-3-1. Beginning Teacher Evaluation Study. San Francisco, California: Far West Laboratory for Educational Research and Development. 1975. *ERIC ED* 124 509. Also, Chicago: Studies of Educative Processes. Report No. 9. University of Chicago. 1975.

Describes a model of teacher behavior and the use of instructional time influencing student achievement, and related to organizational and policy issues.

2461. Harris, Theodore L. "Reading," in *Encyclopedia of Educational Research*. Edited by Robert L. Ebel. pp. 1069-1104. Toronto, Canada: The MacMillan Company. 1969.

Describes aspects of reading, studies of the acquisition of reading skills, factors influencing the acquisition of reading skills and studies of the teaching of reading. For Ebel reference see citation No. 2942.

2462. Kleinman, Gladys S. "Assessing teaching effectiveness: The state of the art," *Science Education 50* (1966): 234-238.

Reviews studies of effects of teachers on students, with discussion of the trend from ratings by supervisors and students to observations of specific behavior.

2463. Klingstedt, Joe Lars. Teachers of middle school Mexican American children: Indicators of effectiveness and implications for teacher education. 1972. *ERIC ED* 059 828.

Summarizes research on teacher effectiveness in terms of teacher behaviors and personality characteristics, and implications for teacher education.

2464. Kulhavy, Raymond W. "Feedback in written instruction," *Review of Educational Research 47* (1977): 211-232.

Reviews studies of effects of feedback, finds feedback is important to student learning if it comes after, not before, student response and if students have the necessary skills to do the work, not simply to guess at answers.

2465. Lavin, David E. *The prediction of academic performance: A theoretical analysis and review of research.* New York: Russell Sage Foundation. 1965.

Describes influences on student achievement, including a brief review of research on teacher influence on student learning.

2466. Lewis, Gertrude M. *The evaluation of teaching.* Washington, D.C.: National Education Association. 1966.

Briefly reviews research on effective teaching, and student, teacher, and parent views of effective teaching, with implications for teacher evaluation.

2467. McDonald, Frederick J. A model of mathemagenic behaviors as intervening variables in classroom communication. Stanford, California: Stanford

Center for Research and Development in Teacher
Education. Stanford University. 1968. *ERIC ED* 053
059.

Essay discusses the impact of teacher discourse
on student behavior and thereby on student
achievement.

2468.   Marksberry, Mary Lee. "Student questioning: An
instructional strategy," *Educational Horizons 57*,
No. 4 (1979): 190-195.

Summarizes research which shows that
instructional behaviors of teachers influence the
questioning behaviors of students.

2469.   Marliave, Richard S. A review of the findings of
Phase II, Beginning Teacher Evaluation Study.
Technical Note V-1. Beginning Teacher Evaluation
Study. San Francisco, California: Far West
Laboratory for Educational Research and
Development. 1967. *ERIC ED* 157 871.

Reviews and summarizes results of the first
portion of a several year study, relating patterns
of teacher behavior to student achievement in
reading and mathematics in second and fifth
grades.

2470.   Marsh, Colin J. An analysis of research findings on
the use of inquiry teaching in social studies
during the last five years (1967-1972). *ERIC ED*
090 118.

Reviews studies from 1967 to 1972 of inquiry
teaching; shows inquiry teaching to be superior to
other strategies but research does not define the
nature of inquiry teaching or measure it.

2471.   Martin, Jeanne & others. The unit of analysis
problem in teacher effectiveness research. Austin,
Texas: Research and Development Center for Teacher
Education. Texas University at Austin. 1979. *ERIC
ED* 174 621.

Reports different patterns of relationship by
level of analysis (student, reading group,
classroom) in analyses of teacher behavior and
student achievement.

2472.   Martin, William R. "Teacher behaviors--Do they make
a difference? A review of the research," *Kappa
Delta Pi Record 16* No. 2 (1979): 48-50, 63.

Reviews research on teacher behaviors and characteristics related to greater student achievement, including warmth, interpersonal communication skill, flexibility, orderliness, sincerity and acceptance of students.

2473.   Medley, Donald M. Indicators and measures of teacher effectiveness: A review of the research. 1971. *ERIC ED* 088 844.

Describes the measurement of teacher effectiveness by evaluating the process and the product of teaching and reviews studies of effectiveness.

2474.   Medley, Donald M. *Teacher competence and teacher effectiveness. A review of process-product research.* Washington, D.C.: American Association of Colleges for Teacher Education. 1977. *ERIC ED* 143 629.

Reviews studies of teacher behaviors related to student learning, summarizes findings which appear to be established, and identifies limitations in the research.

2475.   Morsh, Joseph E. & Wilder, Eleanor W. Identifying the effective instructor: A review of the quantitative studies. 1900-1952. Chanute Air Force Base, Illinois. Air Force Personnel and Training Research Center. 1954. *ERIC ED* 044 371.

Reviews a large number of studies of effectiveness of teachers, based on ratings by supervisors, peers, selves, students, observations, and student gains, with bibliography. Cited for thorough coverage of early period and therefore its value as a historical record.

2476.   Ornstein, Allan C. "Systematizing teacher behavior research," *Phi Delta Kappan 52* (1971): 551-555.

Reviews studies of teaching, discussng research methods and findings of the effects of teacher behaviors on student learning.

2477.   Page, William D. Teaching linguistics to elementary and preschool children: Review of research and comment; and behaviors of teachers teaching linguistics to elementary and preschool children. 1973. *ERIC ED* 078 429.

Review describes studies of teaching of oral language, English grammar, and the behaviors of teachers when teaching English.

2478.   Peterson, Penelope L. "Direct instruction:
        Effective for what and for whom?" *Educational
        Leadership 37* (1979): 46-48.

            Reports that the effects of direct instruction
        vary by student sense of control and student
        ability (better for students with external locus
        of control and lower ability students) and
        objectives of instruction (basic skills, not
        inquiry).

2479.   Peterson, Penelope L. "Direct Instruction
        reconsidered," In *Research on teaching: Concepts,
        findings, and implications.* Edited by Penelope L.
        Peterson and Herbert J. Walberg. Berkeley,
        California: McCutchan Publishing Corporation.
        1979.

            Describes results of studies which show
        different relations between clusters of teacher
        behaviors labelled direct instruction and the
        achievement of different types of students; direct
        instruction is not most effective for all types of
        students. For Peterson & Walberg reference see
        citation No. 3001.

2480.   Powell, William R. & Wenzel, Evelyn L. Indicators
        of learning and teacher competencies in the basic
        skills: Reading and listening. Research Bulletin,
        Volume 12, No. 4. Gainesville, Florida: Florida
        Educational Research and Development Council.
        1979. *ERIC ED* 176 217.

            Reviews studies of teacher behaviors related to
        student learning of the basic skills in elementary
        grades.

2481.   Robinson, H. Alan & Burns, Alvina Trent. Teacher
        effectiveness in elementary language arts: A
        progress report. Urbana, Illinois: ERIC
        CLearinghouse on Reading and Communication Skills.
        1974. *ERIC ED* 089 317.

            Reviews research on teacher behaviors related
        to student learning of reading, writing, spelling,
        from 1966 to 1972.

2482.   Roebuck, Flora N. & Aspy, David N. Polynomial
        representation of teacher behavior. 1975. *ERIC ED*
        106 718.

             Reports that stability of teacher affective
        behavior is related to student outcomes, and
        polynomial models accounted for greater variance
        in student outcomes than linear models of
        analysis.

2483.   Rosenshine, Barak. "Classroom instruction," In *The*
        psychology of teaching methods: 75th Yearbook of
        the National Society for the Study of Education.
        Edited by N.L. Gage. pp. 335-371. Chicago:
        University of Chicago Press. 1976.

             Reviews a number of studies of instruction
        focusing on several variables related to time,
        content covered, work groupings, teacher
        questions, child responses, adult feedback,
        summarized in a model labelled direct instruction.
        For Gage reference see citation No. 1674.

2484.   Rosenshine, Barak V. "Content, time, and direct
        instruction," In *Research on teaching: Concepts,*
        findings, and implications. Edited by Penelope L.
        Peterson and Herbert J. Walberg. Berkeley,
        California: McCutchan Publishing Corporation.
        1979.

             Reviews recent studies which indicate that
        "direct instruction", a collection of patterns of
        teacher behaviors, is related to student
        achievement in the basic skills. For Peterson &
        Walberg reference see citation No. 3001.

2485.   Rosenshine, Barak. "Enthusiastic teaching: A
        research review," *School review 78* (1970):
        499-514.

             Review concludes that teacher ratings as
        enthusiastic, energetic, and animated and
        observations of frequencies of gesture, variation
        in voice, and eye contact are related to pupil
        achievement.

2486.   Rosenshine, Barak. "Experimental classroom studies
        of indirect teaching," *Classroom Interaction*
        Newsletter 5, No. 2 (1969): 7-10.

             Reviews studies in which teachers taught in an
        indirect manner and concludes that the studies
        found no increase in student achievement.

2487.   Rosenshine, Barak. Interpretive study of teaching
        behavior related to student achievement. Final

Report. Philadelphia, Pennsylvania: Temple
University College of Education. 1970. *ERIC ED* 051
116.

Reviews studies from 1956 to 1970 relating
teacher behavior and student achievement, with
studies in four categories: affective variables,
teacher cognitive behaviors, flexibility and
variety, and amount of teacher-student
interaction.

2488. Rosenshine, Barak, "Recent research on teaching
behaviors and student achievement," *Journal of
Teacher Education 27*, No. 1 (1976): 61-64.

Reviews several studies and identifies teaching
behaviors which are consistently related to
student learning of basic skills.

2489. Rosenshine, Barak. "Teacher behavior and student
attitude revisited," *Journal of Educational
Psychology 65* (1973): 177-180.

Describes a relationship between teacher
behaviors and student attitudes toward the teacher
and discusses problems in the measurement of
student attitudes toward the teacher.

2490. Rosenshine, Barak. "Teacher competency research,"
In *Competency assessment, research, and
evaluation.* Edited by W. Robert Houston.
Washington, D.C.: American Association for
Colleges of Teacher Education. 1974.

Reviews studies, identifying teacher behaviors
which are related to student achievement across
studies. For Houston reference see citation No.
2971.

2491. Rosenshine, Barak. *Teaching behaviors and student
achievement*. London: National Foundation for
Educational Research. 1971.

Reviews studies of teacher behaviors and their
relationship to student learning, including
teacher approval, cognitive behaviors,
flexibility, enthusiasm, teacher-student
interaction, time and background variables.

2492. Rosenshine, Barak. "Teaching behaviors related to
pupil achievement," *Classroom Interaction
Newsletter 5*, No. 1 (1969): 4-17. Also in *Research
into classroom processes: Recent developments and
next steps*. Edited by Ian Westbury & Arno A.
Bellack. pp. 51-98. New York: Teachers College
Press. 1971.

Reviews studies of teacher behavior using variables related to teacher approval and disapproval, cognitive aspects of instruction and patterns of teacher behavior. For Westbury & Bellack reference see citation No. 3039.

2493.   Rosenshine, Barak. "Stability of teacher effects upon student achievement," *Review of Educational Research 40* (1970): 647-662.

Reviews long and short term studies of consistency of the relationship of teacher behavior to student achievement, with the greatest stability with short term studies where teachers taught different material to the same students.

2494.   Rosenshine, Barak. "To explain: A review of research," *Educational Leadership 26* (1968): 303-309.

Reviews some initial studies of teacher ability to explain, including use of gestures and vagueness, and discusses the need for further study.

2495.   Rosenshine, Barak & Furst, Norma. "Research in teacher performance criteria," In *Research in teacher education: A symposium*. Edited by B. Othaniel Smith. pp. 37-72. Englewood Cliffs, New Jersey: Prentice-Hall, Inc. 1971.

Reviews studies and discusses results related to a number of variables, such as teacher clarity, enthusiasm, variability of behavior, task-oriented behavior, use of student ideas, student opportunity to learn, general indirectness, criticism, level of difficulty of instruction. For Smith reference see citation No. 3023.

2496.   Rouk, Ullik. "What makes an effective teacher?" *American Educator 4* (1980): 14-17, 33.

Reviews studies and concludes that effective strategies for primary grade reading and math instruction are diverse.

2497.   Rupley, William H. & Blair, Timothy. "Credible variables related to teacher effectiveness in reading instruction," *Reading World 17* (1977): 135-140.

Reviews studies of teaching of reading and the effects of teacher behavior on student learning; identifies variables which are consistent across studies.

2498. Rupley, William H, & Blair, Timothy R. "ERIC/RCS: Teacher effectiveness in reading instruction," *Reading Teacher 31* (1978): 970-973.

    Reviews the studies which are included in the ERIC system on teacher behaviors which are related to effective reading instruction.

2499. Rupley, William H & Blair, Timothy R. "Teacher effectiveness research in reading instruction: Early efforts to present focus," *Reading Psychology 2* (1980): 49-56.

    Reviews studies of effects of methods of teaching reading with an indication of the changes in studies over time.

2500. Saadeh, Ibrahim Q. "Teacher effectiveness or classroom efficiency: A new direction in the evaluation of teaching," *Journal of Teacher Education 21* (1970): 73-91.

    Reviews research on teacher effectiveness and the nature of the teaching-learning process and presents a model of the process which points to variables to be studied.

2501. Sartain, Harry W. The research base for individualizing reading instruction. 1968. *ERIC ED* 024 553.

    Reviews studies and finds that individualized instruction requires highly competent teachers and that less able pupils are less likely to succeed than they would in traditional classrooms.

2502. Sassenrath, J.M. "The logic and validation of teaching tasks in elementary education," *California Journal of Educational Research 18* (Sept. 1967): 168-178.

    Reviews research and finds validation for a number of tasks of elementary teachers, such as the identification of student instructional needs.

2503. Schneyer, J. Wesley. "Classroom verbal interaction and pupil learning," *Reading Teacher 23* (1970): 369-371.

    Reviews studies relating teacher verbal behavior to student reading achievement and ways of observing teaching.

2504.   Snow, Richard E. "Research on aptitude for
        learning: A progress report. In *Review of Research
        in Education, Vol.4* . Edited by Lee S. Shulman.
        pp. 50-105. Itasca, Illinois: F.E. Peacock
        Publishers, Inc. 1976.

        Reviews studies on student aptitude in
        interaction with teaching methods and/or teacher
        behaviors in relation to student learning, with a
        major focus on student characteristics. For
        Shulman reference see citation No. 3018.

2505.   Soar, Robert S. "An integration of findings from
        four studies of teacher effectiveness," In *The
        appraisal of teaching: Concepts and process.*
        Edited by Gary D. Borich. pp. 96-103. Reading,
        Massachusetts: Addison-Wesley Publishing Company.
        1977.

        Describes teacher behaviors and patterns of
        behaviors related to student learning across four
        studies. For Borich reference see citation No.
        2916.

2506.   Soar, R.S. "New developments in effective
        teaching," *American Biology Teacher 30* (1968):
        43-47.

        Describes research using observations in
        classrooms to identify effective teaching.

2507.   Soar, Robert. "Teacher behavior related to pupil
        growth," *International Review of Education 18*
        (1972): 508-528.

        Reviews studies of teacher behavior related to
        student achievement in various skill areas.

2508.   Soar, Robert S. Validity of two sign systems based
        on inductively derived teacher competencies. 1976.
        ERIC ED 135 798.

        Describes some teacher competencies having a
        linear and some a more complex relationship to
        student gain in achievement.

2509.   Soar, Robert S. & Soar, Ruth M. "An attempt to
        identify measures of teacher effectiveness from
        four studies," *Journal of Teacher Education 27*
        (1977): 261-267. 1976. *ERIC ED* 121 854.

        Describes relationships between teacher
        behavior and student learning in four studies
        using the same sets of observations instruments to
        measure teacher behavior.

2510.   Soar, Robert S. & Soar, Ruth M. "Emotional climate
        and management," In *Research on teaching:
        Concepts, findings, and implications*. Edited by
        Penelope L. Peterson and Herbert J. Walberg.
        Berkeley, California: McCutchan Publishing
        Corporation. 1979.

        Reports the results from four studies in which
        teacher behaviors are related to pupil behavior
        and achievement. For Peterson & Walberg reference
        see citation No. 3001.

2511.   Stallings, Jane A. "What teachers do does make a
        difference," In *Perspectives on education*. Edited
        by Allen Calvin. Reading, Massachusetts:
        Addison-Wesley Publishing Company. 1977.

        Reviews studies of teacher behaviors related to
        student achievement, concluding that teachers have
        an effect on student achievement. For Calvin
        reference see citation No. 2921.

2512.   Stallings, Jane A. & Hentzell, Shirley W. *What do
        we know about teaching and learning in urban
        schools?* Volume 10: Effective teaching and
        learning in urban schools. St. Louis, Missouri:
        Central Midwestern Regional Educational
        Laboratory, Inc. 1979. *ERIC ED* 185 165.

        Reviews studies of teacher behaviors and
        student learning, summarizes current knowledge of
        effective teaching. Contains citation No. 2240.

2513.   Thomas, John W. Efficacy and achievement:
        Self-management and self-regard. Philadelphia,
        Pennsylvania: Research for Better Schools, Inc.
        1978. *ERIC ED* 177 712.

        Reviews research on discipline and motivation,
        student self control, achievement motivation
        training, basic skills achievement, and effects of
        teachers.

2514.   Webster, Staten W. Research in teaching reading to
        disadvantaged learners: A critical Review and
        evaluation of research. 1968. *ERIC ED* 024 529.

        Reviews research on the teaching of reading to
        disadvantaged students and identifies variables
        related to achievement, such as teacher behaviors
        and attractiveness of reading materials.

2515.   Wilkinson, Susan S. The relationship of teacher
        praise and student achievement: A meta-analysis of
        selected research. Ed.D. Dissertation. University
        of Florida. 1980.

            A meta-analysis of studies reveals no
        relationship between teacher praise and reading
        achievement, a slight relationship with math
        achievement, across studies at different grades
        with students of different socioeconomic levels.

2516.   Wilson, Janet G. & Black, Alice Brenda. Native
        American Indians and variables that are
        interrelated with academic achievement. 1978. *ERIC
        ED* 165 964.

            Reviews studies of the factors which are
        related to academic achievement of Native American
        students.

2517.   Winne, Philip H. A critical review of experimental
        studies of teacher questions and student
        achievement. Stanford, California: Stanford Center
        for Research and Development in Teaching. Stanford
        University. 1975. *ERIC ED* 107 629.

            Reviews experimental studies of teacher
        questions in which the levels of questioning are
        manipulated.

VI. TEACHER-STUDENT
RELATIONS

2518. Algozzine, Robert. "Perceived attractiveness and classroom interactions," *Journal of Experimental Education 46* (1977): 63-66.

Describes a relationship between student attractiveness and teacher-student interactions.

2519. Algozzine, Robert. "What teachers perceive—Children receive?" *Communication Quarterly 24* (1976): 41-47.

Describes a relationship between student physical attractiveness and student-teacher interactions.

2520. Anderson, J.G. & others. Mexican-American students in a metropolitan context: Factors affecting the social-emotional climate of the classroom. University Park: New Mexico State University. 1969. *ERIC ED* 030 521.

Reports that teacher professional training and the characteristics of a school's students effect teacher-student interaction.

2521. Arnold, Richard D. "The achievment of boys and girls taught by men and women teachers," *Elementary School Journal 68* (1968): 367-372.

Describes differences in marks assigned to boys and girls, with girls receiving higher marks and male teachers assigning higher marks than female teachers.

2522. Baker, Janice Elizabeth. The interaction between selected teaching strategies and content in a Piagetian-based program. Ph.D. dissertation. University of Toronto (Canada). 1980.

Describes differences in the interactions of teachers and students by specific reading content being taught.

2523.   Barnes, Willie J. "Student-teacher dyadic
         interaction in desegregated high school
         classrooms," *Western Journal of Black Studies 2*
         (1978): 132-137.

             Describes a few significant differences in the
         behavior of white teachers with white and black
         students.

2524.   Bauersfield, Heinrich. "Hidden dimensions in the
         so-called reality of a mathematics classroom,"
         Educational Studies in Mathematics 11 (1980):
         23-41.

             Analyzes a classroom teaching episode and
         identifies four dimensions of classroom process
         which are not usually studied.

2525.   Becker, Joanne Rossi, "Differential treatment of
         females and males in mathematics classes," *Journal
         for Research in Mathematics Education 12* (1981):
         40-53.

             Describes greater number and higher quality of
         contacts between teachers and male than female
         students in ten high school geometry classes.

2526.   Becker, Jerome & others. Classroom teaching and
         learning as a complex interactional game. Syracuse
         University. 1968. *ERIC ED* 010 068.

             Describes interactions between teachers and
         students in classrooms as recorded in informal
         observations in inner-city, suburban and rural
         classes.

2527.   Bellack, Arno A. The language of the classroom:
         Meanings communicated in high school teaching." In
         The nature of teaching: A collection of readings.
         Edited by Louis N. Nelson. pp. 93-106. Waltham,
         Massachusetts: Blaisdell Publishing Company.
         1969.

             Describes the language behavior of teachers and
         students in terms of a game with rules and moves,
         based on classroom observations. For Nelson
         reference see citation No. 2997.

2528.   Bellack, Arno A., Davitz, Joel R., Kliebard,
         Herbert M., Hyman, Ronald T. & Smith, Frank L.,
         Jr. "The language of the classroom," In *Teaching:
         Vantage points for study.* Edited by Ronald T.
         Hyman. Philadelphia, Pennsylvania: T.B. Lippincott
         Company. 1968.

Describes the language of the classroom and the rules for teacher and student talk. For Hyman reference see citation No. 2973.

2529. Bellack, Arno A., Kliebard, H.M., Hyman, R.T. & Smith, F.L., Jr. *The language of the classroom*. New York: Teachers College Press. 1966.

Describes the relationships between the verbal behaviors of students and the teacher in the classroom.

2530. Bennett, Roger V. "Curricular organizing strategies, classroom interaction patterns, and pupil affect," *Journal of Educational Research 66* (1973): 387-393.

Describes different teacher student interaction patterns related to differences in curricular approaches.

2531. Biddle, Bruce J., Loflin, M.D., Barron, N., Guyette, T. & Hays, D.G. Race, grade-level, and classroom discourse complexity, Technical Report No. 50. Columbia, Missouri: University of Missouri-Columbia.

Describes the behavior of teachers and students in classroom verbal interaction by grade level and racial mix of students.

2532. Biddle, Bruce J, & Loflin, Marvin D. "Verbal behavior in black-ghetto and white-suburban classrooms: An overview," Columbia, Missouri: Center for Research in Social Behavior, University of Missouri-Columbia. 1971. *ERIC ED* 047 308.

Describes the data collection and the general conclusion of differences in classroom communication of black and white students.

2533. Bidwell, Charles E. "The social psychology of teaching," In *Second Handbook of research on teaching*. Edited by Robert M.W. Travers. pp. 413-449. Chicago: Rand McNally & Company. 1973.

Review of studies of teachers' interactions with individual students and behaviors of teachers working with groups of students and aspects of classroom environment established by teachers. For Travers reference see citation No. 3033.

2534. Boothe, James William, Jr. A study of the relation between classroom verbal interaction patterns and racial coposition, teacher race, and grade level. Ed.D. dissertation. Western Michigan University. 1972.

Describes no difference in the verbal
interaction by race at the elementary level, but
middle school interaction has more volatile and
inconsistent verbal interactions in racially mixed
classrooms.

2535.   Brazil, David. "The teacher's use of intonation,"
         Educational Review 28 (1976): 180-189.

         Describes teacher intonation related to
         teacher-student interaction.

2536.   Bremme, Donald W. & Erickson,
         Frederick. "Relationships among verbal and
         nonverbal classroom behaviors," *Theory into
         Practice 16* (1977): 153-161.

         Describes behavior of teachers and students in
         interactions in kindergarten and grade one
         classrooms.

2537.   Brooks, Douglas M. & others. "The ecology of
         teacher-pupil verbal interaction," *Journal of
         Classroom Interaction 14*, No. 1 (1978): 39-45.

         Describes teacher and student behavior related
         to physical distance; teachers who work at closer
         distances involve students more in discussions and
         decisions.

2538.   Brooks, Robert C. A study to establish behavioral
         and other correlates of the pupil control ideology
         form at the junior and senior high school level.
         Ph.D. dissertation. University of Iowa. 1977.

         Describes custodial teachers having more
         student conflicts than do humanistic teachers.

2539.   Brophy, Jere E. "Interactions between learner
         characteristics and optimal instruction," In
         *Social psychology of education: Theory and
         research*. Edited by Daniel Bar-Tal. pp. 135-148.
         Washington, D.C.: Hemisphere Publishing
         Corporation. 1978.

         Review summarizes the results of several
         studies which report that teacher-student
         interactions vary by teacher and that students
         influence the nature of the interaction.   For
         Bar-Tal reference see citation No. 2907.

2540.   Brophy, Jere E., Evertson, C., Baum, M., Anderson,
         L. & Crawford, W. "Grade level and sex of student
         as context variables in elementary school,"
         Journal of Classroom Interaction 14, No. 2 (1979):
         11-17.

Describes grade level and student sex as related to teacher attitudes and responses to students.

2541. Brophy, J. & Rohrkemper, M. Teachers' specific strategies for dealing with hostile, aggressive students. East Lansing, Michigan: Institute for Research on Teaching. Michigan State University. 1980. *ERIC ED* 196 885.

Describes teacher reports of specific responses to individual student behavior in the classroom, based on written descriptions of possible student behavior.

2542. Brown, Jeannette A. & McDougall, Mary Ann. The impact of teacher consultation on elementary school children," Charlottesville, Virginia: Virginia University. 1972. *ERIC ED* 066 681.

Describes changes in behaviors of teachers trained to observe the behavior of students and changes in student self-perceptions.

2543. Brown, Kelsey Edwin. Differences in kindergarten teachers' behavior toward pupils as a function of sex-role expectations. Ed.D. dissertation. University of Virginia. 1978.

Describes differences in behavior of teachers to boys and girls by teacher expectations for sex roles.

2544. Brown, Richard Campbell. An exploration of teacher-student interpersonal relations. Ph.D. dissertation. Arizona University. 1976.

Describes compatibility of some student and teacher needs, but not others.

2545. Burns, Sandra Kaye. The relationship of pupil self concept to teacher-pupil dyadic interaction in kindergarten. Ph.D. dissertation. University of Texas at Austin. 1975.

Describes student self-concept related to teacher use of praise and teacher behavior in interactions with the student.

2546. Burtt, Merilyn. "The effect of a man teacher," *Young Children 21,* Nov. (1965): 92-97.

Describes experiences of children and teachers with a male teacher in a summer program for grade one and two students from fatherless homes.

2547.   Calonico, James M. Calonico, Beth Ann. "Classroom
         interaction: A sociological approach," *Journal of
         Educational Research*, 66 (1972): 165-168.

             Describes the interactions of students with the
         teacher in different classrooms.

2548.   Carnahan, Richard Stanley. The effects of teacher
         planning on classroom processes. Ph.D.
         dissertation. University of Wisconsin, Madison.
         1980. ERIC ED 189 095.

             Reports that teacher written planning was not
         related to motivational strategies or teacher
         clarity as perceived by students, but student
         engagement was related to teacher clarity.

2549.   Cassandra, S. Levin. "Teaching cues as contoller of
         classroom behavior," In *Focus on classroom
         behaviors: Readings and research*. Edited by W.
         Scott McDonald and others. pp. 7-15. Springfield,
         Illinois: Charles C. Thomas, Publisher. 1973.

             Describes the interaction of one teacher with
         three of the male students in the class. For
         McDonald reference see citation No. 2821.

2550.   Cherry, Louise. "The preschool teacher-child dyad:
         Sex differences in verbal interaction," *Child
         Development 46* (1975): 532-535.

             Describes differences in behavior of female
         preschool teachers toward male and female
         students, with greater verbal initiation and
         interaction and a greater number of
         attention-oriented statements to males and more
         verbal acknowledgements to females.

2551.   Cohen, Ellen Novik. Pupil behaviors as indicators
         of teacher success. Ph.D. dissertation. Columbia
         University. 1978.

             Describes no difference in pupil verbal and
         nonverbal behavior by the indicators which
         teachers use to define success in a lesson.

2552.   Cooper, Harris M. & others. Classroom format as a
         determinant of teacher-student interaction
         patterns and attributions of responsibility for
         performance. 1974. *ERIC ED* 165 085.

             Describes different behaviors of teachers and
         students, in terms of the types of interactions
         and grouping patterns, in open and traditional
         classrooms.

2553. Costales, Ceferino Duran. The congruence of
teacher-student bureaucratic propensities and its
relationship to instructional outcomes. Ph.D.
dissertation. State University of New York at
Albany. 1980.

Reports that student perceptions of classroom
environment are related to outcomes but the
congruence between teacher orientation toward
bureaucratic behavior and student preference for
such behavior is not related to outcomes.

2554. Crist. J. Group dynamics and the teacher-student
relationship: A review of recent innovations.
Stanford, California: Stanford Center for Research
and Development in Teacher Education. Stanford
University. 1972. *ERIC ED 062 292.*

Describes a method for teachers to work with
students and studies of teacher-student
relationships in classrooms.

2555. Daily, Frances MacCannell. A study of female
teachers' verbal behavior and peer-group structure
among classes of fifth-grade children. Ph.D.
dissertation. Kent State University. 1970.

Describes different teacher behavior related to
different interactions among students by student
status.

2556. Davis, Gene & others. "Nonverbal behavior of first
grade teachers in different socioeconomic level
elementary schools," *Journal of the Student
Personnel Association for Teacher Education 12*,
No. 2 (1973): 76-80. By first author only, Ph.D.
dissertation. Oklahoma State University. 1973.

Describes no differences in the nonverbal
behavior of teachers with students from lower and
middle class homes.

2557. Davis, O.L., Jr. & Slobodian, June
Jenkinson. "Teacher behavior toward boys and girls
during first grade reading," *American Educational
Research Journal 4* (1967): 261-269.

Describes teachers interacting equally with
boys and girls during reading instruction.

2558. Davis, William E. "A comparison of teacher referral
and pupil self-referral measure relative to
perceived school adjustment," *Psychology in the
Schools 15*, (1978): 22-26.

Describes the relationship between teacher referral and student self-referral to the school adjustment counselor.

2559. Day, Barbara & Hunt, Gilbert H. "Multiage classrooms: An analysis of verbal communication," *Elementary School Journal 75* (1975): 458-464.

Describes the interactions of students and teachers in multiage classrooms.

2560. Dulay, Heidi & Shultz, Jeffrey. Crosscultural miscommunication in the classroom," Cambridge, Massachusetts: Language Research Foundation. 1972. *ERIC ED* 064 439.

Describes miscommunication between Puerto Rican students and Anglo teachers.

2561. Eder, Donna Jean. Stratification within the classroom: The formation and maintenance of ability groups. Ph.D. dissertation. University of Wisconsin-Madison. 1979.

Describes factors which are related to teacher formation of student ability groups and the impact of the groups on the behaviors of students and teacher.

2562. Ellett, Chad D. & others. "The incremental validity of teacher and student perceptions of school environment characteristics," 1978. *ERIC ED* 169 125.

Reports that teacher and student perceptions of school climate are related to teacher behavior and student achievement.

2563. Emmer, E., Oakland, T. & Good, T.L. "Do pupils affect teachers' styles of instruction?" *Educational Leadership 31*, 700-704.

Summarizes research on the effects of student characteristics on the behavior of teachers.

2564. Fey, James T. *Patterns of verbal communication in mathematics classes.* New York: Teachers College Press. 1970.

Describes rules and patterns of verbal interactions in secondary mathematics classes using the Secondary School Mathematics Curriculum Improvement Study (SSMCIS) materials.

2565. Fiedler, Martha L. "Bidirectionality of influence in classroom interaction," *Journal of Educational Psychology 67* (1975): 735-744.

Describes student influences on student-teacher interactions in seventh-grade classrooms and student perceptions of their control over student-teacher interactions.

2566. Fishman, Harold. The effectiveness of differential social reinforcement strategies in facilitating achievement behavior of lower socioeconomic status, primary grade children. Ph.D. dissertation. University of Maryland. 1971.

Describes no difference by race of student or teacher and socioeconomic status of student in student responses to positive and negative teacher reinforcement.

2567. Flanders, Ned A. "Intent, action and feedback: A preparation for teaching," In *Teachers and the learning process*. Edited by Robert D. Strom. pp. 175-189. Englewood Cliffs, New Jersey: Prentice-Hall, Inc. 1971. Reprinted from *Journal of Teacher Education 14* (1963): 251-260.

Reviews some studies of teacher behaviors and their effects on student behaviors and describes Interaction Analysis. For Strom reference see citation No. 3029.

2568. Flanders, Ned A. "Interaction models of critical teaching behaviors," In *Interaction Analysis: Theory, Research and Application*. Edited by Edmund G. Amidon & John B. Hough. pp. 360-374. Reading, Massachusetts: Addison Wesley Publishing Co. 1967.

Describes several models of the verbal interaction of teachers and students and relates the models to observation categories in Flanders' Interaction Analysis. For Amidon & Hough reference see citation No. 1638.

2569. Gage, N.L. (Ed.) NIE conference on studies of teaching: Panel 2, Teaching as human interaction. Washington, D.C.: National Institute of Education. 1974. *ERIC ED* 111 803.

Summarizes the discussions of the panel of researchers and practitioners about the human interactions in teaching.

2570.   Gallagher, James J. "Analysis of teacher classroom
         strategies associated with student cognitive and
         affective performance. Final Report. Urbana,
         Illinois: Illinois University. 1968. *ERIC ED* 021
         808.

             Reports results of three studies of an
         observation instrument which classifies classroom
         statements by content and concepts and describes
         teacher student interactions in junior and senior
         high classrooms.

2571.   Gallagher, James Joseph. "A pre-scientific study of
         interactions in selected science classes,"
         Cleveland, Ohio: Educational Research Council of
         America. 1969. *ERIC ED* 059 868.

             Describes different agendas of teachers and
         students, with students generally acquiescing to
         teacher agendas.

2572.   Gallagher, James J. & Aschner, Mary Jane. "A
         preliminary report on analyses of classroom
         interaction," In *The nature of teaching: A
         collection of readings.* Edited by Louis N. Nelson.
         pp. 158-169. Waltham, Massachusetts: Blaisdell
         Publishing Company. 1969. Also in *Teaching:
         Vantage points for study.* Edited by Ronald T.
         Hyman. Philadelphia, Pennsylvania: T.B. Lippincott
         Company, 1968. Reprinted from *Merrill-Palmer
         Quarterly 9* (1963): 183-194.

             Describes the process of interaction, including
         teacher and student statements and sequences of
         statements, in terms of the level of cognitive
         processes. For Nelson reference see citation No.
         2997. For Hyman reference see citation No. 2973.

2573.   Galluzzi, Edward Gregory. An investigation of the
         relationship between self-concept and
         others-concept of regular class children and
         student and teacher perceptions of classroom
         environment. Ph.D. dissertation. Indiana State
         University. 1978.

             Describes student self-concept as related to
         student perception of the classroom and the degree
         of similarity between student self-concept and
         teacher perception of student self-concept.

2574.   Garrard, Judy. "Classroom interaction--Review of
         the literature," Austin, Texas: Research and
         Development Center for Teacher Education. Texas
         University at Austin. 1966. *ERIC ED* 013 988.

Reviews the literature on verbal and non-verbal classroom interaction using sign and category systems.

2575. Good, Thomas L., Sikes, J.N. & Brophy, J.E. "Effects of teacher sex and student sex on classroom interaction," *Journal of Educational Psychology 65* (1973): 74-87.

Describes differences in the behavior of male and female teachers with male and female students.

2576. Gordis, Felice Witztum. A Piagetian analysis of the teaching of seriation concepts in four first grade classrooms. 1970. *ERIC ED* 077 756.

Describes teacher and student verbal statements during instruction, with teacher statements dominating.

2577. Grobe, William John, III. Critical teacher and student behaviors in conference settings. Ed.D. dissertation. State University of New York at Buffalo. 1978.

Describes the behavior of students and teachers which result in effect student-teacher conferences.

2578. Guest, Gerald Richard. The teacher-student relationship and student response to double binds. Ph.D. dissertation. University of Victoria, Canada. 1976.

Describes no differences in student observations of contradictory teacher messages in videotapes of teachers by level of student-teacher relationship.

2579. Guthrie, John T. "Research views: Teacher-student interaction," *Reading Teacher 33* (1979): 372-374.

Describes an anthropological study of classroom interaction conducted by Jules Henry.

2580. Hall, Marian D. & others. An experimental assessment program in an inner city school. 1970. *ERIC ED* 042 809.

Describes the students, the classroom climate and teacher-student interaction inner city and suburban classrooms.

2581. Hamilton, Dorothy Gettel. The comparison of student-initiated and teacher-initiated

interaction in an elementary school classroom: A
case study in human differences. Ed.D.
dissertation. University of Southern California.
1978.

Reports that student choice of working groups
results in different patterns of student inclusion
that teacher choice of working groups.

2582.   Hawley, Harold Patrick. The classroom communion: A
study of teacher-student personal relationships in
education with emphasis on secondary education.
Ed.D. Indiana University. 1978.

Reviews the literature on teacher-student
personal relations.

2583.   Hayes, Robert B. & others. The effects of student
reactions to teaching methods, Harrisburg,
Pennsylvania: Pennsylvania State Department of
Public Instruction. Bureau of Research
Administration and Coordination. 1966. *ERIC ED* 010
369. Also 1967 *ERIC ED* 023 619.

Describes no differences in achievement among
classes by the types of feedback to teachers about
student perceptions of teachers.

2584.   Heath, Robert W. "The ability of white teachers to
relate to black students and to white students,"
American Educational Research Journal 8 (1971):
1-10. *ERIC ED* 037 399.

Describes teaching style and student ethnic
background jointly influencing teacher-student
relations.

2585.   Heinig, Ruth Miriam Beall. A descriptive study of
teacher-pupil tactile communication in grades four
through six. Ph.D. dissertation. University of
Pittsburgh. 1975.

Describes different types and amounts of
physical contact by student sex and race and the
match between student and teacher sex in the
elementary grades.

2586.   Hill, John C. Change of content development
patterns observed in classroom communication
behaviors due to in-service training in content
strategies. 1971. *ERIC ED* 049 190.

Describes a system which identifies different
patterns of content communication in classrooms
and differences in communication behavior of
teachers after training.

2587. Hill, John C. The analysis and identification of content development patterns in classroom communication. 1970. *ERIC ED* 043 575.

Describes the content of classroom communication and the development of larger units of sequences for analysis of classroom communication.

2588. Hillman, Stephen B. & Davenport, G. Gregory. "Teacher behavior in desegregated schools," *Journal of Educational Psychology 70* (1978): 545-553. 1977. *ERIC ED* 138 670.

Reports that black students and males receive a greater proportion of teacher interactions than white students and females.

2589. Hillman, Stephan B. & Davenport, G. Gregory. "Teacher-student interaction in desegregated schools," *Journal of Educational Psychology 70* (1978): 545-553.

Describes black and male students as receiving a greater proportion of teacher interactions with students than white and female students.

2590. Hillman, Stephen B. & Elliott, Brownlee. Verbal behavior patterns of teachers in integrated classrooms. 1978. *ERIC ED* 167 921.

Reports that black and male students have a greater rate of interaction than white and female students and white and female teachers have a higher rate of interaction than black and male teachers.

2591. Hoetker, James & Ahlbrand, William P., Jr. "'The persistence of the recitation': A review of observational studies of teacher questioning behavior," *American Educational Research Journal* 6, (1969): 145-167. Occasional Paper Series, No. 3. St. Ann, Missouri: Central Midwestern Regional Educational Laboratory. 1968. *ERIC ED* 036 511.

Reviews research from 1893 to 1963 on classroom observation in terms of Bellack's study of teacher and student talk and the rules for such talk.

2592. Hull, Ray. "Teacher verbal behavior and cognitive interaction," *Clearing House 49* 7 (1976): 307-311.

Describes a relationship between cognitive and social-emotional interactions in classrooms.

2593.   Hunt, David E. "Matching models in education. The
        coordination of teaching methods with student
        characteristics," Toronto, Canada: Ontario
        Institute for Studies in Education. 1971. *ERIC ED*
        053 058.

        Describes studies which match student
        characteristics with teaching styles and train
        teachers to use those styles.

2594.   Hunt, David E. Teachers' adaptation to students:
        Implicit and explicit matching. Research and
        Development Memorandum. No. 139. Stanford,
        California: Stanford Center for Research and
        Development in Teaching. Stanford University. *ERIC
        ED* 117 090.

        Describes teacher adaptations to students and
        the effects of students in defining classroom
        interactions.

2595.   Jackson, Philip W. & Lahaderne, Henriette
        M. "Inequalities of teacher-pupil contacts,"
        Psychology in the Schools 4, (1967): 204-211.

        Describes differences in the number and
        frequency of teacher interactions with individual
        pupils.

2596.   Johnson, Mary Canice. Discussion dynamics: An
        analysis of classroom teaching. 1979. *ERIC ED* 187
        097.

        Describes sequences of interaction in classroom
        discussions, within an interaction and from one
        interaction to the next.

2597.   Jones, Jerry Dale. An investigation of the effects
        of a systematic behavior modification program on
        the verbal interaction of classroom teachers and
        its relationship to teachers' students'
        self-concept. Ed.D. dissertation. Virginia
        Polytechnic Institute and State University. 1978.

        Describes teacher training resulting in
        different teacher and student behaviors and
        interactions.

2598.   Jorgensen, G.W. "Relationship of classroom behavior
        to the accuracy of the match between material
        difficulty and student ability," *Journal of
        Educational Psychology 69,* (1977): 24-33.

        Describes a study of the behaviors of teachers
        and students in terms of the match between the
        ability of students and the difficulty level of
        the materials.

2599.   Kimmel, Melvin J. Correlates of trust of a teacher
        in fourth-grade classrooms. 1977. *ERIC ED* 151
        639.

        Describes a stronger relationship between
        student personality variables and sex and student
        trust of the teacher than between teacher behavior
        and student trust of the teacher.

2600.   Leacock, Eleanor Berke. Teaching and learning in
        city schools: A comparative study. Psychosocial
        studies in education. 1969. *ERIC ED* 033 989.

        Describes the behaviors of middle class
        teachers with lower class black and white
        students, behaviors focusing on academic learning
        and on socialization.

2601.   Lewis, Louisa. Culture and social interaction in
        the classroom: An ethnographic report. Berkeley,
        California: Language and Behavior Research
        Laboratory. University of California, Berkeley.
        1970. *ERIC ED* 044 682.

        Describes an ethnographic study of the
        classroom interaction of black students with their
        teachers.

2602.   Licata, Joseph W. Student brinksmanship: Some field
        observations, findings and questions. 1979. *ERIC
        ED* 174 899.

        Reports that teacher behavior is related to
        student brinksmanship, with less positive rapport
        between students and teacher and low levels of
        routines associated with more brinksmanship.

2603.   Licata, Joseph W. & Wildes, James R. Dimensions of
        robustness in classroom organization. 1979. *ERIC
        ED* 180 703.

        Describes greater robustness with greater
        social interactions in the classroom, and other
        characteristics, such as greater student
        involvement in tasks.

2604.   Lightfoot, Sara Lawrence & Carew, Jean V.
        "Individuation and discrimination in the
        classroom," *American Journal of Orthopsychiatry*
        46 (1976): 401-415.

        Describes three teachers and their attitudes
        toward and interactions with students within the
        context of the school.

2605.   Ludwig, Meredith Jane. Posing the problem ...
        finding the problem: The organization of verbal
        interaction in classroom lessons and its effect on
        successful classroom participation. Ed.D.
        Dissertation. Clark University. 1979.

            Describes the interactive behavior of students
        and teachers in two eighth grade science
        classrooms.

2606.   McCafferty, W. Dean. "Personal-social influences in
        the classroom," *Education 100* (1980): 214-222.
        Reprinted in *Education Digest 45*: 25-28.

            Describes the process of social influence in
        the classroom in terms of compliance,
        internalization, identification and expectations,
        with citations of selected research.

2607.   Mangold, Lana Carole Paremore. Pupil-teacher dyadic
        interaction in desegregated elementary classrooms.
        Ph.D. Dissertation. University of Texas at Austin.
        1974.

            Describes only a few differences in
        interactions between black and white teachers and
        black and white students.

2608.   Martin, Mary Ruth. Analysis of behavior pattern
        composition in the tri student need and behavior
        model as related to behavior problem
        identification and four levels of teacher
        acceptance of the student. Ph.D. dissertation.
        George Peabody College for Teachers of Vanderbilt
        University. 1980.

            Describes patterns of student behavior and
        reports that teachers behave differently toward
        students with different patterns of behavior.

2609.   Martin, Wilfred B.W. "Teachers' perceptions of
        their interaction tactics," *Education 99* (1979):
        236-239.

            Describes teacher student interaction in open
        and traditional elementary school classrooms.

2610.   Mason, Jack Lee. "A study of the relationships
        between the behavioral styles of classroom
        teachers and the quality of teacher-student
        interpersonal relations," *Educational Leadership*,
        28 (1970): 49-56. Ph.D. Dissertation. Syracuse
        University. 1969.

Describes no relationship between observed
teacher behavior and the quality of the
relationship between teacher and students.

2611. Massialas, Byron G. & others. Structure and process
of inquiry into social issues in secondary
schools. Volume 1. Inquiry into social issues.
1970. *ERIC ED* 039 161.

Describes the behavior of teachers and students
in discussing social issues and how students
perceive these discussions.

2612. Measel, Wes & Mood, Darlene W. "Teacher verbal
behavior and teacher and pupil thinking in
elementary school," *Journal of Educational
Research* 66 (1972): 99-102.

Describes a relationship between the level of
student and teacher cognition and response modes
of students.

2613. Metz, Mary Haywood. "Clashes in the classroom: The
importance of norms for authority," *Education and
Urban Society 11*, No. 1 (1978): 13-47. *ERIC ED* 151
340.

Conflicts in classroom result from conflicts
over the appropriate teacher use of authority in
desegregated junior high school classrooms.

2614. Miller, John & Hylton, Cal. "Teacher-student
communication patterns," *Western Speech 38* (1974):
146-156.

Describes classroom communication between
teacher and students.

2615. Montgomery County School System. A comparison of
interaction patterns in an open space and fixed
plan school. Christiansburg, Virginia: Author.
1973. *ERIC ED* 098 721.

Describes different patterns of interaction in
open and traditional schools.

2616. Morine-Dershimer, G., Ramirez, A., Shuy, R. &
Galluzzo, G. How do we know? (Alternative
descriptions of classroom discourse). Syracuse
University. 1980.

Describes teacher and student interaction and
varied views of the purposes for messages
communicated, and the results of classroom
interactions.

2617. Morrison, Virginia B. "Teacher-pupil interaction in
       three types of elementary classroom reading
       situations," *Reading Teacher 22* (1968): 271-275.

       Describes teacher behavior varying by the level
       of the IQ of the class, and the use of a single or
       multiple textbooks.

2618. Munoz-Hernandez, Shirley Ann. A description of
       verbal behaviors of Hispanic teachers and students
       in fifth grade social studies classrooms. Ed.D.
       dissertation. Columbia University Teachers
       College. 1979.

       Describes the verbal interactions between
       teacher and students where teachers and students
       are Hispanic.

2619. Natriello, Gary & Dornbusch, Sanford M. An
       experimental study of the effects of student
       status and performance characteristics on teacher
       standards and warmth. 1979. *ERIC ED* 171 669.

       Describes complex patterns of teacher
       behaviors, as reported by teachers in simulation
       exercises, in response to different student
       characteristics.

2620. Needles, Margaret & Stallings, Jane. Classroom
       processes related to absence rate, Menlo Park,
       California: Stanford Research Institute. 1975.
       ERIC ED 110 199.

       Reports that student absence rate is related to
       teacher behavior and classroom processes.

2621. Novak, John H. A study of the effects of the use of
       a pupil response instrument on the behaviors of
       biological science teachers. Final Report.
       Pittsburgh, Pennsylvania: University of
       Pennsylvania. 1972. *ERIC ED* 069 155.

       Describes changes in teacher behavior as a
       result of feedback from students.

2622. Ortiz, Alba Alicia. A study of teacher-pupil dyadic
       verbal interactions in four first-grade
       classrooms. Ph.D. dissertation. University of
       Texas at Austin. 1976.

       Describes teacher behavior with students as
       related to student sex, readiness level and age.

2623. Palladino, John. "Verbal interaction in urban
       schools," *Urban Education 14* (1979): 353-358.

Describes patterns of verbal interaction in urban classrooms.

2624.   Parakh, Jal Sohrab. "A study of teacher-pupil interaction in high school biology classes. *Journal of Research in Science Teaching 5* (1967-1968): 183-192. Ph.D. dissertation. Cornell University. 1965. *ERIC ED* 013 209. Also under the title, "A study of teacher-pupil interaction in BSCS Yellow version biology classes," *American Biology Teacher 30* (1968): 841-848.

Describes behaviors of teachers and students; during lectures 75% of the time teachers are talking, while in laboratory settings teachers talk 50% of the time.

2625.   Paulissen, Margaret Elizabeth O'Neill. An observational study of the use of time during the designated reading period in first-grade classrooms. Ph.D. dissertation. University of Texas at Austin. 1978.

Describes the behavior of teachers and students during reading periods.

2626.   Perdue, Valerie P. & Connor, Jane Marantz. "Patterns of touching between preschool children and male and female teachers," *Child Development 49* (1978): 1258-1262.

Describes the amounts and patterns of touching between students and teachers in preschool classrooms.

2627.   Perkins, Hugh V. "Classroom behavior and underachievement," *American Educational Research Journal 2* (1965): 1-12.

Describes differences in patterns of on-task behavior for high and low achieving fifth grade pupils and different patterns of student response to teachers and teacher-student interactions.

2628.   Portuges, Stephen H. & Feshback, Norma D. "The influence of sex and socioethnic factors upon imitation by elementary school children," *Child Development 43* (1972): 981-989.

Describes greater student modeling of teacher behavior by advantaged students and girls and in response to positive teacher reinforcment.

2629.   Power, Colin N. "The unintentional consequences of science teaching," *Journal of Research in Science Teaching 10* (1973): 331-339.

Describes four patterns of relations between science teachers and students; the success, the rejection-dependency, person-orientation, and social-alienation.

2630.   Prucha, Jan. "Verbal communication in the classroom--A case for applied psycholinguistics," *Linguistics 112* (1973): 23-38.

Reviews studies of verbal communication between teacher and students in classrooms.

2631.   Ramsey, Gregory A. & Howe, Robert W. "An analysis of research on instructional procedures in secondary school science. Part II--Instructional procedures," *Science Teacher 36*, No. 4, (1969): 72-81.

Reviews studies of teacher student interaction, teaching methods and organization, and laboratory procedures.

2632.   Resnick, Lauren B. Teacher behavior in an informal British infant school. Pittsburgh, Pennsylvania: Learning Research and Development Center. 1971. *ERIC ED* 059 181.

Describes the behaviors of teachers and teacher student interaction in British infant schools.

2633.   Rist, Ray C. *The invisible children: School integration in American society.* Cambridge, Massachusetts: Harvard University Press. 1978.

Describes observations of classrooms in a school which had previously had white students during the first year of integration and the behaviors of students and teachers throughout the year.

2634.   Roecks, Alan L. "Instructional cost and utilization of classroom time for fifth grade students of different achievement levels," *Journal of School Psychology 18* (1980): 381-387.

Reports that fifth grade high achieving students spent less time interacting with the teacher than did low achieving students and therefore had a lower cost for instruction.

2635.   Rosenfeld, Gerry. *"Shut those thick lips!" A study of slum school failure.* Case studies in education and culture series. New York: Holt, Rinehart & Winston, Inc. *ERIC ED* 063 432.

Describes behavior of teachers and students in inner city classrooms and the differences in cultural expectations for behavior.

2636. Rubin, Gary N. A naturalistic study in proxemics: Seating arrangement and its effect on interaction, performance, and behavior. 1972. *ERIC ED* 085 790.

Describes different student and teacher reactions to seating arrangements by student IQ.

2637. Sanchez, Richard Monarrez. Verbal interaction patterns, student opinions, and teacher perceptions in classrooms with Mexican-American student enrollment. Ed.D. dissertation. Western Michigan University. 1972.

Describes differences in interactions of teachers and students by school level, accurate teacher perceptions of student opinion of the teacher and school but not of student opinion of other students.

2638. Schafer, Larry E. & Vargo, Robert A. Students' science attitudes and self-concepts in science as a function of role specific pupil/teacher interpersonal compatibility. 1976. *ERIC ED* 129 592.

Reports that the degree of student-teacher compatibility helped to account for the variance in student attitude toward science and self-concept in science in grade nine.

2639. Schleckty, Phillip C. & Atwood, Helen E. "The student-teacher relationship," *Theory into Practice 16* (1977): 285-289.

Reviews the limited research on the effects of students on the behavior of teachers; the fact that there are so few studies demonstrates the assumption that teachers control the classroom.

2640. Schlegel, Daniel Thomas. The effect of teacher feedback on family attitudes toward school and students' disruptive behavior. Ph.D. dissertation. Saint Louis University. 1980.

Describes no difference in the behavior of students or the attitudes of parents toward school under three conditions of teacher responses to student behavior problems.

2641. Scroggins, Fredna Carlson. An exploratory study of the relationship between teacher reacting moves

and subsequent student verbal participation in
selected ninth grade algebra classes. Ed.D.
dissertation. Southern Illinois University at
Edwardville. 1980.

Describes reactions of teachers to student
initiation of interaction and student reactions to
teacher reactions.

2642.   Sears, Pauline S. & Feldman, David H. "Teacher
interactions with boys and with girls," *National
Elementary Principal 46* (Nov. 1966): 30-35.

Reviews studies of differences and similarities
in teachers' behavior toward and perceptions of
male and female students.

2643.   Seaver, W. Burleigh. "Effects of naturally induced
teacher expectancies," *Journal of Personality and
Social Psychology 28* (1973): 333-342.

Describes a relationship between the
achievement of students and the teacher having
taught an older sibling.

2644.   Shadbolt, D. "Interactive relationships between
measured personality and teaching strategy
variables," *British Journal of Educational
Psychology 48* (1978): 227-231.

Describes a relationship between student
personality variables and teacher behavior.

2645.   Sherman, Thomas More. An examination of the
relationship between student behavior change and
teacher mode of response. Ed.D. dissertation.
University of Tennessee. 1971.

Reports that teacher attitude and behavior
toward problem students changed as student
behavior changed in an experiment.

2646.   Sherman, Thomas M. & others. An investigation of
the influence of student behavior on teacher
behavior. 1973. *ERIC ED* 075 387.

Describes changes in the behavior of problem
students resulting in changes in the behavior of
teachers toward those students.

2647.   Smith, B. Othaniel & Meux, Milton. *A study of the
logic of teaching*. Urbana, Illinois: The
University of Illinois. 1970. Also in *Teaching:
Vantage points for study*. Edited by Ronald T.
Hyman. pp. 101-117. Philadelphia, Pennsylvania:

T.B. Lippincott Company. 1968. Also Cooperative
Research Project No. 258. University of Illinois.
U.S. Department of Health, Education and Welfare.
1962.

Describes the units of language in the
classroom and the percentage of occurance of the
units in the observed classrooms. For Hyman
reference see citation No. 2973.

2648. Smith, B. Othaniel, Meux, M., Coombs, J., Nuthall,
G. & Precians, R.A. *A study of the strategies of
teaching*. Urbana, Illinois: University of Illinois
Press. 1967. *ERIC ED* 029 165.

Describes an analysis of high school classroom
discourse in several subject areas.

2649. Smith, Christine C. "The relationship between
teacher-pupil interaction and progress of pupils
with reading disabilities," *Reading Improvement
17* (1980): 53-65.

Describes teacher pupil interactions, including
teacher praise, task orientation, questions, pupil
initiation and response related to student reading
progress.

2650. Smith, Frank Lester, Jr. Analysis of classroom
discourse: Soliciting moves in the language of
selected classrooms. Ed.D. dissertation. Columbia
University. 1965.

Describes teacher soliciting moves as one third
of all classroom moves, as about one half of all
teacher moves, as related to content of lesson,
and describes other teacher behaviors.

2651. Smith, Louis M. & Geoffrey, William. *The
complexities of an urban classroom: An analysis
toward a general theory of teaching*. New York:
Holt, Rinehart & Winston, Inc. 1968. *ERIC ED* 029
072.

Describes the decision making of one teacher in
an inner-city classroom and the method for
conducting a participant observation study.

2652. Soar, Robert S. "Teacher-pupil interaction," In *A
new look at progressive education*. Edited by J.R.
Squire. pp. 166-204. Washington, D.C.: Association
for Supervision and Curriculum Development. 1972.

Describes observations of interactions of
teachers and pupils in elementary classrooms

with and without special programs such as Follow
Through.

2653.   Spencer, Mima. Bibliography: Teacher
        characteristics. Urbana, Illinois: ERIC
        Clearinghouse on Early Childhood Education. 1969.
        ERIC ED 029 716.

            Presents an annotated bibliography of research
        and other documents on preschool and primary
        teachers and their relationships with students.

2654.   Spring, Martha F. Who's in charge here? Observed
        and perceived patterns of teacher and student
        influence in alternative and traditional classes.
        1974. *ERIC ED* 090 233.

            Describes student influence on the behaviors of
        teachers and student perceptions of the
        classroom.

2655.   Starkel, John Philip. Differences in teacher-child
        verbal interactions due to readiness level, sex,
        and classroom placement in four first grade
        classrooms. Ph.D. dissertation. University of
        Kansas. 1978.

            Describe differences in teacher-student
        interactions due to differences in students and
        teachers, with teachers accounting for the largest
        variation in the interaction patterns in the
        observed classrooms.

2656.   Stayrook, Nicholas G., Corno, Lynn & Winne,
        Phillip. "Path analysis relating student
        perceptions of teacher behavior to student
        achievement," *Journal of Teacher Education 29*, No.
        2 (1978): 51-56.

            Describe student perceptions of teacher
        behavior in experimental lessons related to
        student achievement when teachers' behaviors were
        high in structuring, reacting, but not
        soliciting.

2657.   Stecker, Judith S. A description of teacher verbal
        mediation and of children's verbal coding in
        selected early childhood classrooms. 1976. *ERIC
        ED* 126 733.

            Describe teacher behavior in verbal interaction
        with early childhood students.

2658.   Taba, Hilda & Elzey, Freeman F. "Teaching
        strategies and thought processes. In *Teaching:*

Vantage points for study. Edited by Ronald T. Hyman. pp. 441-458. Philadelphia, Pennsylvania: T.B. Lippincott Company. 1968.

Describes patterns of behavior of teachers and students in terms of the function and the cognitive levels of interactions. For Hyman reference see citation No. 2973.

2659. Talavage, Joseph. A model for the social aspects of classroom organization: Final report. Atlanta, Georgia: Georgia Institute of Technology. 1970. *ERIC ED* 050 047.

Describes the development of a mathematic model of the social interaction in classrooms and relates the model to studies of classroom interaction.

2660. Tenenberg, M., Morine-Dershimer, G. & Shuy, R. What did anybody say? (Salient features of classroom discourse). Syracuse University. 1980.

Describes statements made by teachers and students in various classroom settings.

2661. Thompson, Ray Hadley. Interaction patterns of regular classroom teachers with mildly handicapped students in mainstreamed classrooms. Ed.D. dissertation. Utah State University. 1979.

Describes differences in patterns of teacher-student interactions between groups of high achieving and handicapped third grade students.

2662. Traub, Raymond Gordon. The effect of teacher behavior on patterns of student achievement. Ph.D. dissertation. Ohio State University. 1968.

Describes teacher permissive and punishing behavior related to the degree of student aggressive behavior, with boys more aggressive than girls.

2663. Tretten, Rudolph Weber. Changing status space in Negro teacher-pupil interaction. Ph.D. dissertation. Stanford University. 1970.

Describes an experiment in which teachers used different leadership styles with students of different status and competence.

2664. Trottier, Claude Rene. Teachers as agents of political socialization. Ph.D. dissertation. University of Toronto, Canada. 1980.

Describes limited teacher involvement in
political discussions with secondary school
students.

2665.   Vargo, Robert A. Pupil/science teacher
interpersonal compatibility and science attitudes.
1974. *ERIC ED* 091 203.

Describes no correlation between
teacher-student personal compatibility and student
attitude toward and grade in science.

2666.   Vargo, Robert A. & Schafer, Larry E. Role specific
pupil/science teacher interpersonal compatibility
and science attitudes. 1975. *ERIC ED* 123 031.

Describes no relationship between measures of
interpersonal compatability of teachers and
students in terms of student and teacher roles and
student attitudes toward and achievement in
science.

2667.   Waetjin, Walter B. Recent analyses of teaching.
NASSP Bulletin 50 (Dec. 1966): 17-29.

Reviews several studies which describe the
dominant role of teachers in the classroom and in
interactions with students.

2668.   Walker, Hill M. & Buckley, Nancy K. Assessment and
treatment of deviant behavior in children--Section
five: Investigation of some functional
relationships between teacher consequating
behavior and pupil performance. Final report.
Eugene, Oregon: Oregon University. 1970. *ERIC ED*
049 593.

Describes students exhibiting deviant behavior
receiving more than two times their share of the
teacher's attention, and forty percent of that
attention is due to the deviant behavior.

2669.   Weinstein, Rhone Strasberg. "Reading group
membership in first grade: Teacher behaviors and
pupil experience over time," *Journal of
Educational Psychology 68* (1976): 103-116.

Describes the impact of reading groups on
student teacher interaction, student mobility and
achievement.

2670.   Weiss, Melford S. & Weiss, Paula H. Taking another
look at teaching: How lower-class children
influence middle-class teachers. 1975. *ERIC ED* 137
223.

Describes behavior of students influencing the behavior of teachers; teachers use more violence to resolve problems and are more accepting of obscene language with lower than with middle class children.

2671.   Weiss, Richard L., Sales, Stephen M. & Bode, Shelly. "Student authoritarianism and teacher authoritarianism as factors in the determination of student performance and attitudes," *Journal of Experimental Education 38* (1970): 83-87.

Reports an interaction between student and teacher authoritarianism, with low student attitude toward the teacher and low grades with high student and low teacher authoritarianism.

2672.   Wilcox, Mary Angeline Anastole. Comparison of elementary school children's interaction in teacher-led and student-led small groups. Ph.D. dissertation. Stanford University. 1972.

Describes more student participation, more divergent thinking with trained student leaders than with teachers as leaders of discussion groups.

2673.   Williams, W.C. "Teacher perception and secondary school classroom discussion," *Journal of Educational Research 69* (1976): 296-300.

Describes differences in student talk and teacher and student patterns of responses to talk by students within different role groups in secondary classrooms.

2674.   Woolfolk, Robert L. & Woolfolk, Anita E. "Effects of teacher verbal and nonverbal behaviors on student perceptions and attitudes," *American Educational Research Journal 11* (1974): 297-303.

Describes one teacher and a series of lessons to fourth grade students; student ratings of liking for the teacher related to the degree of teacher positive response to the students.

2675.   Wright, Kathleen Cooper. The relationship of race and sex to grades assigned by high school teachers of English. Ed.D. dissertation. Florida Atlantic University. 1980.

Describes some differences by teacher race and sex and student race and sex in assignment of grades, such as better grades by male than female teachers to boys of both races.

2676.   Yee, Albert H. "Social interaction in classrooms:
         Implications for the education of disadvantaged
         pupils," *Urban Education 4*, No. 3 (1969):
         203-219.

             Describes teacher interaction patterns varying
         by the socioeconomic level of the students.

2677.   Yee, Albert H. "Source and direction of causal
         influence in teacher-pupil relationships," *Journal
         of Educational Psychology 59* (1968): 275-282.

             Describes differences in the influence of
         teachers and students by the class of the
         students, with more mutual influence with middle
         class students.

2678.   Zahorik, John A. The nature and value of teacher
         verbal feedback. 1967. *ERIC ED* 011 526.

             Describes types of teacher feedback to
         students, frequency of use, and student responses
         to feedback in current events discussions.

VII STUDENT

A. PERCEPTIONS

2679.   Anderson, G.J. Student perceptions of their science
        classes: classroom climate differences in physics,
        chemistry and biology. 1970. *ERIC ED* 042 605.

        Describes differences in student perceptions of
        the climate of classrooms by science subject, with
        biology classrooms seen as least like physics
        classrooms.

2680.   Anderson, Gary J. & Walberg, Herbert J. Classroom
        climate and group learning. 1967. *ERIC ED* 015
        156.

        Describes differences in student perceptions of
        science classes by differences in classroom
        achievement, with students in classrooms with
        higher achievement gains perceiving classrooms as
        having stricter control and less stratification.

2681.   Archibald, Robert D. The relationship of teacher's
        cognitive style to minority student satisfaction.
        1975. *ERIC ED* 109 550.

        Describes a relationship between student
        satisfaction with teacher and teacher cognitive
        style.

2682.   Artley, A. Sterl. Identifying good teachers of
        reading. Successful teachers of reading, who are
        they? 1973. *ERIC ED* 074 454.

        Describes the recollections of teacher
        education students of those teachers whom they
        perceived to be good teachers of reading in their
        school experiences.

2683.   Baird, Leonard L. "Teaching styles: An exploratory
        study of dimensions and effects," *Journal of
        Educational Psychology 64* (1973): 15:21.

        Describes student perceptions of teaching
        styles.

2684.   Barnett, Howard Cecil. An investigation of
         relationships among achievement, perception of
         teacher style, and cognitive preferences of
         students in tenth grade biology. 1972. *ERIC ED* 079
         091.

              Describes some relationships between student
         perceptions of teaching style and student
         preferences for cognitive levels of instructional
         tasks.

2685.   Barton, Florence Richter. Do teachers cause
         dropouts? A study to determine attitudes,
         personality characteristics, and teaching
         behaviors of teachers who are effective with
         dropout students. Ph.D. dissertation. University
         of Utah. 1972.

              Describes differences in the attitudes and
         behaviors of teachers who are liked and disliked
         by dropouts.

2686.   Bath, John Barry. The interactions of student
         traits and classroom openness with self-concept,
         attitude toward school, creativity and curiosity
         and persistence in a science exploration lesson.
         Ph.D. dissertation. Syracuse University. 1976.

              Describes student sex, reading achievement and
         teacher use of open classroom teaching methods
         related to student attitude toward and task
         persistence in science tasks.

2687.   Bender, David S. Adolescents' perceptions of
         teachers' caring and achievement press related to
         sex, track, program, and achievement. 1978. *ERIC
         ED* 165 071.

              Describes the attitudes toward and perceptions
         of teachers of junior and senior high school
         students.

2688.   Bishop. W.C. "Successful teachers of the gifted,"
         Exceptional Children 34 (1968): 317-325.

              Reports no differences between teachers whom
         students rated as successful and other teachers in
         terms of background and coursework but differed in
         terms of achievement needs, IQ, and degree of
         interest in students.

2689.   Bledsoe. J. "Personality characteristics and
         teaching performance of beginning teachers as
         related to certification status," *Journal of
         Research and Development in Education 2* (1968):
         3-48.

Describes almost no differences in student perceptions of and the characteristics of first year teachers with full and provisional certificates.

2690. Bohlken, Robert & Giffin, Kim. A paradigm for determining high school teacher effectiveness. 1970. *ERIC ED* 050 119.

Describes a model of teacher behavior in relation to student perceptions and describes the importance of a favorable communications climate.

2691. Borovetz, Frank Charles, Jr. The relationship between sixth grade students' perceptions of their teachers' feelings toward them and reading achievement. Ed.D. dissertation. University of Tulsa. 1975.

Describes student perceptions of teacher feelings toward the students as related to student reading achievement in grade six.

2692. Boyle, Richard Allen. Classroom organizational structure and student alienation. Ph.D. dissertation. St. Louis University. 1978.

Describes differences in student perceptions of the classroom and attitudes toward school by differences in the structure of the classroom.

2693. Bradley, Robert & Teeter, Thomas A. "Perceptions of control over social outcomes and student behavior," *Psychology in the Schools 14* (1977): 230-235.

Describes a relation between student perceptions of teacher control over negative outcomes for students and student behavior.

2694. Bybee, Rodger W. & Chaloupka, Donald W. "Students perceptions of the teacher they like best: A comparison including advantaged-average and disadvantaged students," *Colorado Journal of Educational Research 10*, No.4 (1971): 31-35.

Reports that several groups of students identified interpersonal skills as the most important characteristic of teachers whom they liked best.

2695. Cangemi, Joseph P. "How culturally different, gifted, and creative students perceive their teachers," *Clearing House 52*, No. 9 (1979): 419-420.

Reports that sixth grade students generally
like the behavior of their teachers.

2696.   Carich, Pete Adam. Teacher self-disclosure: A study
of student perceptions of teacher behavior. Ph.D.
dissertation. St. Louis University. 1973.

Describes no differences in student perceptions
of teachers across three levels of teacher
self-disclosure of personal information in class.

2697.   Chaikin, Alan L. & others. "Students' reactions to
teachers' physical attractiveness and nonverbal
behavior: Two exploratory studies," *Psychology in
the Schools 15* (1978): 588-595.

Describes differences in student ratings of
teachers related to teacher behaviors.

2698.   Christensen, Jack Dean. The effects of teacher and
curriculum variables on the self-concept and
school related behavior of Mexican-American
children. Ph.D. dissertation. Stanford University.
1973.

Describes differences in student response rate
but no differences in student perceptions of the
classroom by teacher behaviors.

2699.   Clark, Christopher M., Corno, L., Gage, N.L., Marx,
R.W., Peterson, P.L., Stayrook, N.G. & Winne,
P.H. "Student perceptions of teacher behavior as
related to student achievement," *Journal of
Classroom Interaction 12*, No. 1 (1976): 17-30.

Describes student perceptions of teacher
behavior as related to student achievement.

2700.   Close, Emory Rogers. Relationships between three
facilitative characteristics—empathy, warmth,
genuineness—and selected factors associated with
the secondary teacher. Ed.D. dissertation. North
Texas State University. 1971.

Describes student ratings of teachers as warm
and empathatic related to higher teacher job
satisfaction.

2701.   Cogan, Morris L. "Theory and design of a study of
teacher-pupil interaction," In *Interaction
Analysis: Theory, research and application*. Edited
by Edmund J. Amidon and John B. Hough. pp. 65-88.
Reading, Massachusetts: Addison-Wesley Publishing
Co. 1967. Also printed as, "The verbal behavior of
superior teachers," *Elementary School Journal 65*
(1965): 283-285.

Describes the perceptions of secondary school students of their teachers' behaviors in terms of the extent to which the behavior includes or precludes student interactions. For Amidon & Hough reference see citation No. 1638.

2702. Coley, Richard J. Student evaluation of teacher effectiveness. Tests and Measurements Report 52. Princeton, New Jersey: ERIC Clearinghouse on Tests, Measurement and Evaluation. *ERIC ED* 117 194.

Describes student perceptions of teachers, including perceptions of effective teachers.

2703. Cooper, Charles R. & Petrosky, Anthony. "Secondary school students' perceptions of math teachers and math classes," *Mathematics Teacher 69* (1976): 226-233.

Describes student perceptions of math classes and the behaviors of math teachers.

2704. Coward, Raymond T. & others. "Cognitive style and perceptions of the ideal teacher," *Contemporary Educational Psychology 3* (1978): 232-238.

Describes no relationship between student field dependence-independence and ranking of ideal teacher characteristics.

2705. Crimoli, Felix Gene. Attitudes of eleventh grade students toward union activities of teachers and teacher behavior. Ed.D. dissertation. New York University. 1972.

Describes no relationship between student experiences with teacher union activities but relationship between student home experiences with union activities and student attitude toward teacher union activities.

2706. Davison, Dewitt C. Perceived reward value of teacher-issued reinforcement in relation to student attitude toward teacher, sex, social class background: An application of Newcomb's balance theory. 1971. *ERIC ED* 048 111.

Describes student attitude toward teachers related to student response to teacher reinforcement behaviors.

2707. Ehman, Lee H. "Changes in high school students' political attitudes as a function of social studies classroom climate," *American Educational Research Journal 17* (1980): 253-265.

Describes student perceptions of the social
climate of the classroom and teacher handling of
controversial issues related to student political
interest and trust, with more trust in classrooms
perceived as more open.

2708.   Elliott, Jess Patten. A factor analysis of
teacher-pupil dyads in a Florida high school.
Ed.D. dissertation. University of Florida. 1970.

Describes differences in student preferences by
teacher type as not sufficient to justify matching
students to teacher types.

2709.   Estep, Linda E. Teacher pupil control ideology and
behavior and classroom environmental robustness in
the secondary school. Ed.D. dissertation.
Pennsylvania State University. 1979.

Reports that students considered classrooms
more robust when teachers had a more humanistic
pupil control ideology and behaved in accordance
with the ideology.

2710.   Estep, Linda E. & others. "Teacher pupil control
ideology and behavior as predictors of classroom
robustness," *High School Journal 63* (1980):
155-159.

Describes teachers with more humanistic pupil
control ideology having secondary classrooms which
students perceived to be more robust.

2711.   Etinge, Elias Etongwe. A correlational study of
pupil-teacher relationship and academic
achievement. Ph.D. dissertation. University of
Alabama. 1980.

Describes student perceptions of
teacher-student interactions varying by student
achievement, race, sex.

2712.   Findley, Carpenter & Haddan, Eugene. Effects of
liked and disliked teachers on student behavior.
1966. *ERIC ED* 010 375.

Describes differences by student achievement
level in responses to teachers, in person, on film
and on audiotape.

2713.   Forlenza, Vito A. & Willower, Donald J. "Students'
perceptions of ideal and actual teacher pupil
control behavior and reading achievement," *Child
Study Journal 10* (1980): 49-57.

Describes students' perceptions of teacher behavior and an increase in teacher authoritarian or custodial behavior over the year, as reported by sixth grade students.

2714. Fox, Ronald Bernard. Student evaluation of teachers as a measure of teacher behavior and teacher impact on students. Ph.D. dissertation. University of Texas at Austin. 1980.

Describes student ratings of sixth grade teachers related to observed behaviors of teachers.

2715. French, Yvonne Marie. A study of the relationships between student achievement and student perception of teacher effectiveness. Ph.D. dissertation. Louisiana State University and Agricultural and Mechanical College. 1979.

Describes a correlation between student perception of teacher effectiveness and student achievement.

2716. Gafner, Rosemary S. & others. Nonverbal cues of teacher warmth as perceived by students. 1978. *ERIC ED* 152 749.

Describes student perceptions of teacher warmth and describes the behaviors they identify as indicating teacher warmth.

2717. Gage, N., Zwirner, W.W., Cronbach, L.J. & Beck, W.R. "Pupil perceptions of teachers: A factor analysis of 'About my teacher'," *Western Psychologist* 3 (1972): 78-98.

Describes characteristics of student perceptions their teachers.

2718. Green, Ellen Rosenthal. The relationship between students' recalled and present perceptions of effective teacher practices and appropriate levels of teacher expectations. Ph.D. dissertation. St. Louis University. 1980.

Describes eleventh' grade students' recall of effective teaching and student preference for traditional rather than open practices on classroom management, curriculum and testing and student evaluation.

2719. Griswold, Philip A. & Cox, David L. Perceived classroom climate and cognitive structure of geometry terms as a function of matching

students with teachers on field independence.
1980. *ERIC ED* 189 156.

Describes an experiment in which a class of
field dependent students rated the classroom
climate as more positive than did a class of field
independent students.

2720.   Gustafson, Richard A. & Owens, Thomas. Children's
         perceptions of themselves and their teacher's
         feelings toward them related to actual teacher
         perceptions and school achievement. 1971. *ERIC ED*
         053 848.

Describes differences between Mexican-American
and other elementary students in the degree of
consistency between student perceptions of self
and student reports of how they think their
teacher sees them.

2721.   Harrison, Alton, Jr. & Westerman, John. "An
         assessment of teacher influence," *Clearing House*
         47 (1973): 227-231.

Describes students' attitudes toward their
teachers.

2722.   Herman, Wayne L. "The relationship between
         teachers' verbal behavior and children's interests
         in the social studies," *Peabody Journal of
         Education 43* (1965): 157-160.

Describes the verbal behavior of social studies
teachers in grade five related to the ranking of
student preference for social studies relative to
other subjects.

2723.   Holland, Donald Wayne. An investigation of the
         generality of teacher clarity. Ed.D. dissertation.
         Memphis State University. 1979.

Reports that student ratings of teacher clarity
differ by the subject area and geographic location
of the school.

2724.   Hurewitz, Carol & Hurewitz, Paul. Teacher
         characteristics and their relationship to
         cognitive and/or affective learning in elementary
         school. *ERIC ED* 113 332.

Describes perceptions of college students of
the characteristics of the teachers that they had
in elementary school.

2725. Irilli, Joseph Peter. Third grade students'
       expectations: Ratings of teacher performance as
       biased by teacher physical characteristics. Ph.D.
       dissertation. Kent State University. 1977.

       Reports that teacher attractiveness is related
       to student expectations for teacher performance.

2726. Irilli, Joseph P. & others. Students' expectations:
       Ratings of teacher performance as biased by
       teachers' physical attractiveness. 1978. *ERIC ED*
       155 216.

       Describes student evaluation of teachers
       related to teacher attractiveness.

2727. Jamieson, Judith L. & Brooks, Douglas M. Pupil
       perceptions of teacher presage and process
       variables and their relationship to pupil
       perceptions of instructional effectiveness. 1980.
       ERIC ED 183 554.

       Describes differences by student ability in the
       teacher characteristics which students identify as
       important.

2728. Johnson, Roger T. "The relationship between
       cooperation and inquiry in science classrooms,"
       Journal of Research in Science Teaching 13 (1976):
       55–63.

       Describes differences in student perceptions of
       the classroom by the type of instructional system;
       inquiry-oriented classrooms are viewed as
       cooperative while textbook-oriented classrooms are
       viewed as competitive.

2729. Kennedy, John J., Bush, Andrew, Cruickshank, David,
       and Haefele, D. "Additional investigations into
       the nature of teacher clarity," *Journal of
       Educational Research 72* (1978): 3–10.

       Describes student perceptions of the teacher
       behaviors which compose the variable labelled
       teacher clarity.

2730. Kersting, Joseph Stephan. Congruence of perception
       of the teaching-learning process and it's (sic)
       relation to measured student achievement. Ph.D.
       dissertation. St. Louis University. 1970.

       Describes an inverse relationship between
       student perceptions of teacher affect and student
       achievement, with higher achievement in classrooms
       of teachers whom students rate low in affect.

2731.   Knowling, Winifred Ann. The relationship between
        children's attitudes toward the classroom and
        their perceptions of teacher behavior as
        influenced by the age, sex, and behavior of the
        children. Ph.D. dissertation. University of Iowa.
        1977.

            Describes a correlation between student
        perceptions of teacher behavior and student
        attitude toward the classroom.

2732.   Larson, Wayne L. Discussion of educational plans
        with teachers by Indian and non-Indian high school
        students and type of subject taught by the
        teacher. 1972. *ERIC ED* 072 909.

            Reports that students identified English
        teachers as providing more information than other
        subject teachers.

2733.   Larson, Wayne L. Pygmalion in Native-Indian
        education. 1977. *ERIC ED* 144 744.

            Describes the perceptions of aides and student
        teachers of the behaviors of teachers with Native
        American students.

2734.   Lauren, Paul Martin. Teacher behavior, classroom
        climate, and achievement: An investigation of
        pupil perception of classroom interaction and its
        relationship to achievement within experimentally
        controlled learning environments. Ph.D.
        dissertation. New York University. 1969.

            Describes differences in student reports of
        classroom climate by the degree of teacher direct
        or indirect teaching, and student reports of
        climate related to student achievement.

2735.   Lawson, Dene R. Indicators of teacher ability to
        relate to students. 1971. *ERIC ED* 050 008.

            Describes student ratings of teachers differing
        by teacher behavior, with more positive ratings
        for teachers who allow student questions, lecture
        in response to student questions, and use praise
        extensively.

2736.   Lepard, David Hoyle. Pupil assessment of elementary
        classroom teaching behavior: A study of atypical
        ratings. Ed.D. dissertation. University of
        Massachusetts 1971.

            Describes diversity in student perceptions and
        ratings of teacher behaviors.

2737. Levinthal, Charles F. An analysis of the teacher evaluation process. Final Report. 1974. *ERIC ED 096 341.*

    Describes student evaluation of teachers, with a distinction between student ideal teaching behaviors and the behaviors of their teachers.

2738. Lewis, William A., Lovell, John T. & Jessee B.E. "Interpersonal relationship and pupil progress," *Personnel and Guidance Journal 44* (1965): 396-401.

    Describes greater student achievement when pupils perceived their relationship with the teacher as therapeutic for sixth but not fourth grade boys.

2739. McCann, Mary Margaret. Interpersonal attraction between students and teachers related to their similarity on two dimensions of self-actualizing behavior. Ph.D. dissertation. University of Notre Dame. 1973.

    Describes no relationship between preferred teacher and student level of self-actualization but most students preferred teachers at the highest level of self-actualization.

2740. McDermott, Ray. Kids make sense: An ethnographic account of the interactional management of success and failure in one first-grade classroom. Ph.D. dissertation. Stanford University. 1976.

    Describes the ways that students attribute student success and failure in school tasks.

2741. McFarland, William Joseph. An analysis of the influence of male participation in first grade instruction. Ed.D. dissertation. Indiana University. 1966.

    Reports that boys who identified with a male first grade teacher achieved more than other boys and than girls, but not a statistically significant difference.

2742. McKeown, Robin. "Accountability in responding to classroom questions: Impact on student achievement," *Journal of Experimental Education 45*, No. 3 (1977): 24-30.

    Reports that the degree that students think they have responded to classroom questions is related to student achievement.

2743.   Maffei, Anthony C. "Students' attitudes of a good
        mathematics teacher," *School Science and
        Mathematics 78* (1978): 312-314.

        Reports that students perceive that a good
        secondary math teacher considers student learning
        difficulties.

2744.   Marshall, Jon C. & Watson, Elizabeth P. Level of
        congruity found in students' perceptions of their
        teachers' expectations. 1969. *ERIC ED* 028 968.

        Describes idiosyncratic student perceptions of
        teacher expectations.

2745.   Mason, Jack & Blumberg, Arthur. "Perceived
        educational value of the classroom and
        teacher-pupil interpersonal relationships,"
        Journal of Secondary Education 44 (1969):
        135-139.

        Describes student perceptions of teacher
        personal regard for students as greatest in the
        classes where students felt they were learning the
        most.

2746.   Meighan, Roland. "A pupils' eye view of teaching
        performance," *Educational Review 30* (1978):
        125-137.

        Describes student perceptions of the
        instructional behaviors of teachers.

2747.   Milgram, Robert A. "Perception of teacher behavior
        in gifted and nongifted children," *Journal of
        Educational Psychology 71* (1979): 125-128.

        Describes student ratings of the value of
        different teacher behaviors.

2748.   Morine-Dershimer, Greta & Fagal, Fred. Why do you
        ask? 1980. *ERIC ED* 186 434.

        Describes student perceptions of the purposes
        of classroom questions as instruction, while
        questions asked at home are to obtain
        information.

2749.   Morine-Dershimer, Greta & Galluzzo, Gary. Pupil
        perceptions of teacher praise. 1980. *ERIC ED* 186
        435.

        Describes student perceptions of teacher praise
        and the relationship of those perceptions to

student participation in classroom discussions and
to pupil "success" in school, but no relationship
with student ethnic differences.

2750. Myers, Mary Jayne. A study of the identification of
classroom practices of teachers in the use of
three new junior high school science curriculum
programs. 1971. *ERIC ED* 092 311.

Describes student perceptions of teacher
behavior while teachers are using different
science curricular materials.

2751. Neuberger, Wayne Francis. Student perception of
teacher behaviors as a function of teacher
abstractness and student interpersonal needs.
Ph.D. dissertation. New Mexico State University.
1972.

Describes differences in student perceptions of
teacher behavior by student personality
characteristics.

2752. Norman, Diane E. "Racial classroom composition and
its relationship to students' perception of
teachers," *Negro Educational Review 29* (1978):
47-51.

Describes the racial composition of the
classroom related to student perceptions of the
teacher.

2753. Norton, Linda & Dobson, Russell. "Perceptions of
teachers' nonverbal behaviors by children of
different race, age and sex," *Humanist Education
14* (1976): 94-101.

Describes student perceptions of teacher-
student verbal interaction by student sex, age and
race.

2754. Olson, Miles Curtis. A study of relationships
between student rating of teacher voice and
classroom interaction. Ed.D. dissertation.
University of Nebraska. 1968.

Describes a limited relationship between
student ratings of teachers on what the students
hear and student perceptions of classroom
interaction.

2755. Pearsall, Frank Paul. Some relationships between
pupil sociometric position and pupil perception of
teacher behavior. Ph.D. dissertation. Wayne State

Describes differences in student ratings of teachers, schools, their learning by student characteristics.

2756.   Potter, David, Malin, P. & Lewandowski, A. The relation of student achievement and student ratings of teachers. 1973. *ERIC ED* 090 139.

Reports that a two week experiment found a weak relationship between student achievement and student ratings of teachers.

2757.   Pritchett, Wendell. The relationship between teacher pupil control behavior and student attitudes toward school. Ed.D. dissertation. Pennsylvania State University. 1974.

Describes differences in students' perceptions of teacher control behavior, with student attitude toward the teacher a dominating factor in student attitude toward the school.

2758.   Rapaport, Margaret M. & Rapaport, Herbert. "The other half of the expectancy equation," *Journal of Educational Psychology* 67 (1975): 531–536.

Reports that students receive expectancy information from several different sources.

2759.   Reichle, Alison Lea. Student perceptions of student-teacher relationships in the learning process. Ph.D. dissertation. University of Arizona. 1978.

Describes perceptions of secondary students of student-teacher relationships.

2760.   Rentoul, A. John & Fraser, Barry J. "Predicting learning from classroom individualization and actual-preferred congruence," *Studies in Educational Evaluation* 6 (1980): 265–277.

Describes a relationship between student perception of the degree of individualization and preference for individualization as related to student achievement.

2761.   Ryan, Joseph Francis. The association of teacher-student interpersonal relationship and classroom verbal interaction. Ph.D. dissertation. University of Missouri-Columbia. 1972.

Describes no differences in the behaviors of teachers perceived by students as strong and not strong in interpersonal relationships.

2762. Sabine, Gordon A. How students rate their schools and teachers. 1971. *ERIC ED* 052 533.

Describes variations in student ratings of teachers and schools.

2763. Saklofske, D.H. & others. "A psychometric study of a measure of teachers' directiveness, student perception of teaching style," *Perceptual and Motor Skills 51* (1980): 192-194.

Describes differences in student perceptions of teachers by teacher sex and subject matter (mathematics and English).

2764. Sanders, Askew Squire. Consensual teacher authority as assessed by the determination of the street and cultural value system of the non-conforming students of Forest Park High School. Ed.D. dissertation. University of Pennsylvania. 1980.

Describes attitudes of "street-wise" black urban students toward teacher authority.

2765. Sizemore, Robert Wilson. A comparison of the perceptions of the characteristics of secondary teachers by black and white secondary school students in an urban school district. Ed.D. dissertation. College of William and Mary in Virginia. 1979.

Describes student perceptions of teachers by student characteristics such as sex, grade, race.

2766. Snider, Agnes Marie Nelson. Some relationships between pupil growth in certain basic skills and pupils' perceptions of behaviors of their teachers. Ph.D. dissertation. University of Michigan. 1965.

Describes a relationship between student perception of the teacher and student achievement, with greater liking for the teacher associated with greater student achievement.

2767. Sugrue, Mary A. Shea. Structure and process of inquiry into social issues in secondary schools, Volume II, a study of teacher/student attitude-congruence patterns and student evaluations of controversial social-issue classes and teachers. 1970. *ERIC ED* 039 162.

Describes student evaluations of classes as related to teacher demographic characteristics, student perceptions, and the degree of congruence between teacher and student attitudes.

2768. Susman, Marilyn Ina Epstein. Ideal teacher
       behavior: A comparative study of the perceptions
       of secondary school students. Ph.D. dissertation.
       St. Louis University. 1972.

       Describes student ratings of ideal teachers as
       varying by student sex, grade and ability level.

2769. Thompson, Jack M. "The relationship between Carl
       Rogers' helping relationship concept and teacher
       behavior," *California Journal of Educational
       Research 20* (1969): 151-161. Ed.D. dissertation.
       University of California, Berkeley. 1976.

       Describes a relationship between students'
       perceptions of the quality of student-teacher
       relationships and administrative ratings of
       teacher effectiveness, but not observed behaviors
       of teachers.

2770. Ticknor, George Smith. The effects of positive and
       negative teacher behavior on student ratings of
       teachers. Ed.D. dissertation. Western Michigan
       University. 1972.

       Describes more positive student ratings of
       teachers related to greater teacher use of
       positive evaluative comments about students to the
       students and the class.

2771. Tollefson, Nona. "Selected student variables and
       perceived teacher effectiveness," *Education 94*
       (1973): 30-35.

       Describes student perceptions of effective
       teaching as not related to student
       characteristics.

2772. Townsend, Charles Edwin. Student ratings of
       secondary-school science teachers. Ph.D.
       dissertation. Western Michigan University. 1972.
       ERIC ED 098 032.

       Describes student ratings differing for science
       and non-science teachers.

2773. Tull, Michael J. & Hatley, Richard N. Effects of
       organization development training for teachers on
       teacher effectiveness and teacher-student
       relationships. 1974. *ERIC ED* 088 810.

       Describes student perceptions of teachers
       changing with teacher training.

2774. Walberg, Herbert J. Structural and affective aspects of classroom climate. 1966. *ERIC ED* 015 154.

   Describes a relationship between student perceptions of classroom climate and their perceptions of themselves, with classroom structure influencing the relationship.

2775. Wang, Margaret C. & Stiles, Billie. "An investigation of children's concept of self-responsibility for their school learning," *American Educational Research Journal 13* (1976): 159-179. LRDC Publications Series No. 1975/11. Pittsburgh, Pennsylvania: Learning Research and Development Center. University of Pittsburgh. *ERIC ED* 116 815.

   Describes greater student responsibility for school tasks with a system of self-scheduling of tasks.

2776. Warren, Paul Bauersmith. A study of lower class and middle-upper class students' perception of the behavioral traits of the effective teacher. Ph.D. dissertation. New York University. 1968.

   Describes no differences in the types of teacher behavior selected by lower and middle class students in identifying the "best" teachers.

2777. Weinstein, Rhona Strasberg & Middlestadt, Susan E. Learning about the achievement hierarchy of the classroom: Through children's eyes. 1979. *ERIC ED* 170 071.

   Describes differences between high and low achieving males in perceptions of teacher behavior, such as time for student responses to teacher questions.

2778. Weinstein, Rhona Strasberg & Middlestadt, Susan E. "Student perceptions of teacher interactions with male high and low achievers," *Journal of Educational Psychology 71* (1979): 421-431.

   Describes student perceptions of differences in teacher behaviors toward high and low achievers, with student grade and characteristics related to student perceptions of teachers.

2779. White, William F. & Dekle, Ocie T. "Effect of teacher's motivational cues on achievement level in elementary grades," *Psychological Reports 18* (1966): 351-356.

Describes differences in the way that high and
low achievers perceive the same teachers, in terms
of affective, controlling and subject matter
knowledge behaviors.

2780. Wilson, Bruce L. Classroom instructional features
       and conceptions of academic ability: An
       application of source theory. Ph.D. dissertation.
       Stanford University. 1980.

       Describes no relationship between aspects of
       classroom organization and degree of student
       consensus about the abilities of individual
       students.

2781. Wilson, Eddie Lee. A study of the relationship
       between student perceptions of teachers' classroom
       behaviors and teachers' classroom management
       preferences. Ed.D. dissertation. University of
       Houston. 1978.

       Describes no relationship between student
       perceptions of teacher classroom behavior and
       teacher preferences for classroom control
       behaviors.

2782. Wilson, Willie Leon. The effect of teacher-pupil
       sex interaction and teacher age on pupil
       perception of teacher behavior in junior and
       senior high school classes of English in selected
       Mississippi public schools. Ed.D. dissertation.
       Mississippi State University. 1973.

       Describes differences in student ratings of
       teachers by student and teacher characteristics,
       with senior high students rating teachers more
       favorably, and male and younger teachers rated
       more favorably.

2783. Wright, Benjamin & Sherman, Barbara. "Love and
       mastery in the child's image of the teacher,"
       School Review 73 (1965): 89–101.

       Describes agreement among elementary students
       in ratings of teachers on items related to
       mastery, such as authority and discipline, but
       lack of agreement in ratings of items related to
       teacher sympathy and friendship.

2784. Yeany, Russell H., Jr. & Cosgriff, Stephen J. A
       study of the relationships between perceived and
       observed science teaching strategies and selected
       classroom and teacher variables. 1976. *ERIC ED* 124
       432.

       Describes teacher characteristics and behavior
       related to student perceptions of teaching style.

B. BEHAVIOR

2785. Arlin, Marshall. "Teacher transitions can disrupt time flow in classrooms," *American Educational Research Journal 16* (1979): 42-56.

    Reports more student disruptive behaviors during transitions than during instructional activities.

2786. Ash, Michael J. & Sattler, Howard E. A vidiotape technique for assessing behavioral correlates of academic performance. 1973. *ERIC ED* 074 747.

    Describes student attention to task related to student achievement.

2787. Britan, Ronnie Gail. An analysis of student-pull: student manipulation of teachers in reading classrooms. Ph.D. dissertation. Northwestern University. 1978.

    Describes behaviors of students in well and poorly managed classrooms.

2788. Brody, Celeste Mary. An exploratory study of student classroom behavior as it influences the social system of the classroom. Ph.D. dissertation. Ohio State University. 1971.

    Describes behaviors of students within the classroom social system.

2789. Brophy, Jere E. & Laosa, Luis M. Effect of a male teacher on the sex typing of kindergarten children. *Proceedings of the 79th annual convention of the American Psychological Association, 6* (1971): 169-170.

    Describes no differences in student sex-typed preferences for activities with male and female teachers.

2790. Brown, Carol Wegley & Peters, Donald L. A naturalistic study of the conditions and characteristics promoting social integration of handicapped children in early childhood education classrooms. Final Report. 1979. *ERIC ED* 179 293.

    Describes qualitative differences in the behaviors of handicapped children in the classroom, setting them apart from other students, although they are not isolated in the classroom.

2791.   Brown, Polly Ann Quick. A study of the effects of
        conceptual systems and open vs. traditional
        classroom environments on elementary students'
        locus of control and self-concept. Ph.D.
        dissertation. University of Minnesota. 1978.

            Describes a relationship between student
        self-concept, conceptual level and locus of
        control, with greater student achievement when
        student characteristics are matched with student
        enrollment in an open or traditional classroom.

2792.   Butzow, John W. & Sewell, Leyton E. The process
        learning components of introductory physical
        science: A pilot study. 1971. *ERIC ED* 052 047.

            Describes higher entry level science skills for
        students with higher IQs, but greater student
        gains for lower level students in inquiry science
        classes.

2793.   Carpenter, C. Jan. Relation of children's sex-typed
        behavior to classroom, and activity structure.
        1979. *ERIC ED* 178 173.

            Describes differences in participation in
        free-choice activities by student sex in preschool
        classroom.

2794.   Clifford, Margaret M. "Physical attractiveness and
        academic performance," *Child Study Journal 5*
        (1975): 201-209.

            Describes a relationship between student
        physical attractiveness and academic achievement.

2795.   Cobb, Joseph A. "Relationship of discrete classroom
        behaviors to fourth-grade academic achievement,"
        Journal of Educational Psychology 63 (1972):
        74-80.

            Describes student on-task rates as related to
        student achievement.

2796.   Crumpacker, Carol Bruce. Locus of control and
        classroom structure as they affect student
        competence and self-esteem. Ph.D. dissertation.
        University of Nebraska-Lincoln. 1978.

            Describes no relationship between student locus
        of control and type of classroom and student
        learning competence.

2797.   Day, Barbara D. & Hunt, Gilbert H. Verbal
        interaction across age, race, and sex in a

variety of learning centers in an open classroom setting. Final Report. 1974. *ERIC ED* 105 983.

Describes students as communicating with students of the same sex and race.

2798. deVoss, Gary G. "The structure of major lessons and collective student activity," *Elementary School Journal 80* (1979): 8-18.

Describes collective student activities during instructional periods in first and fifth grades classrooms.

2799. Ferrence, Gary Mark. The quantification and qualification of verbal communication in the high school biology laboratory. Ed.D. dissertation. Indiana University. 1968. *ERIC ED* 043 489.

Describes student interactions in laboratory settings as related to the nature of the laboratory activities.

2800. Forney, Mary Ann & Smith, Lyle R. Teacher grammar and pupil achievement in mathematics. 1979. *ERIC ED* 179 976.

Describes an experiment in which students had higher achievement in the good and the poor than in the moderately good grammar groups, perhaps due to differences in student attention.

2801. Gaver, Donna & Richards, Herbert C. "Dimensions of naturalistic observation for the prediction of academic success," *Journal of Educational Research 72* (1979): 123-127.

Describes student task orientation as related to student achievement.

2802. Glinsky, Mark Warren. The effects of classroom openness on fourth graders' self-concept, school attitude, observing-inferring and question asking behaviors. Ph.D. dissertation. Syracuse University. 1973.

Describes students in open classrooms having a more positive attitude toward school and asking more questions than students in a traditional classroom.

2803. Good, Thomas L. & Beckerman, Terrill M. "Time on task: A naturalistic study in sixth grade classrooms," *Elementary School Journal 78* (1978): 193-201.

Describes student time on task by setting,
subject matter and achievement level of students,
with higher achieving students having higher
engagement rates.

2804.   Grimmett, Sadie & others. Influence of behavior
settings on role of inappropriate and appropriate
behavior. 1969. *ERIC ED* 095 991.

Describes more disruptive student behavior in
large group than in individual choice settings.

2805.   Guilford, Joan S. & others. Relationship between
teacher-pupil value disparities and the academic
achievement, classroom behavior, and school
adjustment of elementary children. Final Report.
1972. *ERIC ED* 064 667.

Describes a relationship between student values
and school adjustment, with better adjustment when
student values are more like teacher values.

2806.   Hays, Daniel G. & others. Manifest characteristics
of interactive sequencing in the classroom. 1971.
ERIC ED 050 399.

Describes differences in student verbal
behavior by student grade, race, socioeconomic
level.

2807.   Horak, Willard Gene. The effects of locus of
control and two types of classroom climate on
student academic achievement and self-concept.
Ed.D. dissertation. Drake University. 1978.

Describes greater student achievement by
students with internal locus of control in both
open and traditional classrooms.

2808.   Jackson, David Ethan. An assessment of the behavior
of children working without direct teacher
supervision alone or in pairs with manipulative
materials on teacher designed tasks self-selected
or teacher-assigned. Ed.D. dissertation. Columbia
University. 1977.

Describes behavior of students differing by
whether students were working alone or in pairs
but not by whether the teacher or the student
selected the task.

2809.   Keane, Edward Joseph. The interactive effects of
global cognitive style and general mental ability
with three instructional strategies on a
mathematical concept task. Ph.D. dissertation.
University of Southern California. 1979.

Describes student mental ability, not the interaction of treatment and student cognitive style, accounting for the variance in student achievement.

2810. Keyes, Judith Droz & Loflin, Marvin D. Prerequisites to the analysis of paraphrase in classroom verbal interaction. 1971. *ERIC ED* 047 310.

Describes differences in the language use of black and white students in the classroom.

2811. Kramer, Shelley Barbara. The relation between pupil on-task behavior and achievement in classroom behavior modification. Ph.D. dissertation. Columbia University. 1971.

Describes rate of student attention related to student achievement, with training of teachers resulting in increased teacher attention to the behaviors of some students and increases in the on-task behavior of those students.

2812. Lahaderne, Henrietta M. Adaptation to school settings--A study of children's attitudes and classroom behavior. Final Report. 1967. *ERIC ED* 012 943.

Describes relationships among student attitude toward school, background characteristics, and attention to tasks.

2813. Lahaderne, H.M. "Attitudinal and intellectual correlates of attention: A study of four sixth-grade classrooms," *Journal of Educational Psychology 59* (1968): 320-324.

Describes a relationship between student attitude and past achievement and attention to assigned tasks.

2814. Lasley, Thomas James, III. Perceived student misbehavior within the context of classroom interactions: A participant observation study. Ph.D. dissertation. Ohio State University. 1978.

Describes types of student classroom misbehavior as defined by teachers and students.

2815. Leviton, Harvey. "The implications of the relationship between self-concept and academic achievement," *Child Study Journal 5* (1975): 25-36.

Review describes a relationship between student
self-concept and achievement.

2816.   Lipe, Dewey & others. Classroom behavior of PLAN
        students compared with control students. 1969.
        ERIC ED 040 567.

        Describes differences in the classroom
        behaviors of students in classrooms where the
        teachers use PLAN as the individualized
        instructional program and other classrooms.

2817.   Lipe, Dewey & others. Varieties of student behavior
        in Project PLAN. 1970. *ERIC ED* 030 413

        Describes no differences in the classroom
        behaviors of students by grade level,
        instructional organization or amount of teacher
        experience with PLAN as a system of individualized
        instruction.

2818.   Loeb, Helen Joan Ward. Social interactions and
        performance under competitive and cooperative
        working conditions: A developmental study of
        elementary school children. Volumes I, II. Ph.D.
        dissertation. Bryn Mawr College. 1975.

        Describes differences in student classroom
        behavior by student age and sex in grades one
        through five.

2819.   Loflin, Marvin D. & others. Implications of the
        linguistic differences between black-ghetto and
        white-suburban classrooms. 1971. *ERIC ED* 047 311.

        Describes earlier development of complex
        language in white students but more complex
        language use by black than white students at the
        peak of development.

2820.   McDonald, Charles Thomas. The influence of pupil
        liking of teacher, pupil perception of being
        liked, and perceived pupil socio-economic-status
        on classroom behavior. Ph.D. dissertation.
        University of Texas at Austin. 1972.

        Describes pupil expression of warmth toward the
        teacher as not related to student perceptions of
        teacher liking or disliking of the student.

2821.   MacDonald W. Scott, & others. *Focus on classroom
        behaviors: Readings and research.* Springfield,
        Illinois: Charles C. Thomas, Publisher. 1973.

Presents a collection of papers on student
behavior and discipline, including Cassandra,
citation No. 2549 & Lens & Gallimore, citation No.
1277.

2822. McElwee, Joy. "Children's questions and
explanations: Interaction in the classroom,"
Claremont Reading Conference 44 (1980): 156-165.

Reviews studies of student questions, including
studies which look at the form and structure and
studies which look at the content and purpose of
questions.

2823. McKeen, Cliff & others. Peer interaction rate,
classroom activity and teaching style. 1972. *ERIC
ED* 070 210.

Describes differences in student rate of
interaction with peers for different classroom
activities.

2824. McKinney, James D., Mason, Jeanne, Perkerson, Kathi
& Clifford, Miriam. "Relationship between
classroom behavior and academic achievement,"
Journal of Educational Psychology 67 (1973):
198-203.

Describes observed behaviors of grade two
students accounting for variance in student spring
achievement after the variance accounted for by
the fall achievement is removed.

2825. Mancini, Dino. An investigation of the
relationships between self-concept of ability,
classroom verbal interaction, and achievement of
seventh grade pupils in biological science in two
suburban schools. Ph.D. dissertation. New York
University. 1972.

Describes differences in student response rate
in classrooms by student sex and achievement
level, with 71% of all students responding at some
time but 17% of the students accounting for 60% of
the student talk.

2826. Murray, Michael Dennis. The relationship of
classroom behavior to academic achievement and
aptitude. Ph.D. dissertation. University of
Tennessee. 1977.

Describes student classroom behavior related to
student achievement in reading and math.

2827. Parakh, Jal Sohrab. A study of relationships among
       teacher behavior, pupil behavior, and pupil
       characteristics in high school biology classes.
       Final Report. 1967. *ERIC ED* 040 070.

       Describes student final achievement related to
       class participation, with eight students
       accounting for 75% of the participation.

2828. Rogers, Carolyn Odom. The relationship between the
       organization of play space and children's
       behavior. 1976. *ERIC ED* 127 011.

       Describes behavior of preschool students and
       the effects of physical space on that behavior.

2829. Ross, Sylvia & Zimiles, Herbert. Children's
       interactions in open versus traditional settings.
       1975. *ERIC ED* 135 468.

       Describes differences in the behaviors of
       children in open and traditional classrooms.

2830. Simmons, Joyce T. & Wasik, Barbara. Small group
       contingencies and special activity times used to
       manage behavior in a first grade classroom. 1971.
       ERIC ED 060 476.

       Describes decreases over time in punishment for
       out-of-center behavior for first grade students
       with the use of peer pressure.

2831. Torop, Nancy R. The effects of adult evaluation on
       elementary school children's work and social
       interaction: An experimental study of affective
       tone and helpfulness. Ph.D. dissertation. Bryn
       Mawr College. 1973.

       Describes student responses to strong criticism
       differing by the type of criticism and student
       sex.

2832. Walberg, Herbert J. "Physical and psychological
       distance in the classroom," *School Review 77*
       (1979): 64-70.

       Describes differences in student character-
       istics related to preferences for seats in the
       front or back of the classroom.

2833. Walberg, Herbert J. & Heise, Kenneth. "The
       distribution of misbehavior," *Psychology in the
       Schools 16* (1979): 306-308.

       Describes the frequency of student misbehaviors
       in classroom settings.

2834. Watson, Elizabeth P. & others. Interrelations of student-teacher agreement of classroom expectations and behavior, program innovations and student satisfaction. 1971. *ERIC ED* 052 129.

Describes student satisfaction as dependent on the role of the student within the teaching approach rather than on the expectations which the teacher communicates to the student.

2835. Way, Joyce W. "Verbal interaction in multiage classrooms," *Elementary School Journal 79* (1979): 178-186.

Describes verbal interactions of students in classrooms with students of several ages.

2836. Weinberg, Susan F. & others. The classroom behavior of students during compensatory reading instruction. 1974. *ERIC ED* 090 277.

Describes behaviors of students during reading in a compensatory education program.

2837. Wyatt, Macy Akel. A study of the interaction between personality traits, IQ and achievement in Negro and white fourth grade children. Ph.D. dissertation. University of Kentucky. 1972.

Describes influences of student sex, race and personality on student achievement.

2838. Zeli, Doris Conti. An analogous study of children's attitudes toward school in an open classroom environment as opposed to a conventional setting. 1975. *ERIC ED* 110 073.

Describes no differences in student attitudes by type of classroom.

VIII METHODOLOGY

2839.   Amidon, Edmund & Simon, Anita. Implications for
        teacher education of Interaction Analysis research
        in student teaching. 1965. *ERIC ED* 012 695.

        Reports the results of a survey of teacher
        educators and supervisors about the strengths and
        weaknesses of the use of Interaction Analysis
        which documents wide use for teacher education.

2840.   Beegle, Charles W. & Brandt, Richard M. (eds.)
        Observational methods in the classroom.
        Washington, D.C.: Association for Supervision and
        Curriculum Development. 1973.

        Presents a series of chapters on observation in
        the classroom, including methods, observation
        systems and results, including Medley, citation
        No. 2875.

2841.   Berliner, David C. "A status report on the study of
        teacher effectiveness," *Journal of Research in
        Science Teaching, 13* (1976): 369-382. *ERIC ED* 114
        261.

        Describes problems encountered in research
        which attempts to relate student achievement to
        the behaviors of teachers.

2842.   Berliner, David C. "Impediments to the study of
        teacher effectiveness," *Journal of Teacher
        Education, 27* (1976): 5-13. Technical Report
        75-11-3. Beginning Teacher Evaluation Study. San
        Francisco, California: Far West Laboratory for
        Educational Research and Development. 1976. In
        The appraisal of teaching: Concepts and process.
        edited by Gary D. Borich. Reading, Massachusetts:
        Addison-Wesley Publishing Co. 1977

        Describes several problems which hinder the
        study of teaching or which limit the
        generalizability of the research results. For
        Borich reference see citation No. 2916.

2843.   Biddle, Bruce J. "Methods and concepts in classroom
        research," *Review of Educational Research, 37*
        (1967): 337-357.

Reviews five areas of research on teaching; aspects of teaching, methods of data collection, unit of analysis, conceptual posture and concepts used.

2844.   Borg, Walter R. "Making the leap from correlational to experimental studies of teacher behavior," 1975. *ERIC ED* 104 844.

Describes different results from correlational and experimental studies of teaching and discusses why such differences exist.

2845.   Borich, Gary D. "Sources of invalidity in measuring classroom behavior," *Instructional Science 6* (1977): 283–318. *ERIC ED* 120 262.

Reviews sources of error in the measurement of teacher behaviors, as measured in studies which relate teacher behavior to student achievement.

2846.   Borich, Gary D. & Madden, Susan K. *Evaluating classroom instruction: A source book of instruments*. Reading, Massachusetts: Addison-Wesley Publishing Company. 1977.

Introduction discusses some issues in observation in classrooms, followed by a collection of instruments.

2847.   Bossert, Steven T. Studying learning environments: Conceptual and methodological issues. 1976. *ERIC ED* 123 145.

Discusses several methodological issues in the study of teaching within classrooms.

2848.   Brophy, Jere E. The student as the unit of analysis. Research Report No. 75-12. East Lansing, Michigan: Institute for Research on Teaching, Michigan State University. *ERIC ED* 147 273.

Essay discusses three major reasons why the student should be the unit of analysis of classroom observation data in studies of teaching.

2849.   Brophy, Jere E. Training teachers in experiments: Considerations relating to nonlinearity and context effects. 1977. *ERIC ED* 150 201.

Discusses the need for teachers to participate in studies to validate the results of correlational studies without the loss of ecological validity which occurs in studies in laboratory settings.

2850.   Burstein, Leigh. "Analysis of multilevel data in
        educational research and evaluation," In *Review of
        research in education* Vol. 8. Edited by David
        Berliner. pp. 158-233. Washington, D.C.: American
        Educational Research Association. 1980.

        Discusses conceptual and statistical issues in
        the use of multilevel data, such as data for
        students and the whole class, with illustrations
        from data sets from studies of teaching. For
        Berliner reference see citation No. 2910A.

2851.   Chapline, Elaine B. "A case study in Interaction
        Analysis matrix interpretation," in *Teaching:
        Vantage Points for Study*, edited by Ronald T.
        Hyman. pp. 265-270. Philadelphia: T.B. Lippincott
        Company. 1968.

        Describes the process of interpreting the
        coding of Interaction Analysis and uses one lesson
        to illustrate both the process and the
        interactions which occur in one classroom. For
        Hyman reference see citation No. 2973.

2852.   Clark, Christopher, M. "Five faces of research on
        teaching," *Educational Leadership, 37* (1979):
        29-32. Occasional Paper No. 24. East Lansing,
        Michigan: Institute for Research on Teaching.
        Michigan State University. *ERIC ED* 180 972.

        Describes five major types of educational
        research: process-product studies, aptitude
        treatment interaction, time for learning (the
        Carroll model), ethnographic studies and cognitive
        information processing studies.

2853.   Doyle, Walter. "Paradigms for research on teacher
        effectiveness," In *Review of research in
        education, Vol. 5*. Edited by Lee Shulman. pp.
        163-198. Itasca, Illinois: F.E. Peacock
        Publishers, 1977. Also, under title, Paradigms in
        teacher effectiveness research. *ERIC ED* 103 390.

        Describes three models for research on
        teaching, process-product, process mediated by
        student behavior, and the culture of the school.
        For Shulman reference see citation No. 3019.

2854.   Doyle, Walter & Ponder, Gerald A. "Classroom
        ecology: Some concerns about a neglected dimension
        of research on teaching," *Contemporary Education
        46* (1975): 183-8.

        Essay identifies inadequacies in research
        methods and measures and identifies areas not
        included within past research.

2855.   Erlich, Oded & Shavelson, Richard. The application
        of generalizability theory to the study of
        teaching. Technical Report 76-9-1. Beginning
        Teacher Evaluation Study. San Francisco,
        California: Far West Laboratory for Educational
        Research and Development. 1976.

           Describes a method for assessing the stability
        of measures of teacher behavior and the number of
        observers and observations necessary to obtain
        stable measures.

2856.   Feldman, Robert S. & Lobato-Barrera, Debra.
        Attitudes, cognition, and nonverbal communicative
        behavior. *ERIC ED* 171 668.

           Reports that raters rating teacher behavior are
        influenced by the behavior of the students in the
        experiment.

2857.   Fisher, Charles W. & Berliner, David C. "Clinical
        inquiry in research on classroom teaching and
        learning," *Journal of Teacher Education 30* (1979):
        42-51.

           Describes types of studies of teaching and the
        need for a new approach to capture the nature of
        interaction in the classroom.

2858.   Furlong, V.A. & Edwards, A.D. "Language in
        classroom interaction: Theory and data,"
        Educational Research 19 (1977): 122-128.

           Argues that assumptions of researchers
        influence findings about classroom language.

2859.   Gage, N.L. (Ed.). NIE conference on studies in
        teaching: Panel 9, Research methodology.
        Washington, D.C.: National Institute of Education.
        1974. *ERIC ED* 111 810.

           Presents a summary of the discussion of a panel
        of researchers about methods for studying
        teaching.

2860.   Gage, N.L., Belgard, Maria, Dell, Daryl, Hiller,
        Jack, Rosenshine, Barak & Unruh, W.R.
        "Explorations of the teacher's effectiveness in
        explaining," *Research in classroom processes*.
        Edited by I. Westbury & A.A. Bellack. pp. 175-217.
        New York: Teachers College Press. 1971. Technical
        Report No. 4, Stanford, California: Stanford
        Center for Research and Development in Teaching.
        Stanford University. 1968.

Presents a review of studies concerned with methods for observing and analyzing observational data and a study of secondary teachers teaching specific units which found good teaching related to cognitive activities within the lesson. For Westbury & Bellack reference see citation No. 3039.

2861. Gage, N.L. & Unruh, W.R. "Theoretical formulations for research on teaching," *Review of Educational Research 37* (1967): 358-370. Also in *Current Research on instruction*. Edited by R.C. Anderson & others. pp. 3-14. Englewood Cliffs, New Jersey: Prentice-Hall. 1969. Also in *School learning and instruction: Readings*. Edited by H.D. Thornburg. pp. 42-53. Monterey, California: Brooks/Cole. 1973.

Describes types of studies, domains addressed in studies, differences in focus between describing and improving teaching, relation of studies of teaching to studies of learning, the need for synthesis and predictions of promising research directions. For Anderson reference see citation No. 2904. For Thornbury reference see citation No. 3031.

2862. Gall, Meredith Damien. "The importance of context variables in research on teaching skills," *Journal of Teacher Education 28*, No. 3 (1977): 43-48. *ERIC ED* 127 265.

Describes problems related to the context in which teaching occurs when researchers use experiments to study teaching.

2863. Galloway, Charles M. An analysis of theories and research in nonverbal communication. Washington, D.C.: ERIC Clearinghouse on Teacher Education. 1972. *ERIC ED* 159 988.

Discusses problems with research and describes one observational system and its development.

2864. Garfunkel, Frank. Observation of teachers and teaching: Strategies and applications. Boston, Massachusetts: Head Start Evaluation and Research Center. Boston University. 1967. *ERIC ED* 023 616.

Reports the development of scales and the observation of classes with participant observers, former teachers who serve to summarize what occurs in the classroom.

2865.   Good Thomas L. & Brophy, Jere E. "Analyzing
        classroom interaction: A more powerful
        alternative," *Educational Technology, 11*, (1971):
        36-41.

            Describes reasons for and results of using the
        student as the unit of analysis for data in
        studies of teaching.

2866.   Hawkins, Edward E. & Stoops, Emery. "Objective and
        subjective identification of outstanding
        elementary teachers," *Journal of Educational
        Research 59* (1966): 344-346.

            Describes consistency in the identification of
        outstanding teachers by ten methods of
        identification.

2867.   Heath, Robert & Nielson, Mark. "The research basis
        for Performance-Based Teacher Education," *Review
        of Educational Research 44* (1974): 463-484.

            Reviews studies of teaching and discusses
        several methodological limitations of models of
        research on teaching currently being used.

2868.   Hill, Russell A. & Medley, Donald A. Goal Oriented
        Teaching Exercise (G.O.T.E.): Methodology for
        measuring the effects of teaching strategies.
        1969. *ERIC ED* 029 846.

            Describes a process of teachers teaching short
        units during which observers record their behavior
        and relate that behavior to student learning on
        the units.

2869.   Lightfoot, Sara Lawrence. A question of
        perspective: Toward a more complex view of
        classrooms. ERIC/Cue Urban Diversity Series,
        Number 58. New York: ERIC Clearinghouse on the
        Urban Disadvantaged, Columbia University. 1978.
        ERIC ED 166 317.

            Discusses the effects of researcher
        perspectives and the limitations of perspectives
        which focus on the teacher and misinterpret the
        role and behavior of students, especially minority
        students.

2870.   Limbacher, Philip C. & Rosenshine, Barak.
        Relationship of high-inference and low-inference
        observation measures. 1972. *ERIC ED* 065 550.

Reports no consistent relationship between high and low inference observations with two groups of teachers teaching social studies.

2871. Lomax, Richard G. & Cooley, William W. The student achievement-instructional time relationship. 1979. ERIC ED 179 598.

Reviews research and discusses problems with studies of instructional time.

2872. McIntyre, D. John. "Teacher evaluation and the observer effect," *NASSP Bulletin 64* (1980): 36-40.

Reviews research findings of the effects of observers on student and teacher behaviors and the implications for administrators.

2873. Marliave, Richard S. & others. Alternative procedures for collecting instructional time data: When can you ask the teacher and when must you observe for yourself? Beginning Teacher Evaluation Study. San Francisco, California: Far West Laboratory for educational Research and Development. *ERIC ED* 137 380.

Describes teacher self-reports of behavior and time allocation which are judged to be accurate and inaccurate on the basis of observations.

2874. Martin, J. Controlled vs. natural settings—Some implications for behavioral analysis and change in classroom situations. *Alberta Journal of Educational Research 21* (1975): 39-45.

Discusses issues which differ between laboratory research settings and classrooms and their effects of research results.

2875. Medley, Donald M. "Measuring the complex classroom of today," In *Observational methods in the classroom.* Edited by C.W. Beegle & R.M. Brandt. Washington: D.C.: Association for Supervision and Curriculum Development. 1973.

Describes the development of methods for observation of teacher behaviors within the classroom. For Beegle & Brandt reference see citation No. 2840.

2876. Millman, Jason. "Teaching effectiveness: New indicators for an old problem," *Educational Horizons 51*, No. 2 (1972-1973): 68-75.

Describes methods available to determine teacher effectiveness.

2877.   Mouly, George J. "Research methods," In
        Encyclopedia of Educational Research. Edited by
        Robert L. Ebel. pp. 1144-1152 Toronto: The
        MacMillan Company, 1969.

        Describes various types of methods for studying
        teaching, including observations, ratings,
        sociometric techniques, anecdotal records and
        longitudinal studies. For Ebel reference see
        citation No. 2942.

2878.   Nixon, Jon. "Classroom research," *Forum for the
        Discussion of New Trends in Education 22* (1980):
        76-77.

        Describes results of a conference on the role
        of teachers in research, including a discussion of
        reasons to involve teachers in research and the
        support needed by teachers who are involved in
        research.

2879.   Ornstein, Allan C. "Can we define a good teacher?"
        Peabody Journal of Education 53 (1976): 201-207.

        Presents a critique of past research which
        identifies problems with the methodology of
        studies of teaching.

2880.   Ornstein, Allan C. Methods for conducting teacher
        behavior research: With implications for teachers
        of the disadvantaged. 1970. *ERIC ED* 046 863.

        Discusses problems in studying teaching,
        including problems in defining effective teaching,
        the rapid sequence of classroom events, the
        non-cumulative nature of past research.

2881.   Rosenshine, Barak, "Evaluation of classroom
        instruction," *Review of Educational Research 40*
        (1970): 279-300.

        Describes types of observation systems and
        issues involved in the selection and use of an
        observation system to study teaching.

2882.   Samph, Thomas & White, Sally A. A factor analysis
        of selected classroom observation systems. Final
        Report. Syracuse, New York: Syracuse University,
        1973. *ERIC ED* 097 299. See also, An analysis of
        selected classroom behavioral category systems.
        Final Report. *ERIC ED* 110 419.

        Discusses overlap in variables measured by nine
        different observation systems.

2883.   Shavelson, Richard, & Dempsey, Nancy.
        "Generalizability of measures of teacher
        effectiveness and teaching process," *Review of
        Educational Research 46* (1976): 553-611. Technical
        Report No. 75-4-2. Beginning Teacher Evaluation
        Study. San Francisco, California: Far West
        Laboratory for Educational Research and
        Development. *ERIC ED* 150 108. also published under
        authors Shavelson, Richard & Attwood, Nancy,
        Educational Research 19 (1977): 171-183.

        Review of studies concludes that few
        observation systems provide measure of teacher
        behavior which are stable or can be generalized
        across teaching contexts such as grade levels, and
        across observers and observation occasions.

2884.   Shymansky, James A. "Assessing teacher performance
        in the classroom: Pattern analysis applied to
        interaction data," *Studies in Educational
        Evaluation 4* (1978): 99-106.

        Describes a method for analyzing observed
        behavior of teachers.

2885.   Simon, Anita & Boyer, E. Gil, (Eds.). *Mirrors for
        behavior: An anthology of classroom observation
        instruments*. Philadelphia, Pennsylvania: Research
        for Better Schools, Inc. & Center for the Study of
        Teaching, Temple University. 1976. *ERIC ED* 029
        833. Also see *ERIC ED* 031 613 and *ERIC ED* 170
        320.

        Presents abstracts of twenty-six classroom
        observation systems and a bibliography on
        observation systems.

2886.   Simon, Anita & Boyer, E. Gil. (Eds.). *Mirrors for
        behavior, An anthology of classroom observation
        Instruments*. Philadelphia, Pennsylvania: Research
        for Better Schools, Inc. 1969. *ERIC ED* 031 613.
        Also see *ERIC ED* 029 833 and *ERIC ED* 179 320.

        In twelve volumes describes seventy-nine
        classroom observation systems.

2887.   Simon, Anita & Boyer, E. Gil. (Eds.). *Mirrors for
        behavior III. An anthology of observation
        instruments*. Philadelphia, Pennsylvania: Research
        for Better Schools, Inc. 1974. *ERIC ED* 1709 320.
        Also see *ERIC ED* 029 833 and *ERIC ED* 031 613.

        Describes classroom observation instruments
        collected since the initial volumes of the
        publication.

2888.   Smith, Louis M. Classroom ethnography and ecology.
         St. Ann, Missouri: Central Midwestern Regional
         Educational Laboratory. 1969. *ERIC ED* 029 009.

             Describes one case study of the use of
             ethnographic procedures to generate and test
             hypotheses.

2889.   Smith, Louis M. Participant observation and
         evaluation strategies. *ERIC ED* 048 339.

             Describes various methods of studying
             classrooms, including participant observation,
             case studies and interviews.

2890.   Smith, Louis M. "The micro-ethnography of the
         classroom," *Psychology in the Schools 4* (1967):
         216-221.

             Describes author's experiences and procedures
             in conducting an ethnographic study in one
             classroom.

2891.   Snow, Richard E. "Representative and quasi-
         representative designs for research on teaching,"
         Review of Educational Research 44 (1974):
         265-292.

             Describes types of research designs used and
             which could be used to study teaching and the
             characteristics of those designs, i.e., degree to
             which sample represents the population with which
             the study is concerned.

2892.   Soar, Robert S. "Classroom observation," In
         Competency assessment, research and evaluation.
         Edited by W. Robert Houston. Washington, D.C.:
         American Association of Colleges for Teacher
         Education. 1974.

             Describes observation procedures,
             characteristics of instruments and some widely
             used instruments. For Houston reference see
             citation No. 2971.

2893.   Soar, Robert S. "Problems in analyzing
         process-product relationships in studies of
         teacher effectiveness," *Journal of Teacher
         Education 160* (1978): 96-116.

             Describes analytic problems and issues in
             analyzing classroom observation data and relating
             measures of behavior to measures of student
             learning.

2894. Soar, Robert S. "Teacher assessment problems and possibilities," *Journal of Teacher Education 24* (1973): 205-212. Also in *The appraisal of teaching: Concepts and process.* Edited by Gary D. Borich. pp. 162-173. Reading, Massachusetts: Addison-Wesley Publishing Company. 1977.

Describes some of the methodological issues in observing teachers in classrooms and analyzing observation data. For Borich reference see citation No. 2916.

2895. Stallings, Jane & Giesen, Phillip A. A study of confusability of codes in observational measures. Menlo Park, California: Stanford Research Institute. 1974. *ERIC ED* 093 944.

Reports a study of observer reliability and a method for conducting such studies, using a videotape, rather than the more difficult paired observer method.

2896. Tikunoff, William J. & Ward, Beatrice A. "Conducting naturalistic research on teaching: Some procedural considerations," *Education and Urban Society 12* (1980): 263-290.

Describes naturalistic research as occurring in field settings, with an emphasis on hypothesis generation for further study with different designs.

2897. Tyler, Ralph W. "Analysis of strengths and weaknesses in current research in science education," *Journal of Research in Science Teaching* (1967-1968): 52-63.

Describes the strengths and weaknesses in and ways to improve research, including research on teaching, on curriculum, and student learning.

2898. Tyler, Ralph W. "Resources, models, and theory in the improvement of research in science education," *Journal of Research in Science Teaching* (1967-1968): 43-51.

Describes current research, including research on teaching, on curriculum and on student learning.

2899. Ward, B., Morine, G. & Berliner, D. "Assessing teacher competence," In *Competency assessment, research, and evaluation.* Edited by R. Houston. Washington, D.C.: American Association of Colleges for Teacher Education. 1974.

Discusses various ways of assessing teacher competence and relates methods to purposes of assessment. For Houston reference see citation No. 2971.

2900.   Wood, Samuel E. & others. A factor analysis of three sets of simultaneously collected observational data: Theory and implications. 1969. *ERIC ED* 028 993. See also *ERIC ED* 038 373.

Reports that using multiple methods for data collection provides for more analyses across the levels of variables within the classroom, such as differences in behaviors of teachers.

2901.   Wood, Samuel E. & others. Collecting and analyzing data yielded by the multidimensional techniques for observing classroom behavior. 1969. *ERIC ED* 038 373. See also *ERIC ED* 028 993.

Reports that use of multiple observation systems at one time provides data in context and broadens our perceptions of the classroom, as illustrated by a study using four observation systems.

IX SUMMARIES AND ESSAYS

2902. Adams, R.S. "Analyzing the teacher's role,"
Educational Research 12 (1970): 121-127.

Discusses aspects of the roles of teachers and
ways to describe the various tasks which teachers
perform.

2903. Anderson, Linda M. Research on teaching:
Applications for the classroom. Research Report
No. 4053. Austin, Texas: Research and Development
Center for Teacher Education. University of Texas
at Austin. 1977.

Discusses the status of research on teaching,
the assumptions, methodologies and future
directions.

2904. Anderson, R.C. & others. *Current research on
instruction*. Englewood Cliffs, New Jersey:
Prentice-Hall Publishing Company. 1969.

Presents a collection of articles on studies of
teaching and student learning, including Gage &
Unruh, citation No. 2861.

2905. Association for Supervision and Curriculum
Development. *The Way Teaching Is*. Washington,
D.C.: Association for Supervision and Curriculum
Development. 1965.

Presents a collection of papers from a seminar,
describing aspects of teaching and the behaviors
of teachers, including Gage, citation No. 2955;
Jackson, citation No. 1032 & Kleibard, citation
No. 1682.

2906. Barr, Rebecca & Dreeben, Robert, "Instruction in
Classrooms," In *Review of Educational Research.
vol. 5*, Edited by Lee Shulman. pp. 89-162. Itasca,
Illinois: F.E. Peacock Publishers, Inc., 1977.

Reviews studies of the effects of schools and
teachers on student learning, including role of
language and management, and identification

of areas needing further research. For Shulman
reference see citation No. 3019.

2907.   Bar-Tal, David & Saxe, Leonard (Eds.). *Social
        psychology of education: Theory and research.*
        Washington, D.C.: Hemisphere Publishing
        Corporation. 1978.

        Presents a collection of articles on research
        and theories of education, including Brophy,
        citation No. 2539.

2908.   Begle, E.G. Critical Variables in mathematics
        education: Findings from a survey of the empirical
        literature. Washington, D.C.: Mathematics
        Association of America. 1979. *ERIC ED* 171 515.

        Reviews research on the teaching and learning
        of mathematics, including studies of effects of
        teachers and teaching approaches.

2909.   Bellack, A.A. "Theory and research in teaching," In
        *Research into classroom processes: Recent
        developments and next steps.* Edited by Ian
        Westbuty & Arno A. Bellack. New York: Teachers
        College Press. 1971.

        Discusses research on teaching and the
        relationship of research to theory development.
        For Westbury & Bellack reference see citation No.
        3038.

2910.   Bennett, S.N. "Recent research on teaching: A
        dream, a belief, and a model," *British Journal of
        Educational Psychology 48,* (1978): 127-147.

        Reviews recent studies describes a model of the
        teaching-learning process and the types of
        teaching skills which are important within the
        model.

2910A. Berliner, David D. (Ed.) *Review of research in
        education Vol. 8.* Itasca Illinois: F.E. Peacock,
        Publishers. 1980.

        Presents a collection of articles reviewing
        research, including Burstein, citation No. 2850.

2911.   Berliner, David C. & Cahen, Leonard S.
        "Trait-treatment Interaction and Learning," In
        Review of Research in Education. vol. 1. Edited by
        Fred N. Kerlinger, pp. 58-94 Itasca, Illinois:
        F.E. Peacock Publishers, Inc., 1973.

Reviews methodological issues and results of research on the interaction of instructional treatment and student traits as the interaction influences student learning, including a brief discussion of studies of interactions of student and teacher traits. For Kerlinger reference see citation No. 2976.

2912. Berliner, David C. & Rosenshine, Barak, The acquisition of knowledge in the classroom. Technical Report IV-1. Beginning Teacher Evaluation Study. San Francisco, California: Far West Laboratory for Educational Research and Development. 1976.

Reviews research and identifies teacher behaviors which studies show to be related to student learning in the elementary grades.

2913. Biddle, Bruce J. & Thomas, Edwin J. *Role theory: Concepts and research.* New York: John Wiley & Sons, Inc. 1966.

Presents a collection of papers on role theory including a chapter relating role theory to teaching, by Biddle, Rosencranz, Tomich & Tugman, citation No. 526.

2914. Birkin, T.A. "Toward a model of instructional processes," In *Research into classroom processes: Recent developments and next steps.* Edited by Ian Westbury and Arno A. Bellack. pp. 119-137. New York: Teachers College Press. 1971.

Describes a model of teacher effects on students and a study of elementary teachers relating teacher behavior to student achievement in three areas, motivation, temperament and cognitive-instructional. For Westbury & Bellack reference see citation No. 3039.

2915. Block, James H. "Success rate," In *Time to learn.* Edited by Carolyn Denham & Ann Lieberman. pp. 95-106. Washington, D.C.: U.S. Government Printing Office. 1980.

Describes research on student rate of success on tasks and the implications for teaching. For Denham & Lieberman reference see citation No. 2933.

2916. Borich, Gary D. (Ed.). *The appraisal of teaching: Concepts and process.* Reading, Massachusetts: Addison-Wesley Publishing Co. 1977.

Presents a collection of chapters on the
evaluation of teachers, including classroom
observations and results of studies relating
teacher behaviors to student achievement,
including Berliner, citaton No. 2842; Good &
Grouws, citation No. 2080; Soar, citations No.
2505 & Soar, citation No. 2894.

2917.   Brophy, Jere E. Recent research on teaching.
Occasional Paper No. 40. East Lansing, Michigan:
Institute for Research on Teaching. Michigan State
University. 1980.

Reviews research on teaching during the 1970's
and discusses of the directions of research on
teaching during the 1980's.

2918.   Brophy, Jere E. "Teacher behavior and its effects,"
Journal of Educational Psychology, 71 (1979):
733-750. Occasional Paper No. 25. East Lansing,
Michigan: Institute for Research on Teaching.
Michigan State University. 1979. *ERIC ED* 181 014.

Describes process-product research on teaching
and discusses the need for focused studies within
defined classroom contexts.

2919.   Broudy, H.S. "Can we define good teaching?"
Teachers College Record 70 (1969): 583-592.

Essay discusses the differences between two
conceptions of teaching, didactic teaching in
which the outcomes can be measured and encounter
teaching in which neither the outcomes nor the
means for teaching can be defined clearly.

2920.   Bush, Robert, "Redefining the role of the teacher,"
In *Teachers and the Learning Process*. Edited by
Robert D. Strom. pp. 142-150. Englewood Cliffs,
New Jersey: Prentice-Hall, Inc. 1971. Reprinted in
From Theory into Practice. pp 246-251.

Describes roles of teacher as conveyor of
knowledge and leader of small group process and
the need to shift from the former to the latter.
For Strom reference see citation No. 3029.

2921.   Calvin, Allen. *Perspectives on education.* Reading,
Massachusetts: Addison-Wesley Publishing Co. 1977

Presents a collection of articles on education
and research, including Stallings, citation No.
2511.

2922.　Campbell, James Reed & Barnes, Cyrus. "Interaction
　　　　analysis--A breakthrough," *Phi Delta Kappan 50*
　　　　(1969): 587-590.

　　　　　　Reviews studies using Interaction Analysis and
　　　　summarizes results and discusses uses of results
　　　　in teacher evaluation and in developing theories
　　　　of instruction.

2923.　Canadian Teachers' Federation. *Teacher evaluation.*
　　　　Bibliographies in Education. No. 52. Ottawa,
　　　　Ontario, Canada: Author. 1975.

　　　　　　Presents a bibliography of students of teaching
　　　　and the relationship of teacher behaviors to
　　　　student achievement.

2924.　Clarizio, F.H., Craig, R.C. & Mehrens, W.A.
　　　　(Eds,). *Contemporary Issues in educational
　　　　psychology.* Boston: Allyn & Bacon. 1977.

　　　　　　A collection of articles discussing issues in
　　　　education, including Gage, citaton No. 2950; Gage,
　　　　citation No. 2951; Good & Brophy, citation No. 459
　　　　& Good, Biddle & Brophy, citation No. 2962.

2925.　Clifford, Geraldine Jancich. "A history of the
　　　　impact of research on teaching," In *Second
　　　　handbook of research on teaching.* Edited by Robert
　　　　M.W. Travers. pp. 1-46. Chicago: Rand McNally &
　　　　Company. 1973.

　　　　　　Discusses issues in identifying the impact, and
　　　　arguments for and against the impact, of research
　　　　on teaching within the context of the impact of
　　　　research in education.　For Travers reference see
　　　　citation No. 3033.

2926.　Cohen, Elizabeth G. "Sociology and the classroom:
　　　　Setting the conditions for teacher-student
　　　　interaction," *Review of Educational Research, 42*
　　　　(1972): 441-452. *ERIC ED* 064 250.

　　　　　　Review identifies four major contributions of
　　　　research to understanding effective teaching
　　　　within classrooms.

2927.　Cooley, William W. Leinhardt, Gaea, & McGrail,
　　　　Janet, "How to identify effective teaching,"
　　　　Anthropology and Education Quarterly, 8 (1977):
　　　　119-126.

　　　　　　Discusses past studies focusing on specific
　　　　teaching behaviors and the need to consider the
　　　　total ecology of the teaching-learning
　　　　environment.

2928. Cooley, William W. & Leinhardt, Gaea. The
       application of a model for investigating classroom
       processes. Pittsburgh, Pennsylvania: Learning
       Research and Development Center. University of
       Pittsburgh. 1975.

           Describes a model of classroom interaction
       which forms the basis for research on the
       relationship between classroom processes,
       including teaching, and student achievement.

2929. Coop, R. & White, K. *Psychological concepts in the
       classroom*. New York: Harper & Row. 1973.

           Presents a collection of articles on teaching
       and research, including Good & Brophy, citation
       No. 460.

2930. Cruickshank, Donald R. "Synthesis of selected
       recent research on teacher effects," *Journal of
       Teacher Education 27*, vol. 1 (1976): 57-60.

           Reviews several studies reported at a
       conference and draws conclusions about aspects of
       effective teaching.

2931. DeBourg, Clyde Emerson, A study of roles for the
       teacher from an historical perspective. Ph.D.
       dissertation. Michigan State University. 1980.

           Describes the roles of teachers at several
       points in history.

2932. DeLapp, Steven Roland. Dilemmas of teaching: A
       self-reflective analysis of teaching in a
       third-fourth grade informal classroom. Ph.D.
       dissertation. Ohio State University. 1980.

           Describes teaching and the tensions between
       teaching and research roles, and identifies
       fifteen dilemmas, such as the desire to provide a
       rich environment for the child but also a limited
       environment in order to focus the child's
       inquiry.

2933. Denham, Carolyn & Lieberman, Ann (Eds.). *Time to
       learn*. Washington, D.C.: U.S. Government Printing
       Office. 1980.

           Presents a collection of papers on the
       implications of studies of teaching, including
       Block, citation No. 2915; Borg, citation No. 2427;
       Fenstermacher, citation No. 2945; Fisher, citation
       No. 2055 & Rosenshine, citation No. 2204.

2934. Denton, Jon J. & McNamara, James F. "Conceptual models for determining the influence of classroom teachers on learner cognitive attainment," *Journal of Experimental Education, 48* (1979-1980): 165-169.

Describes three conceptual models of the effects of teachers on student learning and relates these to theories of instructional design.

2935. Dershimer, Richard A. & Iannaccone, Laurence. "Social and political influences on educational research," In *Second handbook of research on teaching.* Edited by Robert M.W. Travers. pp. 113-121. Chicago: Rand McNally & Company. 1973.

Presents a discussion of the influences on researchers who are studying teaching. For Travers reference see citation No. 3033.

2936. Doyle, Walter, "Classroom Tasks and students' abilities," In *Research on teaching: Concepts, Findings, and Implications.* Edited by Penelope L. Peterson and Herbert J. Walberg. Berkeley, California: McCutchan Publishing Corporation. 1979.

Review describes the need to consider the ways that students influence classroom interaction, the ways students negotiate the tasks of the classroom, different instructional approaches for different types of students and the need to consider contexts in studies of teaching. For Peterson & Walberg reference see citation No. 3001.

2937. Doyle, Walter. "Interpreting teacher effectiveness research," *Viewpoints 54* (1978): 141-153.

Summarizes reearch on teacher effects on student achievement and discusses uses and limitations.

2938. Doyle, Walter, Student mediating responses in teaching effectiveness. Final Report. Denton, Texas: North Texas State University. 1980. *ERIC ED 187 698.*

Describes a model of classroom tasks and student perceptions of those tasks as they mediate the relationship between teaching and student learning.

2939.   Doyle, Walter. The tasks of teaching and learning
        in classrooms. Research and Development Report No.
        4103. Austin, Texas: Research and Development
        Center for Teacher Education. University of Texas
        at Austin. 1979. *ERIC ED* 185 069.

            Analyzes student classroom tasks in terms of
        the learning tasks and the interactions between
        teachers and students which effect student
        learning and teacher behavior.

2940.   Duke, Daniel L. (Ed.). *Classroom Management:
        Yearbook of The national Society for the Study of
        Education.* Part II. Chicago: University of Chicago
        Press. 1978.

            Presents a series of articles on classroom
        management, including Brophy & Putnam, citation
        No. 1649; Calfee & Brown, citation No. 1999;
        Cohen, Intili & Robbins, citation No. 1653; Corno,
        citation No. 1654; Doyle, citation No. 1656; Duke,
        citation No. 131; Feldhusen, citation No. 1775;
        Spady & Mitchell, citation No. 1698; & Ward &
        Tikunoff, citation No. 1632.;

2941.   Dunkin, M. & Biddle, J. *The Study of teaching.* New
        York: Holt, Rinehart & Winston, Inc. 1974.

            Presents a comprehensive review of research on
        teaching as it is related to beliefs about
        teaching, and summarizes research on specific
        topics such as classroom climate, management,
        knowledge, and discusses problems in the
        research.

2942.   Ebel, Robert L. (Ed.). *Encyclopedia of Educational
        Research.* Toronto, Canada: The Macmillan Company.
        1969.

            Presents a collection of brief summary
        articles, including Anderson & Ritsher, citation
        No. 1965; Atkins & Burnett, citaton No. 1641;
        Biddle, citation No. 525; Braddock, citation No.
        1647; Flanders & Simon, citation No. 2947; Gage,
        citaton No. 1673; Harris, citation No. 2461;
        Heathers, citation No. 2969; Massailas, citaton
        No. 1685 & Mouly, citation No. 2877.

2943.   Fenstermacher, Gary D. "A philosophical
        consideration of recent research on teacher
        effectiveness, " In *Review of research in
        education.* Vol. 6. Edited by Lee Shulman. pp.
        157-185. Itasca, Illinois: F.E. Peacock
        Publishers, Inc. 1978.

Describes assumptions underlying research on teaching intended to improve teaching and the direction that such research needs to take to enable the research results to be used to change the behaviors of teachers. For Shulman reference see citation No. 3020.

2944. Fenstermacher, Gary. "Learning from teaching from teachers," *Journal of Teacher Education 31* (1980): 63.

Discusses issues in the study of teaching to identify effective teaching for use in changing the behaviors of teachers.

2945. Fenstermacher, Gary D. "On learning to teach effectively from research on teacher effectiveness," In *Time to learn*. Edited by Carolyn Denham & Ann Lieberman. pp. 127–138. Washington, D.C.: U.S. Government Printing Office. 1980

Discusses the assumptions underlying the uses of results of research on teaching to improve teaching, with illustrations from some research results. For Denham & Lieberman reference see citation No. 2933.

2946. Fisher, Charles, Marliave, Richard & Filby, Nikola N. "Improving teaching by increasing 'Academic Learning Time'," *Educational Leadership, 37.* (1979): 52–54.

Describes research which indicates that teacher and student use of time are related to student learning.

2947. Flanders, Ned A. & Simon, Anita. "Teacher effectiveness," In *Encyclopedia of educational research*. Edited by Robert L. Ebel. pp. 1423–1437. Toronto, Canada: The MacMillan Company. 1969.

Presents a review of studies reported from 1960 to 1966 including process–product, presage–process, presage–setting–product studies, a review of other reviews and a discussion of research terms. For Ebel reference see citation No. 2942.

2948. Flanders, Ned A. & Simon, Anita. "Teacher effectiveness," *Classroom Interaction Newsletter 5*, no. 1 (1969): 18–37.

Reviews studies which look at teacher effectivness, developments in the research such as observation procedures, and process–product studies.

2949.   Fyans, Leslie J. (Ed.) *Achievement motivation:*
         Recent trends in theory and research. New York:
         Plenum Publications. 1980.

              Presents a collection of articles, including
         Wang & Weisstein, citation No. 862.

2950.   Gage, Nathaniel L. "An analytic approach to
         research on instructional methods, " *Journal of*
         Experimental Education, 37 (1967): 119-125. *ERIC*
         ED 011 936. Also in *Phi Delta Kappan 49* (1968):
         601-606. Also in *School learning and instruction:*
         Readings. Edited by H.D. Thornburg. pp. 107-120.
         Monterey, California: Brooks/Cole. 1973. Also in
         Contemporary Issues in Educational Psychology.
         Edited by F.H. Clarizio, R.C. Craig & W. A.
         Mehrens. pp. 67-81. Boston: Allyn & Bacon. 1977.

              Describes emerging categories of research on
         teaching, such as microteaching, and describes
         some studies in progress. For Clarizio, Craig &
         Mehrens reference see citation No. 2924. For
         Thornbury reference see citation No. 3031.

2951.   Gage, N.L. "Can science contribute to the art of
         teaching," *Phi Delta Kappan 49* (1968): 399-403.
         Also in *Contemporary issues in educational*
         psychology. Edited by F.H. Clarizio, R.C. Craig &
         W.A. Mehrens. pp. 27-40. Boston: Allyn & Bacon.
         1977.

              Discusses the role of studies of teaching in
         describing effective teaching and summarizes some
         research. For Clarizio, Craig & Mehrens reference
         see citation No. 2924.

2952.   Gage, N.L. "Desirable behaviors of teachers," *Urban*
         Education 1 (1965): 85-95.

              Describes several desirable behaviors of
         teachers and summarizes research to support them,
         including warmth, cognitive organization,
         orderliness, indirectness, and ability to solve
         instructional problems.

2953.   Gage, N.L. "Models for research on teaching,"
         Stanford, California: Stanford Center for Research
         and Development in Teaching, Stanford University.
         ERIC ED 121 714.

              Discusses models used in studying teaching,
         with implications for research and for what has
         been learned from research.

2954. Gage, N.L. Panel summaries from the national conference on studies in teaching. (June 16, 1974). Washington, D.C.: National Institute of Education, 1974. *ERIC ED* 111 801.

Presents summaries of the discussions of the nine panels of researchers who addressed major topics in the study of teaching.

2955. Gage, N.L. "Research on cognitive aspects of teaching," In *The way teaching is*. pp. 29-44. Washington, D.C.: Association for Supervision and Curriculum Development. 1965.

Reviews earlier studies focusing on teacher personality and teacher interaction with students and discusses a new research focus on cognitive aspects of instruction such as the teacher as explainer. For Association for Supervision and Curriculum Development reference see citation No. 2905.

2956. Gage, N.L. "The generality of dimensions of teaching," In *Research on teaching: Concepts, findings, and implications*. Edited by Penelope L. Peterson and Herbert J. Walberg. Berkeley, California: McCutchan Publishing Corporation. 1979.

Describes research which attempts to find relationships between teacher behavior and student learning across and within settings and predicts an eventual hierarchy of more and less generalizable teaching skills. For Peterson & Walberg reference see citation No. 3001.

2957. Gage, N.L. "Theories of teaching," In *Teachers and the learning process*, Edited by Robert D. Strom. pp. 258-272. Englewood Cliffs, New Jersey: Prentice-Hall, Inc. 1971. Also printed in *Theories of learning and instruction, 63rd Yearbook of the National Society for the Study of Education. Part I*. Edited by Ernest R. Hilgard. Chicago: 1974.

Describes the need for theories of teaching and ways of analyzing teaching in terms of activity, educational objectives, components of the learning process, and families of learning theories. For Strom reference see citation No. 3029.

2958. Gagne, Robert N. "Learning and instructional sequence," In *Review of research in education Vol.1*. Edited by Fred. N. Kerlinger. pp. 3-53. Itasca, Illinois: F.E. Peacock Publishers.

Discusses issues in and research on the
sequencing of instruction in relation to student
learning, including studies of the effects of
types of teacher questions and the transfer of
student cognitive skills. For Kerlinger reference
see citation No. 2976.

2959.   Gall, Meredith D. "The use of questions in
teaching," *Review of Educational Research 40*
(1970): 707-721.

Reviews fifty years of research on teacher and
student questions, effects of teacher questions on
student behavior, and efforts to change teacher
questioning behavior.

2960.   Galloway, Charles, "Nonverbal communication: A
needed focus," 1968. *ERIC ED* 025 484.

Describes a model of teacher nonverbal behavior
and communication.

2961.   Good, Thomas L. Multiple measures of teacher
effectiveness. Technical Report No. 97. Columbia,
Missouri: University of Missouri. 1974.

Describes methods of observing teacher behavior
and relating that behavior to student learning to
identify effective teaching practices.

2962.   Good, T., Biddle, B. & Brophy, J. "Do schools make
a difference," In *Contemporary readings in
educational psychology*. Edited by H. Clarizio, R.
Criag & W. Mehrens. Boston: Allyn & Bacon. 1977.

Summarizes research on teacher effects on
student achievement to argue that schools do have
differential effects on student learning. For
Clarizio, Craig & Mehrens reference see citation
No. 2924.

2963.   Good, Thomas L., Biddle, Bruce J., & Brophy, Jere
E. "The effects of teaching: An optimistic note,"
Elementary School Journal, 76 (1976): 365-372.

Reviews studies of teaching identifying those
teaching behaviors which are related to more
student learning and describing the likely future
success of studies of teaching.

2964.   Good, Thomas L. & Power, Colin. Differential
strategies for classroom success: A theoretical
model. Technical Report No. 100. Columbia,
Missouri: University of Missouri-Columbia, 1974.

Describes a model for mathematics teaching and learning, based on studies of effective teaching, with specific directions to teachers for organizing instruction.

2965. Gordon, Ira J. (Ed.). *Early childhood education: The 71st Yearbook of the National Society for the Study of Education. Part II.* Chicago: University of Chicago Press. 1972.

Presents a series of articles on early childhood education, including Soar & Soar, citation No. 2233.

2966. Hall, Gene E. What context? Is it in use. Research Series No. 3041. Austin, Texas: Research and Development Center for Teacher Education. University of Texas at Austin. 1977.

Discusses the importance of measuring teacher behavior in studies of specific educational programs.

2967. Hamachek, Don. (Ed.) *Human dynamics in psychology and education.* New York: Allyn & Bacon. 1968

Presents a collection of articles, including Hamachek, citation No. 1806.

2968. Harris, Albert J. "The effective teacher of reading, revisited," *Reading Teacher 33* (1979): 135-140.

Summarizes research since 1969 on effective reading instruction, including research on behaviors of reading teachers.

2969. Heathers, Glen, "Grouping," In *Encyclopedia of educational research,* Edited by Robert L. Ebel. pp. 559-570. New York: The McMillan Company. 1969.

Reviews the history of and various methods for grouping students and studies of the effects of grouping, pointing out the absence in those studies of any consideration of instructional activities within groups. For Ebel reference see citation No. 2942.

2970. Hennings, Dorothy G. *Mastering classroom communication: What Interaction Analysis tells the teacher.* Pacific Palisades, California: Goodyear Publishing Company, Inc. 1975.

Discusses teaching as communication and reviews research on various aspects of classroom communication.

2971.   Houston, W. Robert. *Competency assessment, research, and evaluation*. Washington, D.C.: American Association of Colleges for Teacher Education. 1974.

Presents a collection of articles from a conference on teacher assessment, including Soar, citation No. 2892; Rosenshine, citation No. 2490 & Ward, Morine & Berliner, citation No. 2899.

2972.   Hyer, Anna & McClure, Robert M. New patterns of teacher tasks and their implications: The effect of innovations on staffing patterns and teacher roles in the United States. Paris, France: Directorate for Scientific Affairs, Organization for Economic Cooperation and Development. 1973. *ERIC ED* 086 684.

Describes the effects of innovations on the roles that teachers fill and the increasing complexity of the decisions which teachers need to make.

2973.   Hyman, Ronald. T. (Ed.). *Teaching: Vantage points for study*. Philadelphia, Pennsylvania: T.B. Lippincott Company. 1968.

Presents a collection of reprinted articles on teaching and the classroom, usually reporting on or reviewing research, including Bellack, Davitz, Kliebard, Hyman & Smith, citation No. 2528; Chapline, citation No. 2851; Coombs, citation No. 940; Flanders, citation No. 2444; Gallagher & Aschner, citation No. 2572; Galloway, citation No. 990; Huebner, citation No. 1026; MacDonald & Zaret, citation No. 180; Oliver & Shaver, citation No. 2364; Ryans, citation No. 1696; Smith & Meux, citation No. 2647 & Taba & Elzey, citation No. 2658.

2974.   Ivany, J.W. George & Neujahr, James L. "Inquiry into science teaching," *The Science Teacher, 37* (1970): 31-34.

Discusses the need for teachers to study their own teaching, with examples of methods they can use, such as Interaction Analysis and Bellack's language analysis.

2975.   Joyce, Bruce. Variables, designs and instruments in the search for teacher effectiveness. Technical

Report 75-10-4. Beginning Teacher Evaluation
Study. San Francisco, California: Far West
Laboratory for Educational Research and
Development. 1975.

Discusses dimensions of teaching and of
classrooms which need to be considered in a study
of teaching.

2976. Kerlinger, Fred N. *Review of Research in Education
Vol. 1* Itasca, Illinois: F.E. Peacock Publishers,
Inc. 1973.

Presents a collection of reviews, including
Berliner & Cahen, citation No. 2911; Gagne,
citation No. 2958.

2977. Kerlinger, Fred N. *Review of Research in Education
Vol. 3* Itasca, Illinois: F.E. Peacock Publishers,
Inc. 1975.

Presents a collection of reviews, including
Shulman & Elstein, citation No. 1465.

2978. Koehler, Virginia, "Classroom process research:
Present and future," *Journal of Classroom
Interaction 13*, No. 2 (1978): 3-11.

Describes research funded by the National
Institute of Education, including descriptive and
process-product studies.

2979. Koff, Robert H. Dynamics of task and process--the
classroom as social organism. 1967. *ERIC ED* 017
975.

Presents a theoretical model of the classroom
as a work-oriented culture which places demands
upon students and requires teachers to fill
certain roles.

2980. Lanier, Judith E. Research on teaching: A dynamic
area of inquiry. Occasional Paper No. 7. East
Lansing, Michigan: Institute for Research on
Teaching. Michigan State University. 1978.

Discusses the history of research on teaching,
with early emphasis on teacher characteristics,
then teacher behavior and now studies of the
influences on teacher judgements and the complex
interactions of teacher judgements with other
variables.

2981. Levin, H.M. "A new model of school effectiveness,"
In *How do teachers make a difference?* Edited by

A.M. Mood. Washington, D.C.: U.S. Office of
Education. 1970. *ERIC ED* 040 252.

Discusses measures of school effectiveness,
including information about teachers within
schools. For Mood reference see citation No.
2995.

2982. Lucio, William H. "Pupil achievement as an index of
teacher performance," *Educational Leadership 31*
(1973): 71-77.

Reviews the methods for using student learning
and gains in student learning as the basis for
defining teacher effects.

2983. McClellan, James E. "Classroom-teaching research: A
philosophical critique," In *Research in classroom
processes: Recent developments and next steps.*
Edited by Ian Westbury & Arno A. Bellack. pp.
3-15. New York: Teachers College Press. 1971.

Describes research on teaching, critiquing the
assumptions underlying the research. For Westbury
& Bellack reference see caitation No. 3039.

2984. McKenna, Bernard H. & others. Teacher evaluation:
An annotated bibliography. Washington, D.C.: ERIC
Clearinghouse on Teacher Education. 1971. *ERIC ED*
055 988.

Presents an annotated bibliography of teacher
education policies and procedures, observation
methods, and studies relating teacher behaviors to
student learning.

2985. MacMillan J. *The social psychology of teaching.* New
York: Academic Press. 1980.

Presents a collection of articles including
Good, citation No. 456.

2986. McNeil, John D. & Popham, W. James. "The assessment
of teacher competence," In *Second handbook of
research on teaching.* Edited by Robert M.W.
Travers. pp. 218-244. Chicago, Illinois: Rand
McNally and Company. 1973.

Discusses criteria of teacher effectiveness,
including teacher behaviors and student learning,
ratings by students, teachers and administrators,
observations, and identifies important
characteristics of teacher competence measures.
For Travers reference see citation No. 3033.

2987. Magoon, A. Jon. "Sensitive field observation of teaching performance," *Journal of Teacher Education 30*, No.2, (1979): 13-16.

Reviews the state of knowledge of teacher behaviors as related to student learning and as a basis for Performance Based Teacher Education.

2988. Marliave, Richard S. Observable classroom variables. Technical Report I-2. Beginning Teacher Evaluation Study. San Francisco, California: Far West Laboratory for Educational Research and Development. 1976. *ERIC ED* 146 162.

Summarizes research and researcher recommendations for observation of seven domains of variables of teacher behavior and classroom contexts.

2989. Marliave, Richard S., Cahen, Leonard S. & Berliner, David C. Prolegomenon on the concept of appropriateness of instruction. Technical Report IV-1. Beginning Teacher Evaluation Study. San Francisco, California: Far West Laboratory for Educational Research and Development. 1977. *ERIC ED* 146 164.

Discusses the appropriateness of teacher behaviors and the effects of those behaviors on student learning, including the meaning as well as the frequency of behaviors.

2990. Medley, Donald M. "Early history of research on teacher behavior," *International Review of Education 18*: 430-439.

Reviews the history and development of research on teaching from the 1890's to 1955, including a discussion of studies of teacher characteristics, ratings of teachers, and the efforts to measure teacher behaviors.

2991. Medley, Donald M. "Future directions for process-product research," *Journal of Classroom Interaction 13* (1977): 3-8.

Discusses the current status of and directions of needed research on teacher behaviors related to student learning.

2992. Medley, Donald M. "Research in teacher effectiveness: Where is it and how did it get there?" *Journal of Classroom Interaction 13* (1978): 16-21.

Describes the history of research on teaching
and the current state of knowledge about teaching
and its effects on student learning.

2993.   Medley, Donald M. "The effectiveness of teachers."
        In *Research on teaching: Concepts, findings, and
        implications*. Edited by Penelope L. Peterson &
        Herbert J. Walberg. Berkeley, California:
        McCutchan Publishing Corporation. 1979.

Reviews the history of research on teaching
through four stages: teacher personality related
to student outcomes, teaching methods, teacher
behaviors and teacher mastery of sets of
competencies and the appropriate use of those
competencies. For Peterson & Walberg reference
see citation No. 3001.

2994.   Medley, Donald M. "The language of teacher
        behavior: Communicating the results of structured
        observations to teachers," *Journal of Teacher
        Education 22* : 157–165.

Describes procedures used successfully to
describe to teachers their observed behaviors.

2995.   Mood, Alexander M. (Ed.). *How do teachers make a
        difference?* Washington, D.C.: U.S. Department of
        Health, Education and Welfare. 1970. *ERIC ED* 057
        004.

Presents a collection of papers on schools and
teaching, including Levin, citation No. 2981.

2996.   Munby, Hugh. Analyzing teaching: the quality of the
        intellectual experience and the concept of
        intellectual independence. 1977. *ERIC ED* 139 606.

Describes a way to analyze science teaching and
to identify goals and then predict the
relationship between those goals and student
learning.

2997.   Nelson, Lois N. (Ed.). *The nature of teaching: A
        collection of readings*. Waltham, Massachusetts:
        Blaisdell Publishing Company. 1969.

Presents a collection of previously published
papers, several describing studies of teaching,
including Bellack, citaton No. 2527; Flanders,
citation No. 1666; Gallagher, citation No. 989;
Gallagher & Aschner, citation No. 2572 & Nelson,
citation No. 1301.

2998.   Nuthall, Graham & Snook, Ivan. "Contemporary models
        of teaching," In *Second handbook of research on*

teaching. Edited by Robert M.W. Travers. pp. 47-76. Chicago, Illinois: Rand McNally and Company. 1973.

Describes models of teaching and their role in defining research and interpreting the results of studies. For Travers reference see citation No. 3033.

2999. Openshaw, M. Karl & others. The development of a taxonomy for the classification of teacher classroom behavior. Ohio State University. 1966. *ERIC ED* 010 167.

Describes a study in which teacher behaviors from several observation systems were synthesized and modified into a taxonomy of teacher behaviors and then the taxonomy was tested with videotapes of teachers.

3000. Peck, Robert F. "Needed research and development in teaching," *Journal of Teacher Education 27* (1976): 18-21.

Describes a number of important issues in the study of teaching and cites relevant research in discussing each issue.

3001. Peterson, Penelope L. & Walberg, Herbert J. (Eds.). *Research on teaching: Concepts, findings, and implications*. Berkeley, California: McCutchan Publishing Corporation. 1979.

Presents a collection of reviews and reports of research on teaching at the elementary, secondary and college levels, including Borko et al., citation No. 1389; Berliner, citation No. 1977; Clark & Yinger, citation No. 1404; Doyle, citation No. 2936; Gage, citation No. 2956; Medley, citation No. 2993; Peterson, citation No. 2479; Rosenshine, citation No. 2484 & Soar & Soar, citation No. 2510.

3002. Pfau, Richard H. "The comparative study of classroom behaviors," *Comparative Education Review 24* (1980) 400-14.

Describes methods and problems in studies of behaviors of teachers and students, especially in comparative studies across countries.

3003. Phi Lambda Theta. *The Evaluation of Teaching*. Washington, D.C.: author.

Presents a collection of articles discussing studies of teaching, including Ryans, citation No. 1695 & Smith, citation No. 218.

3004. Powell, Marjorie. "Changing conceptions of teaching," *California Journal of Teacher Education 4*, No. 2 (1977): 77-90.

Describes views of teaching and the ways that changes in those views have influenced research and that research in turn has influenced views of teaching.

3005. Powell, Marjorie. "Evaluating classroom information: Methodological concerns," *California Journal of Teacher Education 3*, No. 4 (1977): 20-33.

Discusses methods for compiling information about behaviors of teachers and students in classrooms and problems associated with those methods.

3006. Powell, Marjorie. "New evidence for old truths," *Educational Leadership 37* (1979):49-51.

Describes the results of several years of research, identifying the importance of student attention to task, success rate, time allocation and content coverage, academic focus of the classroom and a cooperative atmosphere.

3007. Powell, Marjorie. "Research on teaching," *Educational Forum 43* (1978): 27-37.

Reviews findings of several studies indicating the teacher behaviors related to direct instruction are related to student learning of reading and mathematics.

3008. Ribotta, Michael, "The teacher: A man for all seasons," *California Journal of Teacher Education 1*, No. 3 (1973): 73-86.

Describes conditions of teaching during the early history of the United States, related to teachers' current status, pay and problems.

3009. Romberg, T.A., Small, M. & Carnahan R. Research on teaching from a curriculum perspective. Theoretical Paper No. 81. Madison, Wisconsin: Wisconsin Research and Development Center for Individualized Schooling. University of Wisconsin-Madison. 1979. *ERIC ED* 193 232.

Discusses the role of curriculum in teaching,
the limited consideration of curriculum in past
studies of teaching, and ways that curriculum may
influence relations between teaching and
learning.

3010. Rosenshine, Barak Victor. Academic engaged time,
content covered, and direct instruction. 1978.
ERIC ED 152 776.

Reviews studies since 1973 and identifies a
shift toward greater observation of students,
researcher attention to seatwork as well as a
discussion of behaviors related to student
learning and a convergence of results toward a
model of teaching called "direct instruction".

3011. Rosenshine, Barak & Furst, Norma. "The use of
direct observation to study teaching," In *Second
handbook of research on teaching*. Edited by Robert
M.W. Travers. pp. 122-183. Chicago, Illinois: Rand
McNally and Company. 1973.

Describes approaches to studying teaching, the
use of observation instruments, types of
instruments, issues in using observations and in
interpreting results and uses of research on
teaching. For Travers reference see citation No.
3033.

3012. Ruff, Frances K. Instructional variables and
student achievement in reading and mathematics: A
synthesis of recent process-product research.
Philadelphia, Pennsylvania: Research for Better
Schools. 1978. *ERIC ED* 189 135.

Summarizes eight reviews and identifies
characteristics of effective instruction for low
socioeconomic status children, with teacher-
directed tasks and information presented in small
steps so that students have a high rate of
success.

3013. Rupley, William H. Credible variable which relate
to teacher effectiveness in reading instruction.
1975. *ERIC ED* 114 768.

Review concludes that researchers should
identify successful and unsuccessful students and
then identify the instructional variables related
to their achievement.

3014. Satz, P. & Ross, J. (Eds.). *The disabled learner:
Early detection and intervention.* Rotterdam:
University of Rotterdam Press. 1972.

Presents a collection of articles including Soar, citation No. 3026.

3015.   Schofield, Hilary L. & Start K.B. "Product variables as criteria of teacher effectiveness," *Journal of Experimental Education 48* (1979–1980): 130–136.

Discusses problems with some current research and areas of needed research related to teacher effectiveness.

3016.   Scott, Myrtle. Teacher effectiveness: A position. George Peabody College for Teachers. *ERIC ED* 039 928.

Reviews research on teacher effectiveness, presents a summary of findings and major problems with the research.

3017.   Shavelson, Richard J. "What is *the* basic teaching skill?" *Journal of Teacher Education 14* (1973): 144–151.

Describes a model of teacher decision making and methods by which teacher decision making can be studied.

3018.   Shulman, Lee S. (Ed.). *Review of research in education Vol. 4.* Itasca, Illinois: F.E. Peacock Publishers, Inc. 1976.

Presents a collection of reviews of research in education, including Snow, citation No. 2504.

3019.   Shulman, Lee S. (Ed.). *Review of research in education Vol. 5.* Itasca, Illinois: F.E. Peacock Publishers, Inc. 1977.

Presents a collection of reviews of research in education, including Barr & Dreeban, citation No. 2906 & Doyle, citation No. 2853.

3020.   Shulman, Lee S. (Ed.). *Review of research in education Vol. 6.* Itasca, Illinois: F.E. Peacock Publishers, Inc. 1978.

Presents a collection of reviews of research in education, including Fenstermacher, citation No. 2943.

3021.   Siegel, Lawrence. *Instruction: Some contemporary viewpoints.* San Francisco: Chandler Publishing Co. 1967.

Presents articles discussing aspects of
teaching, some containing discussions of research,
including Biddle & Adams, citation No. 2425.

3022.   Smith, B. Othaniel, "Recent research on teaching:
An interpretation," *High School Journal* 5 (1967):
63-74.
Reviews types of studies and usefulness of
observational studies in describing and
understanding teaching.

3023.   Smith, B. Othaniel. *Research in teacher education:
A symposium*. Englewood Cliffs, New Jersey:
Prentice-Hall Inc. 1971.

Presents a collection of papers from a
symposium on research on teaching and teacher
education, including Rosenshine & Furst, citation
No. 2495.

3024.   Snow, Richard E. "Theory construction for research
on teaching," In *Second Handbook of Research on
Teaching*. Edited by Robert M.W. Travers. pp.
77-112. Chicago, Illinois: Rand McNally and
Company. 1973.

Discusses types of theories, processes of
theory construction, ways of evaluating theories,
within the context of research on teaching. For
Travers reference see citation No. 3033.

3025.   Snow, Richard E. Toward a model of teacher-learner
interaction. Stanford, California: Stanford Center
for Research and Development in Teaching. Stanford
University. 1978. *ERIC ED* 037 374.

Describes a model of interaction and exchange
of information between teacher and student which
incorporates aspects of information processing,
and relates some experimental studies to the
model.

3026.   Soar, Robert S. "The nature of effective teaching
for young, disadvantages children," In *The
disabled learner: Early detection and
intervention*. Edited by P. Satz & J. Ross.
Rotterdam: University of Rotterdam Press. 1972.

Summarizes results of several studies of
teacher behaviors related to student learning for
disadvantaged students. For Satz & Ross reference
see citation No. 3014.

3027.   Sprinthall, N. *Educational psychology: A
developmental approach*. Reading, Massachusetts

Presents a collection of articles on teaching, including Walberg & Thomas, citation No. 1374.

3028.   Squire, J.R. (Ed.). *A new look at progressive education.* Washington, D.C.: Association for Supervision and Curriculum Development. 1972.

Presents a collection of articles on teaching and schooling, including Soar, citation No. 2652.

3029.   Strom, Robert D. (Ed.). *Teachers and the learning process.* Englewood Cliffs, New Jersey: Prentice-Hall, Inc. 1971.

Presents a collection of articles on pupils, teaching and learning, creative behavior, evaluation of teaching, including Bush, citation No. 2920; Flanders, citation No. 2442; Flanders, citation No. 2567; Gage, citation No. 2957; Hamachek, citation No. 564; Jackson, citation No. 1031. & Rosenthal, citation No. 469.

3030.   Susman, Elizabeth J. & others. Observational child study: An empirical analysis of recent trends and directions. *ERIC ED* 127 013.

Reviews preschool naturalistic observation studies over 15 years with the conclusion that reliability of observations did not increase over that period and that studies focused on 3-5 year old middle class children and did not provide a range of settings to look at developmental processes.

3031.   Thornburg, H.D. *School learning and instruction: Readings.* Monterey, California: Brooks/Cole. 1973.

Presents a collection of articles on instruction and the organization of classrooms, including Gage, citation No. 2861 & Gage, citation No. 2950.

3032.   Tisher, R.P. An alternative conceptualization of teaching with some consequences for research. Technical Report No. 134. Columbia, Missouri: University of Missouri-Columbia. 1978.

Describes a model of teaching and discusses the implications of the model for research methods and knowledge gained from the research.

3033.   Travers, Robert M.W. (Ed.). *Second handbook of research on teaching.* Chicago: Rand McNally and Company. 1973.

Presents a collection of chapters on aspects of research on teaching, including historical perspectives, methodological issues, general findings by subject area and general educational level, including Beller, citation No. 402; Bidwell, citation No. 2533; Clifford, citation No. 2925; Dershimer & Iannaccone, citation No. 2935; Dessart & Frandsen, citation No. 1655; Dreeben, citation No. 1657; Gordon & Jester, citation No. 1678; Khan & Weiss, citation No. 406; Lortie, citation No. 572; McNeil & Popham, citation No. 2986; Nuthall & Snook, citation No. 2998; Riedsel & Burns, citation No. 1693; Rosenshine & Furst, citation No. 3011 & Snow, citation No. 3024.

3034.   Travers, Robert M.W. "Some further reflections on the nature of a theory of instruction," In *Research into classroom processes: Recent developments and next steps*. Edited by Ian Westbury & Arno A. Bellack. New York: Teachers College Press. 1971.

Discusses teaching, research on teaching, and the relationship of research to theory. For Westbury reference see citation No. 3039.

3035.   Walberg, Herbert J. "Decision and Perception: New constructs for research on teacher effects," *Cambridge Journal of Education 7* (1977): 33–39.

Discusses recent studies of teacher perceptions of teaching and planning for and decision making during teaching.

3036.   Ward, Beatrice A. & Tikunoff, William J. Application of research to teaching. Teacher Education Division Publication Series Report No. A-75-2. San Francisco, California: Far West Laboratory for Educational Research and Development. 1975. *ERIC ED* 128 337.

Discusses four ways to apply research to teaching, through development of materials, use of new knowledge by teachers, use of data collection procedures for teacher development, and through teachers conducting research studies to validate other findings.

3037.   Ward, William T. Increasing teacher effectiveness through better use of scientific knowledge. 1969. *ERIC ED* 034 735.

Summarizes research on aspects of teaching and models of teaching with implications of the research for classroom teachers.

3038.   Westbury, Ian. "Problems and prospects," In
         Research into classroom processes: Recent
         developments and next steps. Edited by Ian
         Westbury & Arno A. Bellack. pp. 227–252. New York:
         Teachers College Press. 1971.

         Discusses research on teaching, knowledge about
         teaching gained from research, and problems
         encountered in the research. For Westbury &
         Bellack reference see citation No. 3039.

3039.   Westbury, Ian & Bellack, Arno A. *Research into*
         classroom processes: Recent developments and next
         steps. New York: Teachers College Press. 1971.

         Presents a collection of articles discussing
         studies of teaching, including Adams, citation No.
         1637; Bellack, citatin No. 2909; Birkin, citation
         No. 2914; Gage et al., citation No. 2860; Ginther,
         citation No. 2076; Gump, citation No. 1005;
         McClellan, citation No. 2983; Rosenshine, citation
         No. 2492; Smith, citation No. 590; Travers,
         citaton No. 3034 & Westbury, citation No. 3038.

3040.   Williams, David L. & Herman, Wayne L., Jr. *Current*
         research in elementary school science. New York:
         The Macmillan Company. 1971.

         Presents a collection of articles discussing
         studies of science teaching, including Handley &
         Bledsoe, citation No. 32; Kimball, citation No. 52
         & Rosenshine, citation No. 2492.

3041.   Winne, Philip H. & Marx, Ronald W.
         "Reconceptualizing research on teaching," *Journal*
         of Educational Psychology 69 (1977): 668–679.

         Essay discusses the need to reconceptualize
         research to include studies of human learning,
         information processing and teacher decision
         making.

AUTHOR INDEX

TITLE INDEX

Ability of white teachers to relate to black students and to white students, The, 2584

Academic achievement motivation as a function of classroom responsiveness, 1846

Academic engaged time, content covered, and direct instruction, 3010

Academic expectations and attributed responsibility as predictors of professional teachers' reinforcement behavior, 664

Academic improvement through an experimental classroom management system, 2358

Academic learning time and student achievement in the A-B period, 2149

Academic learning time and student achievement in the B-C period, 2150

Academic objectives in classroom management, 1733

Accountability in responding to classroom questions: Impact on student achievement, 2742

Accuracy of teacher reports of their classroom behavior, 567

Accuracy of teacher reports: Reports and observations of specific classroom behaviors, 579

Accuracy of teacher's predictions on children's learning performance, The, 861

Achievement and student-teacher verbal interactions in high school physics lectures with and without computer simulated demonstration experiments, 1570

Achievement as a function of interactions between student characteristics and teacher behaviors, 396

Achievement correlates, 2430

Achievement, creativity, and self-concept correlates of teacher-pupil transactions in elementary school classrooms, 2238

Achievement motivation: Recent trends in theory and research, 2949

Achievement of boys and girls taught by men and women teachers, The, 2521

Achievement of LSE black children with teachers of different sex and ethnic identity, 2169

Acquisition of knowledge in the classroom, The, 2912

Acquisition of teaching skills in elementary school settings: A research report, The, 1630

Are creative teachers more humanistic in their pupil
    control ideology?, 31
Are good and poor readers taught differently? Is that why
    poor readers are poor readers?, 895
Are the attitudes of teachers related to declining
    percentage enrollments in physics, 1136
Are there great teachers?, 1954
Aspects of teacher discourse and student achievement in
    mathematics, 2389
Assessing classroom incentive practices, 1337
Assessing teacher competence, 2899
Assessing teacher performance in the classroom: Pattern
    analysis applied to interaction data, 2884
Assessing teaching effectiveness: The state of the art,
    2462
Assessment and treatment of deviant behavior in
    children--Section five: Investigation of some
    functional relationships between teacher consequating
    behavior and pupil performance, 2668
Assessment of absenteeism of certificated teacher staff in
    the Robles School District of California, 1978-1979
    school year, An, 1338
Assessment of classroom teachers' attitudes and knowledge
    of gifted and talented students, An, 22
Assessment of relationships between certain personality
    variables and teacher performance in teaching
    assignments of higher and lower difficulty, An, 114
Assessment of student achievement: Evaluation of student
    achievement at the intermediate level, 595
Assessment of teacher competence, The, 2986
Assessment of teacher influence, An, 2721
Assessment of the behavior of children working without
    direct teacher supervision alone or in pairs with
    manipulative materials on teacher designed tasks
    self-selected or teacher-assigned, An, 2808
Assessment of the relationship between birth order and
    classroom teaching practices of secondary teachers and
    a bibliography of birth order research 1866-1977 with
    index, An, 235
Association between certain student responses and certain
    teacher behaviors in classroom settings, The, 1829
Association of teacher-student interpersonal relationship
    and classroom verbal interaction, The, 2761
Attempt to identify measures of teacher effectiveness from
    four studies, An, 2509
Attempt to replicate the teacher expectancy effect, An,
    423
Attending and thinking in the classroom, 739
Attitude change of teachers and students, 339
Attitudes and classroom behaviors of Virginia middle
    school English teachers regarding black English and
    certain other usages, 1291
Attitudes, cognition, and nonverbal communicative
    behavior, 2856
Attitudes of eleventh grade students toward union
    activities of teachers and teacher behavior, 2705

SUBJECT INDEX